JONES & BARTLETT LEARNING INFORMATION SYSTEMS SECURITY & ASSURANCE SERIES

Fundamentals of Information Systems Security

DAVID KIM AND MICHAEL G. SOLOMON

JONES & BARTLETT
LEARNING

World Headquarters
Jones & Bartlett Learning
5 Wall Street
Burlington, MA 01803
978-443-5000
info@jblearning.com
www.jblearning.com

Jones & Bartlett Learning books and products are available through most bookstores and online booksellers. To contact Jones & Bartlett Learning directly, call 800-832-0034, fax 978-443-8000, or visit our website, www.jblearning.com.

Substantial discounts on bulk quantities of Jones & Bartlett Learning publications are available to corporations, professional associations, and other qualified organizations. For details and specific discount information, contact the special sales department at Jones & Bartlett Learning via the above contact information or send an email to specialsales@jblearning.com.

Production Credits
Chief Executive Officer: Ty Field
President: James Homer
SVP, Chief Operating Officer: Don Jones, Jr.
SVP, Chief Technology Officer: Dean Fossella
SVP, Chief Marketing Officer: Alison M. Pendergast
SVP, Chief Financial Officer: Ruth Siporin
SVP, Business Development: Christopher Will
VP, Design and Production: Anne Spencer
VP, Manufacturing and Inventory Control: Therese Connell
Editorial Management: High Stakes Writing, LLC, Editor and Publisher: Lawrence J. Goodrich
Reprints and Special Projects Manager: Susan Schultz
Associate Production Editor: Tina Chen
Director of Marketing: Alisha Weisman
Senior Marketing Manager: Andrea DeFronzo
Cover Design: Anne Spencer
Composition: Mia Saunders Design
Cover Image: © ErickN/ShutterStock, Inc.
Chapter Opener Image: © Rodolfo Clix/Dreamstime.com
Printing and Binding: Malloy, Inc.
Cover Printing: Malloy, Inc.

ISBN: 978-0-7637-9025-7

6048

Printed in the United States of America
16 15 14 13 10 9 8

Contents

This book is dedicated to our readers, students, and IT professionals pursuing a career in information systems security. May your passion for learning IT security help you protect the information assets of the United States of America, our businesses, and the privacy data of our citizens.
—David Kim

To God, who has richly blessed me in so many ways
—Michael G. Solomon

Letter from (ISC)^2 Executive Director W. Hord Tipton

Dear student,

I congratulate you on your decision to advance your knowledge in the rapidly expanding and challenging field of information security. This is currently one of the most in-demand industries in the world and there is an urgent need for qualified information security professionals to secure our systems, networks, and infrastructures.

Fundamentals of Information Systems Security represents (ISC)^2's commitment to providing guidance and support to the information security field through exciting new educational offerings. The information provided in this book highlights the seven domains of (ISC)^2's Systems Security Certified Practitioner (SSCP®) certification: Access Controls; Cryptography; Malicious Code and Activity; Monitoring and Analysis; Networks and Communications; Risk, Response and Recovery; and Security Operations and Administration.

The SSCP is a deeply technical certification, requiring a minimum one year of technical work experience before candidates are able to sit for the examination. Considered an entry-level certification, the SSCP is desirable for those looking to embed the first footprint on their information security career path. SSCPs are often considered the "go-to" practitioners in demanding technical positions such as network security engineers, security systems analysts, and security administrators; however, they also encompass non-security disciplines that require an understanding of security but do not have information security as a primary part of their job description. Due to rapidly emerging technologies, the domains of the SSCP will continue to evolve, which is why it's important to remain vigilant about continuing education throughout your career.

When it comes to educating and certifying information security professionals throughout their careers, (ISC)^2 is acknowledged as the global, not-for-profit leader. We have an elite network of over 72,000 information security professionals worldwide and a reputation built on trust and integrity which has earned our certifications and world-class educational programs recognition as the gold standard of the industry.

Both education and certification create a framework for a successful career in this industry. According to the *2009 Certification Magazine Salary Survey*, with support from (ISC)^2, SSCPs reported earning an average annual base salary of $97,860 in the U.S. A full 96 percent of respondents from the top five countries with the highest salaries said they were certified. Around 47 percent said they think their most recently earned certification played a role in them getting a raise, and more than 85 percent of respondents agreed that since they've become certified, there is a greater demand for their skills.

In closing, let me again thank you for taking this initial step toward a very exciting and rewarding career in information security. I invite you to look to our organization, (ISC)^2, when you are ready to validate your knowledge and experience by obtaining the gold standard of information security certifications.

Be sure to test your knowledge by taking the SSCP practice exam at the end of the book. A tuition grant of \$1,000 toward an SSCP CBK® Review Seminar is available to all students who are enrolled in this course.

I wish you the best of luck in this course and in your future information security career.

Sincerely,

W. Hord Tipton, CISSP-ISSEP, CAP, CISA
Executive Director, (ISC)^2
www.isc2.org

Preface

Purpose of This Book

This book is part of the Information Systems Security & Assurance Series (ISSA) from Jones & Bartlett Learning (*www.jblearning.com*). Designed for courses and curriculums in IT Security, Cybersecurity, Information Assurance, and Information Systems Security, this series features a comprehensive, consistent treatment of the most current thinking and trends in this critical subject area. These titles deliver fundamental information security principles packed with real-world applications and examples. Authored by Certified Information Systems Security Professionals (CISSPs), they deliver comprehensive information on all aspects of information security. Reviewed word for word by leading technical experts in the field, these books are not just current, but forward-thinking—putting you in the position to solve the cybersecurity challenges not just of today, but of tomorrow, as well.

Part 1 of this book on information security fundamentals focuses on new risks, threats, and vulnerabilities associated with the transformation to a digital world. Individuals, students, educators, businesses, organizations, and governments have changed how they communicate and do business. Led by the integration of the Internet and broadband communications into our everyday lives, the digital revolution has created a need for information systems security. With recent compliance laws requiring organizations to protect and secure privacy data and reduce liability, information systems security has never been more recognized than it is now.

Part 2 is adapted from the Official (ISC)^2 SSCP® CBK® Study Guide. It will present a high-level overview of each of the seven domains within the Systems Security Certified Practitioner certification. The SSCP® professional certification requires mastery of the following topics: Access Controls; Cryptography; Malicious Code and Activity; Monitoring and Analysis; Networks and Communications; Risk, Response, and Recovery; and Security Operations and Administration.

Part 3 of this book provides a resource for readers and students desiring more information on information security standards, education, professional certifications, and recent compliance laws. These resources are ideal for students and individuals desiring additional information about educational and career opportunities in information systems security.

Learning Features

The writing style of this book is practical and conversational. Step-by-step examples of information security concepts and procedures are presented throughout the text. Each chapter begins with a statement of learning objectives. Illustrations are used both to clarify the material and to vary the presentation. The text is sprinkled with Notes, Tips, FYIs, Warnings, and sidebars to alert the reader to additional helpful information related to the subject under discussion. Chapter Assessments appear at the end of each chapter, with solutions provided in the back of the book.

Chapter summaries are included in the text to provide a rapid review or preview of the material and to help students understand the relative importance of the concepts presented.

Audience

The material is suitable for undergraduate or graduate computer science majors or information science majors, students at a two-year technical college or community college who have a basic technical background, or readers who have a basic understanding of IT security and want to expand their knowledge.

Acknowledgments

This is the flagship book of the Information Systems Security & Assurance Series (ISSA) from Jones & Bartlett Learning (*www.jblearning.com*). The ISSA Series was designed for IT security and information assurance curriculums and courseware for those colleges and universities needing a hands-on approach to delivering an information systems security and information assurance degree program whose graduates would be ready for the work force.

The entire ISSA series was developed by information systems security professionals, consultants, and recognized leaders in the field of information systems security, all of whom contributed to each word, sentence, paragraph, and chapter. The dedication and perseverance displayed by those involved was driven by a single passion and common goal: "to help educate today's information systems security practitioner" by creating the most up-to-date textbooks, courseware, and hands-on labs to ensure job and skill-set readiness for information systems security practitioners.

Achieving this single passion and common goal involved a collaborative effort with the International Information Systems Security Certification Consortium, Inc. (ISC)^2, to bring the Systems Security Certified Practitioner (SSCP®) Common Body of Knowledge (CBK®) and its seven domains of information systems security responsibility into Part 2 of this book. The seven domains of the SSCP® CBK® encompass what information systems security practitioners must be able to do to implement hands-on security countermeasures in IT infrastructure.

Thank you to Jones & Bartlett Learning for having the vision and patience to underwrite and build the world's best information systems security content and curriculum.

Thank you to (ISC)^2 for recognizing that the SSCP® professional certification is best aligned with programs that incorporate hands-on skills-set readiness aligned to the seven domains of SSCP® CBK.®

Thank you to the many authors, subject matter experts, super subject matter experts, copy editors, development editors, and graphic artists who contributed to this book and entire ISSA Series during the past year of development.

And last but not least, I would like to thank my wife, MiYoung Kim, who is and always will be by my side.

David Kim

I would like to thank Kate Shoup for providing pertinent editorial comments and for helping to fine tune the book's content, and Lawrence Goodrich and Ruth Walker for all your input, work, and patience. All of you made the process so much easier and added a lot to the book. And thanks so much to Stacey and Noah for your help in researching the many diverse topics.

Michael G. Solomon

About the Authors

DAVID KIM (CISSP) is president of Security Evolutions, LLC (*www.SecurityEvolutions.com*), and chief technology officer for vLab Solutions, LLC (*www.vLabSolutions.com*), both located in Tarpon Springs, Florida. Security Evolutions provides IT security training and consulting services for organizations around the world. Security Evolutions has specific expertise and experience in VoIP and SIP layered security solutions where privacy data may encompass both data and voice communications. vLab Solutions is a leading designer and developer of performance-outcome-based, hands-on labs for educational, training, and professional certification requirements. vLearning Cloud,™ vLabSolution's hands-on online labs environment, provides students with secure browser access to complete the lab exercise from a virtual workstation. Mr. Kim's IT and IT security experience encompasses more than 25 years of technical engineering, technical management, and solutions selling and sales management. This experience includes LAN/WAN, internetworking, enterprise network management, and IT security for voice, video, and data networking infrastructures. Previously, Mr. Kim was chief operating officer of the $(ISC)^2$ Institute located in Vienna, Virginia, where he was responsible for content development, educational products, and educational delivery for $(ISC)^2$ (*www.isc2.org*) and its IT security professional certifications.

MICHAEL G. SOLOMON (CISSP, PMP, CISM, GSEC) is a full-time security speaker, consultant, and author, and a former college instructor who specializes in development and assessment security topics. As an IT professional and consultant since 1987, he has worked on projects for more than 100 major companies and organizations. From 1998 until 2001, he was an instructor in the Kennesaw State University Computer Science and Information Sciences (CSIS) department, where he taught courses on software project management, C++ programming, computer organization and architecture, and data communications. Solomon holds an MS in mathematics and computer science from Emory University (1998), a BS in computer science from Kennesaw State University (1987), and is currently pursuing a PhD in computer science and informatics at Emory University. He has also contributed to various security certification books for LANWrights, including *TICSA Training Guide* (Que, 2002) and an accompanying *Instructor Resource Kit* (Que, 2002), *CISSP Study Guide* (Sybex, 2003), as well as *Security+ Training Guide* (Que, 2003). Solomon coauthored *Information Security Illuminated* (Jones and Bartlett, 2005), *Security+ Lab Guide* (Sybex, 2005), *Computer Forensics JumpStart* (Sybex, 2005), *PMP ExamCram2* (Que, 2005), and authored and provided the on-camera delivery of LearnKey's CISSP Prep and PMP Prep e-Learning courses.

PART ONE

The Need for Information Security

CHAPTER 1

Information Systems Security

THE INTERNET HAS CHANGED DRAMATICALLY from its origins. It has grown from a small number of universities and government agencies to a worldwide network with more than two billion users. As it has grown, it has changed how people communicate and do business. It has brought many opportunities and benefits. The Internet continues to grow and expand in new and varied ways. It supports innovation and new services. Like outer space, the maturing Internet is a new frontier. There is no Internet government or central authority. It is full of challenges—and questionable behavior.

The Internet as we know it today has its roots in a computer network called the Advanced Research Projects Agency Network (ARPANET), which the U.S. Department of Defense created in 1969. But the way people use the Internet is new. Today, people working in cyberspace must deal with new and constantly evolving threats. Intelligent and aggressive cybercriminals, terrorists, and scam artists lurk in the shadows. Connecting your computers or devices to the Internet immediately exposes them to attack. These attacks result in frustration and hardship. Anyone whose personal information has been stolen can attest to that. Worse, attacks on computers and networked devices are a threat to the national economy, which depends on **e-commerce**. Even more important, cyberattacks threaten national security. For example, terrorist attackers could shut down electricity grids and disrupt military communication.

You can make a difference. The world needs people who understand computer-systems security and who can protect computers and networks from criminals and terrorists. To get you started, this first chapter gives an overview of information systems security concepts and terms that you must understand to stop these attacks.

Chapter 1 Topics

This chapter covers the following topics and concepts:

- What information systems security is
- What the tenets of information systems security are
- What the seven domains of an IT infrastructure are
- What the weakest link in an IT infrastructure is
- How an IT security policy framework can reduce risk
- How a data classification standard affects an IT infrastructure's security needs

Chapter 1 Goals

When you complete this chapter, you will be able to:

- Relate how availability, integrity, and confidentiality requirements affect the seven domains of a typical IT infrastructure
- Describe the threats and vulnerabilities commonly found within the seven domains
- Identify a layered security approach throughout the seven domains
- Develop an IT security policy framework to help reduce risk from common threats and vulnerabilities
- Relate how a data classification standard affects the seven domains

Information Systems Security

Today's **Internet** is a worldwide network with more than two billion users. It includes almost every government, business, and organization on Earth. Just having that many users on the same network wouldn't have been enough to make the Internet a game-changing innovation, however. These users needed some type of mechanism to link documents and resources across computers. In other words, a user on computer A needed an easy way to open a document on computer B. This need gave rise to a system that defines how documents and resources are related across network machines. The name of this system is the **World Wide Web (WWW)**. You may know it as **cyberspace**, or simply as the Web. Think of it this way: The Internet links communication networks to one another. The Web is the connection of Web sites, Web pages, and digital content on those networked computers. Cyberspace is all the users, networks, Web pages, and applications working in this worldwide electronic realm.

FIGURE 1-1

Cyberspace: the new frontier.

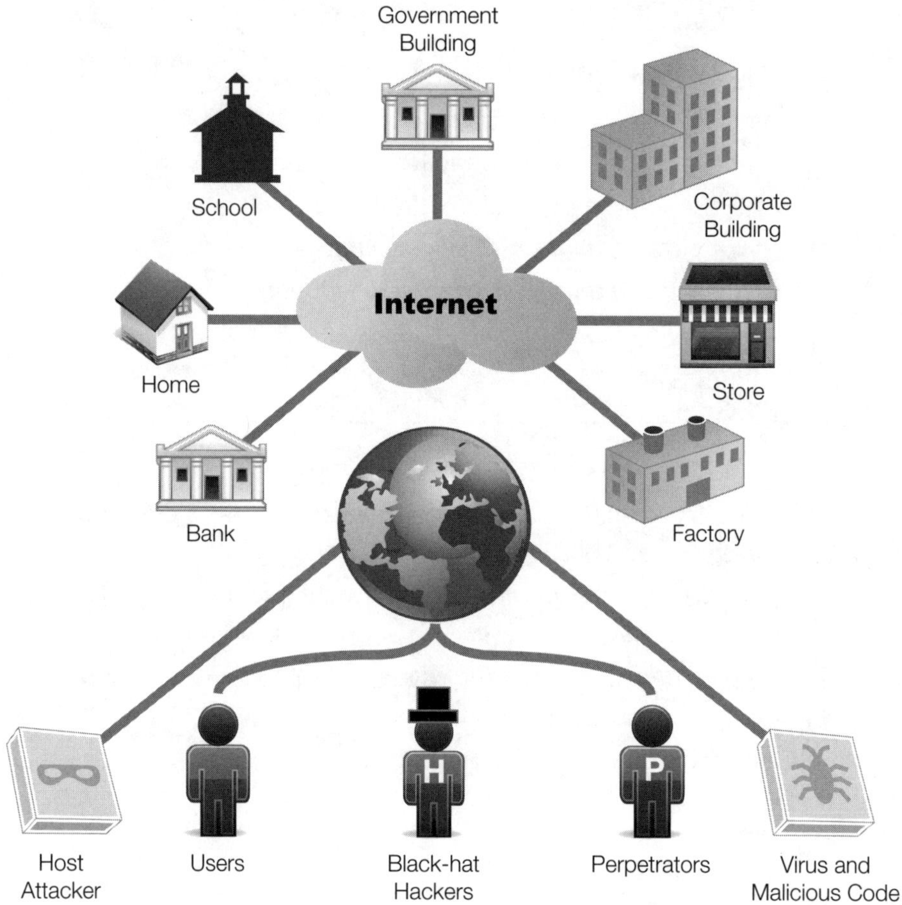

Unfortunately, when you connect to cyberspace, you also open the door to a lot of bad guys. They want to find you and steal your data. Every computer that connects to the Internet is at risk. All users must defend their information from attackers. **Cybersecurity** is the duty of every government that wants to ensure its national security. It's the responsibility of every organization that needs to protect its information. And it's the job of each of us to protect our own data. Figure 1-1 illustrates this new frontier.

The components that make up cyberspace are not automatically secure. These include cabling, physical networks, operating systems, and software applications that computers use to connect to the Internet. At the heart of the problem is the lack of security in the TCP/IP communications protocol. This protocol is the language that computers most commonly use when communicating across the Internet. (A **protocol** is a list of rules and methods for communicating.) TCP/IP is really more than just one protocol. It consists of two protocols, **Transmission Control Protocol (TCP)** and **Internet Protocol (IP)**, that work together to allow any two computers to communicate using a network. TCP/IP, as these two protocols are known collectively, breaks messages into chunks, or packets, to send to another networked computer. The problem is that data is readable within the IP packet. This readable mode is known as **cleartext.** That means you must hide or encrypt the data sent inside a TCP/IP packet to make it more secure. Figure 1-2 shows the data within the TCP/IP packet structure.

All this raises the question: If the Internet is so unsafe, why did everyone connect to it so rapidly? The answer is the huge growth of the Web from the mid 1990s to the early 2000s. Connecting to the Internet gave anyone instant access to the Web and its many resources. The appeal of easy worldwide connectivity drove the demand to connect. This demand and subsequent growth helped drive costs lower for high-speed communications. Households, businesses, and governments gained affordable high-speed Internet access. And as wireless connections have become more common and affordable, it has become easier to stay connected no matter where you are.

Internet growth has also been driven by generational differences. **Generation Y**'s culture is taking over as baby boomers begin to retire. This new generation grew up with cell phones, **smartphones**, and "always on" Internet access. These devices provide real-time communications. Today's personal communications include voice over IP (VoIP), text messaging, and instant messaging (IM), or chatting, as well as audio and video conferencing.

FIGURE 1-2

TCP/IP communications are in cleartext.

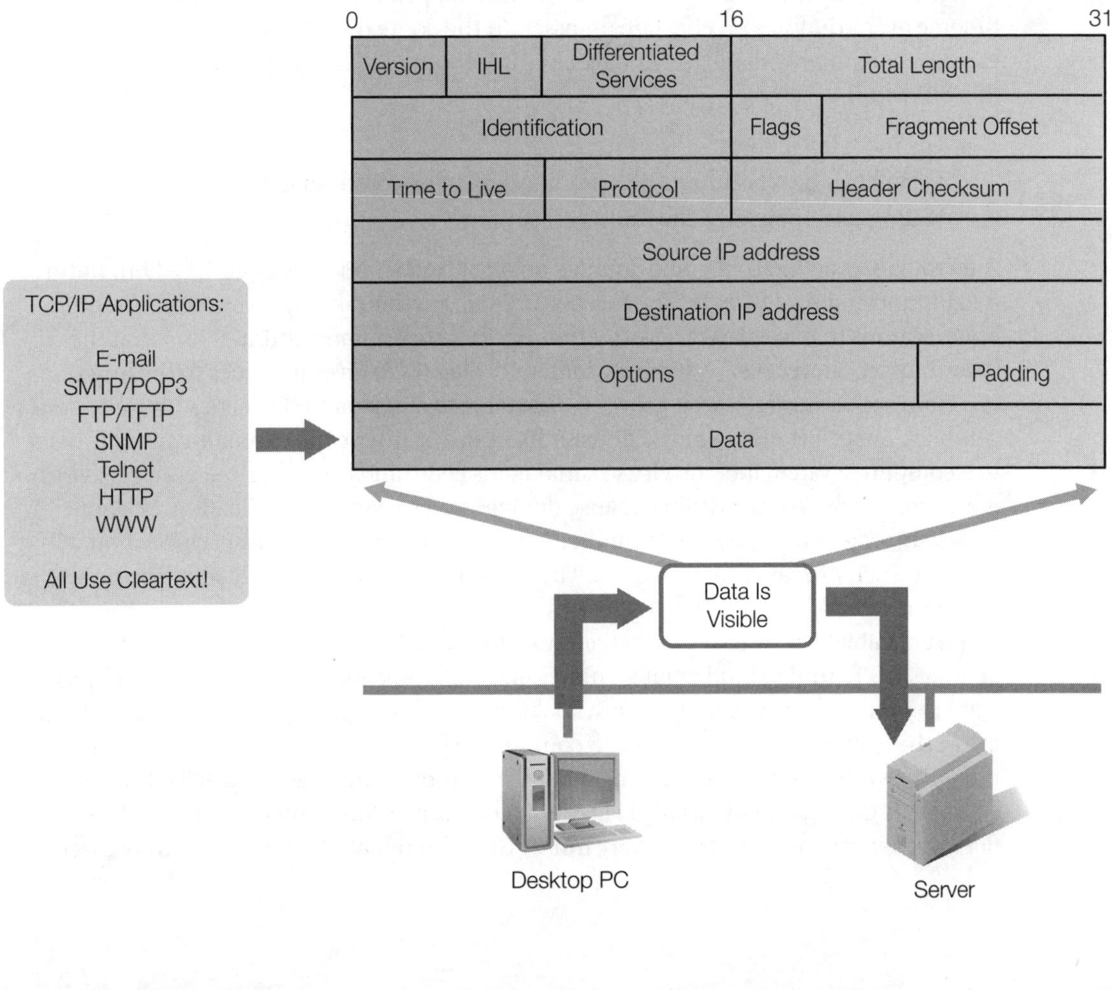

Cyberspace is the new place to meet, socialize, and share ideas. You can chat with friends, family, business contacts, and people from everywhere. But there's a danger: You don't really know who the person at the other end is. Liars and thieves can easily hide their identity. While cyberspace gives you fingertip access to people and information, it also brings along many risks and threats.

An **information security** war is raging. The battlefield is cyberspace and the enemies are already within the gates. To make matters worse, the enemy is everywhere—both in the local area and around the world. Because of this, IT is in great need of proper security controls. This need has created a great demand for information security professionals. The goal is to both protect national security and business information from the enemy.

Risks, Threats, and Vulnerabilities

This book introduces the dangers of cyberspace and discusses how to address those dangers. It explains how to identify and combat the dangers common in **information systems** and IT infrastructures. To understand how to make computers more secure, you first need to understand risks, threats, and vulnerabilities.

Risk is the likelihood that something bad will happen to an asset. It is the exposure to some event that has an effect on an asset. In the context of IT security, an asset can be a computer, a database, or a piece of information. Examples of risk include the following:

- Losing data
- Losing business because a disaster has destroyed your building
- Failing to comply with laws and regulations

A **threat** is any action that could damage an asset. Information systems face both natural and human-induced threats. The threats of flood, earthquake, or severe storms require organizations to have plans to ensure that business operation continues and that the organization can recover. A **business continuity plan (BCP)** gives priorities to the functions an organization needs to keep going. A **disaster recovery plan (DRP)** defines how a business gets back on its feet after a major disaster like a fire or hurricane. Human-caused threats to a computer system include viruses, malicious code, and unauthorized access. A **virus** is a computer program written to cause damage to a system, an application, or data. **Malicious code** or malware is a computer program written to cause a specific action to occur, such as erasing a hard drive. These threats can harm an individual, business, or organization.

A **vulnerability** is a weakness that allows a threat to be realized or to have an effect on an asset. To understand what a vulnerability is, think about lighting a fire. Lighting a fire is not necessarily bad. If you are cooking a meal on a grill, you will need to light a fire in the grill. The grill is designed to contain the fire and should pose no danger if used properly. On the other hand, lighting a fire in a computer data center will likely cause damage. A grill is not vulnerable to fire, but a computer data center is. A threat by itself does not always cause damage; there must be a vulnerability for a threat to be realized.

End User Licensing Agreements (EULAs)

EULAs are license agreements between the user and the software vendor. They protect the software vendor from claims arising from imperfect software. EULAs typically contain a warranty disclaimer. This limits their liability from software bugs and weaknesses that hackers can exploit.

Here is an excerpt from Microsoft's EULA that states the company offers only "limited" warranties for its software. The EULA also advises that the software product is offered "as is and with all faults."

"**DISCLAIMER OF WARRANTIES**. THE LIMITED WARRANTY THAT APPEARS ABOVE IS THE ONLY EXPRESS WARRANTY MADE TO YOU AND IS PROVIDED IN LIEU OF ANY OTHER EXPRESS WARRANTIES (IF ANY) CREATED BY ANY DOCUMENTATION OR PACKAGING. EXCEPT FOR THE LIMITED WARRANTY AND TO THE MAXIMUM EXTENT PERMITTED BY APPLICABLE LAW, MICROSOFT AND ITS SUPPLIERS PROVIDE THE SOFTWARE PRODUCT AND SUPPORT SERVICES (IF ANY) AS IS AND WITH ALL FAULTS, AND HEREBY DISCLAIM ALL OTHER WARRANTIES AND CONDITIONS...."

Microsoft's EULA also limits its financial liability to the cost of the software or $5 (U.S.), whichever is greater.

"**LIMITATION OF LIABILITY**. ANY REMEDIES NOTWITHSTANDING ANY DAMAGES THAT YOU MIGHT INCUR FOR ANY REASON WHATSOEVER (INCLUDING, WITHOUT LIMITATION, ALL DAMAGES REFERENCED ABOVE AND ALL DIRECT OR GENERAL DAMAGES), THE ENTIRE LIABILITY OF MICROSOFT AND ANY OF ITS SUPPLIERS UNDER ANY PROVISION OF THIS EULA AND YOUR EXCLUSIVE REMEDY FOR ALL OF THE FOREGOING (EXCEPT FOR ANY REMEDY OF REPAIR OR REPLACEMENT ELECTED BY MICROSOFT WITH RESPECT TO ANY BREACH OF THE LIMITED WARRANTY) SHALL BE LIMITED TO THE GREATER OF THE AMOUNT ACTUALLY PAID BY YOU FOR THE SOFTWARE PRODUCT OR U.S.$5.00. THE FOREGOING LIMITATIONS, EXCLUSIONS AND DISCLAIMERS (INCLUDING SECTIONS 9, 10 AND 11 ABOVE) SHALL APPLY TO THE MAXIMUM EXTENT PERMITTED BY APPLICABLE LAW, EVEN IF ANY REMEDY FAILS ITS ESSENTIAL PURPOSE."

Vulnerabilities can often result in legal liabilities. Any vulnerability that allows a threat to be realized may result in legal action. Since computers must run software to be useful, and since humans write software, software programs have errors. Thus, software vendors must protect themselves from the liabilities of their own vulnerabilities with an **end user licensing agreement (EULA)**. A EULA takes effect when the user opens the package and installs the software.

All software vendors use EULAs. That means the burden of protecting data falls on systems security professionals.

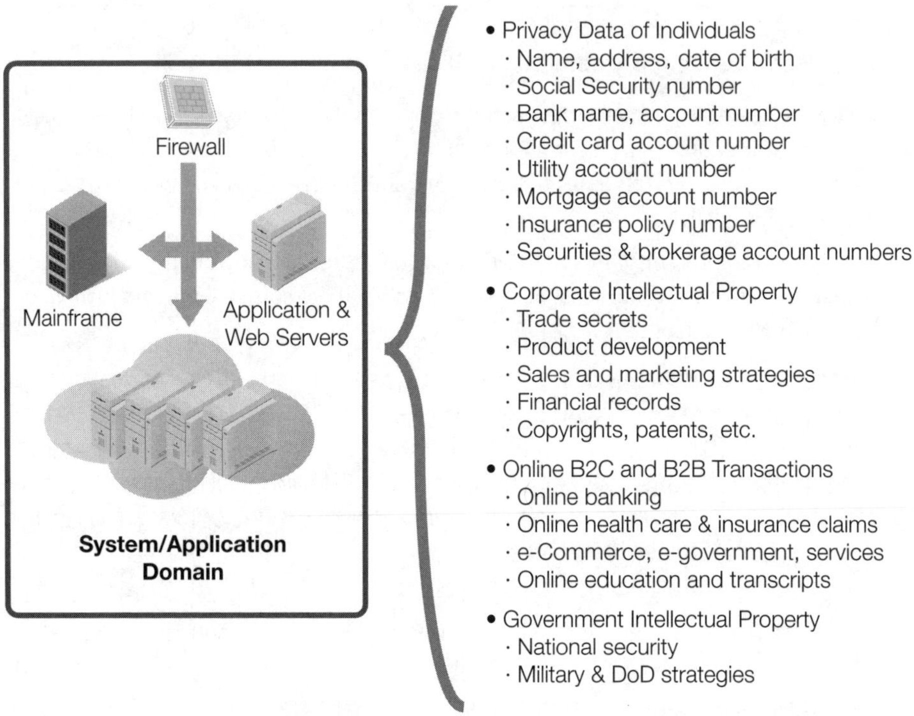

FIGURE 1-3 What are we securing?

Defining Information Systems Security

Security is easiest to define by breaking it into pieces. An information system consists of the hardware, operating system, and application software that work together to collect, process, and store data for individuals and organizations. **Information systems security** is the collection of activities that protect the information system and the data stored in it. Many U.S. and international laws now require this kind of security assurance. Organizations must address this need head-on. Figure 1-3 reviews the types of information commonly found within an IT infrastructure.

U.S. Compliance Laws Drive Need for Information Systems Security

Cyberspace brings new threats to people and organizations. People need to protect their privacy. Businesses and organizations are responsible for protecting both their intellectual property and any personal or private data they handle. Various laws require organizations to use security controls to protect private and confidential data. Recent U.S. laws related to information security include the following:

- **Federal Information Security Management Act (FISMA)**—Passed in 2002, the **Federal Information Security Management Act (FISMA)** requires federal civilian agencies to provide security controls over resources that support federal operations.

- **Sarbanes-Oxley Act (SOX)**—Passed in 2002, the **Sarbanes-Oxley Act (SOX)** requires publicly traded companies to submit accurate and reliable financial reporting. This law does not require securing private information, but it does require security controls to protect the confidentiality and integrity of the reporting itself.
- **Gramm-Leach-Bliley Act (GLBA)**—Passed in 1999, the **Gramm-Leach-Bliley Act (GLBA)** requires all types of financial institutions to protect customers' private financial information.
- **Health Insurance Portability and Accountability Act (HIPAA)**—Passed in 1996, the **Health Insurance Portability and Accountability Act (HIPAA)** requires health care organizations to secure patient information.
- **Children's Internet Protection Act (CIPA)**—Passed in 2000, the **Children's Internet Protection Act (CIPA)** requires public schools and public libraries to use an Internet safety policy. The policy must address the following:
  - Children's access to inappropriate matter on the Internet
  - Children's security when using e-mail, chat rooms, and other electronic communications
  - Restricting hacking and other unlawful activities by children online
  - Disclosing and distributing personal information about children without permission
  - Restricting children's access to harmful materials
- **Family Educational Rights and Privacy Act (FERPA)**—Passed in 1974, the **Family Educational Rights and Privacy Act (FERPA)** protects the private data of students and their school records.

You can find out more about these laws in Chapter 15. Figure 1-4 shows these laws by industry.

FIGURE 1-4

U.S. compliance laws drive the need for information systems security.

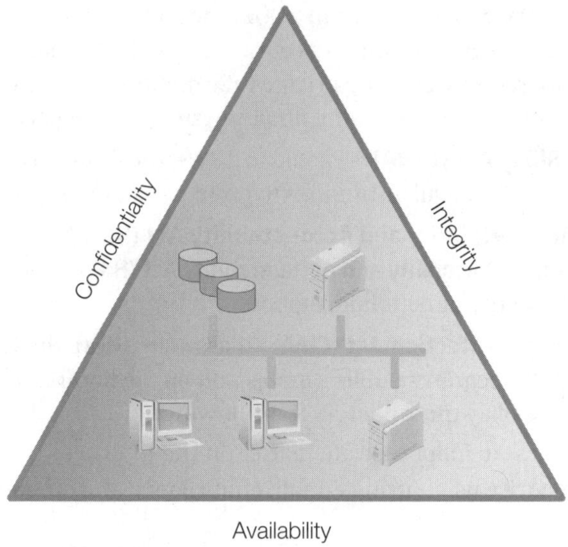

FIGURE 1-5

The three tenets of information systems security.

Tenets of Information Systems Security

Most people agree that private information should be secure. But what does "secure information" really mean? Information that is secure satisfies three main tenets, or properties, of information. If you can ensure these three tenets, you satisfy the requirements of secure information. The three tenets are as follows:

- **Availability**—Information is accessible by authorized users whenever they request the information.
- **Integrity**—Only authorized users can change information.
- **Confidentiality**—Only authorized users can view information.

Figure 1-5 shows the three tenets of information systems security. When you design and use security controls, you are addressing one or more of these tenets.

When finding solutions to security issues, you must use the A-I-C triad. You have to define and achieve your organization's goals for this triad in a typical IT infrastructure's seven domains. Once defined, these goals help you put security controls in place as required for your different types of data.

technical TIP

Some systems security professionals refer to the tenets as the C-I-A triad, but that can lead to confusion with the U.S. Central Intelligence Agency, commonly known as the CIA.

Availability

Availability is a common term in everyday life. For example, you probably pay attention to the availability of your satellite TV service, your cell phone service, or a business colleague for a meeting. In the context of information security, availability is generally expressed as the amount of time users can use a system, application, and data. Common availability time measurements include the following:

- **Uptime**—The total amount of time that a system, application, and data is accessible. **Uptime** is typically measured in units of seconds, minutes, and hours within a given calendar month.
- **Downtime**—The total amount of time that a system, application, and data is not accessible. **Downtime** also is measured in units of seconds, minutes, and hours for a calendar month.
- **Availability**—A math calculation where A = (Total Uptime) / (Total Uptime + Total Downtime).
- **Mean time to failure (MTTF)**—**Mean time to failure (MTTF)** is the average amount of time between failures for a particular system. Semiconductors and electronics do not break and have a MTTF of many years (25+ years, etc.). Physical parts such as connectors, cabling, fans, and power supplies have a much lower MTTF (five years or less) given that wear and tear can break them.
- **Mean time to repair (MTTR)**—**Mean time to repair (MTTR)** is the average amount of time it takes to repair a system, application, or component. The goal is to bring the system back up quickly.
- **Recovery time objective (RTO)**—**Recovery time objective (RTO)** is the amount of time it takes to recover and make a system, application, and data available for use after an outage. Business continuity plans typically define an RTO for mission-critical systems, applications, and data access.

How to Measure Availability

For a given 30-day calendar month, the total amount of uptime equals:

30 days × 24 hours/day × 60 minutes/hour = 43,200 minutes

For a 28-day calendar month (February), the total amount of uptime equals:

28 days × 24 hours/day × 60 minutes/hour = 40,320 minutes

Using the formula Availability = (Total Uptime) / (Total Uptime + Total Downtime), calculate the Availability factor for a 30-day calendar month with 30 minutes of scheduled downtime in that calendar month:

Availability = (43,200 minutes) / (43,200 minutes + 30 minutes) = .9993 or 99.93%

Telecommunications companies offer their customers **service level agreements (SLAs)**. An SLA is a contract that guarantees a minimum monthly availability of service for wide area network (WAN) and Internet access links. SLAs accompany WAN services and dedicated Internet access links. Availability measures a monthly uptime service level commitment. As in the preceding example, 30 minutes of downtime in a given 30-day calendar month equates to 99.993 percent availability. Service providers typically offer SLAs ranging from 99.5 percent to 99.999 percent availability.

Integrity

Integrity deals with the validity and accuracy of data. Data lacking integrity—that is, data that is not accurate or not valid—is of no use. For some organizations, data and information are intellectual property assets. Examples include copyrights, patents, secret formulas, and customer databases. This information can have great value. Unauthorized changes can undermine the data's value. This is why integrity is a tenet of systems security. Figure 1-6 shows what is meant by data integrity and whether that data is usable. Sabotage and corruption of data integrity is a serious threat to an organization, especially if the data is critical to business operations.

Confidentiality

Confidentiality is a common term. It means guarding information from everyone except those with rights to it. Confidential information includes the following:

- Private data of individuals
- Intellectual property of businesses
- National security for countries and governments

U.S. compliance laws require organizations to have controls to keep data private.

FIGURE 1-6
Data integrity.

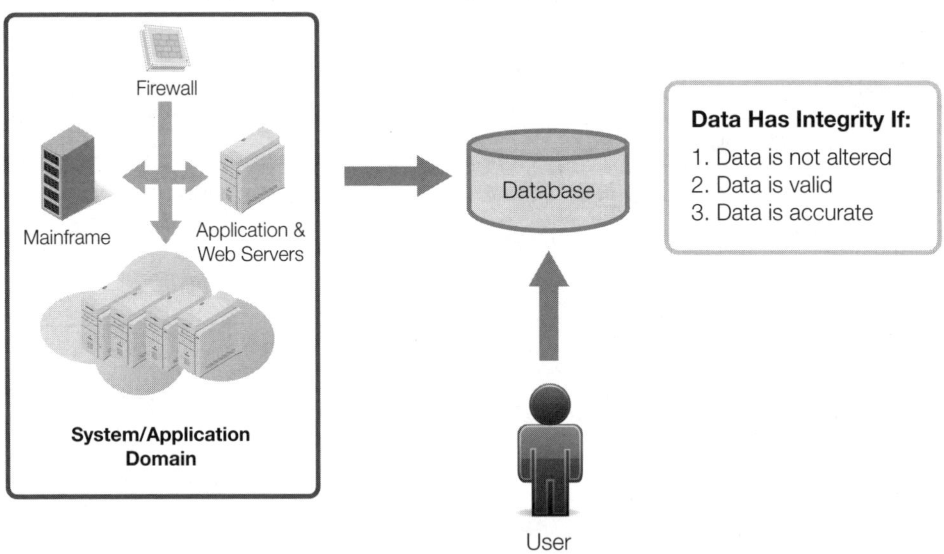

Identity Theft

Identity theft affects about 10 million U.S. citizens each year. It is a major threat to American consumers. Many elements make up a person's identity. These include but are not limited to the following:

- Full name
- Mailing address
- Date of birth
- Social Security number
- Bank name
- Bank account number
- Credit card account number
- Utility account number
- Mortgage account number
- Insurance policy number
- Securities and investment account numbers

An impostor can access your accounts with just your name, home address, and Social Security number.

This threat extends beyond just financial loss. Identity theft can damage your **FICO** personal credit rating. This would stop you from getting a bank loan, mortgage, or credit card. It can take years to clean up your personal credit history. FICO is a publicly traded company that provides information used by Equifax, Experian, and TransUnion, the three largest consumer credit reporting agencies in the United States.

With the growth in e-commerce, more people are making online purchases with credit cards. This requires people to enter private data into e-commerce Web sites. Consumers should be careful to protect their personal identity and private data.

Laws require organizations to use security controls to protect customers' private data. A security control is something an organization does to help reduce risk. Examples of controls include the following:

- Conducting annual security awareness training for employees. This helps remind staff about proper handling of private data. It also drives awareness of the organization's framework of security policies, standards, procedures, and guidelines.
- Putting an **IT security policy framework** in place. This outline is like an instruction manual for security controls.
- Designing a layered security solution for an IT infrastructure. The more layers or compartments that block or protect private data and intellectual property, the more difficult it is to find and steal.

- Performing periodic security assessments and penetration tests on Web sites and IT infrastructure. This is how security professionals verify that they have installed the controls properly.
- Enabling security monitoring at your Internet entry and exit points. This is like using a microscope to see what is coming in and going out.
- Using automated workstation and server antivirus and malicious software protection. This is the way to keep viruses and malicious software out of your computer.
- Using more stringent access controls beyond a logon ID and password for sensitive systems, applications, and data. Logon IDs with passwords are only one check of the user. Access to more sensitive systems should have a second test to confirm the user's identity.
- Minimizing software weaknesses in your computers and servers by updating them with patches and security fixes. This is the way to keep your operating system and application software up to date.

Protecting private data is the process of ensuring data confidentiality. Organizations must use proper security controls specific to this concern. Some examples include the following:

- Defining organization-wide policies, standards, procedures, and guidelines to protect confidential data. These are instructions for how to handle private data.
- Adopting a **data classification standard** that defines how to treat data throughout your IT infrastructure. This is the road map for identifying what controls are needed to keep data safe.
- Limiting access to systems and applications that house confidential data to only those authorized to use it.
- Using cryptography techniques to hide confidential data to keep it invisible to unauthorized users.
    - Encrypting data that crosses the public Internet.
    - Encrypting data that is stored within databases and storage devices.

Sending data to other computers using a network means you have to take special steps to keep confidential data from unauthorized users. **Cryptography** is the practice of hiding data and keeping it away from unauthorized users. **Encryption** is the process of transforming data from cleartext into **ciphertext**. Cleartext data is data that anyone can read. Ciphertext is the scrambled data that is the result of encrypting cleartext. An example of this is in Figure 1-7.

Data privacy is so important that local and state governments are starting to pass laws to protect it by extending federal laws.

WARNING

Never enter private data in an e-mail in cleartext. Remember, e-mail traffic transmits through the Internet in cleartext. Also, never enter private data in a Web site if it is not a trusted host that can be checked by telephone or other means. Never enter private data into a Web site or Web application that does not use encryption.

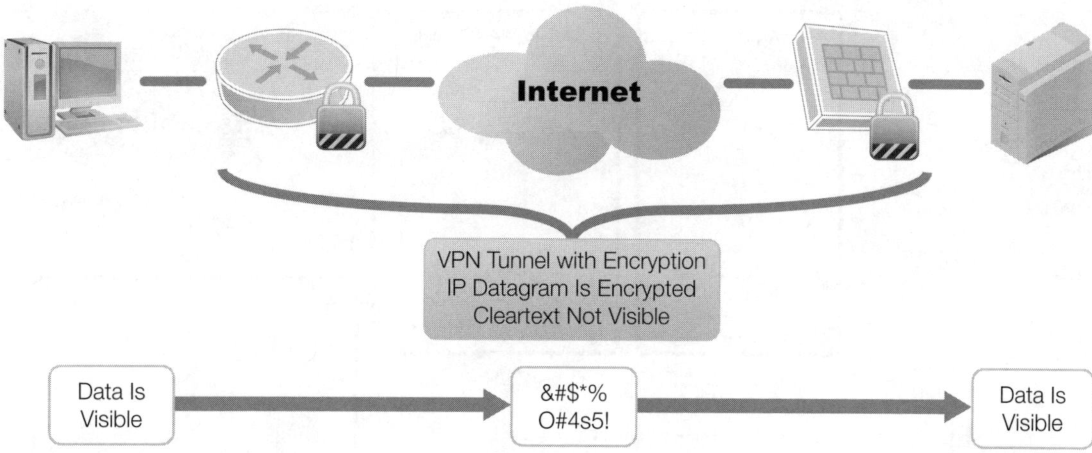

FIGURE 1-7
Encryption of cleartext into ciphertext.

The Seven Domains of a Typical IT Infrastructure

What role do the three tenets of systems security play in a typical IT infrastructure? First, let's review what a typical IT infrastructure looks like. Whether in a small business, large government body, or publicly traded corporation, most IT infrastructures consist of the seven domains shown in Figure 1-8.

A typical IT infrastructure usually has these seven domains. Each one requires proper security controls. These controls must meet the requirements of the A-I-C triad. The following is an overview of the seven domains, and the risks, threats, and vulnerabilities you will commonly find in today's IT environments.

User Domain

The User Domain defines the people who access an organization's information system.

User Domain Roles, Responsibilities, and Accountability

Here's an overview of what should go on in the User Domain:

- **Roles and tasks**—Users can access systems, applications, and data depending upon their defined access rights. Employees must conform to the staff manual and policies. The User Domain is where you will find an **acceptable use policy (AUP)**. An AUP defines what users are allowed to do with organization-owned IT assets. It's like a rulebook that employees must follow. Violation of these rules can be grounds for dismissal. This is where the first layer of defense starts for a layered security strategy.
- **Responsibilities**—Employees are responsible for their use of IT assets. New legislation means that for most organizations it's a best practice to introduce an AUP. Organizations may require staff, contractors, or other third parties to sign an agreement to keep information confidential. Some require a criminal background check for sensitive positions. The department manager or human resources manager is usually in charge of making sure employees sign and follow an AUP.

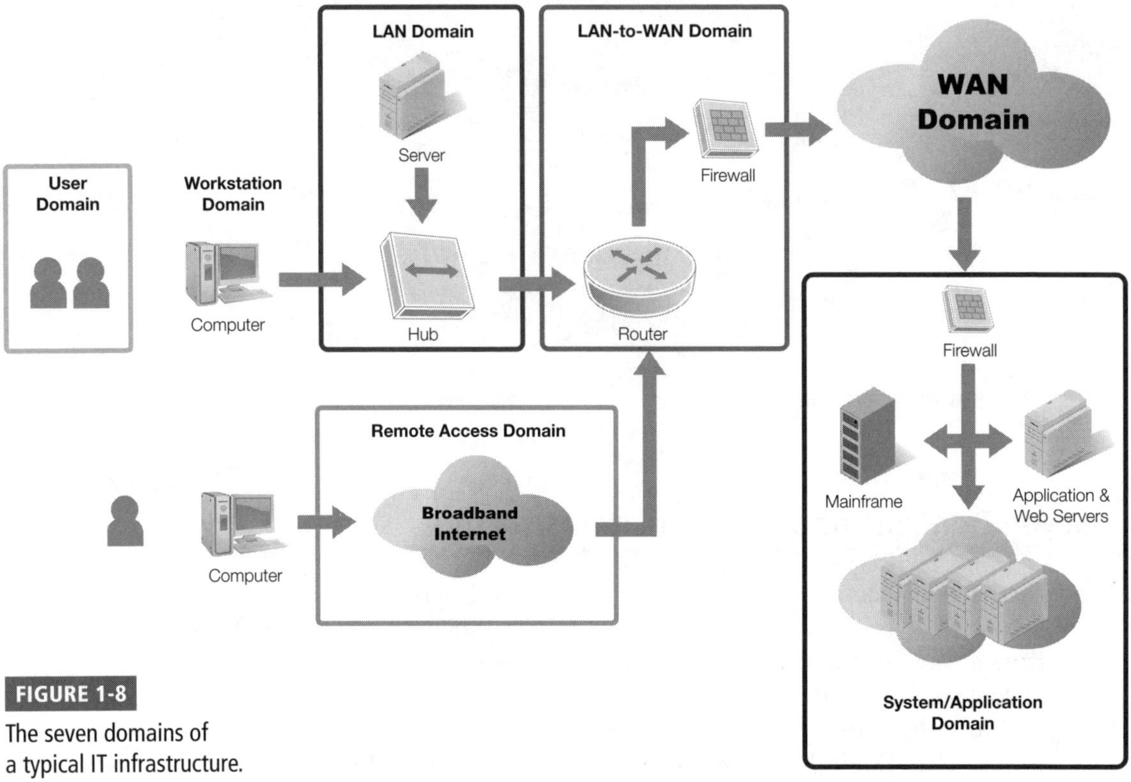

FIGURE 1-8
The seven domains of a typical IT infrastructure.

- **Accountability**—The human resources department must verify an employee's identity before allowing use of the company's computer system. HR must do background checks of any candidate for a job with access to sensitive computer information.

Risks, Threats, and Vulnerabilities Commonly Found in the User Domain

The User Domain is the weakest link in an IT infrastructure. Anyone responsible for computer security must understand what motivates someone to compromise an organization's system, applications, or data. Table 1-1 lists the risks and threats commonly found in the User Domain and plans you can use to prevent them.

TABLE 1-1 Risks, threats, vulnerabilities, and mitigation plans for the User Domain.

RISK, THREAT, OR VULNERABILITY	MITIGATION
Lack of user awareness	Conduct security awareness training, display security awareness posters, insert reminders in banner greetings, and send e-mail reminders to employees.
User apathy toward policies	Conduct annual security awareness training, implement acceptable use policy, update staff manual and handbook, discuss during performance reviews.
Security policy violations	Place employee on probation, review AUP and employee manual, discuss during performance reviews.
User inserts CDs and USB drives with personal photos, music, and videos.	Disable internal CD drives and USB ports. Enable automatic antivirus scans for inserted media drives, files, and e-mail attachments. An antivirus scanning system examines all new files on your computer's hard drive for viruses. Set up antivirus scanning for e-mails with attachments.
User downloads photos, music, and videos.	Enable **content filtering** and antivirus scanning for e-mail attachments. Content-filtering network devices are configured to permit or deny specific domain names in accordance with AUP definition.
User destruction of systems, applications, or data	Restrict access for users to only those systems, applications, and data needed to perform their job. Minimize write/delete permissions to the data owner only.
Disgruntled employee attacks the organization or commits sabotage.	Track and monitor abnormal employee behavior, erratic job performance, and use of IT infrastructure during off-hours. Begin IT access control lockout procedures based on AUP monitoring and compliance.
Employee romance gone bad	Track and monitor abnormal employee behavior and use of IT infrastructure during off-hours. Begin IT access control lockout procedures based on AUP monitoring and compliance.
Employee blackmail or extortion	Track and monitor abnormal employee behavior and use of IT infrastructure during off-hours. Enable **intrusion detection system/intrusion prevention system (IDS/IPS)** monitoring for sensitive employee positions and access. IDS/IPS security appliances examine the IP data streams for inbound and outbound traffic. Alarms and alerts programmed within an IDS/IPS help identify abnormal traffic and can block IP traffic as per policy definition.

Workstation Domain

The Workstation Domain is where most users connect to the IT infrastructure. A workstation can be a desktop computer, laptop computer, or any other device that connects to your network. Other devices might include a **personal data assistant (PDA)**, a smartphone, or a special-purpose terminal. You can find more details about mobile devices in the "Remote Access Domain" section.

Workstation Domain Roles, Responsibilities, and Accountability

Here's an overview of what should go on in the Workstation Domain:

- **Roles and tasks**—An organization's staff should have the access necessary to be productive. Tasks include configuring hardware, **hardening** systems, and verifying antivirus files. Hardening a system is the process of ensuring that controls are in place to handle any known threats. Hardening activities include ensuring that all computers have the latest software revisions, security patches, and system configurations. The Workstation Domain also needs additional layers of defense. Another common defense layer is implementing workstation logon IDs and passwords to protect this entry into the IT infrastructure.
- **Responsibilities**—The desktop support group is responsible for the Workstation Domain. Enforcing defined standards is critical to ensuring the integrity of user workstations and data. The IT security personnel must safeguard controls within the Workstation Domain. Human resources must define proper access controls for workers based on their job. IT security personnel then assign access rights to systems, applications, and data based on this definition.
- **Accountability**—The IT desktop manager is accountable for allowing employees the greatest use of their Workstation Domain. The director of IT security is in charge of ensuring that the Workstation Domain conforms to policy.

Risks, Threats, and Vulnerabilities Commonly Found in the Workstation Domain

The Workstation Domain requires tight security and access controls. This is where users first access systems, applications, and data. The Workstation Domain requires a logon ID and password for access. Table 1-2 lists the risks, threats, and vulnerabilities commonly found in the Workstation Domain, along with ways to protect against them.

TABLE 1-2 Risks, threats, vulnerabilities, and mitigation plans for the Workstation Domain.

RISK, THREAT, OR VULNERABILITY	MITIGATION
Unauthorized access to workstation	Enable password protection on workstations for access. Enable auto screen lockout for inactive times.
Unauthorized access to systems, applications, and data	Define strict access control policies, standards, procedures, and guidelines. Implement a second-level test to verify a user's right to gain access.
Desktop or laptop computer operating system software vulnerabilities	Define workstation operating system vulnerability window policy definition. A **vulnerability window** is the gap in time that you leave a computer unpatched with a security update. Start periodic Workstation Domain vulnerability tests to find gaps.
Desktop or laptop application software vulnerabilities and software patch updates	Define a workstation application software vulnerability window policy. Update application software and security patches according to defined policies, standards, procedures, and guidelines.
Viruses, malicious code, or malware infects a user's workstation or laptop computer.	Use workstation antivirus and malicious code policies, standards, procedures, and guidelines. Enable an automated antivirus protection solution that scans and updates individual workstations with proper protection.
User inserts compact disks (CDs), digital video disks (DVDs), or universal serial bus (USB) thumb drive into organization computer.	Deactivate all CD, DVD, and USB ports. Enable automatic antivirus scans for inserted CDs, DVDs, and USB thumb drives that have files.
User downloads photos, music, or videos via the Internet.	Use content filtering and antivirus scanning at Internet entry and exit. Enable workstation auto-scans for all new files and automatic file quarantine for unknown file types.
User violates AUP and creates security risk for the organization's IT infrastructure.	Mandate annual security awareness training for all employees. Set up security awareness campaigns and programs throughout the year.

LAN Domain

A **local area network (LAN)** is a collection of computers connected to one another or to a common connection medium. Network connection mediums can include wires, fiber-optic cables, or radio waves. LANs are generally organized by function or department. Once connected, your computer can access systems, applications, possibly the Internet, and data. The third component in the IT infrastructure is the LAN Domain.

The physical part of the LAN Domain consists of the following:

- **Network interface card (NIC)**—The interface between the computer and the LAN physical media. The **network interface card (NIC)** has a 6-byte Media Access Control (MAC) layer address that serves as the NIC's unique hardware identifier.
- **Ethernet LAN**—LAN solution based on the **IEEE 802.3 CSMA/CD** standard for 10/100/1000Mbps Ethernet networking. **Ethernet** is the most popular LAN standard. Today's LAN standard is the **Institute of Electrical and Electronics Engineers (IEEE)** 802.3 Carrier Sense Multiple Access/Collision Detection (CSMA/CD) specification. Ethernet is available in 10Mbps, 100Mbps, 1Gbps, and 10Gbps speeds.
- **Unshielded twisted-pair cabling**—The workstation cabling that uses RJ-45 connectors and jacks to physically connect to a 100Mbps/1Gbps/10Gbps Ethernet LAN switch.
- **LAN switch**—The device that connects workstations into a physical Ethernet LAN. A switch provides dedicated Ethernet LAN connectivity for workstations and servers. This provides maximum throughput and performance for each workstation. There are two kinds of LAN switches. A **Layer 2 switch** examines the MAC layer address and makes forwarding decisions based on MAC layer address tables. A **Layer 3 switch** examines the network layer address and routes packets based on routing protocol path determination decisions. A Layer 3 switch is the same thing as a router.
- **File server and print server**—High-powered computers that provide file sharing and data storage for users within a department. Print servers support shared printer use within a department.
- **Wireless access point (WAP)**—For **wireless LANs (WLANs)**, radio transceivers are used to transmit IP packets from a WLAN NIC to a **wireless access point (WAP)**. The WAP transmits WLAN signals for mobile laptops to connect. The WAP connects back to the LAN switch using unshielded twisted-pair cabling.

Ethernet switches typically provide 100Mbps or 1Gbps connectivity for each workstation. Ethernet switches are also equipped with modules that support 1Gbps or 10Gbps Ethernet backbone connections. These backbone connections commonly use fiber-optic cabling.

The logical part of the LAN Domain consists of the following:

- **System administration**—Setup of user LAN accounts with logon ID and password access controls (that is, user logon information).
- **Design of directory and file services**—The servers, directories, and folders to which the user can gain access.

- **Configuration of workstation and server TCP/IP software and communication protocols**—IP addressing, **IP default gateway router**, **subnet mask address**, etc. The IP default gateway router acts as the entry/exit to the LAN. The subnet mask address defines the IP network number and IP host number.
- **Design of server disk storage space, backup and recovery of user data**—User can store data files on LAN disk storage areas where data is backed up and archived daily. In the event of data loss or corruption, data files can be recovered from the backed-up files.
- **Design of virtual LANs (VLANs)**—With Layer 2 and Layer 3 LAN switches, you can configure Ethernet ports to be on the same **virtual LAN (VLAN)**, even though they may be connected to different physically connected LANs. This is the same thing as configuring workstations and servers to be on the same Ethernet LAN or broadcast Domain.

Users get access to their department's LAN and other applications according to what their job calls for.

LAN Domain Roles, Responsibilities, and Accountability

Here's an overview of what should go on in the LAN Domain:

- **Roles and tasks**—The LAN Domain includes both physical network components and logical configuration of services for users. Management of the physical components includes:
    - Cabling
    - NIC cards
    - LAN switches
    - Wireless access points (WAPs)

  LAN system administration includes maintaining the master lists of user accounts and access rights. In the LAN Domain, second-level authentication may be required. Second-level proof is like a gate where the user must confirm who he or she is a second time.
- **Responsibilities**—The LAN support group is in charge of the LAN Domain. This includes both the physical component and logical elements. LAN system administrators must maintain and support departments' file and print services and configure access controls for users.
- **Accountability**—The LAN manager's duty is to maximize use and integrity of data within the LAN Domain. The director of IT security must ensure that the LAN Domain conforms to policy.

Risks, Threats, and Vulnerabilities Commonly Found in the LAN Domain

The LAN Domain also needs strong security and access controls. Users can access company-wide systems, applications, and data from the LAN Domain. This is where the third layer of defense is required. This defense protects the IT infrastructure and the LAN Domain. Table 1-3 lists the risks, threats, and vulnerabilities commonly found in the LAN Domain with appropriate risk-reducing strategies.

TABLE 1-3 Risks, threats, vulnerabilities, and mitigation plans for the LAN Domain.

RISK, THREAT, OR VULNERABILITY	MITIGATION
Unauthorized access to LAN	Make sure wiring closets, data centers, and computer rooms are secure. Do not allow anyone access without proper ID.
Unauthorized access to systems, applications, and data	Define strict access control policies, standards, procedures, and guidelines. Implement second-level identity check to gain access to sensitive systems, applications, and data.
LAN server operating system software vulnerabilities	Define server/desktop/laptop vulnerability window policies, standards, procedures, and guidelines. Conduct periodic LAN Domain vulnerability assessments to find software gaps. A **vulnerability assessment** is a software review that identifies bugs or errors in software. These bugs and errors go away when you upload software patches and fixes.
LAN server application software vulnerabilities and software patch updates	Define a strict **software vulnerability** window policy requiring quick software patching.
Rogue users on WLANs gain unauthorized access.	Use WLAN **network keys** that require a password for wireless access. Turn off broadcasting on WAPs. Require **second-level authentication** prior to granting WLAN access.
Confidentiality of data transmissions via WLAN connections is compromised.	Implement encryption between workstation and WAP to maintain confidentiality.
LAN servers have different hardware, operating systems, and software, making it difficult to manage and troubleshoot.	Implement LAN server and configuration standards, procedures, and guidelines.

LAN-to-WAN Domain

The LAN-to-WAN Domain is where the IT infrastructure links to a wide area network and the Internet. Unfortunately, connecting to the Internet is like rolling out the red carpet for bad guys. The Internet is open, public, and easily accessible by anyone. Most Internet traffic is cleartext. That means it's visible and not private. Network applications use two common transport protocols: Transmission Control Protocol (TCP) and User Datagram Protocol (UDP). Both TCP and UDP use port numbers to identify the application or function; these port numbers function like channels on a TV, which dictate which station you're watching. When a packet is sent via TCP or UDP, its port number appears in the packet header—which essentially reveals what type of packet it is. This is like advertising to the world what you are transmitting.

Examples of common TCP and UDP port numbers include the following:

- **Port 80: Hyper Text Transfer Protocol (HTTP)—Hyper Text Transfer Protocol (HTTP)** is the communications protocol between Web browsers and Web sites with data in cleartext.
- **Port 20: File Transfer Protocol (FTP)—File Transfer Protocol (FTP)** is a protocol for performing file transfers. FTP uses TCP as a connection-oriented data transmission but in cleartext. Connection-oriented means individual packets are numbered and acknowledged as being received to increase integrity of the file transfer.
- **Port 69: Trivial File Transfer Protocol (TFTP)—Trivial File Transfer Protocol (TFTP)** is a protocol for performing file transfers. TFTP utilizes UDP as a connectionless data transmission but in cleartext. This is used for small and quick file transfers given that it does not guarantee individual packet delivery.
- **Port 23: Terminal Network (Telnet)—Telnet** is a network protocol for performing remote terminal access to another device. Telnet uses TCP and sends data in cleartext.
- **Port 22: Secure Shell (SSH)**—This is a network protocol for performing remote terminal access to another device. SSH encrypts the data transmission for maintaining confidentiality of communications.

A complete list of well-known port numbers from 0 to 1023 is maintained by the Internet Assigned Numbers Authority (IANA). The IANA helps coordinate global domain name services, IP addressing, and other resources. Well-known port numbers are on the IANA Web site at this location: *http://www.iana.org/assignments/port-numbers*.

Because the TCP/IP family of protocols lacks security, the need for security controls when dealing with protocols in this family is greater. The LAN-to-WAN Domain represents the fourth layer of defense for a typical IT infrastructure.

LAN-to-WAN Domain Roles, Responsibilities, and Accountability

Here's an overview of what should go on in the LAN-to-WAN Domain:

- **Roles and tasks**—The LAN-to-WAN Domain includes both the physical pieces and logical design of security appliances. It is one of the most complex areas within an IT infrastructure to secure. You need to maintain security while giving users as much access as possible. Physical parts need to be managed to give easy access to the service. The security appliances must be logically configured to adhere to policy definitions.

This will get the most out of availability, ensure data integrity, and maintain confidentiality. The roles and tasks required within the LAN-to-WAN Domain include managing and configuring the following:

- **IP routers**—An IP router is a network device used to transport IP packets to and from the Internet or WAN. Path determination decisions forward IP packets. Configuration tasks include IP routing and access control lists (ACLs). ACLs are used to permit and deny traffic like a filter.
- **IP stateful firewalls**—An **IP stateful firewall** is a security appliance used to filter inbound IP packets based on various ACL definitions configured for IP, TCP, and UDP packet headers. A stateful firewall can examine IP, TCP, or UDP packet headers for filtering.
- **Demilitarized zone (DMZ)**—The **demilitarized zone (DMZ)** is a LAN segment in the LAN-to-WAN Domain that acts as a buffer zone for inbound and outbound IP traffic. External servers such as Web servers, **proxy servers**, and e-mail servers can be placed here for greater isolation and screening of IP traffic.
- **Intrusion detection system (IDS)**—This security appliance examines IP data streams for common attack and malicious intent patterns. IDSs are passive and can be set to trigger an alarm.
- **Intrusion prevention system (IPS)**—An IPS does the same thing as an IDS but can block IP data streams identified as malicious. IPSs can end the actual communication session, filter by source IP addresses, and block access to the targeted host.
- **Proxy servers**—A proxy server acts as a middleman between a workstation and the external target. Traffic goes to the intermediary server acting as the proxy. Data can be analyzed and properly screened before it is allowed into the IT infrastructure.
- **Web content-filter**—This security appliance can prevent content from entering an IT infrastructure based on filtering of domain names or of keywords within domain names.
- **E-mail content-filter and quarantine system**—This security appliance can block content within e-mails or unknown file attachments for proper antivirus screening and quarantining. Upon review, the e-mail and attachments can be forwarded to the user.
- **Internet entry/exit performance monitoring**—This monitoring occurs where the IT infrastructure connects to the Internet through a dedicated Internet access link to maximize availability, and monitor performance and link utilization.

You can find more details about DMZ, IDS, IPS, firewalls, and proxy servers in Chapter 10.

- **Responsibilities**—The network security group is responsible for the LAN-to-WAN Domain. This includes both the physical components and logical elements. Group members are responsible for applying the defined security controls.
- **Accountability**—Your organization's WAN network manager has a duty to manage the LAN-to-WAN Domain. The director of IT security ensures that the LAN-to-WAN Domain security policies, standards, procedures, and guidelines are used.

Risks, Threats, and Vulnerabilities Commonly Found in the LAN-to-WAN Domain

The LAN-to-WAN Domain needs strict security controls given the risks and threats of connecting to the Internet. This domain is where all data travels into and out of the IT infrastructure. The LAN-to-WAN Domain provides Internet access for the entire organization and acts as the entry/exit point for the wide area network (WAN). The LAN-to-WAN Domain is where the fourth layer of defense is required. Table 1-4 lists the risks, threats, and vulnerabilities commonly found in the LAN-to-WAN Domain with appropriate risk-reduction strategies.

TABLE 1-4 Risks, threats, vulnerabilities, and mitigation plans for the LAN-to-WAN Domain.

RISK, THREAT, OR VULNERABILITY	MITIGATION
Unauthorized network probing and port scanning	Disable ping, probing, and port scanning on all exterior IP devices within the LAN-to-WAN Domain. **Ping** uses the Internet Control Message Protocol (ICMP) echo-request and echo-reply protocol. Disallow IP port numbers used for probing and scanning and monitor with IDS/IPS.
Unauthorized access through the LAN-to-WAN Domain	Apply strict security monitoring controls for intrusion detection and prevention. Monitor for inbound IP traffic anomalies and malicious-intent traffic. Block traffic right away if malicious.
IP router, firewall, and network appliance operating system software vulnerability	Define a strict zero-day vulnerability window definition. Update devices with security fixes and software patches right away.
IP router, firewall, and network appliance configuration file errors or weaknesses	Conduct post configuration penetration tests of the layered security solution within the LAN-to-WAN Domain. Test inbound and outbound traffic and fix any gaps.
Remote users can access the organization's infrastructure and download sensitive data	Apply and enforce the organization's data classification standard. Deny outbound traffic using source IP addresses in access control lists. If remote downloading is allowed, encrypt where necessary.
Local users download unknown file type attachments from unknown sources	Apply file transfer monitoring, scanning, and alarming for unknown file types from unknown sources.
Local users receive unknown e-mail attachments and embedded URL links	Apply e-mail server and attachment antivirus and e-mail quarantining for unknown file types. Stop domain-name Web site access based on content-filtering policies.
Local users lose productivity surfing the Web and not focusing on work tasks.	Apply domain-name content filtering at the Internet entry/access point.

WAN Domain

The Wide Area Network (WAN) Domain connects remote locations. As network costs drop, organizations can afford faster Internet and WAN connections. Today, telecommunication service providers sell the following:

- **Nationwide optical backbones**—Optical backbone trunks for private optical backbone networks.
- **End-to-end IP transport**—IP services and connectivity using the service provider's IP networking infrastructure.
- **Multi-site WAN cloud services**—IP services and connectivity offered for multi-site connectivity such as **multi-protocol label switching (MPLS)** WAN services. MPLS uses labels or tags to make virtual connections between endpoints in a WAN.
- **Metropolitan Ethernet LAN connectivity**—Ethernet LAN connectivity offered within a city's area network.
- **Dedicated Internet access**—A broadband Internet communication link usually shared among an organization.
- **Managed services**—Router management and security appliance management 24×7×365.
- **Service level agreements (SLAs)**—Contractual commitments for monthly service offerings like availability, packet loss, and response time to fix problems.

The WAN Domain represents the fifth component in the IT Infrastructure. WAN services can include dedicated Internet access and managed services for customers' routers and firewalls. Management agreements for availability and response time to outages are common. Networks, routers, and equipment require continuous monitoring and management to keep WAN service available.

WAN Domain Roles, Responsibilities, and Accountability

Here's an overview of what should go on in the WAN Domain:

- **Roles and tasks**—The WAN Domain includes both physical components and the logical design of routers and communication equipment. It is the second most complex area within an IT infrastructure to secure. Your goal is to allow users the most access possible while making sure what goes in and out is safe. The roles and tasks required within the WAN Domain include managing and configuring the following:
    - **WAN communication links**—The physical communication link provided as a digital or optical service terminated at your facility. Broadband connection speeds can range from the following:
        - DS0 (64Kbps) to DS1 (1.544Mbps) to DS3 (45Mbps) for digital service
        - OC-3 (155Mbps) to OC-12 (622Mbps) to OC-48 (2,488Mbps) for optical service
        - 10/100/1000Mbps Metro Ethernet LAN connectivity depending on physical distance

- **IP network design**—The logical design of the IP network and addressing schema. This requires network engineering, design of alternate paths, and selection of IP routing protocol.
- **IP stateful firewall**—A security appliance that is used to filter IP packets and block unwanted IP, TCP, and UDP packet types from entering or leaving the network. Firewalls can be installed on workstations, routers, or as standalone devices protecting LAN segments.
- **IP router configuration**—The actual router configuration information needed for the WAN backbone and edge routers used for IP connections to remote locations. The configuration must be based on the IP network design and addressing schema.
- **Virtual private networks (VPNs)**—A **virtual private network (VPN)** is a dedicated tunnel from one endpoint to another. In many applications, the VPN tunnel is encrypted. The VPN tunnel can be created between a remote workstation using the public Internet and a VPN router or a secure browser and **SSL-VPN** Web site.
- **Multi-protocol label switching (MPLS)**—A WAN software feature that allows customers to maximize performance. MPLS labels IP packets for rapid transport through virtual tunnels between designated endpoints. This is a form of Layer 2 switching and bypasses the routing path determination process.
- **SNMP network monitoring and management**—A **simple network management protocol (SNMP)** is used for network device monitoring, alarming, and performance.
- **Router and equipment maintenance**—A requirement to perform hardware and firmware updates, upload new operating system software, and configure routers and ACLs.

- **Responsibilities**—The network engineer or WAN group is responsible for the WAN Domain. This includes both the physical components and logical elements. Network engineers and security practitioners set up the defined security controls according to defined policies. Note that because of the complexities of IP network engineering, many groups now outsource management of their WAN and routers to service providers. This service includes SLAs that ensure that the system is available and that problems are solved quickly. In the event of a WAN connection outage, customers call a toll-free number for their service provider's **network operations center (NOC)**.
- **Accountability**—Your organization's IT network manager must maintain, update, and provide technical support for the WAN Domain. The director of IT security ensures that the company meets WAN Domain security policies, standards, procedures, and guidelines.

Some organizations use the public Internet as their WAN infrastructure. While it is cheaper, the Internet does not guarantee delivery or security. The following presents Internet risks, threats, and vulnerabilities, as well as risk-mitigation strategies.

TABLE 1-5 Risks, threats, vulnerabilities, and mitigation plans for the WAN Domain (Internet).

RISK, THREAT, OR VULNERABILITY	MITIGATION
Open, public, easily accessible to anyone that wants to connect	Apply acceptable use policies, in accord with the document "**RFC 1087: Ethics and the Internet.**" Enact new laws regarding unauthorized access to systems, malicious attacks on IT infrastructures, and financial loss due to malicious outages.
Most Internet traffic is sent in cleartext.	Prohibit using the Internet for private communications without encryption and VPN tunnels. If you have a data classification standard, follow the policies, procedures, and guidelines specifically.
Vulnerable to eavesdropping	Use encryption and VPN tunnels for end-to-end secure IP communications. If you have a data classification standard, follow the policies, procedures, and guidelines.
Vulnerable to malicious attacks	Deploy layered LAN-to-WAN security countermeasures, DMZ with IP stateful firewalls, IDS/IPS for security monitoring, and quarantining of unknown e-mail file attachments.
Vulnerable to denial of service (DoS), distributed denial of service (DDoS), TCP SYN flooding, and IP spoofing attacks	Apply filters on exterior IP stateful firewalls and IP router WAN interfaces to block TCP SYN and ICMP (ping). Alert your Internet service provider (ISP) to put the proper filters on its IP router WAN interfaces in accordance with CERT Advisory CA-1996-21.
Vulnerable to corruption of information and data	Encrypt IP data transmissions with VPNs. Back up and store data in off-site data vaults (online or physical data backup) with tested recovery procedures.
TCP/IP applications are inherently insecure (HTTP, FTP, TFTP, etc.).	Refer to your data classification standard for proper handling of data and use of TCP/IP applications. Never use TCP/IP applications for confidential data without proper encryption. Create a network-management VLAN and isolate TFTP and SNMP traffic used for network management.
Hackers, attackers, and perpetrators e-mail **Trojans**, **worms**, and malicious software freely.	Scan all e-mail attachments for type, antivirus, and malicious software at the LAN-to-WAN Domain. Isolate and quarantine unknown file attachments until further security review is conducted. Provide security awareness training to remind employees of dangers.

Risks, Threats, and Vulnerabilities Commonly Found in the WAN Domain (Internet)

Telecommunication service providers are in the business of providing WAN connectivity for end-to-end communications. Service providers must take on the responsibility for securing their network infrastructure first. Customers who sign up for WAN communication services must review the terms, conditions, and limitations of liability within their service contract. This is important because organizations must figure out where their duties start and end regarding router management and security management.

The most critical aspect of a WAN services contract is how the service provider supplies troubleshooting, network management, and security management services. The WAN Domain is where the fifth layer of defense is required. Table 1-5 lists the risks, threats, and vulnerabilities found in the Internet segment of the WAN Domain and appropriate risk-lowering strategies.

Telecommunication service providers sell WAN connectivity services. Some providers now also provide security management services. The following section presents WAN connectivity risks, threats, and vulnerabilities and risk-reducing strategies.

Risks, Threats, and Vulnerabilities Commonly Found in the WAN Domain (Connectivity)

Telecommunications companies are responsible for building and transporting customer IP traffic. Sometimes this IP traffic is bundled with dedicated Internet access, providing shared broadband access organization wide. If organizations outsource their WAN infrastructure, management and security must extend to the service provider. Organizations must define security policies and needs for their managed security provider to put in place. Table 1-6 lists the risks, threats, and vulnerabilities related to connectivity found in the WAN Domain and appropriate risk-lowering strategies.

TABLE 1-6 Risks, threats, vulnerabilities, and mitigation plans for the WAN Domain (connectivity).

RISK, THREAT, OR VULNERABILITY	MITIGATION
Commingling of WAN IP traffic on same service provider router and infrastructure	Encrypt confidential data transmissions through service provider WAN using VPN tunnels.
Maintaining high WAN service availability	Obtain WAN service availability SLAs. Deploy redundant Internet and WAN connections when 100 percent availability is required.
Maximizing WAN performance and throughput	Apply WAN-optimization and data-compression solutions when accessing remote systems, applications, and data. Enable access control lists (ACLs) on outbound router WAN interfaces in keeping with policy.
Using SNMP network-management applications and protocols maliciously (ICMP, Telnet, SNMP, DNS, etc.)	Create separate WAN network-management VLAN. Use strict firewall ACLs allowing SNMP manager and router IP addresses through the LAN-to-WAN Domain.
SNMP alarms and security monitoring 24×7×365	Outsource security operations and monitoring. Expand services to include managed security.

Remote Access Domain

The Remote Access Domain connects remote users to the organization's IT infrastructure. Remote access is critical for staff members who work in the field or from home—for example, outside sales reps, technical-support specialists, or health care professionals. Global access makes it easy to connect to the Internet, e-mail, and other business applications anywhere you can find a **Wireless Fidelity (Wi-Fi)** hotspot. The Remote Access Domain is important to have, but dangerous to use. It introduces many risks and threats from the Internet.

Today's mobile worker depends on the following:

- **Highly available cell-phone service**—Mobile workers need cell-phone service to get in touch with office and support teams.
- **Real-time access for critical communications**—Use of text messaging or **IM chat** on cell phones provides quick answers to short questions and does not require users to completely interrupt what they are doing.
- **Access to e-mail from a mobile device**—Integration of e-mail with cell phones, smartphones, personal data assistants (PDAs) or **BlackBerry** devices provides quick response to important e-mail messages.
- **Broadband Wi-Fi Internet access**—Some nationwide service providers now offer Wi-Fi broadband access cards. They allow wireless access in major metro areas.
- **Local Wi-Fi hotspot**—Wi-Fi hotspots are abundant, including in airports, libraries, coffee shops, and retailers. While most are free, some require that users pay for access.
- **Broadband Internet access to home office**—Staffers who work from home require broadband Internet access. This is usually bundled with VoIP telephone service and digital TV service.
- **Secure remote access to a company's IT infrastructure**—Remote workers require secure VPN tunnels to encrypt all IP data transmissions through the public Internet. This is critical if private data is being accessed remotely.

The scope of this domain is limited to remote access via the Internet and IP communications. The logical configuration of the Remote Access Domain requires IP network engineering and VPN solutions. This section addresses individual remote access and large-scale remote access for many remote users. The Remote Access Domain represents the sixth layer of defense for a typical IT infrastructure.

Remote Access Domain Roles, Responsibilities, and Accountability

Here's an overview of what should go on in the Remote Access Domain:

- **Roles and tasks**—The Remote Access Domain connects mobile users to their IT systems through the public Internet. The mobile user must have a remote IP device able to connect to the Internet. This can be a smartphone, personal data assistant (PDA), or laptop computer. Telephone, voice mail, e-mail, text messaging, and Web browsing are now possible with mobile devices. Cell phones and PDAs are handheld computers running mobile software.

The Risk from Backdoor Analog Phone Lines and Modems

Some maintenance vendors use analog phone lines and modems to reach equipment. That means they do not use IP or SNMP protocols. While this is convenient, it allows an insecure backdoor into the IT system. Attackers use tools that can get around an analog modem's password. Be alert for user workstations that are equipped with an analog modem connected to a backdoor analog phone line. Your company may not know that IT staff and software developers have set up these back doors. This can be a risk because analog modems generally have few security controls.

The following are some of the best ways to reduce these risk and threats:

- Do not install single analog phone lines without going through a PBX or VoIP phone system.
- Work with local phone-service companies to make sure no single analog phone lines are installed.
- Block unidentified calls from entering your phone system (i.e., calls that appear on caller ID screens as "unknown.")
- Watch call detail record (CDR) reports from PBX and VoIP phone systems for rogue phone numbers and abnormal call patterns.

The roles and tasks required within the Remote Access Domain include managing and designing the following:

- **Cell phones, smartphones, PDAs, and BlackBerry units**—Company-issued devices should be loaded with up-to-date firmware, operating-system software, and patches according to defined policies. Policy should require use of passwords on this equipment.
- **Laptop VPN client software**—When organizations use VPN tunnels between the LAN-to-WAN Domain and remote-user laptop computers, you must select VPN software that meets your organization's specific needs and works with your other software.
- **Secure browser software**—Web pages that use **Hyper Text Transfer Protocol Secure (HTTPS)** need secure browsers. HTTPS encrypts the data transfer between secure browsers and secure Web pages.
- **VPN routers or VPN firewalls**—Remote access VPN tunnels end at the VPN router or VPN firewall usually within the LAN-to-WAN Domain. All data is encrypted between the VPN client (remote laptop) and the VPN router or firewall—hence the name tunnel.
- **Secure Socket Layer (SSL)/VPN Web server**—SSL uses 128-bit encryption between a safe HTTPS Web page and safe browser. This encrypted VPN tunnel gives end-to-end privacy for remote Web page data sharing.
- **Authentication server**—A server that performs a second level authentication to verify users seeking remote access.

- **Responsibilities**—The network engineer or WAN group is usually in charge of the Remote Access Domain. This includes both the hardware components and logical elements. Network engineers and security practitioners are in charge of applying security controls according to policies. These include maintaining, updating, and troubleshooting the hardware and logical remote access connection for the Remote Access Domain. This requires watching the following:
  - IP routers
  - IP stateful firewalls
  - VPN tunnels
  - Security monitoring devices
  - Authentication servers
- **Accountability**—Your organization's WAN network manager is accountable for the Remote Access Domain. The director of IT security must ensure that the Remote Access Domain security plans, standards, methods, and guidelines are used.

Risks, Threats, and Vulnerabilities Commonly Found in the Remote Access Domain

Remote access is dangerous yet necessary for mobile workers. This is true for those organizations that rely on a mobile workforce such as sales reps, consultants, and support staff. As organizations cut costs, many urge staff to work from home. The WAN in this case is the public Internet. Making those connections secure is a top job. You will use your organization's strict data classification standard to verify users and encrypt data.

Remote access security controls must use the following:

- **Identification**—The process of providing identifying information such as a username, a logon ID, or an account number.
- **Authentication**—The process for proving that a remote user is who the user claims to be. The most common authentication method is supplying a password. Many organizations use second-level verifying services such as a **token** (hardware or software), **biometric** fingerprint reader, or smart card. A token can be a hardware device that sends a random number or a software token that text-messages a number to the user. A biometric fingerprint reader grants access only when the user's fingerprint is matched with one stored in the system. A smart card is like a credit card that acts similar to a token. It has a microprocessor chip that verifies the user with a smart-card reader.
- **Authorization**—The process of granting rights to use an organization's IT assets, systems, applications, and data to a specific user.
- **Accountability**—The process of recording user actions. The recorded information is often used to link users to system events.

Table 1-7 lists Remote Access Domain risks, threats, and vulnerabilities and risk-mitigation strategies.

TABLE 1-7 Risks, threats, vulnerabilities, and mitigation plans for the Remote Access Domain.

RISK, THREAT, OR VULNERABILITY	MITIGATION
Brute-force user ID and password attacks	Establish user ID and password policies requiring periodic changes (i.e., every 30 or 60 days). Passwords must be used, passwords must have more than eight characters, and users must incorporate numbers and letters.
Multiple logon retries and access control attacks	Set automatic blocking for attempted logon retries (e.g., block user access after three logon attempts have failed).
Unauthorized remote access to IT systems, applications, and data	Apply first-level (i.e., user ID and password) and second-level (i.e., tokens, biometrics, and smart cards) security for remote access to sensitive systems, applications, and data.
Private data or confidential data is compromised remotely.	Encrypt all private data within the database or hard drive. If data is stolen, the thief cannot use or sell it because it will be encrypted.
Data leakage in violation of existing data classification standards	Apply security countermeasures in the LAN-to-WAN Domain including data leakage security-monitoring tools and tracking as per your organization's data classification standard.
Mobile worker laptop is stolen.	Encrypt the data on the hard drive if the user has access to private or confidential data. Apply real-time lockout rules when told of a lost or stolen laptop by a user.
Mobile worker token or other authentication stolen	Apply real-time lockout procedures if a token is lost or device is compromised.

System/Application Domain

The System/Application Domain holds all the mission-critical systems, applications, and data. Authorized users may have access to many components in this domain. Secure access may require second-level checks.

Examples of applications that may require second-level authentication include the following:

- **Human resources and payroll**—Only staff who work on payroll services need access to this private data and confidential information.
- **Accounting and financial**—Executive managers need access to accounting and financial data to make sound business decisions. Securing financial data requires unique security controls with access limited to those who need it. Publicly traded companies are subject to Sarbanes-Oxley (SOX) compliance law requiring security.

technical TIP

Security controls keep private data and intellectual property safe. Encrypting data can stop bogus users. Hackers looking for data know where people hide it and how to find it. Encrypting the data within databases and storage devices gives an added layer of security.

- **Customer-relationship management (CRM)**—Customer-service reps need real-time access to information that includes customer purchasing history and private data.
- **Sales-order entry**—Sales professionals need access to the sales-order entry and order-tracking system. Private customer data must be kept safe.
- **U.S. military intelligence and tactics**—U.S. military commanders who make decisions on the battlefield use highly sensitive information. Access to it must meet U.S. DoD data classification standards.

The System/Application Domain represents the seventh layer of defense.

System/Application Domain Roles, Responsibilities, and Accountability

Here's an overview of what should go on in the System/Application Domain:

- **Roles and tasks**—The System/Application Domain consists of hardware, operating system software, applications, and data. This domain includes hardware and their logical design. An organization's mission-critical applications and intellectual property assets are here. It must be secured both physically and logically.

  We limited the scope of the System/Application Domain to reducing risks. These include the following:

  - **Physical access to computer rooms, data centers, and wiring closets**—Set up procedure to allow staff to enter secured area.
  - **Server architecture**—Apply a converged server design that employs server blades and racks to combine their use and reduce costs.
  - **Server operating systems and core environments**—Reduce the time operating-system software is open to attack with software updates and patches.
  - **Virtualization servers**—Keep physical and logical virtual environments separate and extend layered security solutions into the cloud. Virtualization allows you to load many operating systems and applications in memory using one physical server.
  - **System administration of application servers**—Provide ongoing server and system administration for users.
  - **Data classification standard**—Review data classification standards, procedures, and guidelines on proper handling of data. Maintain safety of private data while in transport and in storage.
  - **Software development life cycle (SDLC)**—Apply secure software development life cycle tactics when designing and developing software.

- **Testing and quality assurance**—Apply sound software testing, penetration testing, and quality assurance to fill security gaps and software weaknesses.
- **Storage, backup, and recovery procedures**—Follow data storage, backup, and recovery plans as set by the data classification standard.
- **Data archiving and retention**—Align policies, standards, procedures, and guidelines to digital storage and retention needs.
- **Business continuity plan (BCP)**—Conduct a business impact analysis (BIA) and decide which computer uses are most important. Define RTOs for each system. Prepare a BCP focused on those things that are most important for the business to keep going.
- **Disaster recovery plan (DRP)**—Prepare a disaster recovery plan based on the BCP. Start DRP elements for the most important computer systems first. Organize a DRP team and remote data center.

- **Responsibilities**—The responsibility for Systems/Applications Domain lies with the director of systems and applications and the director of software development. This includes the following:
  - Server systems administration
  - Database design and management
  - Designing access rights to systems and applications
  - Software development
  - Software development project management
  - Software coding
  - Software testing
  - Quality assurance
  - Production support
- **Accountability**—The directors of systems and applications and software development are accountable for the organization's production systems and uses. The director of IT security is accountable for ensuring that the System/Application Domain security policies, standards, procedures, and guidelines are in compliance.

Risks, Threats, and Vulnerabilities Commonly Found in the System/Application Domain

The System/Application Domain is where the organization's data is. This data is like treasure. It can be private customer data, intellectual property, or national security information. It is what attackers seek deep within an IT system. Protecting this treasure is the goal of every organization. Loss of data is the greatest threat in the System/Application Domain.

With a data classification standard, types of data can be isolated in like groups. The more important the data, the deeper you should hide and store it. Consider encrypting data to be stored for a long time. Table 1-8 lists common System/Application Domain risks, threats, and vulnerabilities and risk-mitigation strategies.

TABLE 1-8 Risks, threats, vulnerabilities, and mitigation plans for the System/Application Domain.

RISK, THREAT, OR VULNERABILITY	MITIGATION
Unauthorized access to data centers, computer rooms, and wiring closets	Apply policies, standards, procedures, and guidelines for staff and visitors to secure facilities.
Servers must sometimes be shut down to perform maintenance.	Create a system that brings together servers, storage, and networking.
Server operating systems software vulnerability	Define vulnerability window for server operating system environments. Maintain hardened production server operating systems.
Cloud computing virtual environments are by default not secure.	Implement virtual firewalls and server segmentation on separate VLANs. A virtual firewall is a software-based firewall used in virtual environments.
Client-server and Web applications are susceptible to attack.	Conduct rigorous software and Web-application testing and penetration testing prior to launch.
Unauthorized accessed to systems.	Follow data classification standards regarding stringent use of second-level authentication.
Private data is compromised.	Separate private data elements into different databases. For archiving purposes, encrypt data within databases and storage devices.
Data is corrupted or lost.	Implement daily data backups and off-site data storage for monthly data archiving. Define data recovery procedures based on defined RTOs.
Backed-up data may be lost as backup media is reused.	Convert all data into digital data for long-term storage. Retain backups from off-site data vaults based on defined RTOs.
Recovering critical business functions may take too long to be useful.	Develop a business continuity plan for mission-critical applications providing tactical steps for maintaining availability of operations.
IT systems may be down for an extended period after a disaster.	Develop a disaster recovery plan specific to the recovery of mission-critical applications and data to maintain operations.

Weakest Link in the Security of an IT Infrastructure

The user is the weakest link in security. Even information systems security practitioners can make mistakes. Human error is a major risk and threat to any organization. No group can completely control any person's behavior. For these reasons, every organization must be prepared for malicious users, untrained users, and careless users.

The following strategies can help reduce risk:

- Check the background of each job candidate carefully.
- Give each staff member a regular evaluation.
- Rotate access to sensitive systems, applications, and data with different staff positions.
- Apply sound application and software testing and review for quality.
- Regularly review security plans throughout the seven domains of a typical IT system.
- Perform annual security control audits.

To build a respected and effective profession, information systems security professionals must operate ethically and comply with a code of conduct. This section explains why this is the basis of the profession.

Ethics and the Internet

Imagine if there were no air traffic controllers and airplanes flew freely. Trying to take off and land would be extremely dangerous. There would probably be many more accidents. Such a situation would wreak havoc.

Incredibly, cyberspace has no authorities that function like air traffic controllers. To make matters worse, human behavior online often is less mature than in normal social settings. Cyberspace has become the new playground for today's bad guys. This is why the demand for systems security professionals is growing so rapidly.

The U.S. government and Internet Architecture Board (IAB) has defined a policy regarding acceptable use of the Internet geared toward U.S. citizens. It is not a law or a mandate, however; because cyberspace is global and entirely without borders, this policy cannot be enforced. Its use is based on common sense and personal integrity. The box on the following page presents the IAB's standard of ethics and the Internet.

Ethics are a matter of personal integrity. The systems security profession is about doing what is right and stopping what is wrong. Use of the Internet is a privilege shared by all. It is a communications medium with no borders, no cultural bias, and no prejudice. Users have the privilege to connect. This is something to be thankful for. Unfortunately, bad guys use cyberspace to commit crimes and cause trouble. This has created a global need for systems security professionals.

Request for Comment (RFC) 1087—Ethics and the Internet

IAB Statement of Policy

The Internet is a national facility whose utility is largely a consequence of its wide availability and accessibility. Irresponsible use of this critical resource poses an enormous threat to its continued availability to the technical community. The U.S. Government sponsors of this system have a fiduciary responsibility to the public to allocate government resources wisely and effectively. Justification for the support of this system suffers when highly disruptive abuses occur. Access to and use of the Internet is a privilege and should be treated as such by all users of this system.

The IAB strongly endorses the view of the Division Advisory Panel of the National Science Foundation Division of Network, Communications Research and Infrastructure which, in paraphrase, characterized as unethical and unacceptable any activity which purposely:

a) seeks to gain unauthorized access to the resources of the Internet,

b) disrupts the intended use of the Internet,

c) wastes resources (people, capacity, computer) through such actions,

d) destroys the integrity of computer-based information, and/or

e) compromises the privacy of users

$(ISC)^2$: Information Systems Security Certification

One of the most prestigious organizations that certify security professionals is **International Information Systems Security Certification Consortium**, otherwise known as **$(ISC)^2$**.

SSCP Professional Certification

In order to be certified by the $(ISC)^2$, you must agree to its code of ethics. $(ISC)^2$ has two certifications. The first is the **Systems Security Certified Practitioner (SSCP).** It includes the following domains within its common body of knowledge:

- Access controls
- Security operations and administration
- Malicious code and activity
- Monitoring and analysis
- Cryptography
- Networks and communications
- Risk, response, recovery

This certification requires one year of work experience as a security practitioner and a passing grade on the exam. It certifies you to apply security countermeasures.

CISSP Professional Certification

The **Certified Information Systems Security Professional (CISSP)** is a globally recognized and prestigious certification that many systems security professionals seek. CISSP candidates must pass a difficult comprehensive certification exam and have at least five years of professional information security experience. Keeping CISSP certification requires you to conform to its code of conduct. It includes the following domains within its common body of knowledge:

- Access control
- Application development security
- Business continuity and disaster recovery planning
- Cryptography
- Information security governance and risk management
- Legal, regulations, investigations, and compliance
- Operations security
- Physical (environmental) security
- Security architecture and design
- Telecommunications and network security

Refer to the $(ISC)^2$ Web site for additional information (*http://www.isc2.org*).

$(ISC)^2$ Code of Ethics

The box below presents the $(ISC)^2$ code of ethics preamble and canons. The canons define the scope of the profession and personal integrity.

The box on the following page gives the $(ISC)^2$ code of ethics itself. All CISSP and SSCP certified professionals must abide by this code to keep professional certification by $(ISC)^2$.

Code of Ethics Preamble

Safety of the commonwealth, duty to our principals, and to each other requires that we adhere, and be seen to adhere, to the highest ethical standards of behavior. Therefore, strict adherence to this Code is a condition of certification.

Code of Ethics Canons

Protect society, the commonwealth, and the infrastructure.

Act honorably, honestly, justly, responsibly, and legally.

Provide diligent and competent service to principals.

Advance and protect the profession.

Code of Ethics

All information systems security professionals who are certified by $(ISC)^2$ recognize that such certification is a privilege that must be both earned and maintained. In support of this principle, all $(ISC)^2$ members are required to commit to fully support this Code of Ethics (the "Code"). $(ISC)^2$ members who intentionally or knowingly violate any provision of the Code will be subject to action by a peer review panel, which may result in the revocation of certification. $(ISC)^2$ members are obligated to follow the ethics complaint procedure upon observing any action by an $(ISC)^2$ member that breaches the Code. Failure to do so may be considered a breach of the Code pursuant to Canon IV.

There are only four mandatory canons in the Code. By necessity, such high-level guidance is not intended to be a substitute for the ethical judgment of the professional.

Given the sensitivity of systems security, certifications may be required for certain jobs. It is important for you to pursue education, training, and professional certification. You can read more in Chapter 14.

IT Security Policy Framework

Cyberspace cannot continue to flourish without some assurances of user security. Several laws now require organizations to keep personal data private. Businesses cannot operate effectively on an Internet where anyone can steal their data. IT security is crucial to any organization's ability to survive. This section introduces you to an IT security policy framework. It consists of policies, standards, procedures, and guidelines that reduce risks and threats.

Definitions

An IT security policy framework contains four main components:

- **Policy**—A policy is a short written statement that the people in charge of an organization have set as a course of action or direction. A policy comes from upper management and applies to the entire organization.
- **Standard**—A standard is a detailed written definition for hardware and software and how it is to be used. Standards ensure that consistent security controls are used throughout the IT system.
- **Procedures**—These are written instructions for how to use policies and standards. They may include a plan of action, installation, testing, and auditing of security controls.
- **Guidelines**—A guideline is a suggested course of action for using the policy, standards, or procedures. Guidelines can be specific or flexible regarding use.

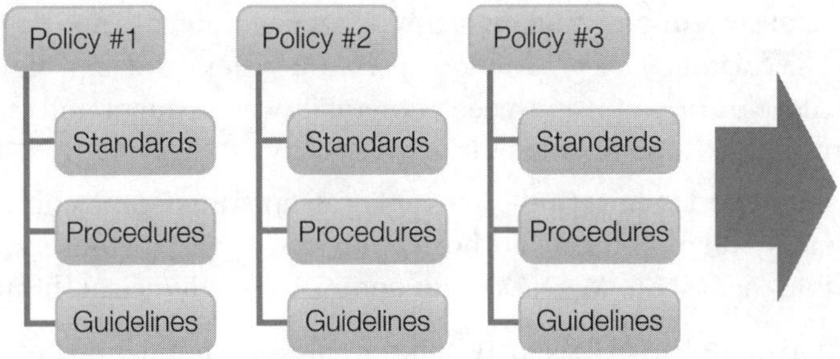

FIGURE 1-9 Hierarchical IT security policy framework.

Figure 1-9 is an example of a hierarchical IT security policy framework. Policies apply to an entire organization. Standards are specific to a given policy. Procedures and guidelines help with use. Within each policy and standard, identify the impact for the seven domains of a typical IT infrastructure. This will help define the roles, responsibilities, and accountability throughout.

Foundational IT Security Policies

The focus of your organization's IT security policy framework is to reduce your exposure to risks, threats, and vulnerabilities. It is important to relate policy definition and standards to practical design requirements. These requirements will properly apply the best security controls and countermeasures. Policy statements must set limits and also refer to standards, procedures, and guidelines. Polices define how security controls and countermeasures must be used to comply with laws and regulations.

Examples of some basic IT security policies include the following:

- **Acceptable use policy (AUP)**—The AUP defines what actions are and are not allowed with respect to the use of organization-owned IT assets. This policy is specific to the User Domain and mitigates risk between an organization and its employees.
- **Security awareness policy**—A policy that defines how to ensure all personnel are aware of the importance of security and behavioral expectations under the organization's security policy. This policy is specific to the User Domain and when you need to change organizational security awareness behavior.
- **Asset classification policy**—This policy defines an organization's data classification standard. It tells what IT assets are critical to the organization's mission. It usually defines the organization's systems, uses, and data priorities and identifies assets within the seven domains of a typical IT infrastructure.
- **Asset protection policy**—This policy helps organizations define a priority for mission-critical IT systems and data. This policy is aligned with an organization's **business impact analysis (BIA)** and is used to address risks that could threaten the organization's ability to continue operations after a disaster.
- **Asset management policy**—This policy includes the security operations and management of all IT assets within the seven domains of a typical IT infrastructure.

- **Vulnerability assessment and management**—This policy defines an organization-wide vulnerability window for production operating system and application software. You develop organization-wide vulnerability assessment and management standards, procedures, and guidelines from this policy.
- **Threat assessment and monitoring**—This policy defines an organization-wide threat assessment and monitoring authority. You should also include specific details regarding the LAN-to-WAN Domain and AUP compliance in this policy.

Organizations need to tailor their IT security policy framework to their environment. Many organizations, after conducting a security assessment of their IT setup, align policy definitions to gaps and exposures. Policies typically require executive management and general legal counsel review and approval.

Data Classification Standards

The goal and objective of a data classification standard is to provide a consistent definition for how an organization should handle and secure different types of data. Security controls protect different data types. These security controls are within the seven domains of a typical IT infrastructure. Procedures and guidelines must define how to handle data within the seven domains of a typical IT infrastructure to ensure its security.

For businesses and organizations under recent compliance laws, data classification standards typically include the following major categories:

- **Private data**—Data about people that must be kept private. Organizations must use proper security controls to be in compliance.
- **Confidential**—Information or data that is owned by the organization. Intellectual property, customer lists, pricing information, and patents are examples of confidential data.
- **Internal use only**—Information or data shared internally by an organization. While confidential information or data may not be included, communications are not intended to leave the organization.
- **Public domain data**—Information or data shared with the public such as Web site content, white papers, etc.

Depending on your organization's data classification standard, you may need to encrypt data of the highest sensitivity even in storage devices and hard drives. For example, you may need to use encryption and VPN technology when using the public Internet for remote access. But internal LAN communications and access to systems, applications, or data may not require use of encryption.

Users may also be restricted from getting to private data of customers and may be able to access only certain pieces of data. Customer-service reps provide customer service without getting to all of the customer's private data. For example, they may not be able to see the customer's entire Social Security number or account numbers. Only the last four digits may be visible.

U.S. Federal Government Data Classification Standard

The U.S. government under Executive Order 13526 defines a data classification standard for all federal government agencies, including the Department of Defense (DoD). President Barack Obama signed this executive order on December 9, 2009. Although the U.S. government and its citizens enjoy the free flow of information, securing information is essential for national security, defense, or military action.

The following defines the U.S. federal government data classification standards:

- **Top secret**—Applies to information that the classifying authority finds would cause grave damage to national security if it were disclosed.
- **Secret**—Applies to information that the classifying authority finds would cause serious damage to national security if it were disclosed.
- **Confidential**—Applies to information that the classifying authority finds would cause damage to national security

While public-domain information is considered unclassified, it is not part of the data classification standard.

The U.S. government does have rules for handling unclassified (posing no threat to national security if exposed) and controlled unclassified information (for official use only, sensitive but unclassified, and law enforcement sensitive). Note this is not included in Executive Order 13562 and was based on previous standards put into use by the administration of President George W. Bush.

technical TIP

Organizations should start defining their IT security policy framework by defining an asset classification policy. This policy, in turn, aligns itself directly to a data classification standard. This standard defines how an organization is to secure and protect its data. Working from your data classification standard, you need to assess whether any private or confidential data travels within any of the seven domains of a typical IT infrastructure. Depending on how you classify and use the data, you will need to employ appropriate security controls throughout the IT infrastructure.

CHAPTER SUMMARY

This chapter introduces information systems security and the systems security profession. You saw a common definition for a typical IT infrastructure. You learned about risks, threats, and vulnerabilities within the seven domains. Each of these domains requires the use of strategies to reduce risks, threats, and vulnerabilities. You saw how IT security policy frameworks can help organizations reduce risk by defining authoritative policies. You also learned that data classification standards provide organizations with a road map for how to handle different types of data.

Qualified systems security professionals are required to create security controls and countermeasures. As a security professional, you must have the highest integrity and ethics.

KEY CONCEPTS AND TERMS

Acceptable use policy (AUP)
Availability
Biometric
BlackBerry
Business continuity plan (BCP)
Business impact analysis (BIA)
Certified Information Systems Security Professional (CISSP)
Children's Internet Protection Act (CIPA)
Ciphertext
Cleartext
Confidentiality
Content filtering
Cryptography
Cybersecurity
Cyberspace
Data classification standard
Demilitarized zone (DMZ)
Disaster recovery plan (DRP)
Downtime
E-commerce
Encryption
End user licensing agreement (EULA)
Ethernet
Family Educational Rights and Privacy Act (FERPA)
Federal Information Security Management Act (FISMA)
FICO
File Transfer Protocol (FTP)
Generation Y
Gramm-Leach-Bliley Act (GLBA)
Hardening
Health Insurance Portability and Accountability Act (HIPAA)
Hyper Text Transfer Protocol (HTTP)
Hyper Text Transfer Protocol Secure (HTTPS)
IEEE 802.3 CSMA/CD
IM chat
Information security
Information systems
Information systems security
Institute of Electrical and Electronics Engineers (IEEE)
Integrity
Internet
Internet Protocol (IP)
Intrusion detection system/intrusion prevention system (IDS/IPS)
IP default gateway router
IP stateful firewall
International Information Systems Security Certification Consortium (ISC)²
IT security policy framework
Layer 2 switch
Layer 3 switch
Local area network (LAN)
Malicious code
Mean time to failure (MTTF)
Mean time to repair (MTTR)
Multi-protocol label switching (MPLS)

KEY CONCEPTS AND TERMS, *continued*

Network interface card (NIC)
Network keys
Network operations center (NOC)
Personal data assistant (PDA)
Ping
Protocol
Proxy server
Recovery time objective (RTO)
"RFC 1087: Ethics and the Internet"
Risk
Sarbanes-Oxley Act (SOX)
Second-level authentication
Secure Sockets Layer virtual private network (SSL-VPN)
Service level agreement (SLA)
Simple Network Management Protocol (SNMP)
Smartphone
Software vulnerability
Subnet mask address
Systems Security Certified Practitioner (SSCP)
Telnet
Threat
Token
Transmission Control Protocol/ Internet Protocol (TCP/IP)
Trivial File Transfer Protocol (TFTP)
Trojan
Uptime
Virtual LAN (VLAN)
Virtual private networks (VPNs)
Virus
Vulnerability
Vulnerability assessment
Vulnerability window
Wireless access point (WAP)
Wireless Fidelity (Wi-Fi)
Wireless LANs (WLANs)
World Wide Web (WWW)
Worm

CHAPTER 1 ASSESSMENT

1. Information security is specific to securing information, whereas information systems security is focused on the security of the systems that house the information.

A. True
B. False

2. Software manufacturers limit their liability when selling software using which of the following?

A. End user licensing agreements
B. Confidentiality agreements
C. Software development agreements
D. By developing error-free software and code so there is no liability
E. None of the above

3. The ________ tenet of information systems security is concerned with the recovery time objective.

A. Confidentiality
B. Integrity
C. Availability
D. All of the above
E. None of the above

4. Encrypting data on storage devices or hard drives is a main strategy to ensure data integrity.

A. True
B. False

5. Organizations that require customer-service representatives to access private customer data can best protect customer privacy and make it easy to access other customer data by using which of the following security controls?

A. Preventing customer-service representatives from accessing private customer data
B. Blocking out customer private data details and allowing access only to the last four digits of Social Security numbers or account numbers
C. Encrypting all customer data
D. Implementing second-tier authentication when accessing customer databases
E. All of the above

6. The ________ is the weakest link in an IT infrastructure.
   A. System/Application Domain
   B. LAN-to-WAN Domain
   C. WAN Domain
   D. Remote Access Domain
   E. User Domain

7. Which of the following security controls can help mitigate malicious e-mail attachments?
   A. E-mail filtering and quarantining
   B. E-mail attachment antivirus scanning
   C. Verifying with users that e-mail source is reputable
   D. Holding all inbound e-mails with unknown attachments
   E. All of the above

8. You can help ensure confidentiality by implementing ________.
   A. An acceptable use policy
   B. A data classification standard
   C. An IT security policy framework
   D. A virtual private network for remote access
   E. Secure access controls

9. Encrypting e-mail communications is needed if you are sending confidential information within an e-mail message through the public Internet.
   A. True
   B. False

10. Using security policies, standards, procedures, and guidelines helps organizations decrease risks and threats.
   A. True
   B. False

11. A data classification standard is usually part of which policy definition?
   A. Asset protection policy
   B. Acceptable use policy
   C. Vulnerability assessment and management policy
   D. Security awareness policy
   E. Threat assessment and monitoring policy

12. The SSCP professional certification is geared toward which of the following information systems security positions?
   A. IT security practitioner
   B. Manager of IT security
   C. Director of IT security
   D. Chief security officer
   E. IT security consultant

13. Maximizing availability primarily involves minimizing ________.
   A. The amount of downtime for a system or application
   B. The mean time to repair a system or application
   C. Downtime by implementing a business continuity plan
   D. The recovery time objective
   E. All of the above

14. Which of the following is not a U.S. compliance law or act?
   A. CIPA
   B. FERPA
   C. FISMA
   D. PCI DSS
   E. HIPAA

15. Internet IP packets are to cleartext what encrypted IP packets are to ________.
   A. Confidentiality
   B. Ciphertext
   C. Virtual private networks
   D. Cryptography algorithms
   E. None of the above

CHAPTER 2

Changing How People and Businesses Communicate

THE TELEPHONE REVOLUTIONIZED COMMUNICATION. Its impact foreshadowed the coming computer revolution. As telephones became more and more common, appearing in nearly every home and workplace, they became *the* way to communicate. Indeed, until the mid 1980s, personal and business communications involved three primary tools:

- **Telephone**—Used for real-time voice communications between people
- **Answering machines and voice mail**—Critical for store-and-forward voice messaging and retrieval
- **Fax**—Real-time data transmission of documents through analog phone lines

In the 1980s, telephones began to evolve from their analog origins into digital devices. Telephone and voice-mail systems became digital. Then the Internet connectivity boom of the 1990s changed communication again. Organizations connected to the World Wide Web (WWW) and began to use this new tool to conduct business. Internet connectivity made electronic mail (e-mail) possible. Almost overnight, it became the predominant personal and business communication tool. Today, with laptops, smartphones, and PDA devices, e-mail communication is almost in real time.

Today's VoIP and **unified communications (UC)** provide several real-time communication options, including the following:

- **Voice communication**—Through VoIP, end-to-end telephony services with integrated voice messaging
- **Availability/presence**—Status update messages in IM chat window
- **IM chat**—Messaging for quick answers to simple questions
- **Conferencing**—Audio and **videoconferencing** for meetings
- **Collaboration**—Document sharing for productive meetings

Chapter 2 Topics

This chapter covers the following topics and concepts:

- How voice communications evolved from analog to digital to VoIP from the 1990s to the 2000s
- What the risks, threats, and vulnerabilities associated with VoIP and Session Initiation Protocol (SIP) applications are
- How the Internet transformed personal and business communications to a TCP/IP world
- What VoIP and unified communications are
- How businesses evolved from brick-and-mortar to e-commerce
- Why today's businesses need an Internet marketing strategy
- What the effects of the Web on people, businesses, and organizations are

Chapter 2 Goals

When you complete this chapter, you will be able to:

- Describe the evolution of voice communications from analog to digital to VoIP to unified communications
- Differentiate store-and-forward communications from real-time communications
- Recognize the impact of the Internet on how people and businesses communicate
- Align risk-mitigation strategies for VoIP and SIP applications
- Understand how brick-and-mortar businesses transform into e-business models with e-commerce

Evolution of Voice Communications

Until January 1, 1984, American Telephone and Telegraph (AT&T) held a monopoly on the telephone-communications industry in the United States. Before 1984, AT&T had no competitors or market pressures. In a settlement with the U.S. Department of Justice, AT&T agreed to split into multiple **Regional Bell Operating Companies (RBOCs)**. This breakup is referred to as the **divestiture** of the Bell System, as AT&T was also known.

For telephone customers, little changed on that date. The dial tone sounded the same. But the newly competitive telecom industry ate away at AT&T's market share. This one event transformed communications. It opened innovation and launched the broadband era.

Specifically, this divestiture resulted in the following:

- **Seven regional bell operating companies (RBOCs)**—Each RBOC was allocated various telephone-operating companies local to its region.
- **A competitive landscape for telecom services**—Obstacles preventing RBOCs from selling outside a given region were removed, allowing RBOCs to provide services outside their regions.
- **Highly competitive long-distance telephone service**—RBOCs and telecommunication service providers competed for the first time against one another for long-distance minutes.
- **Public branch exchange (PBX) phone systems**—Customers now were responsible for **public branch exchange (PBX) phone systems** and wiring inside buildings.
- **Conversion of analog central office (CO) switches to digital central office (CO) switches**—During the late 1980s into the early 1990s, service providers converted their core switches from **analog central office (CO) switches** to **digital central office (CO) switches.**
- **Digital communication services**—When voice signals converted from analog to digital, voice and data communications could travel on the same circuit.
- **The broadband era, driven by fiber-optic backbone networks and wavelength multiplexing**—Nationwide fiber-optic backbone cabling drove broadband Internet and WAN circuit costs down. With **dense wavelength division multiplexing (DWDM)**, light can transmit many data streams down the same fiber-optic path, maximizing bandwidth from a single fiber strand.
- **Broadband IP backbone networks with Internet access**—Organizations installed WANs based on IP networking with dedicated Internet access.
- **Network management and managed services**—With IP network complexity increasing, outsourcing the management of routers and security appliances to service providers made good business sense.

Figure 2-1 depicts the evolution of the U.S. telecommunications industry from divestiture to the present.

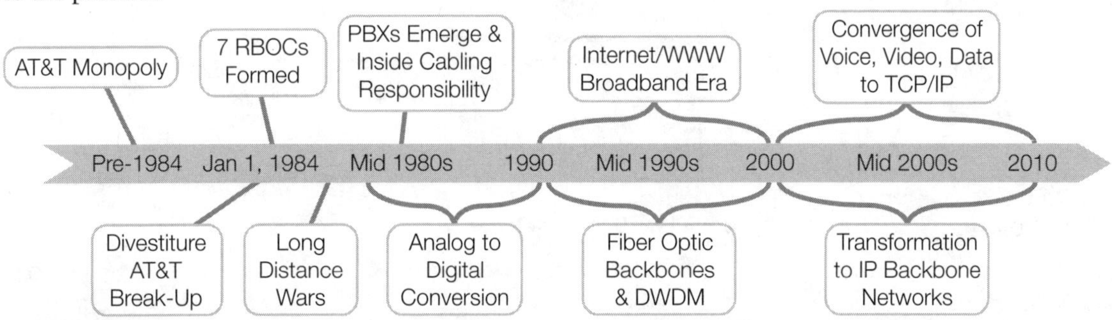

FIGURE 2-1

Evolution of the telecommunications industry in the U.S.

FYI

Time Division Multiplexing (TDM) is a technology that supports the convergence of voice, video, and data communication streams. Time slots split a channel into several segments. Each slot or segment carries voice, video, or data within the communication link. TDM requires the sharing of bandwidth to support voice, video, or data traffic. Because all communication types can share bandwidth using TDM, the new technology made it easier to manage WAN connectivity.

From Analog to Digital

Before fiber optics, most telephone wiring was copper based. It transported analog transmissions. Analog communications have these characteristics:

- **They are based on a continuously generated electrical signal**—Analog transmission requires a continuous but changing electrical signal (positive/negative, etc.).
- **They are susceptible to errors**—Analog communications have a much higher **bit error rate** than digital communications. The bit error rate in analog communications is one error for every 1,000 bits sent; in digital communications, the bit error rate is one error for every 1,000,000 bits sent.
- **They are susceptible to electrical interference and noise**—Interference and noise contribute to slow speeds and throughput for analog communications. Static and noise on the line result in a higher bit error rate.
- **They are slow**—Analog transmissions are capable of reaching speeds of up to 56Kbps but practically range from 9.6Kbps to 38.4Kbps.
- **They have limited bandwidth**—0KHz to 3KHz covers the sound spectrum detectable by the human ear. Phone systems operate within this frequency.

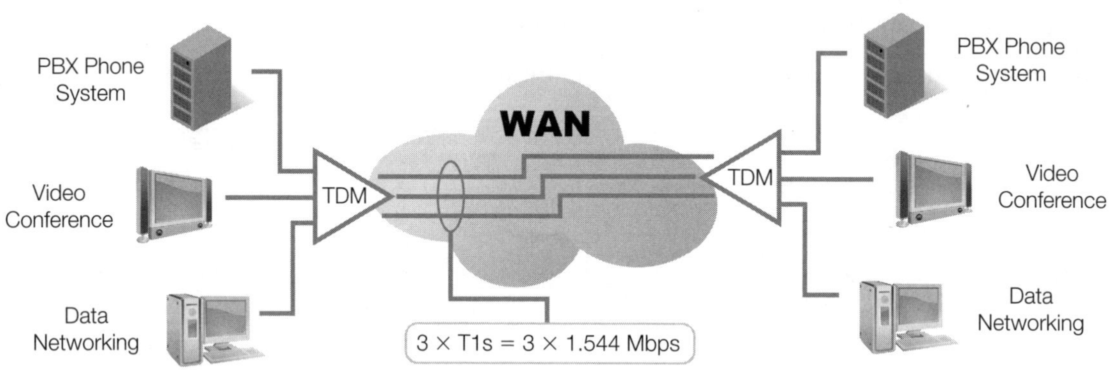

FIGURE 2-2

Convergence of voice, video, and data communications.

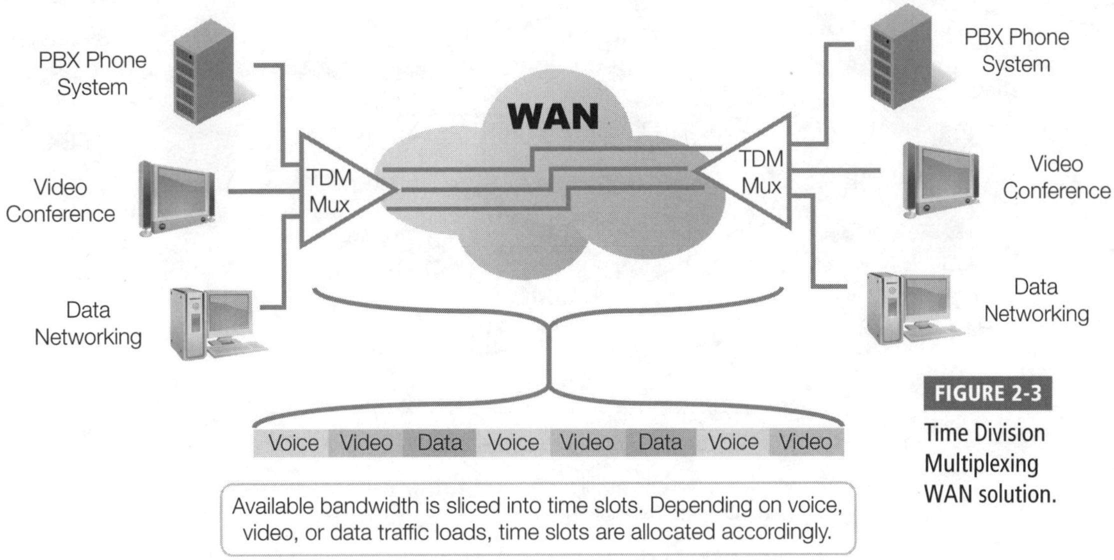

FIGURE 2-3 Time Division Multiplexing WAN solution.

Over time, analog phone lines and fax lines gradually began to disappear. Digital PBX systems began to replace analog phone systems. Voice and data communications converged with data. Digital communication allowed voice, video, and data to share the same bandwidth. WAN consolidation simplified management and lowered operating costs, which made advanced digital communications affordable for many organizations. Figure 2-2 depicts the **convergence** of voice, video, and data communications.

Time Division Multiplexing (TDM) allows voice, video, and data communications to share the same bandwidth. Consolidation lowered operating costs and made blended communication easier to manage, implement, and support. Figure 2-3 shows an example of combining voice, video, and data communications.

Telephony Risks, Threats, and Vulnerabilities

PBX systems, like computers, are vulnerable to malicious attacks by black-hat hackers. These attacks generally take the form of attempts to gain unauthorized access to a computer or other type of electronic device. What do these attackers seek? On PBX systems, attackers often seek free and anonymous long-distance calling or worse, anonymous access to some other networked computer to launch another attack. In other words, someone who compromises your PBX can launch an attack using your system, meaning that the attack will appear to have originated with your PBX.

PBX hackers have been around since divestiture required customers to either lease or purchase a phone system. For the first time, organizations had to manage and maintain their own phone systems. Many PBX systems were designed before security was much of a concern. They lacked proper security controls. Businesses often hired system integrators to do much of the work that AT&T previously performed to install their telecommunications systems. This left many doors open for outside users to gain a dial tone through the phone or voice-mail system. Figure 2-4 shows how PBX systems are susceptible to attack from black-hat hackers.

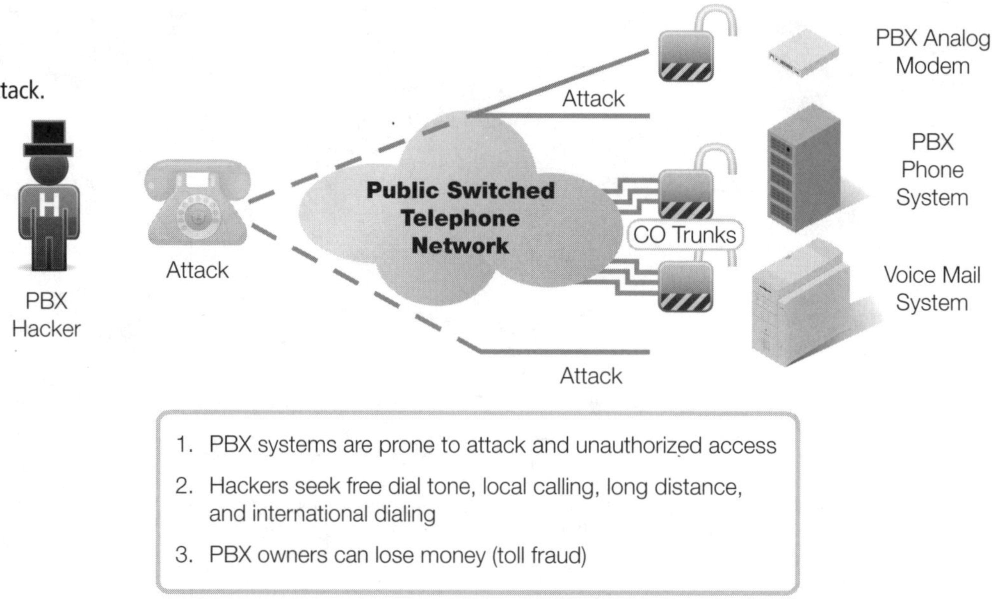

FIGURE 2-4
PBX systems are susceptible to attack.

These attackers are generally organized criminals, drug dealers, and others who want free long-distance privileges and/or an access point they can use to connect to other computers. Once they get into a system, they can sell access to others or use it themselves.

Since the breakup of AT&T, organizations have had to decide whether to lease or purchase their phone systems. In either case, they must hire staff to manage and maintain these systems. Phone systems, like computers, have risks, threats, and vulnerabilities. Table 2-1 lists the risks, threats, and vulnerabilities commonly found in PBX and key phone systems.

Telephony Security Best Practices

A telephony system is open to attack just like any other computer system. The risks that organizations face require proper security controls to avoid suffering successful attacks. Refer to the preceding table for a list of risks.

Organizations tend to forget telephone security. With voice now sent by an IP packet, the same risks, threats, and vulnerabilities apply to both voice and data systems. You must harden your telephony system given the risks from TCP/IP.

Here are the best ways to harden telephony and voice communications security:

- **Telephony system policies**—You must set proper policies, standards, procedures, and guidelines. This includes AUPs for telephone usage and authorization for long-distance dialing.
- **Physical security**—Lock all wiring closets and telephone switch rooms. Document all cabling and cross-connects. Document all new or changed equipment and any equipment location changes.

TABLE 2-1 Risks, threats, vulnerabilities, and mitigation plans for PBX and key phone systems.

RISK, THREAT, OR VULNERABILITY	MITIGATION
Default manufacturer password still in place	Make frequent password changes. Use strong password lengths and character sets.
Social engineering (the act of scamming or manipulating an innocent person); analog modem backdoor access to phone system	Educate employees about scam artists and impostors posing as telephone technicians. Remove remote analog modem access. Enable security controls and dial-back modem dialing.
Auto dialers probing main and **direct inward dialed (DID)** telephone numbers for dial-tone access	Disable **direct inward system access (DISA)** to prevent access to an outside line once inside the switch.
Class-of-service (COS) settings are not secure.	Class-of-service (COS) settings are unique to a specific phone extension or DID number. COS settings enable you to create user profiles with different permissions. COS settings limit access through the phone system. Disable trunk access to override loose COS settings.
Trunk access group restriction (TAGR) settings are not secure.	Trunk Access Group Restriction (TAGR) settings define whether a particular voice line (extension or voice-mail box) can access an outside phone line for outbound dialing. Set security controls to block outside phone-line access.
Outside caller can move from phone system to voice mail and back.	Configure one-way and out-call-not-answered decision paths. Configure COS settings to prevent callers from moving back and forth in the phone system.
Outside caller can gain dial tone from a voice mailbox.	Disable trunk group access completely. Disable voice mailbox to phone-extension access.
Outside caller can gain dial tone from a user's extension.	Disable trunk group access completely. Block access back to phone system once caller transfers to voice-mail systems.
Inside caller can dial long distance or international long distance directly from desktop phone.	Disable long-distance calling on COS types. Disable country codes and international outbound dialing completely. Use **authorization codes** for long distance or international dialing for employees who need it.
Outside caller can dial long distance and international long distance directly once dial tone is accessed through the system.	Disable country codes and international outbound dialing completely. Use authorization codes or passwords for long-distance or international dialing for employees who need it.

- **Disable remote access via the analog modem port**—PBX remote access ports lack proper security. Consider disabling these ports.
- **Harden operating system with updated software patches**—Install all available software patches as soon as possible to reduce exposure.
- **Harden class-of-service definitions for users**—Policies should define classes of service for different user types.
- **Harden trunk access group restrictions**—Policies should define to whom and from what phone you should grant access to a trunk or phone line.
- **Disable trunk access from voice mailboxes**—You should never allow access to an outside phone line from a voice mailbox.
- **Enable system logging and call-detail recording**—These must be part of your security operations and management.
- **Conduct periodic audits and review of call detail records**—You should audit domestic and long-distance calling regularly as part of your security operations and management.

From Digital to Voice over IP (VoIP)

In the 15 years after AT&T was broken up into RBOCs, voice communications switched from analog to digital. This drove the union of voice, video, and data communications using multiplexing technology. In the 10 years after 2000, global acceptance of the Internet and the use of TCP/IP protocols resulted in another major change: Voice communications switched from digital PBX systems to **voice over IP (VoIP)**. Voice now routinely travels with data on LANs and WANs. This radical change in voice communications has its own security implications and affects nearly every IT organization in the following ways:

- **A migration strategy is required to transition from digital PBX to VoIP**—Some PBX vendors developed migration strategies from basic PBX technology to **IP-PBX** hybrid technology (a digital PBX with VoIP capability).
- **Telecom and data networking departments merge**—Barriers between voice and data organizations were torn down, leaving organizations with political battles and downsizing.
- **Management and support responsibilities are consolidated**—IT organizations benefited from management consolidation for both voice and data infrastructures, resulting in simplified operations.
- **LANs and WANs need refreshing**—VoIP needs dedicated, switched Ethernet LAN connectivity. As users upgrade LANs to **GigE** or **10GigE**, switches must support voice and data IP traffic. **Power over Ethernet (PoE)** switches provide electrical power for IP phones from the RJ-45 8-pin jacks directly to the workstation outlet.

- **Quality of service (QoS) is needed on WAN links**—If VoIP traffic needs to traverse through a WAN with congestion, you need **quality of service (QoS)**. QoS reserves some bandwidth for time-sensitive applications such as VoIP or unified communications (which use SIP). Network devices can implement **traffic prioritization** to better support VoIP and SIP IP packets and reduce dropped calls and delays.
- **Voice and data IP traffic converge on the same LAN and WAN infrastructure**—VoIP and unified communications traffic uses 64-byte and 128-byte IP packets.
- Voice and data VLANs must be configured to segment voice and data traffic where needed—Voice and data traffic should be separated onto different VLANs. This isolates VoIP traffic from data traffic, separates small IP packets from large ones, and is easier to manage and troubleshoot.
- **100Mbps or GigE workstation LAN connections should be implemented to support both VoIP and data traffic**—With broadband LAN connections to the workstation, VoIP and data traffic can coexist on the same LAN connection up to the LAN switch where it can be segmented.
- **Voice and data traffic should be segmented on different backbone links**—To optimize performance, segment voice and data traffic on separate GigE or 10GigE fiber-optic trunks.
- **Network should be scaled to support 64-byte VoIP and SIP packets**—VoIP and unified communications are both real-time applications. Unified communications use SIP, which rides inside an IP packet.
- **Security controls should be implemented to secure VoIP and SIP on LANs and WANs**—VoIP and SIP protocols are not secure. You must use security controls to reduce risks, threats, and vulnerabilities associated with them.

Figure 2-5 depicts the evolution of voice communications from analog to digital to VoIP and unified communications.

FIGURE 2-5
Evolution of voice communications.

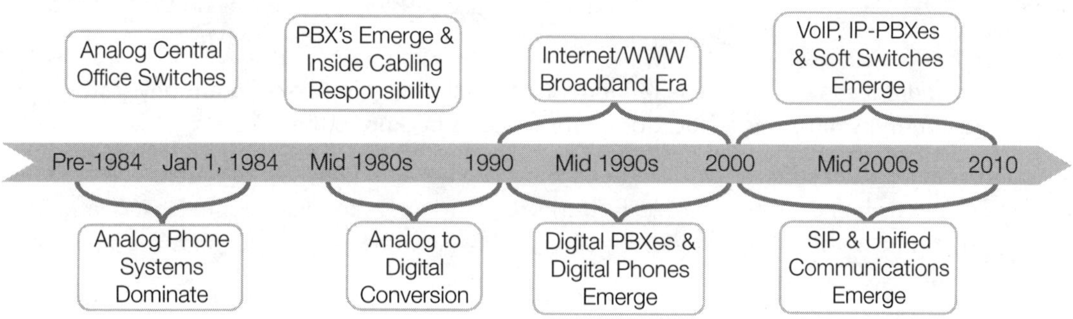

TABLE 2-2 Risks, threats, vulnerabilities, and mitigation plans for VoIP phone systems and SIP applications.

RISK, THREAT, OR VULNERABILITY	MITIGATION
Eavesdropping: Unauthorized parties listening in to phone conversations without permission)	Lock wiring closets, lock down switch LAN attack ports, and house VoIP servers in data center. Deploy separate voice VLANs to minimize access to VoIP traffic. Encrypt VoIP packets where mandated by policy.
Attackers obtaining knowledge about **call control** (VoIP server software), call patterns, and call usage to help them gain unauthorized access	Same as above, plus use strong access controls to the VoIP system. Enable continuous auditing and logging for all system admin access to the VoIP system. Put VoIP call servers on their own firewalled VLAN and encrypt call control.
Attackers impersonating an unauthorized user to gain access to a VoIP phone	Use access controls on VoIP phones to prevent **toll fraud** and non-business use for long-distance and international dialing. Enable second-level authentication on VoIP phones.
Toll fraud or unauthorized use of VoIP phones	Provide users with authorization codes for long-distance and international dialing access.
Brute-force password attacks on VoIP phone systems and phones	Require frequent password-change policies (30/60/90 days). Require long passwords and use of alphanumeric characters.
Denial of service (DoS) and **distributed denial of service (DDoS)** attacks	Put VoIP call servers deep inside your IT infrastructure so that ping or ICMP packets can't move through your IP network. Stop ping or ICMP packets from rogue IP source addresses. Implement an IDS/IPS at the Internet ingress/egress to block ping attacks.
Poor network performance and throughput resulting in dropped VoIP calls	Use separate VLANs for voice and data. Segment voice traffic onto same VLAN with VoIP servers. Use GigE or 10GigE switched LAN connectivity to the desktop. Enable QoS on WAN routers if congestion occurs.
Servers that could fail and disrupt critical business functions	Use redundant VoIP call servers in two different physical locations, one acting as backup to the other.
Disclosure of confidential data because VoIP and data are shared	Isolate departmental VoIP and data VLANs. Enable VoIP and SIP firewalls to secure VLANs that carry confidential information. Remotely access VoIP systems via **secure shell (SSH)**.

VoIP and SIP Risks, Threats, and Vulnerabilities

VoIP and unified communications require real-time support. "Real time" means immediate, as it is happening. VoIP supports voice communications. Unified communications use the SIP multimedia communications protocol. SIP supports the following unified communication applications:

- **Presence/availability**—Within an IM chat box, you can list business, personal, and family contacts, and obtain the current availability status of your contacts.
- **Instant messaging (IM) chat**—This form of real-time communication is used for quick answers to quick questions.
- **Audio conferencing**—**Audio conferencing** is a software-based, real-time audio conference solution for VoIP callers.
- **Videoconferencing**—This is a software-based, real-time video conferencing service.
- **Collaboration**—**Collaboration** allows for software based, real-time, multi-person document and application sharing, with IM chat, audio, and video conferencing functionality.

Although VoIP is a more advanced form of communication, VoIP phone systems suffer from the same risks, threats, and vulnerabilities as digital PBX systems. And because VoIP and unified communications use the TCP/IP family of protocols, they are subject to the same risks, threats, and vulnerabilities as other TCP/IP applications. Table 2-2 lists the risks, threats, and vulnerabilities commonly found in VoIP phone systems and SIP applications, along with risk-mitigation strategies.

VoIP and SIP Security Best Practices

As stated before, VoIP and SIP are not secure protocols. This puts the burden of achieving A-I-C on security personnel using a layered security approach with your IT infrastructure design. A layered security approach means you are placing security countermeasures at multiple domains in the IT infrastructure. In addition, voice and unified communications are real-time applications that use 64-byte IP packets. Lots of these small packets travel the network. This puts a burden on LAN and WAN switches, especially if shared with larger IP packets. One design consideration is to use separate VLANs for voice and data. This practice of segmenting network traffic can help with performance and operational management. Figure 2-6 shows the separation of voice packets from data packets.

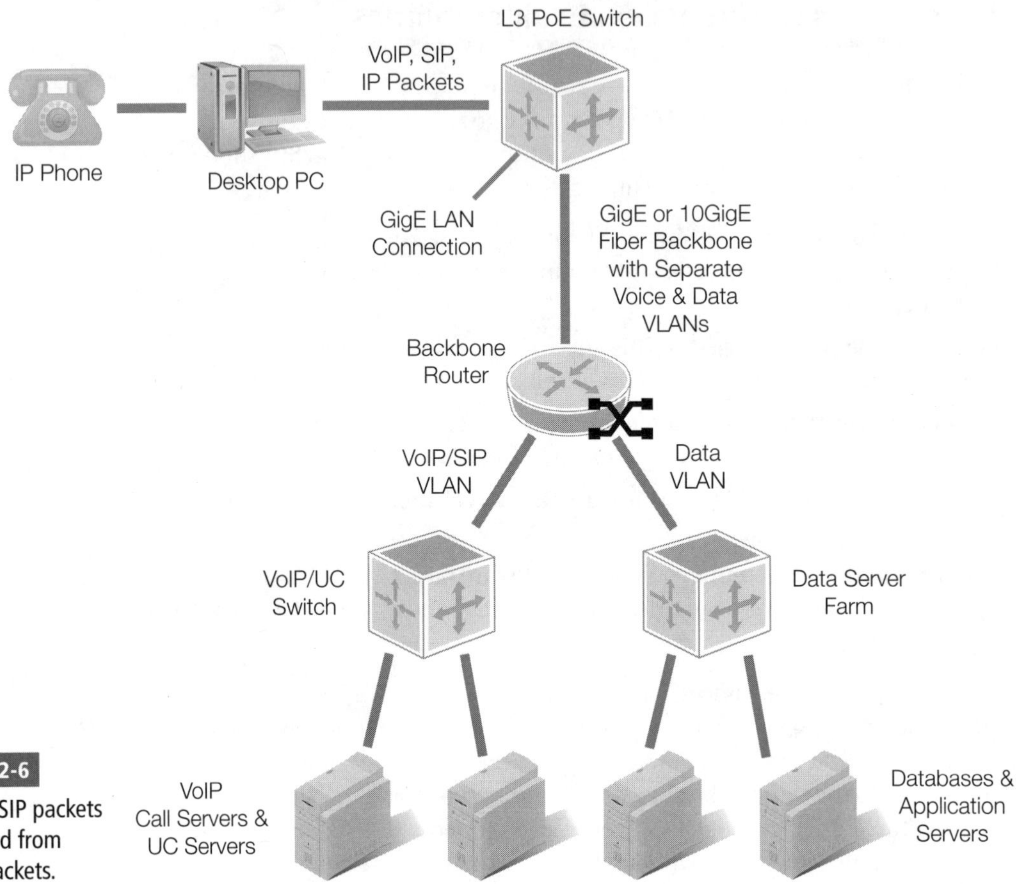

FIGURE 2-6
VoIP and SIP packets segmented from IP data packets.

How can organizations use VoIP and unified communications, knowing the protocols are not secure? The same way organizations use data networking. Proper security controls must protect the organization's voice assets, including long-distance dialing. Remember, VoIP and SIP flow throughout the seven domains of a typical IT infrastructure. This requires a risk assessment of the threats and vulnerabilities that can affect VoIP and SIP applications. Figure 2-7 shows how VoIP and SIP may travel throughout the seven domains of a typical IT infrastructure.

The VoIP Security Alliance (VoIPSA) is a nonprofit organization. It's a leader in providing an open forum for VoIP security, defined by a public domain document called "VoIP Security and Privacy Threat Taxonomy, Release 1.0, October 24, 2005." This document defines the common threats to VoIP and also describes the best ways for reducing then. A list of VoIP security tools and applications is on their Web site: *http://www.voipsa.org*.

As part of its public service, VoIPSA shares these security best practices and useful white papers. The Free Software Foundation provides open source licenses so that anyone can get all the software, documentation, and other materials. The Free Software

Foundation (*http://www.fsf.org*) defined the GNU free software license and documentation license. The URL for GNU is *http://www.gnu.org*. Copies of these public licenses are on their Web site:

- Lesser GNU Public License (LGPL) v3
- GNU Free Documentation License (GFDL) v1.3

When you think of VoIP and SIP best practices for security, you have to examine how A-I-C concerns affect these systems. With VoIP and SIP packets traversing through the IT infrastructure, maintaining A-I-C can be hard. From the risk-reduction strategies listed previously, here are some are best practices for using VoIP and SIP solutions with A-I-C in mind, covering **endpoint security**, physical security, **network infrastructure security**, and **security operations and administration**:

- **Endpoint security**—
    - Before anyone can get a dial tone, IP phones must first logically connect to the IP network; then, users must prove their identity.
    - Enable and run only the minimum functions and features required on the IP phone sets and specific phone extensions.
    - Require passwords or PINs before granting a dial tone for IP phones. Users must enter a valid code to dial long distance. If this is too cumbersome, users must at least be required to prove their identity when using an IP phone prior to getting a dial tone.

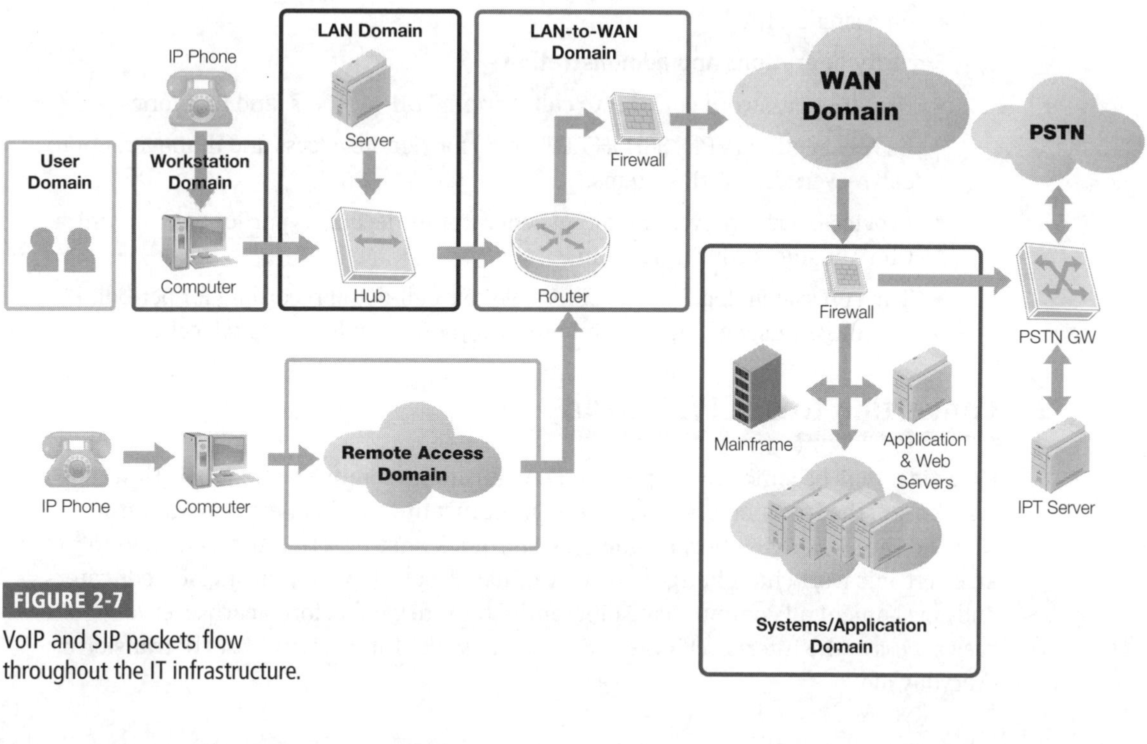

FIGURE 2-7

VoIP and SIP packets flow throughout the IT infrastructure.

FYI

Always turn on **call-detail recording (CDR)** on your phone system. CDR reports give detailed forensics information about the use of your phone system. This is crucial to audit monthly phone bills and long-distance usage, and to identify employee call abuse. CDR is the best way to capture inbound and outbound dialing from each phone extension. Reporting this level of detail tells you everything about the phone system's use. CDR reports help you perform audits of your phone system, phone bill, and employee long-distance use. This helps reduce operating costs through cost consolidation and improved long-distance dialing plans.

- **Physical security**—
  - Lock all doors to phone switch rooms, wiring closets, and cabling systems.
  - Use strict physical access controls to phone switch rooms, wiring closets, and cabling distribution points.
- **Network infrastructure security**—
  - Design and use separate VLANs for voice and data.
  - Use call servers and systems on separate VLANs for proper isolation and security.
  - Harden server operating systems and application software with the latest security patch updates.
  - Encrypt call server signaling if you are not able to isolate call servers on a single VLAN.
- **Security operations and administration**—
  - Use strict password controls to call servers, VoIP systems, and IP phones.
  - Use encryption (VPN, SSH, HTTPS, etc.) for remote access and management to call servers and VoIP systems.
  - Provide backup power or a diesel generator as needed as part of your organization's business continuity plan.
  - Turn on system logging on servers. Enable call-detail recording for periodic auditing of user extensions, inbound/outbound dialing, and **toll calls**.

Converting to a TCP/IP World

How did e-mail become the top personal and business communication tool? How did cell phones, the Internet, and a TCP/IP-communicating world affect Generation Y? How did these changes affect businesses? The quick answer is that the transition to an electronic world has changed our way of life. People, families, businesses, educators, and government all communicate differently than they did before nearly everyone had easy access to the Internet. Figure 2-8 shows how the Internet and TCP/IP transform everyday life.

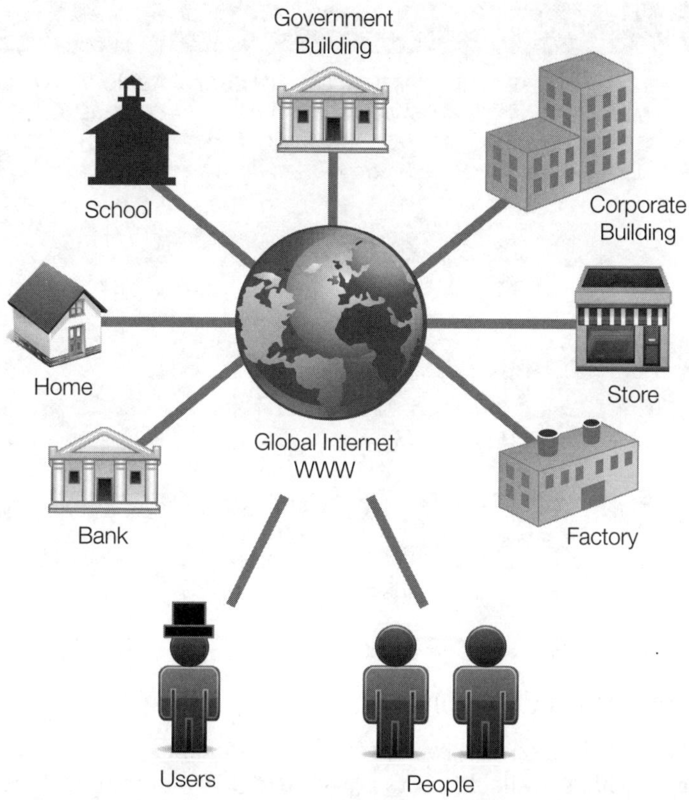

FIGURE 2-8

How the Internet and TCP/IP transform our lives.

Before There Was a World Wide Web

Prior to the widespread use of the Internet—in the dark ages, about 20 years ago—people seemed content to talk on telephones and watch TVs that used analog equipment. No World Wide Web provided instant access to information. News was in newspapers, on television, or on the radio. To talk to people in real time, you had to get them to a telephone. The advent of pagers and voice-messaging systems helped with real-time access and with storing and forwarding information. Eventually, cell phones replaced pagers; people could reach practically anyone, no matter where they were.

In the mid to late 1990s, as use of the Internet and World Wide Web became common, access across the information superhighway began to change everyone's lives. People-to-people communication switched to the Internet, with commerce close behind.

TABLE 2-3 How different types of people communicate.

PERSON	VOICE	TEXT MESSAGING	E-MAIL	PRESENCE/ AVAILABILITY	IM CHAT	AUDIO/VIDEO CONFERENCE	COLLABORATION
Teenage student	L	H	M	H	H	L	L
College student	L	H	H	H	H	L	L
Parent—Gen-Y	M	H	H	H	H	L	L
Parent—Baby Boomer	H	L	M	L	L	L	L
Sales/marketing/ tech professional	H	M	H	H	H	H	H
Sales/marketing/ tech manager	H	M	H	M	M	H	H
Executive manager	H	L	H	L	L	H	H

L = Low Usage, M = Medium Usage, H = Heavy Usage

How Different Groups Communicate

Table 2-3 shows how different types of people communicate.

Depending on what's available, users gravitate to these communication modes. There are two basic ways to communicate:

- **Real-time communications**—When you need to talk to someone right now, **real-time communications** is the preferred mode. It could be to react to a life-threatening situation, to conduct financial transactions like buying stock or securities, or to respond to a security breach.
- **Store-and-forward communications**—When you contact someone via telephone or e-mail and you do not need an immediate response, **store-and-forward communications** may be used. Voice mail and e-mail are examples of store-and-forward communications. You can make store-and-forward communications real time. This is what unified communication does. It converts your voice messages into audio files sent to your e-mail inbox. This is kind of like playing an audio .WAV file, only it's your voice message. You can download your e-mails to your smartphone, PDA device, or BlackBerry device, providing you with immediate access to both voice and e-mail messages.

Broadband Boom of the 1990s

The Internet uses the TCP/IP family of protocols. This information superhighway connects people, families, businesses, organizations, and governments. This transformation to the information superhighway was due to the availability of fiber-optic communication networks built in the 1990s. These networks supported high-speed, broadband Internet access.

The rapidly growing demand for Internet access drove the broadband explosion in the 1990s. Millions of dial-up users started this surge. America Online, EarthLink, AT&T, and other dial-up Internet service providers (ISPs) led the charge. During this dial-up era, service providers laid the nationwide fiber-optic backbone cables.

During the early to mid 1990s, Internet service providers connected the masses with analog dial-up service. Maximum connection speeds ranged from 33.6Kbps to 56Kbps. One of the pioneers of the Internet revolution was America Online. Direct Internet access to residential customers proved to be a winning model. Millions of users signed up for AOL's dial-up access. This led to the explosion of dial-up Internet service providers (ISPs).

Telephone companies found new ways to use existing copper cabling for Internet access. **Digital subscriber line (DSL)** service offered high-speed Internet access. A common DSL service is **asymmetric digital subscriber line (ADSL)**; with ADSL, the bandwidth is different for downstream and upstream traffic. ADSL, which transmits data on telephone lines using different frequencies, can support from 384Kbps to 20Mbps downstream using existing copper facilities, although data travels more slowly upstream. **Symmetric digital subscriber line (SDSL)** is another broadband option that provides two-way communications with equal bandwidth for downstream and upstream communications. (Bandwidth depends on physical distance, line conditions, and the type of DSL technology the carrier uses.)

Cable TV brought the next broadband evolution. The U.S. **Federal Communications Commission (FCC)** opened the market for voice, Internet, cable TV, and data connectivity. Few people foresaw the long-term impact of that decision. Now, cable TV providers, Internet service providers, and telephone companies can provide the following:

- **Voice communication services**—Local and long-distance phone service
- **Internet access**—Dedicated Internet connectivity with service level agreements (SLAs)
- **Cable TV services**—Local cable television service with pay-per-view on-demand movies
- **Residential and business customer service**—Different customer-service departments for residential and business customers

This openness drove the competitive landscape for broadband services. Today, residential and business customers have several choices for communications. Customers can enjoy bundled services from a single service provider with one monthly bill. Another attractive feature of this new approach to service offerings—from the provider's point of view—is that bundling of services makes it difficult for a customer to switch providers. Figure 2-9 shows the evolution of the Internet from dial-up access to broadband.

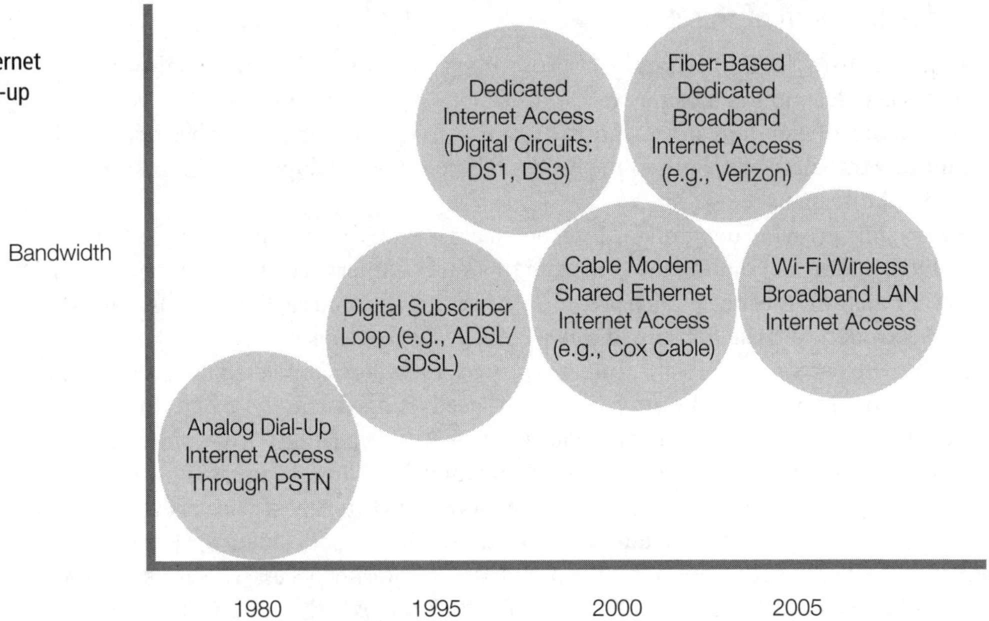

FIGURE 2-9

Evolution of Internet access from dial-up to broadband.

IP Transformation of Telecommunication Service Providers

Before phone companies and service providers could take advantage of new market opportunities, they had a major challenge to overcome. They had to change their legacy circuit-switched networks into next-generation broadband networks. The good news was that these broadband networks used fiber-optic backbones and IP networking. The bad news was that they were being installed and not yet available during the early 1990s. Post-divestiture, copper-based networks changed to fiber-optic networks. As fiber-optic backbone networks became available, they drove down the cost for broadband connections. With more data using the same physical path, the cost per megabit fell.

Service providers raced to change their legacy networks into next-generation broadband networks. This transformation required several important changes, including the following:

- **Maximizing reusability of copper cabling**—Reusing cabling was a critical transition step for service providers to migrate to digital communication systems.
- **Replacing copper cabling with fiber-optic cabling**—Fiber-optic cabling replaced copper, supporting today's broadband networks.
- **Converting from circuit switching to packet switching**—Packet-based networks emerged, like **frame relay** and **asynchronous transfer mode (ATM)**–supporting WAN connectivity.
- **Migrating from packet switching to IP networking**—As Internet access became popular, so did IP networking.

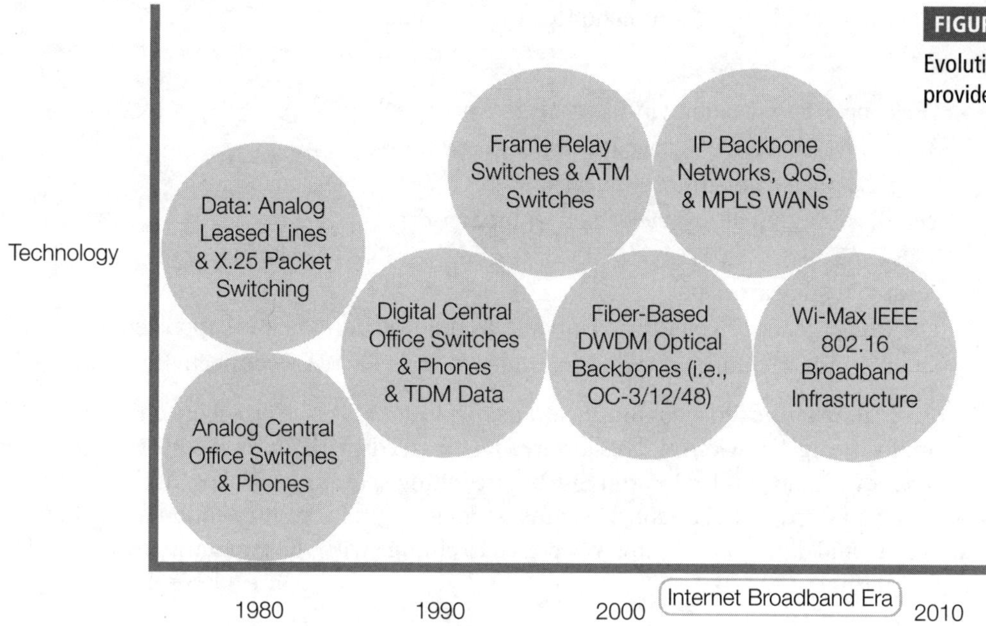

FIGURE 2-10

Evolution of service-provider networks.

New service providers emerged in the early 1990s. These next-generation broadband service providers built nationwide fiber-optic backbone networks. Once in place, IP backbone networks supported Internet access and IP connectivity. Traditional phone companies and service providers had to replace their analog switches with digital switches. This was not easy. Service providers who made the change are still in business. Those that didn't change didn't survive. Figure 2-10 shows the evolution of service-provider networks.

1970s to 1984 (Divestiture): Analog Communications Ruled

During this era:

- Cabling infrastructure was copper based.
- Communication systems were analog.
- Analog transmissions had a high bit-error rate.
- Voice communications were supported by analog switches and phone systems.
- Data communications consisted of analog leased lines and X.25 packet networks.
- Bandwidth ranged from 9.6Kbps to 56Kbps depending on the quality of the physical line.

The era prior to divestiture used analog communications for both voice and data. A common problem with using analog for transmitting data was that analog communications carried high bit-error rates. Service providers used existing copper cabling to design voice and data communication systems. This resulted in bandwidth ranging from 9.6Kbps up to 56Kbps. In most cases, line quality maximized bandwidth at 38.4Kbps. X.25 packet switching was common in WAN technology used in the 1970s and 1980s prior to digital and broadband services being available.

Divestiture to Late 1980s: Transforming to a Digital World

During this era:

- The copper-based cabling infrastructure was reusable.
- Analog systems were replaced with digital switches.
- Long-distance competition was born.
- Digital communications yielded lower bit-error rates.
- **DS0s** (56Kbps), then T-1s (1.544Mbps), and then T-3s (45Mbps) became readily available.
- The convergence of voice, video, and data communications was supported.
- Sharing of bandwidth brought economies of scale for WAN connectivity.

AT&T's breakup launched a communications revolution. Service providers changed from analog to digital switches. This fostered faster speeds with lower bit-error rates. Digital bandwidth expanded beyond 56Kbps, reaching speeds of 45Mbps. In the 1990s, T-1s, or 1.544Mbps digital circuits, became popular. Digital communications combined voice, video, and data. Networking was poised to change with the popularity of TCP/IP and the Internet.

Late 1980s to Mid 1990s: Next-Generation WAN Services

The following bullet points describe communications offerings during this era:

- The copper-based cabling infrastructure was reusable.
- Digital communications supported fixed bandwidth but was not very scalable.
- One-to-many and many-to-many remote connectivity was needed.
- Frame relay switches were used to provide affordable bandwidth.
- Frame relay WAN services provided a bandwidth-on-demand offering.
- ATM switches were deployed providing high-speed backbone networking using fiber-optic backbones (OC-3, OC-12, etc.) with copper-based T-1 (1.544Mbps) or T-3 (45Mbps) endpoint access.
- ATM was a pre-IP solution for supporting real-time applications such as voice and video.

During this time, service providers began offering frame-relay and ATM WAN services. Frame relay is a packet-based WAN service. It can support one-to-many and many-to-many WAN connections and provides for a cloud-service offering. This means organizations can connect to the cloud or network at the closest endpoint and ride on the service provider's backbone network. Frame relay is unique because it offers customers a guaranteed amount of bandwidth. This is defined as a throttle, called a **committed information rate (CIR)**. CIR is like cruise control for a car. When you set the cruise control to a speed limit, the car accelerates to that speed. Likewise, frame relay can support large bursts of traffic while providing a guaranteed CIR or throughput. CIR is the amount of guaranteed bandwidth that frame relay switches can provide through a virtual circuit to a customer's router.

FIGURE 2-11
Frame-relay CIR throttle.

For example, the CIR can be guaranteed up to 256 Kbps as shown in figure 2-11, with bursting supported beyond this committed bandwidth. Figure 2-11 shows how a frame-relay CIR throttle works.

Up to now, data networks have been unable to support time-sensitive applications such as voice and video. Data networking changed into packet-switched types of architectures. Data networking evolved from frame relay to asynchronous transfer mode (ATM) to IP networking. Advances in IP networking allowed support for real-time applications such as VoIP and unified communications (UC). UC applications use the **Session Initiation Protocol (SIP)**.

Service providers liked ATM because it could support voice, video, and data communications. ATM uses 53-byte cells or packets and can support optical broadband speeds. ATM was the front-runner in service-provider networks before the Internet and IP networking boom of the mid to late 1990s. Figure 2-12 shows the format of an ATM cell.

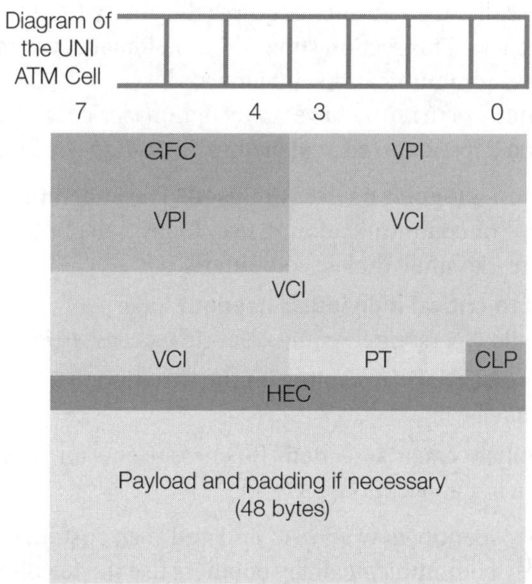

FIGURE 2-12
Asynchronous transfer mode (ATM) and use of 53-byte cells.

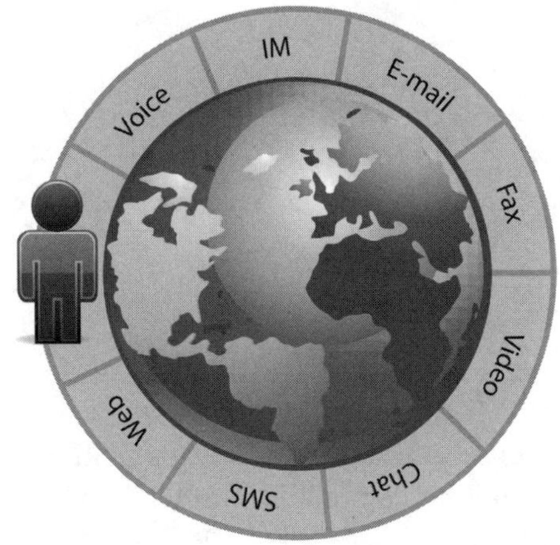

FIGURE 2-13
Multimodal communications.

Multimodal Communications

Today, people use several different types of communication methods. For fast and quick questions, members of Gen Y prefer text messaging via cell phone or smartphone. Baby boomers prefer picking up the phone and calling another person directly. Individuals online can use VoIP or IM chat.

Which communication method should you use? That depends on what you are trying to do as the communicator. Personal communications are usually short and quick—ask a question and get an answer. Business communications can be short or long. When communicating with more than one person, you should consider conducting a meeting or conference call. Business often requires the ability to share documents and review them with others. This section shows how **multimodal communications** can solve unique business communication challenges.

Individuals and businesses currently have many options for communicating. Selecting the best method depends on several factors, including the following:

- **What communication endpoint devices are used?** The endpoint device will determine what type of communication to use. Today, cell phones, smartphones, and PDA devices are like small mobile computers.
- **Is real-time access to critical individuals needed?** Emergency responders such as police, fire, and medical personnel require real-time access to key people.
- **Is real-time access essential?** Depending on the situation, use of store-and-forward communications may be fine.
- **Are productivity enhancements needed?** Business users can benefit from audio- and video-conferencing applications.

Businesses always have to identify new ways to find and keep customers. How they do that depends on how they communicate. Baby boomers use the telephone as the primary business communication tool. Members of Generation Y generally prefer text-messaging, e-mailing, and chatting via IM. Businesses need to know their customers so they can adapt to them. Driving customers to self-serve Web sites helps lower costs. This can also provide 24×7×365 "always-on" customer service. Businesses need VoIP and SIP protocols and applications to enhance customer service. Figure 2-13 shows some of the different components of multimodal communications.

Voice over IP (VoIP) Migration

The early 2000s saw a mass movement from traditional PBX technology to VoIP. What caused this? How did IP packets and IP networking support real-time voice communications? If TCP/IP is insecure, does that mean VoIP also is insecure? In the beginning, VoIP seemed like a square peg in a round hole. How did this perception change? What were some of the business drivers leading this basic shift away from traditional PBXs?

Here are some of the realities that enterprises faced in the mid 1990s into the early 2000s that drove users to VoIP:

- **The communications world was changing to TCP/IP**—The Internet drove people and businesses to change their applications and the way people access them.
- **PBXs could transmit voice with only limited data capability**—Legacy voice PBX systems could not support convergence with data.
- **Convergence of voice, video, and data required updates to IP networking**—Voice and video needed WANs and broadband desktop connectivity to support time-sensitive applications such as VoIP, conferencing, and collaboration.
- **Lower operational and ongoing management costs through consolidation**—Convergence brought consolidation of voice, video, and data communications. All communications were now by TCP/IP.
- **VoIP is insecure**—Like TCP/IP, VoIP and its signaling protocols are not secure. This puts the burden of security on the network and requires a layered security approach.
- **SIP is the basis for unified communications**—SIP is the protocol used by real-time applications such as IM chat, conferencing, and collaboration.

VoIP continues to be the most popular choice for small, medium, and large enterprises because VoIP can ride on the same physical network as data. This gives greater economies of scale. With broadband connected to the desktop, VoIP and workstation connections can share the same LAN connection. VoIP drives convergence. Convergence merges voice, video, and data communications. It encompasses **protocol convergence**, **infrastructure convergence**, and **application convergence**:

- **Protocol convergence**—TCP/IP has become the lowest common denominator for multimodal communications. Many applications have converged on the use of IP as the network layer protocol.
- **Infrastructure convergence**—Using the same 4-pair, unshielded twisted-pair cabling, 100Mbps or GigE workstations can connect to IP phones sharing the same physical cabling. Commingled voice and data IP traffic goes over the shared workstation cabling. Separate voice and data VLANs divide traffic in the wiring closet and building backbone networks.

- **Application convergence**—Applications come together to improve productivity. Unified communications is an example. It integrates recorded voice messages into e-mail. That allows a user to play their voice messages remotely like an audio file sent by e-mail.

Why all the hype, then, about VoIP and convergence? Without convergence, you can never integrate voice with data communications. Today, VoIP provides the basis for integration of enhanced voice communication services with real-time messaging. VoIP supports voice calls and audio conferencing. Figure 2-14 shows an enterprise IP telephony infrastructure.

FIGURE 2-14

Enterprise IP telephony infrastructure.

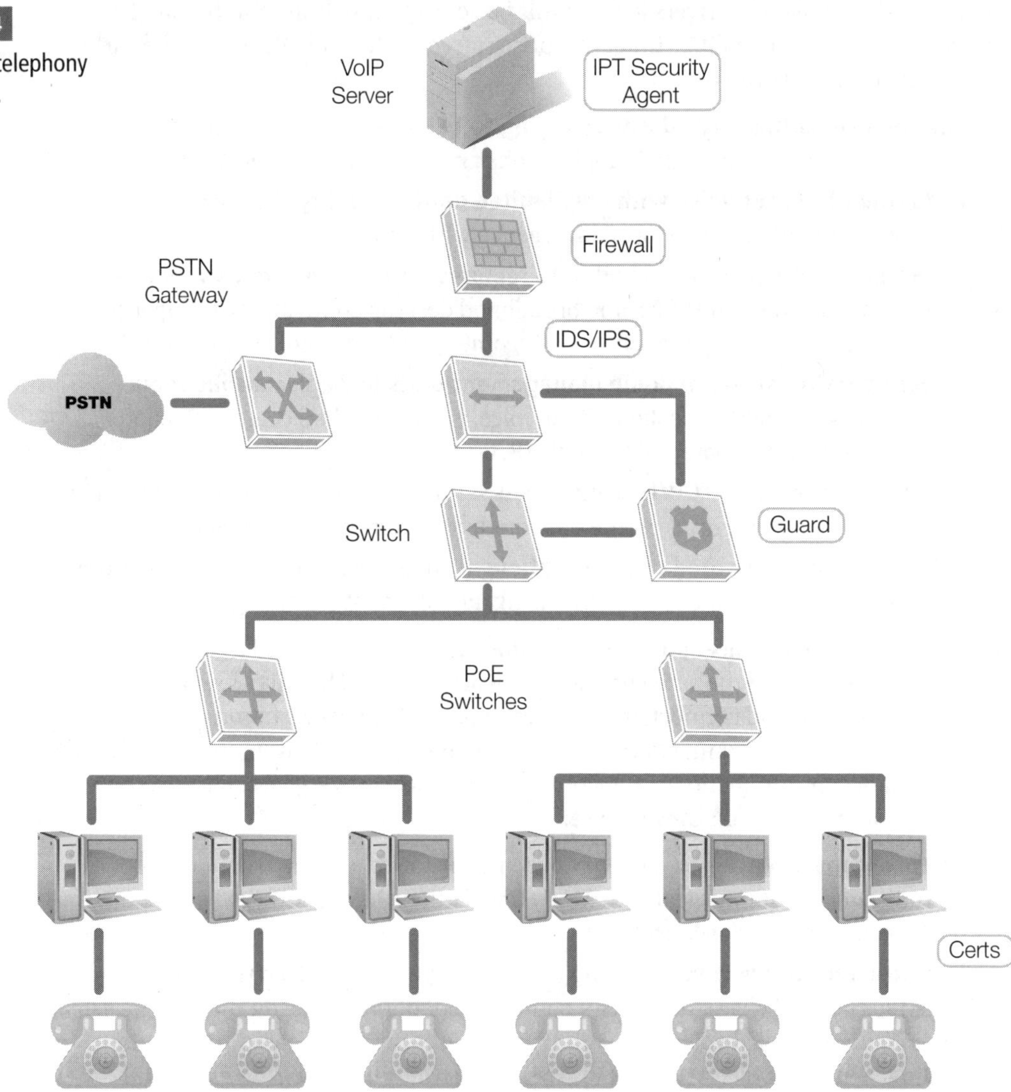

Unified Communications (UC)

Think about the impact that VoIP has made on personal and business communications. Thanks to the Internet, long-distance calls can be free as long as users use VoIP. VoIP is what many popular instant-messaging applications use to support voice communications. Yahoo! Instant Messenger, Microsoft Windows Live, and Skype use VoIP and SIP. Today, desktop computers, laptops, and netbooks come equipped with built-in microphones and Web cams. These VoIP- and SIP-ready tools and applications can support real-time, multimedia communications.

The evolution from analog to digital phone systems was far more than just a format change. Digital telephony migrated to VoIP. As workstation connections reached broadband speeds, VLANs helped separate voice traffic from data traffic. WANs meanwhile needed refining to support time-sensitive uses. This included introducing QoS for setting traffic priorities. IP networks adapted to the onslaught of VoIP traffic. VoIP gave the basis for the advent of unified communications. UC gives several real-time communication solutions, each one unique in the business challenges it solves.

What is unified communications? UC is a suite of real-time communication applications that enhance productivity and support the natural ways we communicate. UC is not new; it has been around since the advent of Instant Messenger. Generation Y users use UC as a social-networking tool. Now, businesses use it to enhance productivity. UC applications provide these features:

- **Presence/availability**—24-hour, always-on contact status.
- **Instant messaging (IM) chat**—IM chat is best for real-time messaging and quick questions. If the user is available, you can get an immediate response. If not, the message is sent to the recipient and is retrieved the next time that user logs in.
- **Audio conferencing**—UC supports audio-conferencing services, enabling multiple users to participate in a conference call.
- **Videoconferencing**—UC supports video-conferencing services enabling multiple users to participate in a videoconference call.
- **Collaboration**—UC supports real-time application sharing for true real-time collaboration among remote users.

Multimodal communications gives you many ways to communicate with customers. These methods include telephone, fax, and e-mail. For example, you can call someone and leave a voice message when the recipient is not there. This is an example of store-and-forward communications, just like e-mail. UC does not focus on leaving messages, however. UC is about communicating in real time. Organizations must define how they want their business partners and customers to contact them while providing the best customer service. With multimodal communications, you must tell your customers how you want them to contact you.

The next section demonstrates how using UC can solve both internal and external business challenges. UC gives users real-time access and communications. You can choose from a variety of devices to support UC, including smartphones, PDA devices, and desktop computers.

Solving Business Challenges with Unified Communications

Business process reengineering is a fancy term for streamlining business processes, eliminating human latency in the decision-making process. **Human latency** is the amount of time humans take to consider input or correspondence, take action, and then respond. It's like building a better mousetrap. To reengineer business processes, you identify the points in a process that require a decision or authorization to continue. Then you suggest changes to streamline the process to reach that decision. UC solves human latency by giving real-time access and communication to key personnel. UC is the opposite of store-and-forward communications, such as voice mail and e-mail. Imagine having to leave a voice message or e-mail message in these situations:

- You are driving on a highway approaching an exit. You call friends for immediate directions and you get their voice mailbox.
- You are in a car accident and are injured. The 911 operator cannot contact an ambulance in real time.
- You are about to close a big sale, but your boss can't be reached to approve a larger discount.
- You cannot contact your spouse to talk about a last-minute change to a contract for buying a house.

Can you think of examples in which human latency can affect human life, cause you to lose money, or diminish business performance? That is the purpose of UC: to solve the human latency problem by eliminating the latency.

FIGURE 2-15

Unified communication can enhance customer-service delivery.

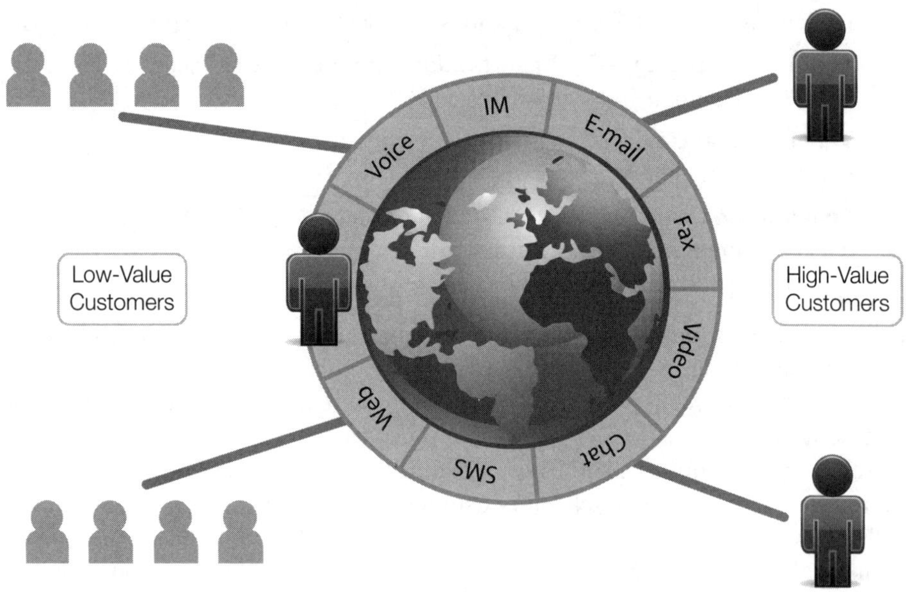

TABLE 2-4 Examples of Unified Communications solutions.

INEFFICIENT BUSINESS PROCESS	UC ENABLEMENT SOLUTION
Cannot find emergency-room doctor or nurse	Emergency medical personnel are "always-on" with a UC-enabled cell phone, smartphone, PDA device, or tablet computer. Real-time presence and availability with IM chat are enabled.
Sales manager is unavailable for approval of a large order with negotiated discount.	Sales managers and outside sales personnel are all UC connected. Real-time presence, availability, and IM chat are enabled.
High-value customers cannot reach a customer-service agent for immediate service.	Preferred customer-service agents are UC-connected to the customer-service call center. When VIP customers call in, real-time access to preferred customer-service agents is enabled.
Just-in-time manufacturing process cannot find factory supervisors to deal with production issues, slowing delivery schedules.	Production supervisors and on-floor supervisor are all UC connected. Real-time presence and availability, IM chat, conferencing, and collaboration for remote discussion are enabled.
Stockbrokers and traders cannot reach supervisors regarding approvals for large buy/sell orders, slowing financial transactions.	Stockbrokers and traders are all UC connected with supervisors for real-time approvals when needed.
Bank sales representatives must share loan documents with financial underwriters, loan officers, and risk assessors.	UC connected loan officers, underwriters, and risk assessors can collaborate in real-time for same-business-day loan-approval decisions.

Examples of Human Latency and UC Enablement

Humans are not the most efficient in streamlining processes. UC can solve this latency with real-time access to key personnel. Table 2-4 lists some examples of UC enablement.

UC is a great way for parents to reach their children in real time. It is an excellent tool for public-safety personnel to communicate during incidents. It can save lives. UC shrinks the time it takes to do anything that involves human communication.

UC can help businesses find ways to improve customer service. Many companies have frequent-buyer programs. They identify high-value customers and offer them incentives. Many businesses conform to the 80–20 rule—80 percent of their revenue is from 20 percent of their customers. The remaining 80 percent are **low-value customers** that you want to convert to high-value customers. Figure 2-15 depicts how UC can enhance customer-service delivery for high-value customers.

UC has many potential benefits for organizations. Led by Microsoft, UC enablement is now a desktop and mobile reality. Workers are always on and connected to the Internet via their cell phone or PDA device. Students are also now UC connected. Securing VoIP and SIP has now become increasingly important. Following are several benefits of using UC:

- **UC supports enhanced parenting**—UC enables parents to keep in touch with their children in real time.
- **UC enhances productivity**—UC enables real-time access to coworkers, audio and video conferencing, and project collaboration.
- **UC saves money**—UC lowers real-estate costs, lowers communication costs, and eliminates travel expenses for face-to-face meetings and training.
- **UC enables employees to work from home**—With broadband Internet access, employees are connected to colleagues and can work from home, reducing costs and saving travel time.
- **UC can deliver real-time or recorded training**—Travel expenses are eliminated, and training can be "just in time," with real-time training and webinar-like deliveries for the masses.
- **UC enhances customer-service delivery**—Real-time access to technical or customer-service specialists helps drive enhanced customer-service support for high-value customers.
- **UC shortens business decision making**—With real-time access to key decision makers, critical business decisions are made more quickly, shortening cycle times.

These benefits demand that VoIP and SIP have proper security controls. You must first address security with VoIP and SIP. This requires a layered security solution to ensure A-I-C.

Evolution from Brick-and-Mortar to e-Commerce

The Internet changed more than how people communicate. It also revolutionized business. Brick-and-mortar businesses now have global reach. E-commerce changed how businesses sell, and the Internet changed how they market.

What is e-commerce? It is the sale of goods and services on the Internet. Online customers buy goods and services from a vendor's Web site. They enter private data and checking account or credit card information.

E-commerce supports two business models, **business to consumer (B2C)** and **business to business (B2B)**:

- **Business to consumer (B2C)**—Businesses create an online storefront for customers to purchase goods and services directly from their Web site, such as *http://www.amazon.com*.
- **Business to business (B2B)**—Businesses build online systems with links for conducting sales with other businesses, usually for integrated supply-chain purchases and deliveries.

E-commerce systems and applications demand strict A-I-C security controls. Organizations must use solid security controls to protect their information from all attackers on the Internet. This is especially true if private data and credit card information crosses the Internet. To comply with the **Payment Card Industry Data Security Standard (PCI DSS)**, businesses must conduct security assessments and use the right controls to protect private customer data.

Solving Business Challenges with e-Business Transformation

The Internet created a global online marketplace nearly overnight. No one foresaw such a large change—or the resulting impact. Once the Internet became ubiquitous, advertising, sales, and marketing were no longer restrained to television, radio, newspapers and magazines, and direct mail. Marketing is about finding new customers, keeping them, and providing better goods and services. The Internet made these activities possible with online convenience. The Internet has realigned business challenges. These new challenges include the following:

- Growing the business through the Internet
- Changing an existing conventional business into an e-business
- Building secure and highly available Web sites and e-commerce portals
- Building a Web-enabled customer-service strategy
- Finding new customers with Internet marketing

Companies like Amazon, DELL, Apple Computer's iTunes, Western Union, e-Bay, Priceline.com, Domino's Pizza, and UPS have created e-business models. Each uses Web sites as the main way to reach global customers. Their customers make purchases with enhanced customer-service delivery built into the Web sites. Self-service is the name of the game. Many online activities, such as account management, can be self-serve. Real-time access to customer-service agents via VoIP and IM chat can enhance the experience for high-value customers.

What is an e-business strategy? It changes business functions and operations into Web-enabled applications. E-business strategies include marketing and selling goods and services on the Internet. An e-business strategy typically includes these elements:

- **E-commerce solution**—This might be an online catalog and system for purchasing goods and services in a secure transaction.
- **Internet marketing strategy**—Internet marketing strategies involve search engine optimization (SEO), which uses embedded meta tags and keywords to help search engines sort results; customer-lead generation, in which marketers request customer information from information Web sites and white-paper downloads; e-mail blasts, in which advertisements and discount coupons are e-mailed directly to prospects; and push marketing, which involves direct sales and marketing based on user interest.

- **E-customer service-delivery strategy**—This is a self-serve and online customer-service strategy.
- **Payment and credit card transaction processing**—Secure online-payment processing and credit card-transaction processing must be encrypted with strict back-end system security controls to prevent unauthorized access to private customer data.

Why Businesses Today Need an Internet Marketing Strategy

Building an e-business strategy is more than just building a Web site. You must understand how to find new business partners and new customers globally through the Internet. Without an e-business strategy or migration plan to get there, businesses will lose to Internet-savvy competitors. An Internet marketing strategy is a key part of a business's success. It is all about getting more eyeballs to your Web sites and keeping them there. Internet marketing strategies use search-engine strategies, joint marketing agreements, and content that is fresh and in demand. Brick-and-mortar business models are out of date as the sole model in today's global market. Businesses must have an online e-business presence that provides customers with continuous access to information, products, and services. Figure 2-16 shows the process of transforming to an e-business model on the World Wide Web.

As businesses include the Internet in their business models, they increase their exposure to online risks, threats, and vulnerabilities. Remember, connecting to the Internet means exposing yourself to hackers and thieves. Secure Web applications, secure front-end and back-end systems, and encryption of private customer data are critical security controls that each organization must implement to reduce risk.

FIGURE 2-16

Transforming to an e-business model on the Web.

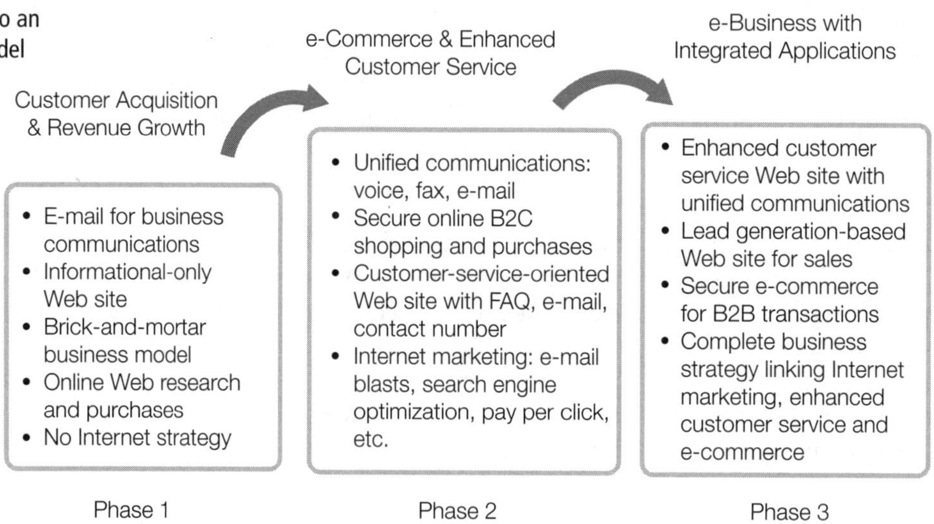

The Web Effect on People, Businesses, and Other Organizations

E-commerce has changed how many businesses sell goods. And other organizations have taken other kinds of transactions online as well. Here are some examples:

- **Buying a computer**—Computers can be ordered online, custom-built to your needs, and sent to your house or business. Boutique computer resellers and system integrators are all but gone.
- **Purchasing recorded music**—You can download digital copies of your favorite recordings. Retail CD and record stores still exist, but in fewer numbers than before.
- **Wiring money globally**—This is now done online with a credit card. Wiring money in person is no longer the only way to complete these types of transactions.
- **Purchasing travel services**—Airplane, hotel, and rental-car purchases have moved to the Internet. Making online reservations is the most popular choice for both businesses and consumers.
- **Purchasing real estate**—Listings have moved to the Internet. Customers can review pictures and videos before e-mailing a real-estate agent to see a property.
- **Donating to charity**—Many organizations find they can reach donors more effectively online than by mail or telephone solicitation; contributors often prefer to be contacted that way, too, and they prefer to give online.
- **Government agencies**—People can renew driver's licenses, download tax forms, or contact officials via the Web.
- **Schools and colleges**—Web sites are critical parts of today's educational institutions, in attracting prospective students, for instance.

CHAPTER SUMMARY

In this chapter, you learned about changes in communication and the impact the Internet has had on people and business. You also learned about the effects of digital protocols evolving and becoming the standard for voice, video, and data communications. These changes led to VoIP- and SIP-based unified communications. Today, VoIP and UC support store-and-forward and real-time communications. Because VoIP and SIP are insecure protocols, it is important to ensure a layered security strategy throughout the IT structure. Security practices for VoIP and SIP reduce risks, threats, and vulnerabilities.

Security for VoIP and SIP is critical as users create real-time communication solutions for customers online and on Web sites. Web-application and Internet security is essential for businesses moving to e-business and e-commerce. As businesses, customers, and applications flock to the Internet, the need for A-I-C to ensure security and compliance continues to grow.

KEY CONCEPTS AND TERMS

10GigE
Analog central office (CO) switch
Application convergence
Asymmetric digital subscriber line (ADSL)
Asynchronous transfer mode (ATM)
Audio conferencing
Authorization codes
Bit error rate
Brute-force password attack
Business process reengineering
Business to business (B2B)
Business to consumer (B2C)
Call control
Call-detail recording (CDR)
Central office (CO)
Class of service (COS)
Collaboration
Committed information rate (CIR)
Convergence
Denial of service (DoS)
Dense wavelength division multiplexing (DWDM)
Digital central office (CO) switch
Digital subscriber line (DSL)
Direct inward dial (DID)
Direct inward system access (DISA)
Distributed denial of service (DDoS)
Divestiture
DS0
Eavesdropping
Endpoint security
Federal Communications Commission (FCC)
Frame relay
GigE
High-value customer
Human latency
Infrastructure convergence
IP-PBX
Low-value customer
Multimodal communications
Network infrastructure security
Payment Card Industry Data Security Standard (PCI DSS)
Power over Ethernet (PoE)
Protocol convergence
Public branch exchange (PBX) phone system
Quality of service (QoS)
Real-time communications
Regional Bell Operating Company (RBOC)
Secure shell (SSH)

KEY CONCEPTS AND TERMS, *continued*

Security operations and administration
Session Initiation Protocol (SIP
Social engineering
Store-and-forward communications
Symmetric digital subscriber line (SDSL)
Toll calls
Toll fraud
Traffic prioritization
Trunk access group restriction (TAGR)
Unified communications (UC)
Videoconferencing
Voice over IP (VoIP)

CHAPTER 2 ASSESSMENT

1. PBX phone systems are susceptible to unauthorized access through the analog modem port connected to the maintenance port.

A. True
B. False

2. Which security control can best reduce toll fraud for PBX systems?

A. Enable trunk access group restrictions and turn off trunk access
B. Define stringent class-of-service definitions for users
C. Turn on authentication for IP phones
D. Turn on encryption for all VoIP communications
E. None of the above

3. Organize the following in the proper sequence of when they happened, 1–5, with 1 being first.

A. ____ Unified communications
B. ____ Divestiture
C. ____ TDM multiplexing
D. ____ Digital PBX
E. ____ VoIP

4. What drove service providers to install fiber-optic backbone networks?

A. Demand for Internet access
B. Broadband growth and expansion
C. Copper transmission capacity was maxed out
D. Lower cost per megabit was needed to support demand
E. All of the above

5. ________ convergence is the combination of voice, video, and data communications using TCP/IP.

A. Application
B. Protocol
C. Infrastructure
D. Voice
E. None of the above

6. Which of the following is *not* an SIP application?

A. Presence/availability
B. SMS text messaging
C. IM chat
D. Conferencing
E. Collaboration

7. Which of the following security controls can help reduce threats to call-control signaling between call servers?

A. Physically placing call servers in locked data centers or phone rooms
B. Updating call servers with system patches and updates
C. Isolating call servers on their own VLAN
D. Enabling firewalls at VLAN edges
E. All of the above

8. Unified communications solves the ________ communication challenge.

A. Human latency
B. One-to-many
C. Many-to-many
D. VoIP
E. SIP

9. Which of the following UC applications can eliminate the need for face-to-face training?

A. Audio conferencing
B. Collaboration
C. IM chat
D. Presence/availability
E. Video conferencing

10. SIP is more secure than VoIP.

A. True
B. False

11. Why do e-commerce systems need the utmost in security controls?

A. PCI DSS
B. Private customer data is entered into Web sites
C. Financial transaction data is entered into Web sites
D. Customer retention requires confidence in secure online purchases
E. All of the above

12. Which of the following is *not* a benefit of using unified communications?

A. Supports work-from-home for employees
B. Shrinks human latency in decision making
C. Enhances productivity with real-time communications
D. Requires a layered security strategy
E. Lowers training and travel expenses through collaboration

13. Unified communications can reduce human latency in business decision making.

A. True
B. False

CHAPTER 3

Malicious Attacks, Threats, and Vulnerabilities

IN PREVIOUS CHAPTERS, you learned about some general security concepts. Now you are ready to learn about the serious problems of malicious attacks, threats, and vulnerabilities. As you learned in Chapter 1, the Internet is an untamed new frontier. Unlike in your everyday life, in cyberspace, there is no real law of the land. Criminal acts that lead to destruction and theft occur regularly. These acts affect businesses, individuals, and governments. The criminals often go unpunished. Sometimes, the acts even go undiscovered.

Malicious attacks result in billions of dollars in damages each year. Fortunately, many companies and individuals like you are working hard to protect IT assets from attacks. In this chapter, you will learn how to identify security vulnerabilities, protect your organization from threats, and keep your computers safe from malicious attacks.

Chapter 3 Topics

This chapter covers the following topics and concepts:

- What the global scope of cyberattacks is
- What you are trying to protect
- Whom you are trying to catch
- What kinds of tools are used to attack computer systems
- What a security breach is
- What vulnerabilities and threats are
- What a malicious attack is
- What malicious software is
- What countermeasures are available

Chapter 3 Goals

When you complete this chapter, you will be able to:

- Identify malicious code and implement countermeasures
- Identify common attacks and develop appropriate countermeasures
- Recognize social engineering and reduce the risks associated with it
- Implement system auditing, logging, and scanning
- Implement basic access controls
- Explain the basics of risk identification
- Explain the importance of end user education and training

Malicious Activity on the Rise

You have probably seen the stories on the news, viewed the humorous ads on TV, or read the headlines about cyberattacks. A case in point: Recently, authorities sent a college student to prison for 20 years for hacking the e-mail account of a U.S. vice presidential candidate. In a similar incident, clothing retailer TJX Companies admitted to carelessness in allowing the theft of millions of payment card numbers. In addition, in a humorous prime-time commercial, a clueless employee sets off a company-wide virus attack by clicking a "harmless" e-mail. Everywhere around you, you find examples of the malicious attacks that security professionals face every day.

While these attacks grabbed the attention of the news media and the public, most victims of cyberattacks don't publicize the incidents at all. Every day, systems around the world are under threat. In most cases, the only people who ever know about these attacks are security professionals and IT personnel. Table 3-1 shows how malicious activity is a worldwide problem.

Security professionals are responsible for protecting their systems from threats and for handling malicious attacks when they do occur. One of the most effective ways to protect computer systems is to make sure that the vulnerabilities that exist in every IT infrastructure don't turn into anything more serious.

TABLE 3-1 Malicious activity by country.

OVERALL RANK			PERCENTAGE OF CYBERATTACKS		2009 RANK BY TYPE OF MALICIOUS ACTIVITY				
2009	2008	COUNTRY	2009	2008	MALICIOUS CODE	SPAM ZOMBIES	PHISHING HOSTS	BOTS	ATTACK ORIGIN
1	1	United States	19	23	1	6	1	1	1
2	2	China	8	9	3	8	6	2	2
3	5	Brazil	6	4	5	1	12	3	6
4	3	Germany	5	6	21	7	2	5	3
5	11	India	4	3	2	3	21	20	18
6	4	Britain	3	5	4	19	7	14	4
7	12	Russia	3	2	12	2	5	19	10
8	10	Poland	3	3	23	4	8	8	17
9	7	Italy	3	3	16	9	18	6	8
10	6	Spain	3	4	14	11	11	7	9

Source: Symantec Corporation

What Are You Trying to Protect?

In a word, you are trying to protect assets. An **asset** is any item that has value. Although all items in an organization have some value, the term asset generally applies to those items that have substantial value. An organization's assets can include the following:

- **IT and network infrastructure**—Hardware, software, and services
- **Intellectual property**—Sensitive data like patents, source code, formulas, or engineering plans
- **Finances and financial data**—Bank accounts, credit card data, and financial transaction data
- **Service availability and productivity**—The ability of computing services and software to support productivity for humans and machinery
- **Reputation**—Corporate compliance and brand image

Let's look at each of these types of assets individually and discuss how they are at risk from malicious attacks.

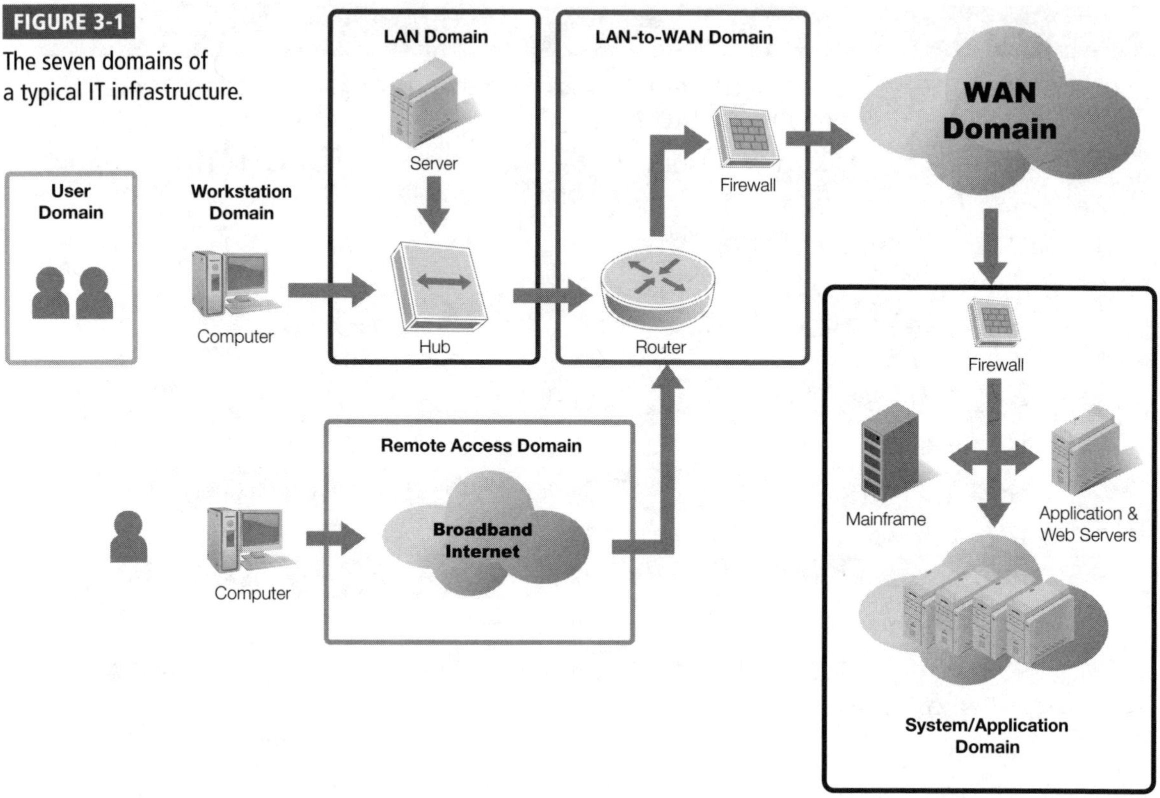

FIGURE 3-1
The seven domains of a typical IT infrastructure.

IT and Network Infrastructure

Hardware and software are key pieces of any organization's infrastructure. Recall the seven domains of the IT infrastructure you learned about in Chapter 1. Figure 3-1 shows the seven domains of the IT infrastructure. Components in each domain may connect to a network or to the Internet, and can be vulnerable to malicious attacks.

Hardware and software damaged by malicious attacks such as Trojan horses or worms cost corporations time and money to fix or replace. Malicious attacks on hardware and software can also lead to more widespread problems. These problems can include loss of critical data or theft of financial information or intellectual property. Unprotected IT and network infrastructure assets can offer attackers and cybercriminals the widest opening to access sensitive resources. The ease of access makes assets that are connected to the Internet the most common first point of attack. That means those same assets should be your first line of defense.

Intellectual Property

Intellectual property (IP) is the center of many organizations. IP is the unique knowledge a business possesses that gives it a competitive advantage over similar companies in similar industries. Examples of IP include such things as patents, drug formulas, engineering plans, scientific formulas, and recipes. In some cases, you can also consider business practices and processes to be intellectual property. Suppose a restaurant chain has a unique process for quickly preparing and delivering food. If the rest of the industry knew about that process, it would remove the restaurant's competitive advantage.

The core issue from an IT security perspective is protecting the theft of intellectual property and preventing its release to competitors or to the public. The theft of intellectual property can nullify an organization's competitive advantage. Imagine that a company called Alpha Drug Company invested $2 billion to develop a new prescription drug, with the expectation that it would earn $10 billion when it releases the drug. Now imagine that just as Alpha Drug Company was set to bring its medication to market, Beta Drug Company obtained Alpha's formulas and rushed its own version to market. Alpha would lose all the money it invested in R&D and a big chunk of the revenue associated with the new drug. Protecting intellectual property is a serious consideration for all IT security professionals.

Finances and Financial Data

Financial assets are among the highest-profile assets in any organization. These assets can take various forms. They can be real financial assets, such as bank accounts, trading accounts, purchasing accounts, corporate credit cards, and other direct sources of money or credit. Alternatively, they can be data that allows access to real financial assets. Financial data can include customer credit card numbers, personal financial information, or usernames and passwords for banking or investment accounts. Other examples include the transaction data that companies and banks use to transfer financial data between themselves. This can include electronic data interchange (EDI) numbers and routing numbers.

Loss of financial assets due to malicious attacks is a worst-case scenario for all organizations. Not only does it represent significant physical loss, but it can also have long-term effects on a company's reputation and brand image.

Service Availability and Productivity

Computer applications provide specific services that help organizations conduct business operations. It is important that critical services be available for use when organizations need them. As you learned in Chapter 1, downtime is the time during which a service is not available due to failure or maintenance. Downtime can be intentional or unintentional. Often, administrators will schedule intentional downtime in advance. For example, when servers need operating-system upgrades or patches, administrators take them offline intentionally so they can perform the necessary work without problems. When administrators schedule intentional downtime, they try to do it so that it has little impact on the rest of the organization. Administrators carefully manage any impact that downtime does have so that it does not disrupt critical business operations. You might be familiar with intentional-downtime scenarios such as weekend upgrades of critical software or overnight application of patches to such things as e-mail systems.

Operation Get Rich or Die Tryin'

In May of 2010, a court sentenced 28-year-old Albert Gonzalez to 20 years in federal prison for breaching security at several well-known retailers and stealing millions of credit card numbers. After stealing the numbers, Gonzalez resold them using a variety of shadow "carding" Web sites. Using a simple packet sniffer, Gonzalez managed to steal payment cards' transaction data in real time. He then parked the card numbers on blind servers in places like Latvia and Ukraine (formerly part of the Soviet Union). Gonzalez, who named his activities "Operation Get Rich or Die Tryin'," enjoyed a lavish lifestyle through the sale of the stolen credit card information. Although the Secret Service eventually tracked him down, Operation Get Rich or Die Tryin' lasted for more than two years. During that period, it cost major retailers like TJX, Office Max, Barnes & Noble, Heartland, and Hannaford more than $200 million in losses and recovery costs. This was the largest computer-crime case ever prosecuted.

At first glance, Operation Get Rich or Die Tryin' seems like an open-and-shut case. An attacker committed a series of cybercrimes, investigators caught the perpetrator, and the authorities successfully prosecuted him. Mr. Gonzalez bore the fault and blame, and the corporations and the millions of cardholders received justice. Not all the blame belongs to the cybercriminal, however. In most cyberattacks, the victim plays a part in the success of the attack. Nearly all cyberattacks use known techniques and organizations can protect their systems from known attacks. Failing to prevent an attack all but invites an attack.

To make this point, shareholders, banking partners, and customers of TJX have filed a series of class-action lawsuits against the company. These lawsuits claim that the "high-level deficiencies" in TJX's security practices made the company at least partially responsible for the damages caused by Albert Gonzalez and his accomplices. The lawsuits point out, for example, that the packet sniffer Gonzalez attached to the TJX network went unnoticed for more than seven months. Court documents also indicate that TJX failed to notice the transfer of more than 80 GB of stored data from its servers using TJX's own high-speed network. Finally, an audit performed by TJX's payment card–processing partners found that TJX failed to comply with nine of the 12 requirements for secure payment card transactions. (You will learn more about the security requirements for payment card vendors in Chapter 12.) TJX's core information security policies were so ineffective that they were unable to place sole blame on Gonzales and have subsequently settled several lawsuits against them.

Along with the lawsuits, TJX faced a serious backlash from customers and the media when the details of the scope of the breaches trickled out. Customers reacted angrily when they learned that nearly six weeks had passed between the discovery of the breach and the company's notification of the public. News organizations ran headline stories that painted a picture of TJX as a clueless and uncaring company. Consumer organizations openly warned people not to shop at TJX stores. TJX's reputation and brand image was shattered in the wake of Operation Get Rich or Die Tryin'. In the end, the real lesson of Operation Get Rich or Die Tryin' may not be the crime itself, but how a lackluster security policy was chiefly responsible for its happening in the first place.

Unintentional downtime is usually the result of technical failure, human error, or attack. Technical failure and human error are the most common causes of unintentional downtime. Although downtime caused by malicious attacks is less common, research indicates that it is growing rapidly. Malicious attacks can occur and cause downtime in all seven domains of an IT infrastructure, but you are more likely to see them in the User, Workstation, LAN, and WAN domains.

Opportunity cost is the amount of money a company loses due to downtime. The downtime can be either intentional or unintentional. Some organizations refer to opportunity cost as **true downtime cost**. It usually measures the loss of productivity experienced by an organization due to downtime. Suppose a major airline's reservation servers fail. While the servers are down, no customers can book flights. You can measure the opportunity cost of that downtime in the dollar amount of the unsold tickets. The opportunity cost of unintentional downtime is usually much higher than the opportunity cost of intentional downtime. Opportunity cost is a serious concern for information security professionals. It comprises a large portion of the $1 trillion estimated yearly cost of dealing with cybercrime and malicious attacks.

Reputation

One of the most important things that information security professionals try to protect is their organization's reputation and brand image. Companies that suffer from security breaches and malicious attacks that expose any assets are likely to face serious negative consequences in the public eye. For example, a security breach that allows attackers to steal customer credit card data and distribute them internationally would do significant harm to that company's reputation and brand image. Even if the response were swift and solved the problem effectively, the negative public perception of the company and its brands could remain for the long term. Among other consequences, this could lead to a decline in the organization's revenue.

Whom Are You Trying to Catch?

In popular usage and in the media, the term **hacker** often describes someone who breaks into a computer system without authorization. In most cases that means the hacker tries to take control of a remote computer through a network, or software cracking. The media and the general public also use the word hacker to describe anyone accused of using technology for terrorism, vandalism, credit card fraud, identity theft, intellectual property theft, or one of many other forms of crime. In the computing community, the term hacker generally describes a particularly brilliant programmer or technical expert who enjoys exploring and learning about computer systems. Because of this conflict, the term hacker is the subject of some controversy.

This book attempts to address the confusion surrounding this term by categorizing hackers as follows:

- **Black-hat hackers**—A **black-hat hacker** tries to break IT security for the challenge and to prove technical prowess. Black-hat hackers generally use special software tools to exploit vulnerabilities. Black-hat hackers generally poke holes in systems, but do not attempt to disclose vulnerabilities they find to the administrators of those systems. They tend to promote the free and open use of computing resources as opposed to the notion of security.
- **White-hat hackers**—A **white-hat hacker**, or **ethical hacker**, is an information security or network professional who uses various penetration-test tools to uncover vulnerabilities so they can be fixed. The difference between white-hat hackers and black-hat hackers is that white-hat hackers are mainly concerned with finding weaknesses for the purpose of fixing them, and black-hat hackers want to find weaknesses just for the fun of it or to exploit them.
- **Gray-hat hackers**—Also called a **wannabe**, a **gray-hat hacker** is a hacker with average abilities who may one day become a black-hat hacker, but could also opt to become a white-hat hacker. (Different people use this term in different ways, by the way.)

> **NOTE**
> Another type of attacker is a script kiddie. A **script kiddie** is a person with little or no skill. This person simply follows directions or uses a cookbook approach to carrying out a cyberattack without fully understanding the meaning of the steps he or she is performing.

Hackers are different from crackers. A **cracker** has a hostile intent, possesses sophisticated skills, and may be interested in financial gain. Crackers, represent the greatest threat to networks and information resources. These threats usually involve fraud, theft of data, destruction of data, blockage of access, and other malicious activity. However, the activities of hackers can also cause damage and loss.

Attack Tools

Protecting an organization's computing resources requires that you have some idea what tools your enemy will be using. Knowing how attackers work makes it possible to defend against their attacks. In fact, many organizations use the same tools that attackers use to help identify weaknesses they need to address. It is always better to find weaknesses in your own environment before an attacker does.

Computer criminals and malicious individuals use a number of hardware and software tools to help carry out attacks. These tools and techniques can include the following:

- Vulnerability scanners
- Port scanners
- Sniffers
- Wardialers
- Keyloggers

Vulnerability Scanners

A **vulnerability scanner** collects information about any known weaknesses on a target computer or network. The scanner works by sending specially crafted messages to select computers. How a computer responds indicates whether a specific weakness exists. Attackers use the results of these scans to decide what types of attacks would work best.

Port Scanners

Attackers also use port scanners to help identify weaknesses. Port scanners connect to a computer to determine which ports are open, or available to access the computer. The port number generally identifies the type of port.

Port scanning enables attackers to see which ports are active on a computer, which helps them figure out which applications are running. Attackers can then use this information to design an attack for that computer. For example, HTTP traffic commonly uses port 80. If a port scanner determines that port 80 is open on a particular computer and that there is a service monitoring that port, then an attacker might deduce that a Web server is likely running on the computer and develop an attack accordingly.

You should disable any unused ports to reduce the information attackers receive during port scans. You can read more ports at the Internet Assigned Numbers Authority (IANA) Web site (*http://www.iana.org*). For a list of available port numbers and their associated services, see Internet Assigned Numbers Authority Request for Comments (RFC) 1700.

Sniffers

A **sniffer** is a software program that captures traffic as it travels across a network. For attackers, passwords and private data are the most valuable information. Sniffers come in hardware versions, software versions, or versions that are a combination or both. Because a sniffer operates in an open mode, it is usually invisible to the user.

Wardialers

Before launching an attack, an attacker must identify the target. One way to do so is use a war dialer. A **wardialer** is a computer program that dials telephone numbers, looking for a computer on the other end. The program works by automatically dialing a defined range of phone numbers. It then logs and enters into a database those numbers that successfully connect to the modem. Some wardialers can also identify the operating system running on a computer, as well as conduct automated penetration testing. In such cases, the wardialer runs through a predetermined list of common usernames and passwords in an attempt to gain access to the system.

A network intruder can use a wardialer to identify potential targets. If the program does not provide automated penetration testing, the intruder can attempt to hack a modem with unprotected logons or easily cracked passwords. A network system administrator can use a commercial war dialer to identify unauthorized modems on an enterprise network. These unauthorized modems can provide attackers with easy access to an organization's internal network and must be controlled or eliminated.

Although wardialing is a rather old attack method, it is still useful for finding access points to computers. Many computer networks and voice systems have modems attached to phone lines. These modems are often attached either for direct access for support purposes or by people attempting to bypass network-access restrictions. Even today's Internet connected environments may have a few modems out there, ready to answer another computer that calls. Successfully connecting to a computer using a modem makes it possible to access the rest of the organization's network.

Keyloggers

A **keylogger** is a type of surveillance software or hardware that can record every keystroke a user makes with a keyboard to a log file. The keylogger can then send the log file to a specified receiver or retrieve it mechanically. Employers might use keyloggers to ensure that employees use work computers for business purposes only. However, spyware can also embed keylogger software, enabling it to transmit information to an unknown third party. (You'll learn about spyware later in this chapter.)

As a piece of hardware, a keylogger is typically a battery-sized plug that serves as a connector between the user's keyboard and computer. Because the device resembles an ordinary keyboard plug, it is relatively easy for someone who wants to monitor a user's behavior to hide such a device in plain sight. Besides, workstation keyboards usually plug into the back of the computer, which makes the keylogger even harder to detect. As the user types on the keyboard, the keylogger collects each keystroke and saves it as text in its own miniature hard drive. Later, the person who installed the keylogger must return and physically remove the device in order to access the information the device has gathered.

A keylogger software program does not require the attacker to physically access the user's computer. Instead, someone wanting to monitor activity on a particular computer can simply download the program. As long as an attacker has network access to a computer, he or she can transfer any file, including executable files, to the target computer. Many attackers then use social engineering to trick users into launching the downloaded programs. Users can also unwittingly download keyloggers as spyware, which an attacker can then execute as part of a rootkit. (You'll learn more about rootkits later in this chapter.) The keylogger program records each keystroke the user types and periodically uploads the information over the Internet to whoever installed the program.

What Is a Security Breach?

In spite of the most aggressive steps to protect computers from attacks, attackers sometimes get through. Any event that results in a violation of any of the A-I-C security tenets is a **security breach**. Some security breaches disrupt system services on purpose. Others are accidental, and may result from hardware or software failures. Regardless of whether a security breach is accidental or malicious, it can affect an organization's ability to conduct business as well as the organization's credibility.

Activities that can cause a security breach include the following:

- Denial of service (DoS) attacks
- Distributed denial of service (DDoS) attacks
- Unacceptable Web-browsing behavior
- Wiretapping
- Use of a backdoor to access resources
- Accidental data modifications

Denial of Service Attacks

Denial of service (DoS) attacks result in legitimate users not having access to a system resource. A DoS attack is a coordinated attempt to deny service by causing a computer to perform an unproductive task. This excessive activity makes the system unavailable to perform legitimate operations. When a disk fills up, the system locks an account out, a computer crashes, or a CPU slows down, the result is denial of service—hence the name. DoS attacks generally originate from a single computer. Once you detect a DoS attack, you can stop it easily.

Two common types of DoS attacks are as follows:

- **Logic attacks**—Logic attacks use software flaws to crash or seriously hinder the performance of remote servers. You can prevent many of these attacks by installing the latest patches to keep your software up to date.
- **Flooding attacks**—Flooding attacks overwhelm the victim computer's CPU, memory, or network resources by sending large numbers of useless requests to the machine.

One of the best defenses against DoS attacks is to use intrusion prevention system (IPS) software or devices to detect and stop the attack. Intrusion detection system (IDS) software and devices can also detect DoS attacks and alert you when they are in progress. Without a defense against DoS attacks, they can quickly overwhelm servers, desktops, and network hardware, slowing computing in your organization to a grinding halt. In some cases, these attacks can cripple an entire infrastructure.

Most DoS attacks target weaknesses in the overall system architecture rather than a software bug or security flaw. Attackers can launch DoS attacks using common Internet protocols such as TCP and Internet Control Message Protocol (ICMP). A DoS attack launched through one of these protocols can bring down one or more network servers or devices by flooding it with useless packets and providing false information about the status of network services. This is a packet flood.

One of the popular techniques for launching a packet flood is a **SYN flood**. SYN is a TCP control bit used to synchronize sequence numbers. In a SYN flood, the attacker sends a large number of packets requesting connections to the victim computer. The victim computer records each request and reserves a place for the connection in a local table in memory. The victim computer then sends an acknowledgment back to the attacker.

The attacker never responds, the result being that the victim computer fills up its connections table waiting for all the request acknowledgments. In the meantime, no legitimate users can connect to the victim computer because the SYN flood has filled the connection table. The victim computer will remain unavailable until the connection requests time out.

Another popular technique is **smurfing**. The smurf attack uses a directed broadcast to create a flood of network traffic for the victim computer.

> **NOTE**
> Request for Comment (RFC) 2827 is a useful source of information for the security administrator. It provides a method for using ingress traffic filtering to prohibit DoS attacks, which often use forged IP addresses.

Both internal attackers and external attackers can launch DoS attacks. However, most attacks come from anonymous outsiders. Network intrusion detection (IDS/IPS) is usually effective at detecting these attacks.

Security personnel routinely take aggressive steps to ensure that attackers cannot use their systems for malicious purposes. In addition, some Web content providers and network-device manufacturers now include new rules designed to prevent DoS attacks in their default configuration tables. Preventing attackers from gaining access to your computers is a full-time effort, but one that is worth the expense.

Distributed Denial of Service Attacks

The DDoS attack is a type of DoS attack. It involves flooding one or more target computers with false requests. This overloads the computers and prevents legitimate users from gaining access. DDoS attacks differ from regular DoS attacks in scope. In a DDoS attack, attackers hijack hundreds or even thousands of Internet computers, planting automated attack agents on those systems. The attacker then instructs the agents to bombard the target site with forged messages. This overloads the site and blocks legitimate traffic. The key here is strength in numbers. The attacker does more damage by distributing the attack across multiple computers.

Larger companies and universities tend to be attractive targets for attackers launching DDoS attacks. Researchers have estimated that attackers issue thousands of DDoS attacks against networks each week. This threat is so serious that preventing such attacks is a top priority in many organizations, including security product vendors. DDoS attacks are more difficult to stop than DoS attacks because they originate from different sources. Protecting computers from DDoS attacks requires several layers of security. Both DoS and DDoS attacks come in many forms and different levels of severity, and can cost millions of dollars in lost revenue.

Unacceptable Web Browsing

Unacceptable Web browsing describes the use of a Web browser in an unacceptable manner. Each organization should have an acceptable use policy (AUP) that clearly states what behavior is acceptable and what is not. Unacceptable use can include unauthorized users searching files or storage directories for data and information they are not supposed to read, or users simply visiting prohibited Web sites. The AUP defines what actions are security breaches.

Wiretapping

Attackers can tap telephone lines and data-communication lines. **Wiretapping** can be active, where the attacker makes modifications to the line. It can also be passive, where an unauthorized user simply listens to the transmission without changing the contents. Passive intrusion can include the copying of data for a subsequent active attack.

Two methods of active wiretapping are as follows:

- **Between-the-lines wiretapping**—This type of wiretapping does not alter the messages sent by the legitimate user, but inserts additional messages into the communication line when the legitimate user pauses.
- **Piggyback-entry wiretapping**—This type of wiretapping intercepts and modifies the original message by breaking the communications line and routing the message to another computer that acts as a host.

Although the term wiretapping is generally associated with voice telephone communications, attackers can also use wiretapping to intercept data communications. When referring to the interception of data communications, however, the more commonly used term is sniffing (although sniffing extends beyond simple wiretapping to include intercepting wireless transmissions).

Backdoor

Software developers sometimes include hidden access methods in their programs, called **backdoors**. Backdoors give developers or support personnel easy access to a system, without having to struggle with security controls. The problem is that backdoors don't always stay hidden. When an attacker discovers a backdoor, he or she can use it to bypass existing security controls such as passwords, encryption, and so on. Where legitimate users log on through front doors using a user ID and password, attackers use backdoors to bypass these normal access controls.

> **NOTE**
>
> Almost every network vendor ships devices with a default username and password, which you must change when setting up the device. Your failure to change these default usernames and passwords when new equipment is deployed will result in a known backdoor in your system—a serious vulnerability!

Attackers can also compromise a system by installing their own backdoor program on it. Attackers can use this type of backdoor to bypass controls that the administrator has put in place to protect the computer system. The **netcat** utility is one of the most popular backdoor tools in use today.

Rootkits commonly include backdoors. Traditional rootkits replace critical programs to give attackers backdoor access and enable them to hide on the host system. Because they replace system software components, rootkits can be more powerful than application-level Trojan horse backdoors. You'll learn more about rootkits later in this chapter.

Data Modifications

Problems with data integrity, including accidental partial data modifications and the storage of incorrect data values, can also cause a security breach. An incomplete modification can occur when multiple processes attempt to update data without observing basic data-integrity constraints. Another example is truncating data because the record field is not large enough to hold the complete data. This can occur with most programming languages and can be difficult to detect. However, the results can be significant. The best way to avoid data-modification issues is to validate data before storing it and to ensure that your programs adhere to strict data-integrity rules.

Additional Security Challenges

Additional challenges to ensuring safe and secure communications can originate from spam, hoaxes, spyware, and even local information stored by Web browsers. A combination of these is also possible.

Spam

Spam is unwanted e-mail or instant messages. Most spam is commercial advertising—often for get-rich-quick schemes, dubious products, or other services. Sending spam costs very little because the recipient covers most of the costs associated with spam. It costs money for ISPs and online services to transmit spam. Processing large volumes of unwanted messages is expensive. ISPs transfer these costs directly to subscribers. In addition, spamming forces the receiving user to waste administrative time on cleanup and monitoring of their received messages.

E-mail spam targets individual users with direct-mail messages. Often, spammers send messages to members of mailing lists associated with public or private e-mail discussion forums. Another popular technique for spammers is to use software to construct e-mail addresses from common user names and domain names and to send messages to those addresses. For example, a spam program might send an e-mail message to the address aaron@yahoo.com, as well as to all other addresses in the yahoo.com domain containing names that start with the letter A. Instant-message spam follows the same approach but uses instant messages to deliver the spam instead of e-mail.

A favorite technique of spammers is to send messages containing an "unsubscribe" link to a set of e-mail addresses. The idea is to use the link to determine whether an e-mail address is valid. That is, instead of unsubscribing users who click the link, spammers simply determine that the e-mail address is valid and therefore an even more attractive target. On a similar note, spam-generating software often includes lists of e-mail addresses. The software makers often assert that these are addresses for people who have "opted in," but in fact, they are typically random addresses from newsgroups or mailing lists. Although spammers often claim to remove addresses from their rolls on request, they almost never do.

According to research by pcpitstop.com (*http://www.pcpitstop.com*), the overall spam volume stabilized in February 2008 for the second month in a row at an estimated 78.5 percent of all e-mail. This is up from a 61 percent average for the first half of 2007. Spam not only reduces a company's productivity, it also wastes valuable resources.

Spam is no longer just a nuisance. The ability to block it is critical for IT security. Recently, spam has become a way for criminals to solicit individual and company information and to plant Trojan horses and other malware onto user computers. In addition, possession of some kinds of spam—for example, spam related to child porn—is illegal.

To fight cybercrime, organizations must tackle spam. Fortunately, many software companies offer effective e-mail and Web-security solutions that provide fail-safe protection against spam, phishing, and other threats. As you investigate software to protect your computers, look at programs designed to protect your servers and clients from message-based attacks.

Hoaxes

A hoax is some act intended to deceive or trick the receiver. In this context, hoaxes normally travel in e-mail messages. Often, these messages contain warnings about devastating new viruses. Although hoaxes do not automatically infect systems like viruses or Trojan horses, dealing with them is time-consuming. In fact, you may wind up spending much more time disproving hoaxes than handling real virus and Trojan horse incidents.

The best way to handle hoaxes is to ask users not to spread them by forwarding them to others. Forwarding a cute message to one or two friends is not a problem. However, sending an unconfirmed warning or plea to everyone in your address book, and asking all those recipients to forward it to everyone in *their* address books, just adds to the clutter that already fills everyone's inboxes. Recipients of this kind of e-mail should not pass it to everyone they know.

> **NOTE**
> If you suspect that a message you received is a hoax, you can visit a Web site called Snopes (*http://www.snopes.com*) to research it. Often, you will find an entry in Snopes that matches the message you received. Snopes isn't the final word on every hoax, but it can provide you with a convenient way to start your research.

Cookies

To help a Web server track a user's history, Web browsers allow the Web server to store a cookie on the user's hard drive. A **cookie** is simply a text file that contains details gleaned from past visits to a Web site. These details might include the user's username, credit card information the user has entered, and so on. Later, when the user sends a request to the Web server, the server can access the cookie instead of requesting that the user reenter the information.

Cookies are sometimes controversial because they allow a Web server to transmit files to a person's computer for storage on his or her hard drive. Because they are text files, though, they generally cannot cause immediate harm. Cookies do not directly perform malicious acts. Cookies cannot spread viruses, nor can they access additional information on the user's hard drive. This does not mean that cookies do not pose a security issue, however. Although cookies cannot gather information from a user's hard drive, as mentioned, they sometimes do store information that is sensitive, such as credit card details.

The problem with cookies is that they store information in cleartext files. That means anyone with access to your computer can potentially read the contents of your cookies. Although Web sites developed in a secure manner would never store information like credit card numbers in a cookie, some sites are sloppy. You never really know what information is stored in the cookies on your computer. The best way to avoid having personal information stored in cookies is to restrict the cookies you allow to Web sites you trust.

As you visit more and more Web sites, you will likely wind up with more and more cookies on your computer. In fact, users may well end up with hundreds of cookies on their computer, which can become a nuisance. Fortunately, you can delete these cookies at any time. In addition, you can prevent your Web browser from allowing cookies in the first place. Check your browser's help information for instructions.

What Are Vulnerabilities and Threats?

As you learned in Chapter 1, vulnerabilities and threats go hand in hand. A threat is any action that could damage an asset. A vulnerability is any weakness in a system makes it possible for a threat to cause it harm. Threats often exploit one or more known vulnerabilities.

If a vulnerability exists in a system, so does the possibility of a threat. Any threat against a vulnerability creates a risk that a negative event may occur. You can't eliminate threats, but you can protect against vulnerabilities. That way, even though a threat still exists, it cannot exploit the vulnerability. The key to protecting assets from the risk of attack is to eliminate or address as many vulnerabilities as possible.

You can find many vulnerabilities in an average organization. Table 3-2 lists some common vulnerabilities as they appear across the seven domains of an IT infrastructure.

Threats can come from an individual, a group of individuals, or an organization. A threat to a computing device is as any action, either accidental or malicious, that can have a negative effect on the assets and resources of an individual or organization. The asset might be hardware, software, databases, files, data, or the physical network itself.

A threat is significant from a security viewpoint. The goal of computer security is to provide insights, methodologies, and techniques that deal with threats. You can achieve this goal by developing policies that help computer and network system administrators, designers, developers, and users avoid undesirable system characteristics and weaknesses.

You can identify threats and rank them according to their importance and impact. You can rank threats by dollar loss, negative reputation created, monetary liability, or how often they are likely to occur. Each organization may rank a threat higher or lower than another organization, based on its importance for that organization. A threat's rank depends on its potential impact.

The most common threats, in no particular order, include the following:

- Malicious software
- Hardware or software failure
- Internal attacker
- Equipment theft

TABLE 3-2 Common vulnerabilities in the seven domains of an IT infrastructure.

DOMAIN	COMMON VULNERABILITY
User Domain	Lack of awareness or concern for security policy Accidental acceptable use policy violation Intentional malicious activity Social engineering
Workstation Domain	Unauthorized user access Malicious software introduced Weaknesses in installed software
LAN Domain	Unauthorized network access Transmitting private data unencrypted Spreading malicious software
LAN-to-WAN Domain	Exposure and unauthorized access of internal resources to the public Introduction of malicious software Loss of productivity due to Internet access
WAN Domain	Transmitting private data unencrypted Malicious attacks from anonymous sources Denial of Service attacks Weaknesses in software
Remote Access Domain	Brute-force attacks on access and private data Unauthorized remote access to resources Data leakage from remote access or lost storage devices
System/Application Domain	Unauthorized physical or logical access to resources Weaknesses in server operating system or application software Data loss from errors, failures, or disasters

- External attacker
- Natural disaster
- Industrial espionage
- Terrorism

Not all threats are malicious. Although some threats may be intentional, others may be accidental. Accidental threats might include hardware failure or a software problem caused by a lack of controls. The results of accidental threats can be just as damaging as malicious threats, however. You must make every effort to minimize all security breaches, whether they are malicious or accidental. The overall goal is to protect the network and computer system from any attack, and to prevent the theft, destruction, and corruption of individual or organizational assets.

FYI

Identifying and responding to threats and vulnerabilities can be a complicated process. In some cases, a threat may be too expensive and time-consuming to eliminate. You should work hard to reduce the occurrence of all threats as much as possible, but you should also carefully assess whether the cost of protecting some assets is more than the value of the assets themselves. You may spend much more time and money identifying and responding to threats than the assets are actually worth.

Threat Targets

Using his or her favorite search engine, an attacker can find precise instructions for breaching nearly any protocol, operating system, application, device, or hardware environment. For this reason, you must monitor all threats very closely. You never know where one might come from next. It may be a professional cybercriminal or someone within your own four walls. The safest bet is to monitor all threat targets constantly and carefully.

The first step in developing a monitoring plan is to identify where in the seven domains of an IT infrastructure threats are likely to occur. Table 3-3 lists many common threat targets as well as where they are found within an IT infrastructure. As you can see, there are many threat targets within the seven domains of an IT infrastructure.

TABLE 3-3 Threat targets in the seven domains of an IT infrastructure.

DOMAIN	THREAT TARGET
User Domain	PCs, laptops, smartphones (BlackBerry, iPhone), personal digital assistants (PDAs), application software (productivity, Web browsing, etc.)
Workstation Domain	Administrative workstations, laptops, departmental workstations and servers, network and operating-system software
LAN Domain	File servers, print servers, e-mail servers, administration servers, database servers, wireless LAN servers (WLANs), hubs, repeaters, bridges
LAN-to-WAN Domain	HTTP servers, e-mail servers, terminal servers (FTP, etc.), IP routers, firewalls, hubs, repeaters
WAN Domain	IP routers, TCP/IP stacks and buffers, firewalls, gateways, switches
Remote Access Domain	Virtual private networks (VPNs), third-party e-mail redirect (i.e., RIM/BlackBerry), laptops with VPN software, SSL-VPN tunnels
System/Application Domain	Desktop operating systems, server and network operating systems, e-mail applications and servers, Enterprise Resource Planning (ERP) applications and systems, Web browsers

From this list, it should be clear that there are many opportunities for an attacker to cause big problems. You should also notice that many of the threat targets appear in different categories. The need for a comprehensive security plan, across all domains, should be clear.

Threat Types

You learned about the A-I-C tenets of security in Chapter 1. To review, in order to secure information, you must protect its availability, integrity, and confidentiality. The three major threat types directly threaten each of the A-I-C tenets. They are as follows:

- Denial or destruction threats
- Alteration threats
- Disclosure threats

Denial or Destruction Threats

Denial or destruction threats make assets or resources unavailable or unusable. Any threat that destroys information or makes it unavailable violates the availability tenet of information security. A denial or destruction attack is successful when it prevents an authorized user to access a resource either temporarily or permanently.

An example of a denial or destruction threat would be a denial of service (DoS) attack. As you learned earlier in this chapter, a DoS attack, which is usually malicious, prevents authorized users from accessing computer and network resources. Many organizations are potential victims of DoS attacks. In fact, any computer connected to the Internet is a DoS threat candidate. This type of attack can represent a minor problem or a great danger, depending on the importance of the blocked asset or resource. For example, suppose an attacker floods a specific port on a server. If the port is not for a critical resource, the impact may be minimal. However, if the port supports authorized user access to your company's Web site, it could prevent customers from accessing it for minutes or hours. In that case, the impact could be severe.

> **WARNING**
> Even if a DoS attack floods a noncritical port, the excess traffic could cause the server to crash or become so slow it cannot service legitimate requests in a timely manner. In this case, the DoS attack is still successful.

Is It Really a DoS Threat?

Poor response time is not always due to a DoS attack. It might be because of oversubscription of network facilities. Oversubscription just means that more computers or processes are using a network than the intended network load. In other words, users are overusing the network. Network vendors use this technique to increase revenue at the user's expense. Alternatively, the provider may be causing a user's inability to reach some network resource. For example, the provider may have taken key resources offline to perform a system update or Web site modifications. Yet another culprit might be throttling, a technique some administrators use to reduce network traffic. On the other hand, it could be simple user error.

Alteration Threats

An alteration threat violates information integrity. This type of attack compromises a system by making unauthorized changes to data on a system intentionally or unintentionally. This change might occur while the data is stored on a network resource or while it is moving between two resources. Intentional changes are usually malicious. Unintentional changes are usually accidental. People can, and often do, make mistakes that affect the integrity of computer and network resources. Even so, unintentional changes still create security problems.

Modifications to the system configuration can also compromise the integrity of a network resource. Such a modification can occur when an unauthorized party tampers with an asset or when an authorized user makes a change that has unintended effects. For example, a user might modify database files, operating systems, application software, and even hardware devices. Modifications might include creating, changing, deleting, and writing information to a network resource. It's a good idea to put techniques in place that enable you to track or audit these changes as they happen. That way, you can have a record of who, what, when, where, and how modifications were made. In addition, change management systems limit who can make changes, how they make changes, and how they document changes. It is very important that only authorized parties change assets, and only in authorized ways.

Advance preparation can reduce the severity of alteration threats. For example, if you have a backup or copy of the data, then the impact of a breach may be less severe than if a backup is not available. However, data recovery should always be the last resort. A far better approach is to avoid an alteration attack in the first place. Protecting your information is always better than repairing or recovering it.

Disclosure Threats

Disclosure occurs any time unauthorized users access private or confidential information that is stored on a network resource or while it is in transit between network resources. Disclosure can also occur when a computer or device containing private or confidential data, such as a database of medical records, is lost or stolen. Two techniques that attackers employ to illegally obtain or modify data are as follows:

- **Sabotage**—Sabotage is the destruction of property or obstruction of normal operations. Technically, sabotage attacks the availability property of information security.
- **Espionage**–Espionage is the act of spying to obtain secret information. Terrorists and enemy agents might well be involved in activities to obtain sensitive government information that they can use to perpetuate future attacks.

> **NOTE**
> An information leak is any instance of someone who purposely distributes information without proper authorization.

Sabotage is not a silent attack, but espionage can occur without any obvious trace.

In many organizations, much stored information is unavailable to the public. This information can include personal information on a user's computer or confidential records stored in a massive database. The effects of the disclosure of this information can vary. For example, where the disclosure of a user's personal information could cause embarrassment, public disclosure of a citizen's private records could result in severe repercussions. In addition, disclosing information could cause even more problems if government secrets or intelligence files are involved.

Information security personnel devote much time and effort to combating disclosure threats. In particular, the U.S. government focuses very closely on disclosure threats because of their potential to cause problems for critical security areas. One of the difficult things about combating these types of threats, however, is that unauthorized users can intercept unprotected data without leaving any trace of their activities. For this reason, security research and development have focused on the disclosure threat and its countermeasures.

What Is a Malicious Attack?

An **attack** on a computer system or network asset succeeds by exploiting a vulnerability in the system. There are four general categories of attacks. An attack can consist of all or a combination of these four categories:

- **Fabrications**—Fabrications involve the creation of some deception in order to trick unsuspecting users.
- **Interceptions**—An interception involves eavesdropping on transmissions and redirecting them for unauthorized use.
- **Interruptions**—An interruption causes a break in a communication channel, which blocks the transmission of data.
- **Modifications**—A modification is the alteration of data contained in transmissions or files.

As you learned earlier, security threats can be active or passive. Both types can have negative repercussions for an IT infrastructure. An active attack involves a modification of the data stream or attempts to gain unauthorized access to computer and networking systems. An active attack is a physical intrusion. In a passive attack, the attacker does not make changes to the system. This type of attack just eavesdrops on and monitors transmissions.

Active threats include the following:

- Brute-force attacks
- Dictionary threats
- Address spoofing
- Hijacking
- Replay attacks
- Man-in-the-middle attacks
- Masquerading
- Social engineering

- Phishing
- Phreaking
- Pharming

Such attacks are widespread and common. A growing number of them appear on an information systems security professional's radar screen every year. Following is a description of several of the most common types of malicious attacks.

Brute-Force Attacks

One of the most tried-and-true attack methods is the brute-force attack. In a brute-force attack, the attacker tries different passwords on a system until one of them is successful. Usually, the attacker employs a software program to try all possible combinations of a likely password, user ID, or security code until it locates a match. This occurs rapidly and in sequence. This type of attack is called a brute-force attack because the attacker simply hammers away at the code. There is no skill or stealth involved; just brute force that eventually breaks the code.

With today's large-scale computers, it is possible to try millions of combinations of passwords in a short period. Given enough time and using enough computers, it is possible to crack most algorithms.

Dictionary Attacks

A **dictionary attack** is a simple attack that relies on users making poor password choices. In a dictionary attack, a simple password-cracker program takes all the words from a dictionary file and attempts to log on by entering each dictionary entry as a password.

Users often engage in the poor practice of selecting common words as passwords. A password policy that enforces complex passwords is the best defense against a dictionary attack. Users should create passwords composed of a combination of letters and numbers, and the passwords should not include any personal information about the user.

Address Spoofing

Spoofing is a type of attack in which one person, program, or computer disguises itself as another person, program, or computer to gain access to some resource. A common spoofing attack involves presenting a false network address to pretend to be a different computer. An attacker may change a computer's network address to appear as an authorized computer in the target's network. If the administrator of the target's local router has not configured it to filter out external traffic with internal addresses, the attack may be successful. Address spoofing can enable an attacker to access protected internal resources.

NOTE

A CERT advisory on IP spoofing reports that the CERT Coordination Center has received reports of attacks in which intruders create packets with spoofed source IP addresses. This exploit leads to user impersonation and elevated privilege access on the target system. This means that the intruder can take over logon connections and create havoc.

Hijacking

Hijacking is a type of attack in which the attacker takes control of a session between two machines and masquerades as one of them. There are a few types of hijacking:

- **Man-in-the-middle hijacking**—In this type of hijacking, discussed in more detail in a moment, the attacker uses a program to take control of a connection by masquerading as each end of the connection. For example, if Mary and Fred want to communicate, the attacker pretends to be Mary when talking with Fred and pretends to be Fred when talking to Mary. Neither Mary nor Fred knows they are talking to the attacker. The attacker can collect substantial information and can even alter data as it flows between Mary and Fred. This attack enables the attacker to either gain access to the messages or modify them before retransmitting.
- **Browser hijacking**—In a browser hijacking, the user is directed to a different Web site than what he or she requested, usually to a fake page that the attacker has created. This gives the user the impression that the attacker has compromised the Web site, when in fact the attacker simply diverted the user's browser from the actual site. Attackers can use this attack with phishing to trick a user into providing private information, such as a password. (You'll learn about phishing in a moment.)
- **Session hijacking**—In **session hijacking**, the attacker attempts to take over an existing connection between two network computers. The first step in this attack is for the attacker to take control of a network device on the LAN, such as a firewall or another computer, in order to monitor the connection. This enables the attacker to determine the sequence numbers used by the sender and receiver. After determining the sequence numbering, the attacker generates traffic that appears to come from one of the communicating parties. This steals the session from one of the legitimate users. To get rid of the legitimate user who initiated the hijacked session, the attacker overloads one of the communicating devices with excess packets so that it drops out of the session.

FYI

Session hijacking reveals the importance of identifying the other party in a session. It is possible for an intruder to replace a legitimate user for the remainder of a communication session. This calls for a scheme to authenticate the data's source throughout the transmission. In fact, authenticating both ends of a connection, a process called mutual authentication, can reduce the potential of an undetected hijack. However, even the strongest authentication methods are not always successful in preventing hijacking attacks. That means you might need to encrypt all transmissions.

Replay Attacks

Replay attacks involve capturing data packets from a network and retransmitting them to produce an unauthorized effect. The receipt of duplicate, authenticated IP packets may disrupt service or have some other undesired consequence. Systems can be broken through replay attacks when attackers reuse old messages or parts of old messages to deceive system users. This helps intruders to gain information that allows unauthorized access into a system.

Man-in-the-Middle Attacks

A **man-in-the-middle attack** takes advantage of the multi-hop process used by many types of networks. In this type of attack, an attacker intercepts messages between two parties before transferring them on to their intended destination.

Web spoofing is a type of man-in-the-middle attack in which the user believes a secure session exists with a particular Web server. In reality, the secure connection only exists with the attacker, not the Web server. The attacker then establishes a secure connection with the Web server and passes traffic between the user and the Web server. In this way, the attacker can trick the user into supplying passwords, credit card information, and other private data.

Attackers use man-in-the-middle attacks to steal theft information, to execute denial of service attacks, to corrupt transmitted data, to gain access to an organization's internal computer and network resources, and to introduce new information into network sessions.

> **NOTE**
> Masquerade attacks can involve other credentials as well. For example, many attackers get free wireless access by capturing wireless packets from paying customers. They use information in the packets to masquerade as a paying customer and connect to the wireless network free of charge.

Masquerading

In a **masquerade attack**, one user or computer pretends to be another user or computer. Masquerade attacks usually include one of the other forms of active attacks, such as address spoofing or replaying. Attackers can capture authentication sequences and then replay them later to log on again to an application or operating system. For example, an attacker might monitor user names and passwords sent to a weak Web application. The attacker could then use the intercepted credentials to log on to the Web application and impersonate the user.

Eavesdropping

Eavesdropping, or sniffing, occurs when a host sets its network interface on promiscuous mode and copies packets that pass by for later analysis. Promiscuous mode enables a network device to intercept and read each network packet, even if the packet's address doesn't match the network device. It is possible to attach hardware and software to monitor and analyze all packets on that segment of the transmission media without alerting any other users. Candidates for eavesdropping include satellite, wireless, mobile, and other transmission methods.

A network protocol specifies how software identifies and labels packets, which enables a computer to determine its destination. Because the specifications for network protocols are widely published, a third party can easily interpret network packets and develop a packet sniffer. A **packet sniffer** is a software application that uses a hardware adapter card in promiscuous mode to capture all network packets sent across a network segment. Because some network applications distribute network packets in plain text, a packet sniffer can yield meaningful and sensitive information, such as user account names and passwords.

Social Engineering

Attackers often use a deception technique called social engineering to gain access to resources in an IT infrastructure. In nearly all cases, social engineering involves tricking authorized users to carry out actions for unauthorized users. The success of social engineering attacks depends on the basic tendency of people to want to be helpful.

Social engineering places the human element in the security breach loop and uses it as a weapon. A forged or stolen vendor or employee ID could provide entry to a secure location. The intruder could then obtain access to important assets. By appealing to employees' natural instinct to help a technician or contractor, an attacker can easily breach the perimeter of an organization and gain access.

Personnel who serve as initial contacts within an organization, such as receptionists and administrative assistants, are often targets of social-engineering attacks. Attackers with some knowledge of an organization's structure will often also target new, untrained employees, as well as those who do not seem to understand security policies.

Eliminating social-engineering attacks can be difficult, but here are some techniques to reduce their impact:

- Ensure that employees are educated on the basics of a secure environment.
- Develop a security policy and computer-use policy.
- Enforce a strict policy for internal and external technical-support procedures.
- Require the use of all identification for all personnel.
- Limit the data accessible to the public by restricting the information published in directories, Yellow Pages, Web sites, and public databases.
- Be very careful when using remote access. Use strong validation so you know who is accessing your network.
- Teach personnel the techniques for sending and receiving secure e-mail.
- Shred all documents that may contain confidential or sensitive information.

> **NOTE**
>
> Many social-engineering activities present today have their basic roots in strategies developed by phreakers. In fact, several current social-engineering attacks bear names that begin with the letters "ph" to pay homage to these social-engineering pioneers.

Phreaking

Phreaking is a slang term that describes the activity of a subculture of people who study, experiment with, or explore telephone systems, telephone company equipment, and systems connected to public telephone networks. **Phone phreaking** is the art of exploiting bugs and glitches that exist in the telephone system.

Phishing

Fraud is a growing problem on the Internet. **Phishing** is a type of fraud in which an attacker attempts to trick the victim into providing private information such as credit card numbers, passwords, dates of birth, bank-account numbers, automated teller machine (ATM) PINs, and Social Security numbers.

> **NOTE**
> Anti-malware programs and firewalls cannot detect most phishing scams because they do not contain suspect code. Some spam filters even let phishing messages pass because they appear to come from legitimate sources.

A **phishing scam** is an attempt to commit identity theft via e-mail or instant message. The message appears to come from a legitimate source, such as a trusted business or financial institution, and includes an urgent request for personal information. Phishing messages usually indicate a critical need to update an account (banking, credit card, etc.) immediately. The message instructs the victim to either provide the requested information or click on a link provided in the message. Clicking the link leads the victim to a spoofed Web site. This Web site looks identical to the official site, but in fact belongs to the scammer. Personal information entered into this Web page goes directly to the scammer, not to the legitimate organization.

A variation of the phishing attack is spear phishing. **Spear phishing** uses e-mail or instant messages to target a specific organization, seeking unauthorized access to confidential data. As with the messages used in regular phishing attempts, spear-phishing messages appear to come from a trusted source.

The best way to protect against phishing of any kind is to avoid supplying personal information when prompted to do so by an e-mail or instant message. If you believe the request might be legitimate, call the company's customer-service department to verify this before providing any information. If you do call the company, do not use phone numbers contained in the message. Even if the request is legitimate, manually enter the Web address in your browser rather than clicking on a link in the message.

The Anti-Phishing Working Group (APWG) is a global, pan-industrial law-enforcement association focused on eliminating fraud and identity theft resulting from e-mail spoofing of all types. For more information, visit the APWG Web site at *http://www.antiphishing.org*. In addition, the Federal Trade Commission (FTC) Web site offers advice for consumers, an e-mail address for reporting phishing activity, plus a form to report identity theft. The FTC Web site is located at *http://www.ftc.gov*.

Pharming

Pharming is another type of attack that seeks to obtain personal or private financial information through domain spoofing. A pharming attack doesn't use messages to trick victims into visiting spoofed Web sites that appear legitimate, however. Instead, pharming uses domain spoofing, "poisoning" a domain name system (DNS) server. The result is that when a user enters the poisoned server's Web address into his or her address bar, that user navigates to the attacker's site. The user's browser still shows the correct Web site, which makes pharming difficult to detect—and therefore more serious. Where phishing attempts to scam people one at a time with an e-mail or instant message, pharming enables scammers to target large groups of people at one time through domain spoofing.

How to Identify a Phishing Scam

It may be difficult to identify a phishing scam simply by looking at the Web page that opens when you click a link in an e-mail message. However, clues in the address can sometimes reveal the deception. Look for the following:

- Phishers often substitute similar-looking characters for the real characters in a URL. For example, you might use a "1" (numeral one) in place of a lowercase "L"—think *paypa1.com* rather than *paypal.com*.
- Phishing scams have become so sophisticated that phishers can appear to use legitimate links, including the real site's security certificate. Before clicking a link, you should preview it to see where it will take you. If you notice that the domain name looks odd, do not click the link. Instead, contact the legitimate Web site's customer-service or technical-support group and ask whether the link is valid. This approach takes more time, but is far safer than just clicking through links without checking them.
- Some phishers purchase domain names that are similar to those of legitimate companies—for example, *walmartorder.com*. The real company is Wal-Mart, but it does not include *order* in its domain name.
- One ploy is to use the same domain name, but with .org rather than .com. The con artists who use these domain names then send out millions of e-mails requesting that consumers verify account information, birth dates, Social Security numbers, and so on. Inevitably, some computer users will respond. Carefully examine the entire domain name!

What Is Malicious Software?

Not all software performs beneficial tasks. Some software infiltrates one or more target computers and follows an attacker's instructions. These instructions can include causing damage, escalating security privileges, divulging private data, or even modifying or deleting data. This type of software is **malicious software**, or **malware** for short.

The purpose of malware is to damage or disrupt a system. The effects of malware can range from slowing down a PC, to causing it to crash, to the theft of credit card numbers, and worse. Simply surfing the Internet, reading e-mail, or downloading music or other files can infect a personal computer with malware—usually without the user's knowledge.

Malware exists in two main categories: infecting programs and hiding programs. Infecting programs actively attempt to copy themselves to other computers. Their main purpose is to carry out an attacker's instructions on new targets. Malware of this type includes the following:

- Viruses
- Worms

Hiding programs hide in the computer, carrying out the attacker's instructions while avoiding detection. Malware that tends to hide includes the following:

- Trojan horses
- Rootkits
- Spyware

The following sections describe each type of malware.

Viruses

A computer virus is a software program that attaches itself to or copies itself into another program on a computer. The purpose of the virus is to trick the computer into following instructions not intended by the original program developer. Users copy infected files from another computer on a network, from a flash drive, or from an online service. Alternatively, users can transport viruses from home and work on their portable computers, which have access to the Internet and other network services.

A computer virus acts in a similar fashion to a biological virus. It "infects" a host program, and may cause that host program to replicate itself to other computers. The virus cannot exist without a host, and it can spread from host to host in an infectious manner.

The first virus recorded was the Creeper virus, written by researcher Bob Thomas in 1971. The Creeper copied itself to other networked computers, displaying the message "I'm the creeper, catch me if you can!" Thomas designed the virus as an experimental self-replicating program to see how such programs would affect computers on a network. Shortly after the Creeper virus was released, researchers unleashed the Reaper program to find and eradicate the Creeper.

Today, thousands of known viruses infect programs of all types. The main concern with viruses is that they often attach themselves to common programs. When users run these infected programs, they are actually running virus code with their user credentials and authorization. The virus doesn't have to escalate privileges; the user who runs the infected program provides the virus with his or her authenticated credentials and permissions.

Over time, viruses have grown smarter. For example, some viruses can combat malware-detection programs by disabling their detection functions. Others compensate for the fact that files infected by a virus typically increase in size, making them relatively easy to detect, by spoofing the preinfected file's size. That way, it appears nothing has changed.

Worms

A worm is a self-contained program that replicates and sends copies of itself to other computers, generally across a network. The worm's purpose may be simply to reduce availability by using up network bandwidth, or it may take other nefarious actions. The main difference between a virus and a worm is that a worm does not need a host program to infect. The worm is a standalone program.

The first worm reported to spread "in the wild" was the Morris worm. Robert Tappan Morris wrote the Morris worm in 1988. The Morris worm attacked a buffer-overflow vulnerability. The original intent of the Morris worm was to estimate the size of the Internet by spreading across the Internet and infecting computers running versions of the UNIX operating system. The worm spread faster than its author expected, however. In the end, the worm infected computers multiple times, eventually slowing each infected computer to the point it became unusable. The Morris worm was the first malware incident to gain widespread media attention and resulted in the first conviction under the U.S. 1986 Computer Use and Fraud Act.

NOTE

A buffer overflow is a condition in which a running program stores data in an area outside the memory location set aside for the data. By storing more data than a program expects, you can insert instructions into a program that alter its behavior at runtime. Buffer overflows are numerous and always result from a programmer neglecting to validate input data.

Trojan Horses

A Trojan horse, also called a Trojan, is malware that masquerades as a useful program. Its name comes from the Trojan horse in *The Aeneid*. In the story, the Greeks, who had been at war with Troy for 10 years, construct a large wooden horse and offer it as a "gift" to the Trojans. The Trojans, viewing the gift as a peace offering, bring the horse into the city. That night, as the Trojans sleep, Greek soldiers hiding in the belly of the hollow horse climb out and open the city gates to admit the rest of the Greek army into the city. The Greeks soundly defeat Troy that night.

Similarly, Trojan horse programs use their outward appearance to trick users into running them. They look like programs that perform useful tasks, but actually, they hide malicious code. Once the program is running, the attack instructions execute with the user's permissions and authority.

The first known Trojan was Animal, released in 1974. Animal disguised itself as a simple quiz game in which the user would think of an animal and the program would ask questions to attempt to guess the animal. In addition to asking questions, however, the program copied itself into every directory to which the user had write access.

Today's Trojans do far more than just save copies of themselves. Trojans can hide programs that collect sensitive information, open backdoors into computers, or actively upload and download files. The list of possibilities is endless.

Rootkits

Rootkits are newer than other types of malware. They did not appear until around 1990. A **rootkit** is a type of malware that modifies or replaces one or more existing programs to hide traces of attacks. Although rootkits commonly modify parts of the operating system to conceal traces of their presence, they can exist at any level—from a computer's boot instructions up to the applications that run in the operating system. Once installed, rootkits provide attackers with easy access to compromised computers to launch additional attacks.

TIP

Rootkits often work with other malware. For example, suppose a program, malware.exe, is running on a Windows system. A simple rootkit might replace the Windows Task Manager with a modified version that does not list any program named malware.exe. Administrators would not know the malware program is running.

Rootkits exist for a variety of operating systems, including Linux, UNIX, and Microsoft Windows. Because there are so many different types of rootkits, and because they effectively conceal their existence once installed on a machine, they can be difficult to detect and remove. Even so, identifying and removing rootkits is crucial to maintaining a secure system. A host-based IDS can help detect rootkit activity, however.

If you do detect a rootkit on your system, the best solution is often to restore the operating system from the original media. This requires rebuilding and restoring user and application data from backups, assuming these exist. This becomes more difficult if you have not completely documented the system. Preventing unauthorized access, which can enable an attacker to install a rootkit, is far more effective than attempting to remove an installed rootkit.

Spyware

Spyware is a type of malware that specifically threatens the confidentiality of information. It gathers information about a user through an Internet connection without his or her knowledge. Spyware is sometimes bundled as a hidden component of freeware or shareware programs that users download from the Internet, similar to a Trojan horse. Spyware can also spread via peer-to-peer file swapping. Spyware has been around since the late 1990s, but increased in popularity after 2000. The rapid growth of the Internet enabled attackers to collect useful information from more and more unsuspecting users.

> **NOTE**
> Licensing agreements that accompany software downloads sometimes warn users that a spyware program will be installed along with the requested software. Often, however, because they are composed in dense legal language, these licensing agreements go unread.

Once installed, spyware monitors user activity on the Internet. Spyware can also gather information such as e-mail addresses and even passwords and credit card numbers. The spyware can relay this data to the author of the spyware. The author might use the data simply for advertising or marketing purposes, but could employ it to facilitate identity theft.

In addition to stealing information, spyware steals from users by using their Internet bandwidth to transmit this information to a third party, as well as by consuming their computers' memory resources. Computers running multiple spyware programs often run noticeably more slowly than clean computers. Furthermore, because spyware uses memory and other system resources, it can cause system instability or even crashes.

Because spyware exists as independent executable programs, it can perform a number of operations, including the following:

- Monitoring keystrokes
- Scanning files on the hard drive
- Snooping other applications, such as chat programs or word processors
- Installing other spyware programs
- Reading cookies
- Changing the default home page on the Web browser

Adware

Adware is similar to spyware, but it does not transmit **personally identifiable information (PII)**—or if it does, the author of the adware promises not to sell it. PII is any information that can help identify a specific person. Examples of PII include driver's license numbers, Social Security numbers, credit card numbers, and so on. Instead, information collected by adware can help deliver pop-ups tailored to purchasing habits or used for market-research purposes. (A **pop-up** is a type of window that appears on top of the browser window. Pop-ups generally contain ads. Although pop-ups are not strictly adware, many adware programs use them to interact with users. Some software products include an option for blocking pop-ups.)

Spyware and adware have rapidly become increasingly common threats to computers, with some experts estimating that more than 90 percent of computers are already infected. Fortunately, a number of software suppliers make anti-spyware and anti-adware software. In fact, many antivirus and general anti-malware software programs also detect and remove spyware and adware. Sorting through these programs to find the right offering for your organization is a challenging task—but an important one.

What Are Countermeasures?

There are no simple measures to protect your organization from computer attacks. You must focus on countermeasures that detect vulnerabilities, prevent attacks, and respond to the effects of successful attacks. This is not easy—but it is better than the alternative. Dealing with computer and network attacks is a cost of doing business in the IT field.

Although smart attackers and intruders continue to invent new methods of attacking computer and network resources, many are well known and can be defeated with a variety of available tools. The best strategy is to identify vulnerabilities and reduce them to avoid attacks in the first place.

Avoiding attacks should be the highest priority. Even so, some attacks will succeed. Your response to attacks should be as aggressive, proactive, and reactive as the attack itself. You can respond to attacks by developing plans to rapidly restore computer and network resources if they are attacked, closing holes in your organization's defenses, and obtaining evidence for prosecution of offenders. Of course, you should use the lessons learned from an attack to protect the network from similar attacks.

Responding to attacks involves planning, policy, and detective work. Fortunately, law-enforcement agencies, forensic experts, security consultants, and independent response teams are available to assist you in responding to a security incident as well as prosecuting the offender. In addition, many organizations have special teams to handle security incidents when they occur. These **incident response teams (IRTs)** know how to recognize incidents and respond to them in a way that minimizes damage and preserves evidence for later action.

As you read the following chapters, you will learn about many countermeasures. To get you started, this section introduces you to a few of the most common countermeasures you can take to protect your IT infrastructure. You may also need to use some of them to respond to threats, vulnerabilities, and malicious attacks in progress.

Countering Malware

Malware provides a platform for attacks on both personal and business networks. Anti-malware measures are the first line of defense against these attacks. You must take steps to prevent the introduction of malware into your environment. It's always better to prevent malware than to have to fix damage caused by malware. You must develop a security program for preventing malware.

Following are six general steps for preventing malware:

- Create an education program to keep your users from installing malware on your system.
- Post regular bulletins about malware problems.
- Never transfer files from an unknown or untrusted source unless the computer has an anti-malware utility installed. You'll learn more about anti-malware utilities in a moment.
- Test new programs or open suspect files on a quarantine computer—one that is not connected to any part of your network—before introducing them to the production environment.
- Install anti-malware software, make sure the software and data are current, and schedule regular malware scans to prevent malicious users from introducing malware and to detect any existing malware.
- Use a secure logon and authentication process.

Another important tactic for countering malware is staying abreast of developments in malware. Keep up with the latest malware information by reading weekly computer journals or joining organizations like the National Cyber Security Alliance (NCSA) or US-CERT. In addition, you should frequently check the following Web sites for information about malware:

- **National Cyber Security Alliance (NCSA)**—*http://www.staysafeonline.org/*
- **Computer Security Institute (CSI)**—*http://gocsi.com/*
- **United States Computer Emergency Readiness Team (US-CERT)**—*http://us-cert.gov/*

In addition, you should use anti-malware software on your system to scan all files introduced to workstations and on mail servers. (Note that the more common name for this type of software is antivirus software. However, because today's antivirus software generally addresses more than just viruses, the term anti-malware software is more accurate.) Most administrators use anti-malware software at many points throughout the network.

There are many anti-malware products available to prevent the spread of all types of malware as well remove malware from infected computers. These include the following:

- **BitDefender**—*http://www.bitdefender.com/*
- **Kaspersky Anti-Virus**—*http://www.kaspersky.com/*
- **Webroot Antivirus**—*http://www.webroot.com*
- **Norton Antivirus**—*http://www.symantec.com/norton/antivirus*
- **ESET Nod32 Antivirus**—*http://www.eset.com/*
- **AVG Anti-Virus**—*http://www.avg.com*
- **G DATA Antivirus**—*http://www.gdatasoftware.com/*
- **Avira AntiVir**—*http://www.avira.com*
- **Trend Micro**—*http://www.trendmicro.com*
- **Microsoft Security Essentials**—*http://www.microsoft.com/security_essentials/*

NOTE

You can find reviews of anti-malware programs on the Web. Two popular review sites, which provide feedback from other users, are *http://www.starreviews.com/* and *http://anti-virus-software-review.toptenreviews.com/*. Checking reviews written by others whose requirements and scenarios are similar to yours can help you select the best products for your organization.

Some anti-malware software works by examining the activity generated by a file to determine whether it is malware. These types of anti-malware programs use an approach called heuristic analysis to see whether programs "act" like malware. Other types of anti-malware software detect malware by comparing programs and files to signatures of known types of malware. The problem is, these programs may not immediately recognize and counteract newly created malware signatures. The anti-malware software must update its signature database to include these new signatures before the software can detect it. Because attackers constantly invent new viruses, it's imperative that you keep your anti-malware software up to date. An effective approach is to run an anti-malware program update and scan with every logon.

Note that even if you detect and eliminate a malware infection on a system, there is still a chance that malware is lurking elsewhere in the organization, ready to reinfect or attack the system. This is especially true in collaborative environments; files containing viruses may be stored in central servers and distributed throughout the network. This cycle of infection, disinfection, and reinfection will continue until you completely purge the malware from the entire system. If you detect malware anywhere in your system, you must scan all your systems, including storage devices, for its existence.

Protecting Your System with Firewalls

A **firewall** is a program or dedicated hardware device that inspects network traffic passing through it and denies or permits that traffic based on a set of rules you determine at configuration. A firewall's basic task is to regulate the flow of traffic between computer networks of different trust levels—for example, between the Internet Domain and the LAN Domain.

There are numerous firewall solutions available. Prominent firewall vendors include the following:

- **Cisco Systems**—*http://www.cisco.com/*
- **SonicWALL**—*http://www.sonicwall.com/*
- **WatchGuard Technologies**—*http://www.watchguard.com/*
- **Check Point**—*http://www.checkpoint.com/*
- **ZyXEL**—*http://www.zyxel.com/*
- **Netgear**—*http://www.netgear.com/*
- **Nortel**—*http://www.nortel.com/*
- **Juniper Networks**—*http://www.juniper.net*
- **DLink**—*http://www.dlink.com*
- **MultiTech Systems**—*http://www.multitech.com*

CHAPTER SUMMARY

Threats to business computers, personal computers, and information assets are an everyday menace. It is essential that organizations and individual users identify existing threats and vulnerabilities and plan for corrective action to address them.

There are many types of threats. These include confidentiality threats, integrity threats, and availability threats. In addition, there is the threat of a malicious attack. Malicious attacks can originate from active threats that include brute-force, masquerading, address spoofing, session hijacking, replay, man-in-the-middle, and dictionary attacks. Passive threats can include eavesdropping and monitoring. Viruses are the most common and frequent type of attack. Anti-malware software is the most effective method of countering a virus attack.

Threat targets are increasing as more users join the Internet community. Common targets include computer systems, network components, software, electrical systems, and databases. Black-hat hackers, white-hat hackers, gray-hat hackers, script kiddies, and crackers can launch attacks.

KEY CONCEPTS AND TERMS

Adware
Asset
Attack
Backdoor
Black-hat hacker
Cookie
Cracker
Dictionary attack
Disclosure
Ethical hacker
Firewall
Gray-hat hacker
Hacker
Hijacking
Incident response team (IRT)
Intellectual property (IP)
Keylogger
Malicious software
Malware
Man-in-the-middle attack
Masquerade attack
Netcat
Opportunity cost
Packet sniffer
Personally identifiable information (PII)
Pharming
Phishing
Phishing scam
Phone phreaking
Phreaking
Pop-up
Replay attack
Rootkit
Script kiddie
Security breach
Session hijacking
Smurfing
Sniffer
Spam
Spear phishing
Spoofing
Spyware
SYN flood
True downtime cost
Vulnerability scanner
Wannabe
Wardialer
White-hat hacker
Wiretapping

CHAPTER 3 ASSESSMENT

1. The main goal of a cyberattack is to affect one or more IT assets.
   A. True
   B. False
2. Which of the following best describes intellectual property (IP)?
   A. The items a business has copyrighted
   B. All patents owned by a business
   C. The unique knowledge a business possesses
   D. The personnel engaged in unique research
3. Which of the following terms best describes a person with very little skill?
   A. Hacker
   B. Script kiddie
   C. Cracker
   D. Wannabe
4. A(n) ________ is a software tool that captures traffic as it travels across a network.
5. Which type if attacks result in legitimate users not having access to a system resource?
   A. DoS
   B. IPS
   C. Man in the middle
   D. Trojan
6. A SYN flood attack floods a target with invalid network packets.
   A. True
   B. False
7. Which type of document defines unacceptable computer behavior?
   A. IDS
   B. DoS
   C. AUP
   D. PII

8. Which of the following steps can best protect your computer from worms?
   A. Installing anti-malware software
   B. Configuring a firewall to block all ports
   C. Encrypting all disks
   D. Enforcing strong passwords for all users

9. A wardialer is a legacy tool no longer in use.
   A. True
   B. False

10. A dictionary attack is a simple attack that primarily relies on users making poor password choices.
    A. True
    B. False

11. Which type of attack involves capturing data packets from a network and transmitting them later to produce an unauthorized effect?
    A. Man in the middle
    B. SYN flood
    C. Replay
    D. Smurf

12. A(n) ________ is any action that could damage an asset.

13. A(n) ________ is any weakness that makes it possible for a threat to cause harm to a computer or network.

14. Which type of malware is a self-contained program that replicates and sends copies of itself to other computers, generally across a network?
    A. Virus
    B. Worm
    C. Trojan
    D. Rootkit

15. Which group is responsible for responding to any reported cyberattack?
    A. Emergency response team
    B. IT security department
    C. Disaster response team
    D. Incident response team

The Drivers of the Information Security Business

CHAPTER 4

EVERY ORGANIZATION CARRIES OUT TASKS to satisfy business objectives. Without objectives, organizations have no purpose. You must identify the elements in your organization that support your business objectives. These elements are your organization's **business drivers**. Business drivers include people, information, and conditions that support business objectives. Information security activities directly support several common business drivers, including compliance and efforts to protect intellectual property. Security activities can also negatively affect business drivers, making it more difficult to satisfy your business objectives.

Some outside requirements direct how your organization carries out its tasks. These requirements can come from legislation, regulation, industry demands, or even your own standards. Every organization has some requirements with which it must comply. There are multiple ways that your organization can meet requirements. Most regulations require that you develop plans to handle business interruptions or disasters. In fact, most activities that restore operations after an interruption support several requirements.

Always consider different controls to satisfy compliance requirements. It's important that you balance security activities with their impact on your business drivers to protect your information's security. In this chapter, you will learn about security-related business drivers and how they support your overall business drivers.

Chapter 4 Topics

This chapter covers the following topics and concepts:

- What risk management is
- How BIA, BCP, and DRP differ from one another, and how they are the same
- How to assess the impact of risks, threats, and vulnerabilities
- How to close the information security gap
- How to mitigate risk and achieve compliance with laws, regulations, and requirements
- How to maintain A-I-C compliance

Chapter 4 Goals

When you complete this chapter, you will be able to:

- Define risk management and the way organizations should approach risk management
- Distinguish BIA, BCP, and DRP from one another and compare them to one another
- Assess the impact of risks, threats, and vulnerabilities on the IT infrastructure
- Define an acceptable level of risk or liability
- Shrink the information security gap based on risk-mitigation strategies
- Adhere to compliance laws and governance (policies, standards, procedures, and guidelines)
- Manage and mitigate risk as part of ongoing security operations
- Determine how to comply with A-I-C goals that are defined for your IT infrastructure

Defining Risk Management

Risk management is the process of identifying, assessing, prioritizing, and addressing risks. Any organization that is serious about security will view risk management as an ongoing process.

Risk management is not something you do just once. Each part of the risk-management process is separate but can occur many times. Risk management ensures that you have planned for risks that are most likely to have an effect on your organization. A secure organization has plans in place to address risks *before* events occur.

In Chapter 1, you learned that risk is the probability that an uncertain event will affect one or more resources. Most people view risks only in terms of negative effects. However, the **Project Management Body of Knowledge (PMBOK)**, maintained by the **Project Management Institute (PMI)**, states that the effects of risk can be positive or negative. PMI bases its risk-management philosophy on a proactive approach, which simultaneously does the following:

- Minimizes the effects of negative risks
- Maximizes the effects of positive risks

Consider the classic view of risks. Figure 4-1 shows the classic relationship between risks, threats, and vulnerabilities.

As shown in Figure 4-1, the risk equation is as follows:

Risk = Threats × Vulnerabilities.

A threat is the frequency of any event. In most cases, the events in the threat equation are negative or adverse events. Vulnerability is the likelihood that a specific threat will successfully be carried out. Multiplying the probability of a threat and the likelihood of a vulnerability yields the risk of that particular event. Risks apply to specific assets. If you multiply the risk probability by the cost of the asset, the result is the exposure to a specific risk.

Many people have never thought of risk as being a positive thing. However, uncertainty can result in events that have negative *or* positive effects. For example, suppose your organization plans to deploy new software to your end users based on projected availability from your software vendor. Your risk-management plan should address the responses to both an early and a late software delivery. If you receive the software early, you can either perform more exhaustive testing or begin deployment early. If your software vendor is late delivering software to you, you may miss your projected deployment date. You should have plans in place to address both the positive and negative effects of a delivery date that does not match your schedule.

A **risk methodology** is a description of how you will manage risk. The risk methodology that your organization adopts should include the approach, required information, and the techniques to address each risk. The approach defines how you will carry out the steps of the risk-methodology process. For example, the approach could state that risk analysis will be conducted at specified intervals. The tools for conducting this analysis can include

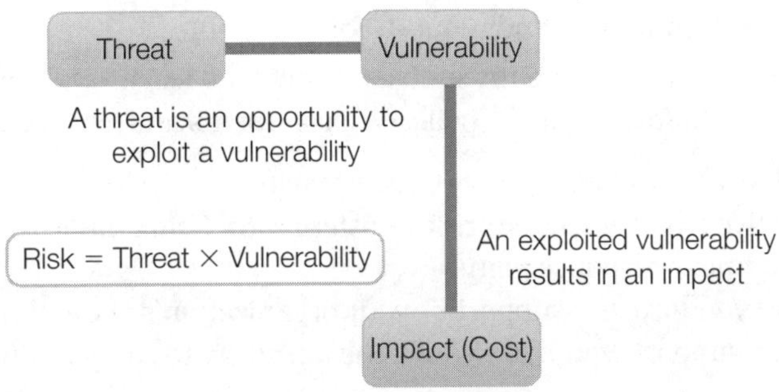

FIGURE 4-1
Risks, threats, and vulnerabilities.

the documents that define, categorize, and rank risks. This approach is consistent with PMI's PMBOK. While the PMI approach isn't the only way to do things, it does provide a prescriptive approach to project management in general, including risk management.

The process of managing risks starts by identifying risks. According to PMI, the steps in the risk-management process are as follows:

- Risk identification
- Risk analysis
- Risk-response planning
- Risk monitoring and control

Risk Identification

Risk identification is the process of determining and classifying the risks that might affect your resources. The ability to identify risks is a key part of an effective risk-management process. Identifying risks should involve as many people working in different roles as possible. Having more people involved enables you to identify risks from multiple perspectives.

The result of the risk identification process is a list of identified risks. PMI calls this list the **risk register**. The risk register can contain many different types of information, but should contain at least the following:

- A description of the risk
- The expected impact if the associated event occurs
- The probability of the event occurring
- Steps to mitigate the risk
- Steps to take should the event occur
- Rank of the risk

You might fill in only part of the risk register during this phase. This goal is to document as many risks as possible. Having too many risks in the risk register is much better than overlooking any severe risk that does occur. You can collect input for the risk register in several ways, including the following:

- Risk-identification brainstorming meetings
- Formal surveys
- Informal polls and requests for comments
- Incentivized events, such as "lunch and learn" sessions that include a forum for collecting comments and feedback

> **NOTE**
> Offering gifts or free food generally encourages a free flow of feedback.

Your organization's ability to respond to any risk starts with how well you identify potential risks. Be creative when asking for risk-register input. Using multiple perspectives will give you a more complete response plan.

It's crucial to ensure you have the support of your organization's upper management. Without management's support, you'll likely lack the authority to carry out the steps needed to develop a good risk-management plan. You will enjoy the benefits of having full management support from the very beginning in these risk-identification activities. Don't bring in management as an afterthought.

As the process of collecting information continues, more and more people should become involved. Larger groups can discourage participants from speaking up about weaknesses within your organization, however. They may fear reprisal, or fear that others will view them as complainers. You may find that one technique in particular produces the candid results you need: the **Delphi method**. This is an approach to using formal anonymous surveys in multiple rounds to collect opinions and information. Because the surveys are anonymous, the method encourages candid responses. A panel reviews each round of survey responses and creates a new survey based on the results of the previous round. Multiple rounds allow you to focus on areas of concern and assemble detailed information from a number of subject-matter experts.

Risk Analysis

The next step is to analyze the identified risks to decide how to rank them. All organizations have limited budgets. They cannot respond to every potential risk. Risk analysis allows organizations to decide which risks require more attention than others do. You shouldn't waste time and resources to mitigate risks that aren't likely to occur and will cause only minimal damage if they do. Mitigating risks that are likely to occur and may cause substantial damage makes the most sense.

Organizations use two common approaches to analyze risk:

- Qualitative risk analysis
- Quantitative risk analysis

Qualitative Risk Analysis

Qualitative risk analysis uses relative ranking to determine risk responses. This technique uses risk probability and risk impact. Risk probability is important because it measures how likely it is a risk will occur. When conducting a qualitative risk assessment, you generally express risk probability as a relative likelihood. You typically express risk probabilities as follows:

- **High probability**—Very likely to occur
- **Average probability**—Neither frequent nor rare
- **Low probability**—Not very likely to occur

A high-probability risk deserves more attention than a low-probability risk.

Another way to assess risk is by risk impact. Risk impact is a measure of how a risk will affect the organization or project. Risk impact can range from low (negligible) to high (substantial). A risk with low impact requires a different response than one with a high impact.

Different organizations may choose different classifications for risk probability and risk impact. Qualitative risk analysis quickly prioritizes risks to conduct response planning and further risk analysis.

Quantitative Risk Analysis

Quantitative risk analysis is another risk-analysis method. It uses mathematical formulas and numbers to rank risk severity. The goal of quantitative risk analysis is to quantify possible outcomes of risks, determine probabilities of outcomes, identify high-impact risks, and develop plans based on risks. Although quantitative risk analysis can be a complex topic, the basic idea is to consider several qualities of risks and the resources the risk may affect.

You can use quantitative risk analysis for all risks on the risk register, but the amount of effort required may be overkill for low-probability or low-impact risks. For this reason, quantitative risk analysis generally starts with those risks you consider high probability during qualitative risk analysis.

Here are the steps involved in performing a quantitative risk analysis for each item on your risk register:

1. Calculate the risk exposure.
   a. Assign a value to each resource.
   b. Determine the percentage of loss for each realized threat. This value is the **exposure factor (EF)** for the threat against a resource.
2. Calculate the loss for a single threat occurrence, called the **single loss expectancy (SLE)**, using the following formula:

   $SLE = \text{resource value} \times EF$
3. Calculate or determine the annual probability of a loss. The estimated annual probability that a stated threat will be realized is called the **annual rate of occurrence (ARO)**.
4. Calculate the annual estimated loss due to a specific realized threat, called the **annual loss expectancy (ALE)**, using the following formula:

   $ALE = SLE \times ARO$

TABLE 4-1 Quantitative risk analysis.

RESOURCE	RISK	VALUE	EF	SLE	ARO	ALE
Building	Fire	$700,000	0.60	$420,000	0.20	$ 84,000
File server	Disk crash	$ 50,000	0.50	$ 25,000	0.20	$ 5,000
Sensitive data	Theft	$200,000	0.90	$180,000	0.70	$126,000
E-business Internet connection	Unavailability for one hour	$ 15,000	1.00	$ 15,000	12.00	$180,000

Table 4-1 contains a few sample risks and the calculated ALE for each risk. Once you have an ALE for each risk, you can determine which risks to address first.

Risk-Response Planning

After you identify and rank as many risks as possible, the next step is to select strategies to address each risk. You should include these strategies in the risk register. Your risk-response plan shows that you have examined risks to your organization and have developed plans to address each risk. It's important that you include a response description for every risk on the risk register. Ignoring a risk is not a valid option. You should assign one or more "owners" to each risk response to carry out the planned actions.

> **NOTE**
> Responding to a risk of any type does not make the risk go away. The risk still exists. Any risk that exists but has a defined response is called a **residual risk**.

There are four responses to negative risks:

- **Avoid**—When you avoid a negative risk, you eliminate the threat by changing resources or the IT infrastructure. For example, you might avoid the risk of a single point of failure for your Internet connection by adding additional gateway devices.
- **Transfer**—When you transfer a negative risk, you shift it to a third party. For example, purchasing fire insurance shifts the associated risk to the company holding the policy.
- **Mitigate**—When you mitigate a negative risk, you reduce the probability or the impact of the risk. For example, to mitigate known attacks, you can harden Web servers by updating software and changing configuration settings.
- **Accept**—When you accept a negative risk, you take no steps in response to that risk. You might accept a risk if the effects of the risk are not worth the expense of a response. An example of a risk you might accept is an unencrypted network connection between your database server and application server. Because setting up an encrypted connection between the two servers involves a cost in terms of both dollars and performance, and because it's very unlikely that an attacker will threaten this network connection, your organization can simply accept the risk.

For positive risks, the responses include the following:

- **Exploit**—When you exploit a positive risk, you take advantage of an opportunity that arises when you respond to that risk. For example, suppose your organization developed training materials for use within your organization to help you address a specific risk. You might exploit the risk by packaging and marketing those training materials to other organizations.
- **Share**—When you share a positive risk, you use a third party to help capture the opportunity associated with that risk. For example, purchasing a group of workstation licenses along with another organization enables both organizations to realize a substantial discount due to the size of the combined order. (In this case, the risk is that the license cost may change.)

- **Enhance**—When you enhance a positive risk, you increase the probability or positive impact of the event associated with the risk. For example, suppose you have a contract to deliver software that includes a $20,000 bonus for early completion. To enhance the positive risk—a delivery date that does not match your schedule—you might offer a subcontractor you've hired a $5,000 bonus for finishing ahead of the deadline.
- **Accept**—When you accept a positive risk, you take no steps to address it because the potential effects of the risk are positive and add value. For example, suppose you have purchased a new automated backup and configuration utility that can help your organization deploy new workstations in half the allotted time. Because the utility is new, it may take some time to learn—meaning it may *not* help your organization save any time deploying new workstations. It's determined that at worst, learning the new utility and using it to manage deployments will take the same amount of time as doing it manually. However, if you realize the positive risk, you will finish the deployments sooner than planned.

Risk Monitoring and Control

You shouldn't perform risk identification and analysis just once. Conditions within an organization constantly change, as do the risks encountered by the organization. You must continually monitor risks and perform additional analysis to develop new risk responses any time you identify new risks. The formal process of monitoring and controlling risk focuses on identifying and analyzing new risks. It also focuses on tracking previously identified risks.

You should reevaluate risks when any of the following events occur:

- You identify evidence that a threat has been realized or is about to be realized.
- Your organization approves a change request to your risk-response plan.
- Any changes occur to your environment that may affect resource risks.
- You apply corrective or preventive actions.

You should continually ensure that your risk-management plan matches your current environment. If your environment changes in any way, you should reevaluate risks to ensure you are best prepared to handle any threats.

Implementing a BIA, a BCP, and a DRP

The primary focus of risk management is to preempt realized threats. It's not possible to foresee and prevent every event that results in loss. That means that the likelihood still exists that any organization will encounter an event that will interrupt normal business operations. Information security requires all information to be available when any authorized user needs it. You'll have to develop and implement methods and techniques for protecting the organization's IT resources and ensuring that events do not interrupt normal business functions.

Business Impact Analysis

The first step in developing plans to address interruptions is to identify those business functions that are crucial to your organization. Some of your organization's activities are critical to the operation of the business and some aren't. When an event interrupts your organization's ability to conduct operations, it's important to restore the most crucial operations first. Before you can do this, you have to identify what those functions are.

A business impact analysis (BIA) is a formal analysis of an organization's functions and activities that classifies them as critical or noncritical. Critical functions are required to run the business. If you cannot carry out a critical function, it causes unacceptable damage. Noncritical functions may be important, and you might miss them if they did not exist, but their absence would not stop an organization from conducting business. A BIA also arranges critical activities based on importance and helps an organization determine which functions to restore in what order if there is a major interruption.

In the BIA, the section for each critical function receives additional information, including a description of recovery goals and requirements for each function. Recovery goals and requirements are expressed as follows:

- **Recovery point objective (RPO)**—The amount of data loss that is acceptable. Depending on the nature of the function, staff members may be able to re-create or reenter data. The RPO provides direction on whether loss prevention or loss correction is a better option.
- **Recovery time objective (RTO)**—The maximum allowable time to recover the function. Many less formal recovery plans overlook RTO. Time may be a critical factor, and specifying the requirements for recovery time helps determine the best recovery options.
- **Business recovery requirements**—Any business prerequisites for the functions—that is, other business functions that must already be in place for the recovery functions to occur. Business recovery requirements help in determining the recovery sequence.
- **Technical recovery requirements**—Any technical prerequisites to support each business function. In most cases, technical recovery requirements dictate which IT infrastructure components must be in place.

Ensuring that operations and functions that are critical to an organization are able to continue is crucial to the organization's survival. The BIA will help identify not only which functions are critical, but also how quickly essential business functions must return to full operation following a major interruption. It will also identify resource requirements for returning each function to full operation. BIAs generally assume a worst-case scenario in which the physical infrastructure supporting each activity or function has been destroyed, along with any data. You can choose to plan for any interruption timeframe, but in many BIAs, restoration plans assume that access to primary resources will not be possible for at least 30 days. In other words, a solid BIA will indicate the requirements necessary to conduct business for an extended period when the normal infrastructure is unavailable.

Business Continuity Plan

A business continuity plan (BCP) is a plan for a structured response to any events that result in an interruption to critical business activities or functions. Performing a BIA is an important first step toward generating a BCP in that the BIA identifies the resources for which a BCP is necessary.

There is generally no reason to develop a BCP for resources that aren't crucial to an organization's survival. The BCP primarily addresses the processes, resources, equipment, and devices needed to continue conducting critical business activities when an interruption occurs that affects the business's viability.

The most important part of any BCP is setting priorities, with the understanding that people always come first. There are no exceptions. Any plan that addresses business interruptions and disasters must place the safety and well-being of the organization's people as the highest priority. All other concerns are secondary. The order of priorities for a well-balanced BCP should be as follows:

- Safety and well-being of all people
- Buildings and facilities
- Infrastructure components, including communications and information systems

You must address the needs of each category before continuing to the next category. If conditions are hazardous for humans, they can't do anything productive. If your people are safe but your building is damaged, you can't replace servers or network hardware. You must wait for the damage to be repaired or for the organization to be relocated to restore infrastructure components. Keep the order of resource priority in mind as you develop plans to avoid business-process interruptions.

> **NOTE**
> Direct costs are immediate expenditures that reduce profit. Indirect costs, such as losing a customer, affect the overall revenue stream but are harder to calculate because there is no expenditure record. In the case of indirect costs, the impact is that potential sales just never happen.

A formal BCP isn't just helpful for many organizations—in some circumstances, it's required. Legislation and regulations often require a BCP to ensure systems are safe. Today's organizations increasingly rely on IT resources and require a solid IT infrastructure to conduct business. The cost for system downtime for these companies can be extreme. Direct and indirect costs associated with downtime can exist in several categories, including:

- Lost customers
- Lost revenue
- Lost market share
- Additional expenses
- Damaged reputation

Organizations must consider contingency and recovery plans from a comprehensive perspective. Plans cannot focus on individual resources to the exclusion of others. While each of the components of contingency and recovery plans do generally address specific resources, they must do so within a larger context. Keeping the larger context in view during plan development enables you to address the risks to an organization as opposed to just fixing a broken resource.

Elements of a complete BCP should include the following:

- Emergency response and protection of life and safety
- Situation and damage assessment
- Resource salvage and recovery
- Alternate facilities for emergency operation and business recovery

Briefly, a BCP directs all activities required to ensure that an organization's critical business functions continue with little or no interruption. The BCP assumes that the infrastructure components needed to support operations are in place. Unfortunately, that is not always the case after a disaster. What happens when a fire destroys your data center? How can you continue business operations in that case? The answer is, you need another plan: a disaster recovery plan (DRP).

Disaster Recovery Plan

A disaster recovery plan (DRP) directs the actions necessary to recover resources after a disaster. A DRP is part of a BCP. It is necessary to ensure the restoration of resources required by the BCP to an available state. The DRP extends and supports the BCP by identifying events that could cause damage to resources that are necessary to support critical business functions. The BCP already contains a list of the resources necessary to support each business function. The next step in developing a DRP is to consider what could happen to each resource.

Threat Analysis

A threat analysis involves identifying and documenting threats to critical resources. Before you can recover from a disaster, you need to consider what types of disasters are possible and what types of damage they can cause. For example, recovering from a data-center fire is different from recovering from a flu epidemic. Some common threats include the following:

- Fire
- Flood
- Hurricane

> **BCP Versus DRP: What's the Difference?**
>
> What is the difference between a BCP and a DRP? A BCP does not specify how to recover from disasters, just interruptions. In general, an *interruption* is a minor event that may disrupt one or more business processes for a short period. In contrast, a *disaster* is an event that affects multiple business processes for an extended period. Disasters often also cause substantial resource damage that you must address before you can resolve the business process interruption.

- Tornado
- Disease
- Earthquake
- Cyberattack
- Sabotage
- Utility outage
- Terrorism

With the exception of disease, each of these threats has the potential to damage an organization's infrastructure. In contrast, disease directly affects personnel. You can address disease with various solutions. If, however, the disease affects people charged with carrying out the recovery plans, the recovery may be unsuccessful.

Note that these threats do not necessarily occur one at a time. One threat may lead to another threat. For example, a flood that introduces contaminated water into an office may lead to disease that incapacitates your staff. As another example, a tornado or earthquake could also result in a fire. Always assume that disasters may occur in groups, not only as single events.

Impact Scenarios

After defining potential threats, the next step in creating a comprehensive DRP is to document likely impact scenarios. These form the basis of the DRP. In most organizations, planning for the most wide-reaching disaster rather than focusing on smaller issues results in a more comprehensive plan. Narrowing the focus on smaller issues can result in a DRP that fails to consider a broader strategy. A broader strategy is necessary to recover from the loss of multiple resources simultaneously. An impact scenario like "Building Loss" will likely encompass all critical business functions and the worst potential outcome from any given threat. A DRP may include additional impact scenarios if an organization has more than one building.

A solid DRP might also contain additional, more-specific impact scenarios. For example, your plan may include a scenario that addresses the loss of a specific floor in a building. Many plans underestimate the resources necessary to move from one location to another. Don't neglect the resources necessary to execute each step of your plan. A recovery plan that fails just because you didn't have access to a truck large enough to move your equipment to an alternate site isn't a very solid plan.

Recovery Requirement Documentation

Once you complete the analysis phase, you should document the business and technical requirements to initiate the implementation phase. You'll likely need access to asset information, including asset lists and their availability during a disaster. Each asset has an owner. The owner of an asset must grant access to it to the disaster relief team. Including at least one member of upper management in BIA, BCP, and DRP planning can help you head off political battles for control over assets during disasters.

The asset information you'll likely need to develop a DRP includes the following:

- The number, types, and locations of desks and other office furniture that can be used to furnish a secondary location
- Personnel necessary for the recovery effort, along with their contact information and their roles in the recovery process
- Application software and data required for critical business functions
- Resources necessary for manual workaround solutions
- Maximum allowable outage time and data loss for each software application
- Required peripherals, such as printers, copiers, fax machines, and other office equipment

Disaster Recovery

It's important to train all personnel on the proper response to any disaster. A common mistake is to be too eager to begin the recovery process. Even though your organization has devoted substantial time and resources to developing a DRP, you must ensure that you react to the disaster, not the plan. The critical steps in responding to a disaster include the following:

- **Ensure everyone's safety first**—No resource is as important as people are.
- **Respond to the disaster before pursuing recovery**—Required response and containment actions depend on the nature of the disaster and may not have anything to do with the recovery effort.
- **Follow the DRP, including communicating with all affected parties**—Once your people are safe and you have responded to the disaster, you can pursue recovery actions.

Disaster recovery is an extension to the DRP. It addresses recovering from common system outages or interruptions. A disaster is generally larger than a common outage, and the resources may not be available to enact simple recovery solutions. For example, most database-management systems enable you to quickly recover the primary database from a replicated copy. However, if a disaster has resulted in the destruction of your database server computer, you'll have to restore the server to a stable state before you can restore your database data.

A disaster may render your data center unusable, forcing you to relocate your operations. Careful planning for such a move makes it viable. Although moving your data center to another location may not sound like a major undertaking, it involves many details—which is why you should devote so much effort to planning. You must install hardware and software, and there are network and telecommunications requirements. Table 4-2 lists several common data-center options for disaster recovery.

TABLE 4-2 Data center alternatives for disaster recovery.

OPTION	DESCRIPTION	COMMENTS
Hot site	Facility with environmental utilities, hardware, software, and data that closely mirrors the original data center	Most expensive option, least switchover time
Warm site	Facility with environmental utilities and basic computer hardware	Less expensive than a hot site, but requires more time to load operating systems, software, data, and configurations
Cold site	Facility with basic environmental utilities but no infrastructure components	Least expensive option, but at the cost of the longest switchover time since all hardware, software, and data must be loaded at the new site
Mobile site	Trailer with necessary environmental utilities that can operate as a warm site or cold site	Very flexible, fairly short switchover time, and widely varying costs based on size and capacity

NOTE

In some industries, cooperative agreements are mandatory. For example, banks are required to maintain cooperative agreements with other banks. They are also required to regularly test their ability to use other banks' facilities to ensure uninterrupted service to their customers.

It may be to your advantage to work out a mutual aid agreement with another company where each organization agrees to provide backup resources in the event of a disaster. The agreement could include after-hours access to computing resources or physical space to use as a temporary data center. Carefully examine all the requirements when considering a cooperative agreement. Providing basic critical functionality for a data center may seem straightforward, but some resources, such as telecommunication service, may not be easy to switch from one location to another. Also, consider how close any alternate location is to your existing location. If your proposed alternate location is too close to your main location, a large disaster such as a flood or an earthquake could affect both.

Disaster recovery is rapidly becoming an increasingly important aspect of enterprise computing. As business environments become more complex, more things can go wrong. Recovery plans have become more complex to keep up. DRPs vary from one organization to another, depending on many factors. These include the type of organization, the processes involved, and the level of security needed. Most enterprises remain unprepared or underprepared for a disaster. And despite recurrent reminders, many companies do not have a DRP at all. Of those that do, nearly half have never tested their plan—which is essentially the same as not having one.

It's crucial to validate your DRP for effectiveness and completeness, and test it for accuracy. It's rare that the first version of a DRP is complete and correct. You must test your DRP to identify weaknesses. You can engage a disaster-recovery firm to assist in such tests. These tests can range from simple reviews to complete disaster simulations. The most effective tests simulate real disasters, including transferring software between computer systems and ensuring that you can establish communications at an alternate location. Following are various different types of DRP tests:

- **Checklist test**—This is the simplest type of DRP test. In a checklist test, each participant follows steps on the DRP checklist and provides feedback. You can use checklist tests for DRP training and awareness.
- **Structured walkthrough**—A structured walkthrough is similar to a checklist test, but the DRP team uses role-playing to simulate a disaster and evaluate the DRP's effectiveness. This type of test is also called a tabletop exercise or conference-room test.
- **Simulation test**—A simulation test is more realistic than a structured walkthrough. In a simulation test, the DRP team uses role-playing and follows through with as much of the effects of a simulated disaster as possible without affecting live operations.
- **Parallel test**—A parallel test evaluates the effectiveness of the DRP by enabling full processing capability at an alternate data center without interrupting the primary data center.
- **Full-interruption test**—This is the only complete test. Full-interruption tests interrupt the primary data center and transfer processing capability to an alternate site.

Not all aspects of DRPs are reactive. Some parts of a DRP are preventative and intended to avoid the negative effects of a disaster in the first place. Preventative components of a DRP may include some of the following:

- Local mirroring of disks systems and use of data-protection technology such as a redundant array of independent disks (RAID)
- Surge protectors to minimize the effect of power surges on delicate electronic equipment
- Uninterruptible power supply (UPS) and/or a backup generator to keep systems going in the event of a power failure
- Fire-prevention systems
- Antivirus software and other security controls

Assessing Risks, Threats, and Vulnerabilities

One of the first steps in developing a comprehensive BCP and DRP is to fully assess the risks, threats, and vulnerabilities associated with your organization's critical resources. You can't protect your environment from every possible threat, so it's necessary to prioritize. Until you know the risks, you can't know which remedies are necessary.

TABLE 4-3 Common risk-assessment methodologies.

NAME	DESCRIPTION	FOR MORE INFORMATION
Risk Management Guide for Information Technology Systems (NIST SP 800-30 and SP 800-66)	Part of the Special Publication 800 series reports, these products provide detailed guidance of what you should consider in risk management and risk assessment in computer security. The reports include checklists, graphics, formulas, and references to U.S. regulatory issues. NIST SP 800-66 specifically addresses HIPAA concerns.	*http://www.csrc.nist.gov*
CCTA Risk Analysis and Management Method (CRAMM)	CRAMM is a risk analysis method developed by the British government. Best practices of British government organizations are the basis of the first releases of the CRAMM method and tool. People around the world use CRAMM. CRAMM is also the British government's preferred risk analysis method. CRAMM is best suited for large organizations.	*http://www.cramm.com*
Operationally Critical Threat, Asset, and Vulnerability Evaluation (OCTAVE)	The OCTAVE approach defines a risk-based strategic assessment and planning technique for security. OCTAVE is a self-directed approach. There are two versions of OCTAVE: OCTAVE and OCTAVE-S. OCTAVE is best suited for large organizations, whereas OCTAVE-S works well for organizations consisting of fewer than 100 people.	*http://www.cert.org/octave/osig.html*
ISO/IEC 27005 "Information Security Risk Management"	An ISO standard that describes information security risk management in a generic manner. The documents include examples of approaches to information security risk assessment and lists of possible threats, vulnerabilities, and security controls.	*http://www.iso.org/*

There are many approaches to assessing risk. Each organization conducts the process in its own unique way. Instead of starting from scratch in the risk-assessment process, you can use one of the many methodologies that are available. At least one of these is likely a good fit for your organization. Investing the time to research the various offerings can make the whole process more effective and efficient. Table 4-3 lists common risk-assessment methodologies.

Closing the Information Security Gap

In spite of all best efforts, no collection of security controls is perfect. There are always some vulnerabilities for which there are no controls. The difference between the security controls you have in place and the controls you need in order to address all vulnerabilities is called the **security gap**.

A valuable tool to help ensure you are satisfying your organization's security policy is a **gap analysis**. From an IT security perspective, a gap analysis is a comparison of the security controls you have in place and the controls you need in order to address all identified threats. Gap-analysis activities should be ongoing. They should consist of regular reviews of day-to-day practices vis-à-vis the latest threat assessment. Threats that you do not address through at least one control indicate gaps in your security.

Gap analysis is an effective method for gauging the overall security of an organization's IT environments. In addition, gap analysis can provide assurances that security implementations are consistent with real requirements. You can conduct many different types of gap-analysis activities. They can be formal investigations or informal surveys. Factors that influence the analysis include the size of your organization, the industry in which you operate, the cost involved, efforts involved, and the depth of the analysis.

Many of the following steps are common when conducting a gap analysis:

- Identifying the applicable elements of the security policy and other standards
- Assembling policy, standard, procedure, and guideline documents
- Reviewing and assessing the implementation of the policies, standards, procedures, and guidelines
- Collecting inventory information for all hardware and software components
- Interviewing users to assess knowledge of and compliance with policies
- Comparing the current security environment with policies in place
- Prioritizing identified gaps for resolution
- Documenting and implementing the remedies to conform to policies

One important aspect of gap analysis is determining the cause of the gap. The fact that a gap exists means there is a lack of adequate security controls, but *why* does the gap exist? There are several common reasons for security gaps in any organization, such as:

- Lack of security training, resulting in noncompliant behavior
- Intentional or negligent disregard of security policy
- Unintended consequence of a control or policy change

- Addition or modification of hardware or software without proper risk analysis
- Configuration changes that lack proper risk analysis
- Changes to external requirements, such as legislation, regulation, or industry standards that require control changes

As you can see, most security gaps relate closely to user actions. One of the first steps you can take to close gaps is to ensure that you fully train personnel on security issues. Well-trained people are your best allies in securing your IT environment. As your security efforts become more sophisticated and your organization's personnel become more security savvy, you should encounter fewer and fewer security gaps.

Adhering to Compliance Laws

The last 20 years have seen an explosion in computing power and in the number of ways computers are used. The increased reliance on networked resources, hardware, and software has created many new opportunities for the malicious use of resources. Information has become a valued asset to organizations and an attractive target to attackers. As information-related crime has grown, so has legislation and regulation to protect organizations and individuals from criminal activity.

Today's organizations are increasingly subject to various laws enacted to protect the privacy of electronic information. Each organization must comply with laws and regulations, although the specific laws and regulations to which an organization is subject depend on its location, the type of information it handles, and the industries in which it operates.

The following list summarizes many of the most far-reaching laws and regulations that affect how organizations conduct IT operations:

- **Sarbanes-Oxley Act (SOX)**—Sarbanes-Oxley, which became law in July of 2002, introduced sweeping changes to how corporate governance and financial practices are regulated. As a direct result of several public financial scandals, SOX established the Public Company Accounting Oversight Board (PCAOB), which is responsible for overseeing, regulating, inspecting, and disciplining accounting firms in their roles as auditors of public companies. SOX also dictates policies that address auditor independence, corporate governance, internal control assessment, and enhanced financial disclosure.
- **Health Insurance Portability and Accountability Act (HIPAA)**—HIPAA, which took effect on April 14, 2006, governs how doctors, hospitals, and other health care providers handle personal medical information. HIPAA requires that all medical records, billing, and patient information be handled in ways that maintain the patient's privacy. HIPAA also guarantees that all patients be able to access their own medical records, correct errors or omissions, and be informed of how personal information is used. To ensure every affected person is aware of HIPAA's requirements, patients must receive notifications of privacy procedures any time they submit medical information.

- **Federal Information Security Management Act (FISMA)**—FISMA officially recognizes the importance of information security to the national security and economic health of the United States. FISMA requires every federal agency to develop and maintain formal information security programs, including security awareness efforts; secure access to computer resources; strict acceptable use policies; and formal incident response and contingency planning.
- **Gramm-Leach-Bliley Act (GLBA)**—GLBA addresses information security concerns in the financial industry. GLBA requires that financial institutions provide their clients a privacy notice that explains what information the company gathers about the client, where the information is shared, and how the company protects that information. Companies must provide clients with this privacy notice prior to entering into an agreement to do business.
- **Payment Card Industry Data Security Standard (PCI DSS)**—Although not a law, PCI DSS affects any organization that processes or stores credit card information. The founding payment brands of the PCI Security Standards Council—including American Express, Discover Financial Services, JCB, MasterCard Worldwide, and Visa International—developed PCI DSS to foster consistent global data-security measures. The PCI DSS is a comprehensive security standard that includes requirements for security management, policies, procedures, network architecture, software design, and other critical protective measures.
- **The Family Education Rights and Privacy Act (FERPA)**—This federal law protects the privacy of student education records. The law applies to all schools that receive funds under an applicable program of the U.S. Department of Education. Under FERPA, schools must receive written permission from a parent or eligible student before releasing any information contained in a student's education record.
- **USA Patriot Act of 2001**—Passed 45 days after the September 11, 2001, attacks on the World Trade Center in New York City and on the Pentagon in Washington, D.C., the Patriot Act substantially expanded the authority of U.S. law-enforcement agencies to enable them to fight terrorism in the United States and abroad. It expands the ability of law-enforcement agencies to access information that pertains to an ongoing investigation.
- **Children's Online Privacy Protection Act of 1998 (COPPA)**—COPPA restricts how online information is collected from children under 13 years of age. It dictates what a Web site operator must include in a privacy policy, when and how to seek verifiable consent from a parent, and what responsibilities an operator has to protect children's privacy and safety online.
- **Government Information Security Reform Act (Security Reform Act) of 2000**—This act focuses on management and evaluation of the security of unclassified and national security systems. It formalized existing Office of Management and Budget (OMB) security policies and restated security responsibilities contained in the Computer Security Act of 1987.

- **California Database Security Breach Act of 2003**—This California act, along with several other similar state acts, requires any company that stores customer data electronically to notify its customers any time there is a security breach. The company must immediately notify any affected customers if someone breaches its computer system and steals unencrypted information. Other similar bills limit the ability of financial institutions to share nonpublic personal client information with affiliates and third parties.

It's the responsibility of each organization to understand which laws and regulations apply to them and to employ necessary controls to comply. This effort often requires frequent attention and results in audits and assessments to ensure the organization remains compliant.

Keeping Private Data Confidential

Many of the compliance requirements you saw in earlier sections address data confidentiality. One of the most important classes of security controls is those that keep information confidential. Ensuring availability and integrity is important, but confidentiality gets the most attention. That's because you cannot undo a confidentiality violation. That is, once someone views confidential data, there is no way to remove it from his or her memory. You must pay careful attention to each of the three tenets of information security to protect your organization's data assets. Figure 4-2 shows the three tenets of information security.

You will learn different techniques in this book to ensure the availability, integrity, and confidentiality of data. At the highest level, data is secure when it is available to authorized users and not available to unauthorized users. You will have to cover many details before you can fully ensure your data's security. Maintaining confidentiality will certainly be a recurring theme. In fact, many controls to ensure confidentiality also ensure other aspects of data security.

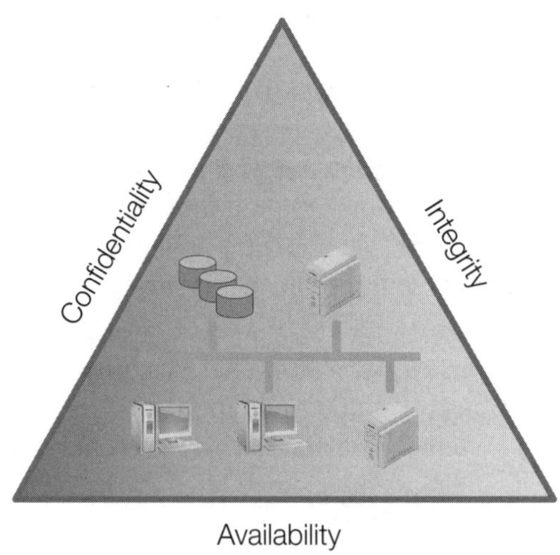

FIGURE 4-2
The three tenets of information security.

As you learn more about various security controls, you will see how they work together to protect data from unauthorized use. Most strategies to secure data use a three-pronged approach that includes the techniques of authentication, authorization, and accounting. These three techniques help ensure that only authorized users can access resources and data. They also ensure that enough information is captured to troubleshoot access issues after the access occurs. Investigations into security incidents rely on accounting information to reconstruct past events.

> **NOTE**
> In the context of monitoring information system activity, the term **accounting** means recording events in log files. You can use computer-event accounting to trace users' actions and determine a sequence of events that is helpful when investigating incidents.

The basic purpose of the three-pronged approach is to maintain security by preventing unauthorized use of any protected resource. Many authentication and access controls can help accomplish this task. Some of the authentication controls you will learn about include the following:

- Passwords and PINs
- Smart cards and tokens
- Biometric devices
- Digital certificates
- Challenge-response handshakes
- Kerberos authentication
- One-time passwords

Once you have authenticated a user, access controls help ensure only authorized users can access the protected resource. Authorization controls you will learn about include the following:

- Authentication server rules and permissions
- Access control lists
- Intrusion detection and prevention
- Physical access control
- Connection and access policy filters
- Network traffic filters

These two lists give a brief overview of some of the security controls that help to ensure your organization's data security. You will learn about the details and implementation techniques of these controls in upcoming chapters.

CHAPTER SUMMARY

In this chapter, you learned that security is much more than a way to keep data secret. Security is an integral part of any organization. A solid security policy ensures that an organization can perform its primary business functions even in the event of a disaster and will do so while protecting all of its assets, including its data. The same solid security policy provides the assurance that the organization has employed the necessary controls to comply with all necessary laws, regulations, and other security requirements. In short, security keeps an organization viable and allows it to conduct business.

KEY CONCEPTS AND TERMS

Accounting
Annual loss expectancy (ALE)
Annual rate of occurrence (ARO)
Business drivers
Delphi method
Exposure factor (EF)
Gap analysis
Project Management Body of Knowledge (PMBOK)
Project Management Institute (PMI)
Qualitative risk analysis
Quantitative risk analysis
Residual risk
Risk management
Risk methodology
Risk register
Security gap
Single loss expectancy (SLE)

CHAPTER 4 ASSESSMENT

1. Risk management is responding to a negative event when it occurs.
   A. True
   B. False
2. With respect to IT security, a risk can result in either a positive or a negative effect.
   A. True
   B. False
3. According to PMI, which term describes the list of identified risks?
   A. Risk checklist
   B. Risk register
   C. Risk methodology
   D. Mitigation list
4. Which type of risk analysis uses formulas and numerical values to indicate risk severity?
   A. Objective risk analysis
   B. Qualitative risk analysis
   C. Subjective risk analysis
   D. Quantitative risk analysis
5. Which type of risk analysis uses relative ranking?
   A. Objective risk analysis
   B. Qualitative risk analysis
   C. Subjective risk analysis
   D. Quantitative risk analysis
6. Which risk-analysis value represents the annual probability of a loss?
   A. EF
   B. SLE
   C. ALE
   D. ARO
7. Which risk-response option would best describe purchasing fire insurance?
   A. Accept
   B. Mitigate
   C. Transfer
   D. Avoid
8. Which risk response would be most appropriate if the impact of a risk becoming a reality is negligible?
   A. Accept
   B. Mitigate
   C. Transfer
   D. Avoid
9. Which of the following statements best describes the relationship of a BCP to a DRP?
   A. A BCP is required but a DRP is not
   B. A DRP is a component of a BCP
   C. A DRP is required but a BCP is not
   D. A BCP is a component of a DRP
10. Which term is used to indicate the amount of data loss that is acceptable?
    A. RAI
    B. ROI
    C. RTO
    D. RPO
11. A(n) ________ identifies processes that are critical to the operation of a business.
12. Which risk-assessment methodology is marketed as a self-directed approach and has two different editions for organizations of different sizes?
    A. CRAMM
    B. OCTAVE
    C. NIST
    D. EBIOS
13. ________ is the U.S. security-related act that governs health-related information.
14. Which U.S. security-related act governs the security of data specifically for the financial industry?
    A. GLBA
    B. SOX
    C. HIPAA
    D. FERPA

PART TWO

The Systems Security Certified Practitioner (SSCP®) Professional Certification from (ISC)²

CHAPTER

5

Access Controls

ACCESS CONTROLS ARE METHODS used to restrict and allow access to certain items, such as automobiles, homes, computers, even your cell phone. Your first experience with access controls might have been when you locked a sibling out of your room or used a combination lock to secure your valuables in your locker at school. Similarly, the key to your car fits *only* your car, so only you can unlock and start it. The same is true of your house or apartment. Perhaps you also use a special code to secure access to your cell phone. Only you know that code, so only you can unlock the phone. Or maybe certain channels on your television cannot be seen without a security code.

Access control is the process of protecting a resource so that it is used only by those allowed to use it. Access controls protect a resource from unauthorized use. Just as the lock-and-key systems for your house or car are access controls, so are the personal information numbers (PINs) on your bank or credit cards.

Businesses use access controls to manage what employees can and cannot do. Access controls define who users (people or computer processes) are, what users can do, which resources they can reach, and what operations they can perform. Access control systems use several technologies, including passwords, hardware tokens, biometrics, and certificates. Access can be granted to physical assets, such as buildings or rooms. Access can also be granted to computer systems and data.

Chapter 5 Topics

This chapter covers the following topics and concepts:

- What the four parts of access control are
- What the two types of access control are
- How to define an authorization policy
- What identification methods and guidelines are

- What authentication processes and requirements are
- What accountability policies and procedures are
- What formal models of access control are
- What threats there are to access controls
- What some effects of access control violations are
- What centralized and decentralized access controls are

Chapter 5 Goals

When you complete this chapter, you will be able to:

- Define access control concepts and technologies
- Describe the formal models of access control
- Describe how identity is managed by access control
- Develop and maintain system access controls

The Four Parts of Access Control

The four parts of **access control** are as follows:

- **Authorization**—Who is approved for access and what, exactly, can they use?
- **Identification**—How are they identified?
- **Authentication**—Can their identities be verified?
- **Accountability**—How are actions traced to an individual to ensure that the person who makes changes to data or systems can be identified? This process of associating actions with users for later reporting and research is known as **accountability**.

These four parts are divided into two phases:

- **The policy definition phase**—This phase determines who has access and what systems or resources they can use. The authorization process operates in this phase.
- **The policy enforcement phase**—This phase grants or rejects requests for access based on the authorizations defined in the first phase. The identification, authentication, and accountability processes operate in this phase.

The Two Types of Access Control

Organizations control access to resources primarily on two levels:

- **Physical access controls**—These control entry into buildings, parking lots, and protected areas. For example, you probably have a key to the door of your office. This key controls the *physical* access to your office.
- **Logical access controls**—These control access to a computer system or network. Your company probably requires that you enter a unique username and password to log on to your company computer. That username and password allow you to use your organization's computer system and network resources. This is an example of a **logical access control**.

Physical Access Control

An organization's facilities manager is often responsible for **physical access control**. This person might give you a security card (also known as a smart card) programmed with your employee ID number. You might need to swipe this card through a card reader to open a gate to the parking lot and swipe it in the elevator to be let off on your floor. You might also need to swipe this card to unlock a door leading to your office. This card allows you to enter these locations because you are an employee. The organization's authorization policy grants you, as an employee, physical access to certain places. People without an authorized card shouldn't get past the front gate. If your organization shares your office building with other organizations, you might even have a second card that grants access into the building after hours. These cards control access to *physical* resources.

Logical Access Control

Computer-system managers use logical access controls to decide who can get into a system and what tasks they can perform. A system manager can also use logical access controls to influence how staff personnel use a system. Examples of system controls for a human resources (HR) system include:

- **Deciding which users can get into a system**—For example, HR employees may be the only employees who are allowed to reach sensitive information stored on an HR server.
- **Monitoring what the user does on that system**—For example, certain HR employees might be allowed to view documents, but other HR employees might be able to actually edit those documents.
- **Restraining or influencing the user's behavior on that system**—For example, an HR staffer who repeatedly tries to get into restricted information might be denied access to the entire system.

These permissions control access to logical (or system) resources.

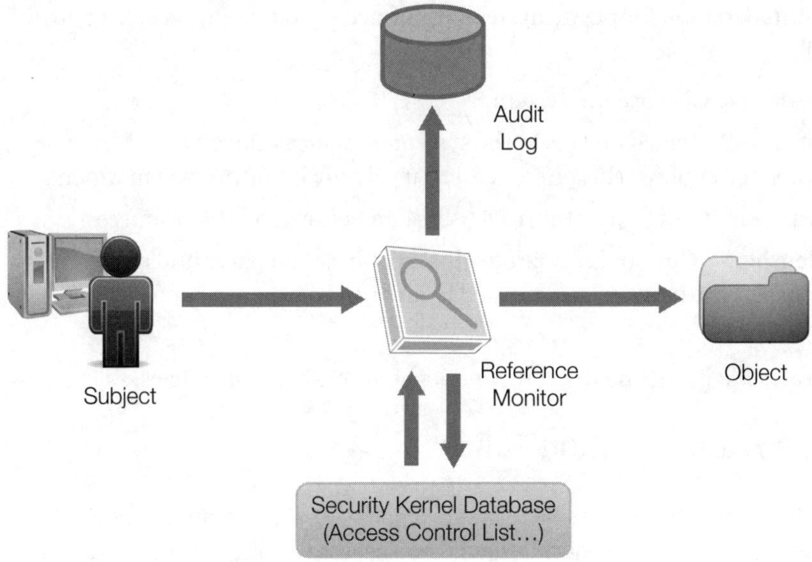

FIGURE 5-1
Enforcing access control.

The Security Kernel

The security kernel is the central part of a computing environment's hardware, software, and firmware that enforces access control for computer systems. The security kernel provides a central point of access control and implements the **reference monitor** concept. It mediates all access requests and permits access only when the appropriate rules or conditions are met. For example:

1. The subject requests access to a particular object. The security kernel intercepts the request.
2. The security kernel refers to its rules base, also known as the **security kernel database**. It uses these rules to determine access rights. Access rights are set according to the policies your organization has defined.
3. The kernel allows or denies access based on the defined access rules. All access requests handled by the system are logged for later tracking and analysis.

Figure 5-1 shows a request for access coming from the subject to a particular object—in this case, a file. The reference monitor intercepts the access request. The access is granted according to the rules in the security kernel database. This rule base might be an access control list (ACL), a directory, or another repository of access permissions. If the rules permit the access request, the reference monitor permits access and creates a log entry.

Access Control Policies

An access control policy is a set of rules that allows a specific group of users to perform a particular set of actions on a particular set of resources. If users aren't authorized, they don't have access to system functions or system resources. You use access control policies to reduce and control security risks. Both automated processes and humans use access control policies.

You must understand four central elements of access to manage access control policies well:

- **Users**—People who use the system.
- **Resources**—Protected objects in the system. **Resources** can be accessed only by authorized subjects. Resources can be used only in authorized manners.
- **Actions**—Activities that authorized users can perform on the resources.
- **Relationships**—Optional conditions that exist between users and resources. **Relationships** are permissions granted to an authorized user, such as *read, write, execute*.

These central elements define the components of access control policies.

Defining an Authorization Policy

The first step to controlling access is to create a policy to define **authorization** rules. Authorization is the process of deciding who has access to which computer and network resources. In most organizations, authorization is based on job roles, background screening, and any government requirements. These conditions or policies are decided primarily by either a group membership policy or an authority-level policy.

In a **group membership policy**, authorization is defined by what group(s) you are in. For example, perhaps only the security cards of staffers in the IT department give access to the room where computer equipment is stored. If you're not a member of this IT group, your security card does not let you enter this room to retrieve a new monitor. If you want to access the computer equipment storage room, you must first contact the IT department, which likely assigns a member of the IT group to help you.

In an **authority-level policy**, you need a higher degree of authority to access certain resources. For example, perhaps only a senior-level member of the IT group has permission to enter the room that houses servers. Servers are often more valuable than computer monitors, so a policy might specify that only a senior staff member can enter the server room.

Identification Methods and Guidelines

Once you define authorization rules in an authorization policy, you can enforce the rules. Each time a user requests access for a resource, the access controls grant or deny access based on the authorization policy.

The first step in enforcing an authorization policy is identification. **Identification** is the method a subject uses to request access to a system or resource. A subject can be a user, a process, or some other entity. There are several methods commonly used to identify subjects. The method you choose depends on your security requirements and the capabilities of your computing environment. In the next section, you'll learn about various methods and guidelines for how a subject identifies itself to a system.

Identification Methods

A username is the most common method to identify a user to a system. A username can be in the form of a user ID, an account number, or a personal identification number (PIN). Some applications identify a user through the use of a **smart card**, which can take the form of a plastic credit card. Just as you might slide your credit card through an electronic card reader to make a purchase, you can swipe a smart card through a card reader that grants access to parking facilities, buildings, and rooms.

Biometrics is another access control method for identifying subjects. Biometrics is used to recognize humans based upon one or more physical or behavioral traits. Examples of biometrics include fingerprints, face or voice recognition, DNA, handwriting, retina scans, and even body odor/scent.

Identification Guidelines

To ensure all **actions** carried out in a computer system can be associated with a specific user, each user must have a unique identifier. The process of associating an action with users for later reporting or analysis is called accounting. You should keep the data used to identify subjects current and monitor it closely. You should disable the IDs of users who leave the organization or who are inactive for an extended time. You should apply standard naming conventions; these should not relate to job functions. The process for issuing IDs should be documented and secure.

Authentication Processes and Requirements

So far in this chapter, you have learned about methods to define authorization rules and identify users. The next step is authentication. In this part of access control, a user validates or proves the identity provided during identification. Authentication answers the question, are users who they say they are? **Authentication** proves that the subject requesting access is the same subject who has been granted access. Without authentication, you could never really know if users are who they say they are.

Authentication Types

There are three types of authentication:

- **Knowledge**—Something you know, such as a password, passphrase, or PIN.
- **Ownership**—Something you have, such as a smart card, key, badge, or token.
- **Characteristics**—Something that is unique to you, such as your fingerprints, retina, or signature. Since the **characteristics** involved are often physical, this type of authentication is sometimes defined as "something you are."

Each type of authentication can be easily compromised on its own. The use of controls from only one category is known as **single-factor authentication**. Systems containing

> **WARNING**
>
> A combination of username password is considered single-factor authentication. This might or might not be adequate for access to more sensitive systems, applications, or data. For example, you might need to swipe a card (something you have) to enter a building, then type a PIN (something you know) to ensure the security of a valuable resource.

> **TIP**
>
> A shorter password lifespan means more protection for the user. To create stronger password controls for users, consider a 30-day password-change policy. A shorter password life means a lower chance an attacker can compromise and use the password before it expires.

sensitive or critical information should use at least two of the three factors. The use of techniques from two or more of these categories is called **two-factor authentication (TFA)** and provides a higher level of security than using only one.

Authentication by Knowledge

Authentication by **knowledge** is based on something you know, such as a password, passphrase, or PIN. Static passwords are those that are seldom, if ever, changed. Passwords are the oldest and most common method of authentication for computer systems. They are also the weakest. You should not use passwords alone to protect valuable resources. As the value of a resource increases, so should the strength of the access controls protecting it. Two-factor authentication should be the minimum requirement for valuable resources.

Attackers often use brute-force or dictionary attacks to crack passwords. These methods can easily crack weak passwords, such as those that are very short or contain dictionary words.

- A brute-force attack involves trying every possible combination of characters. Modern password crackers don't try every combination of letters, numbers, and special characters in alphabetic order. Rather, they first measure the entropy (a measure of randomness) of characters. Then they test low-entropy words first, medium-entropy words next, and then high-entropy words last.
- A dictionary attack works by hashing (hashes are described Chapter 9) all the words in a dictionary (often supplemented with suffixes such as 01, 02, 4u, and so on) and then comparing the hashed value to the system password file to discover a match. Hackers are familiar with all the usual tricks, such as spelling a name backward or simple substitution of characters (such as 3 for e, 0 for o, $ for s, and so on).
- Because most systems store a hash of the password, attackers first precompute these dictionary words and build a table. Then they look up the stored hashed version of the password in the table to discover the word that generated it. These tables, known as rainbow tables, are widely available. For example, a forensic investigator's tool known as FTK (by AccessData Corp.) features a rainbow table with a million words. According to FTK's Web site, the table detects 28 percent of user passwords.

Password Best Practices

For their protection, users should consider the following guidelines when they create and use passwords:

- **Don't use weak passwords**—You should never use a word that appears in the dictionary as your password.
- **Don't store a written copy of the password unless absolutely necessary**—If you must store a written copy, keep it in a secure place. Alternatively, write down a hint for your password instead of the actual password. Destroy any written copies when they are no longer needed.
- **Never share your passwords with anyone**—Even if it is someone you trust, your password should be kept private.
- **Use different passwords for different important user accounts**—Using a single password for all your accounts is like using a single key for your car, your house, your mailbox, and your safety deposit box. If you lose the key, an attacker has access to everything. When you use different passwords for different systems, if one of your passwords is stolen, only that one system is compromised. This strategy prevents intruders from gaining access to accounts and data on other systems. Also, avoid using passwords that are similar to one another—for example, passwords that use the names of your children. If you use the same or similar passwords for more than one system, it makes it easier for an intruder who obtains one of your passwords to figure out the rest.

> **NOTE**
> It's OK to reuse a password for resources that aren't considered critical—for example, to access articles on an online news site. Just don't use that same password for any logons for critical resources.

- **If you think a password is compromised, change it immediately**—Also, change passwords that are assigned to you the first time you use them. Ideally, you should change passwords at least once every 30 days.
- **Be careful when saving passwords on computers**—Some dialog boxes (such as those for remote access and other telephone connections) present options to save or remember passwords. Selecting these options poses a potential security threat because the password is automatically listed when someone opens the dialog box.
- **Choose passwords that are difficult to guess**—Passwords should not be based on personal information. Hackers have easy access to powerful password-cracking tools that use extensive word and name dictionaries. More secure passwords use words that don't make any sense but that are easy to remember. For example, you might create a password using letters from the first words of a poem or song. Or you might substitute obscure characters, such as asterisks (*), dollar signs ($), "at" symbols (@), brackets ({}), mathematical symbols (+), and the like. These can be extremely difficult to guess or crack. Remember: Cracking tools check for simple tricks such as words spelled backwards or simple substitutions for certain characters (for example, where *mouse* becomes *mOus3*).

Tips for Creating Strong Passwords

Don't give the users of your systems the option of creating wimpy passwords for themselves. Everyone is better off if users are held to these principles:

- Passwords must contain at least eight alphanumeric characters.
- Passwords must contain a combination of uppercase and lowercase letters and numbers.
- Passwords must contain at least one special character within the first seven characters of the password.
- Passwords must contain a nonnumeric letter or symbol in the first and last character positions.
- Passwords must *not* contain the username.
- Passwords must never include the name of the user or the names of any close friends or relatives.
- Passwords must never use an employee's ID number, Social Security number, birth date, telephone number, or any personal information that can be easily guessed.
- Passwords must never include common words from an English dictionary (or a dictionary of another language with which the user is familiar).
- Passwords must never employ commonly used proper names, including the name of any fictional character or place.
- Passwords must never contain any simple pattern of letters or numbers, such as *qwertyxx*.

Account Lockout Policies. Many systems are configured to disable a user ID after a certain number of consecutive failed logon attempts. In many cases, user accounts are disabled after three to five attempts. The number of failed logon attempts that trigger an account action is called the **threshold**. The user may be locked out for a few minutes, a few hours, or until the account is reset by a security officer. This helps guard against attacks in which attackers make many attempts to guess a password. It also enables an intruder to lock out users, however—a form of a denial of service attack—by entering groups of incorrect passwords.

Be cautious when defining an account-lockout policy. A restrictive policy increases the probability of preventing an attack on your organization. But with a stringent account-lockout policy, you can also unintentionally lock out authorized users, which can be frustrating and costly. When you apply an account-lockout policy, set the threshold to a high enough number that authorized users aren't locked out due to mistyped passwords.

Auditing Logon Events. One method of keeping track of who is accessing your computing environment is to audit logon events. This provides you with a record of when every user logs in or out of a computer. If an unauthorized user steals a user's password and logs in to a computer, you can determine when that security breach occurred. When you audit failure events in the logon event category (also known as failure auditing), you can see whether the failure event was due to unauthorized users or attackers attempting to log on to a computer or system. This is an example of intrusion detection.

FYI

Although auditing logon events can be helpful for your intrusion detection efforts, be careful. Failure auditing can also expose your systems to a denial of service (DOS) attack. A denial of service attack occurs in one of two ways:

- Attackers fill the security log, possibly causing a system crash or preventing new users from logging on.
- Attackers cause events to be overwritten. They do this by continuously attempting to log on to your network with incorrect usernames or passwords. Purposely overwriting audit events can effectively erase evidence of attack activity.

Password Reset and Storage. When a user forgets a password, or the password must be reset by the help desk, the new password should be valid only for a single logon. It should also expire within a short period of time (generally less than 48 hours).

Never store or transmit passwords in clear text. You should store or transmit only a hash of a password. Note that some systems encrypt these hashes to slow down brute-force attacks. You must take measures to protect your password files from unauthorized access.

Using a Passphrase. A passphrase is a bit different from a password. It is longer and generally harder to guess, so it's considered more secure. Because it usually has more than one word, it is more secure against dictionary attacks. Most often, **passphrases** are used for public and private key authentication. The user uses a passphrase that is known only to the user, and the user uses that passphrase to unlock a private key that gives the user access to information. In most cases, the user converts the passphrase to a password. However, a system can be programmed to automatically convert the passphrase to a password according to an algorithm. A passphrase is stronger than a password, but it takes a bit longer to type. Although passphrases are static, they aren't as susceptible to brute-force attacks as passwords.

FYI

Unless your organization uses an automated password-reset process, your help-desk personnel will likely find that password-reset requests are the most common type of request they receive. When help-desk personnel receive such requests, they should require users to provide information that verifies their identity. For example, the user should provide proof in the form of a driver's license or employee ID. If the request is not made in person, help-desk personnel should use a form of questioning that verifies the user's identity—for example, "What is your mother's maiden name?" A lack of strong identity validation can allow an attacker to request a password change for any user's account and access the account at will.

Authentication by Ownership

Authentication by **ownership** is the second type of verification. This is based on something you have, such as a smart card, a key, a badge, or a token. Tokens can be synchronous or asynchronous.

Synchronous Tokens. A **synchronous token** uses an algorithm that calculates a number at both the authentication server and the device. It displays the number on the device's screen. The user enters this number as a logon authenticator, just as he or she would use a password.

In a **time-based synchronization system**, the current time is used as the input value. The token generates a new dynamic password (usually every minute) that is displayed in the window of the token. To gain access, the password is entered with the user's PIN at the workstation. No token keyboard is required. This system requires that the clock in the token remains in sync with the clock in the authentication server. If the clocks drift out of sync, the server can search three or four minutes on each side of the time to detect an offset. If the difference becomes too great, you must resynchronize them.

An **event-based synchronization system** avoids the time-synchronization problem by increasing the value of a counter with each use. The counter is the input value. The user presses a button to generate a one-time password, and then enters this password with his or her PIN at the workstation to gain access. One common problem with event-based synchronization systems is when a user creates a password using the token but doesn't use the password to log on, the counter in the server and the counter in the token become out of sync.

> **NOTE**
> Synchronous tokens can be used in proximity devices that cause both the PIN and the password to be entered automatically.

Continuous authentication is used by systems that continuously validate the user. This is often done with proximity cards or other devices that continuously communicate with the access control system. If the user walks away from the desktop and steps outside the range of the access control detector, the system locks the desktop.

Asynchronous Tokens. The **asynchronous token** is the second of two types of token-based devices. It looks like a credit card-sized calculator. The authentication server issues a challenge number that the user enters. The token computes a response to the value provided by the authentication server. The user then replies to the server with the value displayed on the token. Many of these systems also protect the token from misuse by requiring the user to enter a PIN along with the initial challenge value.

An asynchronous token device uses challenge-response technology that involves a dialogue between the authentication service and the remote entity that it's trying to authenticate. This requires a numeric keyboard. Figure 5-2 shows an asynchronous token challenge-response process.

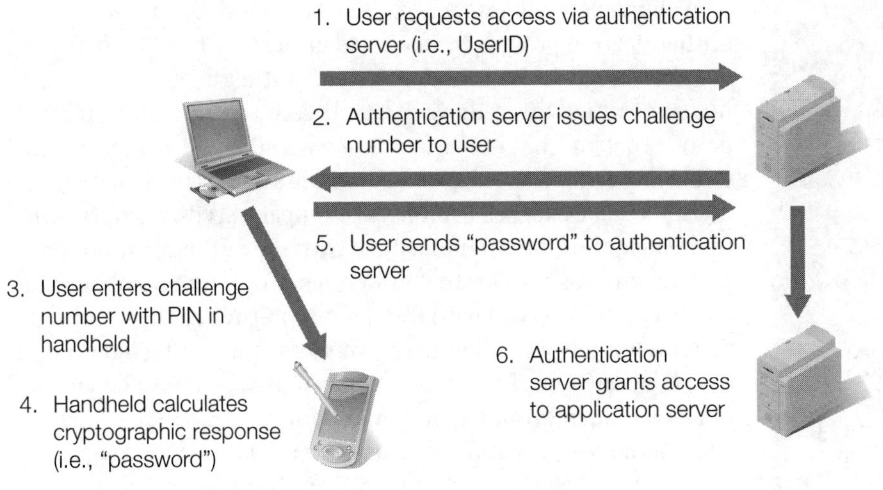

FIGURE 5-2

Asynchronous token challenge-response.

Here are the steps in an asynchronous challenge-response session:

1. The user initiates a logon request.
2. The authentication server provides a challenge (a random number that is the input value) to the user.
3. The user enters the challenge received from the server and a secret PIN known only to the user into the calculation device (a credit card-sized calculator or a software program on a PC or PDA).
4. The token (or program) generates the response (the password) to the challenge, which appears in the window of the token.
5. The user provides the correct password to the authentication server.
6. Access is granted. Without the asynchronous token device and the correct PIN, a correct answer to the challenge cannot be generated.

USB tokens use public key infrastructure (PKI) technology—for example, a certificate signed by a trusted certification authority—and don't provide one-time passwords. A **USB token** is a hardware device that you plug into your computer's USB port. The device is encoded with your digital signature. With it, you don't have to type anything in. The presence of the digital signature on the token is enough to provide proof of possession (something you have).

A smart card is a token shaped like a credit card that contains one or more microprocessor chips that accept, store, and send information through a reader. The information contained within the smart card provides authentication information. Most smart cards need a reader to power the embedded microprocessor. The user inserts the card into the reader to begin communication.

NOTE

One problem with these cards is that some users leave them unattended in the reader. That means any user is authorized as long as the smart card remains in the reader.

> **NOTE**
> For more information about the Common Criteria, visit *www.commoncriteriaportal.com.*

> **NOTE**
> Not all smart cards must be physically inserted into a reader. A contactless smart card contains an embedded radio frequency (RF) transceiver that works when the card is near the reader.

A significant advantage of a smart card is that the user authentication process is completed at the user location between the smart card and the reader. IDs and authentication data are not transmitted to a remove server, thereby avoiding the "trusted path" problem (that is, the fact that when IDs and authentication information are transmitted to a remote server, sensitive information can be exposed to sniffers or tappers). With a smart card, the reader maintains a handshake with the authentication server and directly vouches for the authentication. It then establishes a trusted path in accord with the Common Criteria. The Common Criteria framework allows users, vendors, and testing laboratories to collaborate and share efforts to formally specify, implement, and evaluate information system products.

Finally, many organizations use several varieties of magnetic stripe cards (also known as memory cards) to control access to restricted areas, such as sensitive facilities or parking areas.

Authentication by Characteristics/Biometrics

Biometrics can be used for both identification (physical biometrics) and authentication (logical biometrics). Biometrics involves measuring various unique parts of a person's anatomy or physical activities. The eight common biometric measures you'll learn about in this chapter can be broken into two categories:

- **Static (for example, physiological)**—What you are. Physiological biometrics includes recognizing fingerprints, iris granularity, retina blood vessels, facial looks, hand geometry, and so on.
- **Dynamic (for example, behavioral)**—What you do. Behavioral biometrics includes voice inflections, keyboard strokes, and signature motions.

Concerns Surrounding Biometrics. There are three primary concerns with biometrics:

- **Accuracy**—Biometric devices are not perfect. Each has at least two error rates associated with it. The false rejection rate (FRR) is the rate at which valid subjects are rejected. The false acceptance rate (FAR) is the rate at which invalid subjects are accepted. There is a tradeoff between the FRR and the FAR. The point at which the two rates are equal is called the crossover error rate (CER). The CER is the measure of the system's accuracy expressed as a percentage. In practice, biometric devices that protect very sensitive resources are generally configured to accept a high level of false rejections. Systems that protect less sensitive resources may grant access to potentially unauthorized personnel so as not to excessively slow down access.
- **Acceptability**—Certain biometric measurements, such as retinal scans, are more objectionable to some users than other biometric measurements, such as signature dynamics. If users are not comfortable using the system, they may refuse to submit to it.

- **Reaction time**—Each biometric device requires time for the system to check an identity and give a response. A system that takes too long may not work. For example, consider facial recognition at security airports. If the system needs five minutes to identify a passenger, then passenger checkpoint lines will become far longer than they already are. Reaction time must be fast for most checkpoints. Anything too slow hinders productivity and access.

Types of Biometrics. There are eight types of biometrics:

- **Fingerprint**—This examines the pattern of ridges and valleys on the tip of a finger.
- **Palm print**—This examines the physical structure of the palm. Both palm prints and fingerprints are considered highly accurate for verifying a user. The system reaction time is 5–7 seconds, and people tend to accept them.
- **Hand geometry**—With this type of biometrics, a camera takes a picture of the palm of the hand and, using a 45-degree mirror, the side of the hand. An analysis is made using the length, width, thickness, and contour of the fingers. Hand geometry measurements are highly accurate. System response time is 1–3 seconds and people tend to accept these, too.
- **Retina scan**—This type of biometrics analyzes the blood-vessel pattern of the rear portion of the eyeball area, known as the retina, using a low-level light source and a camera. A retina scan is very accurate for identification and authentication. However, a retina scan is susceptible to changes in a person's physical condition, such as those caused by diabetes, pregnancy, and heart attacks. The emergence of these conditions requires users to enroll again. Many people don't like retina scans because they feel they are intrusive and unsanitary, and because they fear they will have to reveal private medical data. Response time averages 4–7 seconds.
- **Iris scan**—This type of biometrics uses a small video recorder to record unique patterns in the colored portion of the eye, known as the iris, caused by striations, pits, freckles, rifts, fibers, and so on. Iris scans are very accurate for identification and authentication. Iris-scan devices provide the capability for continuous monitoring to prevent session hijacking. Response time is 1–2 seconds. Iris scans are well accepted.
- **Facial recognition**—With facial-recognition biometrics, video cameras measure certain features of the face, such as the distance between the eyes, the shape of the chin and jaw, the length and width of the nose, the shape of cheekbones and eye sockets, and so on. Fourteen common features are selected from about 80 or so features that can be measured. These features are used to create a facial database. Facial recognition is accurate for authentication because face angle can be controlled. However, it's not as accurate for identification in a moving crowd. Because it is passive and nonintrusive, it can give continuous authentication.

- **Voice pattern**—With voice-pattern biometrics, audio recorders and other sensors capture as many as seven parameters of nasal tones, larynx and throat vibrations, and air pressure from the voice. Voice pattern isn't accurate for authentication because voices can be too easily replicated by computer software. Accuracy can be further diminished by background noise. Most users accept this type of biometric. Response time varies up to 10–14 seconds. Because of this long response time, it's not popular in everyday use.
- **Keystroke dynamics**—Here, a user types a selected phrase onto a reference template. The keystroke dynamics measure each keystroke's dwell time (how long a key is held down) and flight time (the amount of time between keystrokes). Keystroke dynamics are considered very accurate. They lend themselves well to two-factor authentication. Because the technology is easy to use when someone is logging in, it combines the ID processes of something you should know with something you own. Keystroke dynamics are well accepted and can give constant authentication.
- **Signature dynamics**—With this type of biometrics, sensors in a pen, stylus, or writing tablet are used to record pen-stroke speed, direction, and pressure. Signature dynamics are accurate and users accept them.

Advantages and Disadvantages of Biometrics. Biometrics offers these advantages:

- A person must be physically present to authenticate.
- There is nothing to remember.
- Biometrics are hard to fake.
- Lost IDs or forgotten passwords are not problems.

Biometrics does have negatives. These include the following:

- Physical characteristics might change.
- Physically disabled users might have difficulty with systems based on fingerprints, hand geometry, or signatures.
- Not all techniques are equally effective, and it is often difficult to decide which technique is best for a given use.
- Response time may be too slow.
- The devices required can be expensive. With methods that require lots of time to authenticate, the organization may have to provide a large number of authentication machines so as not to cause bottlenecks at entry and access.

Privacy Issues. Biometric technologies don't just involve collecting data *about* a person. Biometrics collects information *intrinsic* to people. Every person must submit to an examination, and that examination must be digitally recorded and stored. Unauthorized access to this data could lead to misuse. Biometrics also can be used to watch a person's movement and actions. Lastly, recorded and replayed ID data might be used to allow a person to pretend to be someone else, creating a risk for identity theft.

Single Sign-On (SSO)

A single sign-on (SSO) strategy allows users to sign on to a computer or network once, and have their identification and authorization credentials allow them into all computers and systems where they are authorized. They don't need to enter multiple user IDs or passwords. SSO reduces human error, which is a major part of system failures. It is highly desirable but difficult to put in place.

Advantages and Disadvantages of SSO

Advantages of SSO include the following:

- It's an efficient logon process. The user has to log on only once.
- It can provide for stronger passwords. With only one password to remember, users are generally willing to use stronger passwords.
- It provides continuous, clear reauthentication. The SSO server remains in contact with the workstation and monitors it for activity. This allows timeout thresholds that can be enforced consistently throughout the system near the user entry point. When a workstation is not active for a certain period, it can be disconnected. This protects the system from a user leaving a workstation open to an unauthenticated person who could pretend to be the original user.
- It provides failed logon attempt thresholds and lockouts. This protects against an intruder using brute force to obtain an authentic user ID and password combination.
- It provides centralized administration. It ensures consistent application of policy and procedures.

Disadvantages of SSO include the following:

- A compromised password lets an intruder into all areas open to the password owner. Using dynamic passwords and/or two-factor authentication can reduce this problem.
- Static passwords provide very limited security. Two-factor authentication or, at least, one-time (dynamic) passwords are required for access by the user using SSO.
- Adding SSO to unique computers or legacy systems in the network might be difficult.
- Scripts make things easier to administer, but they expose data. Scripting doesn't provide two-factor authentication to sensitive systems and data.
- The authentication server can become a single point of failure for system access.

SSO Processes

Examples of SSO processes include the Kerberos process and SESAME.

Kerberos. Kerberos is a computer-network authentication protocol that allows nodes communicating over a non-secure network to prove their identity to one another in a secure manner. Kerberos is also a suite of free software published by Massachusetts Institute of Technology (MIT) that applies the Kerberos protocol. Its design is aimed primarily at a client/server model, and it provides mutual authentication—both the user and the server verify each other's identity. Kerberos protocol messages are protected against eavesdropping and replay attacks.

The Kerberos Key Distribution Center (KDC) Server

The Kerberos KDC server serves two functions:

- **It serves as the authentication server (AS)**—An authentication server confirms a user through a pre-exchanged secret key based on the user's password. This is the symmetric key that is shared with the KDC and stored in the KDC database. After getting a request for service from the user, all further dialogue with the user workstation is encrypted using this shared key. The user does not send a password to the KDC. Instead, the authentication occurs at the time the Kerberos software on the user's workstation requests the password to create the shared key to decrypt the ticket from the authentication server. The ticket contains the session key for use in communicating with the desired application server. If the wrong password is supplied, the ticket can't be decrypted and the access attempt fails.
- **It serves as the ticket-granting server (TGS)**—The ticket-granting server (TGS) provides a way to get more tickets for the same or other applications after the user is verified so that step doesn't need to be repeated several times during a day. Tickets usually expire daily or after a few hours.

To get started, the user sends his or her ID and access request through the Kerberos client software on the workstation to the key distribution center (KDC). The authentication server of the KDC verifies that the user and the requested service are in the KDC database and sends a ticket. The ticket is a unique key for the user that is time-stamped for the requested service. If time expires before it's used, it won't work. Included in the ticket are the user ID and the session key, as well as the ticket for the object encrypted with the object's key shared with the KDC.

With Kerberos, security depends on careful execution and maintenance. Lifetimes for authentication credentials should be as short as possible, using time stamps to reduce the threat of replayed credentials. The KDC must be physically secured because it—particularly the authentication server—is a potential single point of failure. Redundant authentication servers can reduce the risk. The KDC should be hardened, meaning it should have a secured operating system and application. It should not allow any non-Kerberos network activity.

SESAME. The Secure European System for Applications in a Multi-Vendor Environment (SESAME) is a research and development project funded by the European Commission. SESAME was developed to address some weaknesses in Kerberos. SESAME supports SSO. Unlike Kerberos, it improves key management by using both symmetric and asymmetric keys to protect interchanged data. It is essentially an extension of Kerberos. It offers public key cryptography and role based access control abilities.

Accountability Policies and Procedures

At this point, you have learned about how users are authorized (step 1), identified (step 2), and authenticated (step 3). Now it's time for the last part of the access control process: accountability. Accountability is tracing an action to a person or process to know who made the changes to the system or data. This is important for audits and investigations, as well as for tracing errors and mistakes. Accountability answers the question, "Can you hold users responsible for what they do on the system?"

Log Files

Log files are a key ingredient to accountability. Log files are records that detail who logged in to the system, when they logged in, and what information or resources they used. In the early days of computing, logs were used on systems that were shared by several users. It was necessary to charge users for the time they used the systems, so logs tracked that data. Log files were also used by companies such as CompuServe and AOL, when Internet use was charged by the hour. On today's networks, this type of fee-based use is rare. Logging now is used mainly as a tool to detect, prevent, or monitor access to a system.

Data Retention, Media Disposal, and Compliance Requirements

Recent laws require that organizations take measures to secure many types of data. The Health Insurance Portability and Accountability Act (HIPAA) is one example of legislation that requires data security. It protects the privacy of personal health data and gives patients certain rights to that information. Another example is the Fair and Accurate Credit Transactions Act (FACTA). FACTA requires any entity that keeps consumer data for business purposes to destroy personal data before discarding it.

These and similar laws require the protection of privacy data with proper security controls. These laws outline the right ways to handle, store, and dispose of data. If these rules and regulations aren't followed, intruders can, for example, simply dive into dumpsters to get sensitive data.

Procedures

Organizations can apply access controls in various forms, providing different levels of restriction, and at different places within the computing system. A combination of access controls provides a system with layered, defense-in-depth protection. A defense-in-depth approach makes it harder for attacks to succeed because the attacker must compromise multiple security controls to reach a resource. An attacker who successfully beats one security control should run into several other controls in a layered system. Security personnel should ensure that they protect every critical resource with multiple controls. Never rely on a single control to protect a resource.

TABLE 5-1 Types of security controls.

CONTROL TYPE	DESCRIPTION
Administrative	These are policies approved by management and passed down to staff in the form of rules. These are a first line of defense to inform users of their responsibilities. Examples include policies on password length.
Logical/technical	These are additional policies that are controlled and enforced automatically. This reduces human error. For example, a computer can check passwords to make sure they follow the rules.
Hardware	This includes equipment that checks and validates IDs, such as Media Access Control (MAC) filtering on network devices, smart-card use for two-factor authentication, and security tokens such as RFID tags. In this instance, MAC is a hardware address that uniquely identifies each node of a network. Media Access Control is not the same as the mandatory access controls discussed later in the chapter.
Software	These controls are embedded in the operating system and application software. They include the Microsoft Windows standard New Technology File System (NTFS) permissions, user accounts requiring logon, and rules restricting services or protocol types. These items are often part of the ID and validation phase.
Physical	These are devices that prevent physical access to resources, including such things as security guards, ID badges, fences, and door locks.

Security Controls

A security control is any mechanism intended to avoid, stop, or minimize a risk of attack for one or more resources. There are several types of security controls; these perform differently based on their purpose. Most organizations need a diverse mix of security controls to protect their systems from all types of attacks. Table 5-1 lists the most common types of security controls.

Media Disposal Requirements

Most security attention tends to focus on securing active resources. Many organizations tend to forget that data still exists on retired media or even in the trash. It is important to ensure that no data leaks out of an organization on discarded media. Media-disposal requirements prevent attackers from getting files, memory, and other protected data. Many organizations allow media to be used again, but only if the original data was not sensitive. As an extreme example, plans for a nuclear missile would not qualify. You could violate the law if you do not destroy data before discarding the media.

NOTE

Methods of destruction include shredding, burning, or grinding of CD-ROMs, hard drives, USB drives, DVDs, paper documents, flash memory, and other forms of media.

It is not always necessary that you physically destroy media. Another method is to use a degausser. A degausser creates a magnetic field that erases data from magnetic storage media. Once data goes through a degausser, the data cannot be recovered. When you use a degausser, not enough magnetic material is left to rebuild the data. If the media-stored information wasn't extremely sensitive, you can use some media to store other data. However, if the media held very sensitive data, it should be destroyed.

Another method used to destroy data without harming the media that stores it is repeated writing. Repeatedly writing random characters over data usually will destroy the data. This is called overwriting. This process works well if the amount of data to be overwritten is fairly small and the overwriting is fairly fast. Large amounts of data or slow writing devices can make this type of data destruction too slow to be useful in a production environment.

Formal Models of Access Control

Some of the most visible types of technical controls are those protecting access to computer resources. Most users have encountered access control restrictions. For example, any user who has typed an incorrect password should have been denied access.

Because there are many ways to restrict access to different resources, it is helpful to refer to models to help design good access controls. There are several formal models of access control, including the following:

- **Discretionary access control (DAC)**—With DAC, the owner of the resource decides who gets in, and changes permissions as needed. The owner can give that job to others.
- **Mandatory access control (MAC)**—With MAC, permission to enter a system is kept by the owner. It cannot be given to someone else. This makes MAC stronger than DAC.
- **Non-discretionary access control**—Non-discretionary access controls are closely monitored by the security administrator, and not the system administrator.
- **Rule-based access control**—A list of rules, maintained by the data owner, determines which users have access to objects.

Other models are based on the work of Biba, Clark-Wilson, and Bell-La Padula. These models describe the use of access controls and permissions to protect confidentiality or integrity.

Discretionary Access Control (DAC)

The Common Criteria define **discretionary access control (DAC)** as follows:

> "a means of restricting access to objects based on the identity of subjects and/or groups to which they belong. The controls are discretionary in the sense that a subject with certain access permission is capable of passing that permission (perhaps indirectly) on to any other subject."

The Common Criteria also note the following:

> "security policies defined for systems ... used to process classified or other sensitive information must include provisions for the enforcement of discretionary access control rules. That is, they must include a consistent set of rules for controlling and limiting access based on identified individuals who have been determined to have a need-to-know for the information."

These definitions apply equally to both public- and private-sector organizations processing sensitive information.

Operating Systems–Based DAC

Operating systems have the primary responsibility for controlling access to system resources such as files, memory, and applications. One of the main jobs for security administrators is to maintain access controls. Access controls are effective when they ensure that only authorized users can access resources. They are efficient when they ensure that users can access all the resources they need. Creating access controls that are both effective and efficient can be challenging. Organizations must decide how they will design and maintain access controls to best meet their needs. Here are a few points organizations must consider when developing access control policies:

- **Access control method**—Today's operating systems contain access control settings for individual users (rule-based) or for groups of users (role based). Which method you use depends on the size of the organization and how specific access rights need to be for individuals or roles.
- **New user registration**—When new users are brought into an organization, their user accounts must be created. This can take a lot of time. It must be done quickly, however, so new people can do their jobs. User registration must be standardized, efficient, and accurate.
- **Periodic review**—Over time, users often get special permission to complete a particular project or perform some special task. These permissions need to be reviewed from time to time to make sure they stop when they are no longer needed. This solves problems of compliance and auditing by making sure people can access only required areas.

Application-Based DAC

Application-based DAC denies access based on context or content. The application presents only options that are authorized for the current user. For example, an ATM machine menu limits access by only displaying options that are available to a particular user. You can apply security controls using these types of DACs based on user context or resource contents:

- In a context-based system, access is based on user privileges as defined in the user's own data records. This is usually granted to persons acting in a certain job role or function.

- In a content-dependent system, access is based on the value or sensitivity of data items in a table. This system checks the content of the data being accessed and allows, for example, a manager of Department A to see employee records for personnel that contain an A in the Department field but not records containing any other value in that field.

Permission Levels

Permission levels indicate a subject's rights to a system, application, network, or other resources. In a DAC environment, the authorization system uses permission levels to determine what objects any subject can access. Permission levels can be any of the following:

- **User-based**—The permissions granted to a user are often specific to that user. In this case, the rules are set according to a user ID or other unique identifier.
- **Job-based or role based access control (RBAC)**—Permissions are based on a common set of permissions for all people in the same or similar job roles.
- **Project-based**—When a group of people (for example, a project team) are working on a project, they are often granted access to documents and data related just to that project.
- **Task-based**—Task-based access control limits a person to executing certain functions and often enforces mutual exclusivity. In other words, if a person executes one part of a task, he or she might not be allowed to execute another related part of the task. This is based on the concepts of separation of duties and need-to-know.

Defeating Separation of Duties and Need-to-Know

Separation of duties is the process of dividing a task into a series of unique activities performed by different people, each of whom is allowed to execute only one part of the overall task. This principle prevents people from both creating and approving their own work. Separation of duties can be a valuable tool to prevent fraud or errors by requiring the cooperation of another person to complete a task. Dual control is an example of separation of duties. Examples include a safe with two combination locks on the door or a missile-control system that requires the simultaneous turning of keys in consoles too far apart for one person to manage.

Need-to-know is the concept of preventing people from gaining access to information they don't need to carry out their duties. Providing access on the basis of need-to-know can reduce the chance of improper handling of data or the improper release of information.

Separation of duties and need-to-know can be defeated by the following:

- **Collusion**—Employees work together (colluding) to avoid the controls and assist each other in performing unauthorized tasks. Job rotation reduces the risk of **collusion**.
- **Covert channels**—These are hidden (covert) ways of passing information against organizational policy. There are two main types of covert channels: timing (signaling from one system to another) and storage (the storing of data in an unprotected or inappropriate place).

FYI

The Trusted Computer System Evaluation Criteria (TCSEC) provides definitions of both DAC and MAC. These definitions fit the needs of public- and private-sector organizations that need to protect sensitive information. TCSEC was a prominent standard in the U.S. Department of Defense's Rainbow Series. The Rainbow Series was a collection of computer-security standards and guidelines published in the 1980s and 1990s. Each book in the series had a different-colored cover, which led to the nickname for each book. The TCSEC had an orange cover, and is often just called *The Orange Book*. The Common Criteria superseded *The Orange Book* in 2005.

Mandatory Access Control (MAC)

Mandatory access control (MAC) is another method of restricting access to resources. You determine the level of restriction by how sensitive the resource is. This is represented by a classification label. Individuals must then be formally authorized (i.e., obtain clearance) to access sensitive information. Security policies defined for systems that are used to process classified information (or any other sensitive information) must include provisions for enforcing MAC rules. That is, they must include a set of rules that controls who can access what information.

NOTE

Remember: sensitivity labels, or classifications, are applied to all objects (resources). Privilege or clearance-level labels are assigned to all subjects (users or programs).

How MAC Works

Under mandatory access control, the system and the owner jointly make the decision to allow access. The owner gives the need-to-know element. Not all users with a privilege or clearance level for sensitive material need access to all sensitive information. The system compares the subject and object labels that go with the terms of the Bell-La Padula confidentiality model, which is covered in the next section. Based on that comparison, the system either grants or denies access.

Temporal isolation restricts access to specific times. It first classifies the sensitivity level of objects. Then it allows access to those objects only at certain times. Temporal isolation is often used in combination with role based access control.

Non-Discretionary Access Control

In non-discretionary access control, access rules are closely managed by the security administrator. They are not managed by the system owner or by ordinary users for their own files.

Non-discretionary access control can be used on many operating systems. This is more secure than discretionary access control. The system doesn't rely only on users' compliance with organizational policies. For example, even if users obey well-defined file-protection policies, a Trojan horse program could change the protection to allow uncontrolled access. This kind of exposure isn't possible under non-discretionary access control.

Security administrators have enough control in non-discretionary access control to make sure sensitive files are write-protected for integrity and readable only by authorized users to preserve confidentiality. The chances that a corrupted program will be used are reduced because users can run only those programs they are expressly allowed to run.

Non-discretionary access control helps ensure that system security is enforced and tamperproof. If your organization needs to manage highly sensitive information, you should seriously consider using non-discretionary access control. It does a better job of protecting confidentiality and integrity than DAC. The data owner, who is often the user, does not make access decisions. This allows you to enjoy some of the benefits of MAC without the added administrative overhead.

Rule-Based Access Control

In a rule-based system, access is based on a list of rules that determine who should be granted access. Data owners make or allow the rules. They specify the privileges granted to users, such as read, write, execute.

The success of rule-based access control depends on the level of trust you have with the data owners. This type of access control pushes much of the administration down to the data owner. For technical and security-conscious users, this type of access control tends to work well. It doesn't work as well in environments with many users or where users lack the necessary technical skills and training. Figure 5-3 shows how individual rules control each user's permissions.

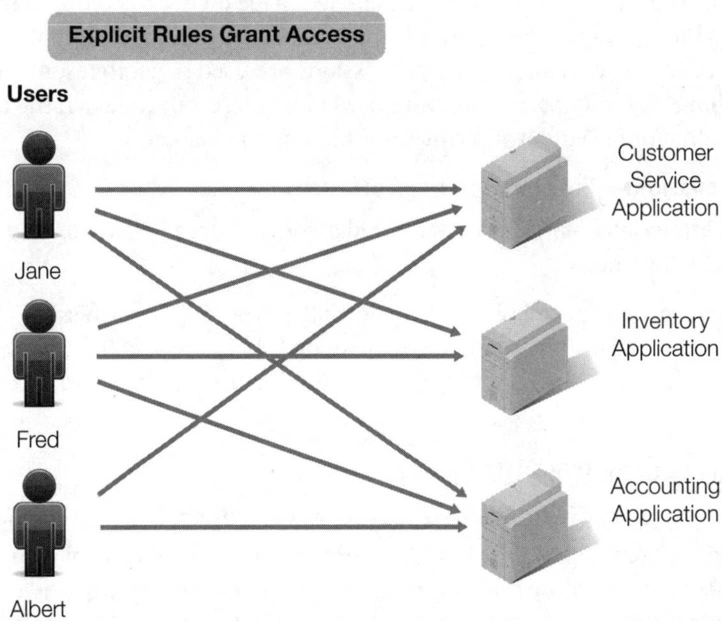

FIGURE 5-3
Rule-based access control.

FIGURE 5-4

An access control list (ACL).

Hal	
User Hal Directory	Full Control
User Kevin Directory	Write
User Kara Directory	No Access
Printer 001	Execute
Kevin	
User Hal Directory	Write
User Kevin Directory	Full Control
User Kara Directory	No Access
Printer 001	No Access
Kara	
User Hal Directory	Write
User Kevin Directory	Full Control
User Kara Directory	No Access
Printer 001	Execute
Printer 002	Execute

Access Control Lists (ACLs)

Most operating systems provide several options to associate lists or permissions with objects. These lists are called access control lists (ACLs). Different operating systems provide different ACL-enabling options. For example, Linux and Apple Macs have read, write, and execute permissions. These can be applied to file owners, groups, or global users. Windows has both share permissions and security permissions, both of which enable ACLs to define access rules. Share permissions are used to get to resources by a network share. Security permissions are used to get to resources when the user is logged on locally. Some Windows permissions include the following:

- **Share permissions**—Full, change, read, and deny
- **Security permissions**—Full, modify, list folder contents, read-execute, read, write, special, and deny

In both share and security permissions, deny overrides every other permission.

Because of the greater number of choices, Windows ACLs are said to be more fine-grained, because they allow a greater level of control. Figure 5-4 shows an access control list (ACL).

Role Based Access Control (RBAC)

Another type of access control is **role based access control (RBAC)**. An RBAC policy bases access control approvals on the jobs the user is assigned. The security administrator assigns each user to one or more roles. Some operating systems use groups instead of roles. The resource owner decides what roles have access to what resource. Microsoft Windows uses global groups to manage RBAC. Figure 5-5 shows role based access control.

Before you can assign access rules to a role, you must define and describe the roles in your organization. The process of defining roles, approvals, role hierarchies, and constraints is called role engineering. Starting with a clear list of role definitions that fit your organization is key to RBAC. The real benefit of RBAC over other access control methods is its ability to represent the structure of the organization and force compliance with control policies throughout it.

Suppose that Jane and Fred in Figure 5-6 should have access to the Inventory application, but Albert should not. As shown in the figure, however, Albert does have access to this application—a need-to-know violation. This is due to the overgeneralizing of roles. Overgeneralizing roles can result in providing more access to individuals than was intended. When you assign roles, consider creating one role for every user or one role for a very small number of users. Windows' "deny permission" makes it possible to create a rule that overrides a role. That would fix Albert's excessive permission. This decision is dependent on risk. A user might be given a role with similar privileges and might be granted access above his need-to-know in order to reduce administrative costs.

Content-Dependent Access Control

Content-dependent access control is based on what is contained in the data. It requires the access control mechanism (the arbiter program, which is part of the application, not the operating system) to look at the data to decide who should get to see it. The result is better granularity than other access control methods you have seen. Access is controlled to the record level in a file rather than simply to the file level. The cost of doing this is higher, however, because it requires the arbiter program. The arbiter program uses information in the object being accessed—for example, what is in a record.

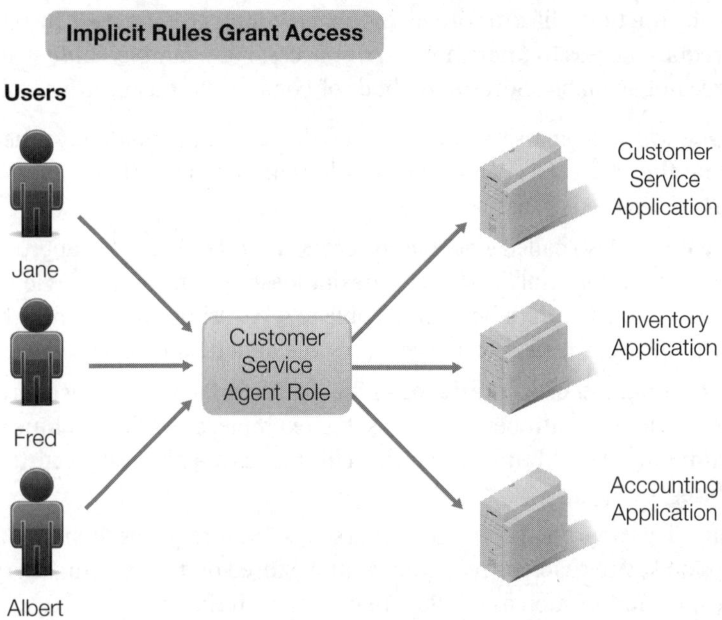

FIGURE 5-5

Role based access control.

FIGURE 5-6
Content-dependent access control.

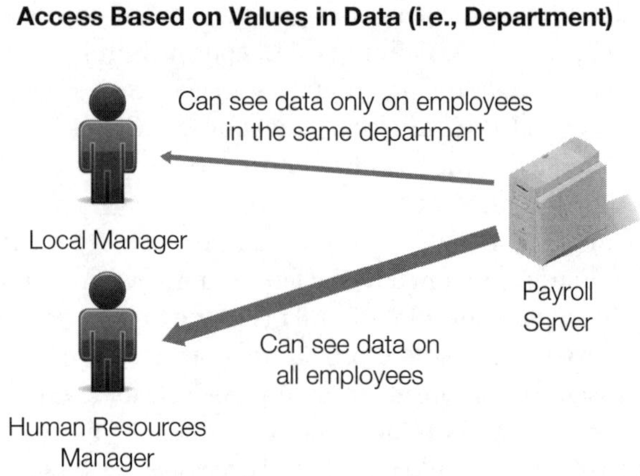

The decision usually comes to a simple if-then question—for example, "If high-security flag equals yes, then check security level of user." Managers might have access to the payroll database to review data about specific employees, but they might not have access to the data about employees of other managers. Figure 5-6 shows how content-dependent access control can protect data.

Constrained User Interface

With a **constrained user interface**, a user's ability to get into—or interface with—certain system resources is restrained by two things. The user's rights and permissions are restricted and constraints are put on the device or program providing the interface. A device such as an ATM or software such as on a public-access kiosk browser lets users reach only specific functions, files, or other resources. It limits their access by restricting their ability to request access to unauthorized resources. For example, some systems grey out icons that are not available. Several methods of constraining users are as follows:

- **Menus**—One way to keep users out of certain data is simply not to give them any idea that the data exists. When the user logs in, the menu that comes up does not include closed areas.
- **Database views**—Also called **view-based access control (VBAC)**, this approach is often used with relational databases. The database system creates a view for each user that limits the data he or she is able to see. Although there may be more data in the database, the user can access only the data defined in the view.
- **Physically constrained user interfaces**—The user interface mechanism presents the user with a limited number of options. For example, an ATM machine offers only a certain number of buttons to push. This makes it a **physically constrained user interface**.
- **Encryption**—This approach constrains users because it requires them to have the decryption key to reach or read information stored on the system. Encryption also hides information such as credit card details from the user.

Other Access Control Models

Other access control models have helped shaped today's access controls. The most prominent access models include the Bell-La Padula Model, the Biba Integrity Model, the Clark and Wilson Integrity Model, and the Brewer and Nash Model. You will learn about each model in the following sections.

Bell-La Padula Model

The Bell-La Padula Model focuses on the confidentiality of data and the control of access to classified information. This model is different from the Biba Integrity Model, covered in the next section, which describes rules to protect data integrity. In the Bell-La Padula Model, the parts of a system are divided into subjects and objects and the current condition of a system is described as its state. The model defines a secure state. The model guarantees that each state transition preserves security by moving from secure state to secure state. This process makes sure the system meets the model's security objectives. The Bell-La Padula Model is built on the concept of a state machine that features a set of allowable states in a computer network system. The transition from one state to another state is defined by what's known as transition functions.

Biba Integrity Model

In 1977, Kenneth J. Biba defined the first model to address integrity in computer systems based on integrity levels. The Biba Integrity Model fixed a weakness in the Bell-La Padula Model, which addresses only the confidentiality of data. The Biba Integrity Model consists of three parts:

- The first part says a subject cannot read objects that have a lower level of integrity than the subject does. A subject at a given integrity level can read only objects at the same integrity level or higher. This is known as a simple integrity axiom.
- The second part says a subject cannot change objects that have a higher level of integrity. A subject at a given integrity level can write only to objects at the same or lower integrity levels. This is known as the (star) integrity axiom.
- The third part says a subject may not ask for service from subjects that have a higher integrity level. A subject at a given integrity level can call up only a subject at the same integrity level or lower.

Clark and Wilson Integrity Model

Published in 1987 by David Clark and David Wilson, the Clark and Wilson Integrity Model focuses on what happens when users allowed into a system try to do things they are not permitted to do. It also looks at internal integrity threats. These two components were missing from Biba's model. This model looks at whether the software does what it is designed to do. That is a major integrity issue. The Clark and Wilson Integrity Model addresses three integrity goals:

- It stops unauthorized users from making changes. (Biba addressed only this integrity goal.)
- It stops authorized users from making improper changes.
- It keeps internal and external consistency.

The Clark and Wilson Integrity Model defines well-formed transactions and constraints on data. For example, a commercial system should allow a new luxury car sale to be entered only at a price of $40,000. It should not be possible to enter the sale at $4,000 or at $400,000. This keeps internal consistency. Internal consistency makes sure the system operates as expected every time.

In the Clark and Wilson Integrity Model, a subject's access is controlled by the permission to execute the program (a well-formed transaction). Therefore, unauthorized users cannot execute the program (first integrity rule). Authorized users can access different programs that allow each one to make specific, unique changes (separation of duties). Two important parts of this model are as follows:

> **NOTE**
> This model is considered a commercial integrity model. Unlike the earlier models, which were designed for military uses, this model was designed to be used by businesses.

- These three access entities—subject, program, and object—combine to form the access triple.
- Integrity is enforced by binding. Subject-to-program and program-to-object binding enforces integrity. This creates separation of duties. It makes sure only authorized transactions can be performed.

Brewer and Nash Integrity Model

The Brewer and Nash Integrity Model is based on a mathematical theory published in 1989 to ensure fair competition. It is used to apply dynamically changing access permissions. It can separate competitors' data within the same integrated database to make sure users don't make fraudulent changes to objects that belong to a competing organization. It's also used to stop users or clients from using data when they have a conflict of interest.

A Chinese Wall security policy defines a wall, or barrier, and develops a set of rules that makes sure no subject gets to objects on the other side of the wall. Figure 5-7 shows a Chinese Wall in action. It illustrates the way an audit company handles audits for competing businesses. In this example, an auditor allowed to work on data related to the Bank of Gloucester is prohibited from getting to any data belonging to the Bank of Norwich. Even though the auditor works for a company that performs the audits for both banks, internal controls at the audit company prevent access between areas that would create a conflict of interest.

> **NOTE**
> Controls can't prevent conflicts of interest. Conflicts of interest have to do with individuals' positions, not with the data itself.

This model makes sure conflicts of interest are recognized and that people are prevented from taking advantage of data to which they should not have access. For example, if a user is allowed into one company's data, the data belonging to that company's competitors can automatically be deemed off limits.

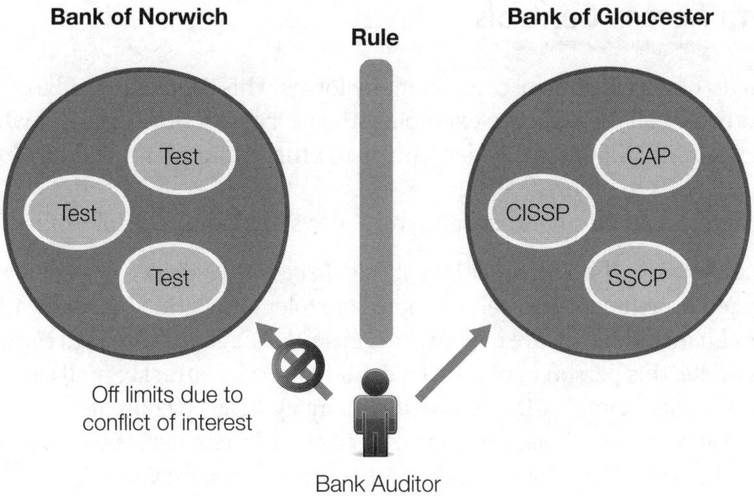

FIGURE 5-7
The Brewer and Nash Integrity Model.

Effects of Breaches in Access Control

Your failure to control access can give your opposition an advantage. That opposition might be a military force, a business interested in competitive intelligence, or even your neighbor. The following list details some of the losses that can occur:

- Disclosure of private information
- Corruption of data
- Loss of business intelligence
- Danger to facilities, staff, and systems
- Damage to equipment
- Failure of systems and business processes
- Denial of service (DoS)

Not all incidents have the same effect. Some are easier to spot than others. For example, losses due to disclosure of business secrets, including business intelligence, often go unnoticed for quite some time. Losses due to corruption of data might make a database and all its backups useless by the time it is discovered. Data corruption can easily cause failures in systems and business processes.

Some types of denial of service (DoS) attacks are short-lived. They are found quickly and can be stopped before they cause serious damage. Other types of DoS attacks take longer to evolve. They can affect the ability of a business to serve its customers. Customers might then take their business elsewhere. This type of DoS attack inflicts more severe damage on an organization.

Threats to Access Controls

The challenges of access control come in many forms. This list can never be complete. New threats evolve all the time. An example is the peer-to-peer (P2P) risk in which P2P users share their My Documents folder with each other by accident. This can expose sensitive documents to others.

Access controls can be compromised several ways, including the following:

- **Physical access**—If an intruder has physical access to a device, logical access control is basically worthless. Data can be copied or stolen outright. Someone with physical access can install hardware or software keystroke loggers or damage equipment. For example, this person could start a denial of service attack. Small removable media, such as writable CDs, DVDs, USB memory sticks, or hard drives create a physical access risk. It's easy to copy data to one of these devices. Mobile phones are another risk. Many have cameras and some can record voices.
- **Eavesdropping by observation**—Sometimes, security staff misses the most obvious breach, allowing information to be seen. Data on papers on an authorized user's desk or screen are open to a spy. Enforcing the right policies and procedures can prevent this kind of data loss.
- **Bypassing security**—Any means of accessing data can lead to a security breach. Developers might think about access via only one method, such as through a Web site. But attackers might easily bypass the security measures in place. The information security team must consider other access paths, such as attackers mapping a drive or logging in at the server's keyboard.
- **Exploiting hardware and software**—Attackers often try to install programs on a system they control. These programs are often called Trojan horses. The network administrator or workstation owner may not even know the attacker is there.
- **Reusing or discarding media**—Attackers can recover erased or altered information from discarded or reused media. It is safer and cheaper to shred documents and physically destroy media than to simply throw them out.
- **Electronic eavesdropping**—Attackers can eavesdrop by wiretapping network cables. Some media are more resistant to eavesdropping than others. For example, fiber-optic cable is safer than copper. However, none provides complete protection. In fact, risks have jumped recently with the widespread use of wireless access points.
- **Intercepting communication**—Another variation of eavesdropping is the physical interception of data communications. This is called sniffing. With sniffing, attackers capture network traffic as it passes by. Sniffing is often used in a man-in-the-middle attack. The attacker inserts himself between two victims and relays messages between them. The attacker makes it seem as if the two victims are talking directly to each other over a private connection. In fact, the attacker is in control of the entire conversation.

- **Accessing networks**—Networks often include unprotected connections. Many organizations build their networks with more drops (female connectors at wall plates) than they need. This allows the organization to add more users in the event of future growth. These unused connection points are often active connections. Intruders can use these connections to gain network access.
- **Exploiting applications**—Several programs and modules have a common programming weakness known as buffer overflow. This happens when an attacker enters more characters than expected into an input field. It allows malicious code throughout the application. There are many other ways to exploit weaknesses in applications, and attackers are always on the lookout to find new ways to compromise applications.

Effects of Access Control Violations

You have seen some of the ways attackers can compromise access controls. But what happens if an attacker is successful? What is the impact of an access control violation? An access control violation can have the following harmful effects on an organization:

- Loss of customer confidence
- Loss of business opportunities
- New legislation and regulations imposed on the organization
- Bad publicity
- More oversight
- Financial penalties

As an example, Egghead Software voluntarily reported a breach in the summer of 2000. The company admitted it hadn't secured customers' credit card information. The trade press praised the company's proactive approach. However, Egghead went out of business within a year of the disclosure. Customers didn't trust the company with their credit cards. They hesitated to purchase Egghead's products. The corporate world took notice. As a result, other companies stopped reporting violations. Finally, the government stepped in with new laws. These laws force companies to reveal access breaches.

In 2003, California passed a mandatory disclosure law that affects all companies that do business in California or with that state's residents. The law protects its residents from disclosure of their personally identifiable information (PII). PII is often the information that bad guys use to steal identities. Note, however, that this law doesn't cover other intrusions, such as theft of intellectual property.

NOTE

You can find a state-by-state summary of similar disclosure laws at the following URL: *http://www.csoonline.com/article/221322/CSO_Disclosure_Series_Data_Breach_Notification_Laws_State_By_State?source=nlt_csoupdate.*

Centralized and Decentralized Access Control

> **NOTE**
> Centralized access control is generally simpler to manage, but the drawback is that if it fails, no one can get into the computer system.

Centralized access control is an access control approach in which a single common entity—such as an individual, department, or device—decides who can get into systems and networks. The access controls are managed centrally rather that at the local level. Owners decide which users can get to which objects. The central administration supports the owners' directives. Centralized authentication services are applied and enforced through the use of authentication, authorization, and accounting (AAA) servers.

The benefits of using AAA servers include the following:

- It involves less administration time because user accounts are maintained on a single host.
- It reduces design errors because different access devices use similar formats.
- It reduces security administrator training because only one system is learned.
- It improves and eases compliance auditing because all access requests are handled by one system.
- It reduces help-desk calls because the user interface is consistent.

Three Types of AAA Servers

In the following sections, you'll read about three leading types of AAA servers: RADIUS, the most popular, along with TACACS+, and DIAMETER.

RADIUS

RADIUS is the most popular AAA service. It is an authentication server that uses two configuration files:

- A client configuration file contains the client address and the shared secret for transaction authentication
- A user configuration file that contains the user identification and authentication data as well as the connection and authorization information

RADIUS follows these steps in the authentication process:

1. The network access server (NAS) decrypts the user's UDP access request.
2. The NAS authenticates the source.
3. The NAS validates the request against the user file.
4. The NAS responds by allowing or rejecting access or by requesting more information.

TACACS+

TACACS+ is an IETF standard that uses a single configuration file to:

- Control server operations.
- Define users and attribute/value pairs.
- Control authentication and authorization procedures.

An Options section contains operation settings, the shared secret key, and the accounting filename. TACACS+ follows these steps in the authentication process:

1. Using TCP, the client sends a service request with the header in clear text and an encrypted body containing the user ID, password, and shared key.
2. The reply contains a permit/deny as well as attribute/value pairs for the connection configuration, as required.

DIAMETER

DIAMETER is based on RADIUS. However, RADIUS works only in a highly fluid or mobile workforce. DIAMETER is not restricted in that way. It works well with a stable or static workforce. DIAMETER consists of the following:

- **Base protocol**—The base protocol defines the message format, transport, error reporting, and security used by all extensions.
- **Extensions**—The extensions conduct specific types of authentication, authorization, or accounting transactions.

DIAMETER also uses **User Datagram Protocol (UDP)**. Computer applications that use UDP send messages, known as datagrams, to other hosts on an Internet Protocol (IP) network. UDP does this without requiring special transmission channels or data paths. As such, UDP's service is somewhat unreliable because datagrams can arrive out of order. They can also seem to be duplicated or even missing. UDP simply relies on applications to fix those issues. That spares UDP the trouble of wasting valuable time and resources fixing those issues itself. That makes UDP faster, which is why it's often used for streaming media and online gaming.

DIAMETER uses UDP in a P2P mode rather than client/server mode. In a P2P mode, a user provides another user with direct access to his hard drive. The second user also has access to the first user's hard drive. No centralized structure exists. Figure 5-8 shows an example of computers connected in P2P mode.

In a client/server mode, the structure is centralized. A client—for example, a user—connects to a server to request access to certain information. Figure 5-9 shows an example of computers connected in client/server mode.

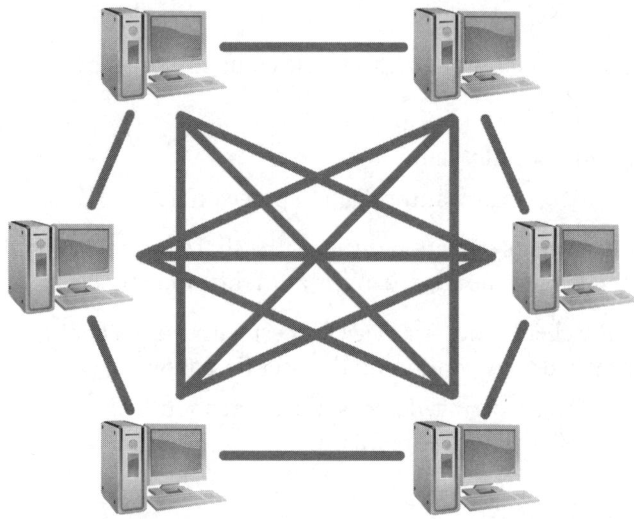

FIGURE 5-8
P2P mode.

This allows servers to initiate requests and handle transmission errors locally, which reduces the time a data packet takes to move across a network connection (latency) and improves performance. The user sends an authorization request containing the request command, a session ID, and the user's user ID and password. This authorization request is sent to a NAS. The NAS approves the user's credentials. If it is approved, the NAS returns an answer packet. The answer packet contains attribute/value pairs for the service requested. The session ID uniquely identifies the connection and resolves the RADIUS problem with duplicate connection identifiers in high-density installations.

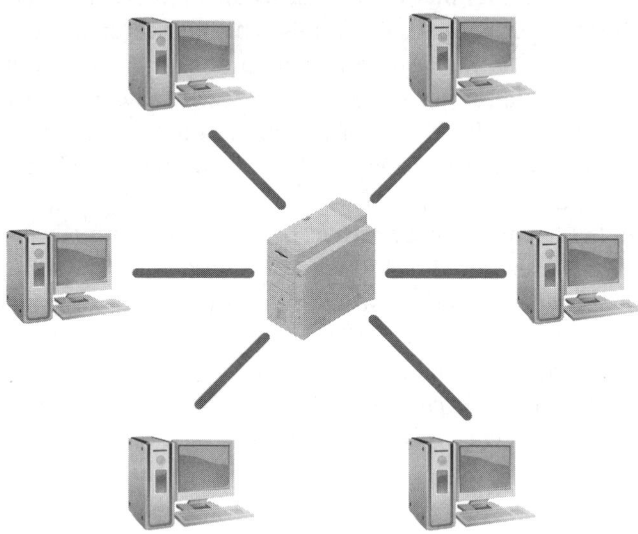

FIGURE 5-9
Client/server mode.

Decentralized Access Control

Another access control approach is to handle access control decisions and administration locally. This approach is called **decentralized access control**. That means access control is in the hands of the people, such as department managers who are closest to the system users. Access requests are not processed by one centralized entity.

On the one hand, decentralized access control often results in confusion. Why? Because it can lead to loss of standardization and to overlapping rights. This might cause gaps in the access control design. On the other hand, a decentralized approach eliminates the single-point-of-failure problem. It ends the perception that a central controlling body cannot respond effectively to local conditions.

The two most common examples of decentralized access control are the Password Authentication Protocol (PAP), which uses cleartext usernames and passwords, and the Challenge-Handshake Authentication Protocol (CHAP). This protocol hashes the password with a one-time challenge number in order to defeat eavesdropping-based replay attacks.

Privacy

One of the most visible security concerns is that of data privacy. The growing awareness of identity theft and the importance of protecting privacy have resulted in new laws and standards to ensure data privacy. Personal data privacy is only one aspect of this. Organizations are becoming more and more aware of the dangers of privacy violations. Organizations often monitor their staff electronically because they are worried about the following:

- Liability in harassment suits
- Skyrocketing losses from employee theft
- Productivity losses from employees shopping or performing other non-work-related tasks online

Electronic monitoring creates its own privacy issues in the workplace. Depending on the country or jurisdiction, the legal levels of staff monitoring might vary widely.

The current thinking is that for employees to have a reasonable expectation of privacy, they must establish two things:

- They have a subjective expectation of privacy.
- This subjective expectation of privacy is reasonable.

If either element is missing, no protected interest is established. This means that if an employee is led to expect that something, such as an e-mail message, is private, his or her employer cannot legally violate that privacy. If, however, the company informs employees that e-mail sent over the company's network is monitored, then the employee can no longer claim to have an "expectation of privacy." In other words, once the company stakes its claim over its cyberdominion, its employees have no right to privacy there.

Companies must clearly communicate their policies for what is acceptable for employees to do and what will be monitored. In many cases, employees cannot expect any privacy while using corporate systems. An organization's acceptable use policy (AUP) is an important document to set the appropriate expectations for, among other things, privacy.

Logon banners are messages that provide notice of legal rights to users of systems and devices. These should be used on your systems and devices. Logon banners are used to gain the following:

- Employee consent to monitoring
- Employee awareness of potential disciplinary action in the event of misuse of the account
- Employee consent to the retrieval of stored files and records

Logon banners are used to legally eliminate any expectation of privacy for employees using corporate systems.

Monitoring in the Workplace

An American Management Association (AMA) survey titled "Workplace Monitoring & Surveillance" found that in 2001, "more than three-quarters of major U.S. firms (77.7%) record[ed] and review[ed] employee communications and activities on the job, including their phone calls, e-mail, Internet connections, and computer files."

Monitoring in the workplace includes but is not limited to the following:

- Opening mail or e-mail
- Using automated software to check e-mail
- Checking phone logs or recording phone calls
- Checking logs of Web sites visited
- Getting information from credit-reference agencies
- Collecting information through point-of-sale terminals
- Recording activities on closed circuit television (CCTV)

> **NOTE**
> Policies alone do not suffice. Employers must clearly communicate what employees can and cannot do. The best way to do this is through training. When systems or policies change, those changes should be communicated to employees.

Employers monitor their staff to check the quality and quantity of their employees' work. Employers are often liable for the actions of their employees, so they need to be sure that their employees are behaving properly.

To make sure the staff understands monitoring, an employer should have a clear code of conduct or policy. Employees should know that they could be disciplined if they do not follow the policy.

CHAPTER SUMMARY

In this chapter, you learned that access controls are ways to permit or deny access to certain resources. Organizations use access controls to manage what staff can and can't do. Access controls specify who users are, what they can do, which resources they can get to, and what operations they can carry out. Access control systems use several technologies, including passwords, hardware tokens, biometrics, and certificates. Access can be granted to physical assets, such as buildings or rooms. Access can also be granted to information systems.

You learned that the four parts of access control are authorization, identification, authentication, and accountability. These four parts create an access control process that can be divided into two phases: the policy-definition phase and the policy-enforcement phase. You learned how you first need to decide who is authorized for access and what systems or resources they are allowed to use. Then you learned how access is granted or rejected based on the authorizations defined in the first phase. You also learned about the formal models of access control, access control methodologies and challenges, and the effects of access control breaches.

KEY CONCEPTS AND TERMS

Access controls
Accountability
Actions
Asynchronous token
Authentication
Authority-level policy
Authorization
Characteristics
Collusion
Constrained user interface
Continuous authentication
Decentralized access control
Discretionary access control (DAC)
Event-based synchronization system
Group membership policy
Identification
Knowledge
Logical access control
Mandatory access control (MAC)
Need-to-know
Ownership
Passphrase
Physical access control
Physically constrained user interface
Reference monitor
Relationships
Resources
Role based access control (RBAC)
Security kernel database
Separation of duties
Single-factor authentication
Smart card
Synchronous token
Temporal isolation
Threshold
Time-based synchronization system
Two-factor authentication (TFA)
USB token
User Datagram Protocol (UDP)
View-based access control (VBAC)

CHAPTER 5 ASSESSMENT

1. Access controls are policies or procedures used to control access to certain items.
   A. True
   B. False
2. Which answer best describes the authorization component of access control?
   A. Authorization is the method a subject uses to request access to a system.
   B. Authorization is the process of creating and maintaining the policies and procedures necessary to ensure proper information is available when an organization is audited.
   C. Authorization is the validation or proof that the subject requesting access is indeed the same subject who has been granted that access.
   D. Authorization is the process of determining who is approved for access and what resources they are approved for.
3. Which answer best describes the identification component of access control?
   A. Identification is the validation or proof that the subject requesting access is indeed the same subject who has been granted that access.
   B. Identification is the method a subject uses to request access to a system.
   C. Identification is the process of determining who is approved for access and what resources they are approved for.
   D. Identification is the process of creating and maintaining the policies and procedures necessary to ensure proper information is available when an organization is audited.
4. Which answer best describes the authentication component of access control?
   A. Authentication is the validation or proof that the subject requesting access is indeed the same subject who has been granted that access.
   B. Authentication is the process of creating and maintaining the policies and procedures necessary to ensure proper information is available when an organization is audited.
   C. Authentication is the process of determining who is approved for access and what resources they are approved for.
   D. Authentication is the method a subject uses to request access to a system.
5. Which answer best describes the accountability component of access control?
   A. Accountability is the validation or proof that the subject requesting access is indeed the same subject who has been granted that access.
   B. Accountability is the method a subject uses to request access to a system.
   C. Accountability is the process of creating and maintaining the policies and procedures necessary to ensure proper information is available when an organization is audited.
   D. Accountability is the process of determining who is approved for access and what resources they are approved for.
6. Physical access controls deter physical access to resources, such as buildings or gated parking lots.
   A. True
   B. False

7. When you log on to a network, you are presented with some combination of username, password, token, smart card, or biometrics. You are then authorized or denied access by the system. This is an example of ________.
   A. Physical access controls
   B. Logical access controls
   C. Group membership policy
   D. The Biba Integrity Model
   E. None of the above

8. Access controls cannot be implemented in various forms, restriction levels, and at different levels within the computing environment.
   A. True
   B. False

9. Which of the following is an example of a formal model of access control?
   A. Discretionary access control (DAC)
   B. Mandatory access control (MAC)
   C. Non-discretionary access control
   D. The Clark and Wilson Integrity Model
   E. All of the above

10. Physical access, security bypass, and eavesdropping are examples of how access controls can be ________.
   A. Stolen
   B. Compromised
   C. Audited
   D. Authorized

11. Challenges to access control include which of the following?
   A. Laptop loss
   B. Exploiting hardware
   C. Eavesdropping
   D. Exploiting applications
   E. All of the above

12. When the owner of the resource determines the access and changes permissions as needed, it's known as ________.
   A. Mandatory access control (MAC)
   B. Discretionary access control (DAC)
   C. Non-discretionary access control
   D. Content-dependent access control
   E. Role based access control

13. The process of identifying, quantifying, and prioritizing the vulnerabilities in a system is known as a ________.
   A. Vulnerability policy
   B. Vulnerability deterrent
   C. Vulnerability authorization
   D. Vulnerability assessment

14. The security kernel enforces access control of computer systems.
   A. True
   B. False

15. When it comes to privacy, organizations are concerned about which of the following?
   A. Liability in harassment suits
   B. Skyrocketing losses from employee theft
   C. Productivity losses from employees shopping or performing other non-work-related tasks online
   D. All of the above

CHAPTER 6

Security Operations and Administration

SECURITY PROFESSIONALS MUST UNDERSTAND how security operations and administration create the foundation for a solid security program. Your role as a security professional is similar to that of a coach. You work with staff to identify the strengths and weaknesses of your "players," or assets. Your goal is to win the game. In the world of the security professional, the "game" is to secure your organization's resources. Your "opponents" are unauthorized users trying to steal your data and use it against you.

As a coach, you have a playbook of strategies. You need to keep these strategies out of the hands of your opponents. You also need to make sure your strategies abide by the rules and regulations of the industry. To prepare them for the challenge, you must educate and train your players. You must give them the skills they need to work together as a team and win the game.

If you are successful, your organization will run as smoothly as a championship team. Everybody will understand the mission and how to work together to complete it. If you fail, your team will appear confused. Each player will seem to do his or her own thing, regardless of the consequences. The next thing you know, your organization's information will fall into the hands of your opponents. Your trade secrets will no longer be secret, your organization will spend a lot of money fixing what's broken, and you and your employees might find yourself "on the bench," or even looking for other jobs.

In this lesson, you'll learn the skills you'll need to develop a strong security administration team.

Chapter 6 Topics

This chapter covers the following topics and concepts:

- What security administration is
- What compliance is
- What professional ethics are
- What the infrastructure for an IT security policy is
- What data classification standards are
- What configuration management is
- What the change management process is
- What the System Life Cycle (SLC) and System Development Life Cycle (SDLC) are
- How software development relates to security

Chapter 6 Goals

When you complete this chapter, you will be able to:

- Manage the security infrastructure
- Create and support policies
- Classify data
- Develop and maintain security programs
- Manage major and minor changes to systems
- Promote user awareness of security
- Understand and use professional ethics

Security Administration

Security administration within an organization is the group of individuals responsible for planning, designing, implementing, and monitoring an organization's security plan. Before you can form an administrative team, your organization must identify its information assets. After your organization identifies and documents the assets, you should assign responsibility of each one to a person or position. Once you have a list of assets and who is responsible for each one, you can form the team. This administrative team then determines the sensitivity of each asset so it can plan how to secure each one accordingly.

Controlling Access

The primary task of an organization's security administration team is to control access to systems or resources. As you learned in the previous chapter, there are four aspects of access control:

- **Identification**—Assertions made by users about who they are
- **Authentication**—The proving of that assertion
- **Authorization**—The permissions a legitimate user or process has on the system
- **Accountability**—Tracking or logging what authenticated and unauthenticated users do while accessing the system

The security administration team leads these efforts by determining the best security controls to put in place to secure your organization's resources.

Documentation, Procedures, and Guidelines

The security administration team handles the planning, design, implementation, and monitoring of your organization's security program. Several types of documentation are necessary to provide the input the security administration team needs to make the best decisions to secure assets. The most common documentation requirements include the following:

- **The organization's security process**—How does it all work?
- **The authority of the persons responsible for security**—Which administrator is responsible or authorized for what assets and what actions?
- **The policies, procedures, and guidelines adopted by the organization**—What information needs to be communicated, how is it communicated, and when is it communicated?

The security administration team puts together all the pieces of a puzzle to ensure your organization complies with stated policies. An organization must comply with rules on two levels:

- **Regulatory compliance**—The organization must comply with laws and government regulations.
- **Organizational compliance**—The organization must comply with its own policies, audits, culture, and standards.

As a result, the security administration team's documentation, procedures, and guidelines focus on compliance and compliance monitoring. They have to make sure the organization follows the various rules and regulations.

Disaster Assessment and Recovery

The security administration team's responsibilities include handling events that affect your computers and networks. These include incidents, disasters, and other interruptions.

The security administration team forms an incident response team to handle any security incidents. This team is composed of individuals who are responsible for responding to incidents and investigating security breaches. Another team managed by the security administration team is the **emergency operations group**. This group is responsible for protecting sensitive data in the event of natural disasters and equipment failure, among other potential emergencies.

Despite the best efforts of the incident response team, the emergency operations group, and system administrators, all systems are subject to failure or attack. The security administration team ensures an organization can respond rapidly and effectively to any event.

Security Outsourcing

Many organizations rely on outside firms to handle security monitoring and analysis. This means you might need to monitor the work of the outsourcing firm or work with it when handling incidents. This approach has both advantages and disadvantages.

- **Advantages**—A security management firm has a high level of expertise because it focuses on security—and security only—every day. Simply put, it will have expertise and experience that your own organization may not have.
- **Disadvantages**—Outsourcing has two primary disadvantages. First, the outsourcing firm may not know your organization well and may not possess internal knowledge. Second, by outsourcing, you won't develop in-house capability or talent, and will therefore need to continue to pay for these services indefinitely.

Outsourcing Considerations

The security administration team must work closely with an outside firm to make sure both agree to specific security requirements. The last thing any organization needs is to find out there isn't a response plan for a specific disaster *after* the disaster occurs. This type of agreement is a service level agreement (SLA). It is a formal contract between your organization and the outside firm that details the specific services the firm will provide. Some examples of services detailed in an SLA can include:

- How and when potential security breaches are communicated
- How logs and events will be reported
- How confidential data will be handled
- What the security system uptime requirements are (for example, you might require that all critical security systems have 99.99 percent reliability)

The SLA should communicate the expectations of both the organization and the outside firm. The SLA should anticipate the needs of both parties. Each member of the security administration team must thoroughly analyze his or her department's risks. Any unaccounted risk is likely to cost your organization in either data loss or expenses to fix it. Think of this as being like maintaining an automobile. Regular oil changes are less expensive than blown head gaskets. Maintaining an engine is cheaper than fixing one.

Compliance

Your organization's security policy sets the tone for how you approach security activities. It also states the rules with which you must comply. Think of a security policy in terms of traffic laws. Traffic laws maintain a certain degree of order and safety on the roads. If these laws aren't enforced, the roads become dangerous. An information security policy is no different. Your security policy isn't much good if it isn't enforced. This is where compliance enters the picture. When policies are enforced, the organization complies with those policies. There are three primary means used to ensure compliance:

- Security event logs
- Compliance liaison
- Remediation

Security Event Logs

Security event logs are records of data that your operating system or application software automatically create. A security event log records which user or system accessed data or a resource and when. You can think of security event logs as being similar to the system a library uses to keep track of who checks out books. When a book is late or missing, the library checks its records to determine who checked out the book last. When an information security breach occurs in your organization, a security event log helps determine what happened to the system and when. It can help you track down the culprit or help you fix the problem.

Compliance Liaison

As organizations and security policies become larger and more complex, it becomes difficult to stay compliant. A **compliance liaison** makes sure all personnel are aware of—and comply with—the organization's policies. Different departments within an organization might have different security ideas or needs. A compliance liaison works with each department to ensure it understands, implements, and monitors compliance. A compliance liaison can also help departments understand how to include information security in their daily operations.

Remediation

You learned in previous chapters how mitigating vulnerabilities reduces the risk of attacks against your computers and networks. In some cases, the best solution is to block an intruder and deny access to a resource. In other cases, it is possible to remove the vulnerability. **Remediation** involves fixing something that is broken or defective. With computer systems, remediation refers to fixing security vulnerabilities.

Of course, some problems are more important than others. You should fix high-risk issues before lower-risk ones. When possible, the best option is to remove vulnerabilities. If you cannot effectively remove a vulnerability, the next best step is to remove the ability of an attacker to exploit the vulnerability. One way to block an attacker's ability to exploit a vulnerability is through aggressive access controls. In either case, the goal is to ensure attackers will not succeed. You should always design security policies to protect your assets from attack. Compliance is extremely important to information technology systems.

Professional Ethics

One of the most important roles security professionals assume is that of a leader in compliant behavior. People won't follow the rules if they don't trust the leaders. Every respected profession has its own code of ethics and conduct. Adhering to such a code fosters the respect of any profession's practitioners. The security profession is no different from other professions in this regard. It is important that security professionals have a definite code of ethics that governs their behavior. $(ISC)^2$ provides a solid set of ethical guidelines. However, guidelines aren't effective unless you adopt and practice them. Here are some tips for practicing strong ethics:

- **Set the example**—Demonstrate strong ethical principles in your daily activities. Users will follow your lead. If you are serious about ethics, your users will be more serious about ethics.
- **Encourage adopting ethical guidelines and standards**—Security professionals must know their ethical boundaries and set an example by adhering to them. This often means making difficult decisions and setting a good example. You must push the organization to define its code of ethics. This helps the staff operate ethically and responsibly.
- **Inform users through security awareness training**—Make sure users are aware of, and understand, ethical responsibilities.

Common Fallacies About Ethics

Simply writing down a list of ethics-oriented rules is not enough. It is important that security professionals actually use ethics in their everyday lives. The first step in adhering to ethics rules is to understand the most common assumptions many computer users hold that may lead them to unethical behavior. Here are some of these common assumptions:

- Users assume that computers should prevent abuse. If they can gain unauthorized access, it's the organization's fault—not theirs.
- Users believe that in some legal systems, they have the right to explore security vulnerabilities as a form of free speech or expression.
- Users think their actions may cause only minor damage. They think that a little damage won't bother anyone.
- Users think that if it's easy to break in, it must be all right to do so.
- Users think that hacking is OK if their motives are not damaging. They think if they are not making any money or otherwise advancing themselves by hacking into a system, they must not be committing a crime.
- Users think information should be free. They think it's OK to look through somebody's system to obtain information.

Codes of Ethics

A code of ethics helps ensure professionalism. Several published codes apply to information security. The focus here is on the (ISC)² Code of Ethics. You will also learn about the published statements from the Internet Architecture Board (IAB). These statements explain what the IAB considers ethical and appropriate behavior.

(ISC)² Code of Ethics

Before you take the SSCP exam, the exam's governing body asks you to sign a statement agreeing to adhere to the following code. Don't just read it; understand it. You will find yourself applying it throughout your workday.

> "Safety of the commonwealth, duty to our principals, and to each other requires that we adhere, and be seen to adhere, to the highest ethical standards of behavior. Therefore, strict adherence to this code is a condition of certification."

The (ISC)² Code of Ethics Canons appear in order of priority. You can't always apply *all* the canons. They might conflict in a particular situation. Just remember that this is the order in which you should apply them to work through difficult ethical challenges.

> "Protect society, the commonwealth, and the infrastructure."
>
> "Act honorably, honestly, justly, responsibly and legally."
>
> "Provide diligent and competent service to principals."
>
> "Advance and protect the profession."

Internet Architecture Board (IAB) Statement of Policy

The IAB has provided this list of unethical and unacceptable practices. In 1989, the IAB issued a statement of policy about Internet ethics. The title of this document is RFC 1087. Although it was one of the first statements on the ethics of Internet use, it still applies today. RFC 1087 states that any activity is unethical and unacceptable that purposely does any of the following:

> "Seeks to gain unauthorized access to the resources of the Internet"
>
> "Disrupts the intended use of the Internet"
>
> "Wastes resources (people, capacity, computer) through such actions"
>
> "Destroys the integrity of computer-based information"
>
> "Compromises the privacy of users"
>
> "Involves negligence in the conduct of Internet-wide experiments"

The key point of the document is this: Access to the Internet is a *privilege*, not a right.

Professional Requirements

In any profession, rules and regulations enforce professional ethics. Those rules might come from the certifying agencies. If you violate them, you risk losing your certification or license.

In other contexts, laws and regulations require ethical behavior. For example, the Organization for Economic Cooperation and Development (OECD) is an organization of more than 30 countries. Its goal is economic cooperation and growth. In 1980, it created eight privacy principles. These principles have formed the basis for much of the world's privacy legislation. Simply put, the principles state the following:

- An organization should collect only what it needs.
- An organization should not share its information.
- An organization should keep its information up to date.
- An organization should use its information only for the purposes for which it was collected.
- An organization should properly destroy its information when they no longer need it.

> **NOTE**
> For more information about the OECD, visit *http://www.cdt.org/privacy/guide/basic/oecdguidelines.html*.

Personnel Security Principles

For all the technical solutions you can devise to secure your systems, the human element remains your greatest challenge. You might be surprised how far a little education can go. If your staff are aware of how security risks can hurt both themselves and the organization, they'll be more likely to help you run a tight ship.

It's important to know what a user should and shouldn't do. The best way is to create well-defined job descriptions, job roles, and responsibilities. When you know what people should be doing, it's easier to identify activities they aren't supposed to do. If their roles or responsibilities are vague, it's more difficult to flag bad behavior—which means they are more likely to get away with things.

Minimizing access to information and assets is an important security control. You have already learned about some concepts related to personnel security. These concepts are very important and bear revisiting. Pay careful attention to any security concepts that directly affect personnel. People are the most important assets in your organization. Ensuring they know how to contribute to your organization's security is important.

Limiting Access

When deciding how to grant access to users, one of the core concepts is limiting access. The idea that users should be granted only the levels of permissions they need in order to perform their duties is called the principle of least privilege. Always use this principle. Otherwise, you run the risk of allowing unauthorized users access to information they shouldn't be able to access. For example, weak access controls may allow a salesclerk to view employee salaries.

> **NOTE**
> Chapter 5 addresses these concepts in more detail.

The need-to-know requirement is another concept that relates to the principle of least privilege. This states that people should have access only to information they need to perform their jobs, regardless of clearance level. Even though a user might have a top-secret security clearance, it doesn't mean he or she should have access to *all* top-secret information. The person needs access to only that information he or she needed to do his or her job.

Separation of Duties

Separation of duties breaks a task into subtasks that different users must carry out. This means a single user cannot carry out a critical task without the help or approval of another user. To put it another way: A user who plans to harm a system must get help from others. A conspiracy is hard to organize and to hide. For example, separation of duties helps ensure that an employee cannot create a new vendor *and* cut a check to that vendor. That prevents an employee from opening a bank account for Acme Consulting, and then going into the system at work to create a new vendor named Acme Consulting and then cutting a check for $1,000 to Acme Consulting.

Job Rotation

Another way to protect your organization from personnel-related security violations is to use **job rotation**. Job rotation minimizes risk by rotating employees among various systems or duties. This prevents collusion, where several employees conspire to commit fraud. It also gives managers a chance to track which users were authorized to take what actions and when. If other security measures have failed, job rotation provides an opportunity to find the security breach before it inflicts more harm. Job rotation also provides trained backup, since several employees learn the skills of specific jobs.

Mandatory Vacations

Much like job rotation, mandatory vacations provide the chance to detect fraud. When users are on vacation, you should suspend their access to your environment. This prevents them from working from home, where they might attempt to cover their tracks. Under U.S. banking rules, certain bank employees must take two consecutive weeks of vacation. Until recently, the law forbade managers from contacting these vacationing employees with work-related matters. That rule has been relaxed to allow for read-only access to systems so they can at least keep up with their e-mail correspondence. However, they still cannot participate in work-related activities while on vacation.

Security Training and Awareness

Because personnel are so important to solid security, one of the best security controls you can develop is a strong security training and awareness program. Security training helps gain the support of all employees. They become security advocates who are motivated to comply with policies that relate to their jobs. They are careful to avoid security breaches. You should train employees, and then train them again at specified intervals. This repeated training refreshes their knowledge and reminds them of the importance of security. Well-trained personnel can make the difference between a secure environment and a collection of attacks and mistakes.

Employees should be aware of security threats to an organization, especially from human factors. These threats include installing rogue technologies, selecting weak passwords, and phishing attacks. These types of threats are common because so many organizations fail to train their personnel on the importance of recognizing them. Simply explaining how weak passwords can endanger personal and business information can often encourage users to create stronger passwords.

A security awareness program should address the requirements and expectations of your security policy. The security policy requires actions and provides authority for security controls. It's one of the best forms of defense. Employees are more likely to comply with a security control if they realize the policy mandates it. In addition to explaining why each part of your policy is necessary, the program should explain the penalties for policy violations.

An awareness program is different from a formal training program. Most users don't understand what security is and why it's necessary. You can use security awareness programs—including posters, e-mails, and employee newsletters, among other tools, to do the following:

- Teach users about security objectives
- Inform users about trends and threats in security
- Motivate users to comply with security policies

Employees generally want to do what's best for the company. When security seems to get in the way of their productivity, however, they'll often bypass security measures to complete their work more quickly. For example, suppose an employee, Bob, is home for the weekend and receives a call from another employee, Sue, at the office. Sue says she needs Bob's password to get to a file or system so she can finish a project. No matter how often you remind employees of the risks of sharing passwords, most people will still be quick to give up their password in this situation. It's your job to reinforce the importance of following security policies. It's also your job to teach them how to solve productivity problems and still maintain a high level of security.

Awareness programs can remind staff about security policies. These programs can also measure how well the staff follows the security policy. The programs provide staff with practical advice on how to deal with security incidents. A good program convinces staff that security is their personal duty. You can help employees change their behavior. Security becomes a part of their daily routine.

Make note of employees who aren't following policies. Use this information in a training session to present employees with scenarios that are specific to their work. Ask employees, "What would you do when ... ?" The information you gather helps identify gaps in your awareness program. Tailor your program with this information.

Social Engineering

One of the most popular types of attacks on computer systems involves social engineering. Social engineering is deceiving or using people to get around security controls. Because most people want to be helpful, it is not too hard for an attacker to convince someone with system access to do something he or she shouldn't do. It is one of the most critical areas of security. As you grant more employees access to systems and data, the risk of security breaches goes up. Technical solutions will not stop an authorized user from calling an unauthorized person and reading sensitive data over the phone. The best way to avoid social engineering is to ensure you train your personnel to recognize it and know how to handle such attacks. Your security training should cover the most common types of social engineering attacks, including:

- **Intimidation**—Using threats or harassment to bully another person for information.
- **Name-dropping**—Using the names of managers or superiors to convince another person that a higher authority has allowed access to information.
- **Appeal for help**—Tugging at a person's sense of compassion or understanding of a difficult, and perhaps unreasonable, situation. The goal of the emotional appeal is to bypass normal procedures or gain special consideration. When combined with an incentive, such as a reward, this type of engineering is very effective. For example, consider the scam in which the scammer promises to send you money if you'll help him transfer money to a disadvantaged person. Unfortunately, this type of emotional appeal fools many people every year.
- **Phishing**—Technology works quite well in social engineering. Take, for example, phishing. In a phishing attack, scammers create an e-mail or Web page that resembles the work of a reputable organization. The scammers want you to believe it's a reputable organization so you'll share sensitive information with them. They use this information to gain access to your financial information or to steal your identity. A phishing attack can also take the form of a survey that asks questions in an effort to capture sensitive information.

> **NOTE**
> For more information about the latest phishing techniques and fraud alerts, see *http://www.fraudwatchinternational.com/*.

The Infrastructure for an IT Security Policy

Every company operates within a complex combination of laws, regulations, requirements, competitors, and partners. In addition, morale, labor relations, productivity, cost, and cash flow affect how a company operates. Within this environment, management must develop and publish an overall security statement and directives. From the security team's perspective, a security program addresses these directives through policies and their supporting elements, such as standards, procedures, baselines, and guidelines. Figure 6-1 shows the elements of a security policy environment.

Each element has a specific requirement for security professionals. You're involved with compliance monitoring, security awareness, training, access control, privacy, incident response, log analysis, and more.

FIGURE 6-1
The security policy environment.

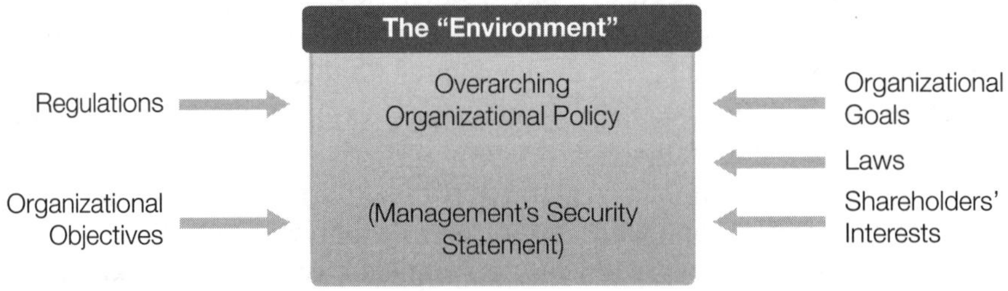

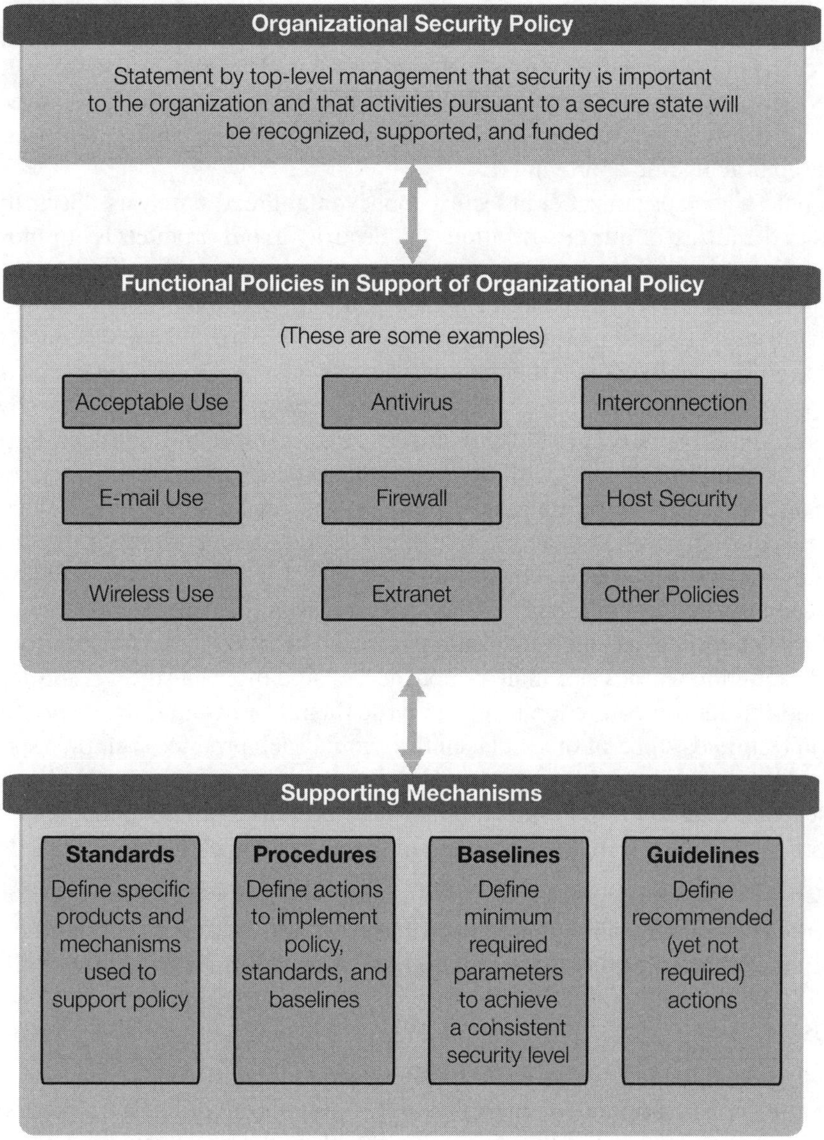

FIGURE 6-2

The security policy hierarchy.

Your security policy sets the organization's tone and culture. As a security professional, you're often required to apply policy intent. You must understand the details of your organization's security policy. The policy is the high-level statement of values and direction. Your organization's standards, baselines, procedures, and guidelines implement your security policy.

The role of the security professional is to provide support for these elements. This support includes informing staff of policies, training, and enforcement. You have a role in any updates or changes. Figure 6-2 shows a typical security policy hierarchy.

Policies

Written security policies document management's goals and objectives. They explain the company's security needs and their commitment to meeting those needs. A security policy should read like a short summary of key facts. If the policy is too complex, management has trouble embracing and approving it.

For example, a good organizational security policy might read simply as, "Security is essential to the future of our organization" or "Security in our products is our most important task." This type of statement provides managers with guidance they need to make a decision. The security policy also helps your organization evaluate how well it is complying with laws, regulations, and standards of due care and due diligence.

Policies aren't of much value if they're not read, available, enforced, and updated. You must post policies in a location available to every employee. For example, you'll often see policies posted in break rooms. Policies must be current, especially with new laws and regulations. You should meet with employees at least once a year to ensure they are up-to-date on the latest policies. Maintain a record of this review with each employee.

A security policy helps all employees understand the assets and principles the organization values. With a clear policy, your staff is more likely to respect the organization's assets. Remember, staff will take policies only as seriously as the organization takes them.

A **functional policy** declares an organization's management direction for security in such specific functional areas as e-mail, remote access, and Internet surfing. The departments responsible for these functional policies write them. For example, human resources, information technology, operations and facilities, would each produce their own specific functional policies. A functional policy should use strong language, such as *will* and *must*. Most people consider a term such as *should* as merely a suggestion, not a mandate. As such, you should not use it. For example, a good access control functional policy reads as follows:

> "All authorized users must be allowed to do *only* their authorized tasks. Unauthorized users must not have access to the company systems or resources."

Standards

Standards are mandated requirements for hardware and software solutions used to address security risk throughout an organization. Standards might refer to a specific antivirus product or password-generation token. Simply put, when a standard is in place, it means the organization has selected a solution—and that solution only—to address a situation.

Adopting standards carries many advantages. Often, standards save an organization money because it can negotiate bulk purchases with vendors. A vendor might sell a single-user license for $29.95. However, that same vendor might sell multiple licenses for only $24.95 per license. If that organization needs multiple licenses to comply with a standard, bulk purchasing can save several thousand dollars. In addition, many vendors offer free training with bulk purchases. This can save the organization the time and trouble of training their staff on how to use the product.

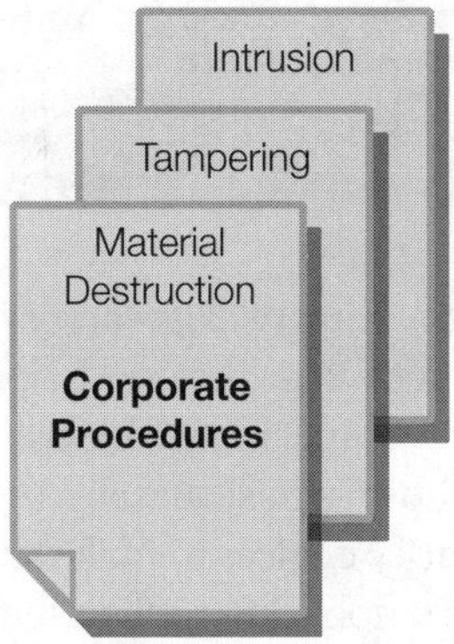

FIGURE 6-3
Systematic actions.

You don't have to develop your own standards for each situation. You can adopt standards created by government, industry, or other sectors and use them as your own. Standards also establish a common basis throughout an organization. This helps keep all departments on the same page. They ensure each department has the blueprints it needs to stay compliant.

The main disadvantage of standards is vulnerability. If the selected product is flawed, the entire organization will be at risk after it installs the product. A single standard cannot work if a vendor doesn't support the product or if it is too expensive to maintain or license. Examine alternatives when evaluating products for standards. Ensure each selection you make comes with a guarantee of support if problems arise.

Procedures

Procedures are systematic actions to accomplish a security requirement, process, or objective. They are one of the most powerful tools available to you. They can provide documentation of the way you do business and ensure no one's critical knowledge remains only in their heads. Procedures cover things such as changing passwords, responding to incidents, and creating backups. Figure 6-3 shows a few sample procedures.

Procedures ensure that you enforce the intent of a policy. They require you to follow a series of steps to complete a task. The following are all true of procedures:

- They reduce mistakes in a crisis.
- They ensure you don't miss important steps.
- They provide for places within the process to conduct assurance checks.
- Like policies and standards, they are mandatory requirements.

Baselines

In many cases, it is helpful to define basic configurations for specific types of computers or devices. For example, having a document that lists the components and configuration settings for a standard workstation makes it easy to ensure all new workstations are the same. Security personnel often create such basic configurations, called **baselines**, to ensure that they enforce the security minimums. Baselines are the benchmarks that

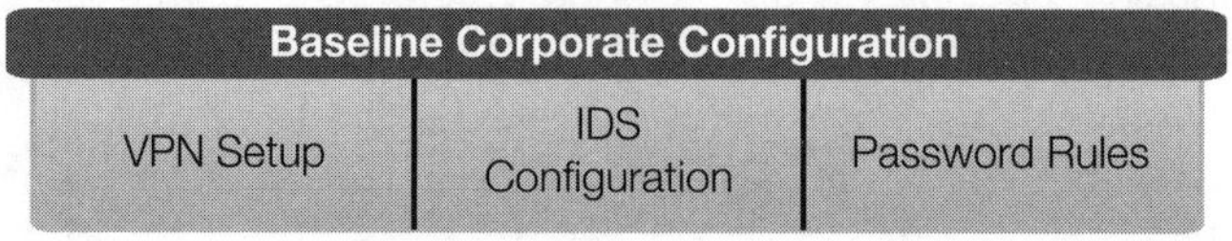

FIGURE 6-4 Baseline corporate configuration.

help make sure a minimum level of security exists across multiple applications of systems and across different products. Baselines are helpful when configuring new computers or devices as well as for comparing with existing systems to see if they still meet the minimums. Figure 6-4 shows a basic baseline corporate configuration.

Baselines tell how to apply security devices to make sure they create a constant level of security throughout the organization. Different systems, or platforms, have different ways of handling security issues. Baselines tell system administrators how to set up the security for each platform. This helps achieve a constant level of security.

Baselines are the great leveler of options offered through different security products, operating systems, and applications. This is becoming more important as more hybrid products enter the security market. These products combine services into multifunctional devices. Organizations often create baseline standards for each operating system in use. You might have different baselines for Windows Vista, Windows 7, Mac OS X, and so on.

Guidelines

Organizations often use **guidelines** to help provide structure to a security program. They outline recommendations for the purchase and use of acceptable products and systems. Guidelines are simply actions that you recommend. They usually exist in the form of white papers, best practices, or other formats defined by an organization's security program.

You must carefully select the language you use in guidelines. A few wrong words can transform a guideline into a company standard. For example, consider the following example of an overarching statement as dictated by the company CEO:

> "This company will follow the recommendations of the ISO 27001 standard."

That statement makes ISO 27001 mandatory within that organization. Make sure that's the intent before you make such a bold statement.

Data Classification Standards

You learned about mandatory access control (MAC) in the previous chapter. MAC involves assigning each object a specific classification. Classifying information often relies on the regulations that apply to the specific type of data. Examples include the protection of personal information, financial information, and health information.

Classification is the duty of the person who owns the data or of someone the owner assigns. You can refer to this person as the data owner. A similar term, system owner, refers to the person or group that manages the infrastructure. System owners are often in control of change or configuration management. System owners are *not* in control of data classification.

It's important to understand the difference between clearance and classification. The authorization grants clearance to *users*. The data owner assigns a classification to *data*. Systems enforce access control by determining that a subject has the right clearance to access a classified object. Operating systems usually enforce access restrictions along with the principles of least privilege or need-to-know.

> **NOTE**
> You can find more information on classification in Chapter 5, which focuses on how organizations use and enforce classification. These pages focus on who makes classification decisions and how they make those decisions.

Organizations take into account three criteria when classifying information:

- **Value**—You can define the value of information by several different measures: the value to the organization, the value to competitors, the cost of replacement or loss, and the value to the organization's reputation.
- **Sensitivity**—Sensitivity is the measure of the effect that a breach of the integrity or the disclosure of information would have on the organization. Organizations can measure sensitivity in many ways, including liability or fines, reputation, credibility, or loss of market share.
- **Criticality**—Criticality is the measure of the importance of the information to the mission of the organization. What would happen to the organization if the information were lost?

Information Classification Objectives

The objectives of classifying information are as follows:

- To identify information protection requirements, which are based on the risk the business faces if the information is disclosed or the data or system is corrupted
- To identify data value in accordance with organization policy
- To ensure sensitive and/or critical information is provided appropriate protection/controls
- To lower costs by protecting only sensitive information
- To standardize classification labeling throughout the organization
- To alert employees and other authorized personnel to protection requirements
- To comply with privacy law and regulations

Organizations can derive many benefits from classifying information:

- Data classified as sensitive or critical gets a level of protection that matches its classification.
- The organization gets more value for its costs because it applies increased controls only where it needs them most. Compare, for example, costs of physical security at an expensive jewelry store, an inexpensive jewelry store, and a costume-jewelry store. None of those stores would operate efficiently with the security system of another. All organizations have data that is of high, medium, and low value. Each classification value warrants a different security level.
- Appropriate markings enable staff to recognize the need to protect classified data.

> **NOTE**
> Compartmentalized information is data that requires special authorization beyond the normal classification system. It is important that your procedures include steps to handle this type of information properly.

Examples of Classification

The U.S. government uses a hierarchical series of classifications that include unclassified, confidential, secret, and top secret. The private sector uses various categories such as public, internal use only, and company confidential.

Government classifications are well known and standardized. Company-related classifications are less well known, and are not standard. This creates issues for the private sector. For example, when an employee changes jobs, the new employer might value "internal use" above "company confidential." In his old job, his employer valued "internal use" below "company confidential." That's confusing. It's even more confusing when this happens within the same company. Part of a security professional's job is to identify these inconsistencies and make recommendations to correct them.

Classification Procedures

Classification procedures are critical to effective data classification. Before implementing these procedures, it's vital that you first determine their scope and process. Classification scope determines what data you should classify and classification process determines how you handle classified data. You must label and mark all resources properly. By adhering to strong procedures, you'll be ready for any upcoming audits.

To determine the scope of your classification plan, you should do a business impact analysis to evaluate all of your organization's data. This determines the data's value and criticality to your organization's operations. Value is determined according to the following:

- Exclusive possession (trade secrets)
- Utility (usefulness)
- Cost to create or re-create the data
- Liability (protection regulations)
- Convertibility/negotiability (financial information)
- Operational impact (if data is unavailable)
- Threats to the information
- Risks

Based on the results of the business impact analysis, you must identify the necessary number of classification levels. You will also standardize the title of each level for use throughout your organization. Send this information to the information owners responsible for assigning the initial classifications. These classifiers must understand the related regulations, customer expectations, and business concerns. The goal is to achieve a consistent approach to handling classified information.

You might find it useful to create a training program so your classifiers handle all data in a consistent manner. The owner is also responsible for a periodic review of classifications to ensure they are still current. This review is particularly critical any time legislators or regulators introduce new government regulations. Finally, the owner is responsible for declassifying information that no longer requires special handling. Government organizations often declare information automatically declassified after a certain number of years.

You must mark all media containing sensitive information according to the organization's classification policy and procedures. That is the only way staff will know what special handling measures to use. You should label magnetic and optical media both electronically and with simple labels. Documents in hard-copy form require labels externally on the cover and internally on the pages.

Assurance

Internal and external auditors should review the organization's information-classification status as a component of their regular audit process. They also should evaluate the level of compliance with the classification policy and procedures. This ensures that all parts of the organization adhere to the process. This review might reveal situations in which information is over classified.

Information security personnel should regularly visit workstations and other areas where users might leave unprotected classified materials. They also should make sure that when violations occur, they submit appropriate reports to supervisors and managers. Ideally, employee performance evaluations should include any instances when they mishandle information. This helps staff understand the importance of this process. The organization should consider implementing a **clean desk/clear screen policy**, which states that users must *never* leave sensitive information in plain view on an unattended desk or workstation.

Configuration Management

It is unusual for any component in a networked computer environment to remain unchanged for a long period. Organizations commonly make modifications to the hardware, software, firmware, documentation, test plans, and test documentation of an automated system throughout the system life cycle. It's important that all configuration changes occur only within a controlled process. Uncontrolled configuration changes often result in conflicts and even new security vulnerabilities. The process of managing all changes to computer and device configurations is configuration management.

From the perspective of a security professional, configuration management evaluates the impact a modification might have on security. Will it affect the availability, confidentiality, or integrity of the system, application, or documentation? Your job is twofold:

- Ensure that you adequately review all system changes.
- Ensure that the change to the configuration will cause unintended consequences on security.

You must control all modifications to ensure that the change will affect your environment as expected and your environment will operate as authorized.

Hardware Inventory and Configuration Chart

Most organizations lack a hardware inventory that tells them what they have, who has ownership or possession of it, and which departments or systems are using it. This is a serious gap in a security program. In the event of a fire, equipment failure, or theft, this lack of documentation can slow the response and extend operational loss. It also makes proper configuration management extremely difficult, if not impossible. A decision to roll out a new patch, service pack, or release will be complicated if you can't find, update, and test every affected device.

Hardware Configuration Chart

You must have an up-to-date map or layout of the configuration of the hardware components. This helps ensure that you configure all systems according to the baseline. It also ensures that you properly review the work completed on a system or network so you can make the correct changes without bypassing any security features. A hardware configuration chart should include the following:

- An as-built diagram of the network, to help you plan the sequence of a change and see the ripple effects it might generate
- Copies of all software configurations so that you can examine changes and updates planned for one device for their impact on other devices. These configurations should include items such as router, switch, and firewall configurations.

Patch and Service-Pack Management

You should regularly check for any available vendor upgrades and service packs. This process may be an involved one if you have many types of software and hardware from different vendors. Nevertheless, it is necessary to address all known vulnerabilities. The organization must have a patch-management process to ensure that it rolls out patches to all computers and devices without causing system outages. You should test every patch prior to rollout to ensure that it will not disable other systems or functions.

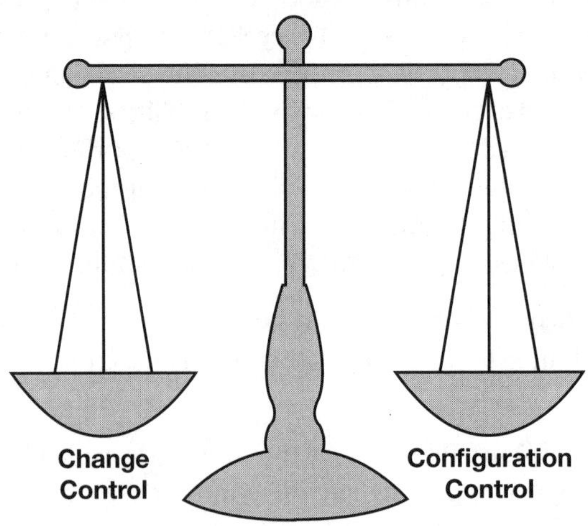

FIGURE 6-5 The complementary balance of change control and configuration control.

The Change Management Process

While it is common to discuss change and configuration control as a pair, they are really two ends of a spectrum. The confusion, of course, is where a particular activity crosses from one to the other. Drawing a sharp line between the two is difficult because different organizations of different complexities will draw the line in different places.

- **Configuration control** is the management of the baseline settings for a system device. The baseline settings meet security requirements. They require that you implement them carefully and only with prior approval.
- **Change control** is the management of changes to the configuration. Unmanaged changes introduce risk, because they might affect security operations or controls. An improper change could even disable the system or equipment. Change control ensures that any changes to a production system are tested, documented, and approved. The change itself must follow a change control process that ensures you make the change correctly and report it to management.

Figure 6-5 shows the balance between change control and configuration control.

Change Control Management

Change control management develops a planned approach to controlling change by involving all affected departments. The objective is to maximize the benefits for all people involved in the change and minimize the risk of failure.

To be effective, change management should be multidisciplinary, touching all aspects of the organization. Nevertheless, an organization should not be constrained so much that it loses all flexibility. Change management should allow organizations to adopt new technologies, improvements, and modifications.

Change management requires a written policy approved by the chief information officer, or the IT director, and the business information security manager. The policy must define all roles, responsibilities, and procedures related to change management. Here are some important things to remember:

- You should communicate change management procedures and standards effectively. They should define the techniques and technologies you'll use throughout the enterprise in support of the policy.
- Change management can be either reactive or proactive. With **reactive change management**, management responds to changes in the business environment. The source of the change is external. Some examples are changes in regulations, customer expectations, and the supply chain. With **proactive change management**, management initiates the change to achieve a desired goal. In this case, the source of the change is internal, such as the adoption of new technology.
- Your organization can conduct change management in several ways. It can occur on a continuous basis, a regularly scheduled basis, a release basis, or when you deem it necessary on a program-by-program basis.

Reviewing Changes for Potential Security Impact

Change creates risk for a business. It might circumvent established security features and it could result in outage or system failure. It might require extensive retraining for employees to learn how to use the new systems. Because of the risk involved, you must include security personnel in the change control process.

The formal change control process should protect the integrity of the IT systems and ensure that all changes in the production environment are properly tested, scheduled, and communicated. Members of the change control committee attend meetings and forums to estimate, plan, review, and prepare for the organization's production environment.

Change Control Committees

A senior manager or business-process owner should lead a **change control committee**. It oversees all proposed changes to systems and networks. The committee approves changes and the schedule for implementing the changes. In this manner, you cannot make changes to a system, application, or network without the proper review, funding, and documentation.

In cooperation with IT, the change control committee—in some cases called a change control board—provides the oversight to protect the computing resources and the data contained within those applications and databases. As part of the change process, key members meet with counterparts from the IT organizations to review upcoming plans and ensure that you properly evaluate all changes. They also make sure the necessary security controls have been applied and evaluated. They communicate their findings to all parts of the organization.

In brief, the primary objectives of the change control committee are to ensure all changes are as follows:

- Properly tested
- Authorized
- Scheduled
- Communicated
- Documented

When you use solid change control, identifying recent changes that might have caused a production problem is easy. That simplifies the problem-resolution process and makes your environment more secure.

Change Control Procedures

Change control procedures ensure that a change does not happen without following the right steps. This helps you avoid problems such as scope creep, which allows unauthorized changes to sneak into a system. It also helps avoid problems caused by lack of oversight, lack of testing, or by making changes without proper authorization. Figure 6-6 shows a sequence of change control procedures.

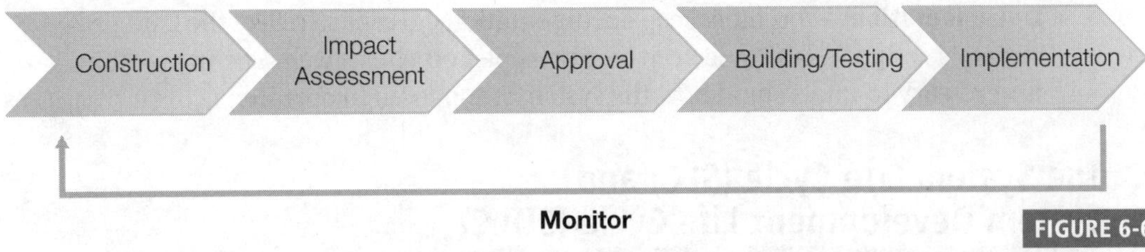

FIGURE 6-6 Change control procedures.

1. **Request**—In the request stage, you should describe all proposed changes in writing and submit the change request to the change control committee for review. You should never make a change to a system without approval.
2. **Impact assessment**—The impact-assessment step evaluates the effect of the change on the budget, resources, and security of the system or project.
3. **Approval**—The approval (or, in some cases, disapproval) stage is the formal review and acceptance (or rejection) of the change by the change control committee.
4. **Build/test**—The build/test step is the actual development or building of the change according to the approved change document. You then must test the change to ensure it does not cause unexpected problems for other systems or components. This testing might include regression testing and an in-depth review of the security of the modified product.
5. **Implement**—Once you test the change and approve it for release, you can schedule the installation process. This is where adequate separation of duties ensures that no one person can make the change without proper review and oversight. The final hurdle is notifying management that you have made the change successfully.
6. **Monitor**—In this step, you must monitor all systems to ensure that the system, program, network, and other resources are working correctly. You should address any user issues or requests using your organization's problem-resolution procedures. Monitoring might identify the need for future changes. This restarts the change control process.

Change Control Issues

Solid change control procedures include the components that tend to identify issues and provide recovery avenues if needed. A successful change control program should include the following elements to ensure the quality of the change control process:

- **Peer review**—This ensures that a peer or another expert double-checks all changes before you put them into production. Peers can often catch problems before they make it to the testing phase.
- **Back-out plans**—This ensures that if the change doesn't work properly, a plan exists to restore the system to a known good condition. In spite of the best control procedures, you may accidentally release changes that have unintended effects. You must know how to undo a destructive change.

- **Documentation**—You must keep documentation current to reflect the true system's design. You should keep backup copies off site as well. Documentation is necessary to understand how the system is supposed to operate.

The System Life Cycle (SLC) and System Development Life Cycle (SDLC)

One critical area of concern is software. Attackers know that the software development process is complex, and that the result of the process is often an application that contains weaknesses. Secure software can be difficult to write. It requires attention to security at every stage of the process, and a structured process to ensure the software does just what it is supposed to do. There are several popular methods to describe and control the systems and software development process. Understanding the process of software development is important to developing software with very few weaknesses. You should be familiar with two of the most popular methods, the System Life Cycle (SLC) and System Development Life Cycle (SDLC). The steps are very similar, except that the SLC includes operations and disposal, and the SDLC ends with the transition to production.

For some organizations, maintenance and new development are done by developers, making them part of SDLC. For others, specialized maintenance teams handle maintenance and development, making it part of SLC. More and more organizations use the term SDLC to describe the entire change and maintenance process for application and system software.

The System Life Cycle (SLC)

This section covers the common steps used in the SLC. The more the security professional can be involved in each step, the more likely the needed security will be built into the system from the start. The main justification for SLC—and for building security in at the start—is reducing or avoiding cost:

- Consumers of commercial software products will see lower costs because you will need to deliver fewer patches and fixes. In addition, there will be fewer losses due to weaknesses in the software, which attackers find and exploit.
- Vendors of commercial software will see lower costs because they require smaller support staffs and have lower warranty and product-maintenance costs.

The common steps used in the SLC are as follows:

1. **Project initiation and planning**—One of the first requirements of a successful project is to have all the necessary resources available. The resources you will need should represent the areas that you need to consider and integrate into the project. Your role is to provide advice on building security into the project from the very beginning. This includes project budgets, system design, maintenance, and the project timeline. You should address threats, vulnerabilities, risks, and controls here first.

2. **Functional requirements and definition**—This is the what-if phase. Always state requirements using positive terms: The program must handle some data or perform some function. You will need to think about what the program should or will do when the data doesn't meet its specifications. What happens when the software receives unexpected input? Are there too many characters? Are fields missing? Are users seeing delayed transmissions? Failure to consider these factors creates a great number of security mishaps.
3. **System-design specification**—In this phase, a project is broken into functions and modules. For that, you must consider the type of hardware on which it is going to run. Security issues here include physical security of the hardware and network. Security also has to account for all the possible platforms. It isn't enough to say the project is limited to Linux or Windows, for example. Each platform features a wide variety of versions and runs on an almost infinite combination of peripherals, chipsets, and drivers.
4. **Build (develop) and document**—Coding standards should include standard libraries of function calls. They should also include industry-standard solutions for items such as cryptography, hashing, and access control. You need to secure code in development so that only developers have access and grant access only on a need-to-know basis. Even developers should have access only to the parts they need to see. You should not leave copies lying around in printed or machine-readable form, such as on CDs or USB memory sticks.
5. **Acceptance testing**—You should create a test plan during the functional design stage. This plan must include testing to make sure the new programs provide necessary security and, where applicable, privacy. The people responsible for the tests should not be the developers. In addition, past-due delivery dates for developers should *not* affect the time allotted for testing.
6. **Implementation (transition to production)**—During this transition, developers will be working on delivery of training and assistance to users and help-desk personnel. Security features need to be carefully explained to both groups. In some organizations, developers also will help manage the turnover of code to maintenance staff.
7. **Operations and maintenance**—When there are problems with the system, it's likely that maintenance, operations, and help-desk personnel will be the first to know. They need to track the issues that come in and be ready to report their results to management. This procedure fuels the change management process. These personnel require training to understand the differences between a request for change, a software malfunction, and a security weakness or breach. In addition, they need to know how to handle each of those cases.
8. **Disposal**—Over time, component parts will reach the end of their life span. You will need to upgrade a backup system or procure a larger disk to replace a smaller one. You should ensure that you have procedures to sanitize the media and then dispose of it in a cost-effective way. In years past, organizations would wipe a disk and resell it. Today, the value of a small used disk is often less than the cost to securely wipe it with a tool such as DBAN and then simply dispose of the disk.

Testing and Developing Systems

Security professionals often help test new systems or upgrades to existing systems. These tests should be thorough enough to ensure that you test for all expected and unexpected actions and that you handle errors correctly. You should also perform tests to test the maximum load on the system, including transaction volume, memory allocation, network bandwidth, and response times. If you use production or sensitive data in testing, make sure you take steps to keep it secure.

Systems Procurement

One common way new vulnerabilities make their way into an environment is through a change that causes unintended side effects. You should thoroughly evaluate any change to your environment to ensure it doesn't introduce new vulnerabilities. Do this with new hardware and software as well. Procuring new equipment is a critical role of the security professional, but can decrease your overall security if not handled well. Any time you need to procure new equipment, you should carefully evaluate which products will meet your requirements. To ensure that new equipment does not expose your environment to any new vulnerabilities, you must do the following:

- Evaluate the various solutions available.
- Evaluate the vendors in terms of maintenance, support, and training.
- Use the Common Criteria to ensure you simplify the evaluation process.
- Monitor vendor contracts and service level agreements (SLAs).
- Correctly install equipment and formally accept it at the end of the project.
- Follow the organization's procurement procedures to ensure a fair purchasing process.
- Monitor systems and equipment to identify equipment that is reaching the end of its lifespan so that you can schedule it for replacement.

The Common Criteria

Because procuring new equipment can lead to security vulnerabilities, it makes sense to formalize the process. The need for a formal approach to evaluate systems and equipment gave rise to several different sets of standards. The U.S. government created a series of computer security standards documents known as the Rainbow Series due to the bold colors on the covers of the documents. *The Red Book* describes components of a trusted network infrastructure (TNI). *The Orange Book* talks about maintaining access control and confidentiality in a classified system. Both used a series of evaluative levels (C2, B3, and so on), and vendors had their products evaluated against these levels. The developers of the Rainbow Series formally called it TCSEC.

Other governments created their own equivalents. Some started with TCSEC and made modifications. Eventually, these merged into what is became ITSEC. The governments of the United States, Britain, Canada, Germany, France, and the Netherlands used ITSEC as a starting point. Then they developed a new procurement standard called the Common Criteria.

The Common Criteria have a series of increasingly more difficult evaluation assurance levels (EALs) numbered from 1 (lowest) to 7 (highest). Evaluation labs are scattered all over the world. Leading vendors within an industry (for example, vendors of firewalls) collectively create a standard, ideal, and perfect solution. Any vendor can have its product evaluated against the standard. An EAL rating assures that the vendor's claims match the collective standard to a defined level of testing. The product's documentation, development, and performance must all match the evaluation claims.

> **TIP**
> The formal name for the Common Criteria is ISO 15408.

Disposing of Equipment

At the opposite end of the life cycle is equipment disposal. Whenever you need to dispose of equipment, you should ensure that you dispose of it in a secure way so that you do not expose any confidential data. There are several options available to you, including the following:

- **Degaussing**—Applying a strong magnetic force to magnetic media usually makes all electronics unusable.
- **Physical destruction**—Physically destroying the media on which data is stored guarantees that you eliminate any confidential material.
- **Removal from inventory**—In order to maintain control over hardware assets, it is important to show that you have removed discarded equipment from inventory and service.
- **Data recovery**—You must take care to ensure that you have backed up all data on discarded media to alternate storage and that it is possible to access or read the data with new equipment.

Certification and Accreditation

Between procurement and disposal, you will need to ensure the components in your computing environment are sufficient to for your requirements. **Certification** is the process of reviewing a system throughout its life cycle to ensure that it meets its specified security requirements. **Accreditation** is the formal acceptance by the authorizing official to accept the risk of implementing the system. The process includes the following:

- **Authorizing official**—The senior manager who must review the certification report and make the decision to approve the system for implementation. The **authorizing official (AO)** officially acknowledges and accepts the risk that the system may pose to agency mission, assets, or individuals.
- **Certifier**—The individual or team that is responsible for performing the security test and evaluation (ST+E) for the system. The **certifier** also prepares the report for the AO on the system operating's risk.
- **System owner**—The person responsible for the daily operations of the system and ensuring that the system continues to operate in compliance with the conditions set out by the AO is the **system owner**.

Certification. Certification is the technical evaluation of a system to provide assurance that the organization implemented a system correctly. It should meet the initial design requirements to ensure that the security controls are working effectively. A certifier or team of certifiers does this task. The certifier should have the skill to perform the verification process and the tests necessary to prove compliance. Certification of a system means the following:

- The system meets the technical requirements.
- The system meets the functional requirements.
- The system provides assurance of proper operation.

In order to certify, the person (or people) involved in the process must first know the technical and functional requirements. They also must know the capabilities of the system they are recommending for purchase or for approval to move into production. These might be software or hardware requirements. You might evaluate them in terms of quantity or quality, such as the ability to authenticate 100 users a minute or to ensure 99.99 percent uptime. You might base them on non-IT factors, such as weight or energy consumption. The accreditors must examine all of the requirements. Many of these testing tasks, whether conducting or managing them will fall to you as a security professional.

Finally, the certifiers must match these lists to make sure the new system meets or exceeds each specification. When they're sure that it does, they recommend management approval. This doesn't mean the system is right for your organization or that it is the best solution available. Certification means only that the product meets its technical and functional specifications and operates as promised.

Accreditation. Accreditation occurs after you certify a system. Accreditation is the process of management officially accepting the system. The accreditor or designated approving authority reviews the certification reports and, based on the operational environment, accepts the system for operation. You can define this process in two ways:

- Accreditation is management's formal acceptance of risk.
- Accreditation is management's permission to implement.

Triggers for New Certification. The certification and accreditation processes ensure a system not only meets the security requirements today, but that it continues to meet them through the operations and maintenance phases of its life cycle. The post-accreditation phase lists the activities required to continue to operate and manage the system so that it maintains an acceptable level of risk. You must continually assess risk to meet this requirement for the following reasons:

- Business needs change due to new products, new processes, mergers, or divestitures.
- Products (solutions) that were once accredited might no longer meet the needs of the business.
- Vendors often upgrade or replace products, and these replacements need to be recertified and reaccredited.

Software Development and Security

You learned earlier in this chapter about the importance of developing secure software. Software development requires specal attention from a security perspective. Applications represent the most common avenue for users, customers, and attackers to access data. That means you must build the software to enforce the security policy and to ensure compliance with regulations, including the privacy and integrity of both data and system processes. Regardless of the development model your organization adopts, you should make sure the application properly performs the following tasks:

- Checks user authentication to the application
- Checks user authorization (privilege level)
- Has edit checks, range checks, validity checks, and other similar controls to prevent the contamination of databases or production data
- Has procedures for recovering database integrity in the event of system failure

Software developed in house will have source code, object code, and runtime executables. You need to manage and protect these with policies, standards, and procedures. For example:

- You should protect source code from access by unauthorized users.
- You should track changes to source code by version control systems so that rollback to a previous version is error-free.
- Programmers should not be able to update production systems directly (programmers to test, then test to production).

Software Development Methods

Many current software development methods base their models on the **waterfall model**. This is a sequential process for developing software. It includes the SDLC and the SLC you learned about earlier. In the waterfall model, progress flows downward, like a waterfall. The essence of the waterfall model is that no phase begins until the previous phase is complete. The phases are as follows:

1. Requirements specification
2. Design
3. Construction
4. Integration
5. Testing and debugging
6. Installation
7. Maintenance

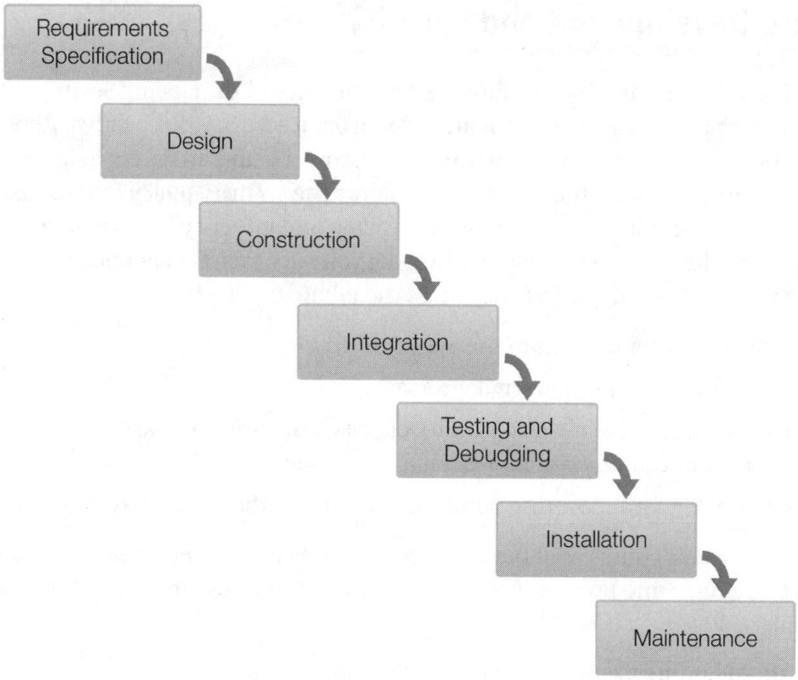

FIGURE 6-7
The waterfall model.

The basic waterfall model originated in the manufacturing and construction industries. It's a feature of highly structured physical environments in which late revisions are very costly, if not entirely prohibitive. When Winston W. Royce devised this model in 1970, no formal software development methods existed. This hardware-oriented model was adapted to software development. Figures 6-7 shows the classic waterfall model.

Because of perceived shortcomings of this model, you'll find modifications of the waterfall model. Most software development models use at least some phases similar to the waterfall model. The importance of the model is in the focus on ensuring that each phase is complete before moving on. While this may be quite difficult in large development environments, always invest the time to properly plan and design your software. Don't just start writing programs!

CHAPTER SUMMARY

In this chapter, you learned that security professionals must understand that security operations and administration are the basis of any solid security program. You learned how security administration works to plan, design, implement, and monitor an organization's security plan. You learned that professional ethics are essential for every solid security plan. You learned what you have to do to make sure your security program is compliant. You learned how the policies, standards, guidelines, and procedures of your plan work together to shape your security program. You learned how data-classification standards affect the decision-making process. You learned how to use configuration management to manage system modifications, and how configuration control and change control affect the change management process. You explored the eight common steps of the System Life Cycle (SLC), the System Development Life Cycle (SDLC), and how these steps reduce costs. You learned why software development methods require special security considerations. Finally, you learned how user awareness is pivotal to the success of your security program.

KEY CONCEPTS AND TERMS

Accreditation
Authorizing official (AO)
Baselines
Certification
Certifier
Change control
Change control committee
Clean desk/clear screen policy
Compliance liaison
Configuration control
Emergency operations group
Functional policy
Guidelines
Job rotation
Proactive change management
Procedures
Reactive change management
Remediation
Security administration
Security event log
Standards
System owner
Waterfall model

CHAPTER 6 ASSESSMENT

1. Security administration is the group of individuals responsible for the planning, design, implementation, and monitoring of an organization's security plan.

A. True
B. False

2. The security program requires documentation of:

A. The security process
B. The policies, procedures, and guidelines adopted by the organization
C. The authority of the persons responsible for security
D. All of the above
E. None of the above

3. An organization does *not* have to comply with both regulatory standards and organizational standards.

A. True
B. False

4. A(n) ________ is a formal contract between your organization and an outside firm that details the specific services the firm will provide.

A. Security event log
B. Incident response
C. Service-level agreement (SLA)
D. Compliance report

5. The (ISC)^2 Code of Ethics Canons include which of the following statements:

A. "Protect society, the commonwealth, and the infrastructure."
B. "Act honorably, honestly, justly, responsibly, and legally."
C. "Provide diligent and competent service to principals."
D. "Advance and protect the profession."
E. All of the above

6. In 1989, the IAB issued a statement of policy about Internet ethics. This document is known as ________.

A. OECD
B. RFC 1087
C. (ISC)^2 Code of Ethics Canons
D. (ISC)^2 Code of Ethics Preamble
E. None of the above

7. ________ is the concept that users should be granted only the levels of permissions they need in order to perform their duties.

A. Mandatory vacations
B. Separation of duties
C. Job rotation
D. Principle of least privilege
E. None of the above

8. Which of the following is an example of social engineering?

A. An emotional appeal for help
B. A phishing attack
C. Intimidation
D. Name-dropping
E. All of the above

9. Policy sets the tone and culture of the organization.

A. True
B. False

10. ________ involve the standardization of the hardware and software solutions used to address a security risk throughout the organization.

A. Policies
B. Standards
C. Procedures
D. Baselines

11. Which of the following is true of procedures?

A. They increase mistakes in a crisis.
B. They provide for places within the process to conduct assurance checks.
C. Important steps are often overlooked.
D. None of the above
E. All of the above

12. Data classification is the responsibility of the person who owns the data.
    A. True
    B. False

13. The objectives of classifying information include which of the following?
    A. To identify data value in accordance with organization policy
    B. To identify information-protection requirements
    C. To standardize classification labeling throughout the organization
    D. To comply with privacy law, regulations, and so on
    E. All of the above

14. Configuration management is the management of modifications made to the hardware, software, firmware, documentation, test plans, and test documentation of an automated system throughout the system life cycle.
    A. True
    B. False

15. The change management process includes ________ control and ________ control.
    A. Clearance, classification
    B. Document, data
    C. Hardware inventory, software development
    D. Configuration, change

16. More and more organizations use the term ________ to describe the entire change and maintenance process for applications.
    A. System Development Life Cycle (SDLC)
    B. System Life Cycle (SLC)
    C. System Maintenance Life Cycle (SMLC)
    D. None of the above

17. When developing software, you should ensure the application does which of the following?
    A. Has edit checks, range checks, validity checks, and other similar controls
    B. Checks user authorization
    C. Checks user authentication to the application
    D. Has procedures for recovering database integrity in the event of system failure
    E. All of the above

18. There are several types of software development methods, but almost all of them are based on the ________ model.
    A. Modification
    B. Waterfall
    C. Developer
    D. Integration

CHAPTER

7 Auditing, Testing, and Monitoring

WHEN YOU AUDIT A COMPUTER SYSTEM, you check to see how it has performed. Simply put, when you audit a system, you see if things on the system work according to plan. Audits also often look at the current configuration of a system as a snapshot in time to verify that it complies with standards.

You can audit a system manually or you can do it using automated computer software. Manual tests include the following:

- Interviewing your staff
- Performing vulnerability scans
- Reviewing application and operating system access controls
- Analyzing physical access to the systems

With automated tests, the system creates a report of any changes to important files and settings. These files and settings might relate to the operating system or to application software. Systems can include personal computers, servers, mainframes, network routers, and switches. Examples of these types of applications include software associated with access to the Internet, databases, or any resources shared by users.

Of course, long before you can audit a system, you need to create the policies and procedures that establish the rules and requirements of the system. That is, before you can determine whether something has worked, you must first define how it's *supposed* to work. This is known as assessing your system. You evaluate all the components of your system and determine how each should work. This sets your baseline expectations. Once you have that, you can audit the system. You compare the system's performance to your baseline expectations to see whether things worked as planned.

Chapter 7 Topics

This chapter covers the following topics and concepts:

- What security auditing and analysis are
- How to define your audit plan
- What auditing benchmarks are
- How to collect audit data
- Which post-audit activities you need to perform
- How to perform security monitoring
- Which types of log information you should capture
- How to verify security controls
- How to monitor and test your security systems

Chapter 7 Goals

When you complete this chapter, you will be able to:

- Describe the practices and principles of system audits
- Review ways to monitor systems, including log management and the use of an intrusion detection system (IDS) or intrusion prevention system (IPS)
- Set metrics for system performance
- Assess an organization's security compliance

Security Auditing and Analysis

The purpose of a security audit is to make sure your systems and security controls work as expected. When you review your systems, you should check for the following:

- **Are security policies sound and appropriate for the business or activity?** The purpose of information security is to support the mission of the business and to protect it from the risks it faces. Your organization's policies and supporting documents define the risks that affect it. Supporting documents include your organization's procedures, standards, and baselines. When you conduct an audit, you are asking the question, "Are our policies followed and understood?" The audit itself does not set new policies. Auditors might, however, make recommendations based on experience or knowledge of new regulations.

- **Are there controls supporting your policies?** Are the security controls aligned correctly with your organization's strategies and mission? Do the controls support your policies and culture? If you cannot justify a control by a policy, you should probably remove it. Whenever a control is explained as "for security," but with no other explanation, you should remove it. Security is not a profit center, and it should never exist for its own sake. It is a support department. Its purpose is to protect the organization's assets and revenue stream.
- **Is there effective implementation and upkeep of controls?** As your organization evolves and as threats mature, it is important to make sure your controls still meet the risks you face today.

If you can answer yes to these questions, you're in good shape. If you can't answer yes, don't worry. You'll develop these skills in this chapter.

Security Controls Address Risk

Security controls place limits on activities that might pose a risk to your organization. (For more details, refer to Chapter 8.) You must review security regularly to make sure your controls are current and effective. This security review includes the following activities:

- **Monitor**—Review and measure all controls to capture actions and changes on the system.
- **Audit**—Review the logs and overall environment to provide independent analysis of how well the security policy and controls work.
- **Improve**—Include proposals to improve the security program and controls in the audit results. This step applies to the recommended changes as accepted by management.
- **Secure**—Ensure that the controls work and protect the intended level of security.

Although security controls protect your computers and networks, you should ensure each one is necessary and is effective. Each control should protect your organization from a specific threat. A control without an identified threat is a layer of overhead that does not make your organization any more secure. Carefully ensure all security controls you have in place address specific threats. It is fine to have multiple controls that address the same threat—just ensure that each control does address at least one threat.

Recall that risk is defined as the probability that a threat will be realized. You can calculate the expected loss by multiplying the risk probability by the asset cost. Identifying risks enables you to measure the validity of the control. When you use a control that costs more than the potential loss if a threat is realized, you may be wasting your organization's resources. One of the best ways to avoid wasting your organization's resources is to ensure you follow the security review cycle. Figure 7-1 shows how each of the steps in the security review cycle fit together.

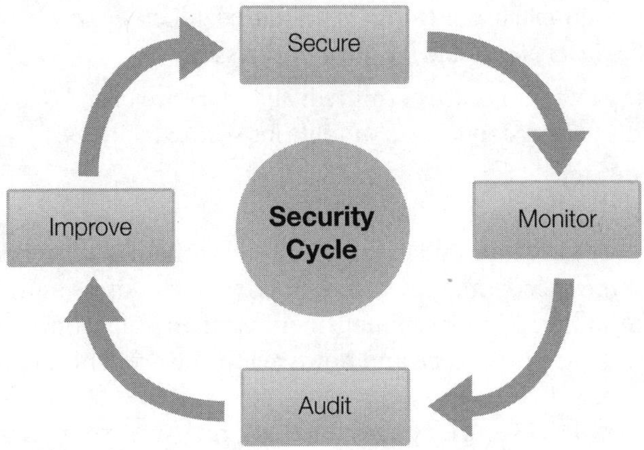

FIGURE 7-1
The security review cycle.

Determining What Is Acceptable

Your first step toward putting the right security controls in place is to determine what actions are acceptable:

- Your organization's security policy should define acceptable and unacceptable actions.
- Your organization might create its own standards based on those developed or endorsed by standards bodies.
- Communications and other actions permitted by a policy document are *acceptable*.
- Communications and other actions specifically banned in your security policy are *unacceptable*. Other communications or other actions may be unacceptable as well. Any action that may cause damage to a system's integrity, reveal confidential information, or make the system unavailable is also unacceptable, even if the policy does not specifically ban it.

NOTE
Chapter 6 covers creating policies and their supporting documents.

Permission Levels

The proper permission level for your organization depends your organization's needs and policies. It's essential to match your organization's required permission level with its security structure. If you don't, you might lose a lot of data, and your reputation could suffer. You could also find that users simply attempt to bypass your security controls if your security controls are tougher than is necessary. The most common permission levels are as follows:

- **Promiscuous**—Everything is allowed. This permission level is suitable for most home users.
- **Permissive**—Anything not specifically prohibited is OK. This permission level is suitable for most public Internet sites, some schools and libraries, and many training centers.

- **Prudent**—A reasonable list of things is permitted; all others are prohibited. This permission level is suitable for most businesses.
- **Paranoid**—Very few things are permitted; all others are prohibited and carefully monitored. This permission level is suitable for secure facilities.

Areas of Security Audits

Audits can be very large in scope and cover entire departments or business functions. On the other end of the spectrum, they can be narrow and address only one specific system or control. An audit provides management with an independent assessment of whether the best controls are in place and how well they work. This helps management understand and address their risks.

For example, a high-level security policy audit is a review of your security policy to ensure it is up to date, relevant, communicated, and enforced. This type of audit also helps ensure that your policy reflects the culture of your organization. These audits may also test whether users or customers accept the controls, or whether they try to bypass the controls they view as unrealistic. In addition, this type of audit tests how well your infrastructure protects your application's data. It ensures that the application limits access to authorized users only and that it hides (encrypts) data that unauthorized users should not see.

You must also audit all your organization's firewalls and other network devices to ensure they function as intended and that their configurations comply with your security policy. Finally, audits can test the technologies themselves. They detect whether all your networked computers and devices are working together according to your policy. They help ensure that your rules and configurations are up to date, documented, and subject to change control procedures.

Purpose of Audits

An audit gives you the opportunity to review your risk-management program and to confirm that the program has correctly identified and reduced (or otherwise addressed) the risks to your organization.

An audit checks whether controls are

- **Appropriate**—Is the level of security control suitable for the risk it addresses?
- **Installed correctly**—Is the security control in the right place and working well?
- **Addressing their purpose**—Is the security control effective in addressing the risk it was designed to address?

The audit report that auditors create should recommend improvements or changes to the organization's processes, infrastructure, or other controls as needed. Audits are necessary because of potential liability, negligence, and mandatory regulatory compliance. Audits can expose problems and provide assurance of compliance. Many jurisdictions require audits by law.

Laws and regulations require some companies that employ a certain number of employees or are in a particular industry to have both internal and external audits. Industries that must conduct these required audits include financial services organizations and any organization that handles personal medical records. Federal laws or vendor standards that require internal and external audits include the Sarbanes-Oxley Act (SOX), the Health Insurance Portability and Accountability Act (HIPAA), and the Payment Card Industry Data Security Standard (PCI DSS). The Personal Information Protection and Electronic Documents Act (PIPEDA) is a Canadian law that protects how organizations collect, use, or disclose personal information in e-commerce transactions. It also includes audit requirements.

An audit might find that an organization lacks sufficiently trained and skilled staff. It might show the company does not do enough to oversee security programs and manage assets. An audit might encourage an organization to provide better staff training. On the other hand, an audit might validate that an organization is meeting or exceeding its requirements.

Many new regulations make management personally responsible for fraud or mismanagement of corporate assets. In the past, corporations were mostly accountable for this; now, individuals are responsible. It is in the organization's best interests to make every effort to be compliant with all necessary requirements to protect itself and its people.

Customer Confidence

Customers will generally do business only with organizations they trust. If customers know you consistently audit your systems for security, they may be more willing to share their sensitive information with you.

An organization that audits itself breeds customer confidence. Many business-to-business service providers use SAS 70 audits to build customer confidence. SAS 70 reports assess and describe an organization's controls and safeguards. These reports provide details that describe the organization's specific controls. Type II reports defined by SAS 70 indicate whether the controls and safeguards work. For example, a company seeking to lease space in a data center might ask the data center to provide the results of a SAS 70 audit to get an independent assessment of the security controls in the data center.

SAS 70 reports are an important tool for an organization's auditors. The reports primarily are used to prepare financial statements for the user organization. The SAS 70 report also can save money because the customer doesn't have to send its own auditors to audit the service provider.

Defining Your Audit Plan

In planning the activities for an audit, the auditor first must define the objectives and determine which systems or business processes to review. The auditor should also define which areas of assurance to check.

An auditor must also identify the personnel—both from his or her own team and from the organization being audited—who will participate in the audit. These people will gather and put together information to move the audit along. The auditor must be sure that everyone has the right skills, is prepared to contribute, and is available when they are needed.

Some auditors include a review of previous audits to become familiar with past issues. Other auditors choose not to review previous audits to avoid being prejudiced by prior conclusions.

Defining the Scope of the Plan

> **NOTE**
> Auditing every part of an organization may not be possible because of resource constraints. Auditors should give the highest risk areas the top priority.

You must define the boundaries of the review at the beginning of the project. It is critical to determine which areas the audit will review and which it will not. You must be sure that the areas not reviewed in the current audit will be subject to another audit and you must set responsibility for those areas. All systems and networks must have a clearly designated owner.

At this point, you need to decide whom to inform that an audit is under way. In many cases, if users know you are auditing them, they may start to follow rules they had previously ignored. If knowing about an audit changes user behavior, your audit will not be accurate. On the other hand, trying to perform an audit without telling staff makes the job more difficult by limiting access to critical information. You have to consider this tradeoff on a case-by-case basis. Figure 7-2 shows how the scope of an audit can span all seven domains in the IT infrastructure.

An auditor should take the time to properly plan an audit before conducting any audit activities. Planning is far more than just listing the files and documents to inspect. In fact, auditors often do a substantial amount of work preparing for an audit. Here's what you can expect from an auditor throughout the planning and execution phases:

- **Survey the site**—An auditor will want to understand the environment and the interconnections between systems before starting the audit activities.
- **Review documentation**—An auditor will want to review system documentation and configurations both during planning and as part of the actual audit.
- **Review risk analysis output**—An auditor will want to understand system criticality ratings that are a product of risk-analysis studies. This helps rank systems into the appropriate order for mitigation in the reporting phase.
- **Review host logs**—An auditor might ask to examine system logs to look for changes to programs, permissions, or configurations.
- **Review incident logs**—An auditor might ask to review security incident logs to get a feel for problem trends.
- **Review results of penetration tests**—When an organization conducts penetration tests, the tester prepares a report listing weaknesses found. The auditor needs to review this report and make sure that the audit addresses all items.

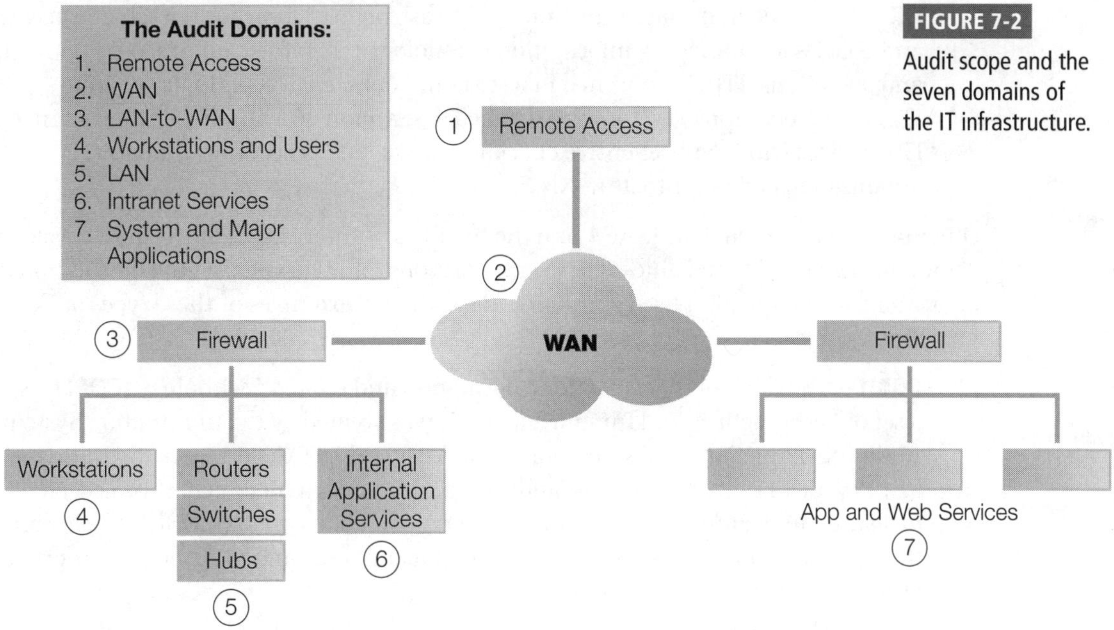

FIGURE 7-2 Audit scope and the seven domains of the IT infrastructure.

Auditing Benchmarks

A **benchmark** is the standard by which your system is compared to determine whether it is securely configured. One technique in an audit is to compare the current setting of a computer or device to a benchmark to help identify differences.

In this section, you will find common ways to audit or review systems, business processes, or security controls. All of these examples are best practices. They often are used as guidelines for auditing a business or business process. Your organization's management may have formally adopted one of the following examples. This can be true especially if your organization is subject to government regulation or legislation. If so, then the benchmark directs the main course of your audit. Otherwise, the auditor, with senior management's approval, decides how an audit is carried out.

- **ISO 27002**—ISO 27002 is a best-practices document that gives good guidelines for information security management. In order for an organization to claim compliance, it must perform an audit to verify that all provisions are satisfied.
- **NIST SP 800**—37-NIST SP 800-37 is a standard published by the U.S. government specifically for computer systems that the government owns or operates. It includes both a best-practices section and an audit section.

> **NOTE**
> NIST SP 800 is a series of best-practices documents. The Web site (*http://csrc.nist.gov/*) is organized with the newest documents listed first. Lower-numbered items might still be current because revisions don't change the number.

- **ITIL**—ITIL is the Information Technology Infrastructure Library. It is a set of concepts and policies for managing information technology (IT) infrastructure, development, and operations. ITIL is published in a series of books, each covering a separate IT management topic. ITIL gives a detailed description of a number of important IT practices with comprehensive checklists, tasks, and procedures that any IT organization can tailor to its needs.

Other organizations, such as ISACA and the Institute of Internal Auditors, have developed commonly used audit guidelines. These organizations might develop a guideline in house or customize an audit plan used elsewhere. Here are two examples of these types of guidelines:

- **COBIT**—The Control Objectives for Information and related Technology (COBIT) is a set of best practices for IT management. It was created by the Information Systems Audit (ISA), the Control Association (ISACA), and the IT Governance Institute (ITGI) in 1996. COBIT gives managers, auditors, and IT users a set of generally accepted measures, indicators, processes, and best practices. You can use COBIT to help obtain the most benefit from the use of information technology and to develop appropriate IT governance and control in a company.
- **COSO**—The Institute of Internal Auditors (IIA) produces the Committee of Sponsoring Organizations (COSO) of the Treadway Commission. This volunteer-run organization gives guidance to executive management and governance entities on critical aspects of organizational governance, business ethics, internal control, enterprise risk management, fraud, and financial reporting. COSO has established a common internal control model. Many companies and other organizations use it to assess their control systems.

Unless a law or regulation prohibits it, organizations are free to choose whatever audit methods make the most sense to them. They might use one of the documents mentioned here, or they might use guidelines from another organization or trade group. They even might develop their own document. Whichever method fits your requirements best, ensure you have an audit method to follow before conducting your first audit.

Audit Data–Collection Methods

Before you can analyze data, you need to identify and collect it. There are many ways to collect data, including:

- **Questionnaires**—You can administer prepared questionnaires to both managers and users.
- **Interviews**—These are useful for gathering insight into operations from all parties. Interviews often prove to be valuable sources of information and recommendations.

- **Observation**—This refers to input used to differentiate between paper procedures and how the job is really done.
- **Checklists**—These prepared documents help ensure that the information-gathering process covers all areas.
- **Reviewing documentation**—This documentation assesses currency, adherence, and completeness.
- **Reviewing configurations**—This involves assessing change control procedures and the appropriateness of controls, rules, and layout.
- **Reviewing policy**—This involves assessing policy relevance, currency, and completeness.
- **Performing security testing**—This testing, **vulnerability testing** and **penetration testing**, involves gathering technical information to determine whether vulnerabilities exist in the security components, networks, or applications.

Areas of Security Audits

Part of the auditing process is to ensure that policy statements exist for all key areas. Auditors document any key areas that your policy does not address. After that, they check to see if all personnel are following policies, procedures, and standards.

You will need a password standard (minimum characters and complexity) and a password procedure (how to set, change, and reset passwords) to support your access control policy. Many organizations use their password policies as their system access policies. This is a dangerous mistake. You should develop a separate access control policy that says something similar to the following:

> "Authorized users should be able to do only that which they are authorized to do. Unauthorized users should be prohibited from doing anything."

Because passwords are so often the targets of attacks, the use of passwords is declining. Instead, many organizations are starting to use tokens, smart cards, or biometrics for authentication. As your IT environment changes, make sure your policies change, too. You don't want all access control policies to dictate password strength when half your systems are using smart cards. A thorough audit ensures that your security policy is up to date and reflects your current environment. You should identify and remove any policies that are out of date.

Table 7-1 shows several of the critical areas that you should include in a security audit.

Control Checks and Identity Management

It's important to ensure that your security controls are effective, reliable, and functioning as you intended. Without monitoring and reviewing, you have no assurance that your information security program is effective or that personnel are exercising due diligence.

TABLE 7-1 Areas that you should include in an audit plan.

AREA	AUDIT GOAL
Antivirus software	Up-to-date, universal application
System access policies	Current with technology
Intrusion-detection and event-monitoring systems	Log reviews
System-hardening policies	Ports, services
Cryptographic controls	Keys, usage (network encryption of sensitive data)
Contingency planning	Business continuity plan (BCP), disaster recovery plan (DRP), and continuity of operations plan (COOP)
Hardware and software maintenance	Maintenance agreements, servicing, forecasting of future needs
Physical security	Doors locked, power supplies monitored
Access control	Need-to-know, least privilege
Change control processes for configuration management	Documented, no unauthorized changes
Media protection	Age of media, labeling, storage, transportation

When auditing an identity-management system, you should focus on these key areas:

- **Approval process**—Who grants approval for access requests?
- **Authentication mechanisms**—What mechanisms are used for specific security requirements?
- **Password policy and enforcement**—Does the organization have an effective password policy and is it uniformly enforced?
- **Monitoring**—Does the organization have sufficient monitoring systems to detect unauthorized access?
- **Remote access systems**—Are all systems properly secured with strong authentication?

NOTE

The audit process should be a cooperative arrangement in which all parties work together to make your organization more secure. You should not view it as "us versus them." The auditors and the audited organization should both be working toward the same goal: a more secure environment.

Post-Audit Activities

After audit activities are completed, the auditors still have more work to do. Additional auditor tasks include exit interviews, data analysis, generation of the audit report, and a presentation of findings to management.

Exit Interview

The auditor performs an exit interview with key personnel to alert them to major issues and recommendations that will come later in the audit report. This enables management to respond quickly and act on serious issues. Aside from these early alerts, auditors should not provide details before the final report. They might give a false view of the organization's security preparedness.

> **NOTE**
> Auditors routinely talk with management during the audit to check what they are finding. Auditors make mistakes too, and this gives management the chance to correct misunderstandings and state their case before the auditors issue their final report.

Data Analysis

Auditors commonly analyze data they collect away from the organizational site. This enables the auditor to review everything learned and to present observations using a standard reporting format. Off-site analysis also enables auditors to remove themselves from the pressure often encountered while on site. Every organization wants to receive a positive audit report, and that desire sometimes translates into subtle pressure for an auditor. Performing data analysis at a different location from the audited organization can help encourage unbiased analysis.

Generation of Audit Report

Most audit reports contain at least three broad sections:

- **Findings**—These are often listed by level of compliance to the standard benchmark. The comparison of audit findings to a stated policy or industry best practices gives a picture of where the organization must improve.
- **Recommendations**—Auditors recommend how to fix the risks they have found. They also tell how the staff may not be complying with a policy or process. In most reports, the recommendations address the most important issues first. Audit recommendations should include the following:
    - **Timeline for implementation**—Change recommendations should not be open-ended. Each recommendation should have a suggested deadline.
    - **Level of risk**—The audit should make clear the level of risk the organization faces from each finding.
    - **Management response**—Auditors should give management an opportunity to respond to a draft copy of the audit report. They should then put that response in the final report. This response often clarifies issues and explains why controls were not used or why recommendations in the draft copy are not necessary. The response can also include action plans for fixing gaps in controls.
- **Follow-up**—When necessary, auditors should schedule a follow-up audit to ensure the organization has carried out recommendations.

> **NOTE**
> Most audit reports get right to the point. An audit report often begins with a summary followed by the details. The summary is often passed around, so be careful not to expose security weaknesses in it. You should include private or confidential information only in the details section of the report.

Presentation of Findings

When the auditors complete the audit report, they present their findings to the organization. Depending on your organization's structure and size, the findings presentation could be a formal meeting or it could be simply delivering the report to a single person. Regardless of how you receive the audit findings, it is important that the audited organization examine the report and make the necessary changes. The findings might lead to changes based on regulatory requirements or available budget.

Security Monitoring

The first goal of a security program is to detect abnormal behavior. After all, you can't respond to behavior that you can't detect! That's where security monitoring comes in. Security monitoring systems might be technical in nature, such as an intrusion detection system (IDS). Or they might be administrative—for example, observing employee or customer behavior on a closed-circuit TV.

When you detect abnormal or unacceptable behavior, the next step is to stop it. Stopping both overt and covert intrusive acts is both an art and a science. **Overt acts** are obvious and intentional. **Covert acts** are hidden and secret.

Many attackers will attempt to avoid detection controls you have in place. In fact, just the presence of security monitoring controls can deter many attackers. On the other hand, it is possible to have too many monitoring devices. Security monitoring must be obvious enough to discourage security breaches but adequately hidden so as not to be overbearing.

Some tools and techniques for security monitoring include the following:

- **Baselines**—In order to recognize something as abnormal, you first must know what normal looks like. Seeing a report that says a system's disk space is 80 percent full tells you nothing unless you know how much disk spaced was used yesterday or even last week. That is, a system that used an additional 1 percent of disk every week and just tipped the alarm is very different from a system that was at 40 percent for the last month but suddenly doubled in usage. Baselines are essential in security monitoring.
- **Alarms**—Alarms notify personnel of a possible security incident, much like a door-open alarm or a fire alarm. Be aware that employees will quickly ignore repeated false alarms. For example, if your neighbor's car alarm goes off repeatedly, you don't run to the window each time. That means employees will likely not respond to a real incident.
- **Closed-circuit TV**—Properly using closed-circuit TV involves monitoring and recording what the cameras see. You must ensure that the security officers monitoring the cameras are trained to watch for certain actions or behaviors. Some jurisdictions prohibit profiling on particular factors, such as race. Others have no such prohibitions. You must know your local laws.
- **Systems that spot irregular behavior**—Examples include IDSs and honeypots—that is, traps set to capture information about improper activity on a network.

Security Monitoring for Computer Systems

Just as there are many types of physical monitoring controls, there are also many ways to monitor computer and network system activity. You must select the controls that monitor the many aspects of your computing environment to detect malicious activity. Many tools exist to help you monitor your system's activities, both as they are occurring and after the fact.

Real-time monitoring provides information on what is happening as it happens. You can use the information from real time–monitoring controls to contain incidents and preserve your organization's business operations. A network intrusion detection system is one example of a real time–monitoring control. It monitors and captures network traffic as it travels throughout your network. Examples of this type of control include the following:

- **Host IDS**—A host intrusion detection system (HIDS) is excellent for "noticing" activity in a computer as the activity is happening. IDS rules help identify suspicious activity in near real time.
- **System integrity monitoring**—Systems such as Tripwire enable you to watch computer systems for unauthorized changes and report them to administrators in near real time.

Non-real-time monitoring keeps historical records of activity. You can use this type of monitoring when it's not as critical to detect and respond to incidents immediately. Examples of this type of control include the following:

- **Application logging**—All applications that access or modify sensitive data should have logs that record who used or changed the data and when. This allows proof of compliance with privacy regulations, investigation of errors or problems with records, and tracking of transactions.
- **System logging**—This type of logging provides records of who accessed the system and what actions they performed on the system.

Following is a partial list of activities that you need to log:

- **Host-based activity**—This includes changes to systems, access requests, performance, and startups and shutdowns.
- **Network and network devices**—This includes access, traffic type and patterns, malware, and performance.

Monitoring Issues

Logging does have its costs. Anytime you choose to log system or application activity, you have to store that information somewhere. Many organizations turn off logs because they produce too much information. After all, without enough staff to review the logs, what's the point of gathering all that data? Without a way to analyze log data automatically, logging just uses up disk space. It doesn't provide any value. Other challenges include the poor quality of the log data and the complexity of attacks. Often, it's difficult to see the value in eating up staff time to analyze logs.

Other monitoring issues that scare off some organizations from aggressive monitoring include the following:

- **Spatial distribution**—Attacks are difficult to catch with logs if they come from a variety of attackers across a wide area. To make matters worse, attackers can use a number of computers managed by different administrators and spread over a large area.
- **Switched networks**—It can be harder to capture traffic on networks that are very segmented through the use of switches and virtual LANs. It will take more work to reconstruct what actually happened from segmented log files.
- **Encryption**—Encrypting data makes logging more difficult because monitors can't see all the data to decide if it is suspicious. Unencrypted parts can be logged, but the rest is virtually invisible. You can encrypt data at various levels:
  - **Link layer encryption (wireless WEP and WPA)**—With this type of encryption, you encrypt everything above the Link layer.
  - **Network layer encryption (IPSec and some other tunneling protocols)**—With this type of encryption, you encrypt everything above the Network layer.
  - **Application layer encryption (SSL and SSH and others)**—This type of encryption encrypts above the Transport layer.

NOTE

Organizations should monitor traffic to ensure that all sensitive data is encrypted as it is transmitted through the network.

Logging Anomalies

One important aspect of monitoring is determining the difference between real attacks in log entries and activity that is merely noise or a minor event. In doing this, monitors of all types make two basic types of mistakes:

- **False positives**—Also known as Type I errors, **false positives** are alerts that seem malicious yet are not real security events. These false alarms are distractions that waste administrative effort. Too many false alarms cause the administrator to ignore real attacks. To combat this, you might decide not to record infrequent or human-error "attacks." You can do this by creating **clipping levels** that ignore an event unless it happens often or meets some other predefined criteria. For example, a failed logon attempt should not be of much interest unless it occurs several times in a short period. A common clipping level for failed logons is five. That means the system will trigger an alarm anytime a user logon fails five times in a row. Clipping levels help reduce the number of false positive errors.
- **False negatives**—The other type of monitoring error is a failure of the control to catch suspicious behavior. **False negatives**, also known as Type II errors, are the failure of the alarm system to detect a serious event. Perhaps the event went unnoticed, or maybe the alarm was fooled into thinking the event was not serious when in fact it was. In some monitoring controls, false negatives are a result of the control being configured incorrectly. The control should be more sensitive to the environment and report more suspect activity.

Log Management

Logging is a central activity for security personnel. Log files can help provide evidence of normal and abnormal system activity. They can also provide valuable information on how well your controls are doing their jobs. The security and systems administrators must consider several things to ensure you are keeping the right information and that information is secure.

First, you should store logs in a central location to protect them and to keep them handy for thorough analysis. Have lots of storage space and monitor your log-file disk-space requirements. If a log file fills up, you're faced with three bad choices:

- Stop logging
- Overwrite the oldest entries
- Stop processing (controlled or crash)

Attackers sometimes purposely fill a log to cause one of these failures. The storage device for your log files must be large enough to prevent this. In addition, your logging settings must not impose artificially low log-file size constraints.

> **NOTE**
>
> To find a list of NTP servers, see Microsoft Knowledge Base article 262680 (*http://support.microsoft.com/kb/262680*).

To link activities between systems and logs, computers and devices on your network must have synchronized clocks. Network Time Protocol (NTP) synchronizes time for all computers and devices that support it. Most modern routers and servers do this. International government-run NTP servers provide an unbiased third party to supply the time.

To prevent overwriting or modification, some systems write logs to a CD-ROM or other write-only device. Protecting logs from modification or read access makes it hard for an attacker to clean up traces of the attack. Log files that are easy to access make it easy for an attacker to remove log-file entries linked to the attack. Log files also often contain confidential information about users or information, which you might need. You must ensure that you protect all your log files from unauthorized access, deletion, or changes.

> **Keeping Log Files**
>
> Regulation, policy, or log volume might dictate how much log information you keep. If a log file is subject to litigation, you must keep it until the case is over. If litigation is not under way, a company can make its own decisions about log quantity and retention. Exceptions to that may be based on laws or regulations. Once litigation begins, providing the data in those logs is a costly process that the company must bear. A company can lower litigation costs by limiting the quantity of data collected in logs only to what is needed and keeping it only for as long as it is likely to be useful.
>
> In some cases, regulations may specify how long you must keep data. For example, the Payment Card Industry Data Security Standard (PCI DSS) requires that logs be kept for at least one year. It's best to have a written retention standard. That way, if necessary, you can explain in court that you deleted logs as part of your normal business practice rather than appearing to have done so in an attempt to destroy evidence.

FIGURE 7-3

Types of log information.

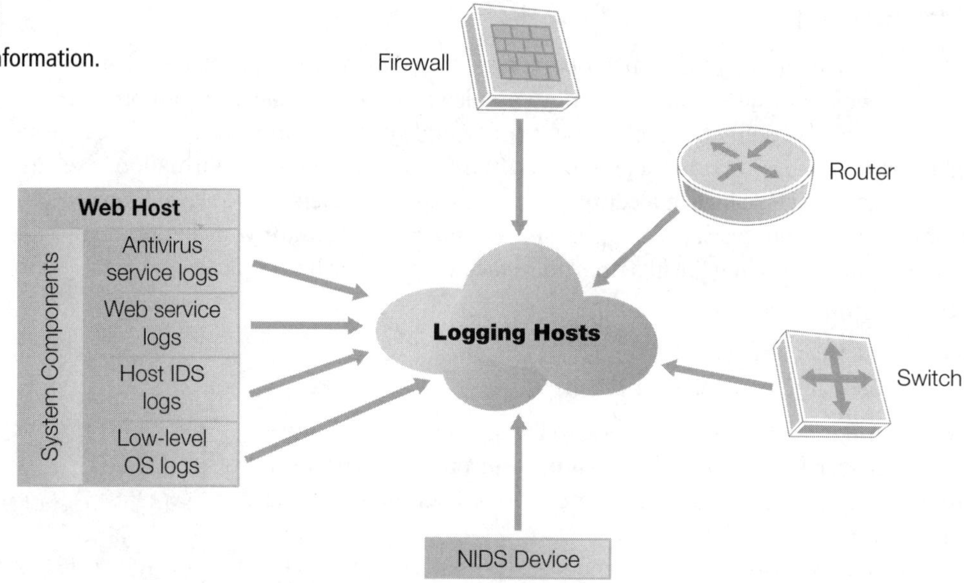

Types of Log Information to Capture

Your organization might need a large number of logs to record all the activity on your systems, networks, and applications. As shown in Figure 7-3, you should record all suspicious activity, errors, unauthorized access attempts, and access to sensitive information. As a result, you will not only track incidents but also keep your users accountable for their activities.

The **Security Information and Event Management (SIEM) system** helps organizations manage the explosive growth of their log files. It provides a common platform to capture and analyze entries. Organizations collect log data from sources such as firewalls, IDSs/IPSs, Web servers, and database servers. In addition, many organizations have multiple brands or versions of these systems. SIEM collection and analysis devices take the log data in whatever format it is created in, from whatever device creates it, and standardize it into a common format. The system stores the standard log messages in a database for easy access. You can run SIEM vendor-supplied reports or custom reports against those databases to access and analyze your log-file information.

As operating-system, application-software, and network-device vendors change products, the new log-file formats may be different from previous products. If your organization uses a SIEM system to handle your log files, such format changes aren't critical. You can merge files from the new products into the same database without limiting the ability to produce reports that cover the before-and-after time period.

SIEM systems monitor user activity and ensure that users act only in accordance with policy. That means SIEM systems are a valuable method of ensuring regulatory compliance. They can also integrate with identity-management schemes to ensure that only current user accounts are active on the system.

How to Verify Security Controls

One specific class of monitoring controls can provide a very good layer of security. This class of controls monitors network and system activity to detect unusual or suspicious behavior. Some controls in this class can even respond to detected suspicious activity and possibly stop an attack in progress. Controls that monitor activity include intrusion detection systems (IDSs), intrusion prevention systems (IPSs), and firewalls.

Intrusion Detection System (IDS)

Layered defense requires multiple controls to prevent attacks. One of the most common layered-defense mechanisms is to place an IDS behind a firewall to provide increased security. A network intrusion detection system (NIDS) monitors traffic that gets through the firewall to detect malicious activity. A host-based intrusion detection system (HIDS)—covered later in this chapter—does the same for traffic aimed at a particular computer or device. Because the HIDS sees a narrower view, you can tune it to detect very specific activities. Unlike the NIDS, the HIDS will also see traffic that originates inside the perimeter. Figure 7-4 shows a network with a NIDS and a HIDS device.

As shown in Figure 7-5, you can connect a NIDS to a switch or hub. The IDS then captures all traffic on the switch and analyzes it to detect unauthorized activity. You can do this analysis in several ways, depending on the type of engine in the IDS.

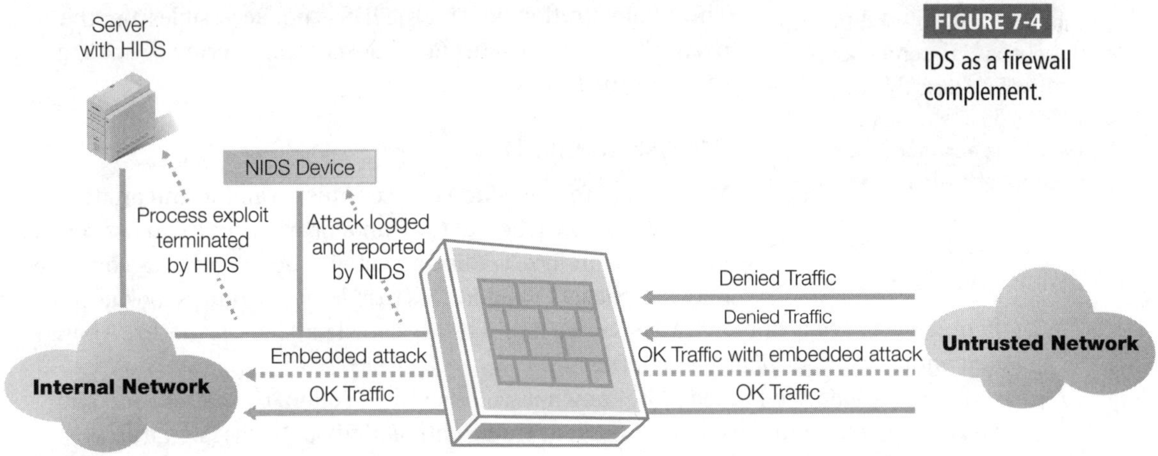

FIGURE 7-4
IDS as a firewall complement.

FIGURE 7-5
Basic NIDS.

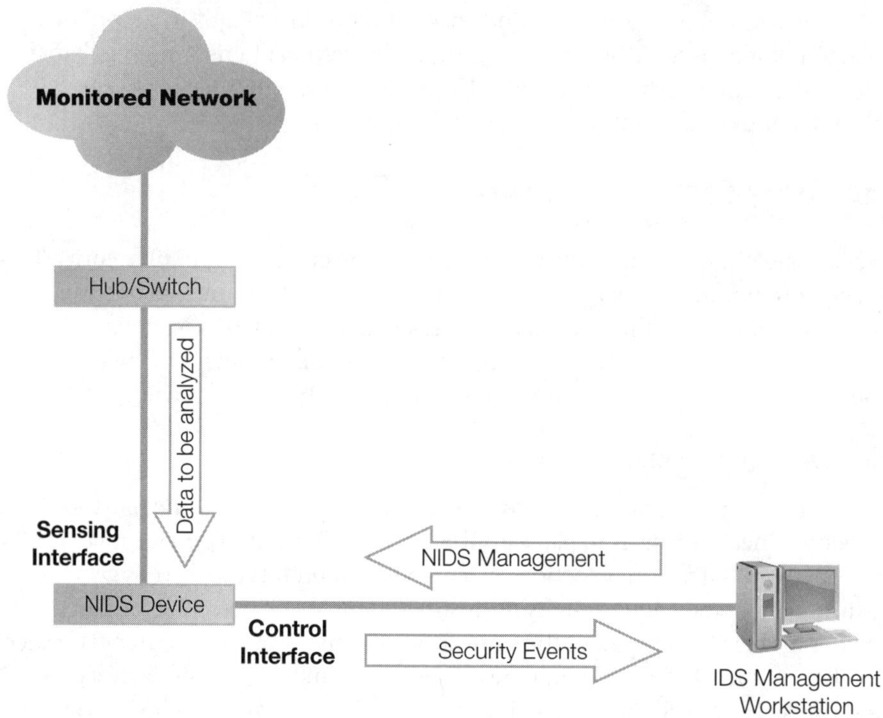

> **NOTE**
> Administrators commonly configure a NIDS without an IP address on its monitoring port. That makes it extremely difficult for the outsider to send packets to or otherwise directly address the NIDS. Administrators reach the device via another interface, which should be on a different subnet. For more information on this, see Chapter 10.

You connect the IDS to a management console that lets the administrator monitor and manage it. Ideally, the IDS will not be detectable from the network. That means attackers will not be able to determine where the IDS is positioned on the network. The administration port on the IDS is not accessible from the network, which prevents an attacker from altering the configuration of the IDS.

Analysis Methods

Monitoring and detection devices must examine and analyze activity to know when to raise an alarm. Devices can use several methods to analyze traffic and activity. Some methods compare network packets or addresses to rules while others look at the frequency and type of activity. These two methods are called pattern- (signature-) based and anomaly- (statistical-) based IDSs.

Pattern- (signature-) based IDSs, known as rule-based detection, use pattern matching and stateful matching to compare current traffic with activity patterns (signatures) of known network attacks. Pattern-matching systems scan packets to see whether specific byte sequences, known as signatures, match the signature of known attacks.

Often, the patterns are related to a certain service and port (source or destination). To avoid this type of control and attempt to escape detection, many attackers change their attacks. You must frequently update your signature files to ensure you can detect the latest known attacks. **Stateful matching** improves on simple pattern matching. It looks for specific sequences appearing across several packets in a traffic stream rather than just in individual packets. Although more detailed than pattern matching, stateful matching can still produce false positives. Like pattern matching, stateful matching can detect only known attacks. It needs frequent signature updates.

> **NOTE**
> False positives are a problem with pattern matching because these systems report close matches, particularly if the pattern lacks granularity—for example, if it's not unique.

Anomaly-based IDSs, sometimes called profile-based systems, compare current activity with stored profiles of normal (expected) activity. These are only as accurate as the accuracy of your definition of "normal activity." Once you define normal system operation, the IDS compares current activity to what you consider normal activity. Anything the IDS considers abnormal is a candidate for analysis and response. The more common methods of detecting anomalies include the following:

- **Statistical-based methods**—These develop baselines of normal traffic and network activity. The device creates an alert when it identifies a deviation. These can catch unknown attacks, but false positives often happen because identifying normal activity is hard.
- **Traffic-based methods**—These signal an alert when they identify any unacceptable deviation from expected behavior based on traffic. They can also detect unknown attacks and floods.
- **Protocol patterns**—Another way to identify attacks without a signature is to look for deviations from protocols. Protocol standards are provided by Requests for Comments (RFCs) memorandums published by the Internet Engineering Task Force (IETF). You can get more information on RFCs at *http://www.ietf.org/rfc.html.* This type of detection works for well-defined protocols, but may cause false positives for protocols that are not well defined.

HIDS

HIDS technology adds to your entire system's protection by keeping watch over sensitive processes inside a computer, also called a host. HIDS systems generally have the following qualities:

- They are usually software processes or services designed to run on server computers.
- They intercept and examine system calls or specific processes (database and Web servers, for example) for patterns or behaviors that should not normally be allowed.
- HIDS daemons can take a predefined action such as stopping or reporting the infraction.

HIDS also have a different point of view than the NIDS. A HIDS can detect inappropriate traffic that originates inside the network. It can also recognize an anomaly that is specific to a particular machine or user. For example, a single user on a high-volume mail server might originate 10 times the normal number of messages for a user in any day (or hour). The HIDS will notice and issue an alert, but a NIDS may not notice a reportable event. To the NIDS, it just looks like increased network traffic.

Layered Defense: Network Access Control

The best defense is to have multiple layers of controls in place. This increases the chances that you'll protect your systems from more attacks than with just a single control. Figure 7-6 shows how network devices work in multiple layers to try to prevent an attack on the internal protected network. The router detects and filters out some traffic, and the firewall detects and stops unwanted traffic.

Control Checks: Intrusion Detection

A NIDS is an important component in any multilayered defense strategy. Figure 7-7 shows how a NIDS can monitor outside attacks as well as insider misuse. A NIDS outside the network gives some idea of the types of attacks faced by the firewall. The internal NIDS detects the types of attacks that may get by the firewall. You can also install this device as an IPS. That way, the device can not only detect a potential attack, but also change its rules to filter traffic to stop the attack. These devices also work well with HIDS devices. While the NIDS helps protect your system from malicious network traffic, the HIDS will see the types of activity being attempted on the host itself.

FIGURE 7-6

Layered network devices trying to prevent an attack on the internal protected network.

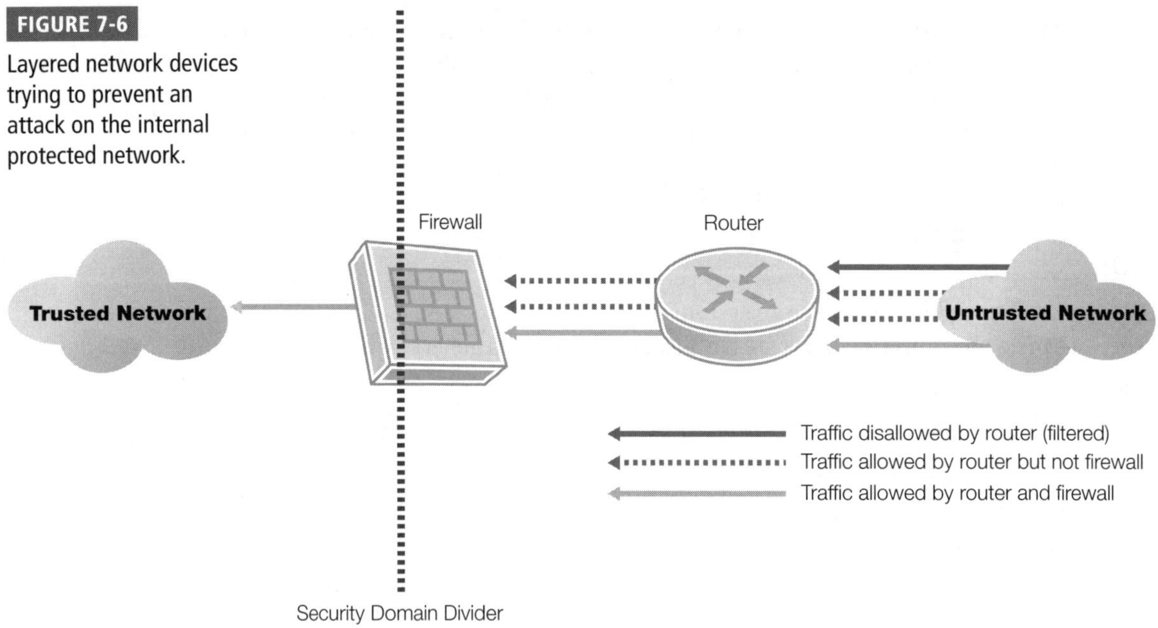

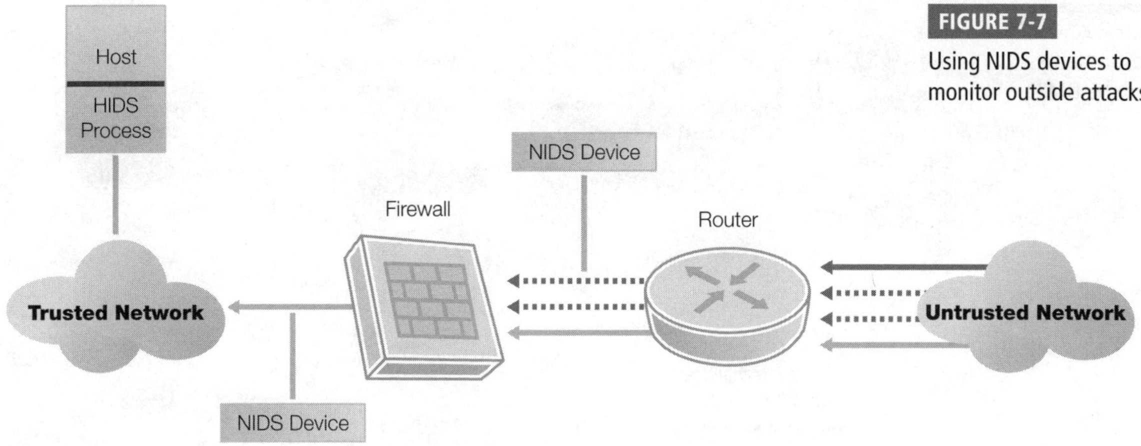

FIGURE 7-7
Using NIDS devices to monitor outside attacks.

Host Isolation

Some servers, or hosts, must be open to the Internet. Web servers are examples of such hosts. You want any user to be able to access your Web server—but you don't want everyone to be able to get to your internal network. A simple solution is to isolate the hosts connected to the Internet from the rest of your network. Host isolation isolates one or more host computers from your internal networks and creates a demilitarized zone (DMZ). Figure 7-8 shows a DMZ with two isolated hosts. A DMZ is a physical or logical subnetwork that contains and exposes an organization's external services to a larger untrusted network, usually the Internet. Outside traffic from the untrusted Internet is allowed only into the DMZ, where it can get to certain company services. The Web applications in the DMZ then access the trusted internal network, but prevent the outside user from getting directly to the internal network.

System Hardening

No computer is completely secure. In fact, very few operating systems or application software packages are secure when you install them. It is important that security administrators go through a process, called hardening, to change hardware and software configurations to make computers and devices as secure as possible. A computer or device with a **hardened configuration** is one on which you have turned off or disabled unnecessary services and protected the ones that are still running. Hardening also requires you to apply the latest software patches available. You should secure all computers and devices from any unauthorized modification. Harden all systems before implementing them. Failure to harden a system before you put it into production almost certainly will result in its compromise.

FIGURE 7-8

Host isolation and the DMZ.

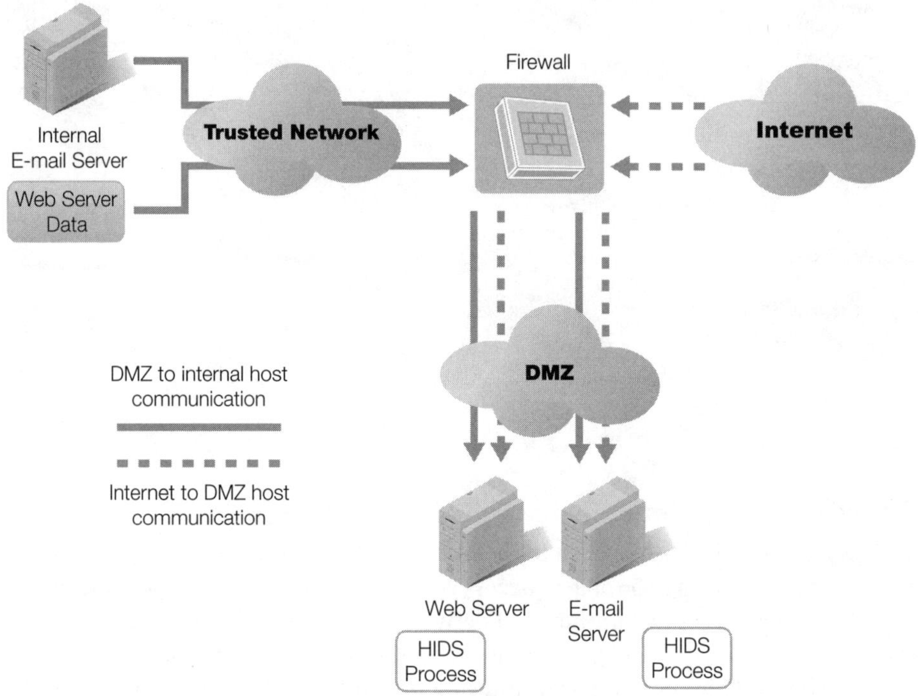

Set a Baseline Configuration

After hardening a computer or device, you must record the hardened configuration settings. That way, you can compare the hardened configuration against known secure configurations. You can also compare the configuration settings in the future with the original settings to see if anything has changed. Creating a baseline makes it easy to ensure security is consistent between the various systems. When it is easy to define standard settings, you can more easily control individual system differences. For example, you can decide whether to allow certain services or applications on an individual computer if you know its basic configuration meets your standards.

Disable Unnecessary Services

One of the easiest and most effective steps to harden computers is to shut down unneeded services and programs. Attackers know that most computers run more services and programs than they really need. For example, many server computers run Web servers even if they don't host a Web site. Attackers search for these unneeded services and try to exploit vulnerabilities in them. You should disable unnecessary services. Even better, uninstall services you don't need. Attackers can't attack programs that aren't there. Close unneeded firewall ports and restrict certain services, such as mobile code, telnet, and FTP. You should configure firewalls to deny anything not specifically allowed. This will stop attackers from secretly adding new and unexpected services.

You should harden all routers and other network devices, too. Protect against unauthorized administrator access and changes to router tables. Network devices ship with either no passwords or default passwords. You should change the default passwords before connecting any device to your network. You manage these device passwords like all passwords. They should be complex and changed regularly. You must document any changes to network devices and log the user ID of the administrator making the changes. You should examine all configuration logs on a regular basis, perhaps by a SIEM implementation.

Servers and network devices aren't the only items you need to harden. Don't forget about workstations. Workstations need a standard configuration and access controls. Organizations should have a hardened image for workstations. You can create a standard image by installing a fresh copy of an operating system and hardening it. Remove unnecessary services and add security products such as antivirus software and personal firewalls. The image also should contain company-standard software such as a word processor, spreadsheet, and browser plug-ins. When you verify that the image meets your organization's standards for workstations, you can use the image as a starting point for all new desktops and laptops. This process can help ensure security compliance and reduce maintenance time.

Physically protect servers, perhaps behind locked doors. Make sure all computers and devices have the latest patches applied. You can use third-party patch-management software to track patches issued by all vendors of all products installed on a company's computers and devices. Some products even have automatic "phone-home" patch management.

In most cases, the best solution for servers exposed to the Internet is to make sure you don't use those servers for any other purpose. For example, a computer that is located in your DMZ and functions as a Web server should not provide any other services.

Review Antivirus Program

An audit of the system should include a review of the antivirus and other anti-malware programs your organization uses. This review should ensure that all software products and their data are up to date. Perform antivirus scans periodically on all network devices and computers. Schedule a full scan of all systems on a regular basis. Scan all application servers, workstations, and gateways.

Monitoring and Testing Security Systems

Securing a closed environment is difficult. Your main goal as a security professional is to protect your organization's sensitive data from attackers. As hard as it is to secure a closed system, the job becomes far more difficult when your network connects to the Internet. Just by connecting to the Internet, you roll out a red carpet for attackers. Your job is to deploy strategies to control access to your systems. Keep in mind that completely securing your system is impossible. Although there are many risks associated with information security, two of the most common risks are as follows:

- Attackers who come in from outside, with unauthorized access, malicious code, Trojans, and malware
- Sensitive information leaking from inside the organization to unauthorized people who can damage your organization

Monitoring

How can you prevent the leakage of sensitive information from your organization? There is no fail-safe method, but monitoring is key. Of course, you can't watch every IP packet on your system. Even if you could train humans to do this mind-numbingly boring work, you wouldn't be able to put enough people on it to keep up. Instead, you must monitor your traffic with an IDS. The premise behind IDS is that you identify abnormal traffic for further investigation. IPSs go a step beyond IDSs by actively blocking malicious traffic. An IDS alerts you to potentially unauthorized activity; an IPS will block it. Of course, before you can use an IDS or an IPS, you must create a baseline definition of normal traffic.

Testing

In addition to monitoring your system, you must test it. The main purpose of any security test is to identify uncorrected vulnerabilities on a system. A system might have been secure at one time, but the addition of a new service or application might have made the system vulnerable. The point of testing is to discover new vulnerabilities so you can address them. Figure 7-9 shows the main goals of security testing.

FIGURE 7-9

Security testing.

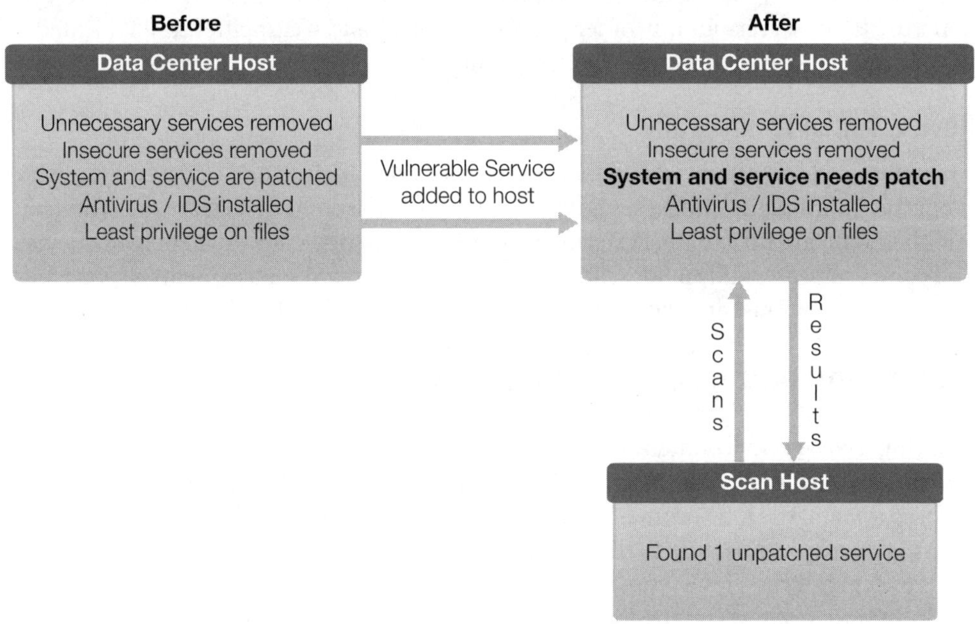

The frequency of your testing depends on such factors as the volatility (rate of changes) of the system and the sensitivity or criticality of the system. Also, policy and regulation often mandate tests. A few of the most common test-schedule trigger points are as follows:

- During the security certification phase
- After major system changes (new technology upgrades, application changes)
- New threats
- During system audits
- Periodically, depending on the nature of the system
- Once a year on critical systems

If none of the other items on the list triggers a test, you should do one at least once a year. Some companies might choose shorter or longer testing intervals, depending on a risk analysis.

A Testing Road Map

No perfect solution exists when it comes to testing, and not every security professional will follow the same path. Figure 7-10 shows a road map for security testing. As shown in the figure, security testing consists of a few common activities that give you a complete view of your system's security. The most common activities include the following:

- **Reconnaissance**—**Reconnaissance** involves reviewing the system to learn as much as possible about the organization, its systems, and its networks. Public resources for the job, such as WHOIS and Dig, are invisible to network administrators—this is a problem when they are used by attackers instead of penetration testers.
- **Network mapping**—This phase uses tools to determine the layout and services running on the organization's systems and networks.
- **Vulnerability testing**—Vulnerability testing involves finding all the weaknesses in a system and determining which places may be attack points.
- **Penetration testing**—In this phase, you try to exploit a weakness in the system and prove that an attacker could successfully penetrate it.
- **Mitigation activities**—**Mitigation activities** reduce or address vulnerabilities found in either penetration tests or vulnerability tests.

> **NOTE**
>
> Vulnerability testing tries to find a system's weaknesses. Penetration testing is a focused attack to exploit a discovered vulnerability. Attackers follow the same steps as penetration testers; the difference between the two is that attackers don't have your consent to penetrate the system.

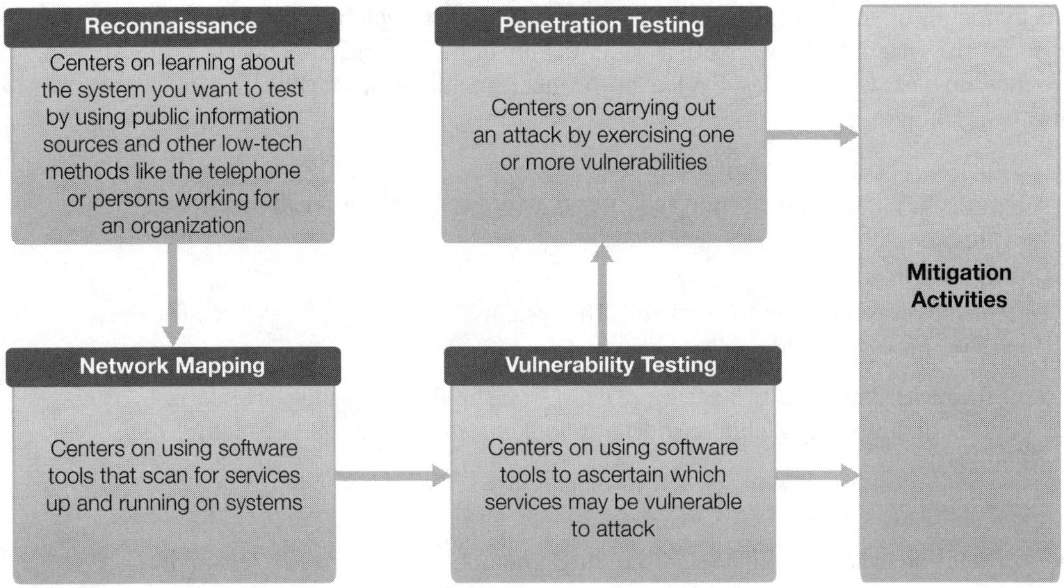

FIGURE 7-10

Security testing might take several paths.

Establishing Testing Goals

Before you run your testing procedures, it's important that you establish your testing goals. Security testing is most concerned with evaluating how well your controls address vulnerabilities. First, identify vulnerabilities and rank them according to how critical they are to your systems. Next, document a point-in-time (snapshot) test for comparison to other time periods. You want to ensure your security controls are working properly regardless of the time of day or volume of activity. Then, prepare for auditor review. This enables your IT staff to tune and test their own procedures using vulnerability analysis in preparation for "real" audits. Finally, find the gaps in your security. This enables covert testers (discussed in a moment) to determine the likelihood of system compromise and intrusion detection.

Reconnaissance Methods

Reconnaissance is the first and most basic of many tests. In the reconnaissance phase, you gather information through techniques such as social engineering or by researching the organization's Web site. Attackers use as many types of reconnaissance as possible to gather information about an organization. You should understand what these attackers are doing and then limit their ability to gather information about you.

Social engineering is a fancy phrase for lying. It involves tricking someone into sharing confidential information or gaining access to sensitive systems. In many cases, the attacker never comes face to face with the victim. Instead, the attacker might phone an employee and pose as a system administrator. All too often, attackers trick employees into sharing sensitive information. After all, employees think, what's wrong with giving your password to an administrator? You should train your users to recognize social-engineering attacks.

Another reconnaissance tool is the WHOIS service. This service provides information that can help attackers, such as names and phone numbers of administrators. Figure 7-11 shows the output from a WHOIS request.

A **zone transfer** is a unique query of a DNS server that asks it for the contents of its zone. The zone is the domain that the server manages. Administrators often use this to synchronize DNS servers within the same organization. If you allow zone transfers without restriction, attackers can use this information to try to figure out the names and types of servers that reside both inside and outside your network. The best defense from this type of information leakage is to lock down your DNS server.

> **NOTE**
> Organizations should be very careful to avoid letting their domain-name registration lapse. Someone else might scoop it up and use it as his or her own. Such an action could cause great cost to the organization's reputation. This type of social engineering is a bit more sophisticated than the run-of-the-mill variety.

WHOIS Search Results

WHOIS Record for

networksolutions.com Back-order this name

```
Registrant:
Network Solutions Registrar (NETWORKSOLUTIONS5-DOM)
  505 Huntmar Park Drive
  Herndon, VA 20170-5142
  US

  Domain Name: NETWORKSOLUTIONS.COM

  Administrative Contact:
    Network Solutions, Inc (NSOL-NOC)          customerservice@networksolutions.com
    Network Solutions, Inc
    21355 Ridgetop Circle
    Dulles, VA 20166
    US
    888-642-9675 fax: 703-326-7000
  Technical Contact:
    idNames Technical Mgr. (ITM-ORG)           tech@IDNAMES.COM
    idNames from Network Solutions, Inc.
    440 Benmar
    Suite #3325
    Houston, TX 77060
    US
    281-447-1044
    Fax- - 281-447-1160

  Record expires on 27-Apr-2011.
  Record created on 27-Apr-1998.
  Database last updated on 9-May-2003 11:19:06 EDT.

  Domain servers in listed order:

  NS1.NETSOL.COM        216.168.229.228
  NS2.NETSOL.COM        216.168.254.69
  NS3.NETSOL.COM        216.168.229.229
```

FIGURE 7-11
WHOIS search results.

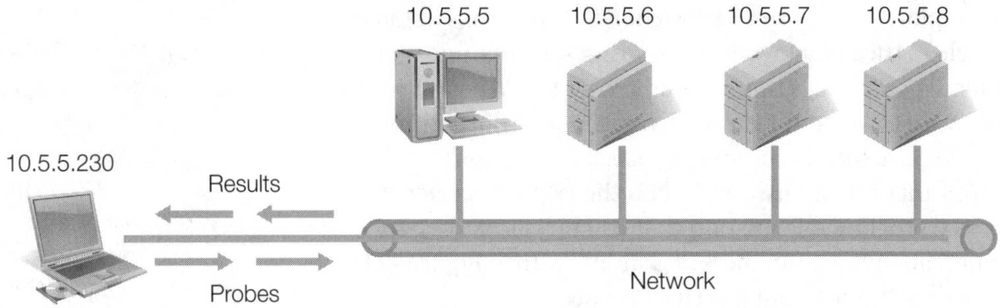

Host Name	IP	Services	OS
user-5	10.5.5.5	http, netbios, ftp	Windows NT4
server-6	10.5.5.6	http, netbios	Windows 2000
server-7	10.5.5.7	telnet, smtp	Linux
server-8	10.5.5.8	dns, finger, telnet	Solaris

FIGURE 7-12

Network mapping.

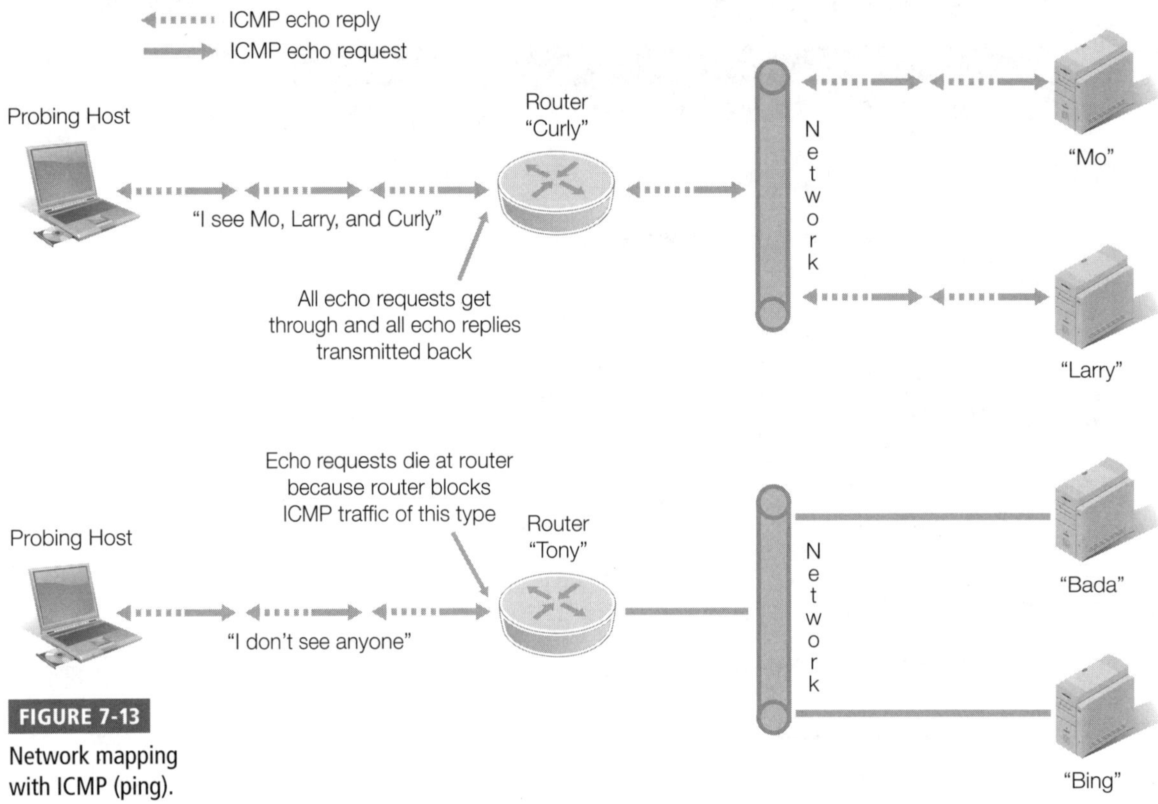

FIGURE 7-13

Network mapping with ICMP (ping).

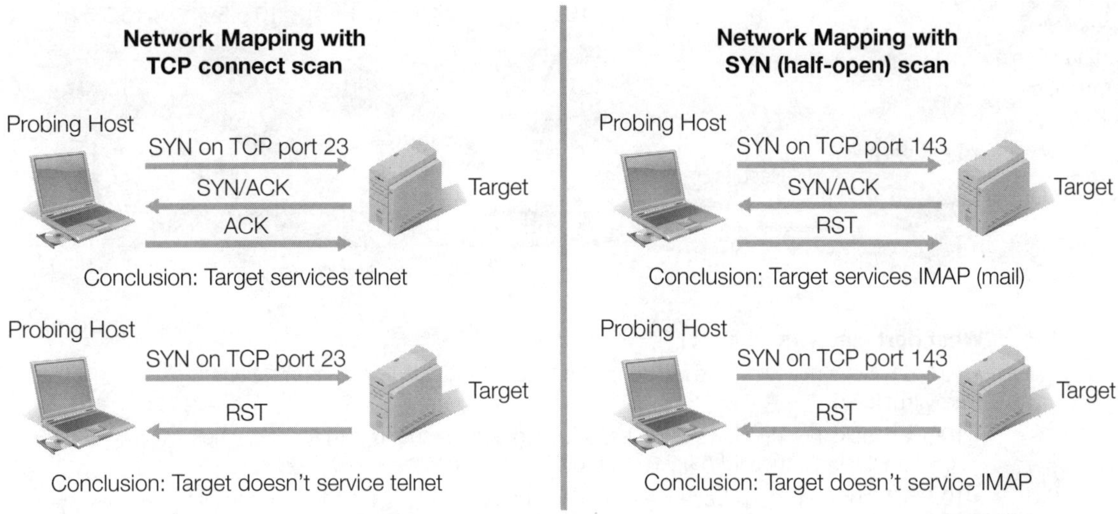

FIGURE 7-14

Network mapping with TCP/SYN scans.

Network-Mapping Methods

Network mapping is an extended type of reconnaissance. Network mapping discovers details about a network, including its hosts and host addresses as well as available services. This might enable attackers to identify certain types of systems, applications, services, and configurations. Figure 7-12 shows some of the information network mapping may provide.

An attacker can use ICMP (ping) packets to discover a network layout. This gives the attacker an advantage in setting up an attack. As shown in Figure 7-13, blocking ping packets, as seen with the Tony router, can prevent the attacker from learning about the network. Of course, this also prevents the administrator from being able to use this valuable tool for network troubleshooting.

Figure 7-14 shows how an attacker can discover the services available on a target host using TCP/SYN scans. The attacker sends packets to common ports and can determine from the response whether the host accepts these services.

Attackers need to know what operating system a potential victim is running. The approach to attacking a system differs based on the target operating system. With **operating system fingerprinting**, an attacker uses port mapping to learn which operating system and version is running on a computer. This can also help an attacker discover computers that might be vulnerable because they don't have patches or may have known exploits. Figure 7-15 shows how operating system fingerprinting can provide attackers with valuable information.

FIGURE 7-15
Operating system fingerprinting.

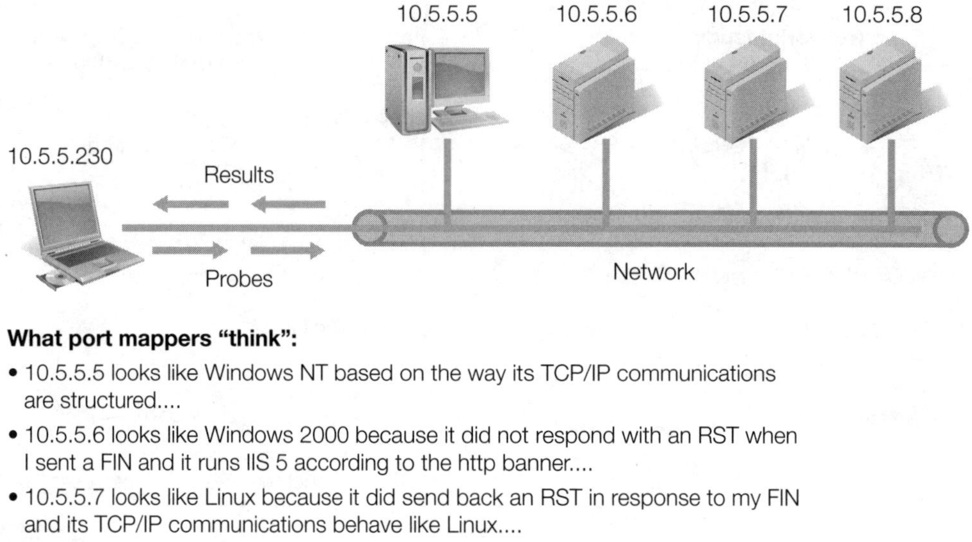

Covert Versus Overt Testers

You can carry out security testing—which can involve both internal and external staff—overtly or covertly. Which personnel and methods you use might depend on regulations or on the skill level of internal staff. Figure 7-16 shows the different types of testers.

Regardless who does the testing, you must consider the potential impact of testing activities:

- **Be aware of the potential for harm**—Some tests might crash a system. Other tests will have little effect. Ensure that all potentially affected parties are aware of which tests you will conduct. Make sure you have agreement from all parties if any tests may cause services interruptions or difficulties. Always make plans to recover if the tests—even the safe tests—crash a system.

FIGURE 7-16
Covert versus overt testers.

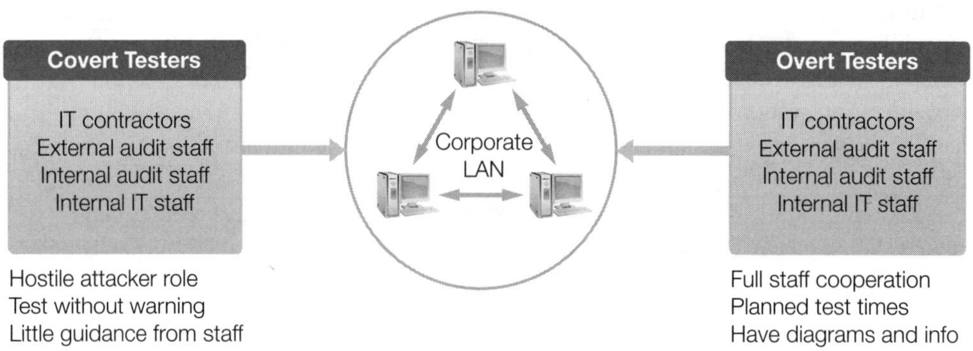

- **Be aware of the time of day and the day of week**—Although it is tempting to test during low-volume times because it won't affect as many users, it might not be a realistic scenario. An alternative is to do more dangerous tests during off times and safer tests during high-volume hours.

Testing Methods

Black-box testing uses test methods that aren't based directly on knowledge of a program's architecture or design. The term implies that either the tester does not have the source code or the details of the source code are not relevant to what is being tested. Put another way, black-box testing focuses on the externally visible behavior of the software. For example, it may be based on requirements, protocol specifications, APIs, or even attempted attacks.

In contrast, **white-box testing** is based on knowledge of the application's design and source code. In fact, white-box tests are generally derived from source code. For example, these tests might target specific constructs found in the source code or try to achieve a certain level of code coverage.

Gray-box testing lies somewhere between black-box testing and white-box testing. It uses limited knowledge of the program's internals. In principle, this might mean the tester knows about some parts of the source code and not others. In practice, it usually just means that the tester has access to design documents that are more detailed than specifications or requirements. For example, the tests might be based on an architecture diagram or a state-based model of the program's behavior.

Security Testing Tips and Techniques

Before you start the testing process, consider these points:

- **Choose the right tool**—Which tools are best for testing your software depends on what is to be tested and how the test plan indicates the tests should be carried out. Keep in mind that tool functions often overlap.
- **Tools make mistakes**—You should view preliminary results with skepticism. Watch for false positives or false negatives. Tool results can vary because detection methods often are not consistent.
- **Protect your systems**—Carrying out tests at the wrong time or in the wrong way can damage systems. Take care to protect your systems.
- **Tests should be as "real" as possible**—Tests should run against production networks and systems to the degree that is possible without impairing system operations. Consider these points when attempting to make your tests as real as possible:
  - You should first run a series of tests that are not likely to crash or have a major impact on a system. Then fix the vulnerabilities those tests detect. After that, you can run tests that might interrupt normal operation during times when an interruption would have the least impact.

- On the most critical systems, you may be able to run these tests at the same time as business continuity plan testing. For example, test at the alternate site or test at the primary site after successfully running the full interruption test, but while still operating at the alternate site.
- Decide whether to include social engineering as part of the penetration test. The tester and management will decide if the test should be limited to technical (remote) means or if the tester should try to take advantage of human behavior to get access. Social engineering tests can be difficult to carry out but can reveal additional vulnerabilities if done well.

CHAPTER SUMMARY

In this chapter, you learned about security auditing. You learned how it's used to help you create safer systems. You explored why you need these audits and how they create a culture of responsibility and accountability. You discovered how to define your auditing plan, including its scope, and how it works to develop secure systems. You learned about auditing benchmarks, and how they help to create the basis for your auditing plan. You also learned about data-collection methods, including how they help you gather information you need to perform a quality audit. You also studied post-audit activities and how they help you complete the process. You explored log collection and analysis, including how they help you monitor your systems. You also learned about log management. You developed an understanding of the types of log information you should capture and the tools that can help you capture it effectively. Finally, you explored monitoring and testing security systems.

KEY CONCEPTS AND TERMS

Anomaly-based IDS
Benchmark
Black-box testing
Clipping levels
Covert act
False negative
False positive
Gray-box testing
Hardened configuration
Mitigation activities
Network mapping
Operating system fingerprinting
Overt act
Pattern- (signature-) based IDS
Penetration testing
Real-time monitoring
Reconnaissance
Security Information and Event Management (SIEM) system
Stateful matching
Vulnerability testing
White-box testing
Zone transfer

CHAPTER 7 ASSESSMENT

1. When you use a control that costs more than the risk involved, you're making a poor management decision.
   A. True
   B. False

2. Which of the following is an example of a level of permissiveness?
   A. Prudent
   B. Permissive
   C. Promiscuous
   D. Paranoid
   E. All of the above

3. An audit examines whether security controls are appropriate, installed correctly, and ________.
   A. Current
   B. Addressing their purpose
   C. Authorized
   D. Cost-effective

4. A ________ is a standard used to measure how effective your system is as it relates to industry expectations.
   A. Control objective
   B. Configuration
   C. Benchmark
   D. Policy

5. Post-audit activities include which of the following?
   A. Presenting findings to management
   B. Data analysis
   C. Exit interviews
   D. Reviewing of auditor's findings
   E. All of the above

6. Some of the tools and techniques used in security monitoring include baselines, alarms, closed-circuit TV, and honeypots.
   A. True
   B. False

7. ________ is used when it's not as critical to detect and respond to incidents immediately.
   A. Non-real-time monitoring
   B. A logical access control
   C. Real-time monitoring
   D. None of the above

8. A common platform for capturing and analyzing log entries is ________.
   A. Intrusion detection system (IDS)
   B. Honeypot
   C. Security Information and Event Management (SIEM)
   D. HIPAA

9. In ________ methods, the IDS compares current traffic with activity patterns consistent with those of a known network intrusion via pattern matching and stateful matching.
   A. Signature-based
   B. Anomaly-based
   C. Heuristic scanning
   D. All of the above

10. Host isolation is the isolation of internal networks and the establishment of a(n) ________.
    A. HIDS
    B. DMZ
    C. IDS
    D. IPS

11. A hardened configuration is a system that has had unnecessary services enabled.
    A. True
    B. False

12. The review of the system to learn as much as possible about the organization, its systems, and networks is known as ________.
    A. Penetration testing
    B. Vulnerability testing
    C. Network mapping
    D. Reconnaissance

CHAPTER 8

Risk, Response, and Recovery

ORGANIZATIONS MUST CONSTANTLY cope with change. Shareholders exert new pressures. Governments pass new legislation and set new standards. Organizations must maintain supply chains linking their suppliers and their customers. Your organization develops strategies to meet its business goals and to remain competitive. Changing these strategies might require shifting personnel, altering the IT organization, and rearranging logistics. Any of these changes can increase risk. The structure of your organization also reflects its culture. Likewise, the culture affects your organization's commitment to protecting information systems as well as people, processes, data, and technology.

How your organization responds to risk reflects the value it puts on its assets. If the risk isn't considered serious, your organization isn't likely to spend a lot to reduce it. The amount of money your organization is willing to spend to protect sensitive data affects the risk. Perhaps your organization understands a risk is important, but it simply doesn't have enough to spend to reduce risk. Or perhaps your organization has a disposable culture. That means it seeks only short-term gains and will cease operation under adversity. If so, it will take only essential steps to meet minimum required standards. If, however, your organization is committed to long-term success, it will invest in cost-effective plans to reduce risk. Either strategy might be right for a particular organization. The only mistake is not matching spending on risk to the company's culture. For example, a disposable organization should not invest in a sustainable plan, and vice versa.

Chapter 8 Topics

This chapter covers the following topics and concepts:

- How risk management relates to data security
- What the process of risk management is
- What a risk analysis is
- What the differences are between the quantitative and qualitative approaches to risk analysis
- How to develop a strategy for dealing with risk
- What countermeasures are, and what factors you must consider when evaluating them
- What the three types of activity controls are and how they correspond to the security life cycle
- What a business continuity plan (BCP) is and how organizations use it to make sure a disaster doesn't put them out of business
- What role backups play in disaster recovery
- What steps you should take to respond to security incidents
- What a disaster recovery plan (DRP) does
- What the primary steps to disaster recovery are

Chapter 8 Goals

When you complete this chapter, you will be able to:

- Understand the principles of risk management
- Understand how to respond to and analyze incidents
- Understand how to prevent and recover from outages using a business continuity plan (BCP)

Risk Management and Information Security

Risk management is a central concern of information security. Every action an organization takes—or fails to take—involves some degree of risk. In the business world, managing risk is the difference between a successful business and a failing business. That doesn't mean you eliminate the risk. Instead, an organization seeks a balance between an acceptable level of a risk and the cost of reducing it. Different organizations have different risk tolerances. For example, a hospital seeks to limit risk to the highest degree possible. On the other hand, some financial institutions accept higher risk levels because taking great risk may result in great rewards.

As a security professional, you will work with others to identify risks and to apply risk-management solutions. You must remember two key risk-management principles:

- Never spend more to protect an asset than it is worth.
- A countermeasure, without a corresponding risk, is a solution seeking a problem; you can never justify the cost.

You play an important role in the risk, response, and recovery aspects of information security. You must help identify serious risks. Some of them could put your company out of business. You also must help create and/or maintain a plan that makes sure your company continues to operate in the face of disaster. This type of a plan is a business continuity plan (BCP). It is an important concept you will learn about in this chapter.

Disasters do happen, so you must expect they will happen to your organization. Planning for disaster is part of your role as a security professional. You must help develop and maintain a disaster recovery plan (DRP).

As a security professional, your goal is to make sure your systems quickly become available to users after an outage and that you recover any lost or damaged data. However, you also play a role in making sure you handle the recovery process correctly.

> **NOTE**
> You should become familiar with the NIST SP 800 series of security practices. You can find it at *http://csrc.nist.gov/publications/PubsSPs.html*. This basic information is the foundation for your understanding of information security. Advanced security professionals use some of the more detailed items.

Definitions of Risk

Risk is the likelihood that a particular threat exposes a vulnerability that could damage your organization. The extent of damage a threat can do determines the level of risk. To fully understand risk, you must understand several key terms. The NIST SP 800-30 publication, *Risk Management Guide for Information Technology Systems*, defines the important risk terms.

If you understand these terms, you will begin to understand how to build an effective IT risk-management program. As a security professional, you must know the bold-faced words that follow:

- **Vulnerability**—A vulnerability is a flaw or weakness in your system security procedures, design, implementation, or internal controls. Attackers can exploit a vulnerability accidentally or intentionally to create a security breach or a violation of a system's security policy.

- **Threat**—A threat is the potential for an attacker or event to exploit a specific vulnerability. An attacker or event that may exploit a vulnerability is also a threat source. A threat source is an intent and method to exploit a vulnerability. A **threat source** can also be a situation or method that might accidentally trigger a vulnerability. Common threat sources are natural, human, or environmental. Note that some security professionals call a threat source a threat agent.
- **Impact**—**Impact** refers to the amount of harm a threat exploiting a vulnerability can cause. For example, if a virus infects a system, the virus could affect all the data on the system.

Some risks are more likely to occur than others are. **Likelihood** is the probability that a potential threat will exploit a vulnerability. For example, there is a high likelihood a virus or other malware will infect an Internet-connected system that does not have antivirus software running.

When a threat is realized, an organization experiences either an event or an incident. An **event** is a measurable occurrence that has an impact on the business. Some events have little effect; others might escalate into incidents. An **incident** is an event that has a negative impact on operations. Incidents are events that justify a countermeasure. For example, employee warehouse theft is an incident.

You will learn more about controls, countermeasures, and safeguards later in this chapter. Many people use these terms interchangeably, although there are subtle differences. They all reduce risk by reducing either a vulnerability or the impact of a threat. Controls include both safeguards and countermeasures. Suffice it to say here that controls are actions taken to limit or constrain behavior. **Safeguards** address gaps or weaknesses in the controls that could otherwise lead to an exploit. **Countermeasures** counter or address a specific threat. A fire sprinkler system is an example of a countermeasure.

Elements of Risk

Assets, vulnerabilities, and threats are all elements of risk. These are component parts rather than a formula. Assets increase or decline in value. Your proactive procedures should discover and patch vulnerabilities. New threats emerge to add to existing ones. As these factors change over time, risk changes as well. You should periodically perform risk reassessments to identify new risks.

Don't assume that all threats come from the outside. In July 2007, Sophos, a security software firm, released a report saying 80 percent of malware caught by its products came from company insiders. They were victims of hackers because they visited inappropriate or corrupted Web sites. A common term for this kind of threat is "drive-by downloading."

New threats appear all the time. The United States Computer Emergency Readiness Team (US-CERT) regularly releases information on new threats by e-mail. You can subscribe to its Technical Cyber Security Alerts, Cyber Security Bulletins, or Cyber Security Alerts through this Web site: *http://www.us-cert.gov/cas/alldocs.html.* Once you sign up, you'll receive regular alerts in your e-mail inbox.

Purpose of Risk Management

The purpose of risk management is to reduce risk to tolerable levels. You must identify risks:

- Before they lead to an incident
- In time to enable you to plan and enact risk-handling activities (controls and countermeasures)
- On a continuous basis across the life of the product, system, or project

You can almost never reduce risk to zero. After identifying the risk culture of an organization, you need to evaluate risks and then reduce the ones that might have a major effect on the organization. You must be able to justify the costs of risk-reduction methods. In many cases, small risk reductions have significantly high costs. Part of your job is to identify the tolerable risk level and apply controls to reduce risks to that level. You must focus some risk-management efforts on identifying new risks so you can manage them before an event. Part of this process will include continually reevaluating risks to make sure you have put the right countermeasures in place.

The Risk Equation

Risk management includes risk assessment, risk mitigation, and risk evaluation and assurance. Note that risk management is a continuous effort. It includes periodic reevaluation of risk and risk assessment in all three phases of the risk-management effort. Figure 8-1 shows the risk equation and the three phases of risk management.

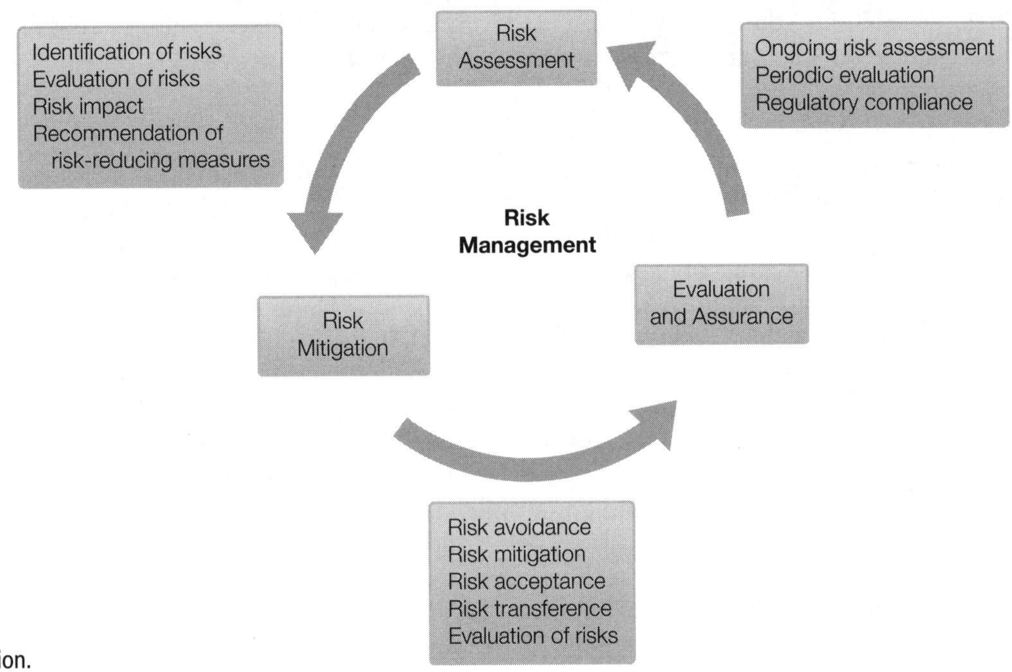

FIGURE 8-1
The risk equation.

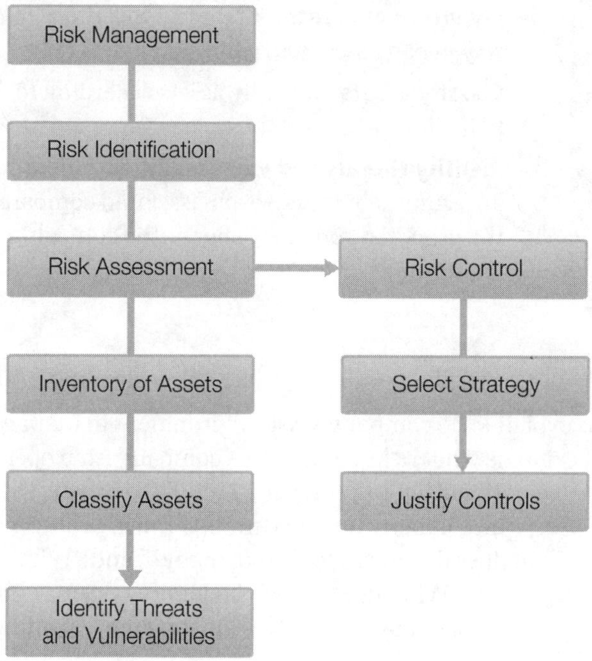

FIGURE 8-2

Flow chart of the risk-management process.

The Process of Risk Management

Figure 8-2 shows a flow chart that outlines the steps in risk management. The left column of the figure outlines the assessment and monitoring of risk. The right column addresses some of the details of the risk-assessment step.

As shown in Figure 8-2, the steps in the risk-management process are as follows:

- **Risk identification**—The first step to managing risk is risk identification. What could go wrong? Answers can include fire, flood, earthquake, lightning, loss of electricity or other utility, strike, and transportation unavailability. You must develop scenarios for each threat to assess the threat.
- **Risk assessment**—Of course, you can't measure all identified risks. Also, not all risks apply to all businesses in all locations. For example, businesses in Montana or Moscow don't need to worry about hurricanes. Of the risks that are possible, impact will be more or less severe depending on the scenario and location. The risk-assessment phase involves the following three aspects, or sub-phases:
  1. Assessment of various types of controls to mitigate the risks that you identify.
  2. Selection of a control strategy—consider reliability, scalability, cost, ease of use, and safety. This will eliminate some options and move others to the forefront.
  3. Justification of choice of controls—compare the cost of all controls with the associated risk. It is not right to spend $100 to protect $10.

NOTE

It is important to avoid "movie-plot" risks. Scriptwriters can create impossible scenarios and make them look possible or even likely. Spending money to protect against these false threats is a waste.

- **Inventory of assets**—Create an inventory of assets so you can assess loss while you assess risk.
- **Classify assets**—Classify assets according to their value to the business.
- **Identify threats and vulnerabilities**—Identify the threats and vulnerabilities to each asset and compare them with the proposed controls to find if the controls are (still) appropriate.

Risk Analysis

A good risk analysis explains the company's risk environment to managers in terms they understand. It explains what risks could stop a company from operating. Sometimes, IT professionals get so emotional about protecting their IT structure, they forget their systems are there to keep the company up and running. During the risk-analysis process, remain focused on "What does this mean to the company?" and "What is the value of this to the company?" rather than "What does this mean for my systems and infrastructure?"

Risk analysis identifies and justifies risk-mitigation efforts:

NOTE

Incidents will occur! Risk analysis, countermeasures, and mitigation, coupled with disaster planning (covered later in this chapter), often mean the difference between a company surviving or failing after a disaster.

- Risk mitigation identifies threats to business processes and data systems.
- Risk analysis justifies the use of specific countermeasures to reduce risk.

While you have many choices to reduce a risk, a key reason for risk assessment and analysis is to provide the data necessary to identify the best choices. That depends on such things as cost, impact on productivity, and user acceptance.

Emerging Threats

You must also perform risk assessment on emerging threats. They can come from many different areas and from both internal and external sources. Some examples of emerging threats include the following:

- New technology.
- Changes in the culture of the organization or environment.
- Unauthorized use of technology (e.g., wireless technologies, rogue modems, PDAs, unlicensed software, iPods). PDA threats include theft of corporate data, poor controls over wireless transmission and traffic, as well as the risk of having multiple copies or versions of data on several devices.
- Changes in regulations and laws.
- Changes in business practices (e.g., outsourcing, globalization).

You should periodically do risk analysis to find emerging threats and vulnerabilities. A proactive security professional watches for new threats that might trigger the need for a new risk review.

Two Approaches: Quantitative and Qualitative

You can approach risk analysis two ways.

- **Qualitative risk analysis**—This type of risk analysis describes a risk scenario and then figures out what impact the event would have on business operations. To do this, you need to talk with division heads who know what would happen if disaster were to strike their departments. This allows the business units and technical experts to understand the ripple effects of an event on other departments or operations. The process of gathering information from these experts is called the Delphi technique.
- **Quantitative risk analysis**—This type of risk analysis attempts to describe risk in financial terms and put a dollar value on all the elements of a risk. One drawback to this approach is that many risks have values that are difficult to measure. These include reputation and the availability of countermeasures. Exact numbers can be difficult to determine, especially the cost of the impact of future events.

Quantitative analysis puts a dollar figure on risk. Qualitative analysis defines risk using a scenario that describes it. Figure 8-3 compares quantitative and qualitative risk analysis. Neither approach is perfect in itself. A solid risk assessment will often combine both techniques.

In most situations, you can combine the two methodologies. Qualitative risk analysis gives you a better understanding of the overall impact a disaster will have as the effects ripple through an organization. It often leads to better communication between departments on how they must work together to reduce damage. However, it lacks some of the solid financial data of a quantitative risk analysis. You often need this cost information to justify the cost of countermeasures. Therefore, you need to consider both techniques.

Calculating Quantified Risk

To calculate quantified risk, you must figure out how much an asset is worth and the probable frequency with which you will encounter a loss. This is the event's loss expectancy. Calculating it is a multistep process:

Quantitative	Numerically Based (Hard) Data	Financial Data Objective
Qualitative	Scenario-Based (Soft) Data	Scenario-Oriented Subjective

FIGURE 8-3
Quantitative versus qualitative risk analysis.

1. **Calculate the asset value (AV)**—An asset is anything of value to an organization. Assets can be tangible (buildings) or intangible (reputation). A first step in risk assessment is to determine all the assets of the organization and their value—that is, the importance of that asset to the organization's ability to meet its mission. Asset value should consider the replacement value of equipment or systems. It should also include factors such as lost productivity and loss of reputation or customer confidence.
2. **Calculate the exposure factor (EF)**—This represents the percentage of the asset value that will be lost if an incident were to occur. As an example, not every car accident is a total loss. Insurance companies have actuaries who calculate the likely percentage loss for every claim. They know the cost of repairs for every make and model and can predict the exposure factor per claim. Their prediction won't be right for any single claim (except by chance), but will be right when grouped by the hundreds or thousands.
3. **Calculate the single loss expectancy (SLE)**—You can calculate the value of a single loss using the two preceding factors. If an actuary calculates that the EF of a late-model SUV is 20 percent, then every time the phone rings, all he needs to do is look up the asset value, multiply by the EF, and he'll have a very good prediction of the payout. This allows the actuary to calculate insurance premiums accurately and reduce the risk of the insurance company losing money.
4. **Determine how often a loss is likely to occur every year**—This is the annualized rate of occurrence (ARO). Some AROs are greater than one. For example, a snowstorm in Buffalo or Berlin will happen many times per year. Others are likely to happen far less often. For example, a warehouse fire might happen once every 20 years. It is often difficult to estimate how often an incident will happen. Sometimes internal or external factors can affect that assessment. Historical data does not always predict the future. An incident such as one stemming from an internal threat is far more likely during times of employee unrest or contract negotiations than at other times.
5. **Determine annualized loss expectancy (ALE)**—The ALE is the SLE (the loss when an incident happens) times the ARO. The ALE helps an organization identify the overall impact of a risk. For infrequent events, the ALE will be much less than the SLE. For example, if you expect an event to occur only once every 10 years, the ARO is .10, or 10 percent. If the SLE is $1,000, the ALE is only $100 ($1,000 × .10). On the other hand, if the ARO is 20, indicating that it is likely to occur 20 times every year, the ALE is $20,000 ($1,000 × 20).

Table 8-1 shows the calculations you can use to determine quantified risk.

The purpose of calculating quantified risk is to find the highest amount that you should spend on a countermeasure. The cost of the countermeasure should be less than the ALE.

TABLE 8-1 Determining quantified risk.

CALCULATION	FORMULA
Single loss expectancy (SLE)	AV × EF = SLE
Annualized rate of occurrence (ARO)	ARO = # incidents/year
Annualized loss expectancy (ALE)	SLE × ARO = ALE

Consider this example. About 100 users in your organization use mobile computers. The value of each mobile computer is $2,000, which includes the cost of the computer, the software, and the data. In the past two years, the organization has lost an average of six computers a year. This information enables you to calculate the SLE, ARO, and ALE.

- SLE is $2,000
- ARO is 6
- ALE is $12,000

Someone has suggested purchasing hardware locks for these systems. Users can use these locks to lock unattended computers to furniture, as bicycle riders lock their bikes to a bike rack. If you purchase the locks in bulk, they cost of $10 each. Additionally, if you purchase and use the locks, you estimate you can reduce the losses from six a year to only one. Is this cost effective?

- Cost of countermeasure is $1,000 ($10 × 100 computers)
- New ARO is 1
- New ALE is $2,000

Clearly, this is cost effective. Instead of losing $12,000 a year, the organization spends $1,000 and only loses $2,000. The total outgoing funds is $3,000. This is much better than the loss of $12,000 you experienced before implementing the new control. On the other hand, if the cost of the countermeasure were $24,000, it wouldn't make sense. You'd be spending $24,000 to potentially save $12,000, which puts you an additional $12,000 in the hole.

Qualitative Risk Analysis

You can judge every risk on two scales:

- **Probability or likelihood**—Some things—for example, the malfunction of a badge reader on the employee entrance—will seldom happen. Other things, such as employees calling in sick, will almost certainly happen.
- **Impact**—Some things—for example, a workstation that fails to boot up—will have an insignificant impact. Other things, such as a production system breaking down, will have a major impact.

FIGURE 8-4
Qualitative risk analysis.

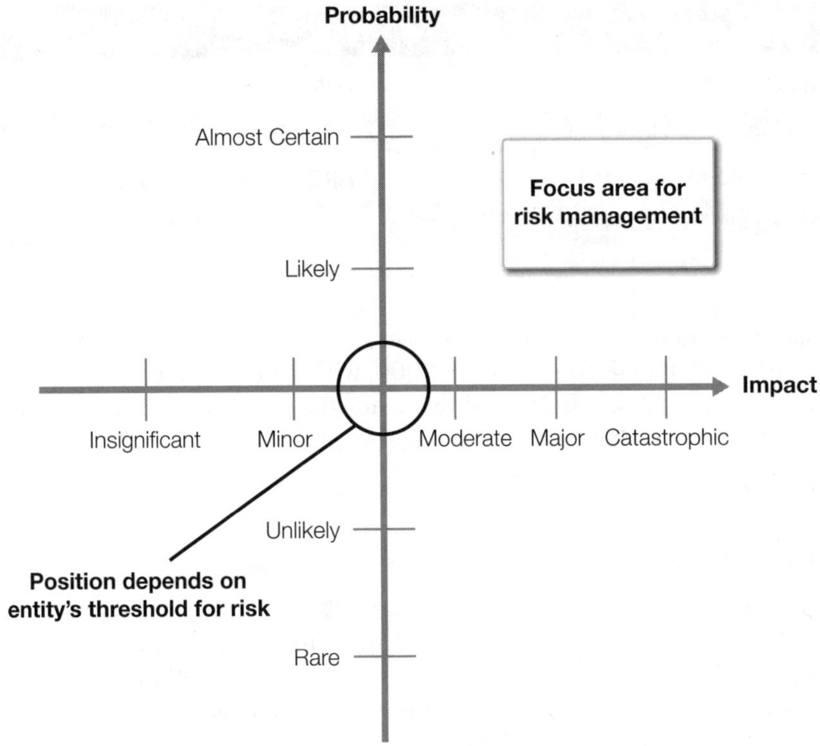

> **NOTE**
> It will often take the opinion of many experts to determine where to place an event on both scales. You must work to get a consensus if the experts disagree. This kind of analysis can account for intangible factors, such as reputation or public interest.

You should evaluate events with respect to both scales and then place them on the chart shown in Figure 8-4.

Notice the quadrant labeled "Focus area for risk management." These are risks with both a high probability and a high impact. You should evaluate these risks first. You can reduce the probability of the risk or its impact if you apply countermeasures to these risks first. You should not conduct risk management solely in the upper right quadrant, but this is where your risk-mitigation efforts should focus. Risk mitigation, transference, acceptance, or avoidance—covered in the next section—reduce the risks in the upper-right quadrant. As a reminder, the goal isn't to eliminate risk, but instead to reduce it to an acceptable level.

Developing a Strategy for Dealing with Risk

As you develop risk-management strategies, you should understand the most common responses. You can reduce, transfer, accept, and avoid risk:

- **Risk mitigation (reduction)**—This approach uses various controls to mitigate or reduce identified risks. These controls might be administrative, technical, or physical. For example, adding antivirus software reduces the risk of computer infection.

- **Risk assignment (transference)**—This approach allows the organization to transfer the risk to another entity. Insurance is a common way to reduce risk. An organization "sells" the risk to an insurance company in return for a premium. Other times, you can transfer risk to insulate an organization from excessive liability. A hotel, for example, engages a separate car-parking corporation to manage its parking lot. Losses are the responsibility of the car-parking corporation, not the hotel. An incident in the parking lot is less likely to put the hotel in jeopardy of a lawsuit.
- **Risk acceptance**—This allows an organization to accept risk. The organization knows the risk exists and has decided that the cost of reducing it is higher than the loss would be. This can include self-insuring or using a deductible. The level of risk an organization is willing to accept depends on the risk appetite of senior management. For example, a physician buys malpractice insurance and accepts the residual risk of loss equal to the deductible. He can decide to pay an even higher premium to reduce his deductible. But he might decide that the higher premium would not be worth the cost because he would rarely need to make a claim.
- **Risk avoidance**—Risk avoidance is just that: deciding not to take a risk. A company can discontinue or decide not to enter a line of business if the risk level is too high. With avoidance, management decides that the potential loss to the company exceeds the potential value gained by continuing the risky activity. For example, a company may decide not to open a branch in a country mired in political turmoil.

Acceptable Range of Risk/Residual Risk

The acceptable range of risk determines how you define activities and countermeasures. The upper bound is the risk impact where the cost would be too great for the organization to bear. The lower bound shows the increased cost of the countermeasures to handle the residual risk. The goal of risk management is to stay inside the acceptable range. See Figure 8-5.

> **NOTE**
> You usually can't eliminate risk entirely. Your organization must select a level of risk it is willing to accept. This is the acceptable range.

The top graph represents the total risk to an organization for a specific vulnerability. The in-place countermeasures are not adequate to reduce the risk from the maximum acceptable residual risk level into the acceptable range. The lower graph shows the proposed countermeasures that will reduce the maximum residual risk level to the acceptable range.

As you now know, threats, vulnerabilities, and asset value comprise risk. Total risk is the combined risk to all business assets. Residual risk is the risk that remains after you have installed countermeasures and controls. Applying countermeasures and controls reduces risk but does not eliminate it. An example would be car insurance. If you purchase a brand-new car, it loses value as soon as you drive it off the dealer's lot because it is now used. If an accident totals the car, insurance may not pay the price you paid for it. The difference between what the insurance company pays and what you actually paid for the car is the residual risk. Other examples include the deductible on insurance or the remaining (but decreased) chance of fire after you implement alarms, sprinkler systems, and training sessions.

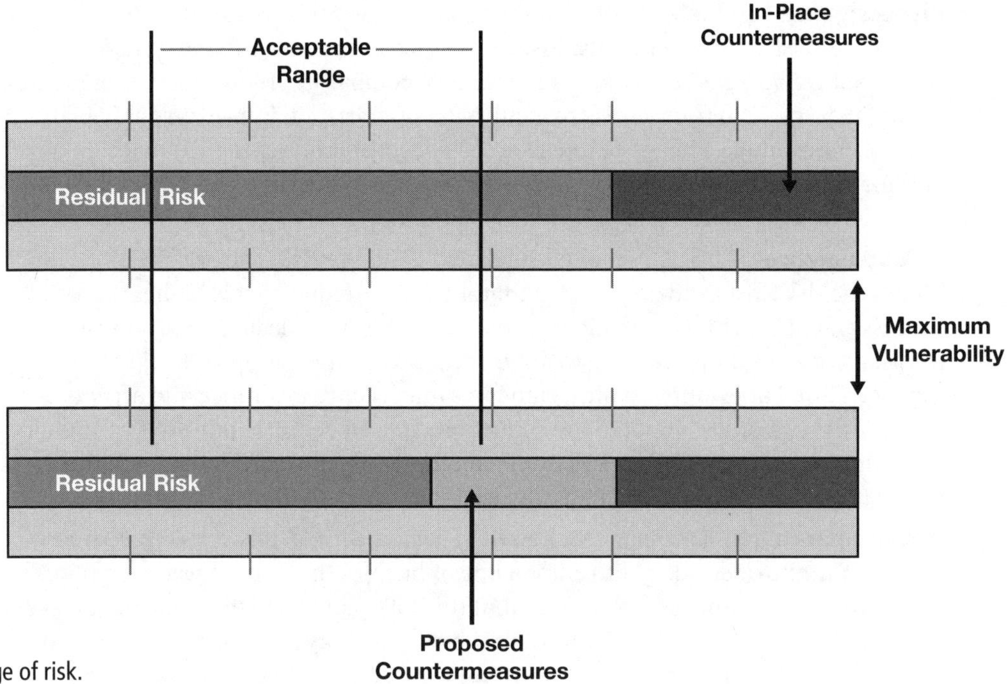

FIGURE 8-5
Acceptable range of risk.

You may choose not to eliminate risk entirely because doing so is impossible or too expensive. When you do not reduced risk to zero, the risk that remains is residual risk. In other words, as shown in Figure 8-6:

risk − mitigating controls = residual risk

You should prepare your organization to accept the cost of residual risk. If its cost is too great, you must either eliminate the risky behavior or use a different countermeasure.

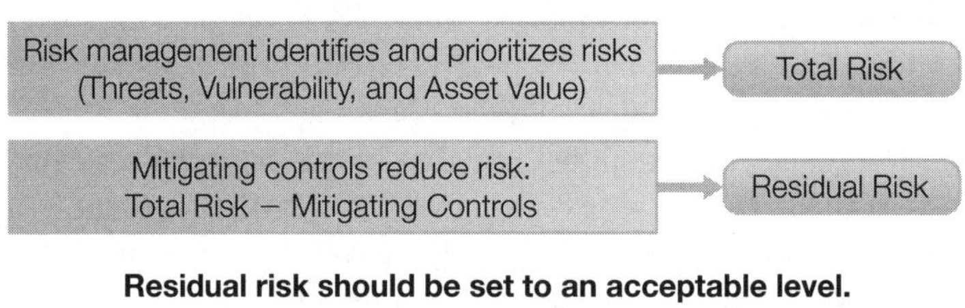

FIGURE 8-6
Total risk and residual risk.

Evaluating Countermeasures

As discussed earlier in the chapter, control, safeguard, and countermeasure are not interchangeable terms. A control limits or constrains behavior. Safeguards and countermeasures are controls that exercise restraint on or management of some activity. For example, a safe for storage of valuables is a control. A guard to watch the safe is a safeguard. Insurance against loss of the valuables, if stolen, is a countermeasure. It counters, or addresses, the loss from a specific incident.

There are an unlimited number of possible countermeasures. A countermeasure must have a clearly defined purpose. It must address a risk and reduce a vulnerability. A countermeasure (or control) without an exposure (risk) is a solution seeking a problem. Some specific purposes of countermeasures include the following:

- Fix known exploitable software flaws.
- Develop and enforce operational procedures and access controls (data and system).
- Provide encryption capability.
- Improve physical security.
- Disconnect unreliable networks.

Everyone needs to be aware of his or her security responsibilities. Security will be a full-time job for some people. Others will have only infrequent responsibilities, such as locking the door on the way out. Some specific security responsibilities that you may hold include the following:

- Delete redundant/guest accounts.
- Train system administrators (specific training).
- Train everybody (general training).
- Install virus-scanning software.
- Install IDS/IPS and network-scanning tools.

Pricing/Costing a Countermeasure

You must consider many factors when evaluating countermeasures:

- **Product cost**—The price of the product will include its base price, the price of additional features, and costs associated with the service level agreement or annual maintenance.
- **Implementation cost**—This refers to costs associated with changes to the infrastructure, construction, design, and training. An example would be the cost of reinforcing a floor to install new equipment.
- **Compatibility cost**—The countermeasure must fit within the overall structure. For example, a Windows-only organization would have to carefully consider the additional costs associated with training and interoperability when installing a Linux-based countermeasure.

- **Environmental cost**—If, for example, a countermeasure uses a lot of energy, you would need to consider whether your electric system would be able to provide it and to offset the waste heat it will generate.
- **Testing costs**—Testing does take time and money, but it is essential. Note, however, that testing also causes disruptions. You must consider all these as costs.
- **Productivity impact**—Many controls affect productivity. They might generate more calls to the help desk, slower response times for users, and so on.

Remember: The cost of a countermeasure is more than just the purchase price of a piece of technology.

Countermeasure Evaluation

The most important part of putting any control or countermeasure in place is making sure it meets its objectives. A countermeasure is of no value if it does not actually provide its intended benefit.

When evaluating a countermeasure, first ask, "What problem is this countermeasure designed to solve?" Then ask, "Does this countermeasure solve this problem?" Here are some other points to consider:

- **Countermeasures might pose a new risk to the organization**—For example, implementing a countermeasure might create a false sense of security. Or the countermeasure itself might become a new point of failure on a critical system. Make sure you continuously monitor the countermeasure. Check it for compliance and good design, and perform regular maintenance.
- **You must perform certification and accreditation of countermeasure programs**—No system, control, or application should go into production without first going through a change control process. This also applies to changes to existing production systems. You must review all controls and countermeasures before performing an installation or making changes. Otherwise, administrators might misconfigure the system or make other errors.
- **You must follow best practices and exercise due diligence**—A good risk-management program tells auditors that the company is taking a prudent and diligent approach to security risks. Due diligence is exercised by frequently evaluating whether countermeasures are performing as expected.

Controls and Their Place in the Security Life Cycle

Security controls are the safeguards or countermeasures that an organization uses to avoid, counteract, or minimize loss or system unavailability. As defined by the Government Accountability Office:

"The control environment sets the tone of an organization, influencing the control consciousness of its people. It is the foundation for all other components of internal control, providing discipline and structure. Control environment factors include the integrity, ethical values, and competence of the entity's people; management's philosophy and operating style; and the way management assigns authority and organizes and develops its people."

Some controls manage the activity phase of security—the things people do. These are administrative controls. **Administrative controls** develop and ensure compliance with policy and procedures. They tend to be things that employees might do, things employees are supposed to do, or things employees are not supposed to do. A control carried out or managed by a computer system is a **technical control**.

Activity phase controls can be either administrative or technical. They correspond to the life cycle of a security program as follows:

- **Detective controls**—These controls identify that a threat has landed in your system. An intrusion detection system (IDS) is an example of a **detective control**. An IDS can detect attacks on systems such as port scans that try to gain information about a system. The IDS then logs the activity.
- **Preventative controls**—These stop threats from coming in contact with a vulnerability. An example of a **preventative control** is an intrusion prevention system (IPS). An IPS is an IDS that you configure to actively block an attack. Instead of just logging the activity, it can change the configuration so that the malicious activity is blocked.
- **Corrective controls**—These reduce the effects of a threat. When you reload an operating system after it is infected with malware, you are using a **corrective control**. Forensics and incident response are other examples of corrective controls.

Planning to Survive

How an organization responds to a disaster might well determine its survival. Poor planning greatly increases the risk. With poor planning, an organization will not be able to respond appropriately and will be unable to return to normal operations. Planning for disasters is part of business continuity management (BCM), which includes both of the following:

- **Business continuity plan (BCP)**—This helps keep critical business processes running in a disaster.
- **Disaster recovery plan (DRP)**—This helps recover the infrastructure necessary for normal business operations.

BCM not only includes BCP and DRP. It also includes crisis management, incident response management, and risk management.

A disaster is a sudden, unplanned, calamitous event. It upsets an organization's ability to provide critical business functions and causes great damage or loss. Examples of disasters include the following:

- **Extreme weather**—Hurricane Katrina is one example.
- **Criminal activity**—This might include the theft of credit card numbers at e-commerce sites.
- **Civil unrest/terrorist acts**—One example is the bombing of World Trade Center on September 11, 2001.
- **Operational**—An example would be the electrical blackout in the northeastern United States during the summer of 2005.
- **Application failure**—One example is the eight-hour delayed opening of the London Stock Exchange on April 5, 2000, due to system failures.

The purpose of BCM is to mitigate incidents. When an incident does occur, however, the first priority must always be to ensure the safety of people. Containing the damage is secondary.

Terminology

As a security professional, you must to understand the following terms:

- **Business impact analysis (BIA)**—An analysis of the business to determine what kinds of events will have an impact on what systems. You should not limit the focus of the BIA to the information systems department and infrastructure! A business with a supply-chain disaster (warehouse fire, trucking strike, etc.) could easily suffer a major impact that has nothing to do with technology at all. Some scenarios will affect some departments, some will affect others, and a critical few will affect the entire business. You will learn more about BIA later in this chapter.
- **Critical business function (CBF)**—Once the BIA has identified the business systems that an incident will affect, you must rank the systems from most to least critical. That ranking determines whether the business can survive—and for how long—in the absence of a critical function.
- **Maximum tolerable downtime**—**Maximum tolerable downtime (MTD)** is the most time a business can survive without a particular critical system. A disaster is any event that makes a CBF unavailable for longer than its MTD. Each of the disaster-planning and mitigation solutions must be able to recover CBFs within their MTDs. Systems and functions with the shortest MTDs are often the most critical. The next section covers this topic in more detail.
- **Recovery time objective (RTO)**—The time frame for restoring a CBF. RTO must be shorter than or equal to the MTD.

- **Recovery point objective (RPO)**—Incidents can cause loss of data. You must calculate the amount of tolerable data loss for each business function. Recovery procedures must be able to meet the minimums defined here. If the business can afford to lose up to one day's data, then nightly backups might an acceptable solution. However, if the business must prevent all data loss, a redundant server or storage solution will be required.
- **Emergency operations center (EOC)**—The place where the recovery team will meet and work during a disaster. Many businesses have more than one **emergency operations center**. One might be nearby—for use in the event of a building fire, for example. Another might be a significant distance away—for example, for use in the event of an earthquake or regional power outage.

Here is how MTD and RTO work together. Suppose power goes out in the data center. It takes six hours to move to the alternate site (RTO). The business can survive for nine hours without a functioning data center. At this point, there is an event, but not yet an incident that you can define as a disaster. If you expect power to return within three hours (MTD–RTO), the business might not declare a disaster in anticipation that it will resume normally. However, if power is still out at the three-hour mark, it is time to declare a disaster.

In this example, the three-hour mark is a critical milestone. Imagine that the organization chose not to switch operations to the alternate site at the three-hour mark. Instead, it waited four hours. Because it takes six hours to switch over to the alternate site, the organization will suffer a total loss of 10 hours. This is beyond the MTD of nine hours. While a single hour may not seem like much, it is based on the established MTD. It may be that the data center provides services to other organizations. Service-level agreements dictate outages no longer than nine hours, with monetary penalties for longer outages. That extra hour could cost the organization tens of thousands of dollars.

Assessing Maximum Tolerable Downtime (MTD)

You determine MTD by business requirements. This is closely associated with the RTOs of several integrated functions. For example, consider a Web site hosted by an organization for e-commerce. The Web servers depend on network services, ISP availability, and electricity. Each of these will have its own incident-dependent RTO, but it will be associated with the MTD.

For example, if you determine that the Web site has an MTD of four hours, the RTO of the failed network services, ISP availability, and electricity all must be less than four hours. Parts of the recovery will be able to take place in parallel, but some might have to be sequential. In this example, you can't recover network services until you've restored the power. However, once you get power back on, you can work on restoring network services and ISP availability at the same time.

The RPO defines the amount of tolerable data loss. The RPO can come from the business impact analysis or sometimes from a government mandate—for example, banking laws or regulations pertaining to pharmaceutical research data retention. Figure 8-7 shows how to assess the MTD, RTO, and RPO.

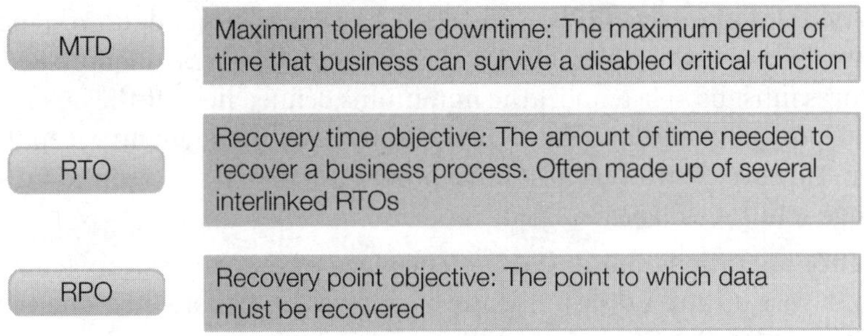

FIGURE 8-7 Assessing maximum tolerable downtime (MTD).

Business Impact Analysis

A BIA determines the extent of the impact that a particular incident would have on business operations over time. The BIA drives the choice of the recovery strategy and the CBFs.

As a security professional, your job is to ask two questions:

- What can affect the business?
- How will it affect the business?

A successful BIA maps the context, the critical business functions, and the processes on which they rely. You should consider all impacts, including those that are hard and less obvious. Different incidents require different recovery strategies. A fire in the accounting department might call for outsourcing and temporary quarters. A flood in the basement might activate a service bureau plan. An earthquake or hurricane might cause a permanent move to a new facility.

You conduct a business impact analysis for three key reasons:

- To set the value of each business unit or resource as it relates to how the entire organization operates
- To identify the critical needs to develop a business recovery plan
- To set the order or priority for restoring the organization's functions after a disruption

Speed of Impact

Some incidents might become more significant over time. The slow deterioration of a critical processing facility might generate a disaster. Continuous installation of new devices in a computer room might overtax the electric supply capacity and eventually cause a blackout or a fire.

Some systems are more important during certain times of the year. A company that supplies heating oil is busier in the winter. Even the smallest outage in the winter can jeopardize its service agreements. That same company might easily withstand far more severe incidents (longer MTDs) in the summer when load is minimal.

Critical Dependencies

The BIA must identify what your organization needs to support a company's critical operations:

- Information processing
- Personnel
- Communications
- Equipment
- Facilities
- Other organizational functions
- Vendors
- Suppliers

Assessing the Impact of Downtime

The BIA will identify critical data and systems. Note that the importance of systems and the importance of data are not always the same. A system might be more critical than the data it contains and vice versa. What is truly important is those systems and data on which the business relies.

Issues you should consider during the BIA fall under the following categories:

- **People**—How will you notify them of the incident and the impact? How will you evacuate, transport, and care for employees (including, for example, paying them)?
- **Systems**—What portions of your computing and telecommunications infrastructure must you duplicate immediately? How long do you have? A minute, an hour, a day?
- **Data**—What data is critical to running your business? How will you recover critical data that is lost?
- **Property**—What items are essential to your business? Things like tools, supplies, and special forms all must be recoverable or easily replaced.

Assessing the impact of downtime is a planning step in the BIA. You are helping to determine what must be done and in what order to accomplish the goals described in these four categories. Figuring out how to do this is the main thrust of BCM.

Plan Review

You must update and regularly maintain the BCP and the inventory and configuration lists for the systems and applications. Some firms do this annually. Others choose different periods. In addition to the scheduled reviews, any major changes to the company should trigger a review. Besides the obvious benefit of having an up-to-date plan, testing and plan revisions are excellent ways to train new employees. Taking new employees through a hands-on process teaches them your procedures and more about your environment.

Testing the Plan

You should not accept any BCP or DRP without thorough testing. This helps ensure the plan will work and that you will meet the CBF, MTD, RPO, and RTO objectives. Each stage of the test must consider the continued need for security and the technical resources required both to perform the test and to handle an actual disaster.

Checklist Test

A checklist test is a simple review of the plan by managers and the business continuity team to make sure that contact numbers are current and that the plan reflects the company's priorities and structure. This kind of check is a desk check. Each team member checks his or her portion of the plan while sitting at his or her desk. As well as checking their contact lists, team members review whether changes in their departments affect the plan. They also look at expected changes in their departments to see if they will trigger a need to update the plan.

Structured Walk-Through Test

A structured walk-through test is a tabletop exercise. During this test, a team of representatives from each department should do the following:

- Present their portion of the plan to the other teams.
- Review goals of the plan for completeness and correctness.
- Affirm the scope of the plan, as well as any assumptions made.
- Look for overlaps and gaps.
- Review the structure of the organization as well as the reporting/communications structure.
- Evaluate the testing, maintenance, and training requirements.
- Conduct a number of scenario-based exercises to evaluate the plan's effectiveness.
- Meet to step through the plan together in a structured manner.

In the case of the final step, team members should act as though they are executing the plan for a certain type of incident. The goal of the structured walk-through is to find errors in each department's plans, such as gaps or overlaps. Gaps are where one department is under the impression a critical task was to be handled by a different department. Overlaps are situations where two departments think they'll have exclusive (or majority) use of the same resource—for example, two departments think they'll have two-thirds of the replacement desktops.

Simulation Test

A simulation test is more than a paper exercise. It requires more planning than a walk-through. All the members of the staff involved in the operations/procedures participate in the test. The test identifies the following:

- Staff reaction and response times
- Inefficiencies or previously unidentified vulnerabilities

You should conduct the simulation on site using only countermeasures defined in the plan. The simulation test involves many of the employees who have not yet participated in plan development. It is common to conduct simulations on an off day, such as a weekend.

The purpose of the simulation test is to identify shortcomings. You should carry out the test as far as possible. If, for example, a critical file is missing, the file should be generated or obtained from the main site and the test should then continue. Ensure you log any on-the-spot corrections for evaluation and plan update later. The test should end only when it is completed or if it becomes impossible to continue.

Parallel Test

Most organizations conduct parallel tests at the alternate site. A parallel test is the same as a full-interruption test (covered in the next section) except that processing does not stop at the primary site. Here are a few key points with respect to parallel tests:

- A parallel test is an operational test, so it will not include representatives from HR, PR, purchasing, facilities, etc.
- Because a parallel test means activating the alternate site, it will cost a significant amount of money. The test must have senior-management approval.
- Compare the results of the test to the processing at the original site.
- A gap analysis exposes any weaknesses or underperformance that requires attention.
- Usually, auditors are involved at every step to monitor the success and to make sure the parallel-run data is not mixed into the normal operational data.

> **WARNING**
>
> This test is high risk! Running a full-interruption test can actually create a disaster. You should run a full-interruption test only after you have successfully run all other types of tests. You must obtain senior-management approval prior to the test!

Full-Interruption Test

The most common way to conduct this type of test is at the alternate site. This type of test is so disruptive that few organizations conduct it. During the test, you must shut down the original system for the duration. You can use only those processes that exist at the alternate site to continue the business operations.

Backing Up Data and Applications

Recovery is possible only if the company has access to backups of its data and applications. Plans must include dealing with backup storage media, location, and access. Tape backup is the traditional choice for backup and still the most common. However, restoration from tape is slow, and many systems have RTOs that are shorter than the tape-restore time. These kinds of sites often use disk-based solutions such as a SAN, NAS, or even off-site network-based storage such as remote journaling. In remote journaling, the system writes a log of online transactions to an off-site location. The log updates a copy of the database. Should the primary site go down, the off-site copy would be current.

Backups Versus Redundancy

Redundancy, or fault-tolerance options, provide for alternate resources if a primary resource fails. In other words, a system can experience a fault but tolerate it and keep operating. However, you must know that redundancies are not replacements for backups.

For example, RAID 1 mirroring writes data to two disks instead of one. Should one disk fail, the system can continue to operate. The data is still available on the second disk. However, imagine that you have a server protected with RAID. If a catastrophic failure in the server destroys all the drives, the data is gone. If you don't have a backup, the data is gone forever.

Similarly, you can set up clustered servers so that standby servers take over if the primary server fails. Again, though, just because a service is using a cluster for fault tolerance, you still need backups.

Backups provide extra copies of needed resources, such as data, documentation, and equipment. You can activate a backup site if a primary site goes down. Similarly, you can restore a backup tape, possibly at an alternate site. Then processing can resume.

Types of Backups

Backups and restores are slow. Businesses have three alternatives for processing them:

- **Full backup**—As its name implies, this backup copies everything to a backup media. It is usually tape, but is sometimes CD, DVD, or disk.
- **Differential backup**—With this type of backup, you start by making a full backup, perhaps on Sunday, when traffic is lightest. On Monday through Saturday, you back up changes made since Sunday's full backup on a daily basis. As the week progresses, each night's backup (the differential) takes a little longer.
- **Incremental backup**—Again, you start with a full backup when traffic is light. Then, each night, you back up only that day's changes. As the week progresses, the nightly (incremental) backup takes about the same amount of time.

It is faster to create the incremental weekday backups than the differential backups. This comes at a price, however. If you need to use the backup images to restore data, systems using differential backups would only need to restore the full backup and then the latest differential. Those using incremental backups would need to restore the full backup and then each day's incremental backups to complete the restore.

You should back up items other than just data. These include router and switch configurations, user access permissions and configurations (e.g., Active Directory), and server/workstation operating systems and configurations. To make this more manageable, most large companies have a standard base configuration for workstations that can be reloaded on demand. As long as you keep these up to date (patched and fixed), this is an attractive solution.

Steps to Take in Handling an Incident

As a reminder, an incident is an event that has a negative impact on operations. When an incident occurs, an organization needs to respond. The incident-handling process includes the following:

- Notification
- Response
- Recovery and follow-up
- Documentation

You will learn about each of these steps in the following sections.

Notification

The first step in an incident-response program is to determine whether an incident has in fact taken place. Not all events are incidents. You must find out if the incident is serious or whether it is a common, benign occurrence. This is triage—prioritizing the incident. You may receive initial notification of an incident from an alarm, a complaint from a user, an alert from a security vendor, or log analysis. Make sure you have the procedures in place to react to any type of notification.

You often will be one of the first people aware of an event and must know how to react. The goal is to contain the incident and, if possible, to improve the situation. Take care not to make the situation worse! You must find out whether the event is a false positive. Be careful to make sure several false positives do not cause you to become desensitized to real events. A series of seemingly individual events taken independently might not justify a response. However, when taken collectively, they might be important.

Courts and Evidence

From time to time, an incident will be the grounds for a civil or even a criminal case. Therefore, you should handle all investigations with care to make sure evidence is not tainted or made inadmissible. Even if an incident does not end up in court, the threat of court action might be enough to meet the company's needs. For example, rather than prosecuting someone, the company might choose to force a resignation.

The laws of individual countries vary, but the following is true nearly everywhere: Once something makes evidence inadmissible, you can't fix it.

In all common law countries (generally, the English-speaking countries) and many countries that follow civil law (generally, mainland Europe and South America), evidence must be shown to be authentic. In other words, you must prove the evidence was not altered after the incident. A chain of custody shows how the evidence was gathered and documented. The document lists everyone who had contact with the evidence since its discovery. It shows how it was handled, what was done to it, and how it was protected from alteration.

You must know how and when to escalate, and whom to notify. This works well when you plan response scenarios and train incident-response team members.

Response

Once you identify an incident, the next phase is to limit the damage. An important aspect of this is containment. Many incidents grow and expand rapidly, possibly affecting other systems, departments, and even business partners. The incident-response plan must outline what steps must be taken to stop the spread of the incident without causing unnecessary outage. For example, if a virus infects a system, a simple way to contain the threat is to unplug the system from the network.

It is essential to have a plan. The odds are slim of correctly guessing the best course of action in the middle of an incident. Remember, people who have the benefit of time and hindsight will evaluate your response after the incident. A preapproved response plan will lead to a better, more effective response while also providing you with blame reduction.

It is essential to identify the source and type of incident so that you can enact proper recovery procedures. Fixing symptoms doesn't solve problems. The responders must find out the extent of the damage and possibly recommend the initiation of the disaster recovery plan if the damage is too severe. A key component of incident management is preventing future incidents. The logs and documentation gathered during the incident must be protected and available for future analysis.

Recovery

After you have contained the incident and eliminated or blocked its source, it is time to recover. Before turning the system over to its normal use, you must deal with the exploited vulnerability so that it doesn't happen again right away. You might need to rebuild systems using uninfected application and data backups. You might also have to clean malicious content from the system to prevent reinfection.

Follow-Up

Learning from the incident will let management establish new procedures and controls to prevent or react to an incident more effectively in the future.

Documentation

Don't ignore the importance of documenting every step in the incident response process. The documentation you create can be very valuable to the quality of future incidents. You can improve your incident response plan any time you document what actions worked well, and those that did not. As you accumulate incident response documentation, you build a valuable resource. You can use this resource to make changes to your incident response plan and your normal security policies and procedures. For example, documenting multiple incidents related to unauthorized personnel in the data center may indicate a need for better controls. Use the information you gain from documenting incident response. It can make your organization more secure.

Recovery from a Disaster

> **NOTE**
> Remember: A disaster is an event that prevents a critical business function (CBF) from operating for a period greater than the maximum tolerable downtime (MTD).

The disaster recovery plan (DRP) does three things:

- It establishes an emergency operations center (EOC) as an alternate location from which the BCP/DRP will be coordinated and implemented.
- It names an EOC manager.
- It determines when that manager should declare an incident a disaster.

A DRP enables you to make critical decisions ahead of time. That way, you can manage and review decisions without the urgency of an actual disaster. If you do not create these plans in advance, you and your managers will have to make best-guess decisions under huge pressure.

DRPs are long-term, time-consuming, expensive projects. The DRP for a large company can cost tens of millions of dollars. It is essential that senior management not only support but also insist upon an effective, well-tested DRP.

> **NOTE**
> DRPs can lower insurance rates, and the preparation of a DRP can assist in risk-management efforts.

The process starts with a business analysis. It identifies critical functions and their maximum tolerable downtimes. Then it identifies strategies for dealing with a wide variety of scenarios that might trigger the plan. As a security professional, you most likely will participate as a member of the disaster-planning and disaster-recovery teams.

Primary Steps to Disaster Recovery

These are the primary steps to disaster recovery (in order of importance):

1. Ensure the safety of individuals.
2. Contain the damage.
3. Assess the damage and begin recovery operations according to the DCP and BCP.

Activating the Disaster Recovery Plan

As a security professional, you will play a key role in reestablishing business operations in a crisis by rebuilding the networks and systems that the business requires. The recovery process involves two main phases. The first phase is to restore business operations. In many cases, the recovery might be at an alternate site. You may be required to build a network rapidly from available backup data, backup equipment, and any equipment that might be available from vendors.

The second phase is to return operations to its original state before the disaster. To return to normal operations, you must rebuild the primary site. The transition back to the normal site and the closure of the alternate site should be part of the "Return to Home Site" portion of the BCP/DRP.

Activate salvage and repair teams. They will do their work before people and data can return to the primary site. Security professionals are often on the repair team to rebuild the damaged parts of the network infrastructure. They will match—or increase—previous security levels. If you need new equipment, use this opportunity to improve security.

Operating in a Reduced/Modified Environment

During a crisis, many of the normal conditions, such as controls, support, and processes, might not be available. You must adapt quickly to ensure the secure operation of systems, including backups and reconciliation of errors. Here are a few points to keep in mind:

- You may want to suspend normal processes, such as separation of duties or spending limits. You should compensate with additional controls or by additional auditing. The DRP should give added privileges or spending authority to certain people or for certain tasks.
- If a number of systems are down, users might need more technical support or guidance on how to use alternate systems or access. The BIAs should have identified minimum recovery resources as part of the recovery needs.
- During a disaster and recovery, it might be good to combine services that were on different hardware platforms onto common servers. This might speed up recovery. However, you must manage this process carefully to make sure the movement and recovery goes smoothly.
- While running at the alternate site, you must continue to make backups of data and systems. This might prevent new disasters if the recovery site fails.

Restoring Damaged Systems

You must plan for rebuilding damaged systems. You need to know where to get configuration charts, inventory lists, and backup applications and data. You must have access control lists to make sure the system allows only legitimate users on it. Keep the following points in mind:

- Once the rebuilding starts, the administrator must make sure to update the operating systems and applications with the most current patches. Backups or installation disks often contain older versions that are not current.
- After you rebuild the system, you must restore the data to the RPO. This includes reconciling books and records. You must make sure the operating systems and applications are current and secure.
- Many organizations overlook access control permissions in recovery plans. You must activate the access control rules, directories, and remote access systems to permit users to get on the new systems. When you are making the plan, be sure that any vendor software will run on alternate processors. Some vendors license their products to operate only on a certain CPU.

Disaster Recovery Issues

This is a short list of disaster recovery issues that are often overlooked in the maintenance and execution of a DRP.

- **Generators**—Ensure all fuel is fresh and contracts are in place to guarantee a supply of fuel in a crisis. Generators must receive routine maintenance and should be run periodically to make sure they are ready to operate and capable of carrying the expected system load.
- **Safety of damaged site**—You must protect the primary (damaged) site from further damage or looting.
- **Reentry**—You must examine the damaged site using people qualified to determine whether it is safe for people to reenter.
- **Transportation of equipment and backups**—The plan must provide safe transportation of people, equipment, and backup data to and from the alternate site.
- **Communications and networks**—Regular telephone service often fails in a crisis. You might need an alternate method of communication, especially among key team members.

Recovery Alternatives

A business continuity (BC) coordinator considers each alternative's ability to support critical business functions, its operational readiness compared to RTO, and the associated cost. He or she examines specifications for workspace, security requirements, IT, and telecommunications.

Three choices usually are considered if a business (or some part of it) has to be moved for recovery:

- A dedicated site operated by the business, such as a secondary processing center
- A commercially leased facility, such as a hot site or mobile facility
- An agreement with an internal or external facility

External commercial providers offer services to many organizations. That means if there is a disaster, it could affect many customers of a commercial provider. What priority will you have if this happens? Know your options (along with prices) for things such as test time, declaration, fees, and minimum/maximum recovery days. Make sure that the specifications for workspace, security requirements, IT, and telecommunications are suitable for your critical business functions. Ensure that suitable accommodations are available for staff including facilities for resting and showering, as well as catering.

No matter what choice your business makes, the IT department's job is to make sure all necessary equipment is available at the alternate site. This includes the critical files, documentation, and other items identified in the recovery categories. Other items can include additional patch cables, USB drives, or other common items IT personnel may use on a daily basis.

Interim or Alternate Processing Strategies

Regardless where you choose to continue operations, you'll need a location to support your IT infrastructure. There are several options available, depending on cost and the time it takes to become operational. Here are the most common recovery location options:

- An alternate processing center or mirrored site is always ready and under the organization's control. It is the most expensive option because it requires fully redundant or duplicate operations and synchronized data. The organization operates it continuously. Its additional costs might be justified by business needs (such as having a duplicate support staff) other than recovery planning. However, making cost allocations is complex.
- A hot site is one that can take over operations quickly. It has all the equipment and data already staged at the location, though you may need to refresh or update the data. There are two kinds of hot sites. One is company owned and dedicated. The other is a commercial hot site. The hot site's advantage is that it can provide alternative computing facilities quickly, allowing rapid recovery. An internally owned hot site will be more expensive than some other alternatives, but no one else will compete for it during a regional disaster.
- A warm site has some common IT, communications, power, and HVAC, but you will have to purchase and deliver IT equipment such as servers and communications. You will have to retrieve and load data as well. Many organizations own warm sites and often use them for off-site data storage.
- A cold site is an empty data center with HVAC and power. It is the least-expensive option. It requires a lot of time to get up and running because you must purchase, deliver, and configure all equipment and telecommunications. Some organizations begin recovery in a hot site and transfer over to a warm site or cold site if the interruption lasts a long time.

Table 8-2 compares the most common recovery site options.

TABLE 8-2 Comparing common recovery site options.

FEATURE	HOT SITE	WARM SITE	COLD SITE	MULTIPLE SITES
Cost	High	Medium	Low	No direct costs
Computer equipped	Yes	Yes	No	Yes
Connectivity equipped	Yes	Yes	No	Yes
Data equipped	Yes	No	No	Yes
Staffed	Yes	No	No	Yes
Typical lead time to readiness	Hours	Hours to days	Days to weeks	Moments to minutes

Processing Agreements

One way to solve recovery problems is to find organizations with similar IT configurations and backup technologies. This could be another company, a contingent carrier, or a service bureau. You then forge an agreement with the other organization to provide support if your company encounters a disaster. IT, security, and legal departments should carefully review draft agreements.

Reciprocal or Mutual Aid

Your company might enter into a reciprocal agreement, also known as mutual aid or a consortium agreement, with a company that has similar technology. In a consortium agreement, a number of companies agree to support each other. You must carefully consider this approach. For example, can each organization continue its primary business while supporting another? Can the equipment and infrastructure support both organizations? You must do tests to confirm that all systems can handle the extra load and that they are compatible. You also must consider the sensitivity of the data and any regulations that apply to it. The partners' administrators or users might be able to access it. Both parties must warn each other if they upgrade or retire technology that could make their systems incompatible.

Reciprocal Centers

Reciprocal centers often involve businesses that do the same type of work, but are not direct competitors. These might include cross-town hospitals or a paperback book publisher paired with a hardcover publisher. Familiarity and commonality have advantages. They may share special codes, industry jargon, and special forms needed in the industry. For example, hospitals use the term "DRG code." It refers to a number that corresponds, in a common database, to a diagnosis, procedure, or disease.

Contingency

An organization might contract for contingency carriers or contingent suppliers if their primary supply method fails. You need to consider maintenance fees and activation time. You also need to check if the carriers, especially communications carriers, share the same cable or routing paths. It is prudent to ask them.

Service Bureau

A service bureau is a service provider that has extra capacity. An example is a call center to handle incoming calls. Your organization can contract for emergency use of it. This can raise the same concerns as those with a reciprocal agreement arrangement. The vendor might increase its business and consume its extra capacity, or the vendor might modify its hardware or configurations.

CHAPTER SUMMARY

You learned three core principles of information security:

- Identify the risks to the organization.
- Prevent damage as much as possible by using controls.
- Have plans and procedures ready to react to incidents that you cannot prevent.

You can express these principles and controls in terms of people, processes, technology, and data.

In this chapter, you learned about the reasons and processes of risk management. You learned how a business continuity plan (BCP) helps you make sure a disaster doesn't put your organization out of business. You learned about risk analysis, including the difference between a quantitative risk analysis and qualitative risk analysis. You learned the most common responses to risk and how they help you develop a risk-reduction strategy. You learned about countermeasures and how to evaluate them.

You learned the three types of activity controls and how they correspond to the security life cycle. You learned how response determines your organization's ability to deal with disasters. You learned the three types of backups and what backup models you can use to recover from a disaster. Additionally, you learned the steps you must take for incident response and the role incident response plays in the risk, response, and recovery processes. Finally, you learned the three main steps to disaster recovery and the roles you play throughout the disaster recovery plan.

KEY CONCEPTS AND TERMS

Administrative controls
Corrective controls
Countermeasures
Detective controls
Emergency operations center (EOC)
Event
Impact
Incident
Likelihood
Maximum tolerable downtime (MTD)
Preventative controls
Safeguards
Technical controls
Threat source

CHAPTER 8 ASSESSMENT

1. A plan that ensures your company continues to operate in the face of adverse circumstances is called a ________.
   A. Disaster recovery plan (DRP)
   B. Business impact analysis (BIA)
   C. Business continuity plan (BCP)
   D. None of the above

2. A plan that ensures your company recovers from a disaster is a ________.
   A. Disaster recovery plan (DRP)
   B. Business impact analysis (BIA)
   C. Business continuity plan (BCP)
   D. None of the above

3. A vulnerability is a flaw or weakness in your system security procedures, design, implementation, or internal controls.
   A. True
   B. False

4. Which of the following is an activity phase control?
   A. Detective controls
   B. Preventative controls
   C. Corrective controls
   D. All of the above

5. ________ is the maximum time that a business can survive without a particular critical system.
   A. Recovery time objective (RTO)
   B. Critical business function (CBF)
   C. Maximum tolerable downtime (MTD)
   D. None of the above

6. The incident-handling process includes which of the following?
   A. Documentation
   B. Response
   C. Notification
   D. Recovery and follow-up
   E. All of the above

7. The primary steps to disaster recovery include the safety of individuals, containing the damage, and assessing the damage and beginning the recovery operations.
   A. True
   B. False

8. An event that has a negative impact on operations is known as a(n) ________.
   A. Countermeasure
   B. Impact
   C. Risk
   D. Incident

9. The process of describing a risk scenario and then determining the degree of impact that event would have on business operations is quantitative risk analysis.
   A. True
   B. False

10. Risk that remains even after risk-mitigation efforts have been implemented is known as ________ risk.
    A. Qualitative
    B. Quantitative
    C. Residual
    D. None of the above

CHAPTER 9

Cryptography

ACCORDING TO *Webster's Revised Unabridged Dictionary*, cryptography is "the act or art of writing in secret characters." The Free Online Dictionary of Computing says cryptography is "encoding data so that it can only be decoded by specific individuals." Encrypting and decrypting data is a cryptosystem. It usually involves an algorithm, known as a cipher. This combines the original data, known as plaintext, with one or more keys. A key is a string of numbers or characters known only to the sender and/or recipient. The secret message is ciphertext.

The security of a cryptosystem usually depends on the secrecy of the keys rather than the secrecy of the cipher. A strong cryptosystem has a large range of possible keys, making it impossible to try them all in a brute-force attack. It should also produce ciphertext that appears random to all standard statistical tests. It resists all known previous methods for breaking codes. The process of breaking codes is cryptanalysis.

Essentially, cryptography conceals information from others. You can find cryptography in business and government, as well as in personal transactions. Cryptography is not the only way to make information secure. Rather, it is a set of tools for IT security.

Cryptography accomplishes four security goals:

- Confidentiality
- Integrity
- Authentication
- Nonrepudiation

The IT security professional creatively uses these cryptographic tools to meet businesses' security goals.

Chapter 9 Topics

This chapter covers the following topics and concepts:

- What cryptography is
- How cryptography can address business and security requirements
- What cryptographic applications are used in information system security
- What cryptographic principles, concepts, and terminology are
- What cryptographic applications, tools, and resources are
- What the principles of certificates and key management are

Chapter 9 Goals

When you complete this chapter, you will be able to:

- Define the basic concepts of cryptography
- Describe symmetric, asymmetric, and hashing algorithms
- Examine the various uses of cryptography
- Understand the challenges of cryptographic uses
- Define certificate management

What Is Cryptography?

Cryptography deals with two types of information:

- **Unencrypted information**—Information in understandable form. Unencrypted information is **plaintext**, or cleartext.
- **Encrypted information**—Information in scrambled form. Encrypted information is ciphertext.

Encryption is the act of scrambling plaintext into ciphertext. **Decryption** is the act of unscrambling ciphertext into plaintext.

Encryption uses a known mathematical process for performing its function. This process is known as an **algorithm**. An algorithm is a repeatable process that produces the same result when it receives the same input. A **cipher** is an algorithm to encrypt or decrypt information. This repeatability is important to make sure that information, once encrypted, can be decrypted. Figure 9-1 shows a cryptosystem at work.

FIGURE 9-1

A cryptosystem at work.

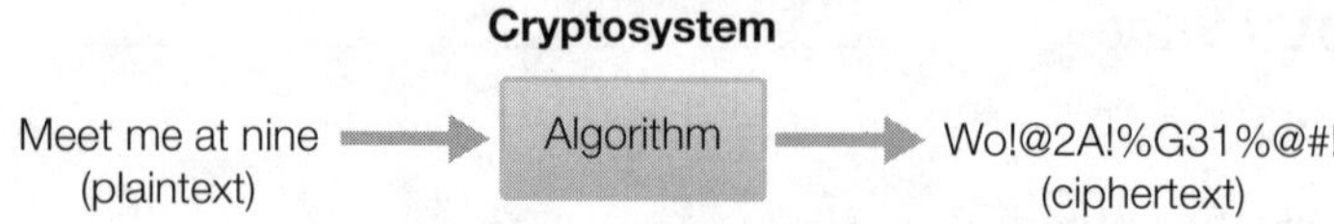

Note that the algorithm you use to encrypt information may or may not be the same one you use to decrypt that information. For example, a simple algorithm that adds X to each value to encrypt would have to subtract X from each value to decrypt. In addition, some encryption algorithms have no decryption algorithms. These are **one-way algorithms**. The output of a one-way algorithm is a **hash**.

Every cipher and any plaintext you want to encrypt needs a **key**. The encryption cipher uses the cryptographic key to vary its output so that two correspondents can protect their information from anyone else who has the same cipher. By changing the key, you change the output of the cryptographic function, even if the plaintext remains the same.

Encryption ciphers fall into two general categories:

- Those that use the same key to encrypt and decrypt are **private (symmetric) key** ciphers.
- Those that use different keys to encrypt and decrypt are **public (asymmetric) key** ciphers.

Sometimes, the terms public key and private key refer to the two different keys in asymmetric ciphers. Together they are a key pair. To avoid confusion, this book uses the symmetric and asymmetric naming convention for ciphers. Note, however, that many sources interchange these terms freely.

Basic Cryptographic Principles

A perfect cipher does not exist. Given sufficient time and resources, an attacker can break any code. The goal of cryptography is to make the cost or the time required to decrypt a message without the key exceed the value of the protected information. Thus, you could effectively protect information that is worth no more than $100 with a cipher that costs $1,000 to break. This is an important concept. It provides one of the basic rationales for selecting cryptographic tools and ciphers.

The number of possible keys to a cipher is a **keyspace**. Without any knowledge of the key, an attacker with access to an encrypted message and the decryption cipher could try every possible key to decode the message. This is a brute-force attack. By making the keyspace large enough, you make the cost of a brute-force attack too high. Assuming the cipher has no mathematical weaknesses, a larger keyspace usually means more security.

There are public (open source) ciphers and hidden (closed-source or proprietary) ciphers. Experts subject open source ciphers to extensive analysis. They find flaws and weaknesses that could diminish the cipher's strength. Although one cannot prove that a cipher is completely secure, a single exception can prove that it is not. A cipher is more secure if it withstands public scrutiny without anyone identifying major flaws.

The most scrutinized cipher in history is the **Data Encryption Standard (DES)**, published in 1977 as Federal Information Processing Standard (FIPS) 46. Modern computing has searched its keyspace of 72 quadrillion keys without finding a single mathematical weakness.

A Brief History of Cryptography

People have used cryptography to protect information for at least 4,000 years. As soon as people learned to write, they sought to protect their words from prying eyes. Early information security was as simple as hiding it. This method is called steganography. For example, legend says that Histiaeus, tyrant of Miletus in the 5th century BCE, sent a message tattooed on the scalp of his slave. Any enemy intercepting the messenger would not likely find the information. However, this was not speedy. Miletus had to wait for the messenger's hair to grow back before sending him with the hidden message. In addition, reusability was somewhat of a problem.

The science of cryptanalysis, or breaking codes, has been important for many years. Queen Elizabeth I had her cousin, Mary Queen of Scots, executed for treason. Why? Because Sir Francis Walsingham cracked the secret code that Mary used to communicate with her co-conspirators. Thus, cryptanalysis altered the course of English history.

Twentieth-Century Cryptography

In World War I and World War II, cryptography played an important role in communications. These were the first major wars fought in which combatants used radios. All countries used codes to protect communications. Many combatants successfully broke their opponents' codes, sometimes more than once. By decrypting the Japanese Purple cipher and the German Enigma, U.S. and British code-breakers gave military decision-makers insight into enemy plans. They helped the Allies win decisive military battles, including the Battle of Midway and the Battle of Britain.

The birth of the digital computer made complex ciphers feasible. Digital computers could perform operations in seconds that would normally take hours or days by hand. As a result, modern cryptography moved quickly into the digital realm. The Munitions Control Act of 1950 specifically classified cryptographic ciphers and equipment as Class 13B munitions. That made them tools of warfare subject to export control and government oversight.

In 1976, Whitman Diffie and Martin Hellman at Stanford University published a paper that revolutionized cryptography. They introduced the concept of asymmetric key cryptography. **Symmetric key cryptography** cannot secure correspondence until after the two parties exchange keys. **Asymmetric key cryptography** uses a cipher with two separate keys. One is for encryption and one for decryption. Correspondents do not first have to exchange secret information to communicate securely. With asymmetric key cryptography, an opponent can intercept everything and still not be able decipher the message.

Consider the four basic goals of encryption: confidentiality, integrity, authentication, and nonrepudiation. Classic computing, before the digital computer, addressed each of these. By encrypting a message, the sender made sure it was secure, as long as an opponent did not have the key and could not find a shortcut to solve it. Integrity often was incidental. If decryption produced gibberish, you knew the message had changed in transit. However, if a forger obtained encryption equipment, a fake message could appear legitimate. Authentication—proving the identity of the sender—was possible if both sender and receiver had the same codebook and exchanged elements of it. However, exchanging this information slowly compromised its contents unless you refreshed the codebook. Lastly, nonrepudiation—proving that a party did indeed originate a message—was not possible with symmetric key cryptography. Anyone with access to the shared key could originate a message. You couldn't "prove" who wrote it before asymmetric key cryptography.

Cryptography's Role in Information Security

When it comes to information security, cryptography can satisfy these requirements:

- Confidentiality
- Integrity
- Authentication
- Nonrepudiation

Confidentiality

Confidentiality keeps information secret from all but authorized people. You can lock safes, post armed guards, or whisper in someone's ear in a remote field to ensure confidentiality. These tactics often are not enough, however. Cryptography makes information unintelligible to anyone who doesn't know the encryption cipher and the proper key. Authorized users can get this knowledge. An effective cryptanalysis also can produce it. The value of confidentiality is straightforward. Disclosing certain communications that contain confidential information could either harm the correspondents or help an opponent.

Integrity

Integrity ensures no one, even the sender, changes information after transmitting it. If a message doesn't decrypt properly, someone or something probably changed the ciphertext in transit. In addition, cryptography can enforce integrity with hashes or checksums. A **checksum** is a one-way calculation of information that yields a result usually much smaller than the original message. It is difficult to duplicate. For example, a simple checksum of the phone number 1-800-555-1212 could be the sum of each digit, 30. You can't re-create the phone number knowing the checksum. Nevertheless, you can tell if the phone number matches the checksum. If you changed one digit—for example you changed 1-800-555-1212 to 1-900-555-1212—the checksum no longer matches the expected value. You would question the data's integrity. Note, however, that this is not a practical security method. You could easily modify the data to produce the correct checksum with the wrong phone number. Integrity verification tends to use robust mathematical processes that are hard to reverse-engineer. These are hashes. You'll learn more about hashes later in this chapter.

Authentication

Authentication confirms the identity of an entity. It can be the sender, the sender's computer, some device, or some information. Humans instinctively authenticate each other based on characteristics such as facial appearance, voice, or skin texture. A traditional military authentication method is a password. If you know it, the sentry lets you pass. If you don't, you're in trouble. In the digital realm, cryptography provides a way to authenticate entities. The most straightforward form is a user ID and password. Note that this is not strong authentication. Anyone else who obtains this fixed information can provide the same information to the recipient, who will think the user is legitimate.

In general, symmetric key cryptography has this problem. If an attacker can listen in on the conversation where the sender and receiver agree on a cipher and key, the attacker can pose as a legitimate user. To be able to authenticate in a symmetric key cryptography world, parties must first securely distribute keys among themselves. For example, they could use asymmetric key cryptography to distribute the symmetric keys. Then they would use the symmetric keys for subsequent correspondence. Another less sophisticated way to distribute keys is to use an unrelated communications method. A physical courier could deliver the key. This is expensive and time-consuming for large numbers of users. However, the value of authenticating all parties is great enough in environments such as the military that it is worth the cost.

Asymmetric key cryptography offers a simpler means of authentication. Along with confidentiality, asymmetric key cryptography is the cornerstone of Internet commerce.

Nonrepudiation

Nonrepudiation enables you to prevent a party from denying a previous statement or action. For example, suppose an investor sends an e-mail to a broker that states, "Buy 1,000 shares of XYZ at 50." Shortly after the exchange executes the order, XYZ stock drops to 20. The investor then denies the buy order and says it was really an order to sell. How does one resolve this he said/she said dilemma?

Using asymmetric key cryptography, one can prove mathematically—usually to the satisfaction of a judge or jury—that a particular party did indeed originate a specific message at a specific time. The fundamental principle of asymmetric key cryptography is that it uses a key pair to encrypt and decrypt. The originator is the only one who knows one of the keys. It has an irrefutable timestamp. The argument in court would go something like this:

FYI

It's easy to confuse public and private keys. If you were encrypting a message to protect its confidentiality and integrity, you would use the recipient's public key. Only the recipient would be able to decrypt the message using the corresponding private key. On the other hand, if you, as the message sender, want to use encryption to enforce nonrepudiation, you would encrypt the message with your private key. Anyone who has access to your public key can decrypt the message, but successful decryption proves that you originated the message.

"Encryption does more than just keep messages secret. It can validate the identity of the sender. This encrypted message decrypts with this public key. Only the holder of the associated private key could have created this message. The message contains a time-based hash produced by a trusted third-party timestamping device. Neither party could have tampered with it. Thus, we know with effective certainty that this message as decrypted is genuine and originated with this known party. This is nonrepudiation."

Business and Security Requirements for Cryptography

In this section, you will learn about information security principles and how cryptography can address them.

Internal Security

A number of security objectives add value to a business. These include the following:

- **Privacy**—Privacy keeps information readable only by authorized people. It keeps that data away from those who are unauthorized. For example, most companies keep salary plans private.
- **Integrity**—Integrity ensures that no one has changed or deleted data. For example, payroll data needs integrity to make sure no one changes a payment after sending it to the check printer.
- **Authorization**—Authorization means approving someone to do a specific task or access certain data. For example, changing salary plans requires proper authorization from management.
- **Access control**—Access control involves restricting information to the right people. For example, you can store salary plans in a locked file cabinet to which only HR employees have the key.

Security Between Businesses

A number of security objectives add value to relationships between businesses. In addition to those listed before, they include the following:

- **Message authentication**—Message authentication confirms the identity of the person who started a correspondence. For example, a broker would like to know that a message to "Buy 1,000 shares of XYZ for account ABC" came from ABC.
- **Signature**—A **digital signature** binds a message or data to a specific entity. Note that this is not a **digitized signature**, which is an image of an electronically reproduced signature.
- **Receipt and confirmation**—E-mail messages often use receipt and confirmation. Receipt verifies that an entity acknowledges information has arrived. Confirmation acknowledges that the provider has provided a service.
- **Nonrepudiation**—Nonrepudiation means that the person who sends a message cannot later deny it. For example, if the person who made the buy order were to dispute it after XYZ dropped 50 percent, nonrepudiation would prove the original message was valid.

Security Measures That Benefit Everyone

Beyond business relationships, certain security objectives add value to information systems. In addition to those items already listed, these include the following:

- **Anonymity**—This disguises a user's identity. For example, a dissident in a repressive country might wish to post information to a Web discussion site without the authorities knowing who he or she is.
- **Timestamping**—This provides an exact time when a producer creates or sends information. For example, people submitting tax returns at the last minute may wish to prove they met the deadline.
- **Revocation**—**Revocation** stops authorization for access to data. For example, a person who loses a credit card calls the issuer to stop use of the card.
- **Ownership**—This associates a person with information to claim legal rights. For example, most documents have copyright notices that tell who wrote them.

Cryptographic Applications and Uses in Information System Security

Information Security magazine prints a yearly "Information Security Buyer's Guide." The 2010 edition lists 15 general classifications of over 1,900 security products and services. These include the following:

- Anti-malware
- Compliance/auditing
- Forensics
- ID management
- Intellectual property
- Managed security service providers (MSSPs)
- Messaging safeguards
- Patch management
- Perimeter defenses
- Security information management (SIM), security event management (SEM), and incident response
- Transaction security (digital certificates, secure file transfer)
- Wireless security

You can find cryptography uses in many of these categories.

Authentication tools include tokens, smart cards, biometrics, passwords, and password recovery. Some tools rely on proximity cards and fingerprint readers. Others use cryptographic techniques such as public key infrastructure (PKI) user authentication and tools that securely send passwords across the Internet. **Public key infrastructure (PKI)** is a set of hardware, software, people, policies, and procedures needed to create, manage, distribute, use, store, and revoke digital certificates.

Access control and authorization includes firewalls, **timestamping**, single sign-on, identity management, and laptop security. These encryption tools have virtual private networks that may be included with firewalls, but not necessarily the firewalls themselves. They also may secure connectivity across the Internet and provide tools that encrypt contents of hard drives.

Assessment and auditing tools include vulnerability-assessment scanners, penetration-testing tools, forensic software, and log analyzers. Assessment scanners and penetration-testing tools that involve password-cracking modules use cryptographic techniques to try to guess passwords.

Security management products include tools for enterprise security management, configuration and patch management, and security policy development. Integrity checking tools use cryptographic methods to make sure nothing and no one has modified the software.

Wireless-security tools encrypt data to protect it in transit and to limit access to authorized people. E-mail security tools often involve encrypting data in transit, and sometimes in storage. Content filtering includes antivirus products, mobile code scanners, Web filters, and spam blockers. They typically do not use encryption, although you may encrypt databases of threat signatures.

Encryption tools include line encryption, database security products, virtual private networks (VPNs), public key infrastructure (PKI), and crypto accelerators. These products use cryptography extensively to do their tasks. A crypto accelerator offloads cryptographic routines from the main processor to cards that have chipsets designed for fast encryption.

technical TIP

The only unbreakable cryptographic cipher is the **Vernam cipher**. Another name for it is a **one-time pad cipher**. You'll read more about that later in this chapter. You can also find out more about the Vernam cipher at: *http://www.pro-technix.com/information/crypto/pages/vernam_base.html*.

Cryptanalysis and Public Versus Private Keys

Encryption makes data unreadable to anyone except an authorized person with the right software and key. If the data is valuable, however, thieves will try to break the code.

You can break a cipher in two ways:

- Analyzing the ciphertext to find the plaintext or key
- Analyzing the ciphertext and its associated plaintext to find the key

A cipher is unconditionally secure if no amount of ciphertext will give enough information to yield a unique plaintext. You can break almost any cipher, given enough time and resources. However, a cipher's main purpose is to make it so difficult to break that it is computationally infeasible to crack. Thus, a cipher that an attacker cannot break economically (relative to the value of the protected data) is strong or computationally secure.

There are four basic forms of a cryptographic attack:

- **Ciphertext-only attack (COA)**—In a ciphertext-only attack, the cryptanalyst has access only to a segment of encrypted data, and has no choice as to what that data may be. An example is the cryptogram in some daily newspapers. Note, however, that by understanding the context of the information, one can infer that certain words or formatting may be present. Figure 9-2 shows a ciphertext-only attack.

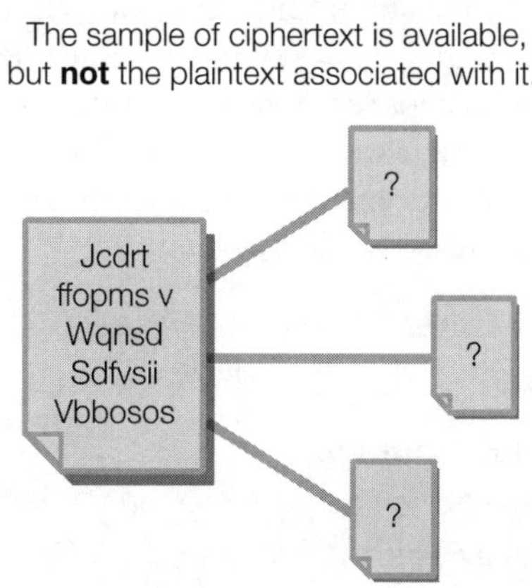

FIGURE 9-2
A ciphertext-only attack (COA).

FIGURE 9-3

A known-plaintext attack (KPA).

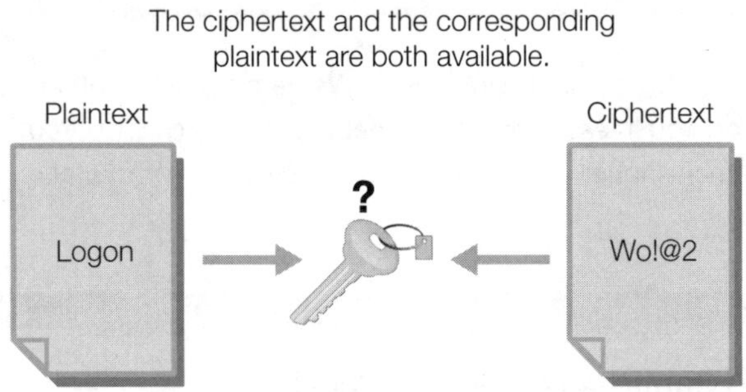

- **Known-plaintext attack (KPA)**—In a known-plaintext attack, the cryptanalyst possesses certain pieces of information before and after encryption. For example, all secure logon sessions may begin with the characters LOGON, and the next transmission may be PASSWORD. A secure encryption cipher should resist an attack by an analyst who has access to numerous plaintext-ciphertext pairs. Figure 9-3 shows a known-plaintext attack.
- **Chosen-plaintext attack**—In a chosen-plaintext attack, the cryptanalyst can encrypt any information and observe the output. This is best case for the cryptanalyst. It offers the most flexibility (and insight) into the encryption mechanism. An example is the encryption offered by older versions of Microsoft Office software applications. One could encrypt only the letter "A," then "B," and so on, to try to discern what the cipher is doing.
- **Chosen-ciphertext attack**—A chosen-ciphertext attack is a special case. It is relevant in asymmetric key systems and hash functions. In a chosen-ciphertext attack, cryptanalysts submit data coded with the same cipher and key they are trying to break to the decryption device to see either the plaintext output or the effect the decrypted message has on some system. As a simple example, consider an owner who trains a guard dog to respond only to commands spoken in Navajo. A burglar doesn't know Navajo, but can make a series of noises and sounds. The dog ignores nonsense (from its perspective), but obeys valid commands. Speaking enough gibberish, the burglar might prompt a response from the dog (even if not the one he seeks). By observing the dog's reaction to various apparently nonsensical commands, the burglar might be able to make the dog lie down and play dead. Chosen-ciphertext attacks have particular uses in attacking encrypted e-mail. Due to the complexity of the mathematics involved, this book does not address them.

Symmetric and Asymmetric Key Cipher Resistance to Attack

Cryptanalysis has several objectives, including the following:

- Derive the plaintext of a target message.
- Determine the key used to encrypt a target message.
- Derive the algorithm used by a particular cipher.
- Solve the general mathematical problem underlying the cryptography.

Cryptographers use many tools in cryptanalysis. They have such names as linear cryptanalysis, differential cryptanalysis, brute force, exhaustive search, and information theory. In the most direct case, the analyst must use an encrypted message to derive its associated plaintext. Many ciphers used today are open source. That means the analyst has access to the logic for the encryption and decryption functions. The security of closed-source or proprietary ciphers stems in part from the fact that the analyst does not necessarily know how the cipher works.

For example, the United States did not have access to a Japanese Purple cipher device in World War II. Code breakers had to determine how the machine worked by analyzing faint patterns in the ciphertext. Once they figured that out, analysts could then change the order of different keys to decrypt message traffic. Once they identified the key, anyone could read all traffic coded for that time period with the same key.

In some cases, analysts found a solution by attacking the underlying mathematics of a cryptosystem. In the late 1970s, some vendors made security products that used asymmetric key cryptography based on a simplified version of the knapsack problem called the subset sum problem. Unfortunately for the vendors, Len Adelman developed a general solution to the subset sum problem in 1982 that could run on an Apple II computer. Overnight, an entire class of products became obsolete.

Today, the basis of most commercial asymmetric key cryptography is the difficulty of factoring large numbers. For example, it is relatively easy with pen and paper to calculate $757 \times 769 = 582{,}133$. Yet, given the result 582,133, deriving its two factors is not as easy. The classic approach would involve trying 2, 3, 5, 7, 11, 13, etc., until a prime factor is found. That would take 134 guesses. Although this becomes much easier with a computer, imagine that the two prime factors are 100 digits each! Just to put this into perspective, here is a 100-digit prime number:

6,513,516,734,600,035,718,300,327,211,250,928,237,178,281,758,494,417,
357,560,086,828,416,863,929,270,451,437,126,021,949,850,746,381

Moreover, the preceding number would only be one of two factors. You'll read more about the mathematics of asymmetric key cryptography later in this course.

Cryptographic Principles, Concepts, and Terminology

You learned in Chapter 1 that there are many information security objectives. It is important to understand these. They represent most of the goals of security initiatives, including cryptography. One of the best summaries of security objectives is in the *Handbook of Applied Cryptography*. Table 9-1 contains the security objectives summary.

When you try to solve a business-security problem, you need to understand these terms. Then you can tell if you could use a cryptographic solution.

Cryptographic Functions and Ciphers

A basic understanding of cryptographic ciphers can tell you how cryptography can satisfy your business needs.

TABLE 9-1 Information security objectives.

OBJECTIVE	STEPS TO TAKE
Privacy or confidentiality	Keep information secret from all unauthorized users.
Integrity	Ensure unauthorized users or unknown processes have not altered information.
Entity authentication or identification	Corroborate the identity of an entity (that is, a person, a computer terminal, a credit card, etc.).
Message authentication	Corroborate the source of information; authenticate the data's origin.
Signature	Bind information to an entity.
Authorization	Convey an official sanction to do or be something to another entity.
Validation	Provide timely authorization to use or manipulate information or resources.
Access control	Restrict access to resources to privileged entities.
Certification	Endorse information by a trusted entity.
Timestamping	Record the time a user created or accessed information.
Witnessing	Verify the action to create an object or verify an object's existence by an entity other than the creator.
Receipt	Acknowledge that the recipient received information.
Confirmation	Acknowledge that the provider has provided services.
Ownership	Grant an entity the legal right to use or transfer a resource to others.
Anonymity	Conceal the identity of an entity involved in some process.
Nonrepudiation	Prevent an entity from denying previous commitments or actions.
Revocation	Retract certification or authorization.

Business-Security Implementations

Here is a review of the general classifications of security products and services:

- Authentication (non-PKI)
- Access control/authorization
- Assessment and audit
- Security management products
- Perimeter/network security/availability
- Content filtering

- Encryption
- Administration/education
- Outsource services/consultants

By cross-referencing them to the information security objectives mentioned before, you can see which business tools and services satisfy which security objectives. Then you can tell which of these objectives cryptography can address. Table 9-2 shows how security products and security objectives relate to one another.

TABLE 9-2 Security objectives and security products.

OBJECTIVE	AUTHENTICATION	ACCESS CONTROL	ASSESSMENT AND AUDIT	SECURITY MANAGEMENT	NETWORK SECURITY	CONTENT FILTERING	ENCRYPTION	ADMINISTRATION	CONSULTANTS
Privacy or confidentiality		X			X		X	X	X
Integrity				X	X		X	X	X
Entity authentication or identification	X	X			X		X	X	X
Message authentication	X				X		X		
Signature	X				X		X	X	
Authorization	X	X			X				
Validation		X	X	X				X	
Access control	X	X		X	X	X	X	X	
Certification			X	X			X		X
Timestamping		X			X		X		
Witnessing			X				X		X
Receipt					X			X	
Confirmation					X			X	
Ownership			X				X	X	X
Anonymity							X	X	
Nonrepudiation					X		X	X	X
Revocation	X				X		X		

As you can see, you can use cryptography to reach many security objectives. Specifically, it offers the following capabilities:

- **Privacy or confidentiality**—Cryptography scrambles information so that only someone with the right cipher and key can read it. Note that this person could include a clever cryptanalyst.
- **Integrity**—Cryptography protects integrity by providing checksums or hashes. You can compare these to a known table of good values to prove the data has not changed.
- **Entity authentication or identification**—Someone's ability to encode or decode a message means that person has the cryptographic key. If a business relationship requires that this key remain secret, possession is proof of valid identity.
- **Message authentication**—Similar to entity authentication, a coded message with a private key proves who the message's writer is. Again, this stipulation should be part of any business contract or formal relationship.
- **Signature**—Cryptography can provide a way to make a digital signature. This can prove that a given person sent a specific message.
- **Access control**—This involves encrypting privileged resources or data so that only authorized people can decrypt them and enforce access to them.
- **Certification**—A trusted entity can certify a message or data by adding a cryptographic checksum and a digital signature.
- **Timestamping**—Using asymmetric key cryptography, a trusted device can issue timestamps that attackers cannot forge. It binds a hash of the timestamped information with the output of a secure, reliable clock.
- **Witnessing**—A third party can add a cryptographic checksum to data to prove it exists in a given format at a particular time.
- **Ownership**—This refers to a cryptographic hash created by an owner and added to the data, and then submitted to a trusted third party for corroboration. This identifies an entity as the data's owner.
- **Anonymity**—Using cryptography, one can conceal the identity of an entity by passing information in an encrypted format that monitors cannot interpret. In addition, using a series of encrypted hops and getting rid of logs can provide an entity with anonymous presence on the Internet.
- **Nonrepudiation**—An asymmetric key signature of data, agreed to as part of a business relationship, can prove the sender's identity to the receiver.

Types of Ciphers

Ciphers come in two basic forms:

- **Transposition ciphers**—A **transposition cipher** rearranges characters or bits of data.
- **Substitution ciphers**—A **substitution cipher** replaces bits, characters, or blocks of information with other bits, characters, or blocks.

1	2	3	4
A	T	T	A
C	K	A	T
D	A	W	N

FIGURE 9-4
A transposition cipher.

Transposition Ciphers

A simple transposition cipher writes characters into rows in a matrix. It then reads the columns as output. For example, write the message "ATTACK AT DAWN" into a four-column matrix as shown in Figure 9-4.

Then, read the information in columns: ACDTKATAWATN. This would be the ciphertext. The key would be {1,2,3,4}, which is the order in which the columns are read. Encrypting with a different key, say {2,4,3,1} would result in a different ciphertext—in this case, TKAATNTAWACD.

Note that in this example, the ciphertext stores the frequency of letters. That is, the most common letters in the English language—E, T, A, O, and N—appear a disproportionate number of times in the transposition ciphertext. This is a clue to the cryptanalyst that this is a transposition cipher.

Transposition ciphers keep all the elements of the original message. They simply scramble the information in a way that they can reassemble later. Some basic digital transposition ciphers will swap bits within bytes to make the data appear unintelligible to the casual reader. An example of a spoken transposition cipher is pig Latin.

Substitution Ciphers

One of the simplest substitution ciphers is the **Caesar cipher**. It shifts each letter in the English alphabet a fixed number of positions, with Z wrapping back to A. Julius Caesar used this cipher with a shift of 3. The following illustrates an encryption using a Caesar cipher:

ATTACK AT DAWN

↓

DWWDFN DW GDZQ

Note that there are 25 possible keys for a Caesar cipher. (The 26th key maps characters back onto themselves.) Note also that this is not a transposition cipher because the letters in the ciphertext were not present in the plaintext.

A popular substitution cipher for children was the Cap'n Crunch decoder ring. The ring was included in specially marked boxes of Cap'n Crunch cereal. This ring consisted of two alphabets (A to Z) written in a circle. The inner circle didn't move, but you could rotate the outer circle. By rotating the outer circle to a set value, you created a one-to-one mapping from one alphabet to the other. To encrypt, you looked up the desired character in the inner circle and read off the character on the outer circle. To decrypt, you reversed the process. (Yes, this is a Caesar cipher!)

A **keyword mixed alphabet cipher** uses a cipher alphabet that consists of a key word, less duplicates, followed by the remaining letters of the alphabet. For example, using the key word CRYPTOGRAPHY, this type of cipher would yield the following:

ABCDEFGHIJKLMNOPQRSTUVWXYZ

↓

CRYPTOGAHBDEFIJKLMNQSUVWXZ

Thus, the plaintext word ALPHABET would encrypt to CEKACRTQ.

Any substitution cipher will use these same basic principles, regardless of complexity. To make it harder to break these codes, you can use multiple encryption schemes in succession. For example, you could encrypt every letter with its own substitution scheme. This is a **Vigenère** (vee zhen AIR) **cipher**. It works like multiple Caesar ciphers, each with its own shift characters. For example, you could use the word PARTY as the key, which would use five Caesar ciphers. Knowing that each character in the alphabet has a value from 1 to 26, you can calculate the encrypted character by adding the value of the plaintext character to the value of the corresponding character in the key. If the sum is greater than 26, just subtract 26 to find the final value. To encrypt the message ATTACK AT DAWN TOMORROW, you would obtain the following:

Plaintext:	ATTACKATDAWNTOMORROW
Key (repeated to match plaintext length):	PARTYPARTYPARTYPARTYPA
Ciphertext (shift chapracters using the key):	PTKTAZAKWYLNKHKDRIHU

This gives more security. The output appears much more random. Increasing the key length generally increases the security of a substitution cipher.

Instead of transforming each letter a fixed number of positions, you can increase the complexity of a substitution cipher by allowing any letter to uniquely map to any other letter. You can find this type of cipher, called a **simple substitution cipher**, in many newspapers as a puzzle called a cryptogram. In this case, A could map to any of 26 letters, B could map to any of 25 remaining letters, C could map to 24 letters, and so on. Thus, there are (26 factorial), or 403,291,461,126,606,000,000,000,000 possible keys that you can use. Even so, breaking these puzzles is straightforward work. This illustrates an important point: One must never confuse complexity with security.

You must do three things to make sure a substitution cipher stays secure. First, make sure the key is a random sequence without repetition. Second, make sure it is as long as the encrypted information. Third, use it only once. Such a cipher is a one-time pad. The first use of this strategy was in computer systems based on a design by an AT&T employee named Gilbert Vernam. A Vernam cipher creates a bit stream of zeros and ones that is combined with the plaintext using the exclusive-or function. The exclusive-or operation is true when one and only one of the inputs is true. The exclusive-or function, represented as $\oplus$, has the following properties:

$$0 \oplus 0 = 0$$
$$0 \oplus 1 = 1$$
$$1 \oplus 0 = 1$$
$$1 \oplus 1 = 0$$

Note that this is equivalent to the not-equal function. Using this approach, you can combine a binary stream of data with a binary keystream (stream of characters from a key) to produce ciphertext. This is how hardware or software uses modern substitution ciphers.

Product and Exponentiation Ciphers

A **product cipher** is a combination of multiple ciphers. Each could be a transposition or substitution cipher. The Data Encryption Standard (DES), or DES, is a product cipher with a 56-bit key consisting of 16 iterations of substitution and transformation. First published as a Federal Information Processing Standard (FIPS) in 1977, DES is still in use. Its developers thought it was highly secure because the computers available in 1977 would take more than 90 years to break an encrypted message. Many civil libertarians and conspiracy theorists, as well as professional cryptographers, think designers built certain weaknesses into DES to let the National Security Agency (NSA) open a backdoor in the algorithm to decrypt messages easily. However, after more than 25 years, no one has found such a weakness. Advances in cryptography—including **differential cryptanalysis**, which involves looking for patterns in vast amounts of ciphertext—actually imply that the DES design was even more secure than first suspected. Nonetheless, advances in computing power have made the 56-bit keyspace (72,057,594,037,927,900 keys) less daunting to search. Finally, in 1998, the Electronic Frontier Foundation built a special-purpose computer called Deep Crack, which can search the keyspace in less than three days. You'll read about DES in more detail later.

Some ciphers rely on the difficulty of solving certain mathematical problems. This is the basis for asymmetric key cryptography. These ciphers use a branch of mathematics known as field theory. Without getting into too much mathematics, a field is any domain of numbers in which every element other than 0 has a multiplicative inverse. For example, all rational numbers form a field. Given $x \neq 0$, one can always compute $1/x$. Fields do not have to be infinite. Instead of counting to infinity, one can restart counting after reaching a particular value. For example, in the United States, we tell time with a 12-hour clock. One hour past 10:00 is 11:00, but one hour past 12:00 is 1:00, not 13:00. Many countries use a 24-hour clock, but the wraparound effect is the same. Things get interesting mathematically when the number of integers in a set is prime. The set of integers from 1 to a prime number represents a finite field.

An exponentiation cipher involves computing exponentials over a finite mathematical field. The Rivest-Shamir-Adelman (RSA) encryption scheme relies on the difficulty of factoring large numbers. As noted earlier, it's straightforward to multiply two numbers together, but very difficult to factor one large number. You'll learn the details of this later in this chapter.

Symmetric and Asymmetric Key Cryptography

In this section, you'll learn the differences between symmetric and asymmetric key cryptography and the relative advantages and disadvantages of both.

Symmetric Key Ciphers

Symmetric key ciphers use the same key to encrypt and decrypt. As a result, they require that both parties first exchange keys to communicate. This represents a basic limitation for these cryptosystems. Before you can send a message to another party, you must first talk securely to exchange keys. This chicken-and-egg problem is what made cryptography difficult in the past for any large, dispersed organization, with the exception of governments, the military, and well-funded people.

In order to illustrate this problem, imagine that two correspondents, Alice and Bob, want to exchange information securely. In this scenario, Alice and Bob work for the ABC Company. They want to exchange pricing information for a proposal to a new client, MNO Plastics. Bob is in the field at the client site, and cannot get to the company's internal network. All information must go back and forth across the Internet.

Eva works for an overseas competitor of ABC. Her job is to gather as much intelligence as she can about ABC's proposal and bid. She has authorization to monitor, disrupt, or masquerade any communications to achieve her mission. (For the purpose of this example, we are not going to address the obvious legal issues.) Assume Eva can monitor all communications to and from Bob. Any messages he sends or receives pass through a node Eva controls.

Here's the problem: How do Alice and Bob create a secure communications session if they have not agreed to anything in advance? Let's say Alice and Bob agree to use DES to encrypt their information. Because DES is a publicly available algorithm, Eva can download a copy of DES software. Alice sends a message to Bob to use BIGBUCKS as the key. Bob acknowledges this convention, and sends his encrypted message to Alice using this key. Eva, listening in on the communications, uses the same key to decrypt Bob's message and sends his information to her company.

Alice and Bob can agree to change keys any number of times, but each time they do, Eva learns of this key change and adjusts accordingly. Using symmetric key cryptography, there is no way around this problem. Each party must exchange keys with the other party to know what key the other is using. Even if you encrypt a key with a special purpose key, or **key-encrypting key**, you must exchange the key-encrypting key at some point. Key-encrypting keys are keys that you use only to encrypt other keys. Exchanging key-encrypting keys means an attacker can intercept the key-encrypting key when you exchange it.

The solution to this dilemma requires a message that travels on a different path that Eva can't monitor. This is out-of-band communication using a secure channel. Let's say in this case that Alice and Bob agree to use DES, and Alice tells Bob to call her on his cell phone and tell her what key to he wants to use. Eva, who can read all Internet traffic, can't monitor cell phones. Alice and Bob agree on a 56-bit key and begin exchanging information. Eva is out of the loop. Of course, before Bob left on the business trip, Alice and Bob could have agreed to use a particular key. This, too, is out-of-band communication. It takes place outside the communications channel used for sending and receiving messages.

Now, ABC Company has a choice to make. It can issue the same key to all employees, which makes correspondence easy. Any employee can correspond securely with any other employee around the world. This model works well until a disgruntled employee quits and joins a competitor, taking the key with him. Now what? ABC has to reissue the key to everyone worldwide. This could be time consuming and expensive.

Alternatively, ABC could decide that a single point of failure is unacceptable and issue separate keys to each employee. However, because both parties have to use the same key with symmetric key ciphers, each employee-employee pair must have its own unique key. Thus, if there were 10 employees, ABC would need 45 key pairs $(9 + 8 + 7 + 6 + 5 + 4 + 3 + 2 + 1)$ to begin this scheme. If ABC had 100 employees, it would need 4,950 key pairs. If ABC had 10,000 employees, it would need 49,995,000 key pairs! The number of key pairs required for n correspondents is $(n(n-1))/2$. Moreover, each time an employee joined or left the company, you would have to add or delete a key pair for each of the other employees. Clearly, symmetric key systems do not scale well.

This remained an intractable problem for cryptologists (and governments, militaries, and businesses) until 1976, when Whitfield Diffie and Martin Hellman published their paper, "New Directions in Cryptography," in the *IEEE Transactions on Information Theory* journal. In this paper, they proposed a radical new approach that offered a potential solution to the scalability problem.

Asymmetric Key Ciphers

In their introduction, Diffie and Hellman pointed out, "The cost and delay imposed by this key distribution problem is a major barrier to the transfer of business communications to large teleprocessing networks." They introduced the concept of **public key cryptography**. (Note that this book refers to this as asymmetric key cryptography.) Public key cryptography is a system that allows correspondents to communicate only over a public channel using publicly known techniques. They can create a secure connection. You do not need to wait until an out-of-band letter arrives with a key in the envelope. Nor do you need to issue and manage millions of key pairs just in case someone wishes to communicate securely with a new correspondent. The impact of this discovery is profound, and has far-reaching effects on cryptography.

Asymmetric key ciphers have four key properties:

- **Two associated algorithms exist that are inverses of each other**—This solution involves two components associated with each other. That means you use one algorithm to encrypt and another to decrypt.
- **Each of these two algorithms is easy to compute**—You can use this approach in computer software without much difficulty. As a result, it becomes a practical approach for secure digital communications.

- **It is computationally infeasible to derive the second algorithm if you know the first algorithm**—You can post one key widely for anyone to use without compromising the contents of its associated key. These are pairs of a public key and its associated private key, or a public-private key pair. Since public key cryptosystems have private keys, you can see why this book has stuck to the asymmetric key naming convention!
- **Given some random input, you can generate associated key pairs that are inverses of each other**—Any party can create public-private key pairs, keep one private, and post the other in a directory for any correspondent to use. Because the private key is secret and never transmitted, an eavesdropper cannot learn this value.

Here's how public key cryptography works. Suppose Bob wants to send Alice a message. Alice has already created her private key, which she keeps safe, and her public key, which she puts on her Web site. Bob uses Alice's public key to encrypt the message "Hi Alice!" Bob then sends the encrypted message to Alice. Because Bob used Alice's public key to encrypt the message, Alice can decrypt it only with her private key. Because she has access to her private key, she uses it to decrypt and read the message, "Hi Alice!" If Alice wanted to respond to Bob's message, she could encrypt her response with Bob's public key and send the message back to Bob.

One of the closest equivalents in the everyday business world to asymmetric key ciphers is the night deposit box at a bank. A merchant takes his receipts to the bank, opens the slot with his key, and drops the money down the chute. The envelope slides down and into the safe. If he turned around and a robber held him up at gunpoint and demanded his key, the merchant can safely surrender the key and run away. The robber can attempt to recover the money, but because the envelope has dropped out of reach, the robber will be unable to access it. The next morning, the bank officer can use her key to open the safe, remove the money, and deposit it into the merchant's account. Each party has a different key, but they are associated with each other. Make this process reversible, where the bank officer could leave messages for the merchant, and you have the equivalent of an asymmetric or public key cryptosystem.

Keys, Keyspace, and Key Management

In this section, you'll learn how to describe the function of keys, the importance of keyspace size, and the requirements for adequate key management.

Cryptographic Keys and Keyspace

You have been reading about keys for some time now. But what are they? A key is a value that is an input to a cryptosystem. The key participates in transforming the message in a particular manner. A well-designed cryptosystem produces different outputs of the same message for each key used. You can think about keys this way: A cipher performs a particular task, and a key gives the specific directions for how to do it.

Physical keys are similar to cryptographic keys, but not the same. Many popular door locks have five tumblers, each with 10 possible positions. Thus, there are 10^5, or 100,000 possible cuts for house keys. This gives a reasonable assurance that a person trying a random key in your front door won't get in. The set of all possible keys is a keyspace. Usually (although not always), the larger the keyspace, the more secure the algorithm. Let's look at an example.

How large is the keyspace for a briefcase with two three-digit locks? Combinations run from 000–000 to 999–999, so there are 1,000,000 keys in the keyspace. Does this mean a thief would have to try one million combinations before guessing the correct combination? Not necessarily. A thief could be incredibly lucky and guess the correct combination on the first try. Alternatively, a thief could be incredibly unlucky and try every possible combination before finding the correct combination on the last try. On average, an attacker will guess the correct combination halfway through searching the keyspace. Does this mean that an attacker would need to try, on average, 500,000 combinations? If each attempt took two seconds, and the attacker worked nonstop day and night, he or she should need more than 11 days to open the briefcase. However, the actual resistance of a briefcase to brute-force attack is closer to 17 minutes! Why is this so?

It has to do with a weakness in the briefcase algorithm. Because there are two separate locks with 1,000 combinations each, on average it takes 500 attempts to guess each sub-combination. After finding the left combination, the attacker proceeds to the right combination. At most, he or she will need to try 1,000 + 1,000, or 2,000, combinations. On average, however, the attacker will need to try only 1,000. At two seconds each, this would take 16 minutes and 40 seconds.

This illustrates nicely that increased keyspace, or even the number of bits in a key, does not necessarily provide much more security. If a briefcase maker wanted to sell you a product with six three-digit locks, would you want to buy it? The company would be correct in claiming that the briefcase had more possible combinations (that is, keys) than DES. However, knowing what you know now, you can calculate that it would take less than an hour to open this secure briefcase.

Key Management

One of the most difficult, and critical, parts of a cryptosystem is key management. Although the mathematics of a cipher might be difficult for an attacker to solve, weaknesses or errors in key management often offer a means of compromising a system. As you have seen, key management of a symmetric cryptosystem can be difficult and complex. As a result, it sometimes leads to shortcuts that can be fatal to the otherwise secure cipher.

World War II history gives an example of how poor key management can wreck a cryptosystem. From 1940 to 1948, the Soviet Union used one-time pads to encode messages sent over commercial telegraph lines. Theoretically, one-time pads are unbreakable. The key is very close to random. It is as long as the information it protects, and it does not repeat. It is not possible to detect a pattern in the ciphertext. However, as you have read, the difficulty of distributing and managing long keys in a worldwide wartime environment led to some places running out of cipher keys. Each location knew better than to reuse its own keys, but what harm could there be in using another station's one-time pad? Plenty, it turns out.

If you use the exclusive-or function to encrypt, then encrypting message A with keystream X becomes:

$$A \oplus X = E\,(A)$$

Where E (A) represents the encrypted message containing A. Remember that the exclusive-or function has the interesting property that anything exclusive-or'd with itself is 0, and anything exclusive-or'd with 0 is itself. To decrypt this message, one recombines it with key X to recover the message:

$$E\,(A) \oplus X = A \oplus X \oplus X = A$$

The problem with reusing keying material from another station is that the United States was trying to capture all encrypted traffic from all locations. It then tried to correlate the messages. For example, a message from New York to Moscow in 1943 might have used the same one-time pad as a message from the embassy in Sydney to the embassy in Cairo in 1944. An interesting thing happens when you combine two messages encrypted with the same key:

$$\begin{aligned} &A \oplus X = E\,(A) \\ &B \oplus X = E\,(B) \\ &E\,(A) \oplus E\,(B) = A \oplus X \oplus B \oplus X \\ &= A \oplus B \oplus \cancel{X \oplus X} \\ &= A \oplus B \end{aligned}$$

Now we're using message A to encrypt message B. If you recall from the discussion on transposition ciphers, the ciphertext stores patterns in plaintext. Using one message to encrypt another also keeps much of the statistical properties of the plaintext. It turns out that breaking these messages is rather straightforward. Note that one is solving for the plaintext, not the encryption key! Once the message is decrypted, you could calculate the key by combining the ciphertext with the plaintext.

The United States code-named this project Venona. It continued trying to break these messages from the 1940s all the way until 1980! There are entire books about this project; the U.S. government declassified the intercepted messages between 1995 and 1997. Just in case you didn't think Julius and Ethel Rosenberg spied for the Soviet Union, you can read the decrypted incriminating messages today.

Key Distribution

Key-distribution techniques typically take one of three forms:

- **Paper**—Paper distribution requires no technology to use. However, it does require a person to do something to install the key. This can introduce errors or give a disgruntled person a chance to compromise a system.

- **Digital media**—Digital distribution can be in the form of CDs, disks, or even e-mail. Note that you must protect the keys in transit. Some form of secure transmission must be used. For physical media, tamperproof cases and registered mail give some level of assurance. For electronic distribution, a higher-level key, known as a key-encrypting key, must protect the keys in transit and storage. This, of course, requires that you first distribute the key-encrypting key by some alternate secure mechanism. You should use key-encrypting keys only to encrypt other keys, not data. Excessive use of any key could lead to it being compromised.
- **Hardware**—You can distribute a key via hardware with a PCMCIA card, a smart card, or a plug-in module. The advantage is that you transfer the keys directly from the key-transport mechanism into the crypto device without anyone viewing them. No copies exist outside of these components.

To protect against key interception in transit, you can split keys. Splitting a key into two equal-sized pieces isn't a good idea. If an attacker intercepts one piece, brute-forcing the other half of the key is much easier (remember the briefcase example). Therefore, one strategy to split a key K is to generate another random key J, which becomes the key-encrypting key. You combine K and J to produce an encrypted key. You would then send this encrypted key on one channel. You would send the key-encrypting key by another channel. If an attacker intercepts one of the two messages, the attacker does not learn the underlying key.

$$\begin{aligned}&\text{Channel 1:} \quad J\\&\text{Channel 2:} \quad K \oplus J\\&\text{Recombine:} \quad J \oplus K \oplus J = K\end{aligned}$$

Note that this scheme requires a new key-encrypting key for every key.

Key-Distribution Centers (KDCs)

Rather than each organization creating the infrastructure to manage its own keys, a number of hosts could agree to trust a common key-distribution center (KDC). All parties must trust the KDC. With a KDC, each entity requires only one secret key pair—between itself and the KDC. Kerberos and ANSI X9.17 use the concept of a KDC.

For example, if Alice wants to initiate a secure communications session with Bob, she sends an encrypted message to the KDC. The KDC picks a random session key, encrypts copies in both Alice's key and Bob's key, and returns both to Alice. Alice decrypts her session key and uses it to encrypt a message to Bob. She sends it, along with the session key encrypted in Bob's key (which Alice can't read), to Bob. Bob gets both messages, decrypts the session key using his secret key, and uses the session key to decrypt Alice's message.

Digital Signatures and Hash Functions

For many business requirements, you should understand the use of digital signatures and hash functions, and what types of ciphers to use.

Hash Functions

To ensure that the values of a message have not changed (either deliberately or through transmission error), you can append some summary of the information that you can verify through a repeatable process. This summary is a checksum. For example, to make sure a string of digits has not changed in transmission, you could append the sum of all the digits to the end of the message. If the recipient adds up the digits and reaches a different value, you can assume there was an error in transmission and request a resend.

Credit cards have a hash digit that validates the card number. The algorithm for calculating this digit is the LUHN formula, based on ANSI X4.13. To calculate whether a credit card number is valid, follow these four steps:

1. Starting with the second digit on the right, multiply every other digit by two.
2. If the result of any doubling is greater than 10 (that is, 8 + 8 = 16), add the digits of this result. Add all the doubled digits.
3. Add all other digits, with the exception of the last digit (the checksum), to this total.
4. The difference between the sum and the next multiple of 10 is the check digit. For example, the correct hash digit for credit card number 5012 3456 7890 123X is 6.

A hash is like a checksum but operates so that a forged message will not result in the same hash as a legitimate message. Hashes are usually a fixed size. The result is a hash value. Hashes act as a fingerprint for the data. Message creators can publish a hash as a reference so that recipients can see whether the information has changed. Software publishers often provide hash values so that customers can check the integrity of the software they receive. To be effective, hashes usually have to be long enough so that creating an alternative message that matched the hash value would take far too much time.

Digital Signatures

Digital signatures are not digitized signatures (electronic images of handwritten signatures). Rather, digital signatures bind the identity of an entity to a particular message or piece of information. They do not provide privacy or secrecy. They ensure the integrity of a message and verify who wrote it. Digital signatures require asymmetric key cryptography. Figure 9-5 shows a digital signature.

FIGURE 9-5

A digital signature.

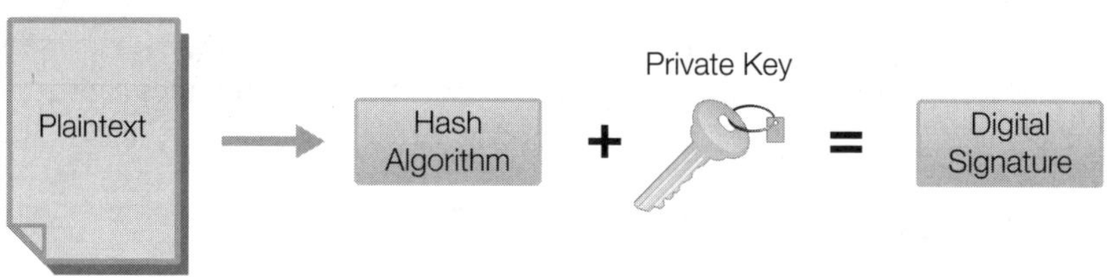

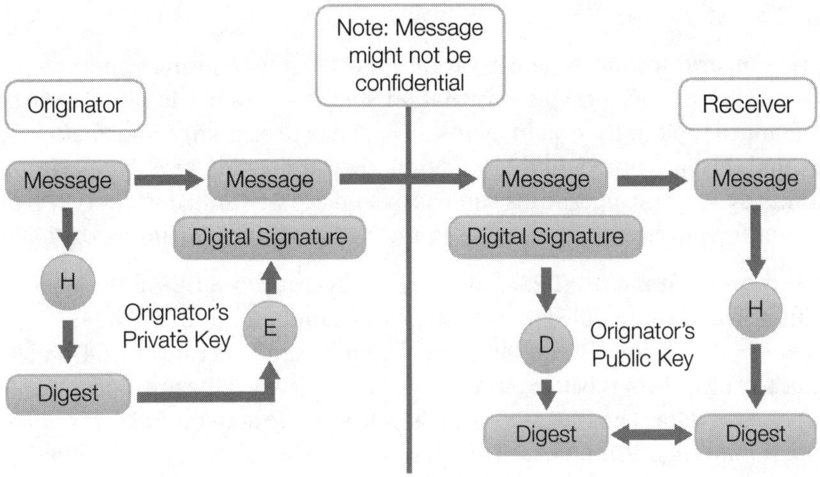

FIGURE 9-6 Operation of a digital signature.

You can construct a digital signature with a private key from an asymmetric key pair. It includes signing a hash of the message. This combination provides dual assurance—that a message originated from a particular entity and that no one has changed the contents. Anyone with access to a signer's public key can verify the digital signature. However, only the holder of the private key can create the digital signature. Figure 9-6 show how a digital signature operates.

Rivest-Shamir-Adelman (RSA) and the Digital Signature Algorithm (DSA) are the most common digital signature algorithms used. The patent on RSA expired in September 2000. It is now in the public domain. The DSA signs the Secure Hash Algorithm (SHA) hash of the message. Although most commercial systems use RSA, the Digital Signature Standard (DSS), DSA, and SHA are U.S. government standards. They are more likely to appear in government products.

Cryptographic Applications, Tools, and Resources

As a security professional, you should understand how to match business needs with cryptographic solutions and select proper tool sets. In this section, you'll learn how to identify tool sets that use symmetric keys and match them to their most common business use. You'll learn how to identify tool sets that can use asymmetric key cryptography and identify the infrastructure required to make a solution. You'll learn how hash functions work, how to identify the ciphers used for hash functions, and how to use them to ensure integrity. You'll learn how to use cryptography to address each issue as well as the differences between each requirement. You'll also learn the differences between digital and digitized signatures and the infrastructure and legal requirements for maintaining digital signatures used for nonrepudiation. Lastly, you'll learn how to design a key-management model that supports your business requirements.

Symmetric Key Standards

Symmetric key algorithms (or standards) are the most common form of encryption used. The same key encrypts and decrypts information. Because symmetric keys can be created easily and changed rapidly, they often are used just once to exchange information between two parties, and then discarded. In this situation, they are session keys. Unlike asymmetric key algorithms, symmetric algorithms can be fast and are well suited to encrypting lots of data. Organizations currently use several symmetric algorithms, including the following:

- **Data Encryption Standard (DES)**—IBM originally developed DES as the Lucifer algorithm. The NSA modified it and issued it as a national standard in 1977. FIPS PUB 46-3 updated its definition. It uses a 56-bit key and operates on 64-bit blocks of data. The algorithm is better for hardware use than for software, and it can rapidly encrypt lots of data. The DES algorithm is in the public domain. DES was once a state-of-the-art algorithm, but with rapid advances in hardware capabilities and attack methods, attackers can now crack it in as little as a few days. It is no longer a secure algorithm.
- **Triple DES**—Triple DES is a protocol that consists of three passes of DES (encrypt, decrypt, encrypt) using multiple keys. It increases the keyspace from 56 to 112 or 168 bits, depending on whether two or three keys are used. Triple DES is computationally secure because of the underlying security of the DES algorithm and the vastly increased keyspace. Note that using the same key three times produces the same result as single DES. It, too, is contained in FIPS PUB 46-3, and is in the public domain.
- **International Data Encryption Algorithm (IDEA)**—Like DES, this block cipher operates on 64-bit blocks. It uses a 128-bit key and runs somewhat faster than DES in hardware and software. Ascom-Tech AG holds a patent for IDEA (U.S. patent 5,214,703), but it is free for noncommercial use.
- **CAST**—The CAST algorithm is a substitution-permutation algorithm similar to DES. Unlike DES, its authors made its design criteria public. This 64-bit symmetric block cipher can use keys from 40 to 256 bits. RFC 2144 describes CAST-128; RFC-2612 describes CAST-256. Although patented (U.S. patent 5,511,123), its inventors, C.M. Adams and S.E. Tavares, made it available for free use.
- **Blowfish**—Blowfish is a 64-bit block cipher that has a variable key length from 32 to 448 bits. It is much faster than DES or IDEA. Blowfish is a strong algorithm that has been included in more than 150 products, as well as v2.5.47 of the Linux kernel. Its author, Bruce Schneier, placed it in the public domain. Schneier's Twofish was a candidate for the Advanced Encryption Standard.
- **Advanced Encryption Standard (AES)**—Also known as Rijndael (RAIN-doll), AES is a block cipher. Vincent Rijmen and Joan Daemen designed AES, and FIPS PUB 197 published it as a standard. The AES algorithm can use cryptographic keys of 128, 192, and 256 bits to encrypt and decrypt data in blocks of 128 bits. The cipher also can operate on variable block lengths. It is both strong and fast.

> **FYI**
>
> To help defend against dictionary attacks, in which attackers try common key values, some algorithms use an additional value called a **salt value**. A salt value is a set of random characters that you can combine with an actual input key to create the encryption key. The combination of the salt value and the input key makes it far more difficult to compromise an encryption key using common key values.

- **RC2**—RC2 is a variable key-size block cipher designed by Ronald Rivest (RC stands for Ron's Code). RC2 operates as a drop-in replacement for DES, and operates on 64-bit blocks. It uses a salt value as part of its encryption routine to make crypt-analysis more difficult. RSA Security owns it.
- **RC4**—Produced by RSA Security, RC4 is a variable key-size stream cipher with byte-oriented operations. Internet browsers often use RC4 to provide a secure sockets layer (SSL) connection.

Wireless Security

With inexpensive high-bandwidth communications technology, wireless local area networks (WLANs) now are a viable strategy for homes and offices that do not wish to link cable to all computers. However, this convenience reduces security.

Many wireless users install their new technology in a plug-and-play fashion. That is, they open the box, connect the pieces, and turn it on and run the installation wizards. If it works, they never touch the manual. Although wireless products have built-in security, the default configuration generally doesn't enable it. Why? Because most consumers expect a product to work when they plug it in. As a result, most vendors that offer security require the customer to turn it on. Many customers never bother. This can create major security problems.

802.11 Wireless Security. The 802.11, or Wi-Fi, wireless standards emerged in 1999. Wi-Fi provides wireless communications at transmission speeds from 11 Mbps for 802.11b to over 150Mbps for 802.11n. The various standards within the 802.11 specification transmit data using either the 2.4GHz or 5GHz band. The ranges of data communications at these bandwidths are advertised to be about 100 meters (over 200 meters for 802.11n). Nevertheless, hackers have used high-gain antennas (including one made from a Pringles can!) to boost reception to several miles. A sort of informal competition is under way worldwide to see who can create the longest 802.11 wireless connection. At last count, the Swedish Space Corporation posted the record with a stratospheric balloon floating at a height of 29.7 km. It achieved a connection with a base station 310 km away.

> **WARNING**
>
> The important lesson to remember is that wireless signals do not stop at a building's perimeter. Therefore, cryptographic protection becomes important to secure your organization's wireless communications.

The 802.11 wireless protocols allow encryption through Wired Equivalent Privacy (WEP) or the newer Wi-Fi Protected Access (WPA). Users need to have a shared secret that serves as the key to begin secure wireless connections. Since most wireless access points (WAPs) generally do not enable wireless encryption by default, most wireless networks operate with no encryption at all. Any attacker can monitor and access these open networks. In 2000, Peter Shipley drove around the San Francisco Bay area with a portable wireless rig. He found that about 85 percent of wireless networks were unencrypted. Of those that were encrypted, more than half used the default password. Although each WAP has its own service set identifier (SSID), which a client needs to know for access, hackers have tools such as NetStumbler that display the names of all SSIDs within range. Windows just connects to the first available network signal. As a result, wireless encryption is a minimum requirement to ensure security on a wireless network.

WEP was the first wireless encryption protocol in widespread use. It has some severe limitations, however. Design flaws exist in the protocol, including some key scheduling weaknesses in the RC4 encryption. A hacker using tools such as AirSnort or WEPcrack can guess the encryption key after collecting approximately 5,000,000 to 10,000,000 encrypted packets. To address these weaknesses, current standards and supported hardware also offer WPA. To provide the best protection for wireless network traffic, always use WPA. Never use WEP. Enable MAC address filtering, which screens out PCs that it doesn't recognize. Place a firewall between the wireless LAN and the rest of the network so that would-be attackers can't get far.

Asymmetric Key Solutions

Recall that **key distribution** issues keys to valid users of a cryptosystem so they can communicate. The classic solution to key distribution is to use out-of-band communications through a trusted channel to distribute keys in advance. This could be by registered mail, by courier, or even by telephone, if you are certain no one is tapping the phone lines. However, this strategy is expensive and slow.

Organizations with the resources and the ability to plan develop ways to do this. For example, the U.S. Navy uses a unique distribution system to make sure their cryptosystems remain secure. It includes strict accountability and control procedures to ensure proper use of cryptosystems. This program is the Communications Security Material System, or CMS. Each command appoints a CMS custodian and an alternate. They are responsible for getting, storing, controlling, installing, removing, and destroying keys for Navy cryptosystems. This involves a lot of overhead and expense. However, the high value of the information justifies it.

An asymmetric key distribution system has no need for couriers, back channels, or expensive storage or inventory plans. That's because it doesn't require each party to first share a secret key. This solves the chicken-and-egg problem of first needing a secure channel before creating a secure channel.

Key revocation occurs when someone is no longer trusted or allowed to use a cryptosystem. In a symmetric key system, where everyone shares the same secret, compromising one copy of the key comprises all copies. This is similar to all employees having the same office key. If a terminated employee refuses to return the key, the organization must change every lock and issue new keys. After a few dismissals, this becomes expensive and cumbersome.

In an asymmetric key environment, the **key directory** is a trusted repository of all public keys. If one person no longer is trusted, the directory's manager removes that public key. No one attempting to initiate communications with that person would be able to find that key. That person still could initiate encrypted communications by using other posted public keys. However, if the protocol requires digital signatures for all messages, the recipient would reject the message because it wouldn't be able to find a valid key to check the signature. For example, you can query the MIT PGP Public Key Server at *http://pgp.mit.edu/*.

Ad hoc secure communications are the basis of Internet e-commerce. This is one of the most frequently used forms of cryptography today. Using a symmetric key would be difficult. It would require each party to make contact some other way and agree on a secret key. If such a channel existed, why not just use that? Practically speaking, it doesn't.

With an asymmetric key, ad hoc communications are straightforward. The most common form of Internet cryptography is Secure Sockets Layer (SSL), or Hypertext Transport Protocol Secure (HTTPS) encryption. The **SSL handshake** created the first secure communications session between a client and a server. The RSA Web site describes this process nicely: *http://www.rsa.com/rsalabs/node.asp?id=2293*.

The SSL Handshake Protocol consists of two phases: server authentication and an optional client authentication. In the first phase, the server, in response to a client's request, sends its certificate (containing the server's public key) and its cipher preferences. The client then creates a master key, which it encrypts with the server's public key. The client then sends the encrypted master key to the server. The server recovers the master key and authenticates itself to the client by returning a message with the master key. The client and server encrypt and authenticate subsequent data with keys derived from this master key. In the optional second phase, the server sends a challenge to the client. The client authenticates itself to the server by returning the client's digital signature on the challenge as well as its public-key certificate.

Digital signatures verify a person's identity or that person's association with a message. They require the use of a **certificate authority (CA)** that can vouch for the validity of a credential. Nonrepudiation verifies the digital signature on a document. It proves who sent a message. In some cases, you can combine this with a tamperproof time source to prove when you sent the message.

Hash Function and Integrity

You should be able to explain in layman's terms how hash functions work, identify the ciphers used for hash functions, and explain their use in ensuring integrity.

Hash Functions

Hash functions help to detect forgeries. They compute a checksum of a message and then combine it with a cryptographic function so that the result is tamperproof. Hashes are usually of a known fixed size based on the algorithm used.

Recall that a checksum is a one-way calculation that yields a result that you can check easily by rerunning the data through the checksum function. For example, given a series of decimal numbers such as the following, a simple checksum could be the two rightmost digits of the sum of these numbers:

71 77 61 114 107 75 61 114 100 121

Therefore, in this case, we add them together to get 901, drop the 9, and our checksum is 01. Now, if you were to send this sequence of 10 numbers to someone over a noisy communications channel, the noise could garble some of the information. By also sending the checksum, the recipient can recalculate to see if the numbers add up. If not, he knows to request a retransmission.

Because checksums are very simple functions, it is possible to have the checksum come out correctly on a garbled message. Of course, it's also possible for someone to deliberately modify the numbers in such a way that the checksum still matches. This illustrates the point that checksums do not ensure security; they ensure reliability.

A hash is a checksum designed so that no one can forge a message in a way that it will result in the same hash as a legitimate message. Hashes are usually a fixed size. The result is a hash value. In general, hash values are larger than checksum values. Hashes act as a fingerprint of the data. You can make hashes available as a reference so that recipients can see if the information has changed. Software publishers often provide hash values so that customers can verify the integrity of the software they receive. To be effective, hashes usually have to be long enough that a hacker would need a long time to create an alternate message that matched the hash value.

Professor Ronald Rivest of MIT (he's the R in RSA) developed the MD5 message digest algorithm. RFC 1321 contains the specifications for the algorithm. It takes an input of any arbitrary length and generates a 128-bit message digest that is computationally infeasible to match by finding another input. This message digest is uniquely associated with its source. You can publish an MD5 hash with information such as compiled source code and then compare the information to the hash. This verifies that no person or process, such as a virus, has modified the information.

Note, however, that the MD5 message digest is not yet a signed hash. Nothing uniquely associates the hash with the originator. That is, if an attacker wanted to modify a program, he or she could easily recalculate a new MD5 hash and post both together on the Web site. The presence of an MD5 hash does not prove authenticity of a file; it only proves that the file hasn't changed since you computed the hash.

The Federal Information Processing Standard Publication 180-1 (FIPS 180-1) defines the Secure Hash Algorithm (SHA-1). SHA-1 produces a 160-bit hash from a message of any arbitrary length. Like MD5, it creates a unique fingerprint of a file that is computationally infeasible to reproduce.

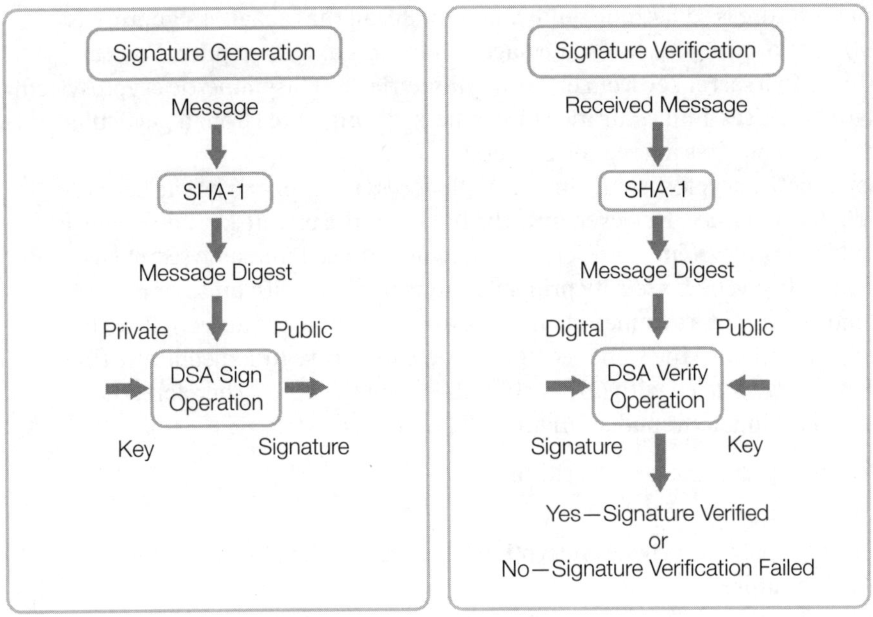

FIGURE 9-7 Relationship between hash and digital signature algorithms.

How do you create a digital signature from a hash? The output from the MD5 or the SHA-1 hash provides input for an asymmetric key algorithm that uses a private key as input. The result of this encryption is a value that is uniquely associated with the file. It is computationally infeasible to forge and provably related to the identity of the entity that signs the file. FIPS 180-1 includes the diagram in Figure 9-7 that shows this relationship.

Someone can digitally sign a message, software, or any other digital representation in a way that anyone can easily verify. Note that this presumes the integrity of the public key directory that the recipient uses to look up the key to verify the signature. If an attacker successfully penetrates the directory, all bets are off. At that point, the fox is vouching for the safety of the henhouse.

Digital Signatures and Nonrepudiation

Given a sample business case, you should understand how to state, in layman's terms, the differences between digital and digitized signatures. You should be able to explain the infrastructure and legal needs for keeping digital signatures for nonrepudiation.

Digital Signatures Versus Digitized Signatures

Earlier in this chapter, you learned about digital signatures and digitized signatures. Although the difference between the two is straightforward, many people often confuse them. To review, a digitized signature is an image of a physical signature stored in digital format. This file could be in JPG, GIF, or BMP format. Theoretically, it could be stored in a digital camera. The chief value of a digitized signature is printing it onto form letters, sometimes in a different color to make it look more like a handwritten ink signature on the printed page.

A digital signature is something quite different. Recall that a digital signature is a combination of a strong hash of a message, which acts as a fingerprint. You can combine this with a secret key from either a symmetric or an asymmetric cryptosystem. This combination gives dual assurance that a message originated from a particular entity and that no one has altered the contents.

In an asymmetric cryptosystem, anyone with access to a signer's public key can verify the digital signature. However, only the holder of the private key can create it. In a symmetric cryptosystem, both sender and recipient need the same secret key.

Think about this: Which security principle can you satisfy with an asymmetric digital signature but not a symmetric one? The answer is nonrepudiation. If both sender and recipient have the same secret key, you can't prove to someone else that a message exchange started with one party rather than the other. Therefore, the conditions for proving nonrepudiation are as follows:

- A effective asymmetric key algorithm
- A strong hash function
- A means to apply the private encryption key to the hash value to produce a digital signature
- A tamperproof or trusted third-party timing device (if desired)
- An agreed-upon protocol for validating digital signatures
- A secure key-management and distribution system
- A public key repository that has an assured level of integrity
- Key escrow to be able to produce public keys from reluctant parties
- Procedures to handle disputes

Organizations must spell out all these steps in writing as part of a business agreement. Then, and only then, are you ready to implement nonrepudiation.

Principles of Certificates and Key Management

You learned about key management earlier in this chapter. It includes creating, distributing, storing, validating, updating, replacing, and revoking keys and keying material.

Here is a sample classic key-management scheme. The Enigma was one of the most famous cryptographic devices of the 20th century. Invented by Arthur Scherbius, it was Germany's chief encryption tool before and during World War II. The machine had more possible keying configurations than the number of atoms in the known universe! In practice, a subset of keys was used to make key changing practical. Nonetheless, the three-rotor Enigma offered a dizzying 158,962,555,217,826,360,000 possible keys at the beginning of World War II.

German Enigma operators got a new codebook monthly. This told which key to use each day. Now, if all messages were encrypted with that same key, Allied cryptanalysts would have a lot of ciphertext, all encrypted with the same key, to attempt to decrypt. This could be a problem. Therefore, the keying protocol required that you use only the key in the codebook as a key-encrypting key. The wartime Enigma had five scramblers. Enigma users used only three scramblers at any time. Users could place each of those scrambler wheels in one of 26 starting positions—one for each letter of the alphabet. Therefore, every message began with the setting of the scramblers. Senders repeated each message to make sure the key got through any radio interference. With 60 different possible scrambler selections and 26 × 26 × 26, or 17,576, possible starting positions, users could encrypt each day's messages with one of 1,054,560 possible keys. Note that without knowing the initial settings, the cryptanalyst still didn't know which of the 159 quintillion keys to use. The Enigma encryption was totally unbreakable, right? The Germans thought so. They were wrong.

Polish cryptographer Marian Rejewski figured it out. There's not enough space to go into detail here about how he did it. You can look up his exploits in a number of books. It's enough to say here that his solution involved a brilliant use of pure mathematics to exploit a weakness in the cipher. The moral of the story is that a key distribution system may appear secure, and the number of keys nearly infinite. However, the best key-management system in the world does not protect against a brilliant cryptanalyst if the encryption algorithm itself has any weaknesses.

Modern Key-Management Techniques

Today, computers handle all business cryptography. Some of the best minds in the field have scrutinized the algorithms of choice, sometimes for decades. Therefore, an attacker most likely will not defeat your cryptography by breaking the mathematics behind it. Human behavior—and most importantly, human error—is much more likely to lead to the compromise. Poor key management is often the cause.

This is not the place to examine the technical complexities of each key-management technique. Instead, you will look at which techniques are right for different business applications. For example, PKI is a technology that absolutely requires effective key management. PKI vendors have promised tremendous growth for years. However, the practicality of using all the key-management components has throttled growth. The rest of this section contains a brief overview of several modern key-management techniques. Use this as a starting point to decide which technique works best for your organization.

AES

The U.S. government currently has no standard for creating cryptographic keys for unclassified applications. However, working groups have been defining an AES key wrap specification that would securely encrypt a plaintext key along with integrity information. This capability would provide a mechanism for key management in unclassified government environments.

IPSec

IPSec protects Internet Protocol (IP) packets from disclosure or change. The protocol provides privacy and/or integrity. Each header contains a security parameter index (SPI) that refers to a particular encryption key. Additionally, the header may contain up to two security headers. The authentication header (AH) provides integrity checking. The encapsulating security payload (ESP) encrypts the packet for confidentiality. Hosts using IPSec establish a security association with each other. This involves agreeing which crypto methods and keys to use, as well as the SPI host. ISAKMP provides key-management services, which you'll learn about next.

ISAKMP

The Internet Security Association and Key Management Protocol (ISAKMP, pronounced ICE-a-camp) is a key-management strategy growing in popularity. RFC 2408 defines ISAKMP as a set of procedures for authenticating a communicating peer, creating and managing security associations, key-generation techniques, and threat mitigation (that is, denial of service and replay attacks). All these are necessary to establish and maintain secure communications (via IP Security Service or any other security protocol) in an Internet environment.

The **security association (SA)** is the basic element of ISAKMP key management. An SA contains all the information needed to perform a variety of network-security services. ISAKMP acts as a common framework for agreeing to the format of SA attributes, and for negotiating, modifying, and deleting SAs. It uses a Diffie-Hellman key exchange signed with RSA.

XKMS

The extensible markup language (XML) key-management specification (XKMS) gives protocols for distributing and registering public keys for use with XML. XML is a markup language for documents containing structured information. It provides syntax that supports sharing complex structured documents over the Web.

Managed PKI

Some vendors offer a managed service to handle issues associated with public key management. Services include centralized key generation, distribution, backup, and recovery. Rather than create a key-management infrastructure, customers can choose to outsource these details.

ANSI X9.17

The financial industry created this standard to define key-management procedures. It defines a symmetric key-exchange protocol that many manufacturers use in hardware encryption devices. Although asymmetric key exchange offers some advantages, the fact that organizations have invested significant amounts of money in X9.17-compliant equipment means they will continue to use it for some time. According to FIPS Pub 171, X9.17 specifies the minimum standards for the following:

- Control of the keying material during its lifetime to prevent unauthorized disclosure, modification, or substitution
- Distribution of the keying material in order to permit interoperability between cryptographic equipment or facilities
- Ensuring the integrity of keying material during all phases of its life, including its generation, distribution, storage, entry, use, and destruction
- Recovery in the event of a failure of the key-management process or when the integrity of the keying material is questioned

When you select a key-management product or technique for your organization, do your homework first. Each method has its advantages and disadvantages. Make sure you understand the up-front cost as well as the ongoing maintenance and administration costs.

CHAPTER SUMMARY

In this chapter, you learned how cryptography works and how it applies to solving business issues. You learned key cryptographic terms and business principles, how to apply cryptography to these principles, and how to identify security tools that rely on cryptography. You also learned the advantages and disadvantages of symmetric and asymmetric ciphers as they pertain to cryptanalysis.

KEY CONCEPTS AND TERMS

Algorithm
Asymmetric key cryptography
Caesar cipher
Certificate authority (CA)
Checksum
Cipher
Data Encryption Standard (DES)
Decryption
Differential cryptanalysis
Digital signature
Digitized signature
Hash
Key
Key directory
Key distribution
Key-encrypting key
Key revocation
Keyspace
Keyword mixed alphabet cipher
Nonrepudiation
One-time pad cipher
One-way algorithm
Plaintext
Private (symmetric) key
Product cipher
Public (asymmetric) key
Public key cryptography
Public key infrastructure (PKI)
Revocation
Salt value
Security association (SA)
Simple substitution cipher
SSL handshake
Substitution cipher
Symmetric key cryptography
Timestamping
Transposition cipher
Vernam cipher
Vigenère cipher

CHAPTER 9 ASSESSMENT

1. ________ offers a mechanism to accomplish four security goals: confidentiality, integrity, authentication, and nonrepudiation.
   A. Security association (SA)
   B. Secure socket layer (SSL)
   C. Cryptography
   D. None of the above

2. A strong hash function is designed so that a message cannot be forged that will result in the same hash as a legitimate message.
   A. True
   B. False

3. The act of scrambling plaintext into ciphertext is known as ________.
   A. Decryption
   B. Encryption
   C. Plaintext
   D. Cleartext

4. An algorithm used for cryptographic purposes is known as a ________.
   A. Hash
   B. Private key
   C. Public key
   D. Cipher

5. Encryption ciphers fall into two general categories: symmetric (private) key and asymmetric (public) key.
   A. True
   B. False

6. An encryption cipher that uses the same key to encrypt and decrypt is called a ________ key.
   A. Symmetric (private)
   B. Asymmetric (public)
   C. Key encrypting
   D. None of the above

7. ________ corroborates the identity of an entity, whether the sender, the sender's computer, some device, or some information.
   A. Nonrepudiation
   B. Confidentiality
   C. Integrity
   D. Authentication

8. Which of the following is one of the four basic forms of a cryptographic attack?
   A. Ciphertext-only attack
   B. Known-plaintext attack
   C. Chosen-plaintext attack
   D. Chosen-ciphertext attack
   E. All the above

9. The two basic types of ciphers are transposition and substitution.
   A. True
   B. False

10. A ________ is used to detect forgeries
    A. Hash function
    B. Checksum
    C. Hash value
    D. KDC

11. DES, IDEA, RC4, and WEP are examples of ________.
    A. Key revocation
    B. 802.11b wireless security
    C. Asymmetric key algorithms (or standards)
    D. Symmetric algorithms (or standards)

12. A ________ signature is a representation of a physical signature stored in a digital format.
    A. Digital
    B. Digitized
    C. Private key
    D. Public key

CHAPTER

10

Networks and Telecommunications

FOR MOST BUSINESSES AND ORGANIZATIONS today, networks and telecommunications are critical parts of business infrastructure. Many organizations could not operate if their networks were unavailable or prone to errors. *Network security* is meeting an organization's essential need for network availability, integrity, and confidentiality. The data transmitted through the network is protected from modification (either accidental or intentional), it cannot be read by unauthorized parties, and its source and destination can be verified (nonrepudiation). Business and security requirements are as follows:

- Access control
- Network stability and reliability
- Integrity
- Availability
- Confidentiality or nonrepudiation

This chapter examines how you can secure networks and telecommunications. It introduces the basic elements of a network and explains the security issues surrounding networks.

As a security professional, you need to understand these elements of the networks and telecommunications world:

- The Open Systems Interconnection (OSI) reference model
- Network topology
- Transmission Control Protocol/Internet Protocol (TCP/IP) networking
- Wireless networking
- Network security

Chapter 10 Topics

This chapter covers these topics and concepts:

- What the Open Systems Interconnection (OSI) reference model is
- What the two types of networks are
- What TCP/IP is and how it works
- What network security risks are
- What basic network security defense tools are
- How wireless networks work and which threats they pose to network security

Chapter 10 Goals

When you complete this chapter, you will be able to:

- Define the OSI reference model
- Understand network types, network protocols, and network security risks
- Understand some basic tools to defend against network security risks
- Understand wireless networking and the threats it can pose to network security

The Open Systems Interconnection Reference Model

The **Open Systems Interconnection (OSI) reference model** is a template for building and using a network and its resources. The OSI reference model is a theoretical model of networking with interchangeable layers. The beauty of it is that you can design technology for any one of the layers without worrying about how the other layers work. You just need to make sure that each layer knows how to talk to the layers above and below it. Figure 10-1 shows each layer of the OSI reference model.

The OSI reference model layers are as follows:

- **Application layer**—This is responsible for interacting with end users. The Application layer includes all programs on a computer that interact with the network. For example, your e-mail software is included, as it must transmit and receive messages over the network. A simple game like Solitaire doesn't fit here because it does not require the network to operate.
- **Presentation layer**—This is responsible for the coding of data. The Presentation layer includes file formats and character representations. From a security perspective, encryption generally takes place at the Presentation layer.

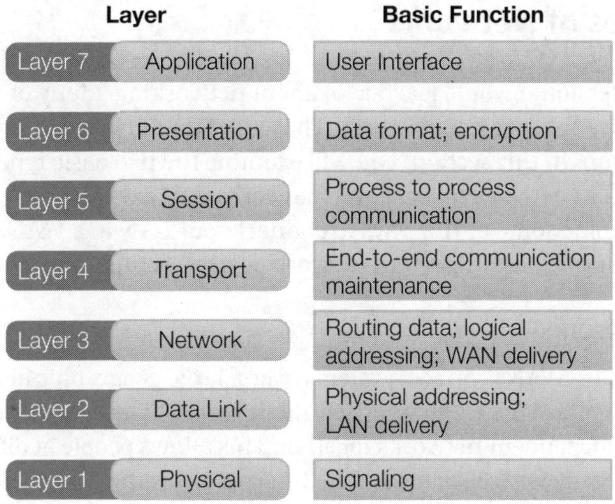

FIGURE 10-1
The OSI reference model.

- **Session layer**—This is responsible for maintaining communication sessions between computers. The session layer creates, maintains, and disconnects communications that take place between processes over the network.
- **Transport layer**—This is responsible for breaking data into packets and properly transmitting it over the network. Flow control and error checking take place at the Transport layer.
- **Network layer**—This is responsible for the logical implementation of the network. One very important feature of the Network layer, covered later in this chapter, is logical addressing. In TCP/IP networking, logical addressing takes the familiar form of IP addresses.
- **Data Link layer**—This is responsible for transmitting information on computers connected to the same local area network (LAN). The Data Link layer uses Media Access Control (MAC) addresses. Device manufacturers assign each hardware device a unique MAC address.
- **Physical layer**—This is responsible for the physical operation of the network. The Physical layer must translate the binary ones and zeros of computer language into the language of the transport medium. In the case of copper network cables, it must translate computer data into electrical pulses. In the case of fiber optics, it must translate the data into bursts of light.

> **TIP**
> An easy way to remember the layers of the OSI reference model is with a mnemonic—for example, "All People Seem To Need Data Processing."

The OSI reference model enables developers to produce each layer independently. If you write an e-mail program that operates at the Application layer, you only need to worry about getting information down to the Presentation layer. The details of the network you're using are irrelevant to your program. Other software takes care of that for you. Similarly, if you're making cables at the Physical layer, you don't need to worry about what Network layer protocols will travel on that cable. You just need to build a cable that satisfies the requirements of the Data Link layer.

The Two Types of Networks

As a security professional, you'll learn a lot about networking. Many of the devices used in the security field protect networks. Those that don't protect networks often rely on them to function. In this section, you will examine the two basic types of networks—wide area networks (WANs) and local area networks (LANs)—and explore their function. You will also examine some of the ways to connect your LAN to a WAN. Finally, you will take a brief look at the most important network devices: routers, switches, and hubs.

Wide Area Networks

As the name implies, WANs connect systems over a large geographic area. The most common example of a WAN is the Internet. As shown in Figure 10-2, the Internet connects many independent networks together. This allows people at different locations to communicate easily with each other. The Internet hides the details of this from the end user. When you send an e-mail message, you don't have to worry about how the data moves. You just click Send and let the network deal with all the complexity.

From a security perspective, it's important to remember that the Internet is an open network. You cannot guarantee data privacy once data leaves your network. The data might travel any path to get to its destination. Anyone might be able to read it along

FIGURE 10-2

Wide area networks.

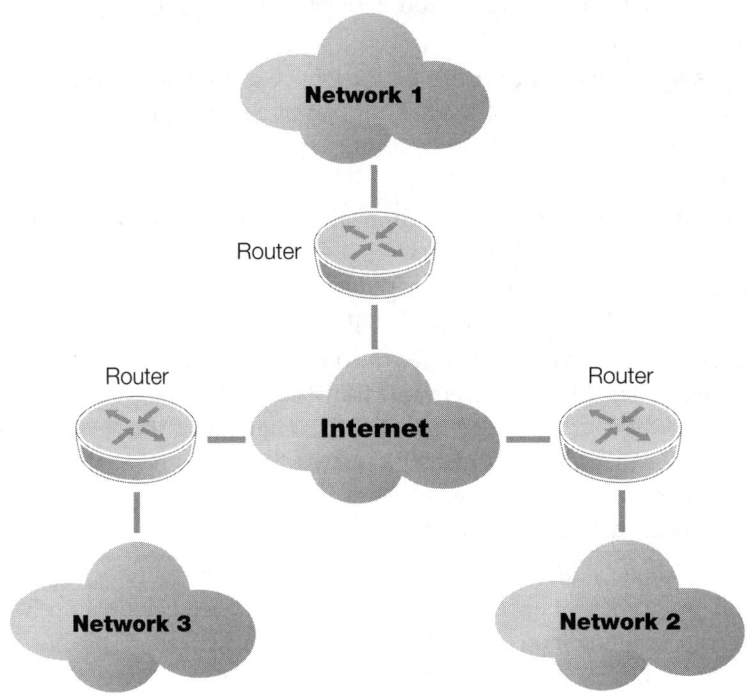

the way. Think of data on the Internet as more like a postcard than a letter in a sealed envelope. Fortunately, security technology such as encryption enables you to hide the meaning of your data when sending it across the Internet. This is similar to sending a postcard but writing the message in a secret code. You'll learn more about network encryption later in this chapter.

Many organizations use the Internet to connect different locations to each other. This is a low-cost way to connect sites, as it is usually easy and inexpensive to connect a network to the Internet. However, you must make sure that you consider the security issues surrounding the use of an open network such as the Internet. Again, encryption technology can help you reduce the risk of using the Internet.

Some organizations prefer to use their own private networks for connecting remote sites. Some choose to do so for security reasons, while others simply want the guaranteed reliability of private networks. Although this is a very good option for security and reliability reasons, it is also very expensive. However, there's no reason you can't work with a communications provider to develop your own private WAN.

Connectivity Options

You can connect to the Internet in many different ways. At home, most people have the choice of a cable modem or a Digital Subscriber Line (DSL) from the telephone company. Depending on where you live, you may also have other options, such as direct fiber-optic connections to your home. Businesses also have many choices for Internet service. Surprisingly, many of them are the same choices available to home users. For example, cable companies offer business service in addition to their consumer offerings. This is often at a much higher speed than home connections to support the needs of business users. DSL connections also are available to business users. Telephone companies offer business-class DSL service that has higher speeds and guaranteed reliability. While cable and DSL connections are suitable for small and medium-sized organizations, larger organizations often need more sophisticated service. A variety of advanced options are available including T1 and T3 lines, frame- relay circuits, IDSN lines, and other technologies.

Think back to the OSI reference model for a moment. The important thing to remember is that the connectivity option you choose will not affect what you can do with your network. The differences relate to how the signal gets into your building (telephone lines, cable lines, or dedicated wires) and the speed and reliability of your service.

Routers

A **router** is a device that connects two or more networks and selectively interchanges packets of data between them. A router connects a LAN to a WAN, as Figure 10-2 shows. A router examines network addresses to decide where to send each packet.

The placement of a router within the network architecture affects configuration choices. You can place routers in two basic locations (see Figure 10-3):

FIGURE 10-3

Router placement.

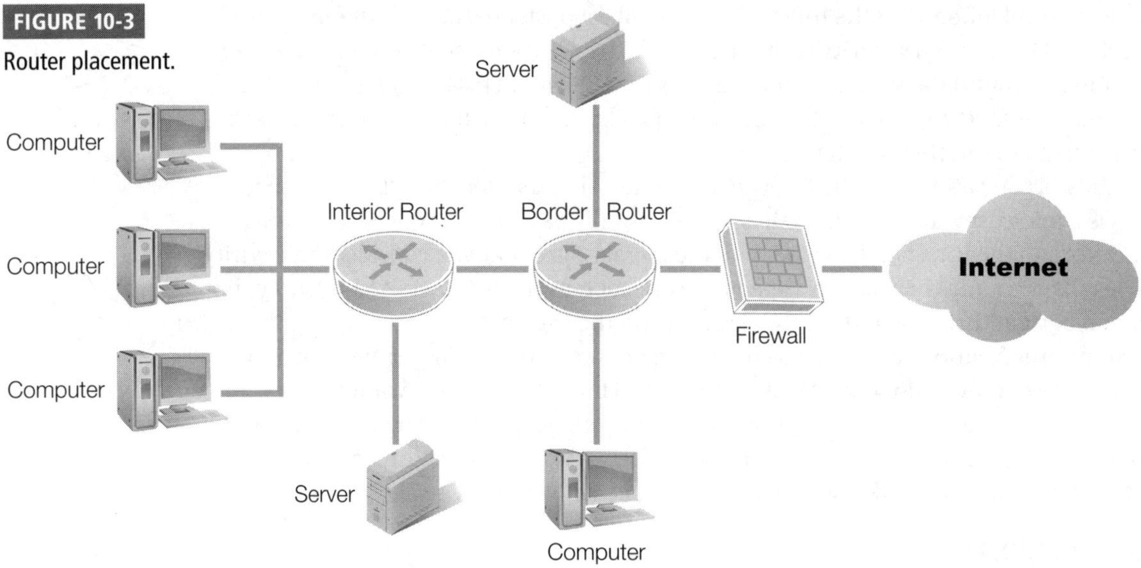

- **Border routers**—A border router is subject to direct attack from an outside source. When you configure any router, you should determine whether it is the only point of defense or if it is one part of a multilayered defense. Of course, a multilayered defense is far better and more secure. The lone defense router can protect internal resources but is subject to attack itself.
- **Internal routers**—An internal router can also provide enhanced features to your internal networks. Internal routers can help keep subnet traffic separate. They can keep traffic out of a subnet and keep traffic in a subnet. For example, an internal router that sits between the network of an organization's research department network and the network for the rest of the organization can keep the two networks separate. These routers can keep confidential traffic inside the research department. They can also keep non-research traffic from crossing over into the research network from the organization's other networks.

You can configure routers to allow all traffic to pass or to protect some internal resources. Routers can use **network address translation (NAT)** and packet filtering to improve security. NAT uses an alternate public IP address to hide a system's real IP address. One of the original purposes of NAT was to compensate for a shortage of IP addresses. Today it helps with security by hiding the true IP address of a device. An attacker will have more difficulty identifying the layout of networks behind a firewall that uses NAT.

Packet filtering is a function of a router or firewall. It happens each time the router or firewall receives a data packet. The device compares the packet to a list of rules configured by the network administrator. The rules tell the device whether to allow the packet into the network or to deny it. If there is not a rule that specifically allows the packet, the firewall blocks the packet.

NAT and packet filtering are two good ways to use your routers to help defend your network. They provide some defense against basic attacks. It is important to remember, however, that no single technology is a "silver bullet." You should still use firewalls to protect your network and other technologies described in this book to secure your data.

Local Area Networks

LANs provide network connectivity for computers located in the same geographic area. These computers typically connect to each other with devices such as hubs and switches. This switching infrastructure is located behind the organization's router, as shown in Figure 10-4.

In many cases, systems on the same LAN do not protect themselves from each other. This is intentional, as collaboration often requires connections between LAN systems that you would not normally allow from the Internet. This is why it is extremely important to have good security on systems located on your LAN. If a virus infects a system on the LAN and the other systems do not protect themselves, the virus can spread quickly to all systems on the LAN.

Ethernet Networks

Until a decade ago, many different types of LANs existed. Now, almost every network has switched to a single technology called Ethernet. In early Ethernet networks, all computers connected to a single wire and had to fight with each other for turns to use the network.

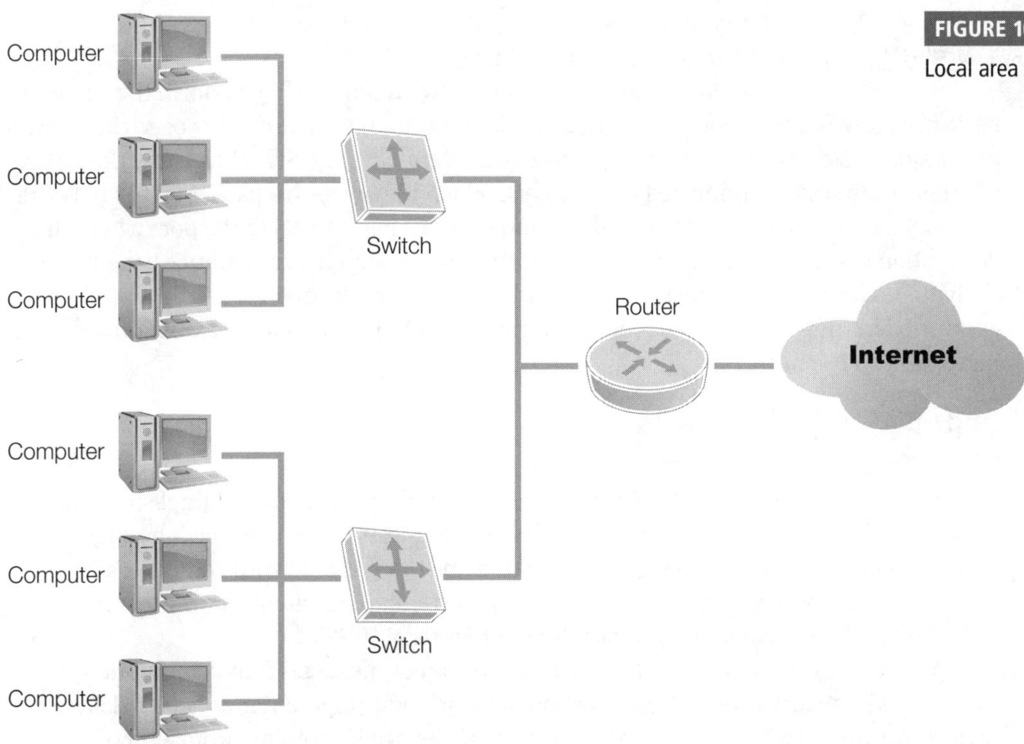

FIGURE 10-4
Local area networks.

This was inefficient. Fortunately, technology evolved. Modern Ethernet networks use a dedicated connection for each system. This wire connects each system back to a **switch**, which controls the LAN.

The Ethernet standard defines how computers communicate on the network. It governs both the Physical and Data Link layers of the OSI reference model. Ethernet defines how computers use MAC addresses to communicate with each other on the network.

LAN Devices: Hubs and Switches

Two main devices connect computers on a LAN: hubs and switches. **Hubs** are simple network devices. They contain a number of plugs (or ports) where you can connect Ethernet cables for different network systems. When the hub receives a packet on any port, it automatically retransmits that packet to all the other ports. In this way, every system connected to the hub can hear everything that every other system communicates on the network. This makes the job of the hub quite simple.

> **WARNING**
>
> Hubs also create a security risk. If every computer can see what every other computer transmits on the network, eavesdroppers have an easy time grabbing all the packets they want.

The simple nature of a hub is also its major disadvantage. A hub creates a lot of network congestion by retransmitting everything it hears. In the last section, you learned how old-fashioned Ethernet networks had every system connected to the same wire. When you use a hub to connect systems, you get the same result. Every system communicates with every other system on the network, making it difficult for a single system to get a packet in edgewise. This causes network congestion and reduces the speed of the network for everyone using it.

Switches are a good alternative to hubs. They perform the same basic function as a hub: connecting multiple systems to the network. However, they have one major added feature: They can perform intelligent filtering. Switches know the MAC address of the system connected to each port. When they receive a packet on the network, they look at the destination MAC address and send the packet *only* to the port where the destination system resides. This simple feature provides a huge performance benefit.

Switches are now inexpensive with greatly improved performance. That's why almost every modern network uses switches to connect systems. Generally speaking, only small networks still use hubs.

TCP/IP and How It Works

Imagine a lunch table with a Chinese speaker, a French speaker, and an English speaker. That would be a confusing conversation! The lunch guests must have one language in common if they want to communicate. The same thing is true with computers. Fortunately, almost every computer now speaks a standard language (or protocol) called the **Transmission Control Protocol/Internet Protocol (TCP/IP)**.

A protocol is a set of rules that governs the format of messages that computers exchange. A network protocol governs how networking equipment interacts to deliver data across the network. These protocols manage the transfer of data from a server

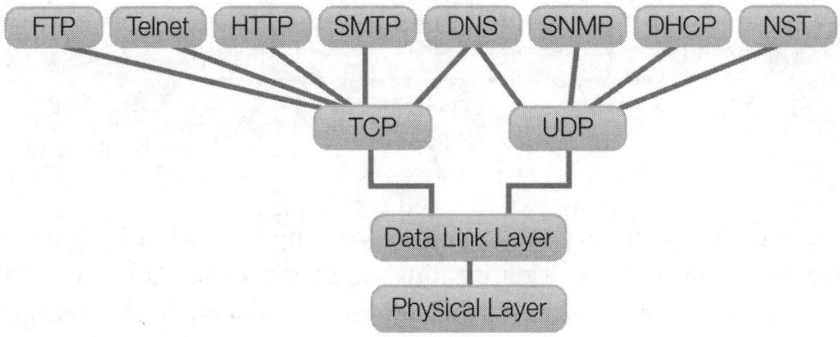

FIGURE 10-5
TCP/IP protocol suite.

to a personal computer from the beginning of the data transfer to the end. In this section, you will learn about the protocols that make up TCP/IP and the basics of TCP/IP networking.

TCP/IP Overview

TCP/IP is actually a suite of protocols that operate at both the Network and Transport layers of the OSI reference model. It governs all activity across the Internet and through most corporate and home networks. The U.S. Department of Defense developed TCP/IP to provide a highly reliable and fault-tolerant network infrastructure. Reliability was the focus, not security.

This suite of protocols has many different responsibilities. Figure 10-5 shows a portion of the TCP/IP suite. In this book, you will look at only a small portion of those protocols that are essential to the operation of the Internet.

IP Addressing

One of the primary functions of Network layer protocols is to provide an addressing scheme. The IP layer contains the addressing scheme in TCP/IP. **IP addresses** are four-byte addresses that uniquely identify every device on the network.

Figure 10-6 shows an example of an IP address. As you can see, IP addresses use the dotted-quad notation. This represents each of the four bytes as an integer between 0 and 255. Each IP address consists of a network address and a host address. For example, the IP address 192.168.10.1 shown in Figure 10-6 is for the network address 192.168 and the host address 10.1. The dividing line between the network and host addresses can change based on the way an administrator configures the network. A network-configuration parameter known as the subnet mask defines this dividing line for a particular network.

NOTE

Figure 10-6 shows the most common type of IP address, IPv4. There is a new IP addressing standard, IPv6, that can address many more computers than its predecessor. IPv4 addresses are 32-bit numbers, where IPv6 addresses are 128-bit numbers. IPv6 has more features but the primary reason for the new standard is the ability to address more computers and devices.

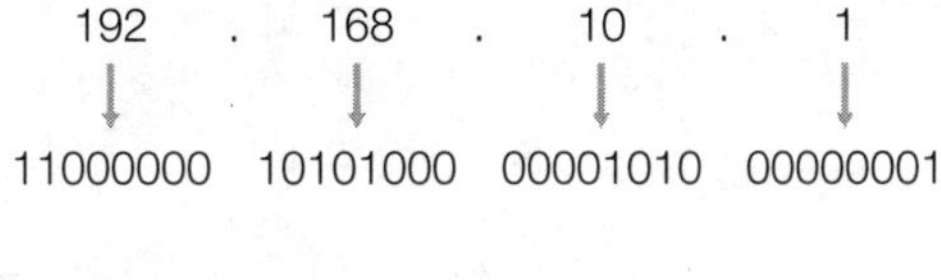

FIGURE 10-6
IP addressing.

FIGURE 10-7
DHCP communication.

Because every computer needs its own IP address, keeping track of address assignments can be time consuming. Many organizations use **Dynamic Host Configuration Protocol (DHCP)** within a network to simplify the configuration of each user's computer. This allows the computer to get its configuration information dynamically from the network instead of the network administrator providing the configuration information to the computer. DHCP provides a computer with an IP address, subnet mask, and other essential communication information. It simplifies the network administrator's job. An example of DHCP communication appears in Figure 10-7.

ICMP

Once you have configured all the network components, you need to monitor your network for health and performance. **Internet Control Message Protocol (ICMP)** is a management and control protocol for IP. ICMP delivers messages between hosts about the health of the network. ICMP messages carry information on hosts it can reach as well as information on routing and updates.

Two ICMP tools are ping and traceroute. The `ping` command sends a single packet to a target IP address called an ICMP echo request. This packet is equivalent to asking the question "Are you there?" The computer on the other end can either answer the request "Yes" with an ICMP echo reply packet or ignore the request. Attackers sometimes use the `ping` command to identify targets for a future attack. Because of this potential vulnerability, many system administrators configure their computers to ignore all ping requests.

The `traceroute` command uses ICMP echo request packets for another purpose: to identify the path that packets travel through a network. Packets may travel many different routes to get from one point on a network to another. The `traceroute` command displays the path that a particular packet follows so you can identify the source of potential network problems.

Attackers can use ICMP to create a denial of service attack against a network. This type of attack is known as a smurf attack, named after one of the first programs to implement it. It works by sending spoofed ICMP echo request packets to a broadcast address on a network, hoping that the hosts on that network will all respond. If the attacker sends enough replies, it is possible to bring down a T1 from a dial-up connection attack. Fortunately, it is very easy to defend against smurf attacks by configuring your network to ignore ICMP echo requests sent to broadcast addresses.

Network Security Risks

Any data in transit is a potential attack target. This makes network security important. So far, in this chapter, you've learned about how networks carry data. You've also learned about a few risks facing networks, such as smurf attacks and eavesdropping. In this section, you will take an in-depth look at some network security risks. You also will cover some of the network security controls that you can put in place to protect your network.

> **NOTE**
> Attackers also want to be able to gain control of systems on your network. They will exploit network security holes. This is beyond the scope of this chapter. You learned about some of these attacks in Chapter 3 and you'll see more of them in Chapter 11.

Three Categories of Risk

The three main categories of network security risks are reconnaissance, eavesdropping, and denial of service. Each of these has different impacts on the availability, integrity, and confidentiality of data carried across a network. They also may affect the security of the network itself. In this section, you will examine some of the most common network security risks.

Network Reconnaissance

Network reconnaissance is gathering information about a network for use in a future attack. Consider an army that wants to attack a country. The attacking army needs a lot of advance information to succeed. Some of the things a commander might want to know are as follows:

- Terrain
- Location of roads, trails, and waterways
- Locations and types of enemy defenses
- Weaknesses in the enemy's perimeter
- Procedures for allowing access through the perimeter
- Types of weapons used by the enemy

Similarly, a network attacker would want to know many things before attacking:

- IP addresses used on the network
- Types of firewalls and other security systems
- Remote access procedures
- Operating system(s) of computers on the network
- Weaknesses in network systems

Normally, you wouldn't just make this information available to an attacker. Unfortunately, however, attackers have many tools to obtain it. You have already learned why it is important to block ICMP echo requests from outside your network. This stops attackers from using the ping and traceroute tools to gather information. You also want to be sure to configure systems to provide as little information as possible to outsiders. This will limit the effectiveness of network reconnaissance attacks.

Network Eavesdropping

Attackers also may want to violate the confidentiality of data sent on your network. Before you learn about network eavesdropping, consider a less complex technology: the phone. If you've seen a spy movie, you know that it's easy to tap a telephone if you can get to the telephone wires. You simply need to hook up a cable to the telephone switch box on the house and connect a handset to listen in on calls.

Network eavesdropping is just as simple. If an attacker has physical access to a cable, he or she can simply tap that cable and see all the data passing through the cable. You have a few options to protect against this type of attack:

- Limit physical access to network cables.
- Use switched networks. The attacker will then see only information sent to or from the computer attached to the tapped cable.
- Encrypt sensitive data. The attacker still might be able to see the transmission but won't be able to make sense of it.

> **NOTE**
> Wireless networking presents a completely new world of eavesdropping challenges. You will learn more about that later in the chapter.

Network eavesdropping is easier than telephone eavesdropping. Physical access to the network makes it easier but is not required. If an attacker compromises a computer on the network, the attacker can use that computer for eavesdropping. Using switched networks and encryption will help limit the effectiveness of this type of attack. You should also secure systems on your network from malicious code. Chapter 11 provides tips on doing this.

Network Denial of Service

Often, an attacker is not interested in gaining access to your network. Rather, he or she simply wants to deny you the use of it. This can be an extremely effective tactic. Many businesses can't operate if they lose their networks. An attacker has two primary methods to conduct a denial of service attack: flooding a network with traffic and shutting down a single point of failure.

Flooding a network with traffic is the simpler method. You can think of a network as a pipe: It can only carry so much data before it gets full. If you send it more data than can fit in the pipe, the network becomes clogged and useless. Attackers can create a denial of service attack by simply sending more data through a network than it can handle. One variation on this theme is a distributed denial of service (DDoS) attack. In this attack, the black-hat hacker uses many systems around the world that he or she has cracked to flood the network from many different directions. It becomes difficult to distinguish legitimate traffic from attack traffic, and the network grinds to a halt.

Several major Internet retailers, including Amazon.com, Wal-Mart, and Expedia, were the victims of a denial of service attack in 2009. The attack shut down all three Web sites for about an hour in the middle of the winter holiday shopping season. The companies lost revenue as customers turned to other retail Web sites.

Protecting yourself against a denial of service attack can be difficult. The most obvious approach is to ensure you have adequate Internet bandwidth to withstand the load. Some new technologies on the market seek to defend against DDoS attacks, but they are unproven and limited in their effectiveness. The best defense is to detect attacks as early as possible and take action to block the incoming traffic before it renders your network unusable.

Basic Network Security Defense Tools

Defense against these kinds of risks begins with some basic hardware and software tools: firewalls, virtual private networks, and network admission control.

Firewalls

A firewall controls the flow of traffic by preventing unauthorized network traffic from entering or leaving a particular portion of the network. You can place a firewall between an internal network and the outside world, or within the internal network to control access to particular corporate assets by only authorized users. Firewalls are critical elements of networking security, but they are just that: elements. Firewalls will not solve all security problems, but they do add a much-needed deterrent.

Figure 10-8 shows the role of a firewall in a network. It separates private networks from the Internet. It also separates different private networks from each other. In this section, you will look at the different types of firewalls and the roles they play in the network topology.

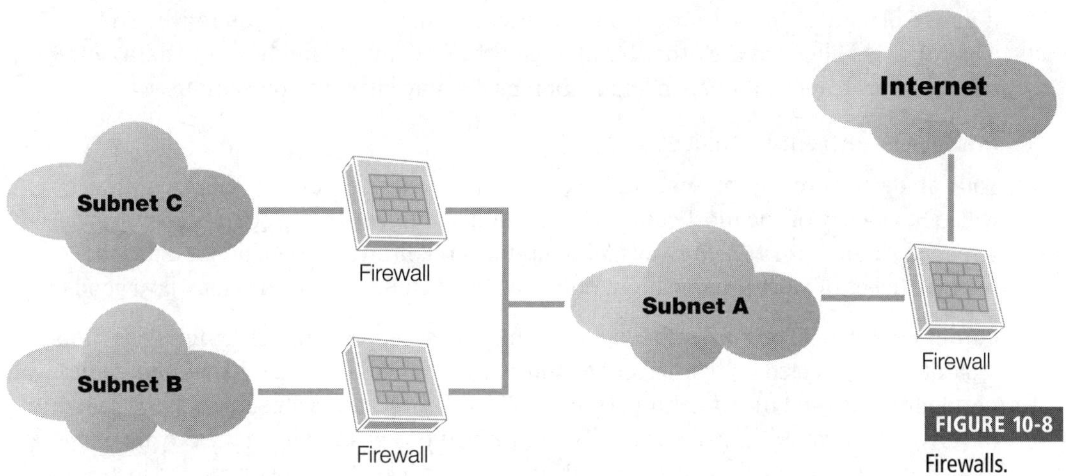

FIGURE 10-8
Firewalls.

Firewall Types

The basic function of a firewall is quite simple. It must block any traffic that you don't explicitly allow. Firewalls contain rules that define the types of traffic that can come and go through a network. Each time the firewall receives a communication, it checks the message against its rules. If the message matches a rule, the firewall allows the message to pass. If the message does not match a rule, the firewall blocks the message.

Going beyond this basic functionality, firewall technology includes three main types:

- **Packet filtering**—A **packet-filtering firewall** is very basic. It compares received traffic to a set of rules that define which traffic it will permit to pass through the firewall. It makes this decision for each packet that reaches the firewall and has no memory of packets it has encountered in the past.
- **Stateful inspection**—A **stateful inspection firewall** remembers information about the status of a network communication. Once the firewall receives the first packet in a communication, the firewall remembers that communication session until it is closed. This type of firewall does not have to check its rules each time it receives a packet. It only needs to check rules when a new communication session starts.
- **Application proxy**—An **application proxy firewall** goes further than a stateful inspection firewall. It doesn't actually allow packets to travel directly between systems on opposite sides of the firewall. The firewall opens separate connections with each of the two communicating systems and then acts as a broker (or proxy) between the two. This allows for an added degree of protection, as the firewall can analyze information about the application in use when making the decision to allow or deny traffic.

The type of firewall you choose for your network will depend upon many different factors. If you're placing a simple firewall at the border of a large network, you may wish to use a basic packet filter. On the other hand, if you're protecting a highly secure data center that hosts Web applications, an application proxy may be more appropriate.

Firewall-Deployment Techniques

You can deploy firewalls in many different ways on your network. In this section, you will look at a few of the most common firewall-deployment techniques: border firewalls, screened subnet (or DMZ) firewalls, and multilayered firewalls. Depending upon the security needs of your organization, one or more of these approaches may be a good fit.

Border Firewall. The border firewall is the most basic approach. Border firewalls simply separate the protected network from the Internet, as shown in Figure 10-9. A border firewall normally sits behind the router and receives all communications passing from the router into the private network. It also receives all communications passing from the private network to the Internet. Border firewalls normally use either packet filtering or stateful inspection.

These are most common for organizations that do not host public services. If you outsource your Web site and e-mail, you may not need to allow the public to get into your network at all. In this case, you may simply block most (or sometimes all) inbound traffic. A border firewall excels in this scenario.

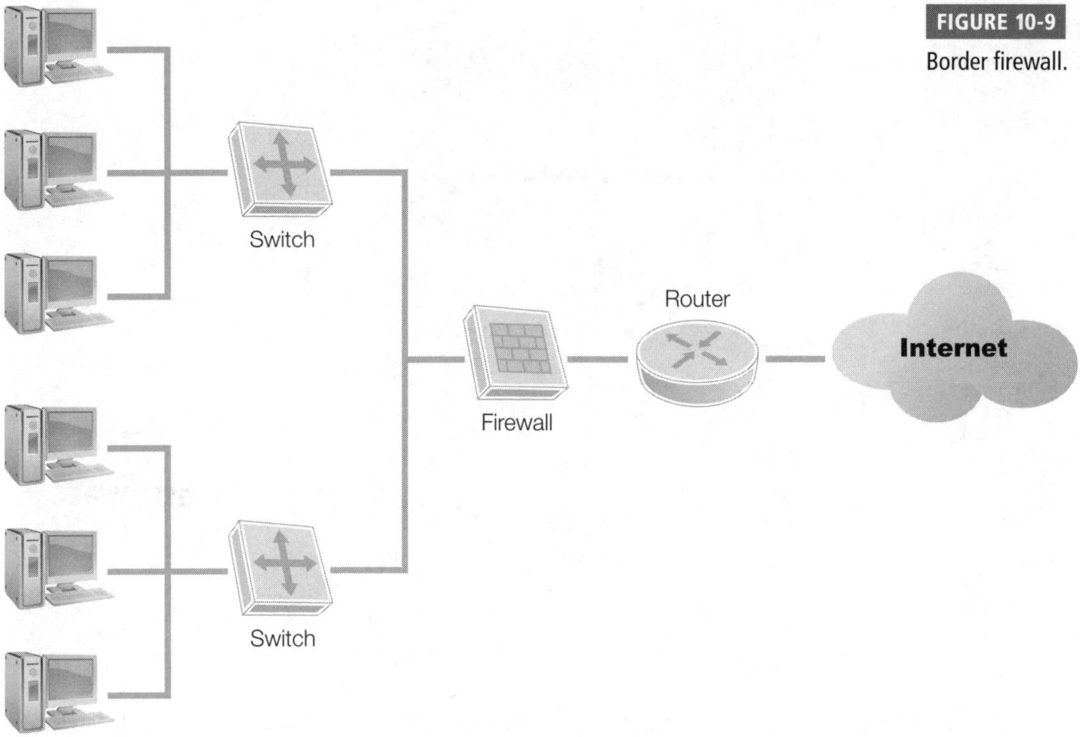

FIGURE 10-9
Border firewall.

Screened Subnet. Often, it's not possible to block all traffic into your network. If you host a public Web site or your own e-mail server, you need to allow inbound connections on a limited basis. The **screened subnet** firewall topology, shown in Figure 10-10, is the best approach for this. The firewall has three network cards. Two are set up identically to a border firewall with one connected to the Internet and another connected to the private network. The third card connects to a special network known as the screened subnet or demilitarized zone (DMZ).

The DMZ is a semiprivate network used to host services that the public can access. Users have limited access from the Internet to systems in the DMZ to access these services. A secure network does not allow direct access from the Internet to the private network.

> **NOTE**
> The screened subnet is the most common firewall topology in use today.

This approach recognizes that systems accessed from the Internet pose a special risk. They are more likely targets of attacks and, therefore, are more likely to suffer successful attacks. If you confine these machines to the DMZ, they can jeopardize only other systems in the DMZ. An attacker who gains access to a DMZ system will not be able to use that system to directly access systems on the private network.

FIGURE 10-10

Screened subnet firewall.

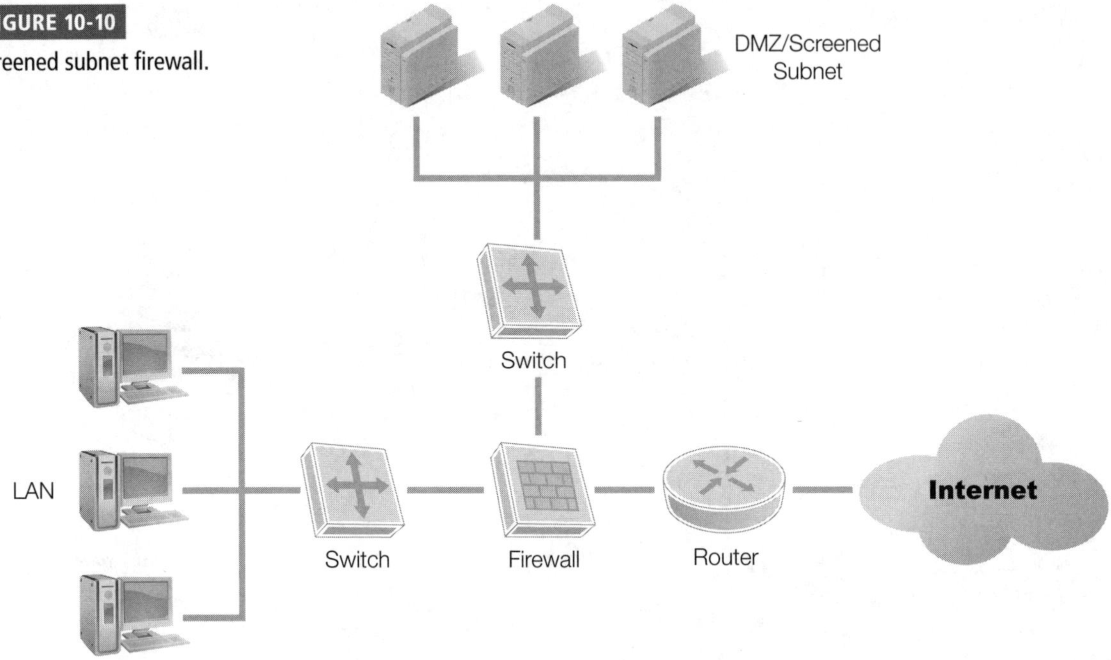

Multilayered Firewalls. In large and/or highly secure environments, organizations often use multiple firewalls to segment their network into pieces. This is the case illustrated in Figure 10-8. In that figure, one firewall acts as the border firewall, protecting subnets A, B, and C from the Internet. However, two other firewalls separate subnets B and C from each other and from subnet A.

Multilayered firewalls are useful when you have networks with different security levels. For example, in Figure 10-8, general users may connect to subnet A. Users working on a secret research project might connect to subnet B. Executives might connect to subnet C. This provides the secret project and the executives with protection from the general user community.

Virtual Private Networks and Remote Access

With the advent of telecommuting, remote access has become a common part of many corporate networks. Today, many companies today have employees who rarely if ever come into the corporate office. These users are at home or on the road. Even so, they still need access to corporate resources. This means opening access to more corporate resources from the Internet than IT professionals want. The trick is to allow corporate employees the access they need but to keep attackers out of these potentially open doors.

Virtual private networks (VPNs) are a good way to increase the security level of data you transmit across the public data network. They normally use encryption to protect all the data they send between a user and the organization's network. Using a VPN for remote access provides security and is cost effective. The cost difference of using a VPN versus paying for a dedicated connection between two sites is significant. Figure 10-11 shows an example of VPN access to a network.

VPNs require your gateway equipment to have a lot of processing power to handle the encryption algorithms. You can offload this processing power to another device by using a dedicated VPN concentrator rather than having your router or firewall terminate the VPN.

When deploying a VPN, you must consider the security of the end users' computers. Once users connect to the corporate network, their PCs could be an open portal into those resources for an attacker who gains access to the PC. For this reason, many organizations require that employees install security software on their home computers. You can also limit VPN access to laptop computers your organization owns and manages.

The three major VPN technologies in use today are as follows:

- **Point-to-Point Tunneling Protocol (PTTP)**—The **Point-to-Point Tunneling Protocol (PTTP)** was once the predominant VPN protocol. For many years, almost all VPNs used PPTP. It is easy to set up on client computers because most operating systems include PPTP support.
- **Secure Sockets Layer (SSL)**—In Chapter 9, you learned about how the Secure Sockets Layer encrypts Web communications. Many VPNs use SSL to provide encrypted communication. Users connect to an SSL-protected Web page and log on. Their Web browser then downloads software that connects them to the VPN. This requires no advance configuration of the system. For this reason, SSL VPNs are quickly growing in popularity.
- **IPSec**—**IPSec** is a suite of protocols designed to connect sites securely. While some IPSec VPNs are available for end users, they often require the installation of third-party software on the user's system and are not popular. Many organizations use IPSec to connect one site to another securely over the Internet. The required IPSec VPN functionality is built into many routers and firewalls, allowing for easy configuration.

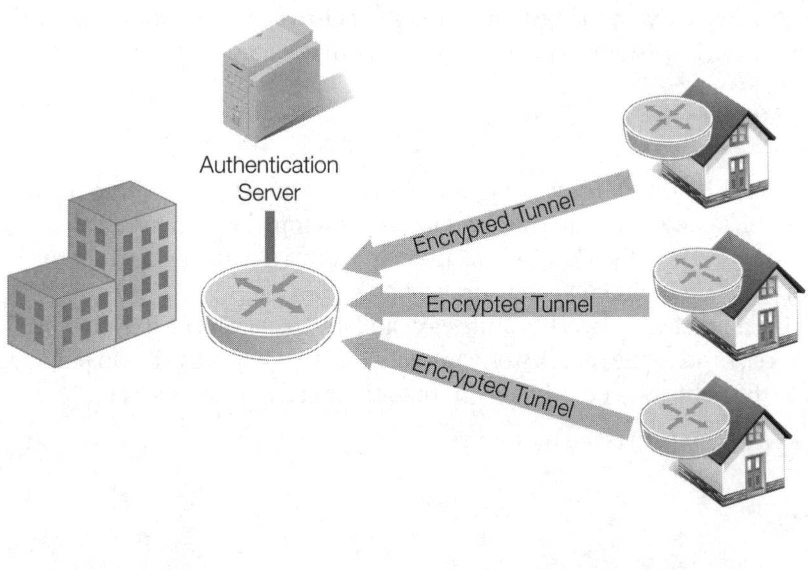

FIGURE 10-11

VPN access.

VPNs provide clear benefit to an organization. They offer an inexpensive, secure replacement for dedicated connections between sites. They also enable users to connect securely to the organization network from remote locations. This promises increased productivity as workers can easily get to resources they need while on the road.

Network Access Control

Network access control (NAC) systems enable you to add more security requirements before allowing a device to connect to your network. They perform two major tasks: authentication and posture checking. Although NAC is a new technology, it is growing in popularity. Many organizations now deploy NAC for both internal users and guests using their network. NAC works on wired and wireless networks.

The IEEE 802.1x standard describes the most common NAC technology. Commonly referred to as simply 802.1x or 1x, this standard tells how clients may interact with a NAC device to gain entry to the network. Software on users' computers prompts them to log on to the network. After verifying the user's credentials, the NAC device instructs the switch (for a wired network) or access point (for a wireless network) to grant the user access to the network. This is the authentication component of NAC.

Posture checking is an optional second use of NAC technology. When used, the NAC device checks the configuration of the user's computer to ensure that it meets security standards before allowing it access to the network. Some things commonly checked include the following:

- Up-to-date antivirus software
- Host firewall enabled
- Operating system supported
- Operating system patched

If users attempt to connect a noncompliant system to a network, the NAC device offers two options. The administrator can decide to block such systems from the network until they are fixed. Alternatively, the system may connect to a special quarantine network where you may fix the system before gaining access to the main network.

Wireless Networks

Wireless networks have become very popular for connecting devices within the home and office. Wireless networks can connect laptops, desktops, smartphones, and many other devices. Wireless networking allows users to work from any location in the building without worrying about finding a network jack.

Configuring a wireless network is quite easy and inexpensive. The question becomes, what does wireless do to the security of your network? If it is so easy for an employee to connect to the network, does that mean that others can connect as well?

Setting up a secure wireless network—at least one as secure as any wired network—is possible. However, it takes careful planning, execution, and testing. Properly configured strong encryption is critical to operating a secure wireless network. In this section, you will examine wireless networking technology and learn how to configure and secure wireless networks.

Wireless Access Points (WAPs)

A wireless access point (WAP) is the connection between a wired and wireless network. WAPs are radios, sending and receiving networking information over the air between wireless devices and the wired network. Anyone within radio range of a wireless access point can communicate with it and attempt to connect to the network.

Attackers who wish to undermine your security can do several things with a wireless network. First, they understand that wireless networks extend the range of your organization's network beyond your walls. While you can easily control physical access to a wired network, walls and fences don't stop wireless signals. Therefore, wireless networks without proper security present an easy target for attackers who wish to connect to your network. Second, they know that it is much easier to eavesdrop on a wireless network than a wired one. It's very simple for anyone within radio range of your network to capture all the data sent on that network. If that data is unencrypted, it's fair game for an attack.

Wireless Network Security Controls

Fortunately, you can do quite a bit to secure your wireless network. In this section, you will look at several examples of wireless network security controls. The most important is the use of wireless encryption to prevent eavesdropping. Other techniques that provide added security include disabling SSID beaconing, implementing MAC address filtering, and adding strong authentication to your wireless network.

Wireless Encryption

Encryption is the single most important thing you can do to secure your wireless network. This makes it impossible for an outsider to view information traveling over the network. Without encryption, all the activity of wireless users is visible to anyone who comes within radio range of your network. It would be possible for an attacker to sit in the parking lot of your building with an inexpensive antenna attached to a standard laptop and monitor everything happening on your wireless network.

You must use strong encryption. In the early days of wireless networking, the industry developed a standard called **Wired Equivalent Privacy (WEP)**, which provided basic encryption. WEP relies on the RC4 encryption algorithm created by Ron Rivest for RSA in the late 1980s. Since its release, security analysts have discovered significant flaws in WEP that make it insecure. With software freely available on the Internet, it is simple to break the encryption on a WEP network in a matter of seconds. In fact, using WEP on a wireless network is probably worse than using no encryption at all because it provides a false sense of security. People feel they are safe because their wireless network encrypts traffic. They don't realize they're using the equivalent of a Cap'n Crunch decoder ring to protect their data.

TJX and WEP

In Chapter 3, you learned about the major security breach experienced by the TJX Companies between 2005 and 2007. Insecure encryption on a wireless network was the culprit. Attackers sat in the parking lot of a single TJX store and, using inexpensive equipment, cracked the WEP encryption key of the store's network. They then used this to access the main corporate network, where they reportedly stole 94,000,000 credit card numbers. This was one of the biggest information security breaches in history. TJX could have prevented this breach by switching from WEP to WPA encryption. Although this might have required an investment to replace some aging equipment, the return would have been invaluable in this case.

Fortunately, there is an alternative. The **Wi-Fi Protected Access (WPA)** standard uses strong AES encryption to protect data on networks and does not share the same vulnerabilities discovered in WEP. WPA is quite easy to configure. In its basic form, it requires entering a shared secret key into the network configuration of every computer on the network. In more advanced forms, you can replace the shared secret key by giving each user a unique user name and password. These passwords can be identical to the user's normal credentials by using a central authentication server, such as a Remote Authentication Dial In User Service (RADIUS) server.

SSID Beaconing

By default, wireless networks broadcast their presence to the public. They send out announcements containing the network's service set identifier (SSID). This is the public name of the network. You've seen these before when you boot up in a coffee shop, for instance, and your computer tells you that wireless networks are available. This notice includes the SSIDs of all available networks.

You can stop your network from announcing itself by disabling SSID beaconing on your wireless access points. If you disable beaconing, users connecting to your network will need to know it is there and provide the network name themselves. This is fine if you have regular users, such as in a corporate environment. It will not work well if you allow guests access to your network.

TIP

Disabling SSID beaconing provides a small degree of protection, but it is not foolproof. In fact, a skilled attacker can easily discover the presence of your network by using freely available software tools. Using this technique simply means you don't advertise the presence of your network, hoping to avoid the casual attacker's interest.

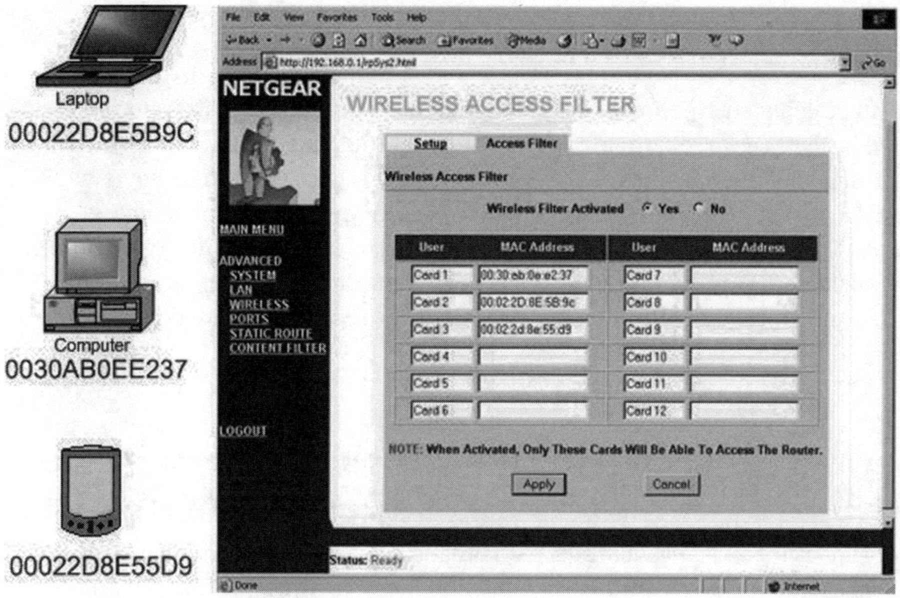

FIGURE 10-12
MAC address filtering.

MAC Address Filtering

WAPs also enable you to apply MAC address filters to control which computers can connect to your network. With this technology, you provide a list of acceptable MAC addresses to your WAP. You should allow only approved computers to connect to your network. Deny all other computers access to your network. Figure 10-12 shows an example of MAC address filtering.

The major disadvantage of MAC address filtering is that it is very complicated to maintain. If you have more than a handful of computers on your network, it quickly becomes a major challenge to update the list of acceptable MAC addresses. Imagine if you worked for an organization with 20,000 users. It wouldn't be unusual to see 100 new computers on the network every week. That's in addition to 100 dropping off the network as you replace them. Can you imagine trying to update 200 MAC addresses every week? Use MAC address filtering in cases where it makes sense.

> **WARNING**
> MAC address filtering is another weak security mechanism. Using free tools, attackers can easily discover an active MAC address on your network and then change their NIC to use a valid MAC address. This is one type of address spoofing.

While no network is totally secure, putting the right security controls in place can make your networks safer. The main point is, never rely on a single control. Always use layered controls. You should always assume a savvy attacker will be able to compromise one or more of the controls you have in place. Ensuring an attacker must compromise multiple controls to get to your data is the best way to make your IT infrastructure as secure as possible.

CHAPTER SUMMARY

In this chapter, you learned about the Open Systems Interconnection (OSI) reference model and how it serves as an example of how you can build and use a network and its resources. You learned what Network layer protocols are, including an overview of TCP/IP. You learned some basic tools for network security. You also learned how wireless networks work and what threats they pose to the security of your organization. Lastly, you gained a better understanding of the need for security policies, standards, and procedures, and how your IT infrastructure is only as secure as its weakest link.

KEY CONCEPTS AND TERMS

Application proxy firewall
Dynamic Host Configuration Protocol (DHCP)
Hub
Internet Control Message Protocol (ICMP)
IP address
IPSec
Network access control (NAC)
Network address translation (NAT)
Open Systems Interconnection (OSI) reference model
Packet-filtering firewall
Point-to-Point Tunneling Protocol (PPTP)
Router
Screened subnet
Stateful inspection firewall
Switch
Transmission Control Protocol/Internet Protocol (TCP/IP)
Wi-Fi Protected Access (WPA)
Wired Equivalent Privacy (WEP)

CHAPTER 10 ASSESSMENT

1. The basic model for how you can build and use a network and its resources is known as the ________.

A. Dynamic Host Configuration Protocol (DHCP) model
B. International Standardization Organization (ISO) model
C. Open Systems Interconnection (OSI) reference model
D. None of the above

2. The basic job of a ________ is to enforce an access control policy at the border of a network.

A. Firewall
B. Router
C. Switch
D. Access point

3. A(n) ________ is a critical element in every corporate network today, allowing access to an organization's resources from almost anywhere in the world.

   A. Local area network (LAN)
   B. Wide area network (WAN)
   C. Dynamic Host Configuration Protocol (DHCP)
   D. None of the above

4. A secure virtual private network (VPN) creates an authenticated and encrypted channel across some form of public network.

   A. True
   B. False

5. ________ is a suite of protocols that was developed by the Department of Defense to provide a highly reliable and fault-tolerant network infrastructure.

   A. DHCP
   B. VPN
   C. PPPoE
   D. TCP/IP

6. A ________ is a device that interconnects two or more networks and selectively interchanges packets of data between them.

7. Which simple network device helps to increase network performance by using the MAC address to send network traffic only to its intended destination?

   A. Hub
   B. Switch
   C. Router
   D. Gateway

8. The three basic types of firewalls are packet filtering, application proxy, and stateful inspection.

   A. True
   B. False

9. What technology is the most secure way to encrypt wireless communications?

   A. TCP
   B. WEP
   C. WPA
   D. UDP

10. IP addresses are assigned to computers by the manufacturer.

    A. True
    B. False

11. Which VPN technology allows users to initiate connections over the Web?

    A. SSL
    B. PPTP
    C. IPSec
    D. ICMP

12. What layer of the OSI reference model is most commonly responsible for encryption?

    A. Application
    B. Presentation
    C. Session
    D. Transport

13. DHCP provides systems with their MAC addresses.

    A. True
    B. False

14. What firewall topology supports the implementation of a DMZ?

    A. Bastion host
    B. Multilayered firewall
    C. Border firewall
    D. Screened subnet

15. What technology allows you to hide the private IP address of a system from the Internet?

    A. SSL
    B. RADIUS
    C. PPTP
    D. NAT

CHAPTER

11

Malicious Code and Activity

MALICIOUS CODE OR SOFTWARE is a threat to any Internet-connected device or computer. You have already learned about the basics of malicious software in earlier chapters. In this chapter, you'll learn more of how malicious code operates and how you can combat it. Simply put, malicious software is any program that carries out actions that you, as the computer user, do not intend. Often, the goal of malicious software is to cause harm to your system. Malicious software moves through the Internet much as a snake slithers through grass. Attackers use malicious software, or malware, to steal passwords, steal confidential information, delete information from your system, or even reformat hard drives. Unfortunately, you cannot control malicious code with antivirus software alone. That's because malicious code includes more than just viruses, and some malware evades detection.

Malicious code attacks all three information security properties:

- **Availability**—Malware can erase or overwrite files or inflict considerable damage to storage media.
- **Integrity**—Malware can modify database records either immediately or over a period of time. By the time you discover the changed data, you may find that the malware has corrupted your backups as well. It is important that you verify all your data's integrity any time you suspect a security breach. The process can be expensive and is likely to be an expense you haven't budgeted for.
- **Confidentiality**—Malware can disclose private information. In this chapter, you will learn how spyware and Trojans, which are other forms of malware, can capture your organization's proprietary information and send it to unauthorized destinations.

As a security professional, you'll find it a challenge to convince your organization's personnel that security is everyone's responsibility. They tend to think it's the responsibility only of the IT department. Not only that, they tend to think your security efforts get in the way of their doing their work. These security efforts include the policies, procedures, and technologies you'll need to use to prevent malware attacks.

Chapter 11 Topics

This chapter covers the following topics and concepts:

- What malware is and how it inflicts harm on your systems
- What the main types of malware are
- What the history of malicious code is
- How malware is a threat to business organizations
- What motivates attackers and what assets they are targeting
- What tools and techniques prevent attacks
- What tools and techniques detect attacks

Chapter 11 Goals

When you complete this chapter, you will be able to:

- Define malicious software and activity
- Define a Trojan, a virus, a worm, spyware, adware, and spam
- Understand malicious software risks and threats to individuals
- Understand malicious software risks and threats to businesses
- Understand the phases of a malicious software attack
- Understand who hackers, crackers, and perpetrators are
- Define social engineering
- Understand incident-detection tools and techniques
- Understand attack-prevention tools and techniques

Characteristics, Architecture, and Operations of Malicious Software

Security professionals know about malicious software. Malicious software, or malware, is set of instructions that run on a computer system and perform operations that you, the user, do not intend. This activity can take several forms:

- An attacker gains administrative controls to your system and uses commands to inflict harm.
- An attacker sends commands directly to your system. Your system interprets these commands and then executes them.

- An attacker uses software programs that harm your system. These programs can come from physical media (such as a USB drive) or a communications process (such as the Internet). Viruses, Trojan programs, and worms are all examples of these types of malicious software programs.
- Attackers use legitimate remote administration tools and security probes to identify and exploit security vulnerabilities in your network.

You must make yourself aware of what kinds of malicious-code threats you may encounter. This understanding will help you develop reasonable countermeasures to protect your organization.

The Main Types of Malware

From a nontechnical perspective, most computer users think all malicious code is a virus. In fact, there are several different types of viruses, as well as many other forms of malicious code. Each type has unique characteristics and architecture. You must design and implement effective countermeasures to detect, mitigate, and prevent malicious-code attacks. To do this, you must develop an understanding of various types of malicious code and how each type is used.

In this section, you learn how to recognize and describe the characteristics and operation of common types of hostile code. You learn how attackers use each type, which helps you understand how to implement appropriate countermeasures.

Virus

A computer virus is an executable program that attaches to, or infects, other executable programs. It then replicates to infect yet more programs. Some viruses also perform destructive activities after they replicate. Good anti-malware controls notice and eliminate most viruses with an obvious or damaging payload. The primary characteristic of a virus is that is replicates and generally involves user action of some type. Not all viruses inflict harm. Some are just annoying or focus on replicating. Other viruses hide their payload and install a backdoor. The victim may not notice the virus or may not immediately notice its damage.

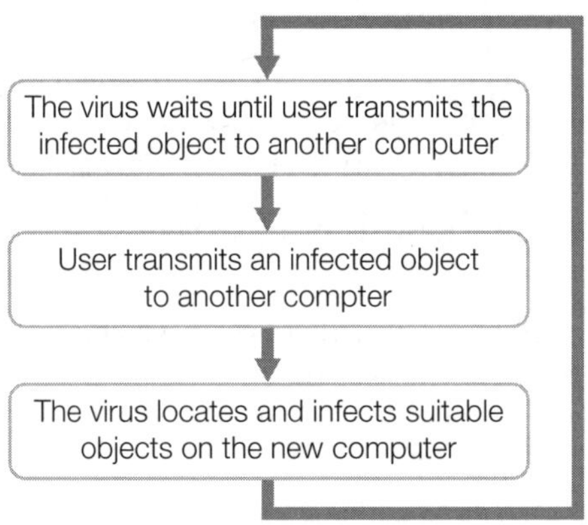

FIGURE 11-1

Typical life cycle of a computer virus.

Evidence of Virus Code Activities

Although you may not always identify every virus, viruses have many telltale signs. Any of the following may indicate an infected computer:

- Deteriorating workstation or server responsiveness
- Unexpected and sustained disk activity levels on workstations (churning)
- Sudden sluggishness of user applications, particularly at startup
- Unexplained freezing of applications or unexpected error messages
- Unscheduled hardware resets and crashes, including program aborts
- Sudden antivirus alarm activity
- Disk error messages, including increased "lost cluster" results from disk scanning
- Unexplained decrease in available space on disk or available memory
- In the case of macro viruses, saved documents that open as DOT files
- Applications (or their icons) that disappear or will not execute

There are three primary types of viruses. **System infectors** are viruses that target computer hardware and software startup functions. **File infectors** are viruses that attack and modify executable programs (like COM, EXE, SYS, and DLL files). **Data infectors** are viruses that attack document files containing embedded macro programming capabilities.

Malicious software activities may occur interactively in real-time sessions between an attacker and the target. Alternatively, they may lie dormant and trigger at some predetermined time or upon some predictable event. They may initiate a destructive action or may simply observe and collect information. Figure 11-1 shows the typical life cycle of a computer virus.

Boot Record Infectors

System infectors are viruses that target key hardware and system software components in a computer. The infected components are usually system startup processes. This type of infection enables the virus to take control and execute before the computer can load most protective measures. The most prevalent types of system infectors include floppy boot record infectors and hard drive master boot record infectors. These viruses travel primarily through media exchange.

Master Boot Record and System Infectors

A master boot record infector moves or destroys the original master boot record, replacing it with viral code. It can then gain control from the bootstrap program and perform its hostile mission. Typically, master boot record infectors perform their tasks and then return control to the legitimate master boot record or the active partition boot record to mask their existence.

FIGURE 11-2
System infector virus.

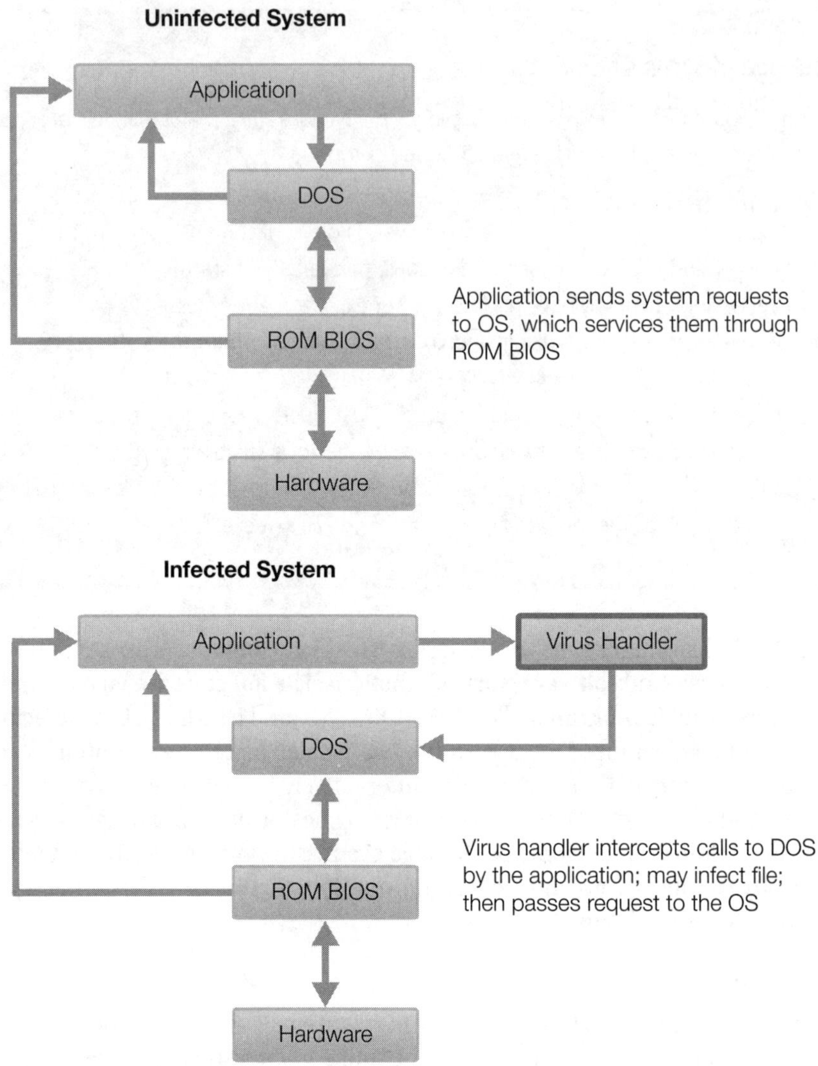

Both types of boot record infectors commonly load instructions that can bypass the ROM-based system services. Loading at this level allows the virus to intercept all normal application and operating system hardware requests. These requests include functions like opening and closing files and file directory services. This type of virus can also execute other types of malicious code routines and cover its own tracks.

A virus with this dual-action capability is a **multipartite virus**. It can subsequently execute file-infection codes as well. Figure 11-2 shows how a system infector virus affects a computer.

File (Program) Infectors

File infector viruses exhibit the classic "replicate and attach" behavior. Because of the wide acceptance and popularity of Microsoft Windows–based operating systems, most well-known file infectors target those systems. They typically attack program files with .com or .exe file extensions. Newer 32-bit virus strains work well with SYS, DLL, and many other file types.

Malware developers write and compile many of these viruses in C++ and other high-level programming languages. In contrast, they often use assembly language to write boot record infectors. While the coding of file infector viruses can be quite complex, the architecture of most executable programs is relatively straightforward.

Viruses of this type attach themselves to the original program file. They control the execution of that file until it can replicate and infect other files, and possibly deliver a payload.

One type of file infector, a companion virus, is really a separate program file that does not attach itself to the original host program. Instead, it creates a new program with a matching file name but with an extension that executes earlier than the original. For example, Windows executes .com files before it executes .exe files. It creates this file in the same directory path as the real program. When the user runs the program, the operating system calls the malware instead of the legitimate program. After the virus finishes its work, it simply executes the command to start the original program. Figure 11-3 shows how a file infector virus works.

Macro (Data File) Infectors

Macro viruses became a problem when software vendors added recording capabilities to popular office applications. Users use macro-recording capabilities to record their actions in a program. The application in which the actions are recorded store these instructions with the data file. The user can then execute the actions automatically when they open

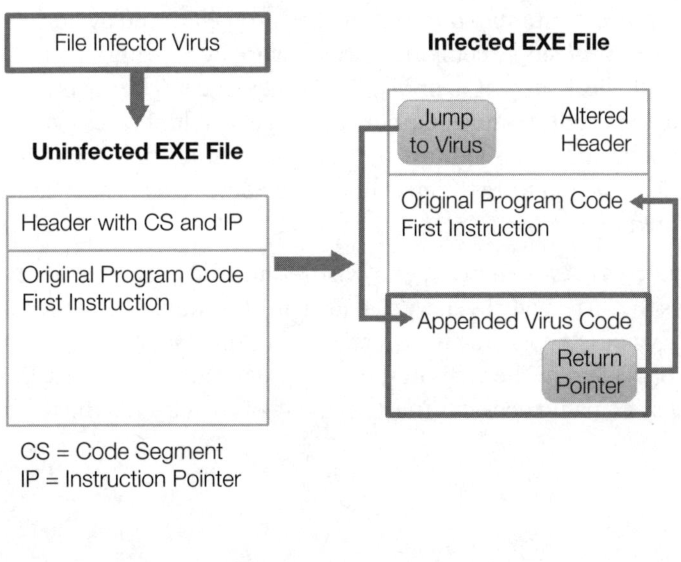

FIGURE 11-3 How a file infector virus works.

FIGURE 11-4

How a macro virus works.

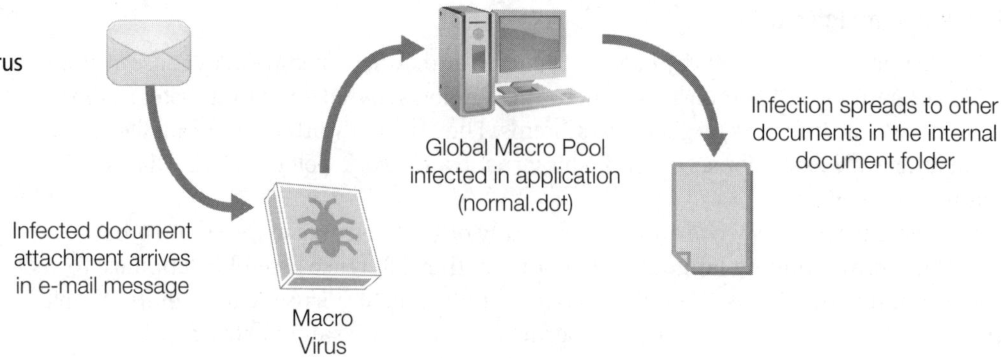

the file or press a predefined keystroke sequence. The original purpose of macros was to automate repetitive processes. Users liked the feature because it made applications more convenient and efficient. However, these macros opened the door for malicious code to carry out its own instructions.

Macro viruses infect these document files and insert their own commands. When users share the infected document with other users, the malware spreads and replicates. The connected nature of most office applications makes it easy for infected documents to spread to other computers and users. Macros can move easily between platforms, and they are quite simple to construct. For this reason, macro viruses are extremely popular.

The electronic mail bomb is a form of malicious macro attack. This type of attack typically involves an e-mail attachment that contains macros designed to inflict maximum damage. Attackers can send the document attachment through anonymous re-mailers to reach its targets with great precision. Someone who receives the e-mail bomb need only open the attachment to launch the macro virus. In some cases, simply previewing the e-mail message activates the e-mail bomb. Figure 11-4 shows how a macro virus works.

Other Virus Classifications

Viruses can use any of a number of techniques to propagate and avoid detection by antivirus software. Most single computer viruses work by copying exact replicas of themselves to each file, boot sector, or document they infect. The virus accomplishes subsequent infections in the same manner, making exact duplicates byte for byte. This predictable action produces a signature pattern. Many antivirus and anti-malware programs look for this signature to detect malware. Some viruses, such as the following, behave differently:

- **Polymorphic viruses**—These types of viruses include a separate encryption engine that stores the virus body in encrypted format while duplicating the main body of the virus. The virus exposes only the decryption routine for possible detection. It embeds the control portion of the virus in the decryption routine, which seizes control of the target system and decrypts the main body of the virus so that it can execute.

FIGURE 11-5 How a polymorphic virus works.

True **polymorphic viruses** use an additional mutation engine to vary the decryption process for each iteration. This makes even this portion of the code more difficult to identify. Figure 11-5 shows how a polymorphic virus infects a computer.

- **Stealth viruses—Stealth viruses** use a number of techniques to conceal themselves from users and from detection software. By installing a low-level system service function, they can intercept any system request and alter the service output to conceal their presence. Stealth viruses can have size stealth, read stealth, or both. Figure 11-6 shows how a stealth virus works.

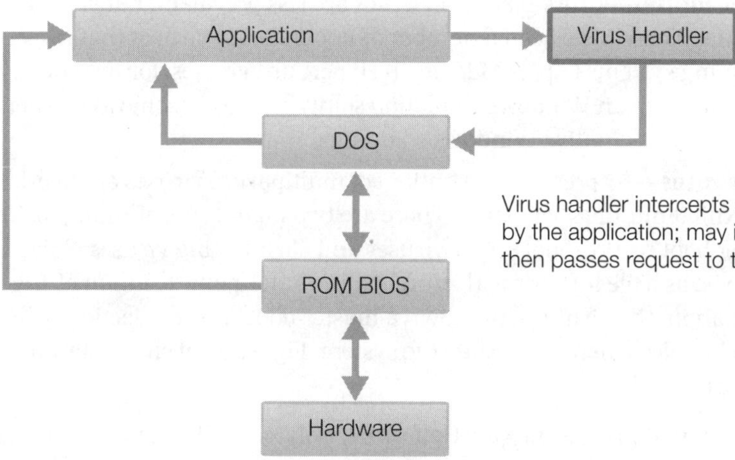

Virus Intercepts File Directory Requests

FIGURE 11-6 How a stealth virus works.

FYI

Size stealth hides the fact that an infected file is bigger than it used to be. The virus intercepts system requests for file information and subtracts its size from the reply before passing it back to the requesting process. Read stealth hides the fact that the virus moved the boot sector code. The virus intercepts read/write requests for the normal boot sector, which the virus has relocated and replaced with the viral code. The virus redirects the request to the new hidden location of the original boot sector code.

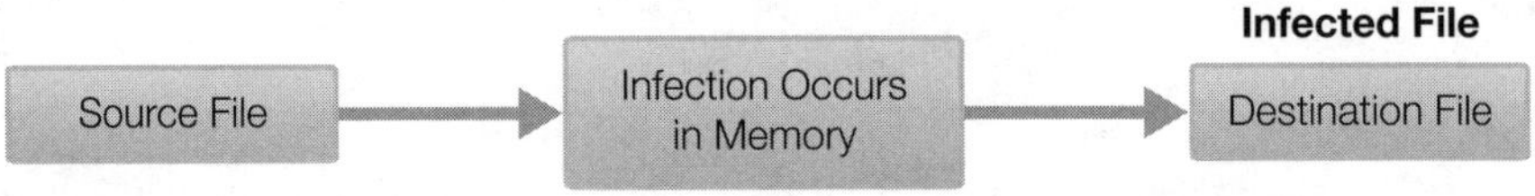

FIGURE 11-7

How a slow virus works.

- **Slow viruses**—Slow viruses counter the ability of antivirus programs to detect changes in infected files. This class of virus resides in the computer's memory, where antivirus software cannot detect it. It waits for certain tasks, like copying or moving files, to execute. As the operating system reads the file into memory, the virus alters it before writing to the output file, making it much harder to detect. Figure 11-7 shows how a slow virus works.
- **Retro viruses**—These viruses attack countermeasures such as antivirus signature files or integrity databases. A retro virus searches for these data files and deletes or alters them, thereby crippling the antivirus software's ability to function. Other viruses, especially boot viruses (which gain control of the target system at startup), modify Windows Registry keys and other key files to disable AV, firewall, and IDS software if found. Figure 11-8 shows how a retro virus works.
- **Cross-platform viruses**—Cross-platform viruses are less prevalent, but can still be potent threats. There have been a number of documented viruses that target multiple operating systems (Apple Macintosh HyperCard viruses, for instance). If those platforms also run Windows emulation software, they become as susceptible to Windows viruses as a native Windows computer.
- **Multipartite viruses**—As previously mentioned, multipartite viruses are hybrid viruses that exhibit multiple behaviors. There are two main types of multipartite viruses: master boot record/boot sector viruses and file infecting viruses. Such viruses may exist as a file infector within an application. Upon execution of the infected application, the virus might spawn a master boot record infection, which then infects other files when you restart the system. Figure 11-9 shows how a multipartite virus works.

Some multipartite viruses, such as the One Half virus, isolated in 1994, may also exhibit both stealth and polymorphic characteristics.

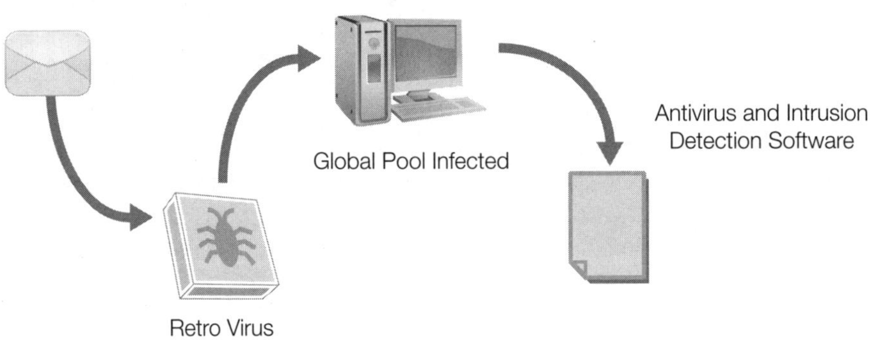

FIGURE 11-8

How a retro virus works.

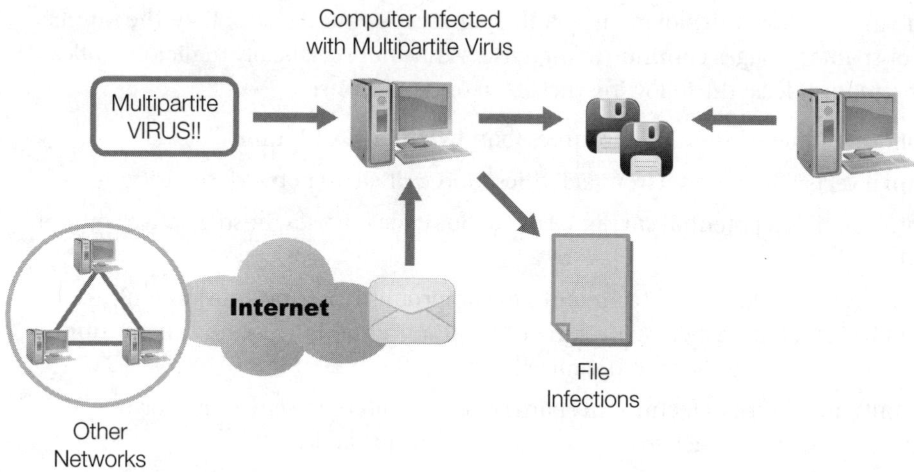

FIGURE 11-9 How a multipartite virus works.

Spam

Spam is one of the most bothersome challenges faced by network administrators. Not only does spam often contain viruses or other malicious code, it congests networks and e-mail servers, and can waste a lot of user time and productivity. Many viruses now carry software to make an infected computer part of a spam botnet. These spam botnets send out new versions of viruses.

Most anti-spam vendors estimate that 70 to 90 percent of all messaging traffic is spam. Simply put, spam is any unwanted message. However, many users still open unwanted e-mails or receive unwanted instant messages. They see the promise of jobs, lottery winnings, or reduced prices on products. This makes it hard to classify the message as strictly "unwanted."

Spam is becoming a major problem for organizations of all sizes. Spam uses bandwidth that organizations need to operate, and it wastes employees' time. Spam is also a breeding ground for viruses and worms. If offensive, spam can expose the organization to financial liability. Fortunately, automated tools are available to assist the security administrator to eliminate these e-mails.

What Is Spam?

SPAM, in all uppercase letters, is a trademark of Hormel Foods. In mixed or lowercase letters, the term refers to unsolicited commercial e-mail. The current use of the term spam originated in a Monty Python comedy skit first televised in 1970. The skit portrayed a waiter in a diner where every dish included the product SPAM. Any time one of the characters uttered the word "SPAM," several Vikings in the diner repeatedly chanted "SPAM, SPAM, SPAM, SPAM!" The Vikings' chanting overwhelmed the main dialogue, making it difficult to understand the other characters. As a result, the term "spam" came to mean any noise or other excessive communication that overwhelms the main message.

Despite the increasing deployment of anti-spam services and technology, the number and size of spam messages continue to increase. While not specifically malicious code, spam represents at least the following threats to organizations:

- Spam consumes computing resources (bandwidth and CPU time).
- Spam diverts IT personnel from activities more critical to network security.
- Spam e-mail is a potential carrier of malicious code (viruses, hostile active content, etc.).
- Spammers have developed techniques to compromise intermediate systems to facilitate remailing services, masking the real source addresses and constituting a denial of service attack for victimized systems.
- Opt out (unsubscribe) features in spam messages can represent a new form of reconnaissance attack to acquire legitimate target addresses.

Worms

Worms are self-contained programs designed to propagate from one host machine to another, using the host's own network communications protocols. Unlike viruses, worms do not require a host program in order to survive and replicate. Originally, the distinction between worms and viruses was that worms used networks and communications links to spread, and did not directly attach to an executable file. The use of the term worm stems from the fact that worms are programs with segments, working on different computers, all communicating over a network.

A worm usually probes network-attached computers to exploit a specific vulnerability. Generally, worms look for a specific piece of server or utility software that will respond to network queries or activity. Examples of worms are the Internet/Morris Worm of 1988.

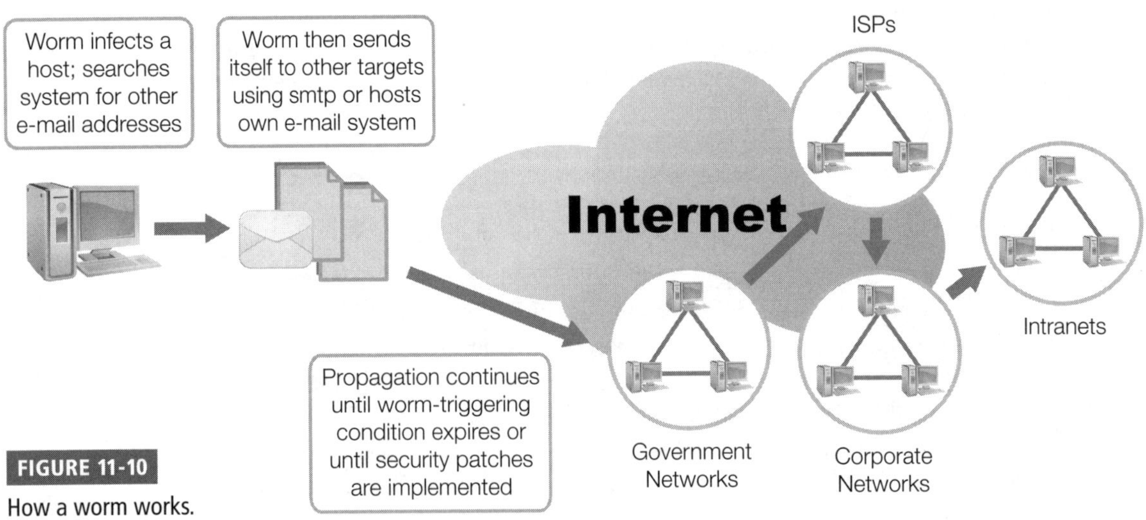

FIGURE 11-10

How a worm works.

Evidence of Worm Attacks

Worms have many telltale signs. Any of the following may indicate an infected computer:

- Unexplained increases in bandwidth consumption
- High volumes of inbound and outbound e-mail during normal activity periods
- Sudden increase in e-mail server storage utilization (this may trigger alarm thresholds set to monitor and manage disk/user partition space)
- Unexplained decrease in available disk space
- Unusual increase in average message size or increase in volume of attachments
- Unexpected SMTP or POP3 daemon responses for nondelivery of message traffic that was not sent by users
- Sudden increase in user response times across the network or sudden congestion at choke points near server farms
- Sudden increase in IDS and firewall threshold alarm activity

Worms that are more recent include the Code Red worm and a number of Linux worms, such as the Lion worm. Figure 11-10 shows how a worm works. Blaster was possibly one of the most successful worms, because the function it used (DCOM) was available on all versions of Windows—desktop as well as server.

A worm may spread rapidly without any user action. A worm often attacks server software. This is because many people who write worms know that servers are on all the time. This allows the worm to spread at a faster rate.

> **NOTE**
> Nimda is another example of a worm. However, it also spreads in a number of other ways, so you could consider it an e-mail virus and a multipartite virus.

Trojan Horses

Trojans, or Trojan horse programs, are the largest class of malware. A Trojan is any program that masquerades as a useful program while hiding its malicious intent. The masquerading nature of a Trojan encourages users to download and run the program. From the cracker's perspective, the advantage to this approach is that the Trojan runs as an authorized process because an authorized user ran it. The success of Trojans is due to their reliance on social engineering to spread and operate. The Trojan has to trick users into running it. If the Trojan appears to be a useful program, it has a better change of spreading. In fact, the most successful Trojans actually do provide useful services, and unwitting users may run the Trojan many times. However, each time the Trojan runs, it also carries out some unwanted action, just like any other type of malware.

Many Trojans spread through e-mail messages or Web site downloads. In years past, Trojan developers posted the programs on electronic bulletin board systems and a file archive sites. Moderators and anti-malware software would soon identify and eliminate

Evidence of Trojans

Trojans have many telltale signs. Any of the following may indicate an infected computer:

- Unrecognized new processes running
- Startup messages indicating that new software has been (or is being) installed (Registry updating)
- Unresponsiveness of applications to normal commands
- Unusual redirection of normal Web requests to unknown sites
- Unexpected or unscheduled modem connection activity
- Unexpected remote logon prompts at unusual times or unfamiliar logon prompt panels (this may result from routine software upgrades or session resets but can also indicate Trojan keylogging or password-capturing software)
- Sudden or unexpected termination of antivirus scanning software or personal firewall software (either at startup or when user attempts to load)

malicious programs. More recently, Trojan programs spread by mass e-mail, Web sites, social-networking sites, and automated distribution agents (bots). Trojan programs can spread in a number of disguises. Identifying their malicious payload has become much more difficult.

Some experts consider viruses to be just a type of Trojan horse program. There is some validity to this view. A virus is an unknown quantity that hides and spreads along with a legitimate program. In addition, you can turn any program into a Trojan by infecting it with a virus. However, the term virus specifically refers to the infectious code rather than the infected host. The term Trojan refers to a deliberately misleading or modified program that does not reproduce itself.

Logic Bombs

A **logic bomb** is a program that executes a malicious function of some kind when it detects certain conditions. Once in place, the logic bomb waits for a specified condition or time. When the specified condition or time occurs, the logic bomb activates, and carries out its tasks. The malicious tasks can cause immediate damage or can initiate a sequence of events that cause damage over a longer period.

Many logic bombs originate with organization insiders. Because people inside an organization generally have more knowledge of the IT infrastructure than outsiders do, they can place logic bombs more easily. In addition, internal personnel generally know more about an organization's weak points and can deduce effective ways to cause damage. For example, a programmer might hide a program within other software that lies dormant. If the company terminates him, he might activate the program. This causes the logic bomb to carry out malicious activities such as deleting valuable files or otherwise causing harm.

Logic bombs can be very difficult to identify because the designer creates them to avoid detection. In addition, the designer generally possesses knowledge of the organization's capabilities and security controls, and can place logic bombs where they will not likely attract attention.

Active Content Vulnerabilities

The term *active content* refers to components, primarily on Web sites, that provide functionality to interact with users. This includes any dynamic objects that do something when the user opens the Web page. Developers can use many technologies to create active content, including ActiveX, Java, JavaScript, VBScript, macros, browser plug-ins, PDF files, and other scripting languages. This code runs in the context of the user's browser and uses the user's logon credentials. These active content threats are considered mobile code because these programs run on a wide variety of computer platforms.

Many Internet Web sites now rely on active content to create their look and feel. For these schemes to operate properly, the user must download these bits of mobile code, where they can gain access to the hard disk. Once they activate, they can potentially do things such as fill up your desktop with infected file icons. These icons will spawn additional copies of the malicious code.

Active content comes in many types, from application macros to applets to background scripts. Java, JavaScript, Visual Basic Script, ActiveX, macros, Adobe Acrobat files, and browser plug-ins can all contain malicious software through well-defined and documented active content features. All these have potential weaknesses that malware can exploit.

Botnets

Hacking groups create **botnets** (short for robotically controlled networks) to launch attacks. The attackers infect vulnerable machines with agents that perform various functions at the command of the bot-herder or controller. (A bot-herder is a hacker who operates a botnet.) Typically, controllers communicate with other members of the botnet using Internet Relay Chat (IRC) channels. IRC is a protocol that enables text conversations over the Internet. Attackers can use botnets to distribute malware and spam, and to launch denial of service attacks against organizations or even countries. Attackers have established thousands of botnets, and they are a real threat to systems. During 2007, the Storm botnet was the second most powerful supercomputer in the world. During 2008, however, even larger botnets superseded it.

Denial of Service Attacks

The purpose of a denial of service (DoS) attack is to overwhelm a server or network segment to the point it becomes unusable. A successful DoS attack crashes a server or network device or creates so much network congestion that authorized users cannot access network resources.

FYI

Botnets are the main source of distributed denial of service (DDoS) attacks and of spam. They are programs that hide on compromised computers and wait for a command to "wake up" and carry out some instructions. Botnets are extremely resistant to takedown and can be hard to detect since they exist on many different computers. Botnet DoS attacks are growing and spreading so rapidly, descriptions such as this one cannot keep up. F-Secure, a vendor of antivirus software, personal-firewalls, and personal IDSs, maintains a series of videos and updates on YouTube: *http://www.youtube.com/fslabs*.

Standard DoS attacks use a single computer to launch the attack. A distributed denial of service (DDoS) attack uses intermediary hosts to conduct the attack. These intermediaries are compromised systems that contain Trojan handler programs. These Trojan programs then act as agents to execute a coordinated attack on a target system or network. The attacker(s) control one or more master handler servers, each of which can control many agents or daemons. The agents receive instructions to coordinate a packet-based attack against one or more victim systems.

There are three parties in these attacks: the attacker, the intermediaries (handlers and agents), and the victim(s). Even though the intermediary is not the intended victim, the intermediary can also suffer the same types of problem that the victim does in these attacks. You can find additional information on DDoS attacks on the CERT Web site (*http://www.cert.org*).

SYN Flood Attacks

As mentioned in Chapter 3, one popular technique for DoS attacks in called a SYN flood. In a SYN flood, the attacker uses IP spoofing to send a large number of packets requesting connections to the victim computer. These appear to be legitimate but in fact reference a client system that is unable to respond to the SYN-ACK messages. The victim computer records each request and reserves a place for the connection in a local table in memory. The victim computer then sends an acknowledgement back to the attacker, called a SYN-ACK message. Normally, the client would finish establishing the connection by responding to the SYN-ACK message with an ACK message. However, because the attacker used IP spoofing, the SYN-ACK message goes to the spoofed system. The result is that the client never sends the ACK message. The victim computer then fills up its connections table waiting for ACK messages for all the requests. In the meantime, no legitimate users can connect to the victim computer because the SYN flood has filled the connection table. The victim computer will remain unavailable until the connection requests time out. Even then, the attacking system can simply continue requesting new connections faster than the victim system can terminate the expired pending connections. Figure 11-11 shows how a SYN flood attack works.

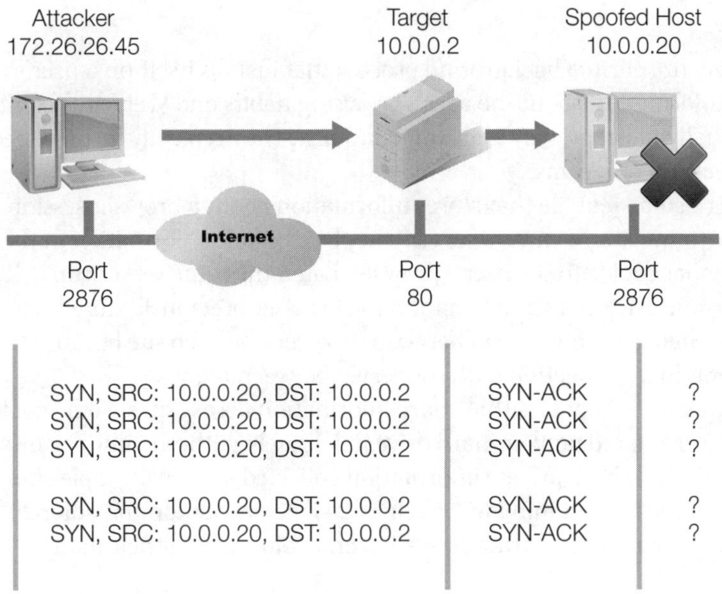

FIGURE 11-11 How a SYN flood attack works.

Smurf Attacks

In a smurf attack, attackers direct forged ICMP echo request packets to IP broadcast addresses from remote locations to generate denial of service attacks. There are three parties in these attacks: the attacker, the intermediary, and the victim. (Note that the intermediary can also be a victim.) The intermediary receives an ICMP echo request packet directed to the IP broadcast address of their network. If the intermediary does not filter ICMP traffic directed to IP broadcast addresses, many of the machines on the network will receive this ICMP echo request packet and send an ICMP echo reply packet back. When (potentially) all the machines on a network respond to this ICMP echo request, the result can be severe network congestion or outages. Figure 11-12 shows how a smurf attack works.

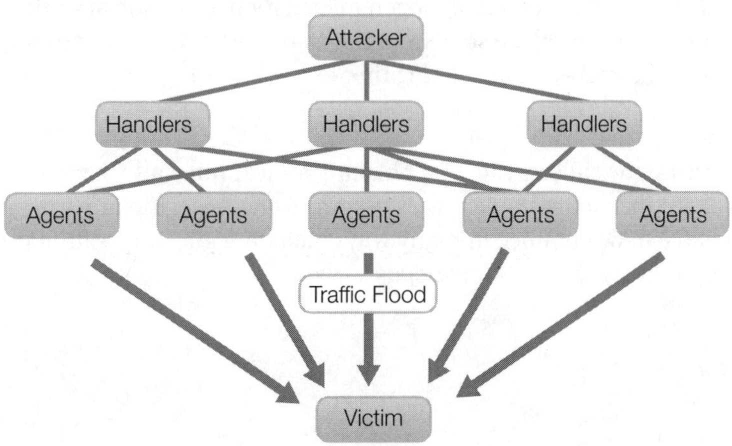

FIGURE 11-12 How a smurf attack works.

Spyware

Spyware is any unsolicited background process that installs itself on a user's computer and collects information about the user's browsing habits and Web-site activities. These programs usually affect privacy and confidentiality. They typically install when users download freeware programs.

A cookie is a small text file that stores information about a browser session. The server side of a user connection to a Web server can place certain information in the cookie, and then transfer that cookie to the user's browser. Later, the same server can ask the browser for the cookie and retrieve the information the browser previously stored. This becomes useful in any intelligent interaction between browser and Web site because the browser does not maintain a connection with the server between requests.

Spyware cookies are cookies that share information across sites. Some cookies are persistent and are stored on your hard drive indefinitely without your permission. They can reveal and share private information collected among multiple sites. Spyware cookies include those containing text such as 247media, admonitor, adforce, doubleclick, engage, flycast, sexhound, sextracker, sexlist, and valueclick in their names.

Adware

Adware programs trigger such nuisances as pop-up ads and banners when you visit certain Web sites. They affect productivity and may combine with active background activities such as home-page hijacking code. In addition, adware collects and tracks information about application, Web site, and Internet activity.

The problem with spyware and adware is distinguishing between legitimate and illicit activities. Spyware and adware companies have taken full advantage of this, often suing anti-spyware companies for labeling their programs as spyware.

Phishing

A phishing attack tricks users into providing logon information on what appears to be a legitimate Web site but is in fact a Web site set up by an attacker to obtain this information. If the attacker can obtain logon information for financial institutions, for example, he or she may be able to steal from the victim. Attackers use very sophisticated technologies to make such sites appear legitimate.

Spear-Phishing

In order to increase the success rate of a phishing attack, some attackers supply information about the victim that appears to come from the legitimate company. This information can be obtained in many ways including guessing, sifting through trash ("dumpster diving"), or sending bogus surveys.

What Is an IP Address?

Every host on the Internet has an IP address. These IP addresses are comparable to the telephone numbers on a telephone system. The most common IP-address format consists of four numbers, each between 0 and 255, separated by dots—for example, 192.0.2.213. Because it is very difficult for people to remember these numbers, Web sites usually also have a domain name—for example wikipedia.org. The domain name server acts like a phone book to match the domain name of a Web site with its IP address, a process known as resolving the domain name.

Pharming

The term pharming originates from the term phishing, which refers to the use of social engineering to obtain access credentials such as user names and passwords. Pharming is possible through the exploitation of a vulnerability in Domain Name System (DNS) server software. DNS servers are the machines responsible for resolving Internet domain names into their real IP addresses. The vulnerability that exists in DNS server software enables an attacker to acquire the domain name for a site and (for example) redirect that Web site's traffic to another Web site. If the Web site receiving the traffic is a fake Web site, such as a copy of a bank's Web site, it can be used to phish or steal a computer user's password, PIN, or account number. For example, in January 2005, an attacker hijacked the domain name for a large New York ISP, Panix, to a site in Australia. Other well-known companies also became victims of this attack. (Note that this is possible only when the original site is not SSL protected or when the user ignores warnings about invalid server certificates.)

Keystroke Loggers

Keystroke loggers are insidious and dangerous tools in the hands of an attacker. Whether software or hardware based, a keystroke logger captures keystrokes, or user entries. The keystroke logger then forwards that information to the attacker. This enables the attacker to capture logon information, banking information, and other sensitive data.

To combat keyloggers, some people have turned to onscreen virtual keyboards. In response, black-hat hackers started distributing malware that would take snapshots of the screen around the area clicked by the mouse. So the battle between security and hackers continues, as each side continues to develop new threats and new solutions.

Hoaxes and Myths

Although virus hoaxes are not always malicious, spreading unverified warnings and bogus patches can lead to new vulnerabilities. Often, the objective of the creator of the hoax or myth is merely to observe how widely the ruse can be propagated. This is a new version of the old chain-letter attack, where an attacker sent a person a letter promising good luck or happiness if the person forwarded the message to a dozen people.

Here are some guidelines for recognizing hoaxes, especially virus hoaxes:

- **Did a legitimate entity (computer security expert, vendor, etc.) send the alert?** Inspect any validation certificates, or at least the source URL of the advisory.
- **Is there a request to forward the alert to others?** No legitimate security alert will suggest that the recipient forward the advisory.
- **Are there detailed explanations or technical terminology in the alert?** Hoaxes often use techno-babble to intimidate the recipient into believing the alert is legitimate. A legitimate advisory will typically omit any details, however. It will simply refer the recipient to a legitimate Web site for details. The Web site will also typically provide a suggestion for protection activities.
- **Does the alert follow the generic format of a chain letter?** In this format, there is a hook, a threat, and a request. The hook is a catchy or dramatic opening or subject line to catch the recipient's attention. The threat is a technical-sounding warning of serious vulnerabilities or damage. The request is a plea to distribute the alert or a suggestion to take some immediate action—for example, to download a patch from a linked Web site.

Home-Page Hijacking

The function of these attacks is to change your browser's home page to point to the attacker's site. There are two forms of hijacking:

- **Exploiting a browser vulnerability to reset the home page**—Many types of active content can change the browser's home page, often without the user's permission. Even without resorting to covert means, it is easy to convince a user to select an action that does more than he or she expects. Just because you click a button that says "Remove Infected Programs from My Computer" doesn't mean that's the action that will occur.
- **Covertly installing a browser helper object (BHO) Trojan program**—This Trojan contains the hijacking code. Once a BHO executes, it can change the browser's home page back to the hijacker's desired site. Typically, hijacker programs put a reference to themselves into the operating system's startup procedures. That way, the hijacker runs every time the computer reboots. If you try to change any of these settings, the hijacker repeatedly changes them back until you find and remove the hijacking software.

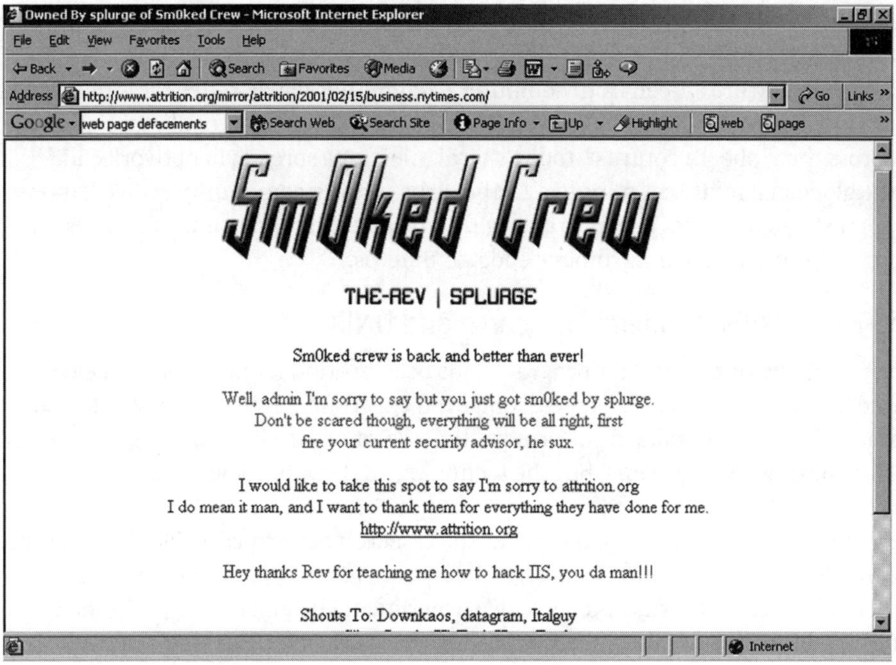

FIGURE 11-13 Defaced *New York Times* Web page (*source*: zdnet.com).

Web-Page Defacements

The term Web defacement or Web graffiti refers to someone gaining unauthorized access to a Web server and altering the index page of a site on the server. Usually, the attacker exploits known vulnerabilities in the target server and gains administrative access. Once in control, he or she replaces the original pages on the site with altered versions. For example, Figure 11-13 shows a defaced *New York Times* Web page.

Typically, the defacement represents graffiti. Most security practitioners consider this form of attack to be merely a nuisance. The potential for embedding malicious active content code into the Web site such as viruses or Trojans does exist, however. Code Red, for instance, included a payload that installed a backdoor Trojan. This Trojan allowed remote access to an infected IIS server, which attackers could use to deface the front page of the Web server. You can minimize the risk of this type of attack by ensuring that you install current software versions and security patches.

FYI

Backdoor programs are typically more dangerous than computer viruses. This is because intruders can use them to take control of a computer and potentially gain network access. These programs are also commonly referred to as Trojan horses because they pretend to do something other than what they actually do. Backdoor programs typically arrive as attachments to e-mails with innocent-looking filenames.

A Brief History of Malicious Code Threats

In the early days, malware spread from computer to computer via diskettes. This manual transmission method was called sneaker net. With sneaker net, a virus could take months to spread across the globe. In contrast, today's viral infections spread via networks and can cross the globe in a matter of minutes. As the virus-writing community evolved, more and more sophisticated viruses began to emerge. Some could spread in multiple ways, and others could spread via e-mail, mobile code, or macros.

1970s and Early 1980s: Academic Research and UNIX

The idea of self-replicating computer programs has been around for decades. This idea has appeared in literature, scientific papers, and even experiments since the early 1970s. Researchers made early attempts to perform routine maintenance tasks on large networks using self-distributing code (worms), but the technology did not become widespread or well known.

A key event in hostile code development was the research performed by Dr. Fred Cohen in 1983. Cohen's paper, "Computer Viruses—Theory and Experiments," published in 1984, defined the computer virus and described experiments he and others performed to prove the viability of viral code. Cohen published this work before anyone observed the first viruses.

The Internet during this period was a network that primarily connected university computers to one another. This network was vulnerable to programs that could propagate using existing communications protocols. A university student named Robert Morris—who unleashed the first major malware incident, the Morris Worm, in November 1988—demonstrated this. This UNIX-based worm overwhelmed almost all computers on the Internet, causing a lot of media interest and many headlines.

1980s: Early PC Viruses

The first personal computers (PCs) hit the market in the early 1980s. Their popularity grew fast. By the late 1980s, the PC was an indispensable and affordable business technology for many companies. This rapid growth also brought computer technology closer to a larger number of individuals.

The PC operating system was disk-based (DOS), and most software and data files migrated between PCs via floppy diskettes. Two primary types of malicious virus code emerged to exploit this: boot sector viruses, which attacked the operating-system components located on disks and in memory, and file infector viruses, which attacked the executable files themselves.

Brain (a boot sector virus), Lehigh, and Jerusalem (a file infector) are examples of the earliest viruses. They propagated primarily via floppy disks and downloads from popular computer bulletin board (BBS) archives. Another early virus, Elk Cloner, which targeted the Apple II computer, also spread by floppy disks.

1990s: Early LAN Viruses

Local area networks (LANs) began to appear in business environments by the early 1990s. This development gave the traditional file viruses a fertile environment to propagate. Very few people understood the virus problem at this time, and finding a virus was a rare event. Interested users collected the samples they found and freely distributed those, giving rise to notorious virus exchange bulletin boards. Some viruses did cause damage and business users started to become aware of the problem. The boot sector virus Form5 became the most widespread virus during this period. Another well-known virus of this era was Dark Avenger, also known as Eddie6. It was a very destructive virus.

By the end of the decade, local area networks had become a key infrastructure in most companies. At the same time, the use of the Internet for communications—particularly e-mail and data file transfer—became widespread. Traditional boot sector and file infector viruses began to diminish in frequency as storage technology advanced with the introduction of CD-ROMs.

Mid-1990s: Smart Applications and the Internet

The popularity of e-mail, combined with the ease of attaching files, gave rise to the extremely widespread distribution of malicious code using the same techniques demonstrated years earlier by Morris: e-mail worms. These programs locate e-mail address files within a user's system and then generate multiple copies of themselves, often disguised as innocent-looking file attachments. The well-known e-mail worms named Melissa and Loveletter are examples of this. Although many of these earlier programs relied upon users to activate the code by opening attachments, newer forms of worms have exploited various security weaknesses in the increasing numbers of always-on computers and servers. For example, Code Red exploited vulnerabilities in Microsoft Web servers (IIS) and had exceptional replication speed.

The Internet provides an environment from which individuals and groups can extend their activities beyond functional and geographic boundaries. During the mid-1990s, hacking (or cracking) became a growing business security concern. Using automated tools and more structured approaches, these individuals and groups have continued to evolve. The inherent resiliency of Internet communications protocols became a way to disrupt normal operations and gave rise to denial of service attacks against popular Web sites.

New forms of malicious code evolved in the 1990s, including Trojan programs like Back Orifice and AIDS. More resilient and stealthy variants of virus code also evolved, including polymorphic versions like Tequila. In addition, new programming languages designed for portability and functionality presented new opportunities to develop additional forms of malicious code. StrangeBrew, while harmless, was the first virus to infect Java files. The virus modifies CLASS files to contain a copy of itself.

With the introduction of advanced programming features into popular application software, the rise of other forms of malicious code appeared to infect document files. The first macro virus, WM/Concept7, was discovered in August 1995. It spread through the transmission of a simple document file.

2000 to Present

As personal and corporate Internet connectivity has continued to increase over the past several years, authors of popular browser technologies have added numerous companion tools, or plug-ins. These tools use specialized scripting codes that can automate common functions. They comprise a generation of active content code that exposes additional opportunities to attackers.

The numbers of computers now connected to the Internet, especially popular server platforms running Windows and other widely distributed software, has created new vulnerabilities. The replication speed of Internet worms coupled with today's high-speed computers, as well as increasing interactive probing for vulnerabilities by hostile groups, mandate continuous improvement, monitoring, and testing of IT security by organizations and user communities.

The W32/Nimda worm, taking advantage of backdoors left behind by the Code Red II worm, is the first to propagate itself via several methods, including e-mail, network shares, and an infected Web site. The worm spreads from client to Web server by scanning for backdoors. The Klezworm infects executables by creating a hidden copy of the original host file and then overwriting the original file with itself.

Threats to Business Organizations

Security threats from malware originate from a variety of sources. These range from isolated incidents involving a single, unsophisticated perpetrator to complex, structured attacks against multiple targets by organized groups. These threats generally originate outside an organization's IT infrastructure and user community. For this reason, organizations make a significant effort to detect, mitigate, and recover from these attacks.

Less publicized yet equally troublesome are threats that originate from within an organization. These threats are due to improper or deficient security policies and unsafe user practices. It is the IT security practitioner's responsibility to understand the nature and significance of any such internal threat and to implement effective countermeasures and practices.

Types of Threats

Malicious code can threaten businesses in the following ways:

- **Attacks against confidentiality and privacy**—These include emerging concerns with respect to identity theft and trade secrets, both at the individual and corporate levels.
- **Attacks against data integrity**—Economic damage or loss due to the theft, destruction, or unauthorized manipulation of sensitive data can be devastating to an organization. Organizations depend on the accuracy and integrity of information. The legitimacy of the source of communications also affects the integrity of the transmitted data.

- **Attacks against availability of services and resources**—Businesses increasingly depend on the Internet as a means of delivery for key network services. As a result, hostile attacks that deny these services to legitimate users have become an increasing concern among IT security practitioners. Early detection and quick recovery are essential to maintaining an acceptable level of service.
- **Attacks against productivity and performance**—Mass bulk e-mail (spam), spyware, persistence cookies, and the like consume computing resources and reduce user productivity. Unnecessary reaction to nonexistent code threats, such as hoaxes, can also affect productivity. Security professionals must make regular efforts to minimize their impact.
- **Attacks that create legal liability**—Unaddressed vulnerabilities can extend beyond the legal boundaries of an organization, creating a potential liability to customers, trading partners, and others.
- **Attacks that damage reputation**—Malicious code attacks can broadcast sensitive information about a company or its customers, or otherwise embarrass a company. Such attacks can damage a company's reputation. This can result in a loss of customers and potential business.

Internal Threats from Employees

Although attackers initiate more notorious security threats from outside a target network, a number of significant vulnerabilities exist inside a trusted network. These require the IT security practitioner's attention.

Perhaps the most common of these vulnerabilities exist because of unsafe computing practices by employees. These include the following:

- The exchange of untrusted disk media among host systems
- The installation of unauthorized, unregistered software (application and OS)
- The unmonitored download of files from the Internet
- The uncontrolled dissemination of e-mail attachments

Security breaches also originate from within the victim organization, perpetrated by current and former employees. These breaches often go undetected due to weak personnel and security policies or ineffective countermeasures. They frequently go unreported by the organization involved. These breaches can include the following:

- Unauthorized access to system and network resources
- Privilege escalation
- Theft, destruction, or unauthorized dissemination of data
- Use of corporate network resources to initiate hostile attacks against outside targets
- The accidental or intentional release of malicious code into internal network segments not protected by perimeter controls and intrusion detection countermeasures

Anatomy of an Attack

To understand threats and developing practical and effective countermeasures, you must understand the objective of malicious code attacks as well as what the attackers are targeting. In this section, you will learn how to identify key targets of malicious code attacks and describe the key characteristics and hostile objectives of each type of attack. This section covers the following:

- What motivates attackers
- The purpose of an attack
- Types of attacks
- Phases of an attack

What Motivates Attackers?

An attacker is no longer simply a social outcast who writes malicious software from his or her parents' basement, with the simple intent of seeing whether he or she can get away with it. Today's attackers are far more sophisticated. They have four primary motivations:

- They want money.
- They want to be famous.
- They want to impose their political beliefs or systems on others.
- They are angry and they want to exact revenge on those who have angered them.

The Purpose of an Attack

There are four main purposes for an attack:

- **Denial of availability**—The goal of some attacks, such as a DoS or DDoS attack, is to prevent legitimate users from accessing a system.
- **Data modification**—The attacker might issue commands to access a file on a local or network drive and modify, delete, or overwrite it with new data. Alternatively, the attacker might modify system settings or browser security settings.
- **Data export**—Attackers might seek to steal information from your computer and forward it over the Internet or e-mail to an attacker. For instance, many Trojan horses forward user names and passwords to an anonymous attacker's e-mail address on the Web. The attacker can then use the password to access protected resources.
- **Launch point**—An attacker might target a computer for use as a launch point to infect and target other computers.

Types of Attacks

There are four primary types of attacks:

- Unstructured attacks
- Structured attacks
- Direct attacks
- Indirect attacks

Unstructured Attacks

Moderately skilled attackers generally perpetrate unstructured attacks against network resources. Often, the initial intent of the attacker is simply personal gratification—the thrill of the challenge—of gaining illegal access. Any level of success can lead to yet more malicious activity, such as defacement or the inadvertent crashing of systems. Occasionally, an unstructured attack exposes an unintended vulnerability; the attacker may then switch to a more methodical approach. All such activity is of concern to IT security practitioners because it represents a compromise of defensive measures.

Structured Attacks

Highly motivated and technically skilled attackers use complex tools and focused efforts to conduct structured attacks. These attackers may act alone or in groups. They understand, develop, and use sophisticated hacking techniques to identify, penetrate, probe, and carry out malicious activities. These attackers' motives may include money, anger, destruction, or political objectives.

Regardless of their motivation, these attackers can and do inflict serious damage to networks. Attackers usually conduct structured attacks in phases after an overall goal is established. An attack might target a specific organization or a specific technology, such as an operating system.

Direct Attacks

Attackers often conduct direct attacks against specific targets, such as specific organizations. They may also conduct direct attacks against target classes—that is, networks using certain hardware, operating system versions, or services. An example might be an IIS Unicode attack against specific Web servers in an organization.

These exploits might be unstructured—for example, when a script kiddie uses well-known hacker tools to uncover vulnerable sites and then conducts random exploits around the compromised network through trial and error. These exploits might also be structured attacks, by individual crackers or by coordinated cyberterrorist groups, and advance methodically through phases to achieve their desired goals.

Typically, an attacker conducts a real-time direct attack by accessing a target system through remote logon exploits—for example, password guessing or session hijacking. Alternatively, the attacker might exploit a known vulnerability in the target operating system, such as a Unicode vulnerability or an active content vulnerability. Figure 11-14 shows a direct attack.

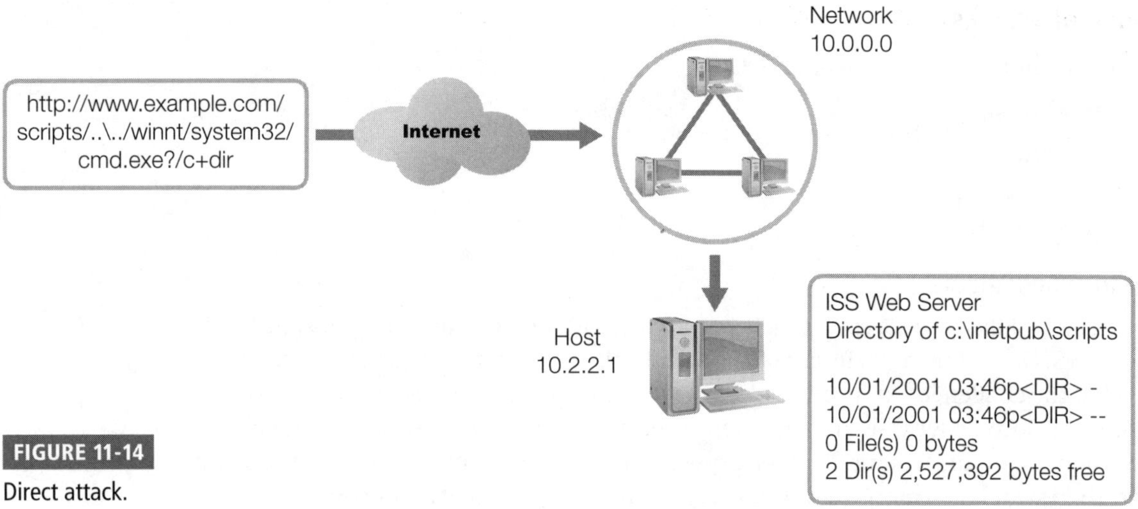

FIGURE 11-14
Direct attack.

The key characteristic is that the attack occurs in real time. Depending on the sophistication of the attacker, the final objective may simply be to deface a Web site. Alternatively, it might be a prelude to more malicious structured attacks. For example, the attacker might seek to locate and compromise a weakly protected target system, and then implant Trojan programs on it to exploit other resources (files or systems) within the compromised network.

Indirect Attacks

Indirect attacks occur as a natural result of preprogrammed hostile code exploits, such as Internet worms or viruses. These attacks are unleashed indiscriminately. Often, they propagate rapidly and widely. Although the worm or virus might exploit a specific system or application vulnerability, its replication and transmission occur indiscriminately.

Most likely, the goal of a direct attack against a specific target might be to establish a starting point for an indirect attack against a more widely dispersed population. For example, the compromise of a single Web server to install an e-mail worm as a denial of service exploit might be the intended goal.

FIGURE 11-15
Phases of an attack.

Phases of an Attack

To develop an attack, attackers need to know the target of the attack. To this end, they develop a strategy. Clever attackers are also concerned about not leaving tracks that allow investigators to identify them. This section details the phases of an attack. Figure 11-15 shows the phases of an attack.

Reconnaissance and Probing

When the overall goal or objective of an attack is clear, the attacker must probe the target network to identify points of possible entry—that is, the vulnerabilities. The reconnaissance and probing phase of an attack is arguably the most important phase. It is in this phase an attacker collects all the information to conduct the attack. In fact, using the information gathered in this phase is the easy part of an attack. Collecting good information is the best starting point for launching a successful attack. This phase generally involves the use of common tools that are readily available on the Internet. These tools are generally part of the underlying protocol suite or are custom developed to exploit specific or potential targets. These can include the following:

- DNS and ICMP tools within the TCP/IP protocol suite
- Standard and customized SNMP tools
- Port scanners and port mappers
- Security probes

Attackers might use these tools independently. Alternatively, an attacker might use them as a coordinated suite to gain a complete understanding of a targeted network. This includes the protocols and operating system used, the server platforms employed, the services and ports that are open, the actual or probable network addressing and naming used, etc.

The Internet and other public sources can provide additional information to profile targets. This information includes the location of facilities, key personnel, and likely business partners. This last piece of information might seem trivial, but an indirect assault committed through a trading partner with serious security breaches is very possible.

DNS, ICMP, and related tools. As you learned, domain name servers act like phone books, matching a Web site's domain name with its IP address. A number of searchable Web sites enable anyone to find information about registered addresses. In addition, TCP/IP supports discovery tools such as WHOIS and finger, which you can use to gather preliminary information in profiling a target site. Figure 11-16 shows the output from a whois lookup.

Reverse DNS lookup and nslookup are additional utility commands that also search DNS information and provide cross-referencing. These services are often free on the Internet. You can locate them by searching on the command name itself.

The Internet Control Management Protocol (ICMP) ping command and several closely related tools are readily available on most computer operating systems. These profiling tools enable attackers to verify that target systems are reachable. For example, attackers can use the ping command with a number of extension flags to test direct reachability between hosts. They can also use the ping command as part of the actual attack plan—for example, to carry out a ping of death attack where an attacker sends specially constructed ping packets that can crash vulnerable computers. Once a target network has been located, many attackers then perform a ping sweep of all (or a range of) IP addresses within the major network or subnet to identify other potential hosts that may be accessible. This information alone sometimes exposes the likely network size and topology. In addition, because many networks use a structured numbering scheme, it may also point to likely server and network device locations.

FIGURE 11-16

WHOIS lookup.

WHOIS information for **boxtwelve.com** :

```
[Querying whois.verisign-grs.com]
[whois.verisign-grs.com]

Whois Server Version 2.0

Domain names in the .com and .net domains can now be registered
with many different competing registrars. Go to http://www.internic.net
for detailed information.

   Domain Name: BOXTWELVE.COM
   Registrar: FASTDOMAIN, INC.
   Whois Server: whois.fastdomain.com
   Referral URL: http://www.fastdomain.com
   Name Server: NS1.HOSTMONSTER.COM
   Name Server: NS2.HOSTMONSTER.COM
   Status: clientTransferProhibited
   Updated Date: 08-mar-2010
   Creation Date: 07-mar-2007
   Expiration Date: 07-mar-2011

<<

NOTICE: The expiration date displayed in this record is the date the
registrar's sponsorship of the domain name registration in the registry is
currently set to expire. This date does not necessarily reflect the expiration
date of the domain name registrant's agreement with the sponsoring
registrar.  Users may consult the sponsoring registrar's Whois database to
view the registrar's reported date of expiration for this registration.

TERMS OF USE: You are not authorized to access or query our Whois
database through the use of electronic processes that are high-volume and
automated except as reasonably necessary to register domain names or
modify existing registrations; the Data in VeriSign Global Registry
Services' ("VeriSign") Whois database is provided by VeriSign for
information purposes only, and to assist persons in obtaining information
about or related to a domain name registration record. VeriSign does not
guarantee its accuracy. By submitting a Whois query, you agree to abide
```

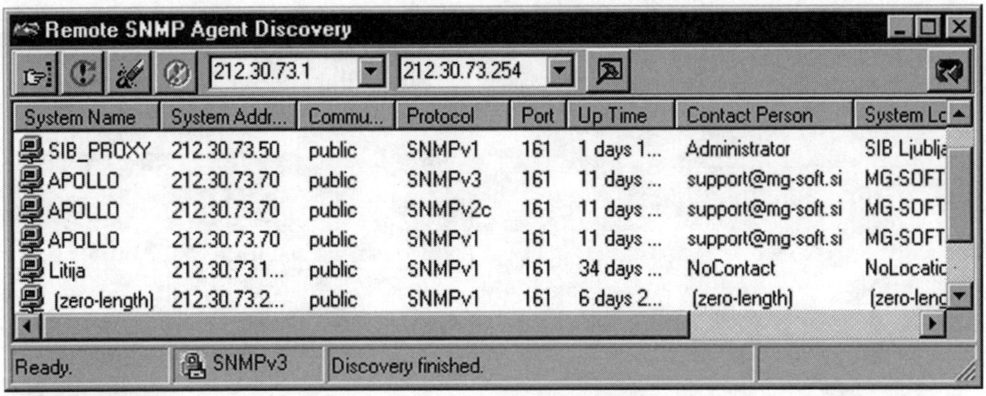

FIGURE 11-17

Remote SNMP Agent Discovery enables you to discover responsive SNMP agents on the network.

If gaining access is one of the objectives, an attacker can attempt a simple telnet logon to test the softness of perimeter controls. An attacker might also use rpcinfo to determine whether the remote procedure call (RPC) service is active for remote command execution.

SNMP tools. The Simple Network Management Protocol (SNMP) is an Application layer protocol that facilitates the exchange of management information between network devices. It is part of the Transmission Control Protocol/Internet Protocol (TCP/IP) suite. SNMP enables network administrators to manage network performance, find and solve network problems, and plan for network growth.

Many popular network-management software suites, like HP OpenView, SunNet Manager, and AIX NetView, are SNMP compliant. They offer full support for managed devices, agents, and network-management systems. In addition, there are many utility programs that can be used to gather network-device information, including platform, operating system version, and capabilities. Poorly configured network-management facilities would allow moderately skilled attackers to gather significant attack profile information. Figure 11-17 shows the Remote SNMP Agent Discovery tool.

Port-scanning and port-mapping tools. After an attacker identifies a target network, the next step might be to explore what systems and services are accessible. To achieve this, an attacker might use several popular port-scanning applications. One of the most popular is Nmap, available for UNIX, Linux, and Windows. Angry IP Scanner is another network reconnaissance tool, this one for Windows, Linux, and OS X. By design, it's fast and easy to use. Figure 11-18 shows the Nmap port-scanning tool for Windows.

These tools permit an attacker to discover and identify hosts by performing ping sweeps, probe for open TCP and UDP service ports, and identify operating systems and applications running.

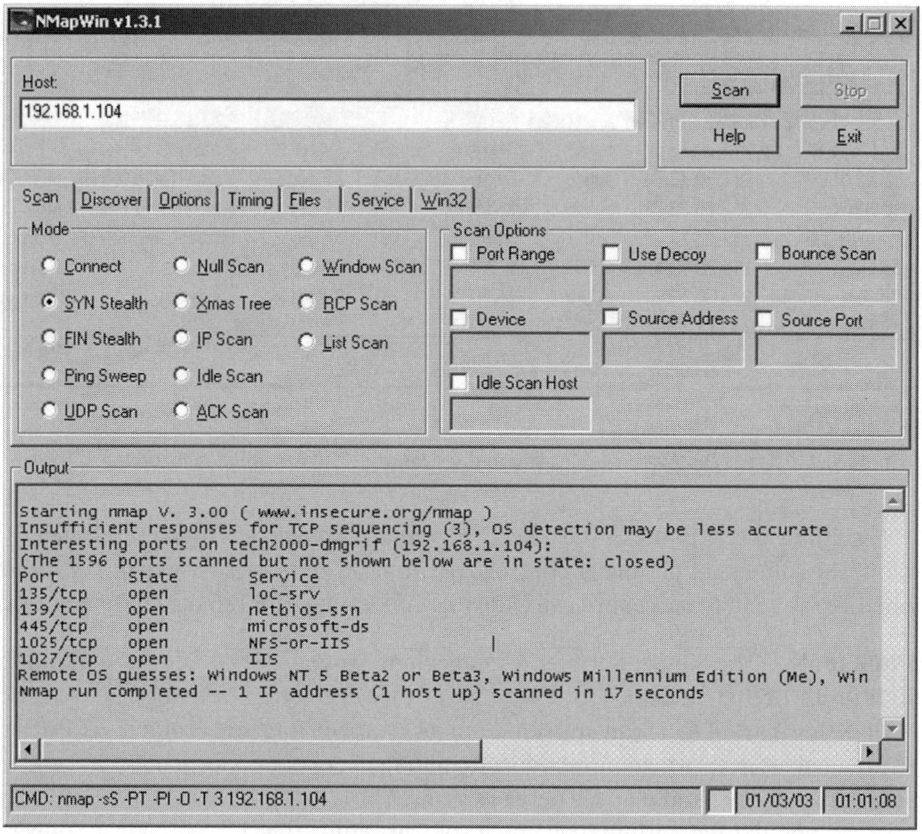

FIGURE 11-18 Nmap port-mapping tool for Windows.

Security probes. SATAN helps security administrators evaluate a number of vulnerabilities. It recognizes several common networking-related security problems and reports the problems without actually exploiting them. SATAN collects information available to anyone with access to the network. With a properly configured firewall in place, you can properly implement policies to protect information from unauthorized access. SATAN is a two-edged sword, however. Like many tools, attackers can use it as easily as security professionals can. It is a good idea to include scanning for evidence of SATAN reconnaissance of your network.

Access and Privilege Escalation

Once an attacker profiles and probes a target network for potential vulnerabilities, he or she must access the target system(s). The primary goal of access is to establish the initial connection to a target host (typically a server platform). In order to conduct additional reconnaissance activities, such as covertly installing hacking tool kits, the attacker must then gain administrative rights to the system.

The method of access depends upon the connection technology necessary to reach the target network. As many organizations evolve to Web-centric business models, they often maintain legacy dial-up access infrastructures, either as secondary remote gateways or due to oversight. In some instances, organizations may not even be aware of modem facilities left connected to outside phone lines or PBXs. Alternatively, they may not consider the security risks of leaving unattended modem connections, which often compromise existing network perimeter defenses. These connections provide another entry point for malicious code attacks.

Password Capturing and Cracking

One method of gaining access is to capture or crack passwords. An attacker can install a password logger as a backdoor Trojan on a target machine and monitor specific protocol and program activity associated with remote logon processes. Alternatively, if the attacker captures logon strings remotely, a program such as LophtCrack (*http://www.atstake.com/research/lc/download.html*) can quickly decrypt and compromise administrator and user passwords.

Maintaining Access Using Remote Administration Tool (RAT)

Remote Access Tool (RAT) is a Trojan that, when executed, enables an attacker to remotely control. RAT allows an attacker to maintain access to a compromised computer. You do this via the following:

- **A server on the victim's machine**—This server listens for incoming connections to the victim. When it receives a connection, it provides remote access for the client that connects. It runs invisibly, with no user interface.
- **A client on the attacker's machine**—This is a GUI front-end that the attacker uses to connect to and manage servers on victim machines.

What happens when a server is installed on the victim's machine depends on the capabilities of the Trojan, the interests of the attacker, and whether another attacker, who might have entirely different interests, manages to gain control of the server.

On Windows machines, infections by remote administration are becoming as frequent as viruses. One common source is through file and printer sharing. Attackers can use file and printer sharing to gain access to the hard drive. He or she can then place the Trojan in the startup folder. The Trojan will then run the next time a legitimate user logs in. Another common attack method is to simply e-mail the Trojan to the user. The attacker then uses social engineering to convince the user to run the Trojan.

Authors of these programs often claim that they are not intrusion tools. Rather, they are simply remote-control tools or tools to reveal weaknesses in an operating system. Based on past activity, however, it's clear that their real purpose is to gain access to computers for unauthorized use.

Covering Your Tracks

One of the most important phases to avoid detection is to remove any traces of the attack. While the specific actions you must take may differ from one attack to another, the basic steps are the same. First, remove any files you may have created and restore as many files to their pre-attack condition as possible. Second, remove any log file entries that may provide evidence of the attack. The second step is generally much more difficult than the first step. Most systems use auditing methods that protect log files from modification. That means you may have to attack the log files or the auditing system to erase your tracks. Regardless of the effort, cleaning any track you left behind greatly increases the likelihood an attack will go unnoticed.

Attack Prevention Tools and Techniques

IT security practitioners must understand how to implement effective countermeasures to defend against malicious code attacks. They must also continuously monitor, test, and improve these countermeasures.

Defense in depth is the practice of layering defenses into zones to increase the overall protection level and provide more reaction time to respond to incidents. Defense in depth combines the capabilities of people, operations, and security technologies to establish multiple layers of protection, eliminating single lines of defense and effectively raising the cost of an attack. By treating individual countermeasures as part of an integrated suite of protective measures, you can ensure that you have addressed all vulnerabilities. Managers must strengthen these defenses at critical locations. They must then monitor attacks and react to them quickly.

With respect to malicious code threats, these layers of protection extend to specific critical defensive zones:

- Application defenses
- Operating system defenses
- Network infrastructure defenses

The goals of defense in depth are as follows:

- There should be layers of security and detection, even on single systems.
- Attackers must break through or bypass each layer undetected.
- Other layers can cover a flaw in one layer.
- Overall system security becomes a set of layers within the overall network security.
- Security improves by requiring the attacker to be perfect while ignorant.

Application Defenses

Software applications provide end users with access to shared data. Some of this data is sensitive or confidential, and is not available to all users. Attackers commonly launch attacks on application software to attempt to access or damage sensitive data. You should deploy appropriate controls to secure all application software running on all computers. Some common controls include the following:

- Implementing regular antivirus screening on all host systems
- Ensuring that virus definition files are up to date
- Requiring scanning of all removable media
- Installing personal firewall and IDS software on hosts as an additional security layer
- Deploying change detection software and integrity checking software and maintaining logs
- Implementing e-mail usage controls and ensuring that e-mail attachments are scanned
- Establishing a clear policy regarding software installations and upgrades
- Ensuring that only trusted sources are used when obtaining, installing, and upgrading software through digital signatures and other validations

Operating System Defenses

The operating system serves as an interface between application software and hardware resources. Any attack that compromises the operating system can yield nearly unlimited access to system resources that store sensitive data. Successful attacks against the operating system can also allow an attacker to own a computer and use it for multiple purposes. Controls to secure the operating system are important. These include the following:

- Deploying change-detection and integrity-checking software, and maintaining logs
- Deploying or enabling change-detection and integrity-checking software on all servers
- Ensuring that all operating systems are consistent and have been patched with the latest updates from vendors
- Ensuring that only trusted sources are used when installing and upgrading OS code
- Disabling any unnecessary OS services and processes that may pose a security vulnerability

Network Infrastructure Defenses

Nearly all computers in today's organizations connect to a network at some point. Most attacks on computers and devices are possible because networks make it easier to access targets remotely. Malicious software often uses networks to spread. Because networks are necessary for end user access, the networks themselves can be targets. You must deploy controls to protect your network, including the following:

- Creating choke points in the network
- Using proxy services and bastion hosts to protect critical services
- Using content filtering at choke points to screen traffic
- Ensuring that only trusted sources are used when installing and upgrading OS code
- Disabling any unnecessary network services and processes that may pose a security vulnerability
- Maintaining up-to-date IDS signature databases
- Applying security patches to network devices to ensure protection against new threats and to reduce vulnerabilities

One of the simplest prevention techniques is to disable unnecessary network services, especially certain TCP and UDP listening ports. This will defeat any attack that focuses on exploiting those services. This may not be efficient if those services are required for legitimate users, however.

You can employ a wide variety of countermeasures and practices to prevent malicious code attacks on network resources. These include the following:

- Employing filtering software that blocks traffic to and from network segments or specific services
- Employing active sensors (intrusion detection, antivirus detection) that react quickly enough to prevent or mitigate damage
- Employing choke points in the network to force traffic to flow through zones of protection
- Allowing sensors and filters to inspect traffic before permitting it to pass into the protected network
- Setting security properties within browsers to prohibit or prompt before processing scripts and active code
- Eliminating unnecessary remote connections to the network and employing effective access control measures to protect those required to remain available
- Avoiding the circumvention of existing control systems and countermeasures

Safe Recovery Techniques and Practices

Regardless how effective your countermeasures are, it is likely you will eventually encounter some type of data loss due to malware. Your ability to recover from data loss depends on how well you have prepared for that situation. You cannot completely recover unless you can ensure a completely malware-free recovery process. Here are a few guidelines to help you ensure your recovery media and procedures do not reintroduce any malware:

- Consider storing OS and data file backup images on CD-ROM to prevent possible malware infection.
- Scan new and replacement media for malware before reinstalling software.
- Disable network access to systems during restore procedures or upgrades until you have re-enabled or installed protection software or services.

Implementing Effective Software Best Practices

All organizations should adopt an Acceptable Use Policy (AUP) for network services and resources. A good AUP includes prohibitions on certain network activities and computer user habits regarding software licensing and installation and procedures for transmitting files and media. Adopt standardized software so that you can control patches and upgrades to ensure you address vulnerabilities.

Consider implementing an ISO 17799 compliant security policy. ISO 17799 is the most widely recognized security standard. Compliance with ISO/IEC 17799, or indeed any detailed security standard, is, therefore, a far from trivial undertaking, even for the most security conscious of organizations. Certification can be even more daunting (*http://www.iso-17799-security-world.co.uk/*).

NOTE

You'll learn more about ISO 17799 and other security standards in Chapter 12.

Incident Detection Tools and Techniques

Intrusion detection tools are an integral component of defense in depth. Each organization should deploy a defense-in-depth approach in critical areas of the network as an early warning system. There are various implementations. Each implementation has features that provide unique capabilities to protect networks and hosts from malicious activity.

A layered defense-in-depth approach would suggest deploying both network-based and host-based intrusion detection. It might also involve deploying products that permit both signature-based and anomaly-based detection schemes.

NOTE

Anomaly detection involves developing a network baseline profile of normal or acceptable activity, such as services or traffic patterns, and then measuring actual network traffic against this baseline. This technique might be useful for detecting attacks such as denial of service or continuous logon attempts, but it requires a learning or preconfiguration period.

Antivirus Scanning Software

Today, most PC users use some form of virus protection to detect and prevent infection. Just as you can layer intrusion detection at the host and network levels, you should deploy antivirus protection on all devices that support it.

The key vulnerabilities to host-based antivirus software are as follows:

- The continuing requirement to keep every host system updated to the most current virus-definition files
- Potential compromise of the protection through unsafe user practices such as installing unlicensed or unauthorized software or indiscriminately exchanging infected e-mail or document files

Network-based antivirus software is an option that permits screening of files and e-mail traffic on servers and provides remote scanning and inoculation of clients on a consistent basis.

Many organizations employ both network and host-based protection; some deploy multiple products in order to maximize detection capabilities. It is imperative that you keep virus definition files up-to-date. Most vendors now offer automatic updating of software as soon as they release new definitions.

Network Monitors and Analyzers

To ensure security practices remain effective, you should regularly monitor network software and appliances, as well as periodically analyze network traffic. Every so often, run a vulnerability scanner such as Nessus, Microsoft Baseline Security Analyzer, or some combination of the two, depending upon your operating systems. Keep in mind that attackers use these tools as well. You should scan the network for unnecessary open service ports on a regular basis; upgrades to software often reset systems to their default settings.

Content/Context Filtering and Logging Software

You must balance privacy and security when implementing countermeasures that filter content. When combined with a clear corporate policy on acceptable use, however, this becomes an additional layer of defense against malicious code. Plug-ins to screen e-mail attachments and content as well as context-based filtering (access control lists) on network routers also permit an additional layer of security protection.

Content-based filtering includes analyzing network traffic for active code (Java, ActiveX) components and disabling script processing on Web browser software. Context-based filtering involves comparing patterns of activity to baseline standards so you can evaluate unusual changes in network behavior for possible malicious activity.

What Is a Honeynet?

A honeynet is a group of honeypots made to simulate a real live network. Honeynets are beneficial because they provide more data and are more attractive to attackers. However, the setup and maintenance requirements of a honeynet are a little more advanced. A honeynet may include many servers, a router, and a firewall. A honeynet may be identical to the production network or it might be a research lab. Either way, honeynets allow for a more real environment for an attacker to attack.

Honeypots and Honeynets

Honeypots are sacrificial hosts and services deployed at the edges of a network to act as bait for potential hacking attacks. Typically, you configure these systems to appear real. In fact, they may be part of a suite of servers placed in a separate network called a **honeynet**, isolated from the real network. The purpose of the honeypot is to provide a controlled environment for attacks. This enables you to easily detect and analyze the attack to test the strength of the network. You install host-based intrusion detection and monitoring software to log activity.

All traffic to and from the honeypot is suspicious because the honeypot contains no production applications. You should produce few logs on the honeypot unless the honeypot is under heavy attack. Logs should be easy to read and understand. When an attacker probes a honeypot, an administrator can place preventive controls on his or her real production network.

A honeypot should contain at least the following elements:

- It looks and behaves like a real host.
- At no point does it disclose its existence.
- It has a dedicated firewall that prevents all outbound traffic in case it is compromised.
- It lives in a network DMZ, untouched by normal traffic.
- It sounds silent alarms when any traffic goes to or from it.
- It begins logging all intruder activity when it first senses an intrusion.

A low-involvement honeypot provides a number of fake services, such as Hypertext Transfer Protocol (HTTP) or Simple Mail Transfer Protocol (SMTP). Low-involvement honeypots allow attackers to connect to services, but do nothing else. With this type of honeypot, an attacker usually cannot gain operating system access. Therefore, the attacker poses no threat.

A high-involvement honeypot produces genuine services and vulnerabilities by providing a real operating system for the attacker. The purpose of this class of honeypot is for attackers to compromise it so you can collect realistic data. The problem with high-involvement honeypots is that you must tightly control the environment. A compromised system can become a host to begin an attack on another system.

CHAPTER SUMMARY

In this chapter, you learned about the different types of malware, and how each type operates. You learned about spam and spyware, and their effect on today's organizations. You learned about different types of network attacks, and methods to protect your networks from attacks. You also learned about the dangers of keyloggers, hoaxes, and Web-page defacements. You learned about the history of malware and how threats have emerged for today's organizations. Lastly, you learned about different types of attacks and how attackers use tools to carry them out.

KEY CONCEPTS AND TERMS

Botnet
Data infector virus
File infector virus
Honeynet
Honeypot
Logic bomb
Macro virus
Multipartite virus
Polymorphic virus
Stealth virus
System infector virus

CHAPTER 11 ASSESSMENT

1. Which type of malware attaches to, or infects, other programs?
   A. Spyware
   B. Virus
   C. Worm
   D. Rootkit

2. ________ is any unwanted message.

3. Which type of malicious software is a standalone program that propagates from one computer to another?
   A. Spyware
   B. Virus
   C. Worm
   D. Snake

4. In the malware context, which of the following best defines the term mobile code?
   A. Web site active content
   B. Malware targeted at PDAs and smartphones
   C. Software that runs on multiple operating systems
   D. Malware that uses networks to propagate

5. A(n) ________ is a network of compromised computers that attackers use to launch attacks and spread malware.
   A. Black network
   B. Botnet
   C. Attacknet
   D. Trojan store

6. What does the TCP SYN flood attack do to cause a DDoS?
   A. Causes the network daemon to crash
   B. Crashes the host computer
   C. Saturates the available network bandwidth
   D. Fills up the pending connections table

7. Which type of attack tricks a user into providing personal information by masquerading as a legitimate Web site?
   A. Phreaking
   B. Phishing
   C. Trolling
   D. Keystroke logging

8. The best defense from keystroke loggers is to carefully inspect the keyboard cable before using a computer because the logger must connect to the keyboard's cable.
   A. True
   B. False

9. How did viruses spread in the early days of malware?
   A. Wired network connections
   B. Punch cards
   C. Diskettes
   D. As program bugs

10. What is the most common first phase of an attack?
    A. Vulnerability identification
    B. Reconnaissance and probing
    C. Target selection
    D. Evidence containment

11. Which software tool provides extensive port-scanning capabilities?
    A. Ping
    B. Whois
    C. Rpcinfo
    D. Nmap

12. The ________ strategy ensures that an attacker must compromise multiple controls to reach any protected resource.

13. A honeypot is a sacrificial host with deliberately insecure services deployed at the edges of a network to act as bait for potential hacking attacks.
    A. True
    B. False

PART THREE

Information Security Standards, Education, Certifications, and Laws

CHAPTER

12

Information Security Standards

IT IS NEARLY IMPOSSIBLE to purchase all hardware and software from one vendor. Today's organizations get parts for their IT infrastructure from multiple vendors—and expect these products to work together.

How can so many products from different vendors together? They work together because of standards. Standards are necessary to create and maintain a competitive market for hardware and software vendors. Standards also guarantee compatibility between products from different countries. They provide guidelines to ensure products in today's computing environments work together.

Several organizations develop and maintain standards for computers. In this chapter, you will learn about the most common standards for computer and networking products and services. You will specifically learn about those standards that relate to security.

Chapter 12 Topics

This chapter covers the following topics and concepts:

- What standards organizations apply to information security
- What ISO 17799 is
- What ISO/IEC 27002 is
- What PCI DSS is

Chapter 12 Goals

When you complete this chapter, you will be able to:

- Identify prominent information security standards organizations
- Summarize what ISO 17799 contains
- Explain how ISO/IEC 27002 pertains to information security
- Describe PCI DSS requirements

Standards Organizations

The earliest computers were custom built for specific purposes. Designers decided how to connect components and how they communicated based on the specific computer's needs. Soon, however, designers realized that by implementing communications standards, they could enable different vendors' components to work together. This increased customer confidence in computers. Customers felt more comfortable buying products based on standards. Some proprietary systems, however, did not support standards.

Adhering to standards is necessary to increase market appeal and, in many cases, to comply with regulations. It is important that you know about the most influential organizations that develop and maintain the standards that govern different aspects of computing and network communications.

NIST

The **National Institute of Standards and Technology (NIST)** is a federal agency within the U.S. Department of Commerce. Founded in 1901 as the National Bureau of Standards (NBS), NIST was America's first federal physical science research laboratory. NIST's mission is to "promote U.S. innovation and industrial competitiveness by advancing measurement science, standards, and technology in ways that enhance economic security and improve our quality of life." NIST provides standards for measurement and technology on which nearly all computing devices rely. In addition, NIST maintains the atomic clock that keeps the United States' official time. Although NIST is a non-regulatory agency, many organizations respect and adopt its publications.

NIST executes its primary mission through four cooperative programs:

- **NIST Laboratories**—Laboratories that conduct research to advance the United States' technology infrastructure. The nation's industry uses this infrastructure to improve the quality of products and services.
- **Baldrige National Quality Program**—A national program that empowers and encourages excellence among U.S. organizations, including manufacturers, service organizations, educational institutions, health care providers, and nonprofit organizations. It also strives to increase quality and recognize organizations that achieve quality goals.
- **Hollings Manufacturing Extension Partnership**—This partnership is a network of centers around the nation that offer technical and business assistance to small and medium-sized manufacturers.
- **Technology Innovation Program**—Another national program that offers awards to organizations and universities to support potentially revolutionary technologies that apply to critical needs of national interest.

NIST maintains a list of standards and publications of general interest to the computer-security community. NIST established this collection of documents, called the Special Publications 800 series, in 1990 to provide a separate identity for information-technology

NOTE

You can find more information about NIST on its Web page (*http://www.nist.gov/*). For more information on NIST special publications, see *http://csrc.nist.gov/publications/PubsSPs.html*.

security publications. The publications in this series report on research and guideline efforts related to computer security in government, industry, and academic organizations.

Many refer to publications in the 800 series by the name NIST SP. For example, many people refer to the document titled "NIST Special Publication 800-66," as NIST SP 800-66. (NIST SP 800-66 contains introductory guidance for complying with HIPAA.)

The NIST Special Publications 800 series contains many standards that provide guidance for information systems security activities. Table 12-1 lists just a few of the resources you can find in the NIST Special Publications 800 series.

TABLE 12-1 NIST Special Publications 800 series sample documents.

NUMBER	TITLE
800-37 Rev. 1	Guide for Applying the Risk Management Framework to Federal Information Systems: A Security Life Cycle Approach
800-46 Rev. 1	Guide to Enterprise Telework and Remote Access Security
800-53 A Rev. 1	DRAFT Guide for Assessing the Security Controls in Federal Information Systems and Organizations, Building Effective Security Assessment Plans
800-61 Rev. 1	Computer Security Incident Handling Guide
800-73-3	Interfaces for Personal Identity Verification (4 Parts) Part 1: End Point PIV Card Application Namespace, Data Model & Representation Part 2: PIV Card Application Card Command Interface Part 3: PIV Client Application Programming Interface Part 4: The PIV Transitional Interfaces & Data Model Specification
800-78-2	Cryptographic Algorithms and Key Sizes for Personal Identification Verification (PIV)
800-85 A-2	DRAFT PIV Card Application and Middleware Interface Test Guidelines (SP 800-73-3 Compliance)
800-115	Technical Guide to Information Security Testing and Assessment
800-118	DRAFT Guide to Enterprise Password Management
800-121	Guide to Bluetooth Security
800-122	Guide to Protecting the Confidentiality of Personally Identifiable Information (PII)
800-128	DRAFT Guide for Security Configuration Management of Information Systems

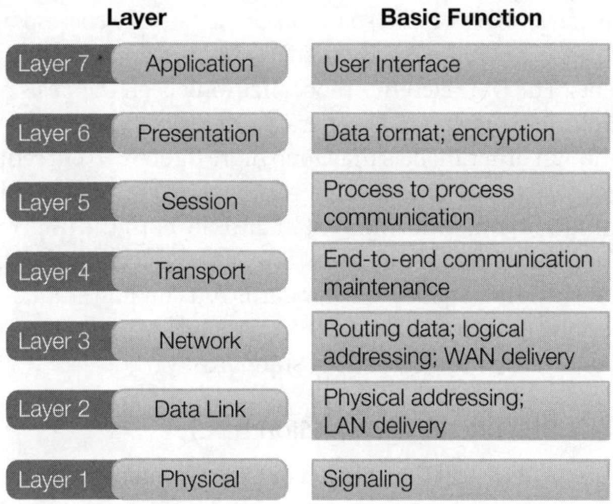

FIGURE 12-1
The OSI reference model.

International Organization for Standardization (ISO)

The **International Organization for Standardization (ISO)** formed in 1946. It is a nongovernmental international organization. Its goal is to develop and publish international standards. ISO, based in Geneva, Switzerland, is a network of 163 national standards institutes. ISO serves as a bridge between the public and private sectors. Some members are governmental entities, while others are in the private sector. ISO's goals are to develop standards that do not cater to either group exclusively, but reach consensus.

Although the organization's short name, ISO, appears to be an acronym, it is not. Because ISO is an international organization, its full name is different depending on the language. ISO members agreed on the short name ISO derived from the Greek word *isos*, which means "equal." ISO strives for consensus, even in the choice of its name. This focus on consensus is what makes ISO such a successful authority in developing and promoting standards in many areas.

ISO publishes many standards for nearly all industries. For example, the International Standard Book Number (ISBN) is an ISO standard. For those in information technology, perhaps the best-known ISO standard is the Open Systems Interconnection (OSI) reference model. This internationally accepted framework of standards governs how separate computer systems communicate using networks. The reference model contains seven distinct layers that address seven different issues related to networked communications. The reference model defines the standards that enable computers and devices from different vendors to communicate. Figure 12.1 shows the OSI reference model.

Each layer in the model represents a collection of related functions. Each function provides services to the layer immediately above it and receives services from the layer immediately below it. For example, the Transport layer (Layer 4) provides error-free communications across a network. It also provides the connections needed by software functions in the Session layer (Layer 5). In addition, it calls functions in the Network layer (Layer 3), the next layer down, to send and receive packets that make up the contents of the network communication.

Although many newer networking solutions do not strictly correspond to a structure of seven distinct layers, the OSI reference model is still the predominant tool used to teach networking concepts. The OSI reference model has long been the basis of understanding how networks provide general services in a standard environment. Even though other models may map more directly to current software, the OSI reference model is still a relevant tool to teach networking fundamentals.

> **NOTE**
> You can browse ISO standards and get more information about the organization at its Web site: *http://www.iso.org*.

ISO organizes its many standards by both the International Classification for Standards (ICS) and the Technical Committee (TC) to which it assigns each standard. You can find standards spread among over 200 different ICSs, assigned to one of 40 TCs. This gives you a feel for the breadth of standards.

International Electrotechnical Commission (IEC)

The **International Electrotechnical Commission (IEC)** is a standards organization that often works with ISO. The IEC is the preeminent organization for developing and publishing international standards for technologies related to electrical and electronic devices and processes. People refer to the collective body of knowledge addressed by the IEC as electrotechnology.

The IEC formed in 1906 to address issues with the expanding technologies related to electrical devices. Today, IEC's standards address a wide variety of areas, including the following:

- Power generation
- Power transmission and distribution
- Commercial and consumer electrical appliances
- Semiconductors
- Electromagnetics
- Batteries
- Solar energy
- Telecommunications

> **NOTE**
> *Gauss* is a measurement of a magnetic field, *hertz* is a representation of cycles per second, and *weber* is a measure of magnetic flux.

The IEC was instrumental in the development of standards for electrical measurements, including the gauss, hertz, and weber. The IEC works closely with ISO and the ITU-T (discussed later in this chapter) to synergize efforts. To ensure international acceptance and maximum usage of its standards, the IEC encourages participation from as many countries as possible. There are 72 full members, also called National Committees (NCs), in the IEC. In 2001, the IEC expanded its membership to include more developing nations. The Affiliate Country Programme includes 81 smaller countries.

As an IT professional, you will most likely encounter IEC standards relating to physical computer and networking hardware. The focus of the IEC has expanded since its inception, as the electrical and electronics industries have changed. Today, much of the IEC's focus includes standards that address emerging power needs and how they affect other functional areas. The IEC is active in developing standards that support safety, performance, environmental responsibility, energy efficiency, and renewable energy sources and use.

> **NOTE**
> You can get more information about the IEC organization and its standards at its Web site: *http://www.iec.ch*.

World Wide Web Consortium (W3C)

The creation of the World Wide Web in 1990 marked a turning point in the way users access resources on the Internet. In the early days of the Internet, competing vendors released their own versions of the primary language of the Web, HTML. These versions were incompatible with those of other vendors. These incompatibilities caused issues with Web browsers and limited the Web's functionality. As interest in the Web grew, the need to standardize the primary language of the Web became clear. Sir Tim Berners-Lee, the computer scientist who wrote the original proposal for what eventually became the World Wide Web, founded the **World Wide Web Consortium (W3C)** in 1994 to address the lack of standards.

The W3C immediately became the main international standards organization for the World Wide Web. The stated purpose of the W3C is to develop protocols and guidelines that unify the World Wide Web and ensure its long-term growth. The W3C currently has 355 members, representing businesses, nonprofit organizations, universities, and various government agencies.

The W3C develops many Web-related standards that govern and coordinate many aspects of Web development and operation. Standards the W3C has developed or endorsed include the following:

- Cascading Style Sheets (CSS)
- Common Gateway Interface (CGI)
- Hypertext Markup Language (HTML)
- Simple Object Access Protocol (SOAP)
- Web Services Description Language (WSDL)
- Extensible Markup Language (XML)

> **NOTE**
> For more information about the W3C, its standards, and its work in providing standards and guidelines for the World Wide Web, see the W3C Web site: *http://www.w3.org*.

Each of these standards and specifications is necessary to ensure that Web applications interact with Web components from other vendors. If you work with any World Wide Web components, you will likely encounter one or more W3C standards.

Internet Engineering Task Force (IETF)

The **Internet Engineering Task Force (IETF)** develops and promotes Internet standards. According to the IETF Web site, the purpose of IETF is to "make the Internet work better." IETF focuses on the engineering aspects of Internet communication and attempts to avoid policy and business questions. The IETF works closely with the W3C and ISO/IEC, focusing primarily on standards of the TCP/IP or Internet protocol suite. IETF is an open organization. There are no membership requirements. All participants, including contributors and leaders, are volunteers. Their employers usually fund their work.

The IETF first met in 1986 as a group of 21 researchers wanting to formalize the main Internet communication protocols. Today, the IETF is a collection of working groups (WGs), with each group addressing a specific topic. There are currently more than 100 WGs. Because WGs tend to operate independently, the IETF sets minimum standards for each group. Each WG has an appointed chair or group of co-chairs and a charter that documents the group's focus and expected deliverables.

Every WG has a dedicated mailing list to which anyone can subscribe. These WG mailing lists serve as the primary communication medium for participants. Most participants get started by simply subscribing to one or more WG mailing lists of interest. WGs also hold periodic meetings, which are open to all participants. While it is generally beneficial to attend meetings, it is possible to participate in a WG by just interacting via the mailing list.

NOTE

For more information on the IETF and its activities, visit the IETF Web page: *http://www.ietf.org/.*

Request for Comments (RFC)

The IETF produces **Requests for Comments (RFCs)**. An RFC is a series of documents that range from simple memos to standards documents. Each RFC's introduction indicates its status. The RFC model allows input from many sources and encourages collaboration and peer review. IETF publishes guidelines for RFCs. Here are a few points about RFCs:

- **Only some RFCs are standards**—Only RFCs that open with phrases like "This document specifies ..." or "This memo documents ..." should be considered standards or normative documents.
- **RFCs never change**—Any changes to an RFC get a new number and become a new RFC. Always look for the latest RFC, because previous documents may be out of date.
- **RFCs may originate with other organizations**—IETF creates only some RFCs. Others may come from independent sources, the IAB, or the Internet Research Task Force (IRTF).
- **RFCs that define formal standards have four stages**—As an RFC moves from one stage to the next, it becomes more formal and more organizations accept it. The stages are as follows:
  - **Proposed Standard (PS)**—The initial official stage of a standard
  - **Draft Standard (DS)**—The second stage of a standard, after participants have demonstrated that the standard has been deployed in working environments

- **Standard (STD)**—The final stage of a standard, after it has been shown to be widely adopted and deployed
- **Best Current Practice (BCP)**—The alternative method used to document operational specifications that are not formal standards

Some examples of IETF standards include RFC 5878 and RFC 5910. RFC 5878, "Transport Layer Security (TLS) Authorization Extensions," contains the specification for extensions to the TLS handshake protocol. RFC 5910, "Domain Name System (DNS) Security Extensions Mapping for the Extensible Provisioning Protocol (EPP)," describes EPP extension mapping for DNSSEC domain names stored in a central repository. Neither of these RFCs is lightweight reading. They contain very technical details that define how the Internet operates.

NOTE
You can find more information about RFCs and access an RFC search engine from IETF's RFC Web page: *http://www.ietf.org/rfc.html*.

NOTE
According to the ISOC's Web site, *http://isoc.org*, the ISOC is "an independent international nonprofit organisation founded in 1992 to provide leadership in Internet related standards, education, and policy around the world."

Internet Architecture Board (IAB)

The **Internet Architecture Board (IAB)** is a subcommittee of the IETF. It also serves as an advisory body to the Internet Society (ISOC). The IAB is composed of independent researchers and professionals who have a technical interest in the well-being of the Internet.

The IAB serves as an oversight committee for many IETF activities. The IAB provides oversight for the following:

- Architecture for Internet protocols and procedures
- Processes used to create standards
- Editorial and publication procedures for RFCs
- Confirmation of IETF chair and technical area directors

The IAB provides much of the high-level management and validation of the processes of conducting IETF business. The IAB is an important committee that has substantial influence over many standards that affect the Internet.

IEEE

According to its Web site (*http://www.ieee.org/index.html*), the Institute of Electrical and Electronics Engineers (IEEE) is "the world's largest professional association for the advancement of technology." The IEEE is an international nonprofit organization that focuses on developing and distributing standards that relate to electricity and electronics. With more than 380,000 members in approximately 175 countries, it has the largest number of members of any technical professional organization in the world. The IEEE formed in 1963 through the merger of two older organizations: the Institute of Radio Engineers, formed in 1912, and the American Institute of Electrical Engineers, formed in 1884.

TABLE 12-2 Common IEEE 802 standard working groups.

WORKING GROUP	DESCRIPTION
802.3	Ethernet
802.5	MAC layer for token ring network
802.6	Defines metropolitan area network (MAN)
802.11	Wireless LAN (802.11a, 802.11b, 802.11g, 802.11n)
802.13	10BASE-X Ethernet
802.14	Cable modems
802.15.1	Bluetooth certification
802.16	Broadband wireless access (WiMAX)

IEEE supports 38 societies that focus activities on specific technical areas. These technical areas include magnetics, photonics, and computers. Each society develops publications, holds conferences, and promotes activities and events to further the knowledge and interest in a specific area. IEEE also provides many training and education opportunities covering a wide number of engineering topics.

IEEE is also one of the largest standards-producing organizations. The IEEE Standards Association (IEEE-SA) manages these standards. IEEE standards cover many industries, including information technology. IEEE currently publishes or sponsors more than 1,300 standards and projects. The best-known standard that relates to information security is the IEEE 802 LAN/MAN standard family. This group of standards defines how different types of local area network (LAN) and metropolitan area network (MAN) protocols work. Table 12-2 lists some of the more recognizable working groups in the IEEE 802 LAN/MAN standard.

> **NOTE**
> The 802 working group takes its name from the date it first convened, in February (month 2) of 1980.

IEEE is open to members from the technical community who meet certain professional requirements. Full members can vote in IEEE elections. Students can obtain student memberships to IEEE; they can enjoy all the benefits of full membership except the right to vote. For interested parties who are not students and do not meet the technical requirement, IEEE offers associate memberships with limited privileges.

International Telecommunication Union Telecommunication Sector (ITU-T)

The **International Telecommunication Union (ITU)** is a United Nations agency. It is responsible for managing and promoting information and technology issues. ITU is a global point of focus for both governmental and commercial development of networks and related services. ITU was formed in 1865 as the International Telegraph Union to develop international standards for the emerging telegraph communications industry. ITU became a United Nations agency in 1947. It was renamed the International Telegraph and Telephone Consultative Committee (CCITT) in 1956, and eventually adopted its current name in 1993. ITU headquarters are in Geneva, Switzerland. Their memberships include 191 member states and more than 700 sector members and associates.

The oldest and most recognizable activity of the ITU is its work developing standards. The **ITU Telecommunication Sector (ITU-T)** performs all ITU standards work. The ITU-T is responsible for ensuring the efficient and effective production of standards covering all fields of telecommunications for all nations. ITU-T also defines tariff and accounting principles for international telecommunication services. Timeliness has become an important focus of ITU-T standards. In 2001, the organization overhauled its antiquated standards-development procedures to reduce the time required to create standards by 95 percent.

ITU-T calls the international standards it produces recommendations. They become mandatory only when adopted as part of a member state's national law. Because the ITU-T is a United Nations agency, its standards carry significant international weight. Even though ITU-T calls its standards recommendations, they tend to carry substantial authority.

ITU-T divides its recommendations into 26 separate series, each bearing a unique letter of the alphabet. For example, switching and signaling recommendations are in the Q series. Data networks, open systems communications, and security recommendations are in the X series. ITU-T has developed and published many communication recommendations that address technical details of all types of communication. Three recommendations of particular interest in information security are X.25, X.75, and X.509. Table 12-3 lists a few details of each of these ITU-T recommendations.

> **NOTE**
> You can find more information about ITU and ITU-T on the ITU Web page: *http://www.itu.int*.

TABLE 12-3 ITU-T recommendations that relate to information security.

ITU-T RECOMMENDATION	DESCRIPTION
X.25	X.25 describes a protocol suite for a packet-switched wide area network communication. X.25 is a Layer 3 (Network layer) protocol that provides a resilient wide area network. Although X.25 is still in use today, most wide area networks use the IP protocol.
X.75	X.75 describes the protocol for connecting two X.25 networks. It defines the requirements for the interface between data communication equipment (DCE) units in a network.
X.509	X.509 is a recommendation for a public key infrastructure (PKI) that addresses single sign-on (SSO) capability and Privilege Management Infrastructure (PMI). The recommendation defines standard formats for public key certificates, certificate-management capabilities, attribute certificates, and a certification path validation algorithm.

ANSI

One of the leading standards agencies on the United States is the **American National Standards Institute (ANSI)**. ANSI's goal is to strengthen the U.S. marketplace within the global economy. At the same time, it strives to ensure the safety and health of consumers and the protection of the environment. It seeks to accomplish this by promoting voluntary consensus standards and conformity assessment systems.

ANSI oversees the creation, publication, and management of many standards and guidelines that directly affect businesses in nearly every sector. ANSI standards cover such business sectors as acoustical devices, construction equipment, dairy and livestock production, and energy distribution.

ANSI was formed in 1918 through the merger of five engineering societies and three government agencies. These groups merged to form the American Engineering Standards Committee (AESC). In 1928, the AESC became the American Standards Association (ASA). In 1966, the ASA reorganized and became the United States of America Standards Institute (USASI). Finally, in 1969, the USASI became ANSI. Today, ANSI is composed of government agencies, organizations, educational institutions, and individuals. ANSI represents more than 125,000 companies and 3.5 million professionals.

> **NOTE**
> You can find more information about ANSI on the organization's Web page: *http://www.ansi.org/*.

ANSI produces standards that affect nearly all aspects of IT. Unlike other organizations that specifically focus on engineering or technical aspects of computing and communication, ANSI primarily addresses standards that support software development and computer system operation. Table 12-4 lists some ANSI standards you will encounter in the information security and software development realms.

TABLE 12-4 Important ANSI standards.

STANDARD	DESCRIPTION
ANSI code	The ANSI code is a standard that defines a set of values used to represent characters in computers. A standard is necessary to enable multiple computers to share data and communicate with each other. The ANSI code set is an extension of the older ASCII seven-bit code set.
American Standard FORTRAN	American Standard FORTRAN was the first standard programming language, also called FORTRAN 66. ANSI published this standard language in March of 1966.
ANSI C	ANSI published ANSI C as a standard version of the programming language C in 1989.

ISO 17799

ISO 17799 is an international security standard. This standard documents a comprehensive set of controls that represent best practices in information systems. The standard actually consists of two separate parts:

- The ISO 17799 code of practice
- The BS 17799-2 specification for an information security management system

The main purpose of the standard is to identify security controls needed for information systems in today's business environments. The standard originally appeared as the "DTI Code of Practice" in Britain and was later renamed BS 7799. It did not gain wide international popularity due to its inflexibility and overly simplistic approach to control. Developers released version 2 in 1999 to address the standard's weaknesses. Developers submitted the standard to ISO for accreditation and publishing. ISO published the standard as ISO 17799 in 2000.

Interest in the standard increased quickly. Several companies began providing tools and services to help implement ISO 17799. It quickly became the predominant information security standard. ISO 17799 gave many organizations a framework on which to build their security policy. Full compliance with the standard quickly became a goal. It also became a differentiator among competitors. The standard enabled potential customers to evaluate organizations on their efforts toward securing data.

The ISO divides the standard into 10 major sections:

- **Security Policy**—A statement of management direction
- **Security Organization**—Governance of information security, or how information security should be enforced
- **Asset Classification and Control**—Procedures to classify and manage information assets
- **Personnel Security**—Guidance for security controls that protect and limit personnel
- **Physical and Environmental Security**—Protection of computer facilities
- **Communications and Operations Management**—Managing technical security controls in systems and networks
- **Access Control**—Controls that limit access rights to network resources, applications, functions, and data
- **System Development and Maintenance**—Guidelines for designing and incorporating security into applications
- **Business Continuity Management**—Protecting, maintaining, and recovering business-critical processes and systems
- **Compliance**—Ensuring conformance with information security policies, standards, laws, and regulations

A newer standard, ISO/IES 27002, has superseded ISO 17799. It provides a generic information security standard accessible by all organizations, regardless of size, industry, or location. Although ISO/IES 27002 replaced ISO 17799, you will still see references to ISO 17799 as a leading information security standard.

ISO/IEC 27002

ISO/IEC 27002 appeared in 2005 as an update to the ISO 17799 standard. Originally named ISO 17799:2005, ISO changed its name to ISO/IEC 27002:2005 in 2007. This was to conform to the naming convention used by other 27000-series ISO/IEC standards. The ISO/IEC 27000 series is a growing family of general information security standards. ISO/IEC 27002 is "Information Technology Security Techniques Code of Practice for Information Security Management."

Like its predecessor, ISO/IEC 27002 provides organizations with best-practice recommendations on information security management. The standard directs its recommendations to management and security personnel responsible for information security management systems. Information security is within the standard in the context of the A-I-C triad:

- **Availability**—Ensuring that authorized users have access to information when it is requested
- **Integrity**—Ensuring only authorized users can modify data, and no one else
- **Confidentiality**—Ensuring only authorized users can access data, and no one else

ISO/IEC 27002 expands on its predecessor by adding two new sections and reorganizing several others. The ISO divides the new standard into 12 major sections:

- **Risk Assessment**—Formal methods of identifying and classifying risks
- **Security Policy**—A statement of management direction
- **Organization of Information Security**—Governance of information security, or how information security should be enforced
- **Asset Management**—Procedures to acquire, classify, and manage information assets
- **Human Resources Security**—Security guidelines for personnel joining, leaving, or moving within an organization
- **Physical and Environmental Security**—Protection of computer facilities
- **Communications and Operations Management**—Managing technical security controls in systems and networks
- **Access Control**—Controls that limit access rights to network resources, applications, functions, and data
- **Information Systems Acquisition Development and Maintenance**—Guidelines for designing and incorporating security into applications

- **Information Security Incident Management**—Anticipating and responding appropriately to information security breaches
- **Business Continuity Management**—Protecting, maintaining, and recovering business-critical processes and systems
- **Compliance**—Ensuring conformance with information security policies, standards, laws, and regulations

The standard specifies and outlines the recommended security controls within each section. Most people regard the information security controls as best practices. These best practices provide methods of achieving each objective. ISO/IEC 27002 also provides guidance for implementing each of the recommended controls.

NOTE

You can find more information about ISO/IEC 27002 at the official ISO Web site: *http://www.iso.org/iso/catalogue_detail?csnumber=50297.*

PCI DSS

The Payment Card Industry Data Security Standard (PCI DSS) is an international standard for handling transactions involving payment cards. The Payment Card Industry Security Standards Council (PCI SSC) developed, publishes, and maintains the standard. PCI DSS is different from other standards you have seen so far. Some of the largest payment card vendors in the world formed PCI DSS. These vendors include the following:

- Visa
- MasterCard
- Discover
- American Express
- Japan Credit Bureau

Each of these organizations had its own standard for protecting payment card information. These organizations combined their efforts and published the PCI DSS in December 2004. They created PCI DSS to protect payment card users from fraud and to preempt legislative requirements on the industry. It requires layers of controls to protect all payment card–related information as it is processed, transmitted, and stored. The standard applies to all organizations that participate in any of the processes surrounding payment card processing.

Compliance with PCI DSS standards is a prerequisite for doing business with any of the member organizations. If any organization violates PCI DSS standards, it could lose its ability to process payment cards. In most cases, noncompliance results in fines and/or audits that are more frequent. Habitual offenders may find their processing privileges revoked. For most organizations that depend on payment cards as a means of receiving payment, compliance is a business requirement.

TABLE 12-5 PCI DSS control objectives and requirements.

CONTROL OBJECTIVE	REQUIREMENT
Build and maintain a secure network.	Install and maintain a firewall configuration to protect cardholder data. Do not use vendor-supplied defaults for system passwords and other security parameters.
Protect cardholder data.	Protect stored cardholder data. Encrypt transmission of cardholder data across open, public networks.
Maintain a vulnerability-management program.	Use and regularly update antivirus software on all systems commonly affected by malware. Develop and maintain secure systems and applications.
Implement strong access control measures.	Restrict access to cardholder data by business need-to-know. Assign a unique ID to each person with computer access. Restrict physical access to cardholder data.
Regularly monitor and test networks.	Track and monitor all access to network resources and cardholder data. Regularly test security systems and processes.
Maintain an information security policy.	Maintain a policy that addresses information security.

The rules with which an organization must comply depend on the number of payment card transactions the organization processes. Organizations assess compliance at least annually. Organizations that handle large volumes of transactions must have their compliance assessed by an independent Qualified Security Assessor (QSA). Organizations that handle smaller volumes of transactions can choose to self-certify using a PCI DSS Self-Assessment Questionnaire (SAQ).

NOTE

You can find more information about PCI DSS at the official PCI Security Standards Council Web site: *https://www.pcisecuritystandards.org*.

PCI DSS version 1.2 defines 12 requirements for compliance, organized into six groups, called control objectives. Table 12-5 lists the 12 PCI DSS control objectives and requirements.

CHAPTER SUMMARY

A number of organizations define standards that document technical specifications or other specific criteria for use as rules, guidelines, or definitions of characteristics. Organizations and industries also use standards to ensure that products and services are consistent. The ability of different products from different organizations to work well together depends on standards. As the IT industry advances, so does the need for new and updated standards. In this chapter, you learned about some of the standards organizations and a few standards that directly affect information security. Research these standards organizations and familiarize yourself with their work. It is likely you will see them again.

KEY CONCEPTS AND TERMS

American National Standards Institute (ANSI)
International Electrotechnical Commission (IEC)
International Organization for Standardization (ISO)
International Telecommunication Union (ITU)
Internet Architecture Board (IAB)
Internet Engineering Task Force (IETF)
ISO 17799
ISO/IEC 27002
ITU Telecommunication Sector (ITU-T)
National Institute of Standards and Technology (NIST)
Request for Comments (RFC)
World Wide Web Consortium (W3C)

CHAPTER 12 ASSESSMENT

1. The earliest digital computers were the result of experimental standards.
   A. True
   B. False
2. Which standards organization's name derives from the Greek word for "equal"?
   A. IEC
   B. ISO
   C. PCI
   D. W3C
3. Which standards organization formed in 1906 and handles standards for batteries?
   A. IEC
   B. ISO
   C. PCI
   D. W3C
4. Which standards organization publishes standards such as CGI, HTML, and XML?
   A. IEC
   B. ISO
   C. PCI
   D. W3C
5. The IETF primarily focuses on standards of the ________ Internet protocol suite.
6. The IETF produces documents called ________.
7. Which of the following is the most well-known ISO standard?
   A. OSI reference model
   B. TCP/IP protocol
   C. TCP/IP reference model
   D. OSI protocol
8. The ________ is the world's largest professional association for the advancement of technology.
9. Which standards organization publishes the 802.11g standard?
   A. ISO
   B. IEC
   C. ITU-T
   D. IEEE
10. Which standards organization publishes American Standard FORTRAN?
    A. IEEE
    B. ANSI
    C. ITU-T
    D. NIST

Information Security Education and Training

CHAPTER 13

AS A SECURITY PROFESSIONAL, your primary job is to protect the availability, integrity, and confidentiality of your organization's data. Executing the tasks to fulfill these goals requires a high level of authority, responsibility, and trust. Security professionals must provide critical services in diverse areas within the IT infrastructure. You must possess specific knowledge and skills to be proactive and to balance competing priorities. Solid security training and education provides a breadth of knowledge to secure existing systems and anticipate future threats. The demand for prepared IT security professionals continues to increase. A steady supply of candidates who possess the skills and education is required to meet the need. In this chapter, you will learn about the many types of security training and education that are available to prepare you to fill the role of security professional.

Chapter 13 Topics

This chapter covers the following topics and concepts:

- How to learn through self-study
- What adult continuing education programs are available
- What post-secondary degree programs are available
- What information security training programs are available

Chapter 13 Goals

When you complete this chapter, you will be able to:

- Identify self-study resources
- Locate adult continuing education programs in information security
- Compare post-secondary higher education degree programs in information security
- Identify which organizations offer information security training programs

Self-Study

The easiest and quickest option for security training is studying materials yourself. Many security resources exist, both online and in book form. Your local bookstore likely carries many books and magazines that cover information security topics. In fact, you may find it difficult to narrow down your choices to just a few.

Before you start learning about security using the self-study method, consider the advantages and disadvantages of the approach. Self-study can be a very cost-effective and convenient option, but it may not be the best solution in all cases.

First, consider some of the advantages of self-study, or self-instruction:

- **Low cost**—Self-study is generally the least expensive training option. You need to buy only those materials required to meet your goals. You can choose the materials that best fit your budget. Some self-study materials are available for no cost.
- **Flexible materials**—With self-study, you select the resource materials you like best. Different people learn in different ways. You might prefer a video course while another person might prefer a printed book. Either way, self-study gives you the option to find the resources that best suit your learning style.
- **Flexible schedule**—You can study when it works best for your schedule. Some people study better in the morning while others study better in the evening. The self-study option lets you decide which study schedule works best for you.
- **Personal pace**—When you're doing it yourself, you get to set the pace. The self-study option lets you decide how fast you want to cover the training material. You may need to explore some topics slowly, and others more quickly. An additional advantage is that you can go back and cover a topic again if you need to.
- **Supplemental materials**—No one is an expert in every area. Most students in any subject benefit from additional materials at one time or another. When you select your own resources, you can decide when to use supplemental materials. Your initial search for primary materials will likely give you a feel for good additional materials if you need them.

There are also some disadvantages to choosing the self-study option. Carefully consider these concerns when deciding if self-study is right for you:

- **Procrastination**—One of the most common pitfalls of self-study is procrastination. There are so many demands on your time, it is often difficult to justify setting aside time to study. Also, you may find that self-study takes more time than you planned. You will need discipline and commitment to stay on schedule. Seriously consider how well you will be able to stick to a study schedule when you're studying on your own time.
- **Resource selection**—Although choosing your own resources can be an advantage, it can also be a disadvantage. It is very difficult to assess the value of a resource without really studying it first. Some resources look great at first glance but don't have the depth or value you need. The large number of options available to you can make the process of identifying the best products difficult.

- **Lack of interaction**—Self-study is a one-way instruction technique. You don't get any feedback from other students or an instructor. If you like learning with others, self-study may not be the best option for you. While most people do benefit from interaction, the inconvenience and cost of other options may limit you to self-study.
- **Quality**—Most self-study resources specifically target the low-cost student market. In other words, they are low-cost products to meet limited budgets. That doesn't mean these products aren't good; it just means they don't have the same appearance as the high-cost products. In some cases, quality directly relates to cost. However, there are very good inexpensive resources, and there are expensive resources that have limited value. Look over the materials you purchase carefully.
- **Validated outcome**—If you are using self-study just to learn about security topics, validation may not be a concern for you. However, it is good to get validation that you successfully completed a study. Most other training methods include some sort of assessment and validation process. Self-study does not have such a process. Your validation is your ability to demonstrate what you have learned. This could be passing a certification exam or just having more knowledge and skills than before you started.

Another important aspect of making a decision to pursue self-study is to decide on the purpose for your study. The specific reasons that you want to study a topic can help you decide the best approach. In most cases, you'll pursue some form of study for at least one reason, including the following:

- **General knowledge**—General security knowledge is necessary to understand the big picture. Security involves all domains of the IT infrastructure and several areas outside the IT infrastructure. As a result, a security professional should have a good understanding of general security topics. Most professionals focus on one or more specific areas of security. These professionals would benefit from a better overall understanding of security works. In addition, many security managers need a more general knowledge set rather than a command of the specific security details.
- **Specific knowledge and skills**—Most security tasks require general knowledge and specific area knowledge. In addition, you may need specific skills to carry out a task. For example, setting up firewall rules can be very complex. You'll need to know the details of firewall configuration and how to maintain rules on your organization's devices. General knowledge is good for a high-level view, but hands-on practitioners need specific knowledge as well. Make sure any self-study materials you use cover the topics you need in sufficient detail.
- **Certification preparation**—One common use for self-study is in preparing for a certification exam. You may meet the requirements to take a certification exam, but want to review the material and fill in any knowledge gaps. Self-study may be a good fit for this need.

TABLE 13-1 Security self-study resources.

RESOURCE	COMMENTS
Bookstore	Visit your local bookstore (or go to its Web site) and browse through information security titles. Check each title's publication date to ensure it contains the latest information.
Library	Your local library can be a good resource, but often contains out-of-date materials. If you do use a library, pay special attention to the publication dates.
$(ISC)^2$ self-paced e-learning	$(ISC)^2$ produces quality materials that help you prepare for $(ISC)^2$ certification exams. See *https://www.isc2.org/self-paced.aspx* for more information.
Jones & Bartlett e-learning	Jones & Bartlett, the publisher of this book, is a leader in providing world-class education products across a wide range of subjects, including information security. See its Web site at *http://www.jblearning.com/elearning/* for a full list of courses and materials.
SANS Institute self-study	The SANS organization produces excellent training products for many security topics. Many SANS courses prepare students to sit for certification exams. Their self-study series provides solid printed and e-learning materials that you can use at your own pace. See *http://www.sans.org/selfstudy/* for more details.
LearnKey, Inc.	LearnKey, Inc. provides a wide range of self-study e-learning titles from different areas. LearnKey's products address both general security and certification preparation topics. See *http://www.learnkey.com* for more information.
Vendor Web sites	Many hardware and software vendors provide training and certification materials for their products. Some examples include Cisco training and certification (*http://www.ciscopress.com*) and IBM education (*http://www-01.ibm.com/software/data/education/selfstudy.html*).

NOTE

Table 13-1 contains only a limited list of self-study resources. An Internet search will produce many additional resources. Try searching for "self-study materials for security." You'll find many resources for materials.

There are many sources for self-study materials. Table 13-1 contains just a few suggestions. This isn't a complete list, but it should help get you started.

Because there are so many providers of self-study material, you have to be careful. Not all products are worth the price. To find the best training materials for self-study learning, follow these guidelines:

- **Reputable sources**—Don't buy resources from just any Web site. Make sure the company has a good reputation. Recognizable companies, such as IBM and Cisco, already have a reputation. Smaller companies may not be so well known. Do some research to find comments and reviews of the company before you buy any products. You should buy materials only from a reputable business that has multiple positive customer reviews.
- **Material reviews**—Even reputable companies can sell training products that don't meet your needs. In addition to checking the reviews for each vendor, look for product reviews too. You should be able to find positive reviews for the book or course you want to buy. A simple Internet search on the product name should provide reviews or comments on its quality.
- **Multiple products**—Retailers that provide multiple products tend to have better-quality training products. It takes a substantial investment to develop and market a range of related products. The product creators want to ensure the quality is high to generate additional sales. Be careful, though. Don't blindly assume that quantity is the same as quality. Some retailers just carry anything they can sell. When in doubt, search for product and vendor reviews.

Whether self-study is a good option for you depends on your situation. Consider your budget, schedule, learning style, and experience before making a decision.

Self-study isn't the only way to go. In the following sections, you'll learn about other options to pursue security training and education.

Adult Continuing Education Programs

An alternative to self-study is a more structured classroom environment. Many colleges and universities host a **continuing education** department. The continuing education group can be part of the school or a closely related educational unit. In some cases, it is actually one of the schools within the university. Regardless of the organization, the purpose of continuing education is to provide formal courses that do not lead to degrees. In many cases the students already have degrees and are looking to update their skills and knowledge. The courses can range from very general topics to highly specific and technical. These courses meet various needs of community members, including the following:

- Preparatory classes for degree programs
- Enrichment classes for adults
- Summertime camp-style classes for children and youth
- Professional training
- Certification preparation

The last category listed above covers both security and many other instructional areas. Continuing education courses often try to meet needs of adult students. Because most adult students have jobs, you'll find that many continuing education classes meet in the evenings or on weekends.

Certificate Programs

Regardless of the schedule, continuing education organizations commonly offer sequences of classes that lead to a **certificate of completion**. A certificate is a document you receive once you meet specific requirements. Certificates attest that you have completed courses and made a sufficient score on an assessment. Although some continuing education courses prepare students for certification exams, many more lead to certificates of completion. The biggest difference between a certificate and a certification is the formal nature of the certification and the weight it carries. Certificates show the student has completed specific training and possesses a general level of competence in a specific area. It also verifies that the student should be able to perform at an entry or intermediate level.

Certificate programs are commonly specific to the educational institution. Similar programs at different schools may have different requirements. Each institution also dictates its own methods of delivery. It is very common to see blended programs that include both traditional classes and online offerings. If a certificate program interests you, start by contacting your local colleges and universities. Many continuing education providers work closely with practitioners in each subject area to ensure their classes meet the needs of local employers and other organizations. You may find that the classes you take at local institutions provide specific content encouraged by local organizations. That can help you gain the specific knowledge and skills local companies need and want.

Because many continuing education providers have online programs, you don't have to limit your search to local providers. An Internet search will show you many continuing education offerings for nearly any interest area. Try searching for "continuing education in information security." You'll find many institutions that provide certificate programs.

CPE Credits

Continuing education programs also include courses that don't lead to a certificate. Many courses exist just to keep practitioners current and informed. Another name for these types of courses is continuing professional education courses. These courses generally target practitioners who are already working in their chosen fields. Most certifications require certification holders to pursue additional education each year to keep their certification current. Certifications that require additional education generally specify the number of credits each certificate requires. If a certificate holder fails to earn the minimum number of credits, he or she may lose the certification.

To make the process of validating continuing education easier, most institutions offer credit for courses in a standard unit. Institutions assign each course a **continuing professional education (CPE)** value. Each CPE credit represents 50 minutes of classroom instruction. Students can select courses based on the number of CPEs credits they can earn. Students who hold certifications can prove they completed a course and then claim the CPEs toward their certification maintenance requirements.

> **NOTE**
> Make sure you note the CPE requirements for each certification you hold and keep track of the CPEs you earn. You'll need CPEs each year to maintain most certifications.

A continuing education program is a great way to pursue new knowledge and keep certifications current. Contact your local colleges and universities to find out what courses they offer. As you look for continuing education course offerings, don't forget to search online. You may find just what you're looking for in an online course. If you're just looking for online courses, you can look beyond your local colleges and universities.

Post-Secondary Degree Programs

Colleges and universities also provide degree programs related to information security. While the number of security-related degrees was small even a few years ago, that number is rapidly growing. And proprietary (for-profit) institutions are in many cases offering more degree programs for hands-on security professionals than traditional nonprofit colleges are. Today, you can find programs in **traditional classrooms** and **distance learning** environments for degrees ranging from the associate level up to PhDs. Each degree has a specific focus and appeals to a different group of people. Consider your background, interests, and career plans when deciding what degree fits best.

> **WARNING**
>
> Before you select a program of study, investigate whether the program is **accredited**. Most prospective employers value accredited programs more than unaccredited ones.

Nearly any college or university can offer a security-related degree. It can be difficult to determine which program is best for you. In February 2003, The U.S. President's National Strategy to Secure Cyberspace called for a program to recognize educational and research institutions that provide quality security education and conduct pertinent research. In response to that strategy, the U.S. National Security Agency (NSA) and the Department of Homeland Security (DHS) jointly sponsor two important programs:

- **The National Centers of Academic Excellence in Information Assurance Education (CAEIAE) program**—The **National Centers of Academic Excellence in Information Assurance Education (CAEIAE)** program identifies educational institutions that meet the program's information assurance educational guidelines.
- **The National Centers of Academic Excellence in Research (CAE-R) program**—The **National Centers of Academic Excellence in Research (CAE-R)** program identifies institutions that meet the research guidelines.

Together, these two programs help identify the best institutions in the U.S. in information assurance education and research. Four-year colleges and graduate-level universities can apply to be CAEIAE or CAE-R designated institutions. Some institutions apply to both programs. The approval process requires each institution to pass a rigorous review demonstrating its commitment to academic excellence in the field of information security. This list is a good place to start when looking for a good education in information security.

> **NOTE**
>
> You can find out more information on CAEIAE and CAE-R and see a list of institutions that offer these programs on the NSA Web site: *http://www.nsa.gov/ia/academic_outreach/nat_cae/index.shtml*.

TABLE 13-2 Associate's degree programs.

INSTITUTION	DESCRIPTION
ITT Tech	ITT offers online and campus-based associate's degrees in computer network systems. The program explores a variety of computer networks. Students investigate these topics through classroom theory and practical applications. For more information, visit *http://www.itt-tech.edu/programs/*.
Anthem Education Group	Anthem Education Group offers career-focused diplomas, degrees, and training programs. These are available at campuses across the United States as well as online. For more information, visit *http://www.anthemcollege.edu/programs/computer-networking-security/associate-of-science-degree/*.
University of Phoenix	The University of Phoenix offers online associate's degrees in various IT disciplines that support security functions. For more information, visit *http://www.phoenix.edu/degrees/associate.html*.
Everest University	Everest University offers an online program with comprehensive computer courses built around real-world experience. For more information, visit *http://www.everestonline.edu/online-degrees/computer-information-science*.
Strayer University	Strayer University offers online and campus-based information systems degrees. For more information, visit *http://www.strayer.edu/degree_guide*.
Herzing University	Herzing University offers online and campus-based associate's degrees in computer science. For more information, visit *http://www.herzing.edu/academics/computer-networking-and-security-technology/programs*.
South University	South University offers online degrees with fundamentals of IT with knowledge and capabilities for which corporations and organizations are searching. For more information, visit *http://online.southuniversity.edu/degrees/associate-science-information-technology.aspx*.
Edmonds Community College	Edmonds Community College offers online and campus-based associate's degrees in computer information systems, information security, and digital forensics. For more information, visit *http://catalog.edcc.edu*.

Associate's Degree

One type of degree that many institutions offer is the associate's degree. This degree is the most accessible because it generally represents a two-year program. Some institutions offer accelerated programs that allow students to complete the degree in less than two years. Either way, an associate's degree provides a basic education for people who want to enter the information security field without spending four or more years in school. These programs can prepare you for a wide range of entry-level positions in IT and information security.

Different institutions offer different types of associate's degrees. Just to name a few, you can pursue an associate of science (AS), associate of technical arts (ATA), or an associate of applied sciences (AAS). You can find both traditional and online degree programs at every level. Table 13-2 lists some associate's degree programs offered by different institutions.

Bachelor's Degree

The bachelor's degree is the next type of degree many institutions offer. The standard bachelor's degree is a four-year degree program. Many institutions offer accelerated programs to complete the degree requirements in less than four years, however. The bachelor's degree is often a requirement for any information security position other than entry-level positions. In fact, some entry-level positions even require a bachelor's degree as a minimum.

There are many types of bachelor's degree programs. Some degree programs focus on knowledge breadth, while others focus on knowledge depth. In general, liberal arts institutions and larger universities offer programs that focus on breadth. Technical institutions generally focus more on depth. Consider the various degree programs offered by institutions and compare the courses you'll take to satisfy the degree requirements. Find a program that fits your professional goals.

As with other degree programs, you can find institutions that offer both traditional and online programs of study. The current term for online study is distance learning. If this type of study interests you, try searching for "information security distance learning degree programs" online. You'll find that there are many choices available.

You can pursue several different types of bachelor's degrees. Some of the choices include bachelor of science (BS or BSc), bachelor of science in information technology (BScIT), bachelor of applied science (BASc), and bachelor of technology (B.Tech). The degree programs differ in the courses you must take and in the subject matter on which the degree programs focus. For example, a BS degree would likely focus more on a wide breadth of subjects, where a B.Tech degree would likely consist of mostly technical courses. Again, select the program of study that best fits your plans. Table 13-3 lists some of the bachelor's degree programs offered by different institutions.

TABLE 13-3 Bachelor's degree programs.

INSTITUTION	DESCRIPTION
ITT Tech	ITT Tech offers online and campus-based degrees in information systems security. For more information, visit *http://www.itt-tech.edu/programs/*.
Capella University	Capella University offers online degrees in information technology with information assurance and security specialization. Capella University has earned an NSA and Homeland Security designation. For more information, visit *http://www.capella.edu/schools_programs/undergraduate_studies/technology/information_assurance_security.aspx*.
Kaplan University	Kaplan University offers online degrees in information technology with the opportunity to focus on security and forensics. For more information, visit *http://online.kaplanuniversity.edu/information_technology/Pages/Information_Technology.aspx*.
University of Phoenix	The University of Phoenix offers online and campus-based IT degrees. These apply information technology theory and principles to address real-world business opportunities and challenges. For more information, visit *http://www.phoenix.edu/programs/degree-programs/technology/bachelors/bsit-iss/v006.html*.
Strayer University	Online and campus-based degrees in computer security and forensics, as well as computer security. For more information, visit *http://www.strayer.edu/degree_guide*.
Herzing University	Herzing University offers online or campus-based (or combination) degrees in computer networking and security or technology management. A networking security minor is available. For more information, visit *http://www.herzing.edu/academics/computer-networking-and-security-technology/programs*.
South University	South University offers online and campus-based degrees in information technology. For more information, visit *http://www.southuniversity.edu/college-of-business/information-technology-28711.aspx*.
Westwood College	Westwood College offers online and campus-based degrees in information security. It offers training in advanced security skills to manage the deployment of security solutions. For more information, visit *http://www.westwood.edu/programs/school-of-technology/information-technology-major-in-systems-security/*.

Master's Degree

The next type of academic degree is the master's degree. A master's degree program goes beyond the level of a bachelor's degree program. It generally consists of two years of study beyond a bachelor's degree. Some institutions offer accelerated programs that enable students to earn a master's degree more quickly than two years. A master's degree shows that the person who holds it possesses a deeper level of knowledge than the general population of information security practitioners.

Master's programs are generally very specific to a field of study. When you enter a master's program you normally spend most your time focusing on a specific are of study. Programs at this level focus more on depth of knowledge than on breadth of knowledge.

There are several different master's degrees available. These include master of science (MS or MSc), master of science in information technology (MScIT), and master of business administration (MBA). There is a definite difference in degree programs at this level. The main difference exists between the MS and MBA degrees. Each one has a different focus and targets a different group of students.

Master of Science Degree

The master of science degrees—MS, MSc, and MScIT—focus on the technical aspects of information security. In other words, these degrees are appropriate for security practitioners. If you want to work in a hands-on environment and perform security-related work, these degrees may be good choices. These types of degree programs detail how the IT infrastructure operates and how to design and implement proper security controls. Master of science degree programs prepare you to enter the field of information security and perform the work of securing systems. Table 13-4 lists some master of science degree programs offered by different institutions.

Master of Business Administration

The master of business administration degree—MBA—focuses on managing the process of securing information systems. Where MS programs prepare students to perform information security work, MBA programs prepare students to manage and maintain the people and environment of information security. A person who holds an MBA degree in information security fields will be prepared to manage information security or IT groups. The skills necessary to manage any technical environment are different from the skills necessary to perform technical work. A separate degree program prepares students to enter the specific field of their choice. Table 13-5 lists some master of business administration degree programs offered by different institutions.

TABLE 13-4 Master of science degree programs.

INSTITUTION	DESCRIPTION
SANS Institute	SANS Institute offers online, self-study, and classroom-based information technology degrees. SANS enables students to master communications, project management, teaching, mentoring, and persuasive skills. For more information, visit *http://www.sans.edu/.* Note: SANS, highly regarded in the field, is authorized by the State of Maryland to grant master's degrees. As of this writing, regional accreditation for the SANS degree is pending.
Capella University	Capella University offers online degrees in information security and assurance. It has earned an NSA and Homeland Security designation. For more information, visit *http://www.capella.edu/schools_programs/business_technology/masters/information_assurance_security.aspx*.
Kaplan University	Kaplan University offers online degrees in information science with the opportunity to specialize in information security and assurance. For more information, visit *http://online.kaplanuniversity.edu/information_technology/Pages/Information_Technology_MS.aspx*.
University of Phoenix	The University of Phoenix offers online and campus-based management of information degrees. These programs examine key IS technologies, such as IT infrastructure, enterprise models, and emerging technologies. For more information, visit *http://www.phoenix.edu/colleges_divisions/technology/master-information-systems.html*.
Strayer University	Strayer University offers online and campus-based degrees in computer security management. For more information, visit *http://www.strayer.edu/online_programs*.
South University	South University offers online degrees in information systems and technology. For more information, visit *http://www.southuniversity.edu/college-of-business/information-systems-and-technology-37811.aspx*.

TABLE 13-5 Master of business administration degree programs.

INSTITUTION	DESCRIPTION
Herzing University	Herzing University's online MBA program explores the cornerstones of business. It provides instruction in analyzing issues with technology systems facing companies in today's market. For more information, visit *http://www.herzingonline.edu/graduate/mba-technology-management*.
James Madison University	James Madison University offers a blended MBA, with online courses and meetings with faculty every eight weeks. All graduates receive the NSA-approved certificate: Information Systems Security (INFOSEC) Professionals. For more information, visit *http://www.jmu.edu/cob/mba/aboutinfosec.shtml*.
Keller University	Keller University offers an online and campus-based MBA, with a concentration in information security. For more information, visit *http://www.keller.edu/graduate-degree-programs/mba-information-security.jsp*.
Southern New Hampshire University	Southern New Hampshire University offers an online and campus-based MBA in information security and assurance. No GRE or GMAT required. For more information, visit *http://www.snhu.edu/9497.asp*.
Jones International University	Jones International University offers an online MBA in information security management. It is designed to provide realistic recommendations for improving the information security of an organization. For more information, visit *http://www.jiu.edu/specializations/mba-information-security-management*.

Doctoral Degree

The highest level of academic degree is the doctoral degree. This degree represents the most respected academic honor and is the most difficult to obtain. A doctoral program goes even further than the level of study required for a master's degree. Depending on the type of degree, requirements normally include rigorous course work and extensive research that makes a meaningful contribution to the field. Unlike other degrees, doctoral degrees do not involve a set amount of time. While many doctoral programs take from three to five years, there is no standard time frame to complete the degree.

A doctoral degree identifies a person as one who values extensive education in their chosen field of study. This person will possess the ability to function at a level that requires exceptional abilities and insight. In the field of information security, people who hold doctoral degrees often work in research, in large enterprise information security management, or in academic roles.

TABLE 13-6 Doctoral degree programs.

INSTITUTION	DESCRIPTION
Nova Southeastern University	Nova Southeastern University offers an online program in computer and information sciences. It is a National Center of Academic Excellence in Information Assurance, and is endorsed by the NSA and the Department of Homeland Security. For more information, visit *http://www.scis.nova.edu/*.
Capella University	Capella University offers an online PhD in information technology with a specialization in information assurance and security. This degree provides opportunities for advanced skill development and doctoral research in such topics as information confidentiality, integrity, governance, compliance, and risk management. For more information, visit *http://www.capella.edu/schools_programs/business_technology/phd/information_security.aspx*.
Northcentral University	Northcentral University offers an online PhD in business administration with a concentration in computer and information security. The specialization focuses on developing best practices for forensic investigations and evidence handling, federal and state privacy, intellectual property, search and seizure process, and cybercrime laws. For more information, visit *http://www.ncu.edu/northcentral-programs/specializations/BUS/phd-ba/computer-and-information-security*.
Walden University	Walden University offers an online PhD in management and a doctor of business administration with a concentration in information systems management. For more information, visit *http://info.waldenu.edu/business.php*.
Colorado Technical University	Colorado Technical University offers an online program in computer science with a digital systems security concentration. It develops leaders in the implementation, evaluation, and analysis of digital systems in which security is a primary component. For more information, visit *http://www.coloradotech.edu/Degree-Programs/Doctor-Of-Computer-Science-In-Digital-Systems-Security*.

There are several types of doctoral degrees available, depending on whether you want to pursue an academic, technical, or management path. Some of the available doctoral degrees in the areas of information security include doctor of science (DSc), doctor of information technology (DIT), doctor of technology (DTech), and the most widely recognized doctoral degree, the doctor of philosophy (PhD). Even at this level, institutions offer degree programs in both traditional and online formats. Table 13-6 lists some of the doctoral degree programs offered by different institutions.

Information Security Training Programs

Traditional education programs normally focus on students learning a bulk of information through a quarter or semester. Although some programs do introduce hands-on skills, educational institutions focus on complete coverage of topics. They want students to understand the reasons behind decisions and topics. Sometimes, all students want is to learn skills or acquire very specific knowledge. Security training programs fill this need with many different offerings.

In general, security training programs differ from security education programs in their focus on skills and in their duration. While education classes generally meet for a few hours a week over several months, security training classes often meet for intensive sessions lasting from a few hours to several days. The main purpose of security training courses is to rapidly train students in one or more skills, or to cover essential knowledge in one or more specific areas. Many security training courses specifically prepare students for certification exams.

Security Training Requirements

You learned about the NIST 800 Series publications in Chapter 12. The 800 Series publications cover all NIST-recommended procedures for managing information security. The publications also provide guidelines for enforcing security rules. These publications set forth many procedures that are necessary to keep IT environments secure. It is important that users receive training to ensure they understand the security procedures and can implement them.

The U.S. Office of Personnel Management (OPM) requires that federal agencies provide training suggested by the NIST guidelines. It requires agencies to train all current employees and to train all new employees within 60 days of the employee's hire date. Under the OPM requirements, agencies must also provide training whenever any of the following conditions occur:

- There is a significant change in the agency's IT security environment.
- There is a significant change in the agency's security procedures.
- An employee enters a new position that deals with sensitive information.

Agencies must also provide periodic refresher training at specified intervals. In addition, the regulations require that all employees or other personnel receive specialized security training before they receive access to secure IT applications and systems.

The Health Insurance Portability and Accountability Act (HIPAA) also includes directives that require security awareness and training. Implementation specifications include the following:

- Establishing a security awareness program.
- Providing training in malicious software.
- Providing training on logon monitoring procedures.
- Providing training on password management.

The Computer Security Act of 1987 mandated that NIST and OPM create guidelines on computer security awareness and training. It directed these agencies to create training that is specific to an agency's functional organizational roles. NIST Special Publication 800-16,

"Information Technology Security Training Requirements: A Role- and Performance-Based Model," includes these guidelines. The publication also contains a methodology that some organizations use to develop training courses for different audiences that have significant information security responsibilities. Special Publication 800-50, "Building an Information Technology Security Awareness and Training Program," is another NIST document related to information security awareness and training. The four areas main areas in NIST SP 800-50 are as follows:

- **Awareness**—A continuous process to help keep all personnel vigilant. This can include acceptable usage policy (AUP), reminders, logon banners, posters, e-mail messages, and any other techniques to keep personnel thinking about security.
- **Training**—Teach necessary security skills and competency to the staff as a whole as well as those whose jobs are in IT.
- **Education**—Integrate security skills and competencies into a common body of knowledge.
- **Professional development (organizations and certifications)**—Meet a standard by applying evaluation or measurement criteria.

These are just a few examples of regulations that require an ongoing security training and awareness program. Many organizations also include security awareness and training in their security policy. Ensuring that your personnel are aware of the security policies and procedures is a primary responsibility of your organization's management. Security and training personnel may develop and deliver the security message, but management is responsible for ensuring they communicate their policy.

And by the way: Just providing security training isn't enough. Each organization should provide training that is specific to each job function. Some job functions, such as data owners, need different training from other job functions, such as managers. You should ensure all personnel receive the training that is specific to their job functions.

Security Training Organizations

Some organizations cannot provide the level and amount of security training their personnel need. Separate security training organizations play a major part in providing the necessary training and certification for security personnel. Some organizations provide specific security training and others provide certification programs. You'll learn more about the security certifications available in Chapter 14.

Many vendors provide security training. As with educational institutions, you can find vendors that will provide classroom, online, and prepackaged study options. Choose the course-delivery option that works best for your budget, learning style, and schedule. There are many options for you, so take some time to evaluate the available products. Table 13-7 lists some of the larger security training vendors.

You can choose from among many quality training organizations. Visit each one's Web site to look at current course offerings. You'll probably be able to find a class and delivery method that fits your needs.

TABLE 13-7 Security training vendors.

VENDOR	DESCRIPTION
SANS Institute	SANS is one of the largest and most trusted sources for information security training in the world. It offers classes on many security topics that cover development, implementation, management, and auditing roles. SANS classes range from one half day to six days, are available globally, and tend to be very hands-on and focused. For more information, visit the SANS Web site at *http://www.sans.org*.
Computer Security Institute (CSI)	CSI is an educational membership organization that holds conferences and provides online training courses for its members. CSI serves its members by providing high-quality, focused training courses to keep members current with security-related topics. Visit the CSI Web site for more information: *http://gocsi.com*.
InfoSec Institute	InfoSec Institute is a large security training organization that holds regular classes across the U.S. Their goal is to provide the best possible hands-on training for students in topics ranging from certification preparation to very specific technical security topics. You can get more information at the InfoSec Institute's Web site: *http://www.infosecinstitute.com*.
Information Systems Audit and Control Association (ISACA)	ISACA is a nonprofit global organization that promotes "the development, adoption, and use of globally accepted, industry-leading knowledge and practices for information systems." They hold conferences and training events related to information systems auditing and management around the world. Visit the ISACA Web site for more information: *http://www.isaca.org*.
Security University	Security University offers a wide range of certification preparation courses in various locations in the U.S., although most courses run in the state of Virginia. More than just certification prep, their courses are very hands-on. They focus on getting personnel to a point of being extremely competent in specific areas. For more information on Security University, visit its Web site: *http://www.securityuniversity.net*.
MIS Training Institute	MIS Training Institute offers a wide range of live and online courses and training events that cover areas including information security management and auditing. MIS Training Institute holds training events in several major cities and provides opportunities for attendees to earn CPEs and prepare for certification exams. For more information on MIS Training Institute, visit its Web site: *http://www.misti.com/*.

CHAPTER SUMMARY

Being a qualified security professional requires pertinent knowledge and skills. You have to understand security issues and be able to act on that understanding. Education and training organizations can provide you with the necessary knowledge and help to develop required skills. You explored several different options to learn more about information security. You learned that self-study is a viable choice in some cases. It is also the least expensive. You learned about continuing education offerings for informal education and degree programs for varying levels of formal education. You also learned about some of the organizations that offer focused training in short courses. Regardless of where or how you acquire additional knowledge and skills, you should have a better understanding of what's out there.

KEY CONCEPTS AND TERMS

Accredited
Certificate of completion
Continuing education
Continuing professional education (CPE)
Distance learning
National Centers of Academic Excellence in Information Assurance Education (CAEIAE)
National Centers of Academic Excellence in Research (CAE-R)
Traditional classroom

CHAPTER 13 ASSESSMENT

1. One of the disadvantages of self-study is that the materials are generally expensive.
   A. True
   B. False

2. Which of the following would be the least likely resource to have current self-study materials?
   A. Online bookstore
   B. Local bookstore
   C. Local library
   D. Online e-library

3. When selecting self-study materials, a vendor that sells many products always has higher-quality products.
   A. True
   B. False

4. Which of the following generally holds classes that do not lead to a degree but is associated with a college or university?
   A. Associate program
   B. Extension program
   C. Continuing education
   D. Professional training organization

5. Which term refers to the unit of credit many certifications require to keep current?
   A. Credit hour
   B. Quality point
   C. GPA
   D. CPE

6. A ________ classroom is one in which students and at least one instructor are all in the same room.

7. Which two organizations sponsor the National Centers of Academic Excellence? (Choose two.)
   A. NSA
   B. HHS
   C. DOD
   D. DHS

8. Which term means that an educational institution has successfully undergone evaluation by an external body to determine whether the institution meets applicable standards?
   A. Certified
   B. Accredited
   C. Audited
   D. Accepted

9. Which U.S. agency requires that all federal agencies provide security training to their employees?
   A. DOD
   B. NIST
   C. OPM
   D. NSA

10. Which of the following is *not* one of the main areas in NIST Special Publication 800-50?
    A. Responsibility
    B. Awareness
    C. Training
    D. Professional development

CHAPTER 14

Information Security Professional Certifications

INFORMATION SECURITY is continually becoming more complex. As more software and hardware products emerge, it becomes more difficult to stay current. In addition, it becomes difficult for employers to identify qualified people they need to keep systems secure.

Today, one of the most common methods for identifying what skills a security professional possesses is certification. A certification proves that the holder has obtained some training. It also may prove that the holder has a certain level of experience and has passed an examination. Each certification attests to a different skill set and has different requirements.

More than 100 certifications relate to information security. These certifications are for personnel ranging from high-level security management to very detailed technical practitioners. Regardless of your interest or experience in the information security field, it is likely there is a certification for you. Certifications can help identify you as someone who has pursued training and complies with industry standards in your chosen specialty. In this chapter, you will learn about the most popular information security certifications and their requirements.

Chapter 14 Topics

This chapter covers the following topics and concepts:

- What vendor-neutral professional certifications are
- What vendor-specific professional certifications are
- What DoD/Military 8570.01 requirements are

Chapter 14 Goals

When you complete this chapter, you will be able to:

- Describe popular vendor-neutral professional certifications
- Identify popular vendor-specific professional certifications
- Explain the DoD/Military 8570.01 requirements

Vendor-Neutral Professional Certifications

A **certification** is an official statement that validates a person has satisfied specific requirements. These requirements often include the following:

- Possessing a certain level of experience
- Completing a course of study
- Passing an examination

An organization that is empowered to state that an individual has met the certification's requirements issues the certification.

While certifications are not perfect, obtaining them is a standard way for security professionals to further their security education and training. Certifications show that a security professional has invested time, effort, and money into learning more about security. Many prospective employers consider security certifications as they screen job applicants. True security expertise involves more than just holding a certification. However, certification preparatory organizations have developed curriculum that does a good job of educating certification candidates as well as preparing them for an exam.

> **NOTE**
>
> A certification does not guarantee that a person is good at a specific job. Unfortunately, there are bad security professionals with certifications. There are also excellent security professionals who hold no certifications.

Certifications target specific areas of knowledge and expertise. There is at least one certification for most security-related job functions and expertise levels. The first type of certification is the **vendor-neutral certification**. This type of certification covers concepts and topics that are general in nature. It does not focus on a specific product or product line. Several organizations provide certifications that the security community recognizes as having high value. The following sections cover some of the many certification organizations and their credentials.

$(ISC)^2$

The International Information Systems Security Certification Consortium, Inc. $(ISC)^2$ is one of the most respected global certification organizations. $(ISC)^2$ is a not-for-profit organization that focuses on educating and certifying security professionals from all experience levels. $(ISC)^2$ offers four main credentials, each addressing a different security professional role. The four main $(ISC)^2$ credentials are as follows:

- Systems Security Certified Practitioner (SSCP)
- Certified Information Systems Security Professional (CISSP)
- Certified Authorization Professional (CAP)
- Certified Secure Software Lifecycle Professional (CSSLP)

Systems Security Certified Practitioner (SSCP)

The Systems Security Certified Practitioner (SSCP) credential enables security practitioners to demonstrate their level of competence. The SSCP covers the seven domains of best practices for information security. $(ISC)^2$ publishes the security best practices in the SSCP Common Body of Knowledge (CBK). The SSCP credential is ideal for those who are working toward or already hold positions as senior network security engineers, senior security systems analysts, or senior security administrators.

Certified Information Systems Security Professional (CISSP)

$(ISC)^2$'s flagship credential is the Certified Information Systems Security Professional (CISSP). The CISSP was the first ANSI/ISO-accredited credential in the field of information security. The CISSP provides information security professionals with an objective measure of competence and a globally recognized standard of achievement. The CISSP credential demonstrates competence in the 10 domains of the $(ISC)^2$ CISSP CBK. The CISSP credential targets middle and senior-level managers who are working toward or already hold positions as chief information security officers (CISOs), chief security officers (CSOs), or senior security engineers.

$(ISC)^2$ offers three CISSP concentration credentials. Each credential enables CISSP credential holders to demonstrate deeper knowledge and skills in a specific area. Each concentration has its own additional requirements and exam. The three CISSP concentrations are as follows:

- Information Systems Security Architecture Professional (ISSAP)
- Information Systems Security Engineering Professional (ISSEP)
- Information Systems Security Management Professional (ISSMP)

Certified Authorization Professional (CAP)

The Certified Authorization Professional (CAP) credential provides a method to measure the knowledge and skills necessary for professionals involved in the process of authorizing and maintaining information systems. The best fits for the CAP credential are personnel responsible for developing and implementing processes used to assess risk and for establishing security requirements. Professionals seeking the CAP credential could include authorization officials, system owners, information owners, information security officers, and certifiers. This credential is appropriate for both private-sector and U.S. government personnel.

Certified Secure Software Lifecycle Professional (CSSLP)

The Certified Secure Software Lifecycle Professional (CSSLP) is one of the few credentials that address developing secure software. The CSSLP credential evaluates professionals for the knowledge and skills necessary to develop and deploy secure applications. This credential is appropriate for software developers, software architects, and anyone involved in the software development and deployment process.

> **NOTE**
> For more information on (ISC)^2 credentials, visit the (ISC)^2 Web site at *http://www.isc2.org*.

GIAC/SANS Institute

The next major certification organization is also a global organization that is ANSI accredited. The Global Information Assurance Certification (GIAC) offers more than 20 individual credentials. These credentials span several information security job disciplines:

- IT audit
- Forensics
- Legal
- Security management
- Security administration
- Software security

GIAC has a close relationship with the SANS Institute. In fact, the SANS Institute provides specific training that prepares students for each of the GIAC credentials. You can pursue individual GIAC credentials or follow a path to earn higher-level credentials.

Anyone who holds a GIAC credential can submit a technical paper that covers an important area of information security. An accepted technical paper adds the Gold credential to the base GIAC credential. The Gold credential enables security professionals to stand out from other credential holders. The GIAC Security Expert (GSE) credential provides another method for security professionals to stand apart from other credential holders. The GSE requirements include holding three GIAC credentials (with two of the credentials being Gold), passing a GSE exam, and completing an intensive two-day hands-on lab. The GSE represents the highest-level credential within GIAC.

Table 14-1 lists the current GIAC credentials.

> **NOTE**
> For more information on GIAC credentials, visit the GIAC Web site at *http://www.giac.org*.

TABLE 14-1 GIAC credentials.

JOB DISCIPLINE	CREDENTIAL
Audit	GIAC Certified ISO-17799 Specialist (G7799) GIAC Systems and Network Auditor (GSNA)
Forensics	GIAC Certified Forensics Examiner (GCFE) GIAC Certified Forensic Analyst (GCFA) GIAC Reverse Engineering Malware (GREM)
Legal	GIAC Legal Issues (GLEG)
Security management	GIAC Information Security Professional (GISP) GIAC Security Leadership Certification (GSLC) GIAC Certified Project Manager Certification (GCPM)
Security administration	GIAC Information Security Fundamentals (GISF) GIAC Security Essentials Certification (GSEC) GIAC Web Application Penetration Tester (GWAPT) GIAC Certified Enterprise Defender (GCED) GIAC Certified Firewall Analyst (GCFW) GIAC Certified Incident Handler (GCIH) GIAC Certified Windows Security Administrator (GCWN) GIAC Certified UNIX Security Administrator (GCUX) GIAC Certified Penetration Tester (GPEN) GIAC Assessing Wireless Networks (GAWN)
Software security	GIAC Secure Software Programmer—.NET (GSSP-NET) GIAC Secure Software Programmer—Java (GSSP-JAVA)

NOTE

For more information about CIW credentials and current requirements, see the CIW Web site at *http://www.ciwcertified.com*.

CIW

Certified Internet Webmaster (CIW) offers several credentials that focus on both general and Web-related security. Several of CIW's advanced credentials require a combination of passing an exam and holding at least one recognized credential from another vendor. CIW uses this blended approach to encourage a breadth of security knowledge and skills. Table 14-2 lists the CIW security-related credentials and their general requirements.

TABLE 14-2 CIW credentials.

CREDENTIAL	REQUIREMENTS
CIW Web Security Associate	Pass Web Security Associate exam (1D0-571)
CIW Web Security Specialist	Pass Web Security Associate exam (1D0-571), plus earn one credential from the CIW-approved credential list
CIW Web Security Professional	Pass Web Security Associate exam (1D0-571), plus earn two credentials from the CIW-approved credential list
CIW Security Analyst	Pass Security Associate exam (1D0-470), plus earn two credentials from the CIW-approved credential list

The CIW-approved credential list contains the credentials from other vendors that satisfy the CIW Web Security Specialist, CIW Web Security Professional, and CIW Security Analyst credentials. Other credentials that satisfy CIW requirements include the following:

- $(ISC)^2$ SCCP or CISSP
- Various GIAC credentials, such as GSE, GCFW, GCIH, etc.
- CompTIA Security+
- Several vendor-specific credentials

CompTIA

CompTIA administers a testing process to validate knowledge within specific IT support functions. Candidates who pass the CompTIA exam can earn a CompTIA credential. Subject-matter experts develop all CompTIA exams. These exams are standard for proving foundation-level skill sets. CompTIA's Security+ certification has become the entry-level information security certification of choice for IT professionals who want to pursue further work and knowledge in this area.

> **NOTE**
> For more information on CompTIA's credentials, visit their Web site at *http://www.comptia.org/certifications.aspx.*

SCP

The Security Certified Program (SCP) is another popular certification organization. SCP offers three certifications for IT security professionals, as well as a separate Security Awareness program for general audiences. The SCP certification programs apply mainly to network security topics and are most appropriate for professionals involved in securing network components within the IT infrastructure. The SCP credentials include the following:

> **NOTE**
> SCP's credentials cover a range of IT network security needs. For more information on SCP's certifications and requirements, visit their Web site at *http://www.securitycertified.net/Certifications.aspx.*

- **Security Certified Network Specialist (SCNS)**—A credential for IT professionals entering the network security environment. The SCNS is a foundational credential that covers important knowledge and skills necessary for solid network security.
- **Security Certified Network Professional (SCNP)**—An intermediate credential for experienced network security professionals. The SCNP goes beyond the scope of the SCNS. It covers prevention techniques, risk analysis, and security policy to address a complete network security environment.
- **Security Certified Network Architect (SCNA)**—A credential primarily targeted for IT managers and advanced IT security professionals. The SCNA focuses on more than just the technical aspects of security. It tackles management and environmental issues such as legal, forensics, organization security policy, and security architecture.

TABLE 14-3 ISACA certifications.

CERTIFICATION	DESCRIPTION
Certified Information Security Manager (CISM)	The CISM certification program is a credential for experienced information security professionals who are involved in security management. It provides a way to measure the knowledge and skills necessary to design, implement, and manage enterprise security programs.
Certified Information Systems Auditor (CISA)	The CISA certification program targets information systems audit, control, and security professionals. It defines and promotes the skills and practices that are the building blocks of success in the IT audit and control field.
Certified in the Governance of Enterprise IT (CGEIT)	The CGEIT is a new ISACA certification program. It targets security professionals who ensure their organization satisfies IT governance requirements. The CGEIT bases its requirements on the ISACA and the IT Governance Institute's (ITGI's) audit and control guidelines, which come from global subject-matter experts.
Certified in Risk and Information Systems Control (CRISC)	The CRISC certification applies to a wide range of security professionals. This certification focuses on the knowledge and skills required to design, deploy, monitor, and manage security controls to address risk. CRISC addresses all risk-management areas, including identification, assessment, response, and monitoring.

ISACA

The Information Systems Audit and Control Association (ISACA) is a nonprofit global organization that promotes "the development, adoption, and use of globally accepted, industry-leading knowledge and practices for information systems." ISACA provides security training at conferences and training events. The organization offers four certification programs for IT security professionals. Table 14-3 lists the ISACA certifications.

> **NOTE**
> You can learn more about ISACA's certifications and their requirements at the ISACA Web site. Visit *http://www.isaca.org* for more information.

Vendor-Specific Professional Certifications

Several vendors of hardware and software products also offer certification programs. These **vendor-specific certifications** help identify professionals who possess in-depth product knowledge. Many organizations use these certifications, along with vendor-neutral certifications, when evaluating prospective employees and personnel. As with vendor-neutral certifications, holding a certification for a specific vendor does not guarantee competence, but it does imply it. If an applicant meets the requirements for a certification, it means he or she has a certain level of knowledge and skills.

In this section, you'll learn about some of the vendor-specific certification programs. Certification programs change frequently. You should visit the vendor Web site for each of the software and hardware products active in your IT infrastructure. You will find that many vendors offer certifications. The following sections introduce a few of the many vendor-specific certifications for security personnel.

Cisco Systems

Cisco Systems is one of the largest manufacturers of network security devices and software. Cisco Systems offers a range of certifications for its networking products. Its training and certification process helps ensure that security professionals who work with Cisco products possess the knowledge and skills they need to secure their environments. Cisco offers several different certification levels along different tracks. These options enable security professionals to focus their efforts on the specific knowledge and skills they need to get the most out of their Cisco equipment.

Cisco offers certifications at five different levels to address the needs of professionals with different experience levels. Entry-level professionals can work their way up the sequence with additional training and experience. Those who already possess substantial Cisco equipment experience may choose to start with a higher level. Cisco offers certifications at these levels:

- Entry
- Associate
- Professional
- Expert
- Architect

Cisco challenges applicants differently depending on the level of certification. Entry-level certifications require only a single exam, while more advanced certifications require multiple courses and exams. Cisco also offers multiple paths for associates, professionals, and experts. These paths enable Cisco credential holders to specialize in specific areas. You can earn a Cisco certification in the following paths:

- Design
- Security
- Voice
- Wireless
- Routing and switching
- Service provider operations

Table 14-4 lists the Cisco certifications.

> **NOTE**
> For more information on Cisco's certification programs, visit the Cisco Web site at *http://www.cisco.com/web/learning/le3/learning_career_certifications_and_learning_paths_home.html.*

TABLE 14-4 Cisco certifications.

LEVEL	CERTIFICATION
Entry	Cisco Certified Entry Networking Technician (CCENT)
Associate	Cisco Certified Design Associate (CCDA) Cisco Certified Routing and Switching Associate (CCNA) Cisco Certified Security Associate (CCNA Security) Cisco Certified Service Provider Operations Associate (CCNA SP Ops) Cisco Certified Voice Associate (CCNA Voice) Cisco Certified Wireless Associate (CCNA Wireless)
Professional	Cisco Certified Design Professional (CCDP) Cisco Certified Routing and Switching Professional (CCNP) Cisco Certified Security Professional (CCSP) Cisco Certified Service Provider Professional (CCIP) Cisco Certified Service Provider Operations Professional (CCNP SP Ops) Cisco Certified Voice Professional (CCVP) Cisco Certified Wireless Professional (CCNP Wireless)
Expert	Cisco Certified Design Expert (CCDE) Cisco Certified Service Provider Operations Expert (CCIE SP Ops) Cisco Certified Routing and Switching Expert (CCIE Routing and Switching) Cisco Certified Security Expert (CCIE Security) Cisco Certified Service Provider Expert (CCIE Service Provider) Cisco Certified Storage Network Expert (CCIE Storage Network) Cisco Certified Voice Expert (CCIE Voice) Cisco Certified Wireless Expert (CCIE Wireless)
Architect	Cisco Certified Architect

TABLE 14-5 Juniper Networks certification levels and tracks.

TRACK	JUNIPER NETWORKS CERTIFIED INTERNET ASSOCIATE (JNCIA)	JUNIPER NETWORKS CERTIFIED INTERNET SPECIALIST (JNCIS)	JUNIPER NETWORKS CERTIFIED INTERNET EXPERT (JNCIE)
Enterprise Routing	Offered	Offered	Offered
Junos Security	Offered	Offered	
Enterprise Switching	Offered		
Enterprise Routing and Switching	Offered	Offered	
Firewall/VPN	Offered	Offered	
Intrusion Detection and Prevention (IDP)	Offered		
Secure Sockets Layer (SSL)	Offered	Offered	Offered
WAN Acceleration (WX)	Offered		
Unified Access Control	Offered		

Juniper Networks

Juniper Networks manufactures a variety of network security hardware and software. Juniper also offers a varied range of certifications for their networking product line. Like Cisco, Juniper Networks offers multiple certification levels and different tracks. Its certifications help personnel who work for organizations that use Juniper Networks hardware to get the most from the products.

Certification candidates can take courses and exams to qualify for certifications at three levels from 10 different tracks. Juniper Networks does not offer certifications at all levels for every track. Table 14-5 shows the Juniper Networks certification levels and the tracks available at each level.

NOTE

For more information on Juniper Networks certifications, visit the Juniper Networks Web site at *http://www.juniper.net/us/en/training/certification/*.

RSA

RSA is a global provider of security, risk, and compliance solutions for enterprise environments. RSA products include identity assurance, data loss prevention, encryption, and tokenization devices. They also provide specific training and certifications to help security professionals acquire and demonstrate the knowledge and skills to use RSA products effectively. Because organizations commonly use RSA products in various capacities in an enterprise environment, RSA offers several certification options. The available RSA certifications include the following:

- RSA SecurID Certified Systems Engineer (CSE)
- RSA SecurID Certified Administrator (CA)
- RSA enVision Certified Systems Engineer (CSE)
- RSA Access Manager Certified Systems Engineer (CSE)
- RSA Digital Certificate Management Solutions Certified Systems Engineer (CSE)
- RSA DLP Suite Certified Systems Engineer (CSE)

> **NOTE**
> For more information on RSA certifications, visit their Web site at *http://www.rsa.com/node.aspx?id=1261*.

> **NOTE**
> At the time of this writing, Symantec was in the process of integrating the Altiris certification program with its own. Be sure to check the Symantec certification Web site, *http://www.symantec.com/business/training/certification/index.jsp*, for the latest list of certifications.

Symantec

The Symantec Corporation provides a wide range of security software products. Like previous vendors, Symantec also offers certifications for its product lines. These certifications provide specific product training and validate practitioners' knowledge and skills related to the Symantec product line.

Here is a list of the available certifications in the Symantec Certified Specialist (SCS) program:

- Symantec Backup Exec for Windows Servers
- Symantec Enterprise Vault
- Veritas Storage Foundation for UNIX
- Veritas Storage Foundation for Windows
- Veritas Cluster Server for UNIX
- Veritas Cluster Server for Windows
- Symantec Endpoint Protection
- Veritas NetBackup for UNIX
- Veritas NetBackup for Windows

> **NOTE**
> For more information about Symantec certifications, visit its Web site at *http://www.symantec.com/business/training/certification/index.jsp*.

Check Point

Check Point is another global manufacturer of network and security devices and software. Check Point provides training and certification paths for security professionals to encourage the highest level of knowledge and skills in the use of Check Point products. Security professionals have several certification options and can choose from among three tracks and three levels. Check Point certifications require that applicants pass an exam that involves 80 percent study materials and 20 percent hands-on experience. Table 14-6 shows the Check Point certifications for each level and track.

> **NOTE**
> For more information on Check Point certifications, visit their Web site at *http://www.checkpoint.com/services/education/certification/index.html*.

TABLE 14-6 Check Point certifications.

LEVEL	SECURITY GATEWAYS TRACK	SECURITY MANAGEMENT TRACK	ENDPOINT SECURITY TRACK
Administrator	Check Point Certified Security Administrator (CCSA)	Offered	Offered
Expert	Check Point Certified Security Expert (CCSE)	Check Point Certified Managed Security Expert (CCMSE)	Check Point Certified Endpoint Expert (CCEPE)
Master	Check Point Certified Master Architect (CCMA)	Check Point Certified Master Architect (CCMA)	

DoD/Military—8570.01

The U.S. Department of Defense (DoD) has developed many standards and requirements to govern nearly every aspect of daily operation and behavior. While not all DoD standards apply directly to information security, some do. The DoD Directive 8570.01, "Information Assurance Training, Certification and Workforce Management," defines many requirements for DoD personnel and contractors with respect to information security. DoD Directive 8570.01 requires "all DoD personnel and contractors who conduct information assurance functions in assigned duty positions to achieve very specific levels of certification." Different jobs carry different certification requirements.

The Gov IT Wiki, *http://govitwiki.com/wiki/8570.01*, is a great resource for additional information on DoD Directive 8570.01. Here, you can find more details about the specific certification requirements for each job type. You can also find explanations of how the requirement may affect your organization or job. In general, DoD Directive 8570.01 affects any DoD facility or contractor organization. It ensures all personnel who are directly involved with information security possess security certifications. The purpose of this directive is to reduce the possibility that unqualified personnel can gain access to secure information.

DoD Directive 8570.01 has created a new segment of opportunity for training and certification organizations. Many providers of security training and certifications target DoD employees and contractors to offer paths to DoD Directive 8570.01 compliance. This mandatory certification requirement has increased the number of personnel who pursue certifications. It also maintains a steady flow of students through security classes to earn CPEs to keep credentials current. While some have questioned its effectiveness, DoD Directive 8570.01 has increased the number of security personnel seeking ongoing security training.

CHAPTER SUMMARY

In this chapter, you learned about some of the available security certifications. Although security certifications don't guarantee competence, they can provide employers with confidence that the credential holder possesses a standard level of knowledge and skills. Most organizations issue credentials for limited periods, so you can also determine that a current credential relates to current knowledge and skills. You learned about vendor-neutral and vendor-specific certifications. You also learned about DoD Directive 8570.01 and how it has increased demand for certification.

You should use certifications to help direct your learning and measure your knowledge and experience in information security. However, don't measure your value or abilities only by the number of certifications you hold. Employers do use certifications to help assess prospects, but the best assessment is the prospect's actual performance.

KEY CONCEPTS AND TERMS

Certification
Vendor-neutral certification
Vendor-specific certification

CHAPTER 14 ASSESSMENT

1. A certification is an official statement that validates a person has satisfied specific requirements.

A. True
B. False

2. Which (ISC)^2 certification covers seven domains of security for practitioners?

A. CISM
B. CCNA
C. SSCP
D. GSEC

3. Which (ISC)^2 certification specifically addresses developing secure software?

A. CISSP
B. CSSLP
C. GSEC
D. CISA

4. Which certification is the highest level GIAC credential?

A. CAP
B. GSEC
C. GCIH
D. GSE

5. The ________ Specialist, Professional, and Analyst certifications require that you hold one or more certifications from other vendors.

6. Which CompTIA certification targets foundational security topics?

A. Security+
B. TIA practitioner
C. TIA+
D. InfoSec practitioner

7. Which ISACA certification applies to security auditors?

A. CISSP
B. CISA
C. GSEC
D. CCNA

8. Which network device manufacturer offers certifications in five levels: entry, associate, professional, expert, and architect?

A. Cisco
B. Check Point
C. Juniper Networks
D. Symantec

9. Which vendor offers separate certifications for its products in UNIX and Windows environments?

A. Cisco
B. Check Point
C. Juniper Networks
D. Symantec

10. What is the main purpose of DoD Directive 8570.01?

A. It requires personnel to acquire security training.
B. It requires personnel to acquire security certifications.
C. It requires DoD facilities and contractors to provide security training.
D. It requires DoD facilities and contractors to enforce security policies.

CHAPTER

15 U.S. Compliance Laws

CYBERSPACE BRINGS NEW THREATS to U.S. citizens and organizations. People are sharing more data than ever before. People share data online to purchase goods and services. They also share data to network with colleagues and connect with friends. Organizations collect and use data to conduct business. Federal and state governments collect and use information to provide for their citizens.

With the increased collection of data come questions about proper use of it. People demand that the organizations entrusted with their sensitive data take steps to protect it. If the organizations don't voluntarily protect that data, people often say, "There ought to be a law." The United States doesn't have one comprehensive data protection law. Instead, many federal data protection laws focus on specific types of data. These laws require organizations to use security controls to protect the different kinds of data that they collect. Laws aren't optional. If a law applies to an organization, the organization must follow it. Sometimes organizations must follow a number of data protection laws. This chapter discusses the major federal data protection laws. It focuses on the information security protections that those laws require.

Chapter 15 Topics

This chapter covers the following topics and concepts:

- What compliance is
- What the Federal Information Security Management Act is
- What the Health Insurance Portability and Accountability Act is
- What the Gramm-Leach-Bliley-Act is
- What the Sarbanes-Oxley Act is
- What the Family Educational Rights and Privacy Act is
- What the Children's Internet Protection Act is
- How to make sense of information security compliance laws

Chapter 15 Goals

When you complete this chapter, you will be able to:

- Explain what compliance is and how it's related to information security
- Describe the main features of the Federal Information Security Management Act
- Describe the main features of the Health Insurance Portability and Accountability Act
- Describe the main features of the Gramm-Leach-Bliley Act
- Describe the main features of the Sarbanes-Oxley Act
- Describe the main features of the Family Educational Rights and Privacy Act
- Describe the main features of the Children's Internet Protection Act

Compliance and the Law

Organizations use and store a lot of data. For many, information is one of their most important assets. They use it to conduct business. They use large and complex databases to keep track of customer product preferences. They use these same information technology (IT) systems to manage the products and services that they offer customers. Organizations also transfer data to other businesses. They often collect data that most people consider sensitive. This is data that you can use to identify a person. It's called **personally identifiable information (PII)**. PII includes the following:

- Social Security numbers
- Driver's license numbers
- Financial account data, such as account numbers or personal identification numbers (PINs)
- Health data and biometric data
- Authentication credentials, such as logon or usernames and passwords

Unfortunately, organizations sometimes don't do a very good job of protecting PII. They might lose the data in a security breach. They also could use it in ways their customers and clients don't approve. When organizations don't voluntarily protect PII, governments create laws that force them to. Once the laws are enacted, these organizations must follow them. This is called compliance.

Compliance is an important concept. In the legal system, compliance is the act of following laws, rules, and regulations that apply to you. For an organization, compliance involves not only following laws and regulations, but also following the organization's own policies and procedures. An organization must document its compliance activities. It's not enough for an organization to say that it's compliant with the laws. It must prove that it's compliant.

Organizations use a number of different activities to show compliance, including:

- Creating policies and procedures to comply with legal or regulatory requirements
- Comparing compliance requirements against the organization's daily practices, and modifying those practices as needed
- Developing and using monitoring systems in computer systems to alert the organization if legally required security controls are compromised
- Creating training and awareness activities that educate employees about compliance requirements

> **TIP**
>
> An organization must show that it's complying with laws every day. It does this through its policies and operating procedures.

Compliance not only includes the actual state of being compliant, it also includes the steps and processes taken to become compliant. Compliance usually asks the questions: What are the rules? How must the rules be followed? If an organization fails to meet its obligations, it can be subject to penalties.

The United States doesn't have one comprehensive data protection law. Instead, many laws focus on different types of data found in different industries. These laws contain privacy and information security concepts. They also focus on how that data is used. A number of federal agencies regulate compliance with these types of laws. You will learn briefly about these laws in this chapter. Each one of these laws is long and detailed. Each one could easily be a book topic on its own. Table 15-1 lists these laws, the type of data they address, and the federal government authority that regulates compliance with them.

As a systems security professional, you must be familiar with these laws. You must understand how they affect your organization. Knowing about these laws won't make you qualified to practice law. That's the job of an attorney. However, you should be able

TABLE 15-1 Laws that influence information security.

NAME OF LAW	INFORMATION REGULATED	REGULATING AGENCY
Children's Internet Protection Act	Internet access in certain schools and libraries	FTC
Family Educational Rights and Privacy Act	Student educational records	U.S. Department of Education
Federal Information Systems Management Act	Federal information systems	Office of Management and Budget
Gramm-Leach-Bliley Act	Consumer financial information	FTC
Health Insurance Portability and Accountability Act	Protected health information	Department of Health and Human Services
Sarbanes-Oxley Act	Corporate financial information	Securities and Exchange Commission

How Are Privacy and Information Security Related?

Most federal data protection laws contain both privacy and information security requirements. Information security and privacy are closely related. However, it's important for you to know that they're not the same. Privacy is a person's right to control the use and disclosure of his or her own personal information. It means that people have the opportunity to assess a situation and determine how their data is used. Information security is the process used to keep data private. Security is the process; privacy is a result.

Privacy is a simple term that describes a number of different but related concepts. At its core, privacy means that a person has control of his or her personal data. "Control" means that a person can decide how his or her data can be collected, used, and shared. It means that a person gets to decide how to share his or her personal data with third parties.

Most traditional views on privacy also include the belief that the government's power to interfere in the privacy of its citizens is limited. This means that people and their information must be free from unreasonable government intrusion. The government must not investigate people or their personal information without a good reason. Courts spend a lot of time defining the reasons to allow governments to investigate their citizens. This is a core privacy concept for most Americans.

Information security is about protecting IT systems and data to ensure their confidentiality, availability, and integrity for an organization's business purposes. Just because information is secure doesn't mean it's private. Many people can have access to electronic data that is considered "secure" for information security purposes.

Privacy with respect to IT systems means that people have control and can make choices about how their information will be used by that system. Security is used to carry out those choices. Privacy can't exist in information systems without security.

to identify which laws apply to your organization. You also must be able to discuss these laws with attorneys. Many organization's executive management and attorneys aren't familiar with how the organization's IT systems operate. It will be up to you to help bridge the gap to make sure that your organization understands how the law influences systems security decisions.

The Federal Information Security Management Act

The federal government is the largest creator and user of information in the United States.[1] Government IT systems hold data that's critical for government operations. They contain data that's important for running the business of the federal government. They also hold sensitive military data. These systems also hold personal information about U.S. citizens. All of this personal data is very sensitive, too.

Federal IT systems and the data in them are attractive criminal targets. In 2010, the federal chief information officer (CIO), Vivek Kundra, said that the government's computers are attacked millions of times each day.[2] This isn't very surprising.

Congress created the Federal Information Security Management Act (FISMA) in 2002.[3] This Act was created partly in response to the September 11, 2001, terrorist attacks. The attacks stressed the need for better information security in the federal government. After the attacks, the government realized that computer security for federal IT systems wasn't what it should be. FISMA changed the government's approach to information security. It superseded most of the federal government's previous computer security laws. It's now the main law that defines how federal agencies must secure their IT systems.

FISMA applies to federal agencies and their IT systems. Federal agencies fall under the executive branch of the U.S. government. They report to the president. The Office of Management and Budget (OMB) is responsible for FISMA compliance.

Purpose and Main Requirements

FISMA defines "information security" as protecting federal agency IT systems to provide confidentiality, integrity, and availability.[4] Agencies must protect their IT systems (and data in those systems) from unauthorized use, access, disruption, modification, and destruction.

FISMA requires each federal agency to create an agency-wide information security program that includes:

- **Risk assessments**—Agencies must perform risk assessments. They must measure the harm that could result from unauthorized access to or use of their IT systems. Agencies must base their information security programs on the results of these risk assessments.
- **Annual inventory**—Agencies must inventory their IT systems. They must update it each year.
- **Policies and procedures**—Agencies must create policies and procedures to reduce risk to an acceptable level. The policies must protect IT systems throughout their life cycles. Agencies also must create configuration management policies.
- **Subordinate plans**—Agencies must make sure they have plans for securing networks, facilities, and systems or groups of IT systems. These plans are for technologies or system components that are a part of the larger information security program.
- **Security awareness training**—Agencies must give training to employees and any other users of their IT systems, including contractors. This training must make people aware of risks to the agency's IT systems. It also must make them aware of their duties to protect these systems.
- **Testing and evaluation**—Agencies must test their security controls at least once a year. They must test management, operational, and technical controls for each IT system.

- **Remedial actions**—Agencies must have a plan to fix weaknesses in their information security program.
- **Incident response**—Agencies must have an incident response procedure. They must state how the agency detects and resolves incidents. Agencies also must report incidents to the Department of Homeland Security (DHS).
- **Continuity of operations**—Agencies must have business continuity plans as part of their information security programs.

An agency's information security program applies to any other organization that uses the agency's IT systems or data. An agency must protect the IT systems that support its operations. It must protect them even if another agency or contractor owns the IT systems. This can broaden the scope of FISMA beyond a federal agency. This is important because IT systems and functions are often outsourced. Systems security professionals must know if any of their organization's IT systems use or process information belonging to federal agencies. If they do, then FISMA may apply.

One of the most important parts of a FISMA information security program is that agencies test and evaluate it. FISMA requires agencies to test their IT systems at least yearly. They must test IT systems with greater risk more often. Agencies also must review the information security controls on these systems. FISMA requires agencies to apply some types of controls, such as access control measures. Agencies must make sure their controls work. Yearly testing recognizes that security is an ongoing process. Agencies must always monitor their security risk. They also must monitor the controls put in place to address that risk.

> **NOTE**
> Under FISMA, agencies must name a senior official in charge of information security. In most cases, this is the chief information security officer (CISO). These officials must be information security professionals with security experience.[5]

Each agency must report yearly to the OMB on its FISMA compliance work. The report must review the agency's information security program. It also must assess the agency's progress on fixing any weaknesses in the program or security controls. An agency's report is shared widely. An agency must send a copy to certain congressional committees and other federal agencies. The OMB says that agencies shouldn't include too much information about actual IT system operations in their reports. It's possible that criminals could learn about weaknesses in federal IT systems by reading the reports.

The FISMA yearly reporting process is time consuming. Agencies spend a lot of time creating their reports. The OMB spends a lot of time reviewing them. It takes almost three full-time employees over a month to review the reports.[6] The process also is very paper-intensive. For example, in six years the Department of State spent $133 million to produce 95,000 pages of paper to meet its reporting requirements.[7] In 2010, the OMB began requiring all federal agencies to file their reports electronically. The new electronic reporting tool will allow agencies and the OMB to assess quickly the agency's information security posture.[8]

> **NOTE**
> You can read the OMB's 2010 FISMA report instructions at *http://www.whitehouse.gov/omb/assets/memoranda_2010/m10-15.pdf.*

The Role of the National Institute of Standards and Technology

FISMA requires the U.S. Department of Commerce to create information security standards and guidelines. The Department of Commerce delegated this duty to one of its agencies, the National Institute of Standards and Technology (NIST). It creates guidance that all federal agencies use for their information security programs. NIST creates standards that agencies use to classify their data and IT systems. It also creates guidelines and minimum information security controls for IT systems. Agencies must follow these standards and guidelines.

> **NOTE**
> Generally, a *standard* states mandatory actions that an organization must take to protect its IT systems. A *guideline* states recommended actions that an organization should follow.

NIST creates two different types of documents. They are called Federal Information Processing Standards (FIPSs) and Special Publications (SPs). FIPS are standards. SPs are guidelines. Under FISMA, federal agencies must follow both FIPS and SPs.

FIGURE 15-1

Risk management framework process.

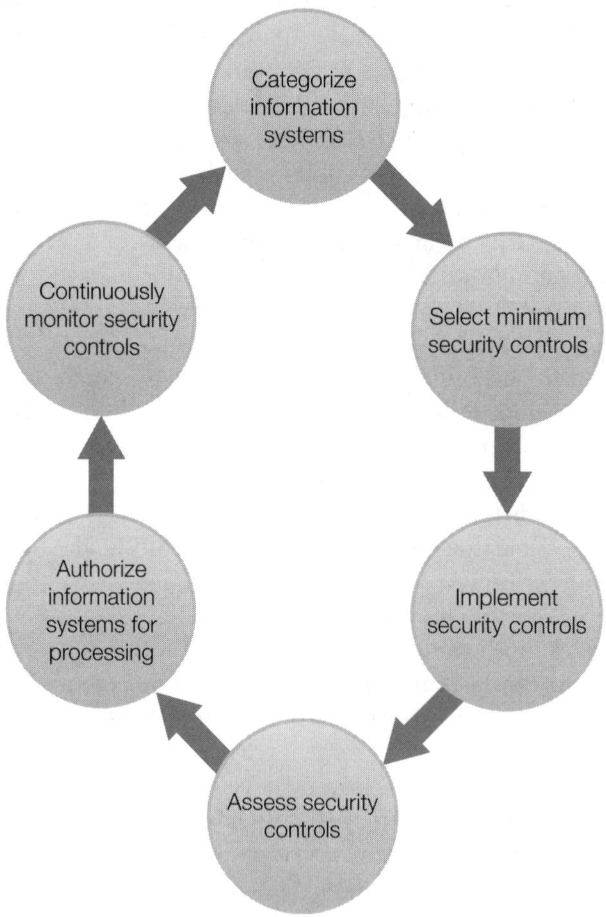

United States Computer Emergency Readiness Team (US-CERT)

Under FISMA, the government must have a federal incident response (IR) center. The OMB is responsible for this. In 2003, the Department of Homeland Security was given the responsibility to run a federal IR center. It absorbed its predecessor into a new IR center. The DHS center is called the United States Computer Emergency Readiness Team, or US-CERT.

Under FISMA, all federal agencies must report security incidents to the US-CERT. This includes incidents involving national security systems. An incident is a violation of computer security policies or practices. It also includes an imminent threat of violation of these policies or practices. The government has six incident response categories. Agencies must report incidents within certain time periods. The reporting period depends upon the incident category. Some incidents must be reported as soon as they are discovered.

From October to December 2008, agencies reported scans, probes, and attempted access incidents to the US-CERT the most often. They were 74 percent of all reported incidents. You can read the report at *http://www.us-cert.gov/press_room/trendsanalysisQ109.pdf*.

NIST recommends using a risk management framework (RMF) approach to FISMA compliance.[9] It approved this framework in February 2010. This approach helps protect IT systems during their whole life cycle. The NIST RMF outlines six steps to protect federal IT systems. They are:

- **Categorize information systems**—An agency must sort its IT systems based on risk.
- **Select the minimum security controls**—An agency must select controls for its IT systems based on their risk category.
- **Implement security controls in IT systems**—An agency must apply controls in certain areas that are specified by NIST. Included in these areas are access control, contingency planning, and incident response.
- **Assess security controls for effectiveness**—An agency must assess its controls on a continuous basis to make sure that they're effective in reducing risk.
- **Authorize the IT system for processing**—An agency must test its IT systems and approve their operation. An agency specifically must accept the risks of operation prior to allowing a system to operate. This process used to be known in FISMA terminology as "certification and accreditation."
- **Continuously monitor security controls**—An agency must monitor its security controls continuously to make sure they're effective. They also must document any changes to their IT systems. They must assess changes for new risks.

NIST's RMF recommends a continuous process of categorization and assessment. It also requires continuous monitoring. Figure 15-1 shows the RMF process.

National Security Systems

FISMA requires federal agencies to secure national security systems (NSSs) using a risk-based approach. These systems are used for:

- Intelligence activities
- National defense
- Foreign policy
- Military activities

These systems must be specially protected due to their national security significance.

The Committee on National Security Systems (CNSS) oversees FISMA activities. The CNSS reports to the president of the United States. It has 21 voting members. They include officials from the National Security Administration (NSA), Central Intelligence Agency (CIA), and Department of Defense (DoD). You can learn about the CNSS at *www.cnss.gov*.

Federal agencies with national security systems must follow CNSS policies, which use a six-step process for protecting these systems. This process is the same as the NIST RMF. NIST and the CNSS worked together to create them.

Oversight

The OMB is responsible for making sure that federal agencies meet their FISMA obligations. It has broad powers. It can withhold funding from agencies that fail to follow the law. The OMB shares some oversight responsibility with other agencies. The responsibility is shared for NSSs. For example, the DoD has FISMA responsibility for NSSs that hold military data. The CIA has responsibility for NSSs with intelligence data.

The Future of FISMA

Even as this book is being written, the federal government's approach to FISMA is changing. In late 2009, the government began to review how it protects data in federal IT systems. The government wants to move from a compliance-based approach to a risk management approach. The new electronic reporting tool introduced in 2010 is part of this new, comprehensive approach. In addition, agencies with FISMA oversight responsibilities are starting to work together. They want to create a unified government-wide

FYI

In 2009, President Barack Obama ordered a review of cyberspace policy. The final report is called the "Cyberspace Policy Review." This review is influencing the government's new information security strategy. You can read it at *http://www.whitehouse.gov/administration/eop/nsc/cybersecurity*.

information security risk management structure. This will help eliminate confusion and complexity. It will allow agencies to help one another with information security.

The government is expected to make more changes in IT security. A House Oversight and Government Reform subcommittee held a FISMA hearing in March 2010. It focused on federal information security challenges. Witnesses said that FISMA did improve federal information security. They also said more work must be done to protect the government's IT systems. At this writing, Congress is considering possible FISMA amendments. Both the House and the Senate introduced bills in early 2010 to amend it.

As a systems security professional, you must keep up with changes to the law because they could affect the information systems you protect.

The Health Insurance Portability and Accountability Act

Most people consider their health information to be among the most sensitive types of personal information. It can be full of private details. People share this information with health care providers to receive treatment. Their medical records include details on illness diagnoses, lab results, and treatment options. These records also contain details about lifestyle, chronic conditions, or mental health counseling.

People fear they will be embarrassed if their health data isn't kept secret. Some people may even fear for their lives if particularly intimate facts, such as reasons for health counseling, are disclosed. Other people may fear that insurance companies or employers could reject them because of information in their health records.

People often feel that they have little control over how their health information is shared and protected. Almost every day media reports confirm that these are valid concerns. For example, in November 2009, Health Net of the Northeast, Inc. reported that 1.5 million patient records were affected when it lost an external hard drive. The hard drive also contained the personal information of physicians who participated in its network. The data on the drive wasn't encrypted.

The federal government recognizes that health information is highly sensitive. It created the Health Insurance Portability and Accountability Act to protect it.

Purpose and Scope

Congress passed the Health Insurance Portability and Accountability Act (HIPAA) in 1996. It was amended in 2009 by the Health Information Technology for Economic and Clinical Health (HITECH) Act. HIPAA is best known for its data protection rules. They address the security and privacy of personally identifiable health information. The Department of Health and Human Services (HHS) makes these rules and oversees their compliance.

> **NOTE**
> PHI includes notes that your doctor puts in your medical record. It also includes any conversations your doctor has with anyone else about your health care. Billing information for health care goods and services provided to you is PHI. Information that your health insurance company has about your health care may also be PHI.

HIPAA applies to **protected health information (PHI)**. PHI is any individually identifiable information about a person's health. It includes mental and physical health data. PHI includes past, present, or future information.[10] It also includes information about paying for health care. PHI can be in any form. It's commonly considered to be all information that is put in a person's medical record.

Under HIPAA, covered entities may only use PHI in certain ways. The term **covered entity** is defined by the law. It refers to very specific types of entities that must follow HIPAA. They include:

- Health plans
- Health care clearinghouses
- Any health care provider that transmits PHI in an electronic form

Determining which entities are covered under HIPAA can be complicated. Generally speaking, HIPAA covers most health care providers. HHS provides tools to help entities determine whether they're covered by HIPAA. Those tools are available at *http://www.hhs.gov/ocr/privacy/hipaa/understanding/coveredentities/index.html.*

HIPAA also applies to the **business associates** of covered entities. A business associate is an organization that performs a health care activity for a covered entity. Covered entities may outsource some health care functions, such as claims and billing, to these organizations. They must comply with HIPAA. Under the HITECH Act, HHS may directly require business associates to comply with HIPAA.

Covered entities that use PHI must follow the HIPAA Privacy and Security Rules.

Main Requirements of the HIPAA Privacy Rule

The Privacy Rule determines how covered entities must protect the privacy of PHI. HHS published the final Privacy Rule in December 2000. Compliance with the Privacy Rule was required in April 2003. The Privacy Rule is the first time the U.S. government has specified federal privacy protections for PHI.

Under the Privacy Rule, covered entities may not use or disclose a person's PHI without his or her written consent. The term **use** refers to how a covered entity shares or handles PHI within its organization. **Disclosure** refers to how a covered entity shares PHI with other organizations that may not be affiliated with it.

There are some exceptions to the Privacy Rule. These exceptions allow a covered entity to share a person's PHI without a person's written consent. The main permitted use and disclosure of PHI under the Privacy Rule is for the entity's own treatment, payment or health care operations. A covered entity doesn't need a person's written consent to share PHI for this purpose because it's assumed that most people want their health care providers to use their PHI to provide medical treatment. Treatment, payment and health care operations are common covered entity activities. Requiring a person's written consent to complete these functions would be inefficient.

There are other times a covered entity may disclose PHI without consent such as reporting victims of child abuse and neglect. The rules for disclosing PHI without consent are complicated. Covered entities must analyze the rules carefully to make sure that they follow them.

Even if a covered entity is allowed to use or disclose PHI without written consent, it must follow the **minimum necessary rule**.[11] A covered entity may disclose the amount of PHI necessary to satisfy the reason why the information is being used or disclosed, but no more. A covered entity must use its professional judgment and make reasonable efforts to limit its use or disclosure. A health care provider shouldn't disclose a person's entire medical record if only a portion of it is needed to respond to a request.

A covered entity must inform people about how it uses and discloses PHI.[12] It does this in a privacy notice. The covered entity must only use and disclose PHI in the ways described by this notice. The Privacy Rule has many requirements for how these notices must be written. The most important requirement is that a covered entity use plain language to draft its notice. An average person must be able to understand it.

The Privacy Rule requires covered entities to mitigate an unauthorized use or disclosure of PHI.[13] Prior to the HITECH Act, a covered entity didn't have to notify people if their PHI was used or disclosed in an unauthorized manner. The HITECH Act now requires them to do so. It creates notification requirements that covered entities must follow in the event of a breach of unsecured PHI.[14] PHI must be encrypted through an HHS-approved process to be considered secure.

NOTE

Under HIPAA, a "breach" is any impermissible use or disclosure of unsecured PHI that harms its security or privacy. The use or disclosure must cause a significant risk of harm to the affected person. The harm can be financial or reputational.[15]

Both covered entities and business associates must follow the breach notification rules. If a covered entity has a breach of unsecured PHI, it must notify the victims within 60 days of the discovery. A breach is "discovered" on the first day that the covered entity knows about it. Individuals must be notified without "unreasonable delay." A covered entity may delay notification if a law enforcement official requests it. HIPAA has many rules for how notice of a breach must be given.

Under the breach notification rules, business associates also are required to notify covered entities following their discovery of a breach of unsecured PHI. The business associate must tell the covered entity no later than 60 days after it discovers the breach. It must help the covered entity notify victims.

TABLE 15-2 Security Rule administrative safeguards.

SAFEGUARD	REQUIRED SPECIFICATIONS	ADDRESSABLE SPECIFICATIONS
Security Management Process	• Risk Analysis • Risk Management • Sanction Policy • Information System Activity Review	
Name an Official Responsible for Security Rule Compliance	Required	
Workforce Security Measures to Protect EPHI		• Authorization and/or Supervision • Workforce Clearance Procedure • Termination Procedures
EPHI Access Management	• Isolating Health Care Clearinghouse Function	• Access Authorization • Access Establishment and Modification
Security Awareness and Training		• Security Reminders • Protection from Malicious Software • Log-in Monitoring • Password Management
Security Incident Procedures	• Response and Reporting	
Contingency Plan	• Data Backup Plan • Disaster Recovery Plan • Emergency Mode Operation Plan	• Testing and Revision Procedure • Applications and Data Criticality Analysis
Evaluation of Security Safeguards Program	Required	
Business Associate Contracts and Other Arrangements	• Written Contracts or Other Arrangements	

Main Requirements of the HIPAA Security Rule

Since 2005, the Health and Human Service Department's Security Rule requires covered entities to protect the confidentiality, integrity, and availability of electronic PHI. This rule requires covered entities to use security safeguards to protect **electronic protected health information (EPHI)**. EPHI is PHI that is stored in electronic form.

Like the Privacy Rule, the Security Rule was the first time the federal government addressed security safeguards for electronic PHI. The rule requires covered entities to protect all EPHI they create, receive, or maintain. They also must protect EPHI they transmit.[16] They must protect EPHI from reasonably anticipated threats. They also must guard it from uses or disclosures that aren't allowed by the Privacy Rule.

The Security Rule requires covered entities to create an information security program.[17] They have flexibility in creating these programs. They don't have to use specific types of security technology. To create its program, the covered entity must consider:

- Its size and complexity
- Its technical infrastructure, hardware, and software security resources
- The costs of security measures
- The potential risks to EPHI[18]

The Security Rule also requires covered entities to use information security principles to protect EPHI. They must use administrative, physical, and technical safeguards. The rule contains instructions on each type of safeguard. Some safeguards are "required." Covered entities must implement them. Others are "addressable." Covered entities have discretion in implementing addressable specifications. For addressable specifications, the entity must assess whether the control is reasonable and appropriate in its environment.[19] If it is, then the covered entity must use it. If it isn't, the covered entity doesn't have to use it.

> **NOTE**
> An information security safeguard is also called an information security control. Different laws use either the term safeguard or control. Sometimes laws use these terms interchangeably. They mean the same thing.

Half of the safeguards required by the Security Rule are administrative controls. They are actions, policies, and procedures that a covered entity must implement to follow the Security Rule. There are nine different administrative safeguards. Table 15-2 summarizes them.

Physical safeguards are controls put in place to protect a covered entity's physical resources. They protect information systems, equipment, and buildings from environmental threats. The Security Rule contains four physical security standards. Table 15-3 summarizes the required and addressable physical safeguards required by the Security Rule.

TABLE 15-3 Security Rule physical safeguards.

SAFEGUARD	REQUIRED SPECIFICATIONS	ADDRESSABLE SPECIFICATIONS
Facility Access Controls		• Contingency Operations • Facility Security Plan • Access Control and Validation Procedures • Maintenance Records
Workstation Use	Required	
Workstation Security	Required	
Device and Media Controls	• Disposal • Media Reuse	• Accountability • Data Backup and Storage

TABLE 15-4 Security Rule technical safeguards.

SAFEGUARD	REQUIRED SPECIFICATIONS	ADDRESSABLE SPECIFICATIONS
Access Control	• Unique User Identification • Emergency Access Procedure	• Automatic Logoff • Encryption and Decryption
Audit Controls	Required	
Integrity		• Mechanism to Authenticate Electronic Protected Health Information
Person or Entity Authentication	Required	
Transmission Security		• Integrity Controls • Encryption

Technical safeguards are applied in the hardware and software of an information system. The Security Rule contains five technical security standards. Table 15-4 summarizes the required and addressable technical safeguards required by the Security Rule.

Oversight

HHS oversees compliance with the HIPAA Privacy and Security Rules. It delegated this function to its Office for Civil Rights (OCR). The OCR enforces both rules against covered entities and against business associates. The OCR investigates and responds to complaints from people who claim that a covered entity has violated HIPAA.

The OCR can fine covered entities that don't comply with these rules. The HITECH Act created a new penalty structure. It allows the OCR to fine a covered entity up to $1.5 million a year for Security or Privacy Rule violations. Minimum fines range from $100 to $50,000 per violation.

> **NOTE**
> A flowchart of the OCR complaint process is available at *http://www.hhs.gov/ocr/privacy/hipaa/enforcement/process/index.html*.

The Gramm-Leach-Bliley Act

In 2008, 285 million records were compromised in data breaches. Credit card data and personally identifiable information were the top two types of compromised records. This is because of their sensitivity. These records can be used to commit identity theft. Almost all of the compromised records—93 percent—were in the financial industry. Organized crime committed almost all of the thefts—91 percent.[20] Criminals hoped to gain consumer financial information.

Consumer financial information is personally identifiable information. It's information that a person provides to a vendor to get a good or service. Customers can provide it to get services from banks or other financial institutions. These institutions collect and use this data to provide home or car loans, credit cards, or to open checking accounts. Consumers demand that their financial institutions protect it.

> **NOTE**
> A study estimated that identity theft cost the U.S. economy $54 billion in 2009. This is the cost to consumer victims, financial institutions, and merchants.

The Gramm-Leach-Bliley Act (GLBA) addresses the privacy and security of consumer financial information. GLBA is also known as the Financial Services Modernization Act of 1999. This law made great changes in the banking industry. Its main purpose was to allow banks, securities, and insurance companies to merge. This wasn't allowed before GLBA. The financial industry urged Congress to pass GLBA so that customers could use one company for all their financial service needs.

After GLBA, these new, larger corporations would have access to large amounts of consumer financial information. People feared that their privacy would suffer. To help ease that fear, Congress included privacy and security protections in GLBA.

Purpose and Scope

Financial institutions must follow GLBA because they engage in financial activities. They include borrowing, lending, credit counseling, debt collection, or similar activities. They are transactions that have to do with money or investments. This definition is very broad. Any institution that engages in these activities must follow GLBA. GLBA applies to consumer financial activities only. They're transactions made for personal, family, or household services. GLBA doesn't apply to business transactions.

GLBA requires financial institutions to protect consumers' nonpublic financial information. **Nonpublic personal information (NPI)** is personally identifiable financial information that a consumer gives to a financial institution. It's the data that a consumer shares during a financial transaction. NPI also includes PII that an institution gets from sources other than a consumer. NPI can be in paper or electronic form. Under GLBA, NPI includes:

> **NOTE**
> NPI doesn't include a consumer's publicly available information. For example, a person's address in a phone book is publicly available.

- Social Security number
- Financial account numbers
- Credit card numbers
- Date of birth
- Name, address, and phone numbers when collected with financial data
- Details of any transactions or the fact that an individual is a customer of a financial institution

GLBA is a complicated law. Compliance can be tricky. One reason is that different federal agencies have GLBA oversight responsibilities. Their responsibilities are based on the type of financial institution under review. The agencies with GLBA oversight responsibilities are:

- **The Securities and Exchange Commission (SEC)**—Oversees securities brokers and dealers.
- **The Federal Reserve System (the Fed)**—Oversees state-chartered member banks and bank holding companies.
- **The Federal Deposit Insurance Corporation (FDIC)**—Oversees state-chartered banks that aren't members of the Fed.
- **The National Credit Union Administration (NCUA)**—Oversees federally insured credit unions.
- **The Office of the Comptroller of the Currency (OCC)**—Oversees nationally chartered banks.
- **The Office of Thrift Supervision (OTS)**—Oversees all nationally chartered and some state-chartered thrifts.
- **Federal Trade Commission (FTC)**—Oversees GLBA for any financial institution that isn't regulated by one of the other agencies.

Main Requirements of the GLBA Privacy Rule

The GLBA Privacy Rule[21] went into effect July 1, 2001. All of the GLBA regulatory agencies worked together to create it. Under this rule, a financial institution may not share a consumer's NPI with nonaffiliated third parties. A financial institution can share this information only when it first provides the consumer with notice of its privacy practices. This notice must tell consumers about the types of data that the institution collects. It also must state how the institution uses the collected information. The notice also must describe how the institution protects a consumer's NPI. The Privacy Rule requires that consumers have a chance to opt out of certain types of data sharing with nonaffiliated third parties.

> **NOTE**
>
> A "nonaffiliated party" is an entity that isn't legally related to a financial institution. It is not the same as an affiliated party. Affiliated parties have a legal relationship. They are members of the same corporate family. An "affiliated party" is any entity that controls, is controlled by, or is under the common control of another entity. Nonaffiliated parties don't have these legal relationships with one another.

GLBA distinguishes between customers and consumers for its notice requirements. A "consumer" is any person who gets a consumer financial product or service from a financial institution. A "customer" is a consumer who has a continuing relationship with the institution. An example of a consumer without a customer relationship is a person who withdraws cash from an ATM that doesn't belong to his or her personal bank. The person is a consumer of the bank's ATM service, but he or she is not a customer of that bank. Customers must receive the financial institution's privacy notices. A financial institution doesn't have to give a privacy notice to a consumer if it doesn't share the consumer's NPI with nonaffiliated parties.

An institution must give a customer notice of its privacy practices as soon as the customer relationship begins. Customers also must receive a copy of the privacy notice each year for as long as the relationship continues. The notice must be provided in writing and be understandable.

Financial institutions must give their privacy notice to consumers if they plan to share the consumer's NPI with nonaffiliated parties. The privacy notice must give the consumer a chance to stop the financial institution from sharing the consumer's NPI with nonaffiliated third parties. This is called an "opt out" provision. The privacy notice must tell consumers how to opt out. If a consumer doesn't opt out, then the financial institution can share NPI in ways described by its privacy notice.

GLBA doesn't give consumers the right to opt out of situations where a financial institution shares NPI with its affiliates. In some instances consumers don't have the ability to opt out at all. For example, consumers can't opt out of a disclosure that is required by law.

Main Requirements of the GLBA Safeguards Rule

GLBA requires the agencies that regulate financial institutions to issue security standards for those institutions to follow. This requirement is called the Safeguards Rule. The law requires each agency to create security standards that:

- Protect the security and confidentiality of customer data.
- Protect against threats to the security or integrity of customer data.
- Protect against unauthorized access to or use of customer data that could result in harm to a customer.[22]

Unlike the Privacy Rule, the agencies with GLBA oversight responsibilities didn't work together to create one safeguards rule. The SEC issued its rule in June 2000. The Fed, FDIC, NCUA, OCC, and OTS worked together to issue a joint rule in early 2001. The FTC issued its Safeguards Rule in May 2002. These rules are all very similar to one another. For simplicity's sake, this section will refer to the FTC Safeguards Rule.

The FTC Safeguards Rule[23] requires a financial institution to create a written "information security program." The program must state how the institution collects and uses customer data. It also must describe the controls used to protect that data. Financial institutions must use administrative, technical, or physical controls. The program must protect information in paper and electronic form.

The Safeguards Rule allows financial institutions some flexibility. It doesn't have general security program requirements that all institutions must follow. Instead, it requires financial institutions to have programs that are a good fit for their size and complexity. The programs also must be suitable for the sensitivity of the customer data that the institution uses. Data that is more sensitive requires more protection. The rule also requires institutions to:

- Assign an employee to run the program.
- Conduct a risk assessment to identify risks to customer information.
- Assess current safeguards to make sure they're effective.
- Design and implement safeguards to control risks.
- Select service providers and make sure that contracts with them include terms to protect customer information.
- Review the information security program regularly to account for changes in business.

The Safeguards Rule allows financial institutions to pick the controls that best protect its customer data. It specifies three areas that institutions must review for their programs:

- Employee management and training
- Information systems design
- Detecting and responding to attacks and system failures

Institutions must be sure to address these areas when conducting their risk assessments. They also must make sure that these areas are addressed in their information security program.

Oversight

The agencies that oversee GLBA compliance may take action against the financial institution that they regulate. Institutions that violate GLBA can be subject to both criminal and civil penalties. Monetary fines can be substantial.

GLBA requires financial institutions to follow privacy and security rules. If your organization is a financial institution or engages in financial activities, you need to know about these rules. You will want to make sure your organization's IT systems operate in a way that complies with the law.

The Sarbanes-Oxley Act

Many large corporate scandals rocked the early 2000s. Companies such as Enron, Adelphia, and WorldCom made news for their inaccurate and misleading financial reporting practices. These practices duped investors by making the corporations look more successful than they actually were. Many of these investors, which included corporate employees, lost large amounts of money. By the time everyone knew the truth, it was too late to recover investment losses. When these scandals came to light, they shook investor confidence in the U.S. economy. As a result, the decade from 2000 to 2009 had some of the worst stock market performance ever.[24]

Accurate information is the "investor's best tool."[25] People need accurate financial information so they can invest wisely and make money. Investors have a hard time detecting fraud. Congress passed the Public Company Accounting Reform and Investor Protection Act in 2002 to help protect investors.[26] This law is more commonly known as the Sarbanes-Oxley Act of 2002. It's called SOX or Sarbox in many resources. President George W. Bush signed SOX into law on July 30, 2002. At that time, he called SOX "the most far-reaching reforms of American business practices since the time of Franklin Delano Roosevelt."[27]

Purpose and Scope

The main goal of SOX is to protect investors from financial fraud. SOX supplements other federal securities laws. It applies to **publicly traded companies** that must register with the Securities and Exchange Commission. Investors own a publicly traded company by buying its stock on a stock exchange. SOX doesn't apply to **privately held companies**.

> **NOTE**
> The two most popular U.S. stock exchanges are the New York Stock Exchange (NYSE) and the NASDAQ Stock Market. National securities exchanges are registered with the SEC. You can learn more at *http://www.sec.gov/divisions/marketreg/mrexchanges.shtml*.

SOX is a very detailed act with many provisions. When it was first enacted, most companies assumed that it didn't have any IT components. Congress didn't mention IT anywhere within the act. This opinion changed as companies began to study SOX more carefully. Many SOX provisions require companies to verify the accuracy of their financial information. Since IT systems hold many types of financial information, companies and auditors quickly realized that these systems were part of SOX compliance. That meant that the way those systems are used and the controls used to safeguard those systems had to be reviewed for SOX compliance.

The relationship between IT and SOX compliance continues to evolve. This section focuses on SOX Section 404 certification requirements. This section requires an organization's executive officers to establish, maintain, review, and report on the effectiveness of the company's internal controls over financial reporting (ICFR). An organization's executives must understand how its IT systems work in order to make these certifications. This section has caused compliance headaches for IT professionals.

SOX Control Certification Requirements

SOX Section 404 requires a company's executive management to report on the effectiveness of the company's internal controls over financial reporting (ICFR). Management makes this certification to help ensure that a company's financial reports are accurate. It helps protect investors from fraudulent financial activities. Management must make this certification on documents that a company files with the SEC.

A company must create, document, and test its ICFR. It must report on its ICFR every year. After a company makes its yearly report, outside auditors must review it. The outside auditors must verify that the ICFR specified in the report actually work.

Under SEC rules, ICFR are processes that provide reasonable assurance that an organization's financial reports are reliable. ICFR provide management with reasonable assurance that:

- Financial reports, records, and data are accurately maintained
- Transactions are prepared according to accounting rules and are properly recorded
- Unauthorized acquisition or use of data or assets that could affect financial statements will be prevented or detected in a timely manner

Companies trying to comply with Section 404 quickly learned that they needed to review their IT systems. Specifically, they needed to review the ICFR on their IT systems. An Ernst & Young survey found that public companies spent 70 percent of their time addressing IT controls in their first year of SOX compliance.[28] Companies spent a lot of time on IT controls because their IT systems contain financial data. An error in these systems could cause financial statements to contain errors or mistakes. To comply with Section 404, companies had to make sure that system data were accurate. They had to make sure that they had processes in place to detect inaccurate data.

SOX Section 404 compliance isn't easy. Section 404 is very general about the types of ICFR that companies must implement. It doesn't give a good definition for ICFR generally. It doesn't address IT controls at all. In 2007, the SEC issued additional guidance to help companies assess ICFR during their Section 404 review. It did this in response to many complaints about the large scope of a Section 404 review. Many of these complaints focused on how to address IT controls.

The SEC stated two broad principles in its guidance:

- Management should assess how its internal controls prevent or detect significant deficiencies in financial statements.
- Management should perform a risk-based review of the effectiveness of these controls.

TABLE 15-5 Internal controls and information security goals.

STEPS TAKEN TO MEET INTERNAL CONTROLS	INFORMATION SECURITY GOALS
Financial reports, records, and data are accurately maintained.	Integrity
Transactions are prepared according to GAAP rules and properly recorded.	Integrity, availability
Unauthorized acquisition or use of data or assets that could affect financial statements will be prevented or detected in a timely manner.	Confidentiality, integrity, availability

The SEC also said that management must exercise its professional judgment to limit the scope of a Section 404 review. It reminded companies that SOX applies to internal controls, including IT controls that affect financial reporting only.[29] This means that a Section 404 review certainly applies to IT systems that process financial data. It might not apply to IT systems that process non-financial data.

> **NOTE**
> SOX doesn't specify the IT controls that companies need to implement. Instead, companies must determine the best controls for their systems.

Management must review general IT controls to make sure that IT systems operate properly and consistently. Organizations use many approaches to evaluating their IT controls. The controls must provide management with reasonable assurance that IT systems operate properly to protect financial reporting. Table 15-5 shows how the goals of ICFR match up with information security goals.

A company can't escape SOX Section 404 liability by outsourcing financial functions. SOX requires companies to monitor ICFR for outsourced operations as well. Many companies do this by asking their outsourcing companies to provide them with a special audit report about the outsourced operations. A company must review this report to determine if the outsourcing company's controls are sufficient.

SOX Records Retention Requirements

SOX contains some records retention provisions. As a systems security professional, you must know about these requirements. This is because most companies store many of their records electronically. Some studies estimate that 93 percent of all business documents are created and stored electronically.[30] Companies must understand how their IT systems work in order to meet SOX retention requirements. You will be instrumental in helping your organization understand how to manage and secure its electronic records.

SOX requires public companies to maintain their financial audit papers for seven years.[31] Audit papers are most documents used in an audit. They're the materials that support the conclusions made in an audit report. SOX takes a very broad view of the type of records that must be saved. This includes work papers, memoranda,

> **FYI**
>
> Many federal and state laws contain records retention requirements. SOX is another law to add to that list. Organizations should develop document retention policies to help them track their different obligations.

and correspondence. It also includes any other records created, sent, or received in connection with the audit. SOX includes electronic records.

SOX requires that a public company retain the records and documentation that it uses to assess its internal controls over financial reporting.[32] Guidance issued by the SEC recognizes that this documentation takes a number of different forms. It also includes electronic data. Companies must permanently retain this information.

The penalties for failing to retain records for the right amount of time can be severe. SOX makes it a crime for a person or company to violate its records retention provisions knowingly and willfully. A person who violates this provision can face fines and up to 10 years in prison.

Oversight

The Securities and Exchange Commission oversees and enforces most SOX provisions. The SEC was created under the Securities and Exchange Act of 1934. Its mission is to protect investors and maintain the integrity of the securities industry. The SEC has the power to investigate and sanction public companies that don't comply with SOX.

The SEC has five commissioners. The U.S. president appoints them. They serve for five-year terms. No more than three of the commissioners may belong to the same political party. The SEC has 11 regional offices in the United States.

SOX requires the SEC to review a public company's yearly and quarterly reports at least once every three years.[33] It must do this to try to detect fraud and inaccurate financial statements that could harm the investing public. The SEC has discretion in deciding how often to review companies.

The Family Educational Rights and Privacy Act

Educational institutions such as colleges, universities, and grade schools have access to lots of information about their students. They can collect and store the following types of student data:

- Demographic information
- Address and contact information
- Parental demographic information
- Parental address and contact information
- Grade information
- Disciplinary information

This data is useful to educational institutions. It helps them educate students. This information also is very sensitive. Privacy concerns are raised if an educational institution improperly discloses this information to third parties. It could be embarrassing for the student and his or her family. The Family Educational Rights and Privacy Act (FERPA) is the main federal law protecting the privacy of student information.

Purpose and Scope

Congress created FERPA in 1974.[34] It applies to any education agency or institution that receives federal funding. Educational institutions include:

- Community colleges
- Colleges and universities
- Primary and secondary schools (kindergarten through twelfth grade)
- State and local educational agencies (such as a school board)
- Schools or agencies offering a preschool program
- Any other educational institution that receives federal funding

In this section, these educational institutions are collectively referred to as "schools."

Most educational institutions receive some kind of funding from the U.S. Department of Education. If a school chooses not to comply with FERPA, it can't receive any federal funds. Federal funding is very important to most schools. As a result, almost all of them comply with FERPA. It's possible that some small private schools don't receive federal funds. If they don't receive federal funds, they don't have to comply with FERPA.

FERPA is a very detailed act with many provisions. Its primary goal is to protect the privacy of student records. A "student record" includes any data about a student that a school keeps. These records include written documents, computer media, video, film, and photographs. They also include any records maintained by an outside party acting on a school's behalf. They can be in paper or electronic form.

FERPA doesn't require that specific information security controls be implemented to protect student records. However, systems security professionals must be aware of FERPA's requirements. If an organization is an educational institution, or maintains records for a school, then FERPA may apply to the data it uses. The organization must then implement security controls in IT systems to protect the privacy of electronic student records.

Main Requirements

Under FERPA, students (or their parents if the student is under 18) have the following rights:

- The right to know what data is in the student's "student record" and the right to inspect and review that record
- The right to request that a school correct errors in a student record
- The right to consent to have certain kinds of student data released

FYI

Unlike the generic definition for personally identifiable information that has been used throughout this section, FERPA specifically defines personally identifiable information. When you read any law, you always must be sure to check how that law defines specific terms. Sometimes a word's legal definition can be very different from its generic definition.

A school must protect its student records. In particular, it must protect the personally identifiable information that is located in the records. Under FERPA, personally identifiable information includes direct identifiers such as a student's name, Social Security number, and student number. It also can include indirect identifiers when they're matched with a student name. "Indirect identifiers" are personal characteristics that can be used easily to identify a student. A school can't release a student's records to a third party without the student's written consent.

There are some exceptions when a school can release student records without the student's consent. For example, some school officials can view student records when required by their job duties. In addition, a school can transfer a student's record from the old school to a new school without the student's consent. Schools can transfer student records for some financial aid or accreditation purposes. Schools can disclose some student information in order to comply with a court order or lawful subpoena.

FERPA allows a special category of personally identifiable information to be disclosed without student consent. A school can do this so long as it has given notice to the student that it will disclose this information. This category of information is called **directory information**. Directory information is information that is publicly available about all students. Directory information includes information such as a student's name, address, or telephone number. Many schools give out this information. Colleges and universities often provide this type of information in an online directory.

A school can release directory information without a student's consent. A student can choose to forbid the release of this type of information. The student must tell the school not to release this type of information. If a student tells a school not to release directory information, the school must put measures in place to make sure that this information is not released.

NOTE

The Education Department's Family Policy Compliance Office has prepared a model FERPA notice form. You can read it at *http://www2.ed.gov/policy/gen/guid/fpco/ferpa/mndirectoryinfo.html.*

FERPA requires schools to give students and parents an annual notice about the school's FERPA practices. This notice informs students and parents about their FERPA rights. It tells students about the school officials who have access to records without student consent. For example, FERPA allows any official who has a legitimate educational interest in the school record to view it without the student's consent. The school must identify these officials. They could be teachers, instructors, and professors. They also could be administrative personnel such as principals or provosts.

Systems security professionals must understand these FERPA requirements. If student records are stored electronically, access controls must be used to make sure that only officials who have a right to those records actually do have that access. This protects the confidentiality of the records. Where student data is transferred electronically, systems security professionals must make sure that it's transmitted in a secure way. If students forbid a school from sharing their directory information, then a systems security professional must be able to advise the school on how to suppress that information in online databases.

Oversight

The Family Policy Compliance Office (FPCO) oversees FERPA compliance. The FPCO has the authority to review and investigate FERPA complaints. Schools that violate FERPA can lose their federal funding. Students who have had their FERPA rights violated aren't allowed to sue a school for that violation. Only the FPCO is allowed to sanction schools that violate FERPA.

The Children's Internet Protection Act

Most societies have laws to protect children from inappropriate, or adult, material. Systems security professionals need to be aware of these laws so that their organizations can comply. The Children's Internet Protection Act (CIPA) protects children from viewing obscene or objectionable material on certain school or library computers. These computers must implement technology to make sure that objectionable content is filtered.

Purpose and Scope

Congress passed CIPA in 2000.[35] It requires certain schools and libraries to filter offensive Internet content so that children can't access it. CIPA defines a minor as anyone under the age of 17. Offensive content includes any visual depictions that are obscene, child pornography, or harmful to minors (if the computers are accessed by minors). CIPA defines the phrase "harmful to minors" as any visual picture that:

- Appeals to a prurient interest in nudity, sex, or excretion with respect to what is suitable for minors
- Depicts, describes, or represents sexual acts, contact, or genitalia in a patently offensive way with respect to what is suitable for minors
- Taken as a whole, lacks serious literary, artistic, political, or scientific value with respect to what is suitable for minors

> **NOTE**
> The law refers to anyone who is not of legal adult age as a minor. A minor is a child. Different laws may state different ages for determining when a person is a minor and when he or she is not.

Not every school or library has to comply with CIPA. But any school or library receiving federal funding from the E-Rate program must do so. The E-Rate program provides discounts to most primary and secondary schools and libraries for Internet access. Discounts range from 20 percent to 90 percent of the actual costs. Schools and libraries

Defining Obscene and Objectionable Material

Most people agree that children should be protected from obscene material. However, the definition of "obscene material" is complex. A 1973 U.S. Supreme Court case helps define what is obscene. The court case is called *Miller v. California*. The Supreme Court said that for material to be identified as "obscene," it must meet three conditions. The conditions are based on the average person applying contemporary community standards. Under the test, material is obscene if it:

- Appeals predominantly to prurient interests; "prurient" indicates a morbid, degrading, and unhealthy interest in sex
- Depicts or describes sexual conduct in a patently offensive way
- Lacks serious literary, artistic, political, or scientific value

This test is commonly known as the "Miller test." Courts use it to determine whether material is obscene.

don't have to accept these funds. They can either pay for the Internet access with private funds, or choose not to use the Internet. The Federal Communications Commission (FCC) manages the E-Rate program.

CIPA was quickly challenged. The American Library Association and the American Civil Liberties Union claimed CIPA violated the free speech rights of adults. They also claimed the law could prevent minors from getting information about topics such as breast cancer. A federal court agreed that CIPA violated free speech rights. That court temporarily overturned CIPA in 2002.

NOTE

The First Amendment of the U.S. Constitution sets forth the right to freedom of religion, speech, the press, and assembly. Within these rights is the implicit right of freedom of thought, which has a privacy component. Censorship actions can violate the First Amendment.

The government appealed the decision of the federal court to the U.S. Supreme Court. The case is called *United States et al. v. American Library Association, Inc. et al.* In 2003, the Supreme Court overturned the lower court and upheld the law. The Supreme Court held that only schools and libraries that receive E-Rate funding for Internet access must comply with CIPA. A school or library can choose not to accept the funding, if desired. The case also specifically held that CIPA applies to minors only. Schools and libraries must have some way to allow adults unfiltered Internet access. If they don't, then they face scrutiny for censorship and violating the First Amendment rights of the adult.

Main Requirements

CIPA requires covered schools and libraries to filter offensive Internet content so that children can't get to it. Schools and libraries can use technological tools to meet this requirement. CIPA identifies these tools as a **technology protection measure (TPM).** A TPM is any technology that can block or filter the objectionable content. A proxy server used to filter content is an example of a TPM.

> **NOTE**
> Many companies use proxy servers for various purposes. Their use isn't restricted to CIPA compliance. For example, they can be used to restrict employees' access to different Internet Web sites.

The FCC recognizes that a TPM cannot be 100 percent effective. However, neither CIPA nor the FCC defines what level is acceptable. A third-party company may claim its filter is CIPA compliant. However, no certification process exists to verify a filter is CIPA compliant. The FCC has stated that local authorities should determine which measures are most effective for their community.

CIPA states what must be filtered but not how to filter it. In addition to the TPM, the school or library must create an Internet safety policy and identify a method to address filtering exceptions.

School and libraries must adopt and enforce an Internet safety policy to comply with CIPA. Provisions in this policy must be able to monitor the online activity of children. The policy also must state how the school or library will restrict access to objectionable online materials. It must address the safety and security of children when using e-mail, chat rooms, or other electronic communications. It must address situations where a child uses the Internet for unlawful activities, and it must address the unauthorized use of a child's personal information.

Under CIPA, a library or school must be able to disable the TPM for any adult. If an adult needs to use a computer, you can disable the TPM for him or her. This is an important point. If you can't disable the TPM for an adult, you run the risk of violating the adult's First Amendment rights. Adults should be able to use the system without any filtering.

Libraries can use any method to disable the TPM that works best for their location. For example, library personnel could label some computers as "adult only." Librarians would prevent minors from using these computers. Librarians also could log onto a program designed to disable the TPM. Only personnel with the proper credentials could disable the TPM. Another method is to require an administrator to disable the TPM. Upon request by a patron, the librarian could contact an administrator to disable the TPM for the patron.

Oversight

The FCC has oversight for CIPA. However, little oversight action is required. When a public school or library requests E-Rate funding, they must certify that they comply with CIPA. This certification is usually all that's required.

If a TPM fails, the school or library is expected to take steps to resolve the failure. If the library doesn't resolve them, the patron can file a complaint with the FCC. If the FCC receives complaints that too many objectionable images are getting through, it may investigate.

The FCC presumes that Congress never intended libraries to be fined if they don't comply with CIPA. At most, the FCC may require a library to refund the E-Rate discount for the period of time it wasn't in compliance.

Making Sense of Laws for Information Security Compliance

The United States doesn't have one single data protection law. As a result, many laws focus on different types of data. This chapter focused specifically on federal data protection laws. You must remember that states have data protection laws too. Discussing all of the different kinds of state data protection laws could be a book in itself. It's important to remember that organizations must comply with federal laws AND laws of the states where they are located. When systems security professionals work on compliance projects, they must be aware of both kinds of laws.

It's not practical to have separate information security programs for each law an organization must follow. IT systems can hold many different types of data. It's possible that an organization will need to make sure that its systems are compliant with a number of laws. As a result, an organization's information security program must be comprehensive. It must be able to accommodate a general response to many laws. To do this, systems security professionals must understand what each law has in common from an information security standpoint.

For example, many of the laws discussed in this chapter require an organization to assess the security of its IT systems. To do this the organization must perform a risk assessment. This is a stated requirement of many laws. FISMA, GLBA, HIPAA, and SOX all contain this requirement. Systems security professionals often are responsible for performing these risk assessments. They help organizations identify where their IT systems are vulnerable. They allow the organization to take steps to reduce any risks. The process of performing a risk assessment and taking steps to reduce risk is known as risk management. Risk management concepts are discussed in Chapter 8 of this book.

System security professionals are in a unique position. They must appreciate the impact these laws and regulations have on how IT systems operation. They also must appreciate how the basic tenets of information security influence these laws. Confidentiality, availability, and integrity are discussed in Chapter 1. For instance, almost all of the laws discussed here focus on protecting the confidentiality of certain types of data. FISMA, HIPPA, GLBA, and FERPA all have confidentiality requirements. These laws prove that information security isn't just a good idea. It's the law.

Some of the laws have integrity requirements. Both FERPA and HIPAA require organizations to have a way to identify inaccurate data. They also must be able to correct it. SOX requires that organizations test and certify the internal controls on their IT systems. These controls must protect financial data from being modified without proper authorization.

Other laws have availability requirements. CIPA requires that certain types of online materials be available to one population (adults). Those same materials must be denied to another population (children). This is an availability concept. An organization will need to use access control measures to comply with CIPA. FISMA requires federal agencies to create contingency plans for their IT systems. HIPAA has a similar requirement. These plans ensure that IT systems are available during and after an incident or disaster. Even if a law doesn't specifically address availability, it's an important requirement for almost every organization. Organizations need their data and IT systems to be available in order to conduct business.

NOTE

Contingency plans include incident response and disaster recovery plans. These kinds of plans are discussed in Chapters 4 and 8.

Table 15-6 shows how you can think about the laws discussed in this chapter with respect to information security concepts. This chart shows the laws as they are discussed in this chapter.

As a systems security professional, you will possess the skills needed to make sense out of these compliance laws. You will understand how IT systems must be configured in order to meet your organization's compliance requirements. You will be able to explain how these laws affect IT systems. You also will be able to explain the steps that your organization took to be compliant with these laws.

TABLE 15-6 Laws and information security concepts.

CONFIDENTIALITY	INTEGRITY	AVAILABILITY
FISMA	FISMA	FISMA
HIPAA	HIPAA	HIPAA
GLBA	SOX	GLBA
FERPA	FERPA	SOX
		CIPA

CHAPTER SUMMARY

This chapter reviews U.S. federal data protection laws. They are industry based and apply to different types of information. Organizations that use and handle certain types of data must comply with these laws. Compliance with federal law isn't optional; it's mandatory. An organization must document its compliance with these laws.

These laws affect the daily activities of a systems security professional. Systems security professionals must understand what these laws require. They must be able to implement them in IT systems. Systems security professionals must be able to translate the laws' requirements into information security controls and safeguards. They help an organization show compliance with the law.

KEY CONCEPTS AND TERMS

Business associates
Covered entity
Directory information
Disclosure
Electronic protected health information (EPHI)
Minimum necessary rule
Nonpublic personal information (NPI)
Personally identifiable information (PII)
Privately held companies
Protected health information (PHI)
Publicly traded companies
Technology protection measure (TPM)
Use

CHAPTER 15 ASSESSMENT

1. An addressable implementation specification under HIPAA must be used if it's ________.

2. What elements must a written GLBA information security program include?

A. Technical safeguards
B. Physical safeguards
C. Administrative safeguards
D. A designated employee to run the program
E. All of the above

3. What types of companies must follow all Sarbanes-Oxley Act provisions?

A. Public
B. Private
C. Nonprofit
D. Governmental
E. None of the above.

4. CIPA requires a library to be able to disable the TPM for some situations.

A. True
B. False

5. What law governs the release of student information?

A. HIPAA
B. SOX
C. FERPA
D. CIPA
E. None of the above.

6. What is the maximum yearly fine for a violation of the HIPAA Privacy or Security Rule?

A. $100
B. $1,500
C. $1 million
D. $1.5 million
E. It is unlimited

7. The U.S. has one comprehensive data protection law.

A. True
B. False

8. What must an educational institution get prior to releasing student personal information to a third party?

A. Verbal consent
B. Notarized consent
C. Signed affidavit
D. Written consent
E. None of the above

9. Who is considered a "minor" under CIPA?

A. Anyone under the age of 13
B. Anyone under the age of 17
C. Anyone under the age of 20
D. Anyone under the age of 21
E. None of the above

10. What is personally identifiable information?

11. FISMA requires federal agencies to test their information security controls every six months.

A. True
B. False

12. What is the main goal of the Sarbanes-Oxley Act?

13. What option must be included in a GLBA privacy practices notice?

A. Disclosure
B. Opt out
C. Opt in
D. Notice
E. None of the above

14. A HIPAA breach is a breach of ________ PHI.

15. How many steps are there in the NIST Risk Management Framework?

A. Six
B. Five
C. Four
D. Three
E. None of the above

ENDNOTES

1. U.S. Office of Management and Budget, Circular No. A-130, "Management of Federal Information Resources," December 2000, http://www.whitehouse.gov/omb/circulars_a130_a130trans4/ (accessed April 21, 2010).

2. Committee on Oversight and Government Reform, "Federal Information Security: Current Challenges and Future Policy Considerations," March 24, 2010, http://oversight.house.gov/images/stories/Hearings/Government_Management/032410_Federal_Info_Security/2010.FISMA.Kundra.testimony.final.pdf (accessed April 21, 2010). *See* prepared testimony of Mr. Vivek Kundra.

3. Federal Information Security Management Act, Title III of the E-Government Act of 2002, P.L. 107-347; U.S. Code Vol. 44, sec. 3541 et seq.

4. U.S. Code Vol. 44, sec. 3542(b)(1).

5. U.S. Code Vol. 44, sec. 3544(a)(3)(A)(ii).

6. GovInfoSecurity.com, "Automated FISMA Reporting Tool Unveiled," October 30, 2009, http://www.govinfosecurity.com/articles.php?art_id=1894 (accessed April 24, 2010).

7. Committee on Oversight and Reform, "Federal Information Security: Current Challenges and Future Policy Considerations," March 24, 2010. *See* prepared testimony of Mr. Vivek Kundra.

8. The White House Blog, Vivek Kundra, "Faster, Smarter Cybersecurity," April 21, 2010, http://www.whitehouse.gov/blog/2010/04/21/faster-smarter-cybersecurity (accessed April 23, 2010).

9. National Institute of Standards and Technology, SP 800-37, "Guide for Applying the Risk Management Framework to Federal Information Systems: A Security Life Cycle Approach" February 2010, http://csrc.nist.gov/publications/nistpubs/800-37-rev1/sp800-37-rev1-final.pdf (accessed May 21, 2010).

10. Code of Federal Regulations, Title 45, sec. 160.103.

11. Code of Federal Regulations, Title 45, sec. 165.502(b).

12. Code of Federal Regulations, Title 45, sec. 164.520.

13. Code of Federal Regulations, Title 45, sec. 164.530(f).

14. Health Information Technology for Economic and Clinical Health Act (2009), Pub. L. No. 111-5, sec. 13402.

15. Ibid.

16. Code of Federal Regulations, Title 45, sec. 164.306.

17. Code of Federal Regulations, Title 45, sec. 164.316.

18. Code of Federal Regulations, Title 45, sec. 164.306.

19. Ibid.

20. Verizon Business, *2009 Data Breach Investigations Report*, April 15, 2009, http://www.verizonbusiness.com/resources/security/reports/2009_databreach_rp.pdf (accessed March 1, 2010).

21. U.S. Code Vol. 15, sec. 6801-6803.

22. U.S. Code Vol. 15, sec. 6801(b).

23. *Standards for Insuring the Security Confidentiality, Integrity and Protection of Customer Records and Information* ("Safeguards Rule"), Code of Federal Regulations, Title 16, sec. 314.

24. *The Wall Street Journal*, "Investors Hope the '10s Beat the '00s," December 20, 2009, http://online.wsj.com/article/SB10001424052748704786204574607993448916718.html (accessed April 16, 2010).

25. U.S. Security and Exchange Commission, "Information Matters," February 22, 2006, http://www.sec.gov/answers/infomatters.htm (accessed April 16, 2010).

26. Sarbanes-Oxley Act of 2002, Pub. L. No. 107-204, 116 Stat. 745 (codified as amended in scattered sections of U.S. Code Vol. 15).

27. *The New York Times*, "Bush Signs Bill Aimed at Fraud in Corporations," July 30, 2002,http://www.nytimes.com/2002/07/31/business/corporate-conduct-the-president-bush-signs-bill-aimed-at-fraud-in-corporations.html?pagewanted=1 (accessed April 16, 2010).

28. Ernst & Young, "Emerging Trends in Internal Controls: Fourth Survey and Industry Insights," September 2005, http://www.sarbanes-oxley.be/aabs_emerging_trends_survey4.pdf (accessed April 16, 2010).

29. *Commission Guidance Regarding Management's Report on Internal Controls Over Financial Reporting*, Code of Federal Regulations, Title 17, sec. 241.

30. Marcella, Albert J., "Electronically Stored Information and Cyberforensics," Information Systems Control Journal, Vol. 5 (2008). Available at http://www.isaca.org/Template.cfm?Section=Home&CONTENTID=52106&TEMPLATE=/ContentManagement/ContentDisplay.cfm (accessed April 16, 2010).

31. U.S. Code Vol. 15, sec. 7213m.

32. *Commission Guidance Regarding Management's Report on Internal Controls Over Financial Reporting*, Code of Federal Regulations, Title 17, sec. 241.

33. U.S. Code Vol. 15, sec. 7266.

34. U.S. Code Vol. 20, sec. 1232g.

35. The Children's Internet Protection Act, Pub. L. No. 106-554, 114 Stat. 2763A-335 (codified in scattered sections of U.S. Code).

APPENDIX A

Answer Key

CHAPTER 1 Information Systems Security

1. A 2. A 3. Availability 4. B 5. B 6. E 7. E 8. D 9. A
10. A 11. A 12. A 13. E 14. D 15. B

CHAPTER 2 Changing How People and Businesses Communicate

1. A 2. A 3. A: 5; B: 1; C: 3; D: 2; E: 4 4. E 5. B 6. B 7. E
8. A 9. B 10. B 11. E 12. D 13 A

CHAPTER 3 Malicious Attacks, Threats, and Vulnerabilities

1. A 2. C 3. B 4. Sniffer (or packet sniffer) 5. A 6. B 7. C
8. A 9. B 10. A 11. C 12. Threat 13 Vulnerability 14. B. 15. D

CHAPTER 4 The Drivers of the Information Security Business

1. B 2. A 3. B 4. D 5. B 6. D. 7. C 8. A 9. B 10. D
11. Business impact analysis (BIA) 12. B 13 HIPAA 14. B

CHAPTER 5 Access Controls

1. A 2. D 3. B 4. A 5. C 6. A. 7. B 8. B 9. D 10. B
11. E 12. B 13 D 14. A 15. D

CHAPTER 6 Security Operations and Administration

1. A 2. D 3. B 4. C 5. E 6. B 7. D 8. E 9. A 10 B
11. B 12. A 13 E 14. A 15. D 16. A 17. E 18. B

CHAPTER 7 Auditing, Testing, and Monitoring

1. A 2. E 3. B 4. C 5. E 6. A. 7. A 8. C 9. A 10. B
11. B 12. D

CHAPTER 8 Risk, Response, and Recovery

1. C. 2. A 3. A 4. D 5. C 6. E 7. A. 8. D. 9. B 10. C

CHAPTER 9 Cryptopgraphy

1. C 2. A 3. B 4. D 5. A 6. A 7. D 8. E 9. A 10. C
11. D 12. B

CHAPTER 10 Networks and Telecommunications

1. C. 2. A 3. B 4. A 5. D 6. Router 7. B 8. A 9. C 10. B 11. A 12. B 13 B 14. D 15. D

CHAPTER 11 Malicious Code and Activity

1. B 2. Spam 3. C 4. A 5. B 6. D 7. B 8. B 9. C. 10 B. 11. D 12. Defense in depth 13 A

CHAPTER 12 Information Security Standards

1. B 2. B 3. A 4. D 5. TCP/IP 6. Requests for Comments (RFCs) 7. A 8. IEEE 9. D 10. B

CHAPTER 13 Information Security Education and Training

1. B 2. C 3. B 4. C 5. D 6. Traditional 7. A and D. 8. B 9. C 10. A

CHAPTER 14 Information Security Professional Certifications

1. A 2. C 3. B 4. D 5. CIW 6. A 7. B 8. A 9. D 10. B

CHAPTER 15 U.S. Compliance Laws

1. Reasonable and appropriate 2. E 3. A 4. A 5. C 6. D 7. B 8. D 9. B 10. Data that can be used to individually identify a person. It includes Social Security numbers, driver's license numbers, financial account data, and health data. 11. B 12. To protect shareholders and investors from financial fraud. SOX also was designed to restore investor faith in American stock markets. 13. B 14. Unsecured 15. A

APPENDIX

B

Standard Acronyms

3DES	triple data encryption standard
ACD	automatic call distributor
AES	Advanced Encryption Standard
ANSI	American National Standards Institute
AP	access point
API	application programming interface
B2B	business to business
B2C	business to consumer
BBB	Better Business Bureau
BCP	business continuity planning
C2C	consumer to consumer
CA	certificate authority
CAP	Certification and Accreditation Professional
CAUCE	Coalition Against Unsolicited Commercial Email
CCC	CERT Coordination Center
CCNA	Cisco Certified Network Associate
CERT	Computer Emergency Response Team
CFE	Certified Fraud Examiner
CISA	Certified Information Systems Auditor
CISM	Certified Information Security Manager
CISSP	Certified Information System Security Professional
CMIP	common management information protocol
COPPA	Children's Online Privacy Protection
CRC	cyclic redundancy check
CSI	Computer Security Institute
CTI	Computer Telephony Integration
DBMS	database management system
DDoS	distributed denial of service
DES	Data Encryption Standard
DMZ	demilitarized zone
DoS	denial of service
DPI	deep packet inspection
DRP	disaster recovery plan
DSL	digital subscriber line
DSS	Digital Signature Standard
DSU	data service unit
EDI	Electronic Data Interchange
EIDE	Enhanced IDE
FACTA	Fair and Accurate Credit Transactions Act
FAR	false acceptance rate
FBI	Federal Bureau of Investigation
FDIC	Federal Deposit Insurance Corporation
FEP	front-end processor
FRCP	Federal Rules of Civil Procedure
FRR	false rejection rate
FTC	Federal Trade Commission
FTP	file transfer protocol
GIAC	Global Information Assurance Certification
GLBA	Gramm-Leach-Bliley Act
HIDS	host-based intrusion detection system
HIPAA	Health Insurance Portability and Accountability Act
HIPS	host-based intrusion prevention system
HTTP	hypertext transfer protocol
HTTPS	HTTP over Secure Socket Layer
HTML	hypertext markup language
IAB	Internet Activities Board
IDEA	International Data Encryption Algorithm
IDPS	intrusion detection and prevention
IDS	intrusion detection system

IEEE Institute of Electrical and Electronics Engineers
IETF Internet Engineering Task Force
InfoSec information security
IPS intrusion prevention system
IPSec IP Security
IPv4 Internet protocol version 4
IPv6 Internet protocol version 6
IRS Internal Revenue Service
(ISC)² International Information System Security Certification Consortium
ISO International Organization for Standardization
ISP Internet service provider
ISS Internet security systems
ITRC Identity Theft Resource Center
IVR interactive voice response
LAN local area network
MAN metropolitan area network
MD5 Message Digest 5
modem modulator demodulator
NFIC National Fraud Information Center
NIDS network intrusion detection system
NIPS network intrusion prevention system
NIST National Institute of Standards and Technology
NMS network management system
OS operating system
OSI open system interconnection
PBX private branch exchange
PCI Payment Card Industry
PGP Pretty Good Privacy
PKI public-key infrastructure
RAID redundant array of independent disks
RFC Request for Comments
RSA Rivest, Shamir, and Adleman (algorithm)
SAN storage area network
SANCP Security Analyst Network Connection Profiler
SANS SysAdmin, Audit, Network, Security
SAP service access point
SCSI small computer system interface
SET Secure electronic transaction
SGC server-gated cryptography
SHA Secure Hash Algorithm
S-HTTP secure HTTP
SLA service level agreement
SMFA specific management functional area
SNMP simple network management protocol
SOX Sarbanes-Oxley Act of 2002 (also Sarbox)
SSA Social Security Administration
SSCP Systems Security Certified Practitioner
SSL Secure Socket Layer
SSO single system sign-on
STP shielded twisted cable
TCP/IP Transmission Control Protocol/Internet Protocol
TCSEC Trusted Computer System Evaluation Criteria
TFTP Trivial File Transfer Protocol
TNI Trusted Network Interpretation
UDP User Datagram Protocol
UPS uninterruptible power supply
UTP unshielded twisted cable
VLAN virtual local area network
VOIP Voice over Internet Protocol
VPN virtual private network
WAN wide area network
WLAN wireless local area network
WNIC wireless network interface card
W3C World Wide Web Consortium
WWW World Wide Web

APPENDIX

C

Become an SSCP®

About (ISC)²®

(ISC)² is the largest not-for-profit membership body of certified information security professionals worldwide, with over 70,000 members in more than 135 countries. Globally recognized as the gold standard, (ISC)² issues the Certified Information Systems Security Professional (CISSP®) and related concentrations, as well as the Certified Secure Software Lifecycle Professional (CSSLP®), Certified Authorization Professional (CAP®), and Systems Security Certified Practitioner (SSCP®) credentials to qualifying candidates. (ISC)²'s certifications are among the first information technology credentials to meet the stringent requirements of ANSI/ISO/IEC Standard 17024, a global benchmark for assessing and certifying personnel. (ISC)² also offers education programs and services based on its CBK,® a compendium of information security topics. More information is available at *www.isc2.org*.

About SSCP®

If you are currently working in the information security field or IT with some responsibilities or even interest in security, then you should be seriously considering the Systems Security Certified Practitioner (SSCP®) credential from (ISC)²®. With one year's work experience you can become certified and be on your way down a meaningful career path.

The SSCP certification is the ideal credential for those who are hands-on practical technicians, the enforcers everyone goes to for answers. You would implement the plans and policies designed, planned, and managed by the CISO or CSO, who would typically hold the more advanced Certified Information Systems Security Professional (CISSP®) gold standard certification from (ISC)² and operate in a managerial capacity, as opposed to hands-on like you.

The SSCP is ideal for those working toward positions such as Network Security Engineers, Security Systems Analysts, or Security Administrators. This is also the perfect career path for personnel in many other non-security disciplines that require an understanding of security but do not have information security as a primary part of their job description. This large and growing group includes information systems auditors; application programmers; system, network, and database administrators; business unit representatives and systems analysts.

SSCP experience includes:

- Work requiring special education or intellectual attainment, usually including a technical school, liberal education, or college degree.
- Work requiring habitual memory of a body of knowledge shared with others doing similar work.
- Management of projects and/or other employees.
- Supervision of the work of others while requiring only a minimum of supervision oneself.
- Work requiring the exercise of judgment, management decision-making, and discretion.
- Creative writing and oral communication.
- Teaching, instructing, training, and the mentoring of others.
- Research and development.
- The specification and selection of controls and mechanisms (i.e., identification and authentication technology, not the mere operation of these controls).

SSCP candidates must meet the following requirements prior to taking the SSCP examination:

- Subscribe to the (ISC)² Code of Ethics.
- Have at least one year of cumulative work experience in one or more of the seven domains in information security.

(ISC)² SSCP CBK® topics are:

- Access Controls
- Cryptography
- Malicious Code and Activity
- Monitoring and Analysis
- Networks and Communications
- Risk, Response and Recovery
- Security Operations and Administration

If you're working on building your experience right now, you may earn the Associate of (ISC)² designation by subscribing to the code of ethics and by passing the required SSCP examination. As an Associate, you receive member benefits that are afforded to our certified members. Having passed the three-hour, 125-question multiple-choice SSCP examination, completed the endorsement process, attained the relevant experience, and paid the annual maintenance fee (AMF), you will hold the SSCP credential. For more details, see the "About the Associate of (ISC)²" section.

Because the SSCP certification can be used to waive one year of experience for the CISSP credential, SSCP is frequently viewed as the first step on an information security career path leading to CISSP and the more advanced concentrations. However, for many professionals, having a more vibrant, hands-on participation in company security, as an SSCP, is even more challenging. It all depends on which part of the (ISC)^2 career path best suits your goals and personality.

Maintenance Requirements

To remain in good standing with (ISC)^2, you must recertify every three years to maintain your SSCP credential. This is accomplished primarily by acquiring 60 continuing professional education (CPE) credits every three years, with a minimum of 10 CPEs earned each year after certification. You must also pay an annual maintenance fee of US$65. For more information on the SSCP certification, visit *www.isc2.org/sscp*.

About the Associate of (ISC)^2®

You don't have to spend years in the field to demonstrate your competence in information security. Become an Associate of (ISC)^2, and you're already part of a reputable and credible organization, earning recognition from employers and peers for the industry knowledge you've already gained.

Participation Requirements

Associate of (ISC)^2 status is available to those knowledgeable in key areas of industry concepts but lacking the work experience. As a potential candidate, you may take the SSCP® examination and subscribe to the (ISC)^2 Code of Ethics; however, to earn the SSCP credential, you will have to acquire the necessary years of professional experience, provide proof, and be endorsed by a member of (ISC)^2 in good standing. Therefore, if you are working toward this credential, you have a maximum of two years from your exam pass date to acquire the necessary one year of professional experience. An Annual Maintenance Fee (AMF) of US$35 applies, and 10 Continuing Professional Education (CPE) units must be earned each year to remain in good standing.

The Advantages of Becoming an Associate of (ISC)^2

Prior to earning the SSCP certification, becoming an Associate of (ISC)^2 demonstrates your competence and commitment to the profession, helping attract employers early in your career. (ISC)^2 provides a wide variety of benefits for CPEs for Associates, such as discounts on industry conferences, free educational events, networking opportunities, and more. Don't miss opportunities like:

- **Discounts on Industry Conferences**—(ISC)^2 Associates receive discounts on industry conferences, which means you'll earn valuable CPEs while learning about cutting-edge developments in the field. For more information, visit *www.isc2.org/industry*.
- **Member Receptions**—(ISC)^2 also hosts networking receptions at industry events. It's not often that you get the chance to share opinions and observations with your peers and (ISC)^2 management in an informal social setting. As the gold standard in information security credentials, we believe this kind of idea exchange is part of what makes the (ISC)^2 membership renowned and respected worldwide.

- **Security Leadership Series Events**—Stay current on emerging security issues through events like the (ISC)^2 Security Leadership Series. Hosted worldwide by (ISC)^2, this series consists of local and online events.
  - **Local Information Security Education Events**—These one-day or multipe-day local events are either free to members or offered at a reduced fee respectively. The knowledge and exposure you'll gain is well worth the price of admission. "For more details, visit *www.isc2.org/events*.
  - **Online Events**—(ISC)^2 offers two different online event seminars for you to learn and earn CPEs from the convenience of your computer at work or home. The *(ISC)^2 e-Symposium Seminar Series* consists of free, half-day events on hot industry topics and live interaction with industry experts. The *(ISC)^2 ThinkTank Roundtable Webinar Series* consists of one-hour seminars. For more details, visit *www.isc2.org/e-symposium*.
- **Member Web site**—Gives you access to a suite of resources, such as industry developments, research, upcoming event details and private news sections.
- **InterSeC**—The community where secure minds meet. Collaborate with other security professionals for career advice, projects, best practices through groups, wiki's, blogs, etc. InterSeC is the place where you can be sure that everyone you meet online is governed by a similar code of ethics and has the same passion and interest driving their quest for shared knowledge in application and information security. *www.isc2intersec.com*
- **The (ISC)^2 Journal**—*Information Security Journal: A Global Perspective* is the official bi-monthly journal of (ISC)^2. Associates pay only US$55 for one year for essential information on managing the security of a modern, evolving enterprise. To subscribe, visit *www.isc2.org/journal*. To submit articles, please contact *journaleditor@isc2.org*.
- **(ISC)^2 Magazine**—Published in response to member demand, (ISC)^2 provides a members-only online publication called *InfoSecurity Professional*, distributed quarterly. For news on the latest industry topics, current happenings within organizations and CPE opportunities, this is the magazine you've been waiting for.
- **SecurityTALK**—From one convenient location, you'll have access to presentations, Podcasts and research reports that come to you, courtesy of information security associations and the vendor community and (ISC)^2.

Hold Yourself to Globally Recognized Standards

(ISC)^2 is the global leader in information security education and certification. As an Associate, you're aligning yourself with an organization that offers information security credentials that are accredited to ANSI/ISO/IEC Standard 17024, such as the CISSP and SSCP. And since (ISC)^2 created the CBK® and updates it annually, no one else is better equipped to offer reviews of the subject matter. All told, the Associate of (ISC)^2 gets your career off to a solid start with the tools you'll need to succeed along the way. For additional information and member benefits, visit *www.isc2.org/advantages*.

APPENDIX D

SSCP® Practice Exam

Test your SSCP® knowledge and gauge your readiness.

Complete the SSCP practice exam below, visit *www.isc2.org/student* to review the answers and rationale, and get a $1000 Tuition Grant on any 5-day Official SSCP CBK® Review Seminar.

Offer can't be combined with any other offer and is exclusive to the purchaser of this textbook.

OFFER CODE: STUDENT

1. When an administrator provisions a new account, what is a typical step?

A. Creation of an e-mail account
B. Auditing of passwords
C. Assignment of rights
D. Resetting password

2. In biometric systems, false acceptance rate (FAR) is also known as:

A. False positive rate (FPR)
B. False rejection rate (FRR)
C. Cross-over error rate (CER)
D. True positive rate (TPR)

3. Which concept of access control is used to set up privileges such that no one person should be able to execute a critical task, and the likelihood of abuse of the system is minimized?

A. Process control
B. Least privilege
C. Separation of duties
D. Change management

4. Disabling write or modify permissions to an executable file is done to prevent:

A. Unauthorized use of an authorized application
B. Unauthorized use of an unauthorized application
C. Unauthorized access to an authorized application
D. Unauthorized replacement of an authorized application

5. Which of the following describes the process of recording the exact state of the IT environment at any point in time?

A. Configuration management
B. Classification management
C. Change management
D. Content management

6. You have recently been appointed the Chief Information Security Officer (CISO) of a large health care organization. During the first week, you notice that when many members of the organization leave for the day, they leave their computers unlocked and also leave sensitive information on paper unprotected. One day you also hear staff discussing a health claim loudly at a nearby coffee shop.

   You realize that the staff violating the security policies have been with the organization for more than five years, whereas the newer employees are following the security policies. Also, you notice that only the new hires undergo security awareness training.

   What should the Chief Information Security Officer (CISO) do to help increase the employees' knowledge of security practices within the organization?

   A. Implement and track mandatory security awareness training for all experienced staff
   B. Implement and track mandatory security training for executive management
   C. Implement and track mandatory periodic security awareness training for all staff
   D. Implement and track mandatory periodic security training for management

7. One of the *best* ways to prevent a network from compromise is to:

   A. Develop a rigorous audit program
   B. Run monthly penetration tests and vulnerability scans
   C. Allow only secure protocols on the network
   D. Ensure that endpoints that are attached to the network are secure

8. When designing a change management process, what element has to be designed to help notify all teams within the organization about future system changes such as software patches, fixes, or updates?

   A. A change priority scheme
   B. A change request form
   C. A change review methodology
   D. A change control board

9. The intrusion prevention system (IPS) takes the network monitoring process one step further by:

   A. Making access control decisions through traffic analysis
   B. Alerting directly to law enforcement
   C. Writing malware content directly to disk, for later analysis
   D. Alerting the networking monitoring team when an incident occurs

10. A company has been receiving a high volume of attacks on their Web site. The network administrator wants to be able to collect information on the attacker(s) and mitigate the effect of the attack. What should be implemented?

    A. A honeypot
    B. A firewall
    C. A demilitarized zone (DMZ)
    D. An intrusion detection system (IDS)

11. A system has a vulnerability and a patch is available for download. The system administrator goes to the Web site where the patch is being hosted and downloads the patch. Then the hash is recalculated and compared with that which is hosted on the Web site. When file hashing is being done, what state is being confirmed?

    A. File confidentiality is being verified.
    B. File sensitivity is being verified.
    C. File integrity is being verified.
    D. File availability is being verified.

12. What is the minimum that a computer incident response team (CIRT) must do when responding to a new incident?

    A. Verify that an incident has actually occurred.
    B. Start an investigation immediately.
    C. Inform management that an incident occurred.
    D. Formulate a response strategy.

13. Emergency response plans often depend upon alternative processing procedures:

A. Because they allow for the absence of non-critical systems
B. Because of mandates from a government agency
C. Because of insurance requirements to file a claim
D. Because of the need to keep things simple in a time of crisis

14. The record of the chain of custody is used to:

A. Trace the location of the evidence from the moment it was collected to the moment it was presented in a judicial proceeding
B. Trace the location of the evidence from the moment it was collected to the moment it was presented to management
C. Trace the location of the evidence from the moment it was authorized to the moment it was presented in a judicial proceeding
D. Trace the location of the evidence from the moment it was authorized to the moment it was presented to management

15. A secure communication's session commonly uses both public and private key encryption algorithms. This is due to:

A. The higher speed of symmetric key algorithms for data transfer
B. The key negotiation properties of private key algorithms
C. The increased integrity provided by a private key algorithm
D. The convenience of using shorter keys for public key algorithms

16. In order to establish a secure connection between two end points over a public network, the router at each location should be configured to use IPSec (Internet Protocol Security) in:

A. Secure mode
B. Transport mode
C. Tunnel mode
D. Data Link mode

17. A one-way function that compresses a message of arbitrary size into a fixed length output is commonly referred to as:

A. A symmetric algorithm
B. An asymmetric algorithm
C. A public key algorithm
D. A hashing algorithm

18. An organization encrypts its data in order to achieve Payment Card Industry Data Security Standard (PCI DSS) compliance, this supports the security principle of:

A. Need-to-know
B. Availability
C. Data integrity
D. Nonrepudiation

19. What technology was originally designed to decrease broadcast traffic but is also beneficial in reducing the likelihood of having information compromised by sniffers?

A. Remote Authentication Dial In User Service (RADIUS)
B. Demilitarized zone (DMZ)
C. Virtual local area network (VLAN)
D. Virtual private network (VPN)

20. 802.11g devices can receive unintentional interference that resembles a Layer 1 denial of service attack from

A. 802.11n devices
B. Bluetooth devices
C. Cell phones
D. Radio transceivers

21. What is a key disadvantage of using a circuit level gateway?

A. It checks the initial connection but none of the subsequent packets.
B. In order to work with new services the kernel would have to be modified.
C. It is slower as a result of in-depth packet analysis.
D. It is new technology, and is relatively untested.

22. A logic bomb differs from a Trojan insofar as:
   A. A logic bomb will destroy the application in which it was hidden.
   B. A logic bomb will destroy the operating system in which it was hidden.
   C. The actions of a logic bomb are logical and therefore more dangerous.
   D. The actions of a logic bomb take place only under certain conditions.

23. If a malware scanner's detection threshold is set too low, the system's administrator could be overwhelmed by:
   A. Administrative alerts
   B. False negative alerts
   C. False positive alerts
   D. Log file entries

24. A common method used by malware to identify and disable anti-malware software is to:
   A. Locate and run the software's uninstaller program
   B. Locate and alter the software's configuration information
   C. Locate the software's process in memory and terminate it
   D. Locate and erase the software's Malware signature file

25. Why might a business be very reluctant to submit malware samples to its anti-malware vendor?
   A. The samples most likely do not contain malware.
   B. The vendor charges a fee to examine malware samples.
   C. The malware samples might contain private information.
   D. The possession of malware may be considered illegal.

Information Systems Security Professionals, NSTISSI No. 4011

APPENDIX E

In June 2012 Jones & Bartlett Learning, publishers of this book, received an award and recognition from the National Security Agency for the Information Systems Security & Assurance (ISSA) curriculum. The ISSA curriculum mapped 100 percent to both the National Security Agency (NSA) Information Systems Security Professionals 4011 Standard and also the National Information Assurance 4013 Standard for System Administrators. This recognition places the ISSA curriculum at the forefront of supporting undergraduate and graduate degree programs in cybersecurity and information assurance.

This supplement that you are reading, coupled with the ISSA curriculum, provides students with content, courseware exercises, and hands-on labs to fulfill the requirements of both the learning objectives and the performance competences of the NSA Information Systems Security Professional 4011 Standard. The terms and concepts presented in this supplement were not originally contained in the ISSA curriculum.

After reviewing this supplement, you will be well versed in the electromagnetic and electrical transmission topics that are required within the 4011 Standard, including the TEMPEST security section. TEMPEST refers to the electrical signaling that is generated by analog and digital communication systems. In addition, this supplement presents information systems terms and concepts in order to provide the student with a historical perspective on information systems and evolution toward digital communications.

Scope

This supplemental booklet fulfills the requirements of the National Training Standard for Information Systems Security (INFOSEC) professionals in the disciplines of telecommunications and automated information systems (AIS) security.

Applicability

National Security Telecommunications and Information Systems Security Directive No. 501 established the requirement for federal departments and agencies to train INFOSEC professionals. As defined in NSTISSD 501, an INFOSEC professional is an individual responsible for the security, oversight, or management of national security systems during all phases of the life cycle.

Federal agencies must satisfy these INFOSEC education and training requirements as effectively and efficiently as possible. This instruction is the first in a series of minimum training and education standards to assist departments and agencies in meeting their responsibilities in these areas.

Training Standards

The curriculum provides two levels of knowledge:

- Awareness level: This creates a sensitivity to the threats and vulnerabilities of national security information systems and a recognition of the need to protect data, information, and the means of processing them. Awareness builds a working knowledge of principles and practices in INFOSEC.
- Performance level: This provides the employee with the skill or ability to design, execute, or evaluate agency INFOSEC security procedures and practices. Performance-level knowledge ensures that employees can apply security concepts while performing their jobs.

System Operating Environment

Communications Security (COMSEC)

Communications Security (COMSEC) refers collectively to all methods used to secure all forms of communications. COMSEC prevents an attacker from intercepting or detecting any sent signals containing sensitive or secure data but still ensures that the data gets to the correct recipient. COMSEC is not a single security method, but a variety of combined methods.

COMSEC protects any government secret or secure data. COMSEC is the safest way to send and receive secure or sensitive data across any communication system that the military uses to send data.

When you combine several different security methods to send and receive critical government information, you are using COMSEC. COMSEC makes it much harder for an attacker to detect and intercept data sent from one piece of equipment or system to another.

You use COMSEC as part of the TEMPEST security policy. COMSEC applies to transmitted or received data considered critical government information. COMSEC combines a number of methods at the same time to provide the most secure transmission possible.

FIGURE E-1 An example of virtual private networks over the public network.

Automated Information Systems (AIS)

An automated information system (AIS) is the assembly of various hardware and software components. The hardware components of an AIS can be a personal computer, minicomputer, or mainframe computer. The US government uses many automated information systems. These systems can support desktop, client/server, and mini- or mainframe applications. The evolution of automated information systems includes the following:

- Mainframe computing
- Minicomputer processing
- Personal computer processing
- Local area networking
- Client/server processing
- Distributed processing
- Virtualization processing
- Cloud computer processing

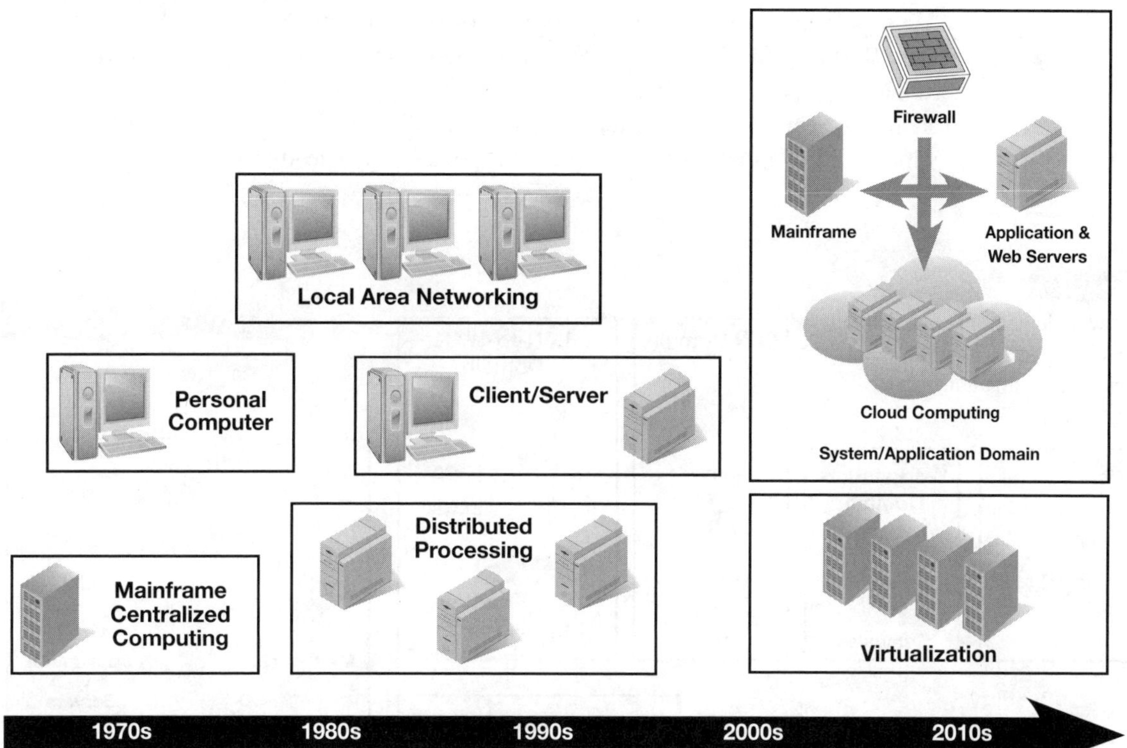

FIGURE E-2 A timeline of computing and computer networking.

US government agencies require automated information systems. Throughout the history of information systems, agencies' computer and data processing systems have evolved to meet the demands of users and their agency directives. Federal agencies need computing and data processing systems to serve the needs of the citizens of the US. This need drives automated information systems for government agencies. Servicing enhanced, secure, and high-performing computer systems requires information system and information systems security professionals.

Automated information systems require information systems, information technology, and security professionals. Use of AIS must start with user requirement definitions, system design, procurement, and deployment. Along each step in the process, information system professionals must not only design and build but manage and maintain computing and data processing systems. This requires program management, system administration, and ongoing technical support to maximize availability, confidentiality, and integrity.

Use of US government automated information systems must adhere to compliance laws and mandates. For the military, the Department of Defense (DoD) has defined the Department of Defense Certification and Accreditation Process (DIACAP). Civilian agencies must comply with the Federal Information Systems Management Act (FISMA). These laws and mandates require information systems security and information assurance. Without this, US government automated information systems would be vulnerable to risks, threats, and attacks.

To ensure the confidentiality, integrity, and availability of US federal government agency information and data, you must use proper security throughout your

FIGURE E-3

The seven domains of a typical IT infrastructure or automated information system (AIS).

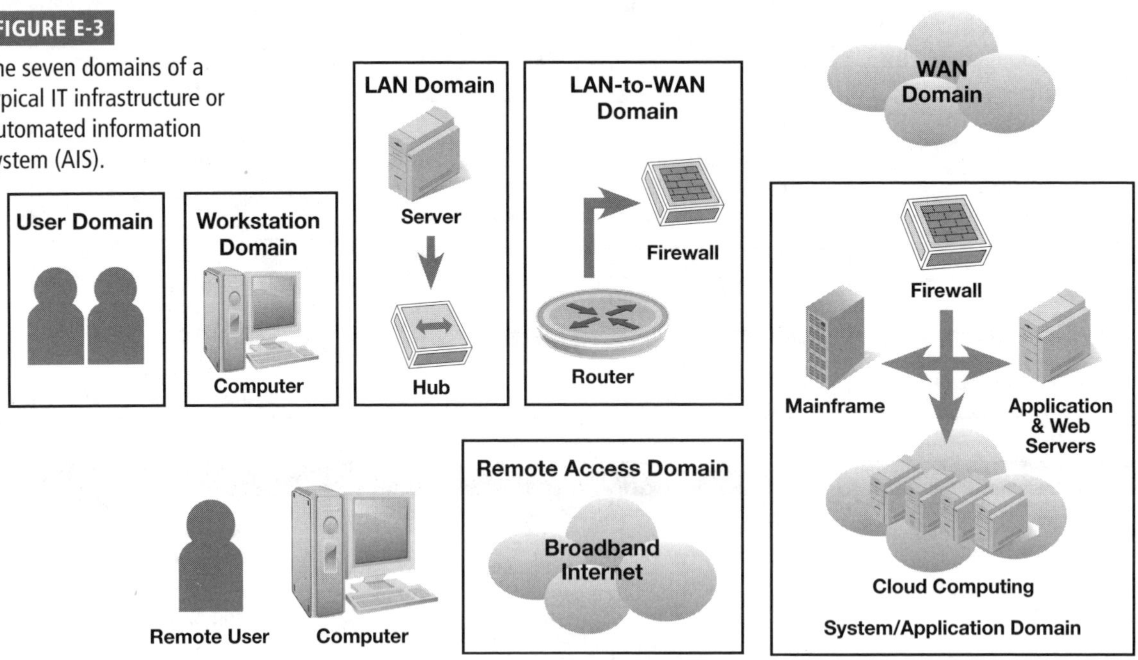

IT infrastructure. Your IT infrastructure consists of the seven domains of a typical IT infrastructure. Use defense in depth or a layered security strategy. Layered security is like an onion with many layers. By implementing layered security controls, you ensure information security throughout your infrastructure.

Hardware

Distributed Versus Standalone Systems

A distributed system is any computer connected to another computer system or group of computers that transmit, exchange, share, or use the same software applications. A standalone system is a computer system that is not attached to any other computer or group of computer systems.

Distributed computer systems communicate from one computer or computer system to another and provide additional computer services or features that would be unavailable or not cost effective on a single standalone computer. Distributed systems also allow easier, more cost-efficient maintenance of the software or computer applications.

Use distributed systems when you have two or more computers doing the same tasks or using the same software and applications. If you use standalone systems instead, it might take more time, space, power, and maintenance to provide the same results as you using the distributed system.

Use a distributed computer system instead of a standalone computer whenever a new computer function or task will run on several different computers. The distributed system lets you keep costs down by setting up the computers in different areas and still have them perform as if they were physically next to each other.

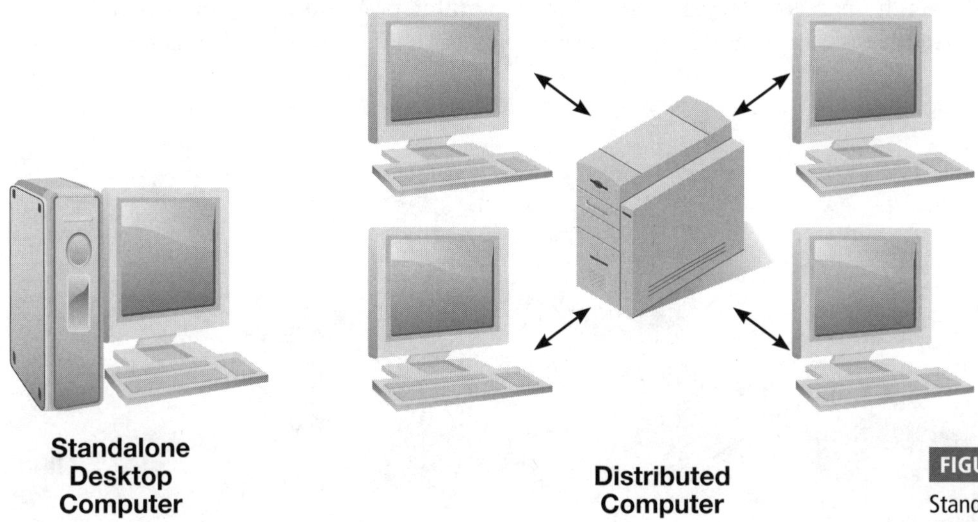

FIGURE E-4 Standalone and distributed systems.

Microcomputers and Miniframe and Mainframe Computers

The terms microcomputer, miniframe, and mainframe refer to certain types of computers and usually refer to the computer's size or processing power. A microcomputer is a computer with a microprocessor as its central processing unit. Such computers are usually small compared to miniframe and mainframe computers. A miniframe computer is a computer that allows up to six users to work on the same physical PC hardware all at the same time, but running different programs from each other. Mainframe computers are powerful computers used mainly by corporate and government organizations for critical applications, bulk data processing, and large transaction processing. The term originally referred to the large cabinets containing the central processing unit and main memory of early computers. Later, the term was used to distinguish high-end commercial machines from less powerful units.

Different sizes or processing capabilities are necessary to fill the different requirements of federal agencies throughout the country. Not every agency or branch has to have the processing power of a mainframe, and some are more apt to use a miniframe for their applications. Moreover, the cost difference between the different computer platforms allows just about every federal agency to take advantage of today's computer technology.

Use this range of computer system configurations to perform the functions and tasks of your agency much faster and more accurately. The use of these computers not only speeds up the calculating processes and functions, but also helps you become more efficient and more accurate in accomplishing daily tasks. These systems can eliminate just about all errors caused by users performing the same tasks and calculations manually.

Use this range of configurations whenever you are building an office or location where users will have to perform many repetitive daily tasks. These computers perform these tasks faster and with less error and are less expensive over long periods when compared with their human counterparts. A single micro-, mini- or mainframe computer can perform the tasks of several hundred users doing the same task with fewer errors.

FIGURE E-5

A microcomputer, a miniframe, and a mainframe computer.

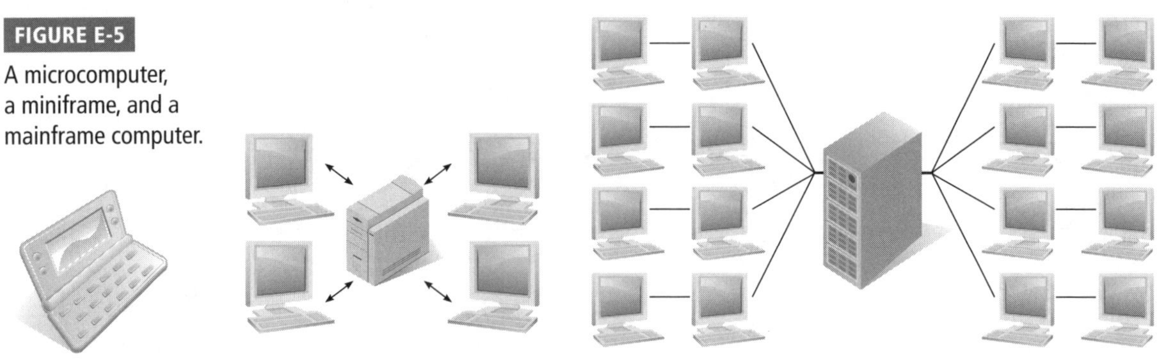

Storage Devices

Storage devices or data storage—often called simply storage—refers to numerous types of physical computer components and recording media that retain digital data. Storage devices or data storage is a core function and fundamental component of computers, computer systems and/or computer networks. Common storage devices are always tied to hard drives, whether they are regular or solid state drives.

Storage devices are necessary as a means to securely store or collect as well as retrieve electronic digital data written, gathered or obtained. Storage devices can hold small to very large amounts of digital data information. Storage devices eliminate the use of traditional paper documents that take up much more physical space than a standard storage device. Storage devices can be internal, external, fixed, and portable.

Use storage devices whenever you need to keep the information or a copy of information on a computer system or computer network. You can keep this copy as long as necessary, or archive it as a permanent record as long as you maintain the condition and security of the storage device. Follow the critical applicable FISMA or DIACAP mandates, depending on your federal agency.

Federal agencies must follow strict data classification standards to safeguard information stored on its automated information systems. Pay particular attention to compliance laws, because you use storage devices whenever a new computer or computer network is being set up. The storage device is typically installed within the computer system itself, or the computer is connected to a computer network that has one or multiple storage devices located on that network for use by multiple computers.

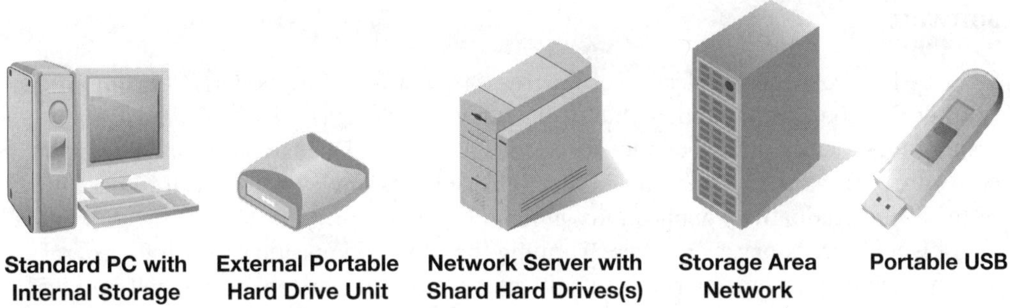

FIGURE E-6 Several different types of storage devices.

Components

Components are the physical pieces assembled to make up a computer or computer system. Components may be internal or external parts and pieces of the computer and are usually referred to as hardware. The number of components in a computer is limited to the number of slots provided by the main component or motherboard.

Components allow the computer to perform the various tasks required by a user or facility working with the computer or computer system. Certain components are specifically designed for specific tasks and technologies. Without these different components, a computer or computer system can be very limited in the tasks it can perform and the speed at which it performs them.

Use components to perform the functions and tasks that you need a computer or computer system to perform. Build or install the correct components so the computer can perform the tasks quickly and correctly. If you use incorrect components, the computer cannot handle the required tasks or will perform very slowly. The computer may even shut down or lock up all together.

Use components whenever you are building a computer or computer system to perform a set of tasks. Use of the correct components is largely determined by the main component or motherboard. The motherboard is set up with various slots that the other components can connect to in order to perform tasks and use certain technologies.

FIGURE E-7

Some of the components in a computer system.

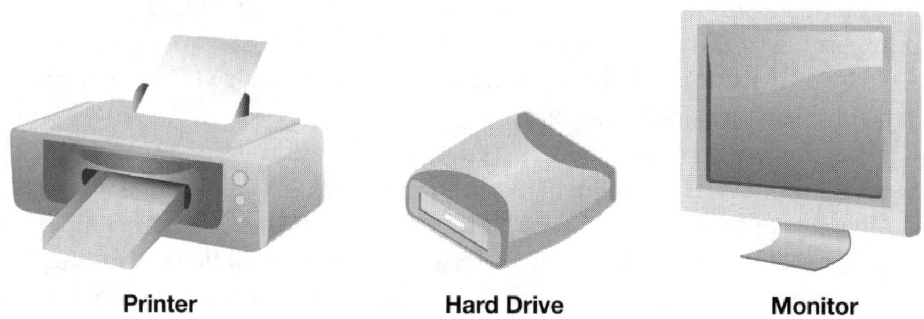

Software

Software is a program or collection of programs that provide instructions to a computer or other electronic device about what to do and how to do it. Think of software as the brain of most devices and appliances or as the fundamental instructions that make all the hardware parts work together and do their jobs. Some examples are firmware, operating systems, and productivity applications, among others.

Software is necessary everywhere: running the workstations and servers of a federal agency, making printers and routers do their jobs, powering custom productivity applications for services, or coordinating data transmissions between the battlefield and a satellite during warfare. Nowadays, every electronic computing device runs on some sort of software. This particular fact opens the door to one of the most critical problems in information systems security: software vulnerabilities. US government agencies need stringent best practices to manage software application vulnerabilities. These best practices allow an organization to minimize any risk or threat to an installed software application.

Software applications support government agencies in providing citizen services. The use of the software applications depends on the task that the agency is working to accomplish. This includes protecting medical records, filing IRS returns, or providing military intelligence support. The critical task is to eliminate risk and vulnerability by using a comprehensive software management cycle and assessment.

Use of software applications for the US government must comply with applicable laws and mandates. For the military, the Department of Defense (DoD) has defined the Defense of Defense Certification and Accreditation Process (DIACAP). Civilian agencies must comply with the Federal Information Systems Management Act (FISMA). These laws and mandates dictate the need for software security and information assurance. Without this oversight, US government automated information systems would be vulnerable to risks, threats, and attacks.

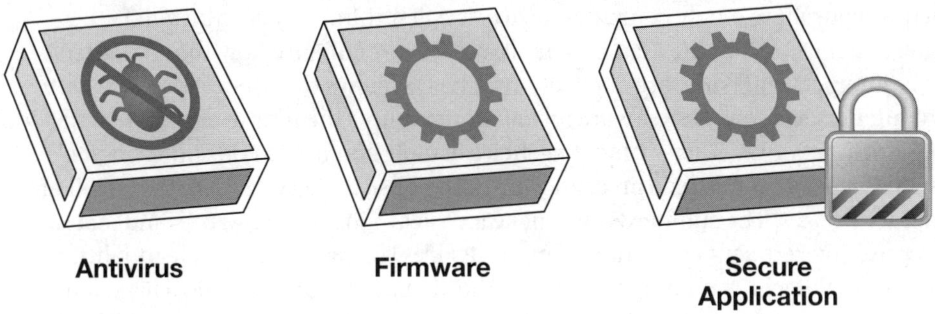

FIGURE E-8
The following figures illustrate different types of software.

Operating Systems

An operating system (OS) is the heart of a computer. Operating systems run in any device with a computer processing unit (CPU). The operating system is what controls the computer's hardware and allows software applications to run in the computer's memory. Employees who use software applications are dependent on the operating system of their computers. Think of the operating system as the set of instructions that runs the computer hardware and software applications. Devices with CPUs that need operating systems include smartphones, laptops, workstations, servers, minicomputers, and mainframe computers.

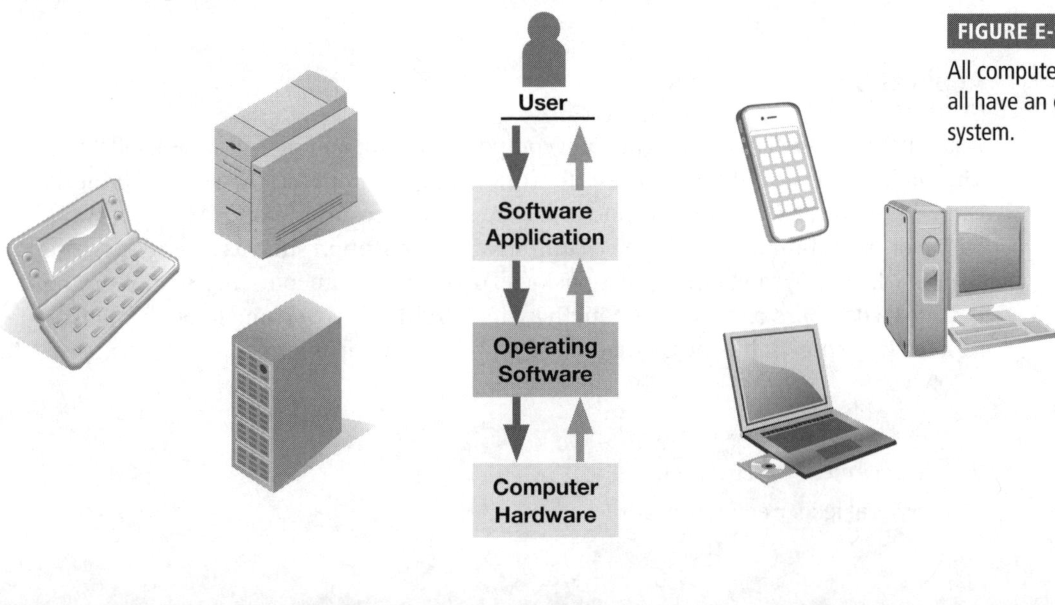

FIGURE E-9
All computer devices all have an operating system.

Operating systems enable CPUs to run within commonly used devices. Without an OS, computer devices cannot function. An OS makes computer hardware and software applications function. This represents the greatest opportunity for an attacker trying to compromise a computer device. Attacking an electronic device's OS, an attacker can take control of the hardware and software. This means an attacker can compromise all data on that device. It is important, therefore, to secure the OS within an electronic device. Securing or hardening the OS means you install software updates and security patches as soon as they are released.

When you purchase a new computer device, the first thing you do is install the operating system. OS software installation allows you to configure how the computer hardware interacts with software applications. The OS allows the user to interface with the computer device. New OS software installation requires the user to enable desired features and functions. US government agencies usually conform to OS configuration standards. These standards help an agency install a consistent OS environment in all of its computer devices. The standards also make it easier to install, configure, and manage an enterprise environment consisting of many devices. To ensure the confidentiality, integrity, and availability of computer devices, hardening the OS is a critical first step. Hardening means you install the latest software updates and security patches to eliminate bugs and vulnerabilities.

You harden computer devices whenever you find a software vulnerability. A software vulnerability is a weakness in the OS. These weaknesses are usually found and fixed by the software vendor as soon as possible. Attackers perform software vulnerability scans to find weaknesses or old OS software in an attempt to exploit a vulnerability. You can perform periodic software vulnerability assessment scans to find OS bugs and weaknesses. After finding a software bug or vulnerability, install software updates and security patches to eliminate these vulnerabilities.

US government agencies must use stringent best practices to manage software OS vulnerabilities. These best practices allow an organization to minimize any risk or threat in an OS.

Applications

If an operating system is the heart of a computer system, an application is its lifeblood. The application is what the user uses to work with the computer. On a smartphone, it can be a phone call, e-mail, IM chat, or a browser to access the World Wide Web. On a laptop or workstation, it can be office automation application such as a word processor, a spreadsheet program, or graphics package. In a server, minicomputer or mainframe, it can be a database or custom productivity tool. In the US government, applications support government business functions. Examples of government applications include the following:

- IRS tax return processing
- government procurement
- general ledger accounting

- electronic medical records
- building facilities management
- network management
- military intelligence
- terrorist tracking

Think of an application as software that enhances human productivity by automating a manual function. Software applications support government agencies in providing citizen services. Without applications, the US government would operate in manual mode. Productivity would be hindered. Things like tax returns, tax refunds, or military intelligence, and terrorist tracking would be at a standstill. Think of a software application as the tool that automates and enhances government business operations. Software is critical in military warfare, terrorist intelligence gathering, and satellite reconnaissance.

If the operating system is the heart of a computer, the software application is its lifeblood. It provides productivity enhancement, rapid analysis, and access to databases and information in real-time. Software applications install on newly purchased computer devices. In addition, new software applications install on existing computer devices. You need proper software application installations and configurations to ensure proper operation. US government agencies usually conform to certain software application purchasing and configuration standards. This helps an agency install consistent software applications on all of its computer devices. This also makes it easier to install, configure, and manage an enterprise environment of many devices. To ensure the confidentiality, integrity, and availability of computer devices, hardening software applications is a critical first step. Hardening means you install the latest software updates and patches to eliminate bugs and vulnerabilities found in the software application.

You must harden software applications—like a word processor, spreadsheet, browser or database—whenever you find a software vulnerability. A software vulnerability is a weakness or bug in the software application. Software vendors usually identify and fix these weaknesses or bugs as soon as they are able. Attackers perform software vulnerability scans to find weaknesses or old software applications in an attempt to exploit that vulnerability. You can perform periodic software vulnerability assessment scans to eliminate the software application's bugs and weaknesses. After you find a software bug or vulnerability, you must install software updates and security patches to eliminate these vulnerabilities. This update is critical for database software applications that work with confidential data.

US government agencies follow stringent best practices to manage software application vulnerabilities. These best practices allow an organization to minimize any risk or threat in an installed software application.

Memory

Computer memory is like your own memory. You have short-term memory for things that occur in real time. You also have long-term memory for things that occurred in the past. Sometimes the memory can remember things in sequence. Other times your memory can remember things randomly without sequence. Every computer device has different types of memory to function effectively and efficiently. For example, when you power up a computer, it also powers up the device's random access memory (RAM). RAM is the amount of built-in computer data storage that your computer device has. RAM helps load a real-time operating system and software applications required by the user. Sequential access memory (SAM) is still in use today. Examples of SAM devices include hard disks, CD-ROMs and magnetic tape where the user accesses data on the storage device in sequence. Non-volatile RAM (NVRAM) is a hard drive or storage device like a USB thumb drive. The data saves and stores in NVRAM even when you power the computer device down.

FIGURE E-10

All computer devices have memory.

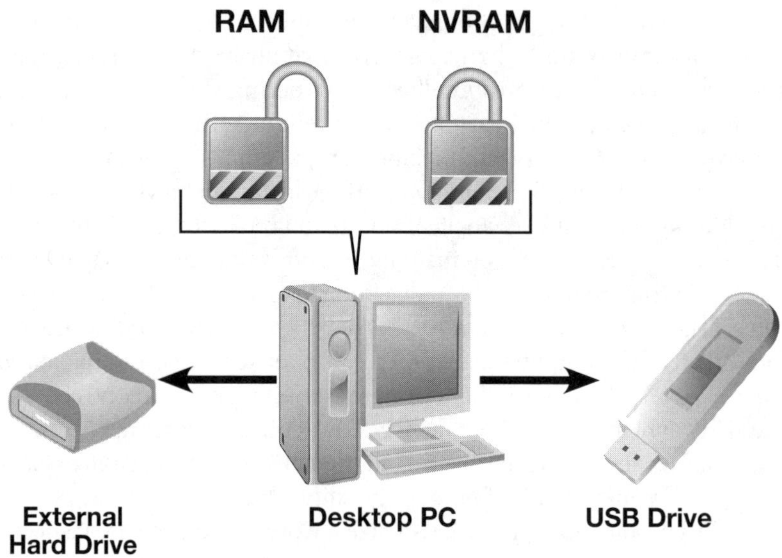

Memory is what makes a computer operate efficiently. With RAM, a computer can load its operating system and software applications. RAM allows a computer to store short-term data and allows it to perform additional functions. This is what allows a computer to multitask using many software applications at once. NVRAM is a hard drive or external USB hard drive. It allows you to store configurations or data on a computer device even after you power down. Sequential access memory (SAM) means you must access that data in sequence from a hard drive, CD, or magnetic tape drive. You must access the memory sequentially to get to the part of the data you need.

Use of memory—no matter what kind—requires proper security controls. This is especially important if your computer is accessing confidential data or information. This confidential data is stored in RAM while your computer device is running, leaving the data fully exposed. NVRAM or storage of confidential data can also be subject to compromise. This is particularly true if that data is unencrypted in its storage state. Use of SAM for storing confidential data requires unique security controls, especially if this data resides on a hard drive, CD, or magnetic tape. Proper security safeguards, including encryption, are necessary for confidentiality.

It's possible to extract RAM, NVRAM, and SAM memory from a computer device. How this data gets stored in its normal state or encrypted state depends on whether that data must be secure. Proper security controls are necessary depending upon the type of data accessed. US government agencies have a data classification standard that defines how data stores both short-term and long-term memory. Confidential data might need to be to be encrypted or stored in memory devices that are inaccessible without proper controls, such as a secure storage area network (SAN) device or encrypted hard drive.

US government agencies use stringent security controls for memory containing confidential data. This data classification dictates how you handle a computer's access to stored data. You may need to ensure proper removal of confidential data from RAM and NVRAM before you power down a computer, for instance. This includes SAM devices and the use of encryption to protect unauthorized access to confidential data. Depending on the computer, use of RAM, NVRAM, SAM and the removal of storage devices and memory may be necessary. Thin clients, for example, lack hard drives; this prevents their users from storing confidential data locally on them. You can disable the USB ports of computers for which you are responsible, in order to prevent transfer to data onto a USB thumb drive. US government agencies must use best practices on their computers whenever a new installation occurs. This includes proper removal of confidential data on RAM, NVRAM, SAM or other memory storage device. This may also include the disabling USB ports, hard drives, and other external data storage devices.

Policies and Procedures

Emission Security (EMSEC)

Emission Security (EMSEC) refers to federal and Defense Department rules and regulations to keep secure and safe information that might be sent from any equipment or system. These rules focus on providing confidentiality by including protocols to determine if nearby equipment or systems can intercept or detect a signal from secure equipment or systems.

EMSEC is critical to provide confidentiality, one of the three pillars in information security. EMSEC is mandatory for any military agency working under DIACAP. You must implement EMSEC on any piece of equipment or system that sends, receives, or holds sensitive information, to protect it and keep it secure from crosstalk. This is particularly important because it helps prevent and control unintended information leakage.

In addition, test all equipment and systems for EMSEC or signal crosstalk in accordance with TEMPEST security and EMSEC policies.

TEMPEST security and EMSEC policy require that you test all equipment, computer systems, power wires, and data cabling within a building or an area for signal crosstalk. You must implement EMSEC in any federal agency building that holds equipment or systems that send, receive, or hold sensitive data.

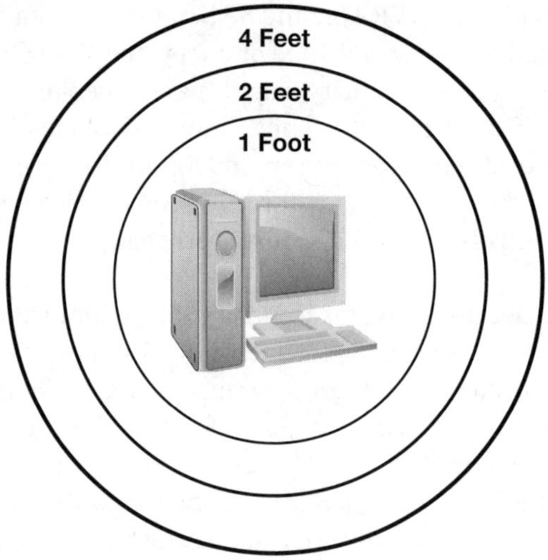

FIGURE E-11

An illustration of the distance a typical device might emit signals. The rings represent the electronic emissions given off by a given piece of equipment. The farther away you get from the computer, the lower the emissions.

Transmission Security

Transmission security keeps information from being intercepted or detected as a signal is being sent from one piece of equipment or system to another. It also defines ways to check whether an unauthorized party can detect and intercept a signal.

The flow of traffic may reveal a lot about activities that should be kept secure. A careful attacker can figure out from the amount of data and the direction of data flow the different types of activities you are hosting.

Transmission security uses different signal patterns when sending secure data or information from one piece of equipment or system to another. These hide the patterns in a signal when they are sent, so that the patterns can't reveal information.

Another form of transmission security is to monitor the electrical voltage going across a wire or cable to detect whether someone is tapping into the wire or cable. It is harder to tap into fiber cables than into copper cables.

Transmission security is part of the TEMPEST security policy. You must implement transmission security any time one piece of equipment or system sends secure information or data to another. Follow the TEMPEST Black/Red cable policy in place.

Line Authentication

Line authentication means verifying that the transmission line or method is secure—that security controls are in place as required if you are transmitting confidential data. You must perform this verification before sending or communicating confidential data.

You must be authorized to send the data in question. This requires verifying your identity. Likewise, the identity of the data receiver must be verified, to ensure that the person is who he says he or she is and that he or she is authorized to receive the data being sent.

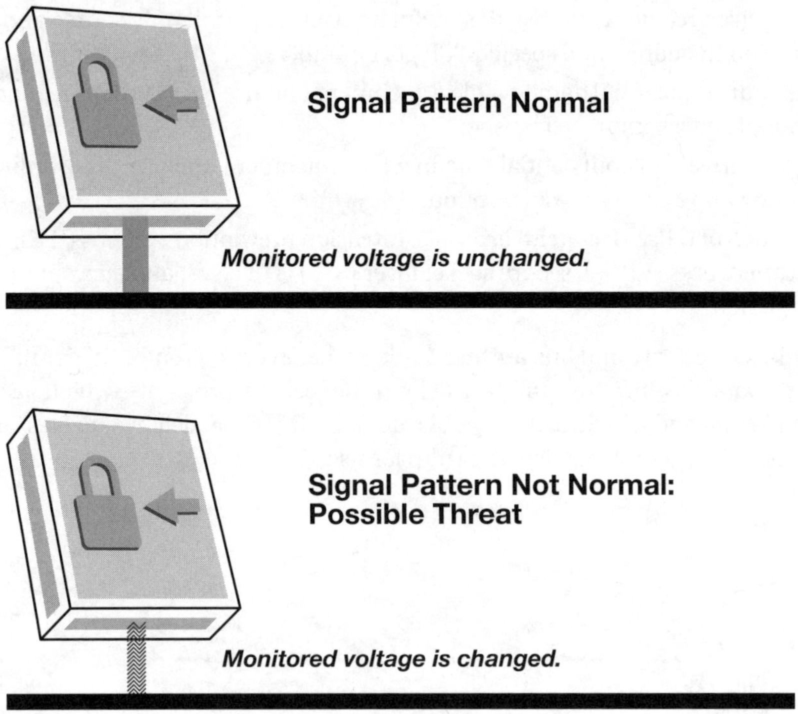

FIGURE E-12 An illustration of how transmission security can monitor a cable or wire.

Transmission security pertains to how you send data and what medium you use, such as:

- analog voice conversation
- digital voice conversation
- analog or digital communication circuit
- private wide area network
- e-mail
- USB hard drive
- public Internet

FISMA (for civilian agencies) and DIACAP (for military agencies) define security controls for transmitting confidential data. Agency data classification standards define types of data—these types include confidential data and data in the public domain. Confidential transmission requires proper security controls, including authenticating the user and the transmission method.

The methods for ensuring that the user and the transmission line are secure include:

- Voice conversation: Confirm caller and receiver via voice verification and number dialed.
- Analog or digital communication circuit: Confirm that the source and destination is valid and test the link.

- Private wide area network: Use IP stateful firewalls to permit only source and destination IP address and specific TCP port numbers.
- E-mail: Put confidential data in a file attachment and use password protection and appropriate encryption via transport.
- USB hard drive: Put confidential data in a file attachment and use password protection and appropriate encryption.
- Public Internet: Use IP stateful firewalls, intrusion prevention systems (IPS), virtual private networks (VPNs), secure socket layer (SSL) HTTPS://, and appropriate encryption.

Use transmission security and line authentication whenever you send confidential data. The agency's data classification standard defines the security protocol—which agency data is confidential and which is in the public domain. Once you define data classification, the agency and the user must follow the rules for use.

FIGURE E-13 An example of virtual private networks (VPNs) over the public network.

Frequency Hopping

Frequency hopping is a way to protect information that might be vulnerable to interception as a signal is being sent from one piece of equipment or system to another. You usually use it during radio transmissions or other transmission through the airwaves.

Frequency hopping keeps information from being intercepted, detected, or jammed by an unauthorized party. You use frequency hopping so that an attacker cannot figure out the signal from a single frequency. To intercept the data, an attacker must monitor multiple frequencies constantly, which is costly and requires more equipment and time.

Frequency hopping divides the data into many smaller pieces and sends the pieces across many frequencies simultaneously. The pieces are then put back together on the receiving side to make a complete piece of data. The sending and receiving equipment or system uses the same frequencies so that the information is always sent, received, and read correctly by your equipment or systems.

Use frequency hopping any time a piece of equipment or system sends sensitive or secure data to another piece of equipment or system using radio or the airwaves.

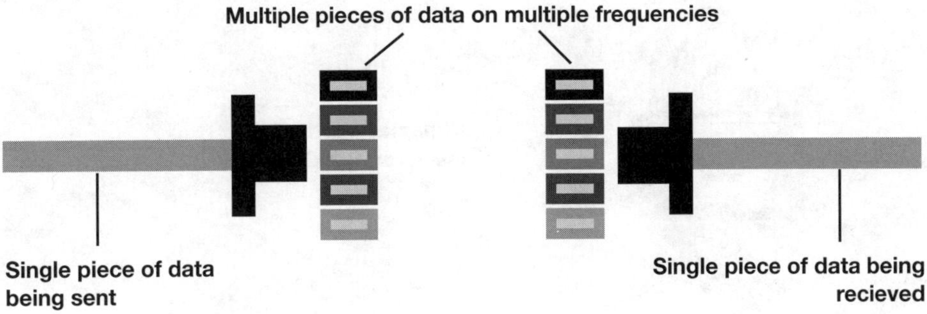

FIGURE E-14 An illustration of frequency hopping sending data as pieces across several frequencies and then putting them back together on the other side as a single piece of data.

Masking

Masking is concealing or hiding something. The most popular known form of masking is using a password to log in to a computer or piece of equipment or system. The typed letters appear as symbols only and do not reveal the password on the screen.

Masking ensures that the signal and its information will reach its intended destination without an attacker detecting, intercepting or jamming it during transmission.

Masking originally set up devices to send out signals that didn't differentiate between different data values. Early masking attempts operated several devices at once, so that their combined output would mask individual signals. This approach rarely worked. Typically, a device had to be redesigned to radiate a uniform signal.

This original masking method is now obsolete and has been replaced by newer techniques that include:

- Lower-power output signal: This keeps the output signals so low that adversaries can't detect them and target them for jamming.
- Burst transmissions: These avoid two-way radio transmissions and rely instead on brief, highly compressed messages. Each message is transmitted in a very brief burst that is hard to detect and jam before the transmission ends.
- Directional transmissions: These use either directional radio transmissions or optical techniques, like a directed laser, to hinder interception, detection, and jamming. These often are restricted to line-of-sight transmissions.
- Spreading spectrum transmissions: These send the transmission across a range of frequencies to make it harder to detect. Noise is mixed in with the transmission to make it harder to distinguish the communication traffic from random noise.

Use masking any time you transmit sensitive or secure data by radio or airwaves. Include it as part of a secure transmission whenever a radio or airwave transmission takes place.

FIGURE E-15

The typical password masking on a computer system.

Directional Signals

Directional signals are signals sent in a single direction. The most common directional signal today is the microwave antenna transmission. You commonly use directional antennas to provide reliable transmission and communication security over long distances.

Directional signals keep information from being intercepted, detected, or jammed by an unintended party. US federal government agencies must comply with all applicable laws and mandates. Civilian agencies must comply with the Federal Information Systems Management Act (FISMA). Military agencies must comply with the Department of Defense Information Assurance Certification and Accreditation Process (DIACAP). These requirements define security controls for transmission of confidential data.

Directional signals use either directional radio transmissions or optical techniques, like a directed laser, to minimize the chance of interception, detection, and jamming. These directional signals often are restricted to line-of-sight transmissions. The main purpose is to provide confidentiality and integrity for all communications, which is particularly critical in warfare, intelligence-gathering, and defense operations.

Use directional signals any time you transmit sensitive or secure data by radio or airwaves. Include it to provide secure transmission whenever transmitting by radio or airwave over long distances.

FIGURE E-16

A directed microwave tower and an optical laser.

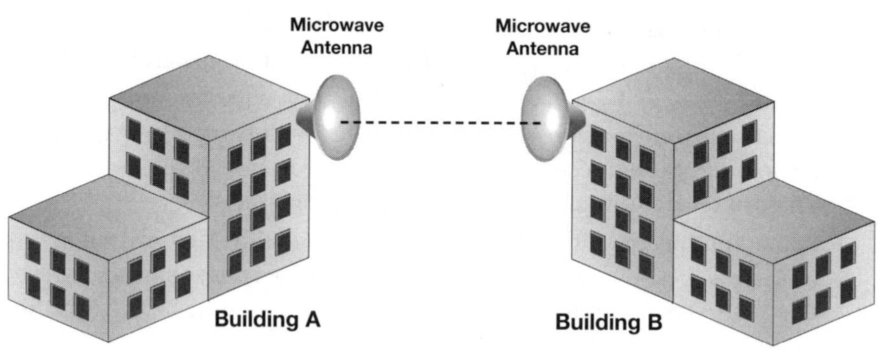

Burst Transmission

A burst transmission is a transmission that combines a very high data signaling rate with very short transmission times. Burst transmission usually uses compressed messages. This is popular with the military and spies, who wish to minimize the chances of detection of their transmissions.

Burst transmissions keep information from being intercepted, detected, or jammed by an unauthorized party. Burst transmissions are another way of masking data during radio or airwave transmissions.

Use a burst transmission as a way to avoid two-way radio transmissions and rely instead on brief, highly compressed messages. A burst transmission sends each message in a very brief signal that is hard to detect and jam before the transmission ends.

Use burst transmission any time you transmit sensitive or secure data by radio or airwaves. Use it to provide a secure transmission whenever you use a radio or airwave transmission.

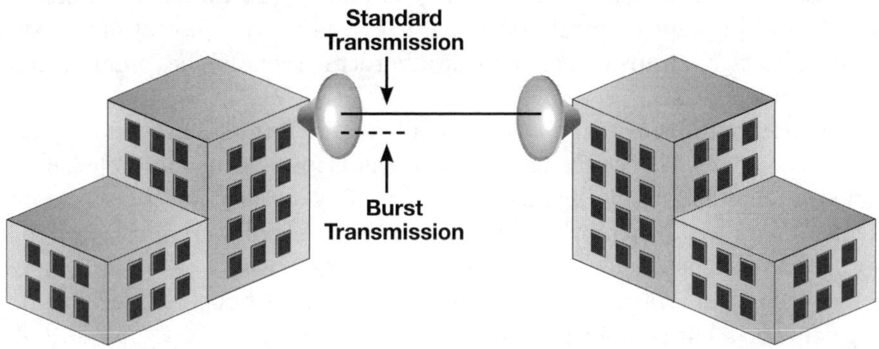

FIGURE E-17

A typical burst transmission.

Optical Systems

Early optical systems transmitted data using a waving flag or a flashing light. These forms of optical systems disappeared in the mid-1800s with the rise of electrical telegraph networks. Optical systems today use fiber optic cabling as a way to transmit data over greater distances than traditional copper cabling techniques. The fiber optic cabling serves as a "light pipe" to carry the signal. In addition, because the fiber carries "light pulses," the signal does not bend in the same way as traditional copper wire.

Optical systems using fiber cabling keep information more secure than traditional copper cabling. They keep the signal from being intercepted, since they are harder than copper cables to tap. Optical systems are immune to electromagnetic and radio interference—signal induction problems that usually arise in copper connections. A signal can travel greater distances using optical systems than traditional copper cabling. One critical thing is that fiber optic connections are more delicate to handle than regular copper wire. In this regard, US federal agencies must comply with laws and mandates regarding the protection of their cable infrastructure to guarantee availability of services. Civilian agencies must comply with the Federal Information Systems Management Act (FISMA). Military agencies must comply with the Department of Defense Information Assurance Certification and Accreditation Process (DIACAP). These compliance requirements define security controls for transmission of confidential data.

Use optical systems in the same way you use all copper telecommunications cabling. Optical systems can transmit the same services provided across copper cabling such as data, voice, and video. They require different end or connection devices but provide larger bandwidth capacity (the amount of data that can travel through the system at any given moment).

Use optical systems any time the distance for signal transmission exceeds its copper counterpart. You can also boost service availability in areas where radio interference and induction problems exist. In addition, since optical systems are harder to tap, federal agencies can improve confidentiality by switching from legacy copper infrastructure to fiber optic systems.

Spread Spectrum Transmission

Spread spectrum transmission is a radio signal technology that sends a transmission across a range of frequencies, making it harder to detect. This technology may also mix noise in with the signal transmission to make it harder to separate the communication traffic from random noise.

Spread spectrum transmission keeps information more secure than standard radio or airwave transmissions. The technology keeps the signal from being intercepted, detected, or jammed by an attacker while maintaining your ability to transmit between equipment or systems. Spread spectrum provides the most effective general-purpose protection for both security and availability.

Use spread spectrum transmission as part of the frequency hopping technology for masking data and securing information. Use the technology whenever you transmit secure data or information using radio or airwaves from one piece of equipment or system to another. The receiving equipment or system uses the same frequencies as the sending equipment or system, so that the information is always sent, received, and read correctly by the receiving equipment or systems.

Use spread spectrum transmission any time you use radio or airwave transmissions. Spread spectrum is one of the most effective forms for securing radio or airwave signals. It provides a very secure information or data link between equipment or systems.

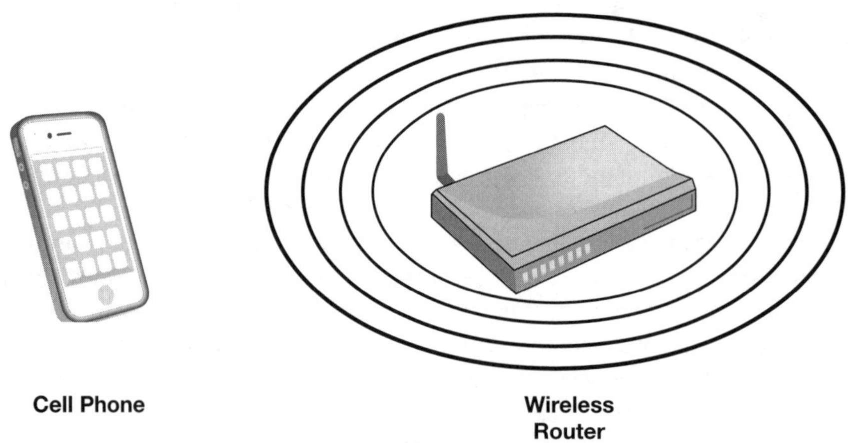

FIGURE E-18 Spread spectrum technology is used in devices such as cell phones and wireless access points/routers.

Covert Channel Control

Covert channel control prevents or inhibits crosstalk. Crosstalk occurs when the energy produced by a signal on one wire produces a detectable signal in another wire. In most cases, the problem is a bother—crosstalk allows noise into a clean signal—but in TEMPEST, crosstalk may allow data leakage. This may leak data from a higher-classified communications line to a lower-classified one.

Covert channel control ensures that a signal containing secure or sensitive data is safe or secure from interruption. Covert channel control typically is a function of copper wiring or cabling.

Use covert channel control to avoid crosstalk whenever possible. By its nature, fiber optic cabling is one way to help with covert channel control to halt crosstalk, since such cabling doesn't leak signal as copper wiring does. Optical systems can transmit the same services as copper cabling such as data, voice, and video more securely and at greater distances than copper cabling.

Covert channel control or crosstalk is part of the TEMPEST security policy. Use covert channel control every time a building or area within a building has wire or cabling installed and secure or sensitive data is to travel across that wiring or cabling. Careful attention to TEMPEST Black/Red cabling standards is a large piece of making sure that covert channel control succeeds and crosstalk is avoided.

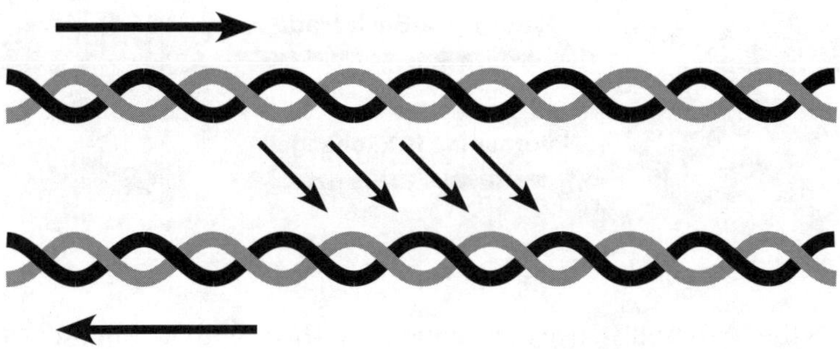

FIGURE E-19

Crosstalk over twisted copper wiring: Signal on one cable affects the other.

Dial-Back

Dial-back is a legacy end-to-end authentication method in which a dial-in request to a server, equipment, or system travels by a return call to the original number to verify the requester. The connection takes place only after both ends have been verified and proper credentials validated. The idea is to avoid spoofing and provide some level of confidentiality. The server, equipment, or system will not dial back to the original number unless that number is on a specific list or has made the correct exchange of a security key.

Dial-back authenticates both ends before communication takes place. This provides critical confidentiality and ensures the messages travel to the intended parties. In other words, dial-back ensures that data travels only to equipment and systems "approved" to receive such data. Remember that the system will dial back only to a known secure number or system that provides the correct security ID or key. This is particularly critical since civilian federal agencies must comply with the Federal Information Systems Management Act (FISMA) and military agencies must comply with the Department of Defense Information Assurance Certification and Accreditation Process (DIACAP) for transmission of confidential data.

Dial-back was an early way of trying to limit or securing a system and the data it contained. Dial-back is a common authentication feature available in most servers, equipment, and systems. It usually requires only connecting the system to a telephone line with a specific telephone number. The telephone number is available only to those parties or systems using, sending, and receiving information to and from that specific system.

Use dial-back as a way of securing a piece of equipment or system if the only connection available to the equipment or system is a standard telephone line. Dial-back is not the most secure or effective way to transmit secure or sensitive data currently used today. Use it only if no more secure transmission method is available. If you use dial-back, install the telephone line according to the TEMPEST Black/Red cabling procedures and test the line.

FIGURE E-20

A typical dial-back session.

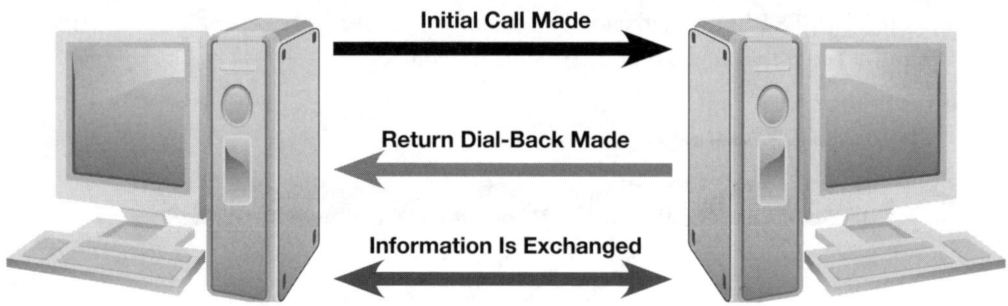

Line of Sight

Line of sight is the farthest distance information can travel with an unobstructed view from one point, place, or object to another point, place, or object. You typically use line of sight in microwave and laser transmitting situations. Infrared also uses line of site, but infrared bounces or reflects off other surfaces.

Line of sight ensures a clear transmission path from one piece of equipment or system or antenna to another when no copper or fiber cabling is present. In this case, the signal travels from one antenna to another antenna for either microwave or laser transmission.

Use line of sight by installing antenna towers to a certain height allowing the signal to travel on an uninterrupted path to the next antenna at great distances away. The terrain and location of a given antenna restricts the line-of-sight transmissions, as does, of course, the curvature of the earth. If you use an infrared signal, contain it within a building or room, because infrared signals can bounce or reflect off other surfaces and escape the area of transmission.

Use line of sight when standard copper or fiber cabling is not available or possible. Line of sight is not the most secure way to transmit secure or sensitive information unless you add other TEMPEST masking techniques to the signals.

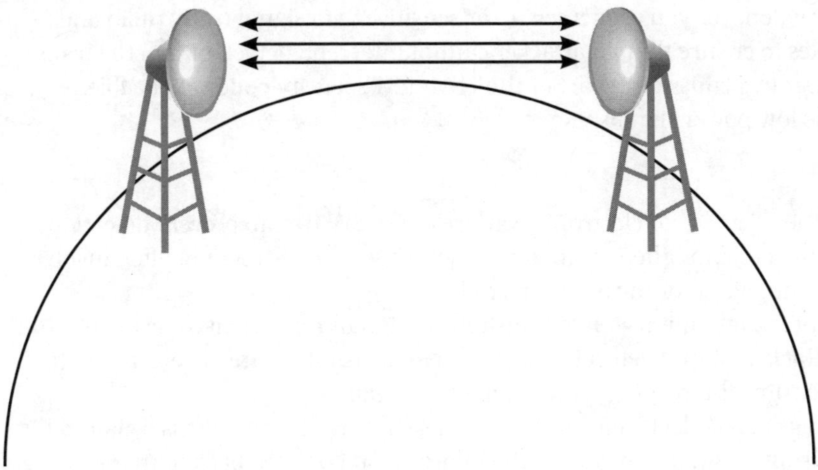

FIGURE E-21
An illustration of how antenna height compensates for the curvature of the earth and achieves a greater distance for transmission over line of sight.

Low Power

Low power is exactly that—the use of lower power when transmitting or when sending secure or sensitive data signals from one piece of equipment or system to another. Low power is particularly critical in military warfare, satellite reconnaissance, or intelligence gathering.

The use of low power ensures that an attacker cannot detect, intercept, or jam a transmitted signal containing secure or sensitive data. Low power transmitting is part of transmission security.

Use low power as part of electronic warfare (EW) and to secure transmitted data. Use low power when you transmit a signal by radio or airwave. Radio and airwave signals can include microwave or laser transmissions from one antenna to another that provide a way for a piece of equipment or system to send the data.

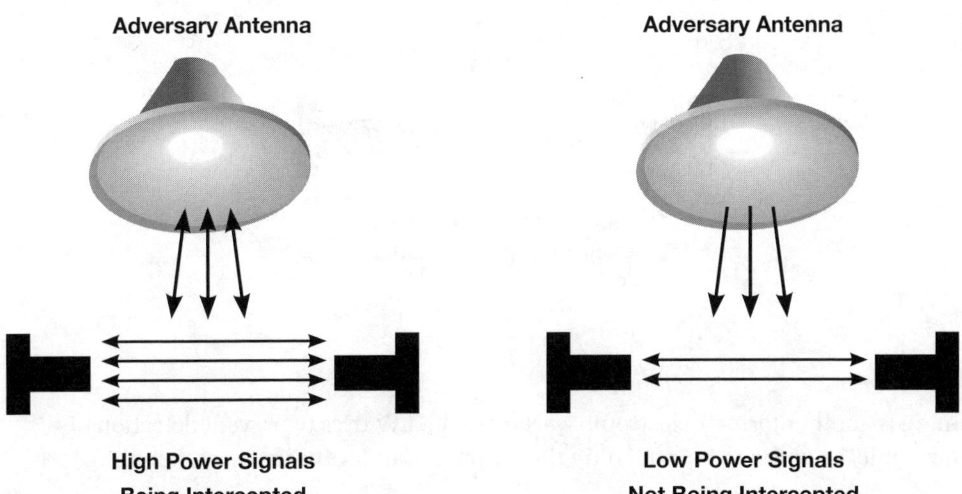

FIGURE E-22
High power and low power signals.

Use low power whenever you send a secure or sensitive data signal using radio and airwave techniques to ensure that an attacker cannot intercept, detect, or jam the transmission. Low power transmission is part of the TEMPEST security policy applicable whenever you use low power signals.

Screening

Screening is another element of electronic warfare (EW). EW tries to prevent detection of military units by screening them from radar or other sensors. Screening often involves active jamming or deception of the attacker's radar.

Screening ensures that military units transmitting signals remain invisible to an attacker. If the attacker cannot detect the unit used to transmit secure or sensitive data, they have a harder time intercepting or jamming the signals.

Use screening as part of electronic warfare (EW). One way of screening is by jamming. Suppose you transmit a signal that garbles the information bounced back to the radar. Instead of seeing a clean radar signal that indicates the target's direction, distance, and speed, the attacker sees a noisy bar that indicates only the general direction of the jammer itself. A more sophisticated jammer might actually adjust the radar signal either to indicate a target that's not really there or to hide the target entirely.

Use screening whenever you are trying to conceal or hide the location of a military device. In other others, use screening whenever you are placing a military transmission device somewhere.

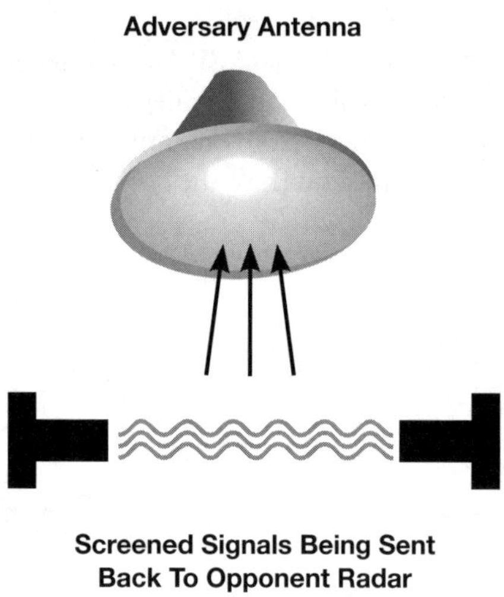

FIGURE E-23
A screened signal transmitted to secure the location of a device from an attacker.

Jamming

Jamming is another form of electronic warfare (EW). EW tries to prevent detection of military units by jamming or screening them from radar or other sensors. Jamming is the intentional use of radio frequency signals to interfere with the operation of a radar by saturating its receiver with noise or false information. Mechanical and electronic are two types of radar jamming.

Jamming ensures that military units transmitting signals remain undetected by an attacker. If the attacker cannot detect the unit transmitting secure or sensitive data, they have a harder time intercepting or jamming the signals.

Use jamming as part of electronic warfare (EW). One way of jamming is to transmit a signal that garbles the information bounced back to the radar. Instead of seeing a clean radar signal that indicates the target's direction, distance, and speed, the attacker sees a noisy bar that indicates the general direction of the jammer itself. A more sophisticated jammer might actually adjust the radar signal either to indicate a target that's not really there or to hide the target entirely.

Attackers can seriously disrupt operations if they block messages from commanders or from surveillance systems that detect and report targets. To counter an EW attack, try to avoid jamming by masking your transmitter from the opposition. Use jamming whenever masking is not a good option and you are trying to conceal the location of a military device.

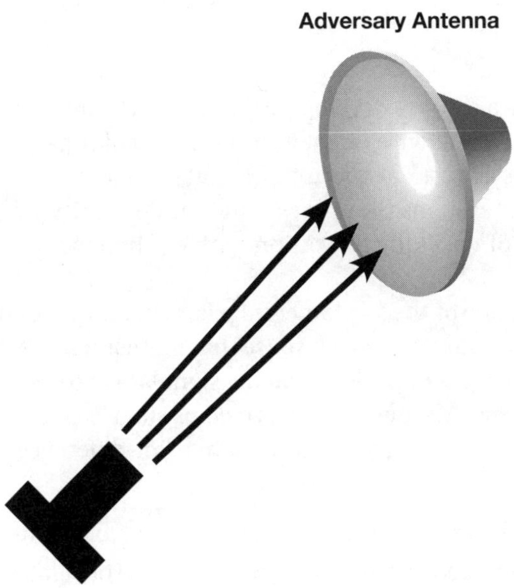

FIGURE E-24
Signals being sent out to jam a radar system.

Protected Wireline

Protected wireline is part of a protected distribution system (PDS). A PDS is a wireline or fiber-optic system that includes terminals and good sound electrical and physical safeguards to allow the standard transmission of classified information.

Protected wireline or PDS is required to transmit plaintext-classified information through an area of lesser classification or control. All three components of the information systems security triad are important. However, confidentiality is particularly critical during military warfare, counterterrorism intelligence gathering, and defense operations. Military agencies and branches must comply with the Department of Defense Information Assurance Certification and Accreditation Process (DIACAP), which defines security controls for transmission of confidential data.

Use PDS to safeguard physical access to electrical or electronic signals. In practice, a PDS primarily serves to slow down such an attack and to make the attack visible. You can find National PDS guidance in NSTISSI-7003. Protected wireline provides physical security of the transmission media—protecting all cables and terminals involved in the process. PDS improves and protects the medium's availability, as well.

The simplest way to use PDS consists of a single piece of pipe, conduit, or other uncut enclosure. The pipe carries the cables through the less-cleared area between the closed areas. Run the cables inside the pipe. The cables must reach the full transmission length unbroken to be protected. The PDS process also applies to civilian federal agencies since they must comply with the Federal Information Systems Management Act (FISMA) regarding secure transmission of confidential data.

TEMPEST Security

TEMPEST is a codename for a process developed by the Department of Defense for checking and studying leaking wire or cabling signals. Leaking signals consist of electrical, mechanical, or acoustical energy given off—accidentally or otherwise—by equipment or systems that process national security information. TEMPEST security is a way of checking a location with equipment or systems that may be leaking signals.

To provide confidentiality, one of the fundamental pillars in information security, TEMPEST sets the rules for checking any given space that has equipment or systems that can leak signals. It studies all forms of possible leaking signals because such signals may arise in many unexpected forms. Although many problems stem from unintended noise, you also face risks from other signals and even from power-line differences. Eight ways to stop the leakage are:

- Shielding: putting metal shields around the equipment to block out signals.
- Grounding: using proper electrical grounding to stop noise or signals and block possible signal crosstalk or interference between systems.
- Attenuation: adjusting the device so it uses less power and a weaker signal.
- Banding: limiting the number of frequencies you use to transmit a signal
- Using filtered power: putting filters on power lines and other wiring to stop signal leakage and secure the data.
- Cabling: using copper or fiber cables to send and receive voice, data, or video signals to a building or an area within a building.

- Using "zone of control" or zoning: establishing a safe area between the secure data and possible attackers.
- Providing TEMPEST separation: a gap between cables, wires, or equipment and systems in a building or area.

The rules defining TEMPEST zones, a Defense Department standard, are found in NSTISSAM TEMPEST/2-95. This document explains three zones and the three critical distances for equipment that define them:

- Zone A: a controlled area within a radius of 66 feet (20 m) or less
- Zone B: larger than Zone A but within a radius of less than 328 feet (100 m)
- Zone C: a controlled area at a distance of 328 feet (100 m) or more

To implement TEMPEST security, you must test individual equipment or systems for TEMPEST signal leakage and sort it into different levels. Then set up zone requirements according to equipment TEMPEST levels.

Your use of TEMPEST will depend on which laws and regulations directly apply to your federal agency. For example, agencies dealing with military information must follow the Department of Defense's Information Assurance Certification and Accreditation Process (DIACAP). Deploying TEMPEST begins with setting up a secure area. The specific requirements for TEMPEST protection vary from one application to another. The rules vary among agencies and projects and according to the sensitivity and possible site risks.

Shielding

Shielding refers to methods for reducing the signal or interference a piece of equipment, a system, or cabling gives off in a building or area within a building. Any piece of equipment or system giving off a signal or interference requires shielding.

Shielding prevents a signal from one piece of equipment or system from interfering with the signal of another piece of equipment or system in the same area. Shielding also helps separate the signals so that a signal from one system is not picked up by another system, creating a security risk.

In shielding, you measure how much signal crosstalk or interference a piece of equipment or system gives off. Then you place a metal cover or caging over equipment or system. This usually blocks the interference or signal crosstalk. Sometimes you ground the shielding to a common or earth ground to clear of all the interference present. Interference can also occur on the cables or wiring connected to a piece of equipment or system. You also shield the cable and wiring to help block the interference or signal crosstalk it gives off, if necessary.

Shielding is part of the TEMPEST security policy. Use shielding any time a building or area within a building houses a piece of equipment or system. Test all equipment or systems, power, and cabling within a building or area for interference or signal crosstalk, as required by TEMPEST security policies. Implement the TEMPEST shielding requirements if interference or signal crosstalk occurs on any piece of equipment or system or on its wiring and cabling.

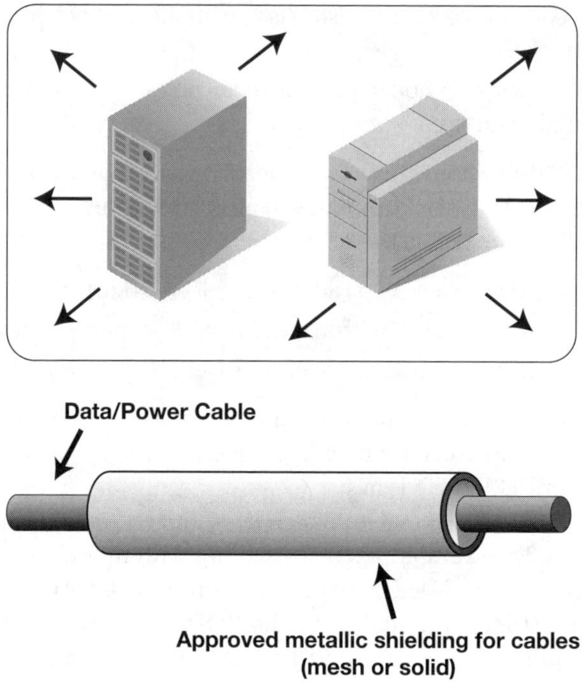

FIGURE E-25
An illustration of the basic idea behind shielding.

Grounding

Grounding or ground refers to a point in an electrical circuit were voltages are measured, to a common return path for electric current, or to a direct physical connection to the earth. All electrical circuits on alternating current (AC) or standard voltage (found within in a home or business) or on direct current (DC) voltage (for batteries or vehicles) need a ground or common return path for proper operation.

Grounding completes the voltage circuit for equipment or a system to work correctly. If equipment or a system is not grounded, it will not work because of insufficient voltage. In alternating current (AC), a grounding point or common to complete the circuit also prevents electrical shock to anyone touching the electrically charged wire.

Grounding completes the electric circuit to a common, negative, or earth ground point. Voltage is the difference between a given point in the circuit and the ground. A proper ground is also a way to stop noise or signals in an electrical wiring system. Separating the grounds for different systems also helps block possible signal crosstalk in the system or interference between one system and the other.

Grounding is part of the TEMPEST security policy. Use proper grounding any time you cable a building or area within a building with power. Install all power cabling according to the TEMPEST Black/Red policy. If it's not possible to implement the TEMPEST Black/Red cabling policy, you might need separate grounding of the different Black/Red circuits to block signal crosstalk or interference.

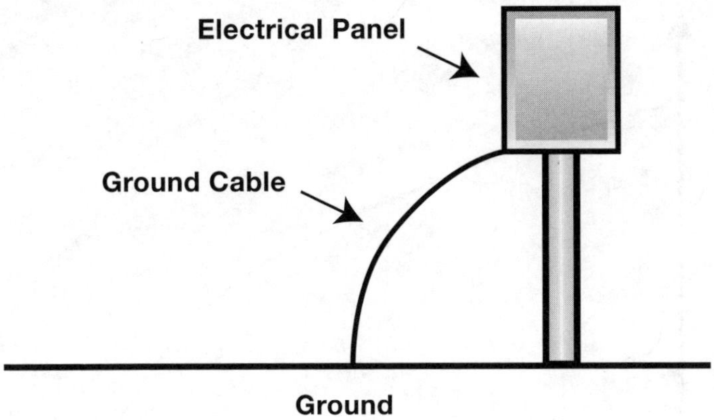

FIGURE E-26
A standard or typical earth grounding point for an AC electrical circuit or panel for a building.

Attenuation

Attenuation is the reduction of signal strength during transmission. Attenuation is of normal appearance when a signal is sent from one point to another. However, if the signal strength decreases too much, then the end device can't decode it. Protecting signals is particularly critical for military operations, intelligence agencies, and reconnaissance tasks.

Attenuation is necessary because it affects the distance a signal can travel on wires and fiber cables, as well as in the air (as radio waves). Decreased attenuation on a piece of equipment or system reduces the signal's ability to travel via other equipment or systems and/or to crosstalk to other wires or cables. This is useful when you are trying to conceal and protect information from unintended leakage.

To make use of attenuation, you adjust a given piece of equipment or system so that it uses less power and gives off a weaker signal. In some cases, you redesign the equipment or system to lower its signals without reducing its transmitting effectiveness. The goal is always to comply with federal laws, regulations, and mandates—in this particular case, the rules set by the Department of Defense.

Attenuation serves as a part of TEMPEST security when signals are leaking through wiring or cabling. Use attenuation whenever transmitting secure or sensitive information or data. You may not be able to adjust attenuation to get rid of all signal leakage or crosstalk, so attenuation, as a tactic, may leave the piece of equipment or system less useful or effective than you need it to be.

Banding

Banding, or frequency banding, is limiting the number of frequencies you use to transmit a signal and keeping other signals from interfering with those frequencies. It's also a way to keep someone else from intercepting or jamming the signal.

Banding is necessary because it secures a signal that may be carrying sensitive information. Frequency banding also makes sure the data travels only on those

FIGURE E-27

An attenuation curve for a signal sent from Building A to Building B.

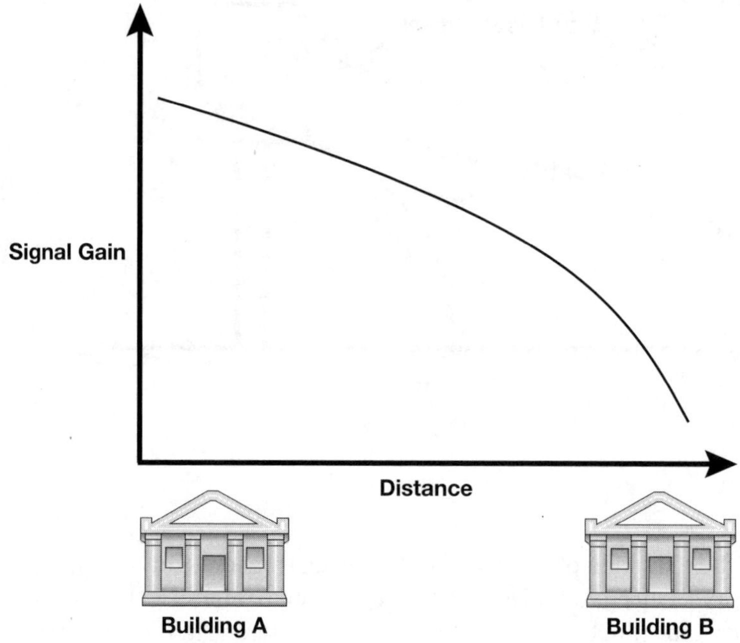

frequencies you allow and consider safe. Strict rules apply to open or public frequencies. These are compatible with Department of Defense rules. US federal agencies must comply with the laws and mandates regarding secure data transmission.

Frequency banding or banding uses filters on the wires or cables sending the data. You adjust the filters to allow the data to travel only across the frequencies that are secure for that data or information. Different filters serve for sending different types of data along copper wire or fiber-optic cable or over the airwaves (radio).

Use banding as a part of TEMPEST security to help secure a signal that's sending data. Start using banding as soon as you determine that the other methods used for TEMPEST security are not viable. Other TEMPEST security methods that may not be viable might include shielding, signal leaking, attenuation, or zoning.

FIGURE E-28

Frequency banding.

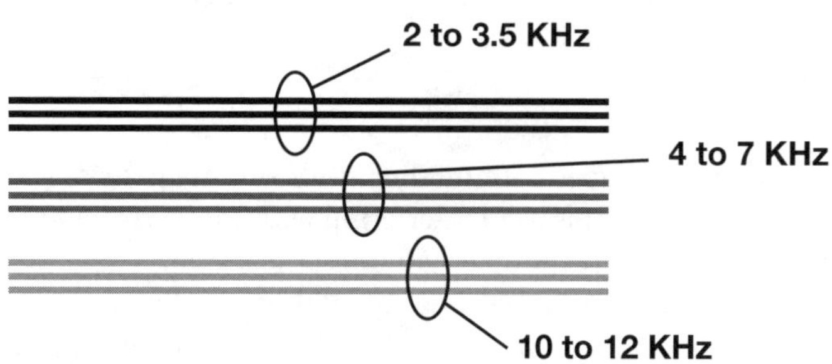

Filtered Power

Filtered power refers to filtering the signal of the power wires that feed equipment and systems. Filtering keeps power wires from sending out any signals and provides a much cleaner signal. Filtering protects one of the three pillars of information systems security: confidentiality. Use filtered power for an entire building or for individual power cords, if necessary.

Protecting power wires is critical, not only for day-to-day operations, but for compliance with federal mandates and regulations as well. Strict federal rules apply to agencies, mandating both filtered power and backup power for critical systems. Filtered power ensures that data or information signals containing confidential information cannot travel outside an area or building on the power wires in that area or building. This is particularly critical because power lines become vulnerable to leaking when they connect to the public grid or to a different area of the building.

Types of power filters vary, from internal or external filters to filters for a particular device or building class. Filtered power works the same way as any other traditional power source. The only difference is in the filter installed to prevent the signals from being sent across the power cables. Your agency must comply with any mandatory requirement from FISMA or DIACAP. The cables, plugs, and voltages on filtered power are all the same as other power sources. Equipment or systems connected to filtered power will not operate any differently.

Filtered power is part of TEMPEST security and Emission Security (EMSEC) policies. Use it any time a building or area within a building is about to be cabled with power. Install all power cabling within a building or area within a building following TEMPEST specifications.

Cabling

Cabling refers to any copper and fiber cables you use to provide power or send and receive voice, data, or video signals to a building or an area within a building. Cables can be aluminum, copper, or fiber optic, depending on building construction. As the default medium for transferring data and voice, cables need protection following the strict rules and mandates for your federal agency.

Eventually all data communication will pass through cables, whether aluminum, copper, or fiber. Proper and approved cabling is necessary to protect all three components of the information systems security triad: confidentiality, integrity, and availability. Cabling is usually necessary to connect critical services to a building or an area within a building. Strict rules apply to proper cabling and protection, depending on the federal agency. INFOSEC professionals, for example, must abide by and comply with the Federal Information Systems Management Act (FISMA) or DIACAP.

Cabling provides power, telecommunications, and video to a building or an area in the building. You must follow federal mandates and regulations regarding the installation and protection of cabling infrastructure. Civilian agencies must comply with FISMA. Military agencies must comply with FISMA or DIACAP.

FIGURE E-29

Dedicated cabling between government buildings. It could be carrying analog voice, digital voice, or data.

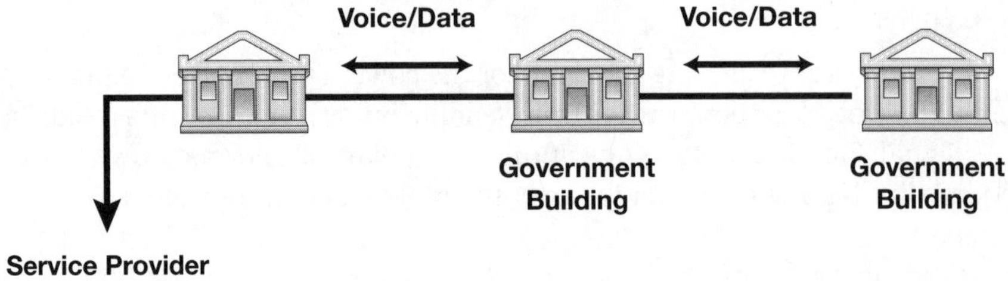

You must establish a cabling policy any time a building or an area within a building is cabled. Install all cabling according to the manufacturer's specifications. Follow the TEMPEST Black/Red cabling policy.

Zone of Control or Zoning

Zone of control, or zoning —also called TEMPEST zones—is a security strategy that establishes a zone of control around sensitive equipment or systems and restricts access to that area. You measure this zone in all dimensions: side to side, back to front, and up and down.

Implementing a zone of control keeps secure a piece of equipment or a system that sends, receives, or holds sensitive information. It bars any unauthorized person from access to that information for security reasons.

You implement a zone of control or TEMPEST zone by creating a secure area around a building or an area that contains sensitive equipment, systems, or information. Zone of

FIGURE E-30

An illustration of the zones around a device. Zones could include adjacent rooms.

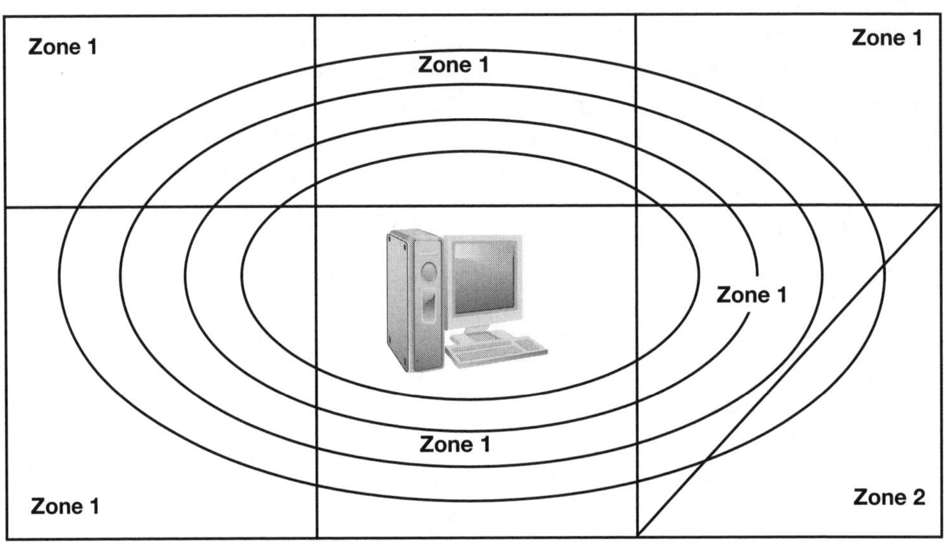

control/zoning began with the US Army and was originally set at 100 feet. The following lists the current zones of control or TEMPEST zones in place:

TEMPEST zones are defined in NSTISSAM TEMPEST/2-95. There are three critical measures:

- Zone A: a controlled area within a radius of 66 feet (20 m) or less
- Zone B: larger than Zone A and within a radius of less than 328 feet (100 m)
- Zone C: a controlled area at a distance of 328 feet (100 m) or more

You check each piece of equipment or system for TEMPEST output signals and sort them into different levels.

Zone of control or zoning is part of the TEMPEST security policy. Use it any time a building or an area contains a piece of equipment or system that sends, receives, or holds sensitive data. Test all equipment, systems, power, wires, and cabling within a building or an area for interference or signal crosstalk as required by the TEMPEST security policy.

TEMPEST Separation

TEMPEST separation is the gap between cables, wires, and equipment or systems in a building or an area created by the shielding on the equipment. TEMPEST separation keeps a signal from one piece of equipment, a system, wires, or cables from interfering with the signal of other equipment, systems, wires, or cables in the same area.

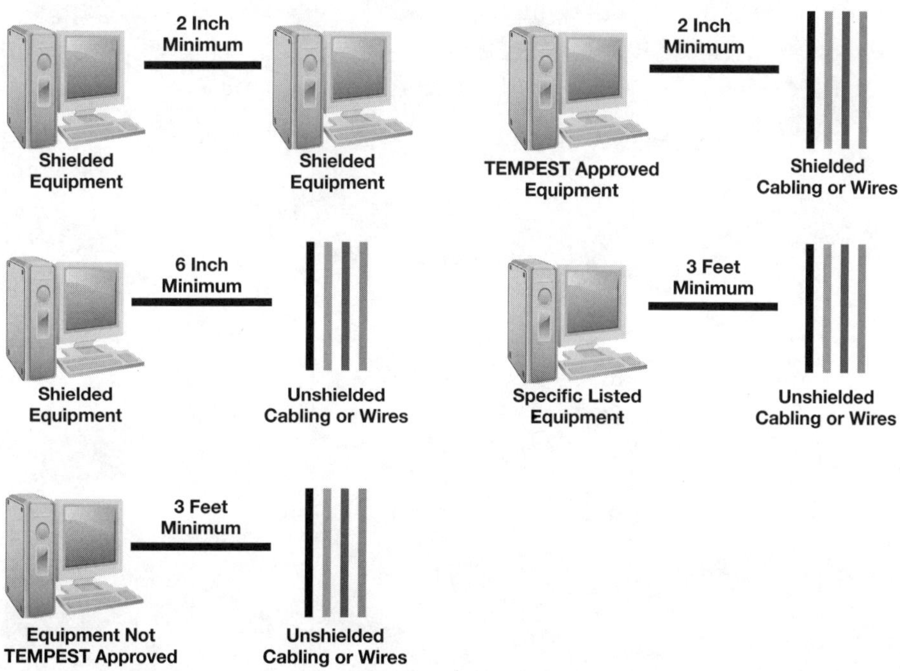

FIGURE E-31 An illustration of TEMPEST separation gaps.

Implement TEMPEST separation by following the policy for TEMPEST Black/Red installation. Here are the TEMPEST Black/Red separation gaps required for cable, equipment, or systems:

- Two inches between shielded equipment or systems, including shielded cables and TEMPEST-approved equipment
- Six inches between unshielded cables and shielded equipment or system
- Three feet between specific listed equipment and unshielded cables
- Three feet between equipment or systems without TEMPEST approval and unshielded cables

TEMPEST separation is part of the TEMPEST security policy. Use it any time a building or area within a building holds a piece of equipment or a system. Test all equipment, systems, power, wires, and cabling within a building or an area for interference or signal crosstalk as required by the TEMPEST security policy.

System Administrators, CNSSI No. 4013A

APPENDIX F

Scope

This supplemental booklet fulfills requirements of the National Information Assurance Training Standard for Systems Administrators (NIATS_SA 4013). This document provides minimum standards for administrators of unclassified systems. Some departments or agencies may require more stringent standards.

Applicability

The President's National Strategy to Secure Cyberspace, Feb 03; National Security Telecommunications and Information Systems Security Directive (NSTISSD) No. 501, 16 Nov 92; Department of Defense Directive (DoDD) 8000.1, 27 Feb 00; DoDD 8500.1, 24 Oct 02; Department of Defense Instruction (DoDI) 8500.2, 6 Feb 03; and DoDI 5200.40, 30 Dec 97, establish the requirements for DoD and other federal departments and agencies to use for training programs for IA professionals. As defined in NSTISSD 501, an INFOSEC professional is an individual who is responsible for the security, oversight, or management of national security systems during all phases of the system's life cycle.

Federal agencies are charged with satisfying these INFOSEC education and training requirements as effectively and efficiently as possible. This instruction starts with the minimum training and education standards to help departments and agencies meet their responsibilities in these areas. Please check your agency's policies for applicable documentation.

Training Standards Terminal Objectives

The curriculum provides three levels of knowledge:

- **Entry level:** Given various scenarios and typical situations containing information systems security issues, the security administrator (SA) will be able to describe and apply the appropriate actions to manage and administer an information system (IS) in a secure manner. To be acceptable, the description and application align with applicable information assurance (IA) regulations, policies, and guidelines.
- **Intermediate level:** Given various scenarios and typical situations containing information systems security issues, the SA will be able to explain and use the appropriate actions to manage and administer an IS securely. To be acceptable, the explanation and use must align with applicable IA regulations, policies, and guidelines.

- **Advanced level:** Given various scenarios and typical situations involving information systems security issues, the SA will be able to take the appropriate actions to manage and administer an IS securely. To be acceptable, verification must align with applicable IA regulations, policies, and guidelines.

Secure Use: General Security Policy

The National Security Telecommunications and Information Systems Security Policy (NSTISSP)

The NSTISSP is the National Security Telecommunications and Information Systems Security Policy, No. 11. This policy governs the purchase of information assurance (IA) services and IA-enabled information technology products. US federal government and Department of Defense (DoD) agencies must abide by this policy to ensure the purchase of IA services and products. Procurement and contracting officers define an evaluation process to ensure the purchase of only approved IA services and products.

The NSTISSP is necessary because, with so many IT- and security-related services and products on the market, it's sometimes difficult for an IA professional or purchasing officer to know what to buy. Two approaches can help meet this challenge. You achieve IA by purchasing pre-approved government off-the-shelf (GOTS) or commercial off-the-shelf (COTS) products. IA-approved products ensure availability, integrity, and confidentiality for IT infrastructures. This policy helps ensure that agencies purchase only approved IT services and IA products.

As of Jan. 1, 2001, those making purchases have been required to review and validate purchases of GOTS or COTS according to the following standards:

- **Common Criteria for Information Security Technology Evaluation Mutual Recognition Arrangement**—this policy provides assurance that you specify, use, and evaluate IA products in a standardized manner.
- **National Security Agency (NSA)/National Institute of Standards and Technology (NIST) IA Partnership Evaluation and Validation Program**—this policy defines a process for cost-effective security testing, evaluation, and validation.
- **NIST Federal Information Processing Standard (FIPS) validation program**—FIPS validation assures users that cryptography solutions have passed rigorous testing as defined by NIST.

Government agency procurement and contracting officers must develop a plan and process for ensuring that all services and products are IA-enabled. As long as this plan and process incorporate the review and validation processes above, that agency is compliant with this policy. This policy ensures that GOTS and COTS purchases are IA-enabled.

NSTISSP is an acquisition policy. Therefore, during the requirements definition and design phase, aligning requirements with GOTS and COTS IA solutions is a first step. The process should include this step in the initial design. That way, IA professionals can be sure to purchase IA-enabled products. The Common Criteria GOTS and COTS product lists can help guide the selection of IA products. This policy took effect on July 1, 2002.

Information Assurance

Department of Defense (DoD) Directive 8500.1 is the parent DoD document regulating information assurance. This policy requires all Department of Defense agencies and contractors to meet certain minimum guidelines regarding use of confidentiality, integrity, and availability protection for information systems. You can find this policy at http://diacap.org/DoDD 8500_1.pdf.

Information assurance guarantees that all Department of Defense agencies and contractors meet a certain level of protection in a standard way. Given the sensitive nature of information handled by DoD personnel and equipment, having all administrators meet a common standard in a similar fashion allows them to achieve and maintain protection of confidentiality, integrity, and availability. Specifically, this policy requires a defense-in-depth approach to IA.

IA professionals in DoD agencies and contractors must, when designing their networks, make sure that they incorporate a defense-in-depth approach to IA. This procedure includes technical and non-technical controls such as firewalls, DMZs, access control, and training and awareness programs.

You must use the IA policy at the planning stage for network design. Since this policy covers both technical and non-technical approaches, administrators must build the entire network around it and adhere to it throughout the life of the network.

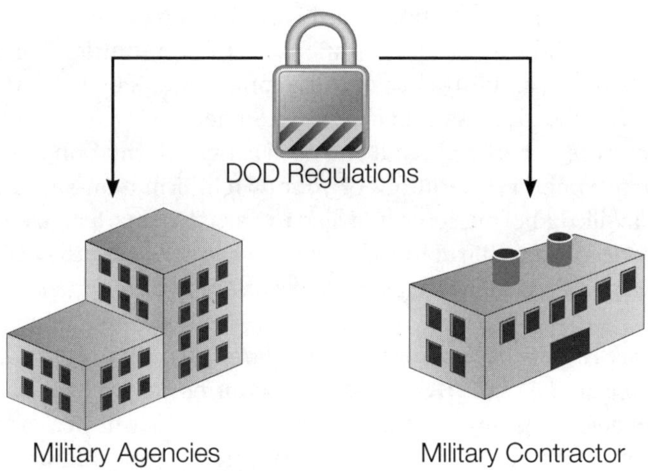

FIGURE F-1 Most DoD regulations apply to both military agencies and contractors.

TEMPEST/Emission Security (EMSEC)

TEMPEST is a Department of Defense code name for a practice of checking and studying leaking wires or cabling signals. Leaking signals consist of electrical, mechanical, or acoustical energy given off intentionally or accidentally by equipment and systems that process national security information. TEMPEST security is an approach to checking a location housing equipment or systems for leaking signals.

All electronic devices give off electromagnetic radiation (EM) while in use with the proper equipment. Adversaries can capture and analyze this radiation to recreate the activity of the computer releasing it. TEMPEST refers to a series of studies of how to prevent such capture. EMSEC stands for "emission security," or "emanation security," the process that prevents capture and analysis.

EMSEC rules and regulations are created by the Department of Defense and other agencies of the federal government to keep information that might travel from any equipment or system secure and safe. These rules focus on providing confidentiality by including protocols that determine if any other nearby equipment or system can intercept or detect a signal.

For more information on EMSEC/TEMPEST, see Appendix for Information Systems Security Professionals, NSTISSI No. 4011.

Information Operations

Information operations (IO) is an umbrella term for all forms of information attack and defense. It involves the integration of all information assurance (IA) activities with misinformation campaigns, operational security procedures, and other concerns. The goal of an IO is to disrupt or stop enemy activities and protect your own. The protection of your own assets is the everyday goal of the IA professional. As such, you play a key role in IOs on a day-to-day basis. When active operations occur, IA personnel become even more important.

Attempts to steal classified national security information occur every day. Hostile nations and rogue individuals and organizations operate continuously in attempts to secure any data they can. It's the job of the IA professional, using all the means introduced in this guide, to prevent their success. Sometimes the defensive actions of IA personnel alone are not enough, and you need active information operations to support either active military operations or your own information-gathering efforts. Compromised classified information could lead to harm to American citizens, failure of military or other operations, harm to American businesses, or other serious outcomes. The role of the IA professional lies in electronic warfare and computer network operations.

IA personnel are responsible for electronic warfare and computer network operations within an IO. These are tasks the IA professional performs on a regular basis. Electronic warfare activities defend agency systems daily. EMSEC-certified devices protect from eavesdropping. Encryption of sensitive data renders any intercepted communication illegible. Proper access control procedures prevent unauthorized access. VPN tunnels provide secure communications. Should the agency be involved in an outside operation, the techniques that secure the agency internally can secure it externally, too. Vulnerability and port scanning, penetration attempts, DDoS attacks, ping sweeps, and SYN floods are all techniques you can use to protect your systems from attacks.

The protective side of IOs is a daily activity for IA professionals. The agency must continuously monitor its resources for unauthorized access attempts. Use controls where necessary and revise them regularly to retain relevance.

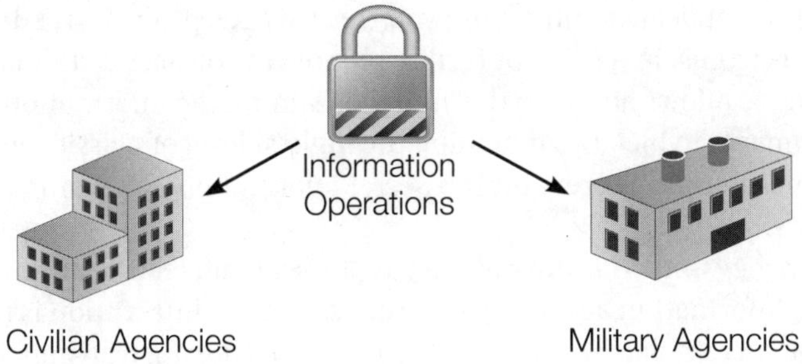

FIGURE F-2 Information operations is an important concept for both civilian and military agencies.

Records Management

Electronic records management (ERM), sometimes referred to as electronic recordkeeping, is the use of automated techniques to manage records regardless of the format of the actual records. They could be, for example, paper, microform, or electronic. ERM is part of day-to-day procedure in any modern federal agency, where databases hold all kind of records, including personal identifiable information, military secrets, and all kinds of sensitive material.

ERM helps the federal government collect, organize, and categorize information, as well preserve, retrieve, and dispose of critical data. ERM is critical for operations; however, it's equally critical, from an information systems security perspective, to have controls in place to protect those databases.

ERM is the handling of all electronic information, including archived information. Regulations require agencies to retain certain kinds of information for up to several years. You must establish policies and procedures to keep these records secure and accessible, if necessary. Backups play a large role in this process for both active and archived data.

Electronic information is in some ways more permanent than hard copy. Even information deleted or erased from a computer's memory is not actually necessarily lost. With regulations regarding the storage and maintenance of electronic records, you need to make plans to secure them. Keep personally identifiable information confidential while you have it on hand. Backups and archives should meet federally mandated retaining periods. Such archives are often kept offsite, but the data must remain both secure and accessible—to those who are authorized, that is. Carefully protect this archived data from unauthorized access.

US federal government agencies must comply with all laws and mandates. Civilian agencies must comply with the Federal Information Systems Management Act (FISMA). Military agencies must comply with the Department of Defense Information Assurance Certification and Accreditation Process (DIACAP). These compliance requirements define security controls for transmission of confidential data. Agency data classification standards define these types of data. This includes confidential data and public domain data. Use proper security controls as necessary for confidential transmission. This process includes authenticating the user and the transmission method.

These requirements complicate maintaining your records. Keep Top Secret documents, whether physical or electronic, in a room or facility secured to Top Secret standards. Only Top Secret clearance allows access to the areas containing the information. Keep mixed clearance documents in facilities matching the highest level of classification of the document. A document that has Secret and Top Secret information, for example, requires Top Secret conditions.

ERM requires firm policy and procedure as well as physical and technical controls. Protect onsite current information according to its classification. Encryption is the most effective protection for current data. Keep records confidential during transmission. VPNs and encryption apply here as well. Regulations also require that you keep backups for mandated periods for any future need. Keep these records both secure and intact in case the need to access them should arise. Encrypting the backups helps to maintain their security. Information storage requires well-maintained, ventilated, and dry locations. Humidity, disaster, theft, and degradation are all issues to consider when planning for storage. Establish well-defined procedures to protect the information in compliance with standards.

You might need multiple locations for different levels of classification. You cannot store documents labeled confidential in the same room as unclassified material, for example. You cannot store confidential material in the same room as secret material. Managing material of mixed clearance levels requires either a facility with varying levels of physical access, or multiple storage facilities.

You can use several solutions already available to handle electronics record management. However, any record management system used by a federal agency must, at minimum, meet the Department of Defense 50115.2 Standard for Records Management for federal agencies to ensure sufficient authenticity and reliability to meet all the agency's recordkeeping needs.

FIGURE F-3

IA professionals implementing secure electronic records management practices might need multiple locations for different levels of classification.

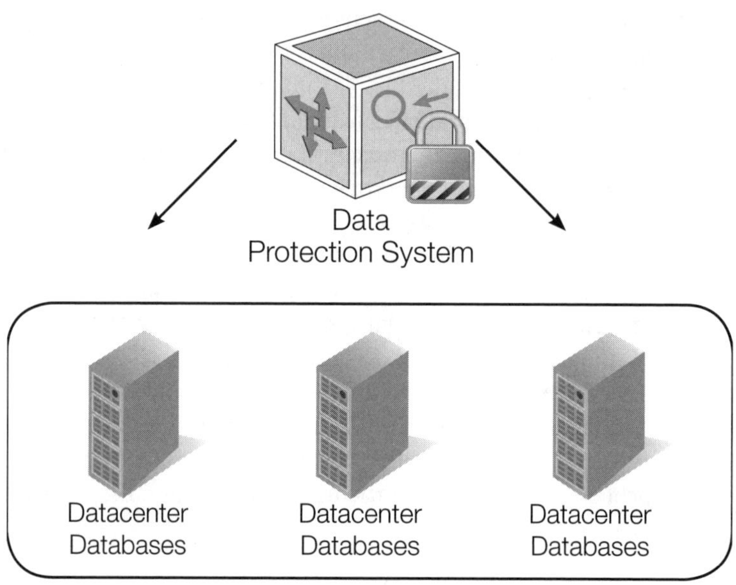

Establish electronics record management procedures before archiving and storing any information. Define policies and procedures for the storage and maintenance of all archived records. Update these policies regularly to ensure best practices.

Strict rules and mandates apply regarding the protection of sensitive and confidential information. The use of a secure electronic records management system is a priority for any civilian or military agency all across the federal government.

Secure Use: General Procedures

Aggregation

Aggregation relates to the consolidation of resources. Under current Department of Defense standards, you must certify and accredit every information system (IS) individually, as well as monitor and audit it from a security standpoint. This policy applies even if the different ISs are in the same location, such as on a Navy ship. Aggregation is a way to simplify certification and accreditation, reduce associated costs, and enhance security levels by checking whole systems rather than individual chunks.

Imagine a small agency with twenty or thirty computers. It's easy to make sure that those computers are up to standard from a security standpoint. Now imagine the agency has grown to a 500-employee, 300-system, multilevel building. The agency has multiple departments within one location with computers on every floor, as well as laptops, PDAs, and smartphones connected to services. If a system administrator is still checking every computer individually, not only is the task exponentially more difficult, but there is also risk of overlooking problems due to inter-network connections. Now imagine the agency has grown to have 35 sites, located in 10 states and two other countries as well. The task becomes nearly impossible, and the costs have skyrocketed. Aggregation is a way of checking and handling each location as a whole, instead of checking every piece of equipment individually.

Using this policy requires a modification of existing certification and accreditation procedures. Using aggregation requires looking at a single location as a whole system, and securing it as a whole. For this to work, the systems must be logically connected and have uniform policies and procedures throughout and between different departments. Once

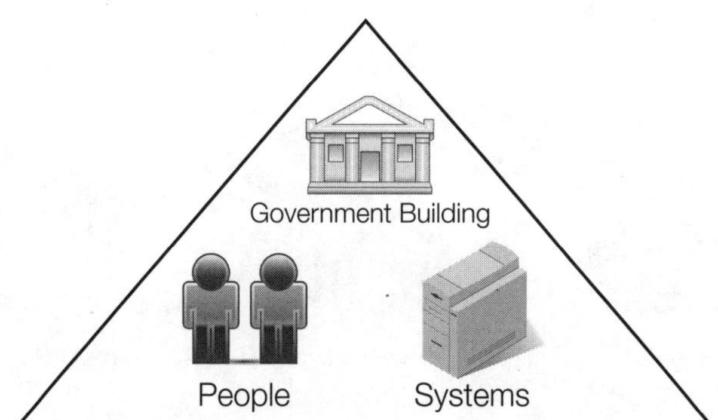

FIGURE F-4

The concept of aggregation applies to agencies, employees, and networks.

this is in place, you can develop appropriate metrics to analyze multiple systems within locations and streamline the certification process.

Aggregation applies to existing networks that have grown too large, with too many discrete locations to easily manage individually. However, if you apply the concept from the design stage for policies, procedures, and infrastructure onward, then it becomes much easier to scale up the operation long term.

Facility Management

Facility management is the care and management of the actual building in which you do business. It includes such things as changing light bulbs, keeping fire suppression and alarm systems tested and functional, maintaining heating and air conditioning systems, and managing anything else related to the actual building. This policy relates to physical security and response to natural and human-generated emergencies.

For an information security professional, facility management is an availability concern. Proper redundancy in the case of power outages is a concern. You have to plan for sufficient airflow in the server room to prevent equipment overheating. You need proper fire suppression equipment to prevent damage in case of a fire. If you use a "wet" system to suppress a fire near electronics, fire damage may be completely prevented, but the equipment may be completely ruined. The safety and well-being of personnel are also of paramount importance to any business professional. Facility management may also relate to information security, including the storage and disposal of sensitive documents.

Facility management is a physical security concern. Carefully consider computer and server placement. Install proper fire suppression systems per code and need. Route wiring properly per code and standard procedure. Make sure you have backup electricity. Consider ventilation and heating. How will you handle sensitive documents? Secure disposal may require allowing outside personnel into the facility. This requires planning to keep them away from classified information. Maintain locks and other physical security checkpoints.

Certain aspects of facility management are crucial at the construction or renovation of the building, such as the fire suppression system. Once these systems are in place however, you need to maintain and test them regularly throughout the life of the system. Proper upkeep and maintenance are paramount to protect the personnel and equipment the information security specialist manages.

FIGURE F-5

Facilities management policies apply to all federal buildings, agencies, and facilities:

Fax Security

Fax systems, though an old technology, are still in use. Consider security for use of these machines. This includes such issues as who has access to the room containing the device, who retrieves documents from the machine, when is it checked, and more. A fax machine represents another possible vulnerability with specialized security requirements. This particular policy is critical since it protects one of the three components of the information systems security triad: confidentiality. It's imperative to make sure that the hands picking up sensitive information are hands authorized to do so.

There are still times when you have to transmit a document by fax. Sometimes a document requires a physical signature and no scanner is available. A fax machine operates separately from other aspects of the network. It uses the phone lines, so network controls may not apply to fax transmissions. Also, fax machines require or produce physical copies of possibly sensitive information. An unauthorized user might look at documents in a fax machine or even take them. Employees might fax classified information out of the building without permission. An adversary might tap the transmission and siphon off sensitive information. Civilian agencies must ensure that their practices for handling fax transmissions comply with the Federal Information Systems Management Act (FISMA). Military agencies must ensure that their fax practices comply with the Department of Defense Information Assurance Certification and Accreditation Process (DIACAP).

Fax security is largely a physical concern. You should develop a fax policy regarding use, disposal, and other concerns. When the fax transmission finishes, what happens to the physical document? Are incoming faxes allowed at all times, or must they be arranged? What level of classification is fax-permissible? Who has access to the room where the fax machine is located? How do you secure the fax line from tapping? If you send classified information, how do you ensure confidentiality? Remember, the use of this policy must focus on federal compliance. Civilian and military agencies must not only adhere to laws and mandates, but also show constant due diligence in information assurance.

Whenever there is a fax machine present in your facility, consider the policies you have in place for it. Update proper training on the policy regularly. Keep in mind that strict rules, federal mandates, and regulations apply to both civilian and military agencies.

Housekeeping Procedures

Housekeeping procedures are for the management of personnel. They include procedures for hiring, transfers, promotions, and termination. Do not forget: Users are the weakest link within the information security and assurance chain.

US federal government agencies must comply with laws and mandates. Civilian agencies must comply with the Federal Information Systems Management Act (FISMA). Military agencies must comply with the Department of Defense Information Assurance Certification and Accreditation Process (DIACAP). Most DoD regulations apply to both military agencies and contractors.

Proper access control security requires procedures to handle hiring, transfers, promotions, and termination of employees. For example, if an employee is terminated, how quickly do you remove access? Disgruntled employees may perform malicious acts when informed of a termination. New employees need proper access rights and no others. Promotions and transfers require the modification of access rights to reflect only the new duties.

Housekeeping procedures are policies that involve human resources as well as security. At the surface, they are administrative controls, but require some technical control to execute. The company must decide how to process incoming and outgoing employees. When you hire a new employee, what access rights do you grant that employee? What groups should the employee belong to? What does the employee need to do the job? When promotions or transfers occur, how do you go about assigning new rights and removing old? When an employee is terminated, how quickly do you remove access?

Define housekeeping procedures before hiring begins. However, you should regularly review procedures to keep them up to date with current requirements.

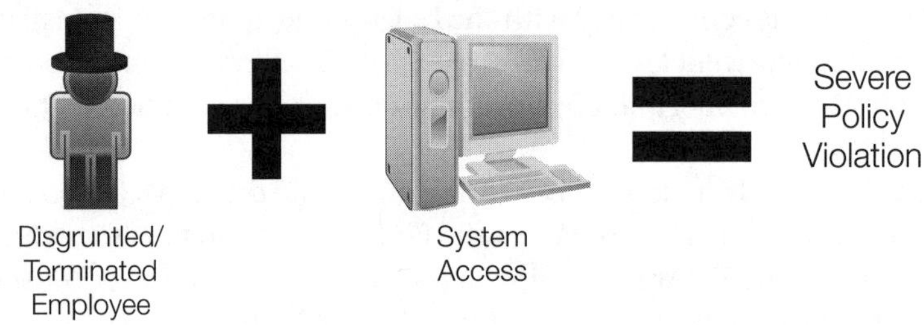

FIGURE F-6 Leaving employees with access to your systems even after they've been terminated could become a serious policy violation.

Inference

Inference means drawing a conclusion from limited information. From an information security standpoint, this means that unauthorized adversaries gain access to enough information to allow them to make proper conclusions about the network to permit further intrusion. This usually happens when a control presents information in a way that tells a malicious user more than you want him or her to know. A primary example of inference is what happens when a person learns and enters the wrong password, telling attackers that they have found a valid user ID. Even without a password, knowledge of a valid user ID can be of interest to a malicious user.

You reduce or eliminate problems stemming from inference by maintaining policies that limit the information available to unauthorized users. Such policies protect data by making certain actions more difficult. The more information an unauthorized user has, the greater the risk of leakage of information. Eliminating this threat includes using procedures to prevent users at lower clearance levels from deducing information at higher clearance levels.

Preventing inference has various components. You should develop policies about how exactly to develop controls. One way you can prevent inference is to set up your system so that if a login attempt fails, the would-be user gets no indication whether it was the username or the password that was was wrong. Another way to block inference is not to give away what access rights are required to access a particular object. You can change default response messages so that remote unauthorized users cannot guess application names or OS types.

Use policies to limit inference-granting information when you put the controls in place. Test and revise controls already in place for unintended inference. Update these controls regularly to maintain classification standards.

FIGURE F-7 A basic picture of what might happen due to inference.

Object Reuse

Object reuse is what occurs when a computing device is repurposed. Sometimes when you purchase new equipment, you don't dispose of the old equipment but move it to another location, department, or company altogether. When this happens to an object that has handled sensitive information, you must follow pre-established policies on reuse.

First you must establish a policy and procedure for determining how you will clear information from objects being repurposed. This becomes more complicated if you have both classified and unclassified equipment on site. Files on a computer or server, network information on a router or switch, or print history on an old printer must all be securely cleared to allow reuse in another situation or location. Residual data left over from a prior use of the object can provide an unauthorized user with access to sensitive information. This is particularly critical when dealing with military systems where proper data sanitizing is part of the mission.

Object reuse policies are administrative controls. The company must make plans on the reuse of equipment at other locations, in other departments, or by other companies. When you give equipment to other companies, ensure that no sensitive information remains. Secure drive wiping procedures can help with this, but which one should your organization use? What standards do you need to meet with regard to the level of confidentiality? Is even secure drive wiping secure enough if you want to repurpose a machine from a classified network? Should you ever repurpose a machine from classified to unclassified use under any circumstance?

Object reuse policies must be in place before you repurpose any object. Review these policies regularly to make sure they are being applied consistently.

FIGURE F-8

A basic example of repurposing a server.

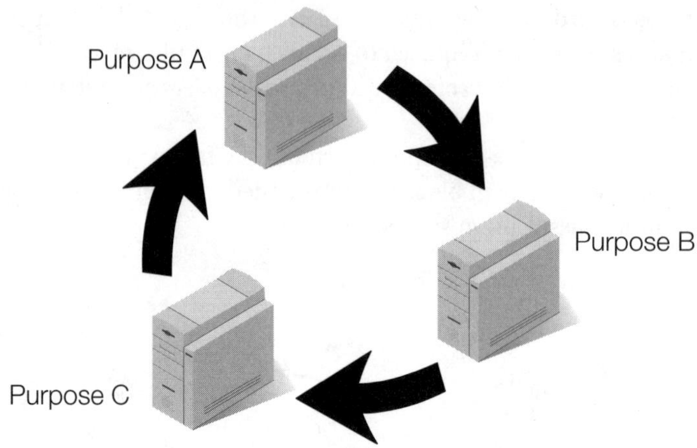

Polyinstantiation

Polyinstantiation is a method database managers use to prevent inference of information. It involves coding a database to allow for multiple records with similar primary keys at different clearance levels. For example, a database of military units with unit ID as primary identifier could have two units with the same unit ID if they were at different security clearance levels.

Polyinstantiation means that lower-clearance-level employees do not have access to information that would allow them to deduce the existence of information at higher levels of clearance. For instance, if a user attempts to enter a Unit ID for a new unit that exists above his clearance, he is told that ID is in use. While he cannot see it, he can deduce that the unit exists at a higher level than his clearance will allow. To maintain classification integrity, work to eliminate errors like this. Allowing for multiple records with the same ID at different clearance levels helps to maintain information security.

Polyinstantiation is a database coding technique. Tables must allow for different objects that have different clearance levels to share primary keys. This prevents users from becoming aware of information for which they have no clearance. Objects that share clearance levels would not allow shared keys, as this is information allowed to the user entering it.

UNIT ID	CLEARANCE
03-01a	S
03-01a	TS
03-01f	S

Use this technique any time you need to enforce separate levels of data classification. For it to function properly, use it at setup of the database and review the technique regularly. Remember that civilian agencies must comply with the Federal Information

Systems Management Act (FISMA). Military agencies must comply with the Department of Defense Information Assurance Certification and Accreditation Process (DIACAP). These compliance requirements define security controls for transmission of confidential data. Agency data classification standards define types of data. This includes confidential data and public domain data. Polyinstantiation is a technique that helps meet these security goals.

Open Systems Interconnection (OSI): Internet Protocol (IP)

Internet Protocol (IP) is a suite of protocols that operates on the network layer of the OSI model. It is also known as TCP/IP. IP is the primary protocol suite for network communication. Its use grew from the old ARPANET to encompass many of the features of the current Internet. As the Internet grew, so did use of its primary communication method, TCP/IP. IP is also the source of all addressing for the Internet. Virtually all communication, whether from private enterprise, public users, or the federal government, travels across WAN links using IP packets. IPv4, the current addressing scheme, began to run out of addresses due to the rapid increase in network devices. The introduction of Class A, Class B, and Class C private addresses and Network Address Translation (NAT) delayed this event. During the extra time provided by the introduction of NAT, IPv6 was developed. IPv6 allows for much greater numbers of network devices and addresses helping eliminate the lack of security present in the IPv4 protocol.

The IP suite actually is inherently insecure. It takes relatively little to reproduce information sent across the Internet with TCP/IP. So the question is less why we need it for security and more why we need security for TCP/IP. Given the fact that TCP/IP provides not only virtually all communication over the Internet, but all addresses, the need arose to secure an inherently insecure system. Sensitive and classified information must be protected, and Information Assurance was created to provide this. Encryption, tunneling, DMZs, NAT, firewalls, and routing policies are all techniques developed to secure data due to the limitations of TCP/IP.

The IP suite is the default and primary protocol suite for WAN communication. All transmissions over the Internet ordinarily go out using TCP/IP. All the network addressing is based on IP as well. IP addressing means that any IPv4 or IPv6 network layer address is required for any IP host device that must be recognizable on an IP network. This addressing is required for IP host devices to communicate with other devices. This includes communication between computers, laptops, network printers, fax machines, copiers, routers, Web servers, etc. Because TCP/IP is inherently insecure, you must take steps to ensure information security. A large percentage of the work by information assurance personnel relates to the nature of TCP/IP and efforts to overcome its limitations.

TCP/IP is necessary whenever you are dealing with WAN communication. Develop IP addressing policies during the design of your network. As you add and remove devices from the network, keep your network up to date with any protocol changes.

Secure Use: General Countermeasures and Safeguards

Due Care

"Due care" has been a familiar term in the fields of finance, securities, and law for a long time. In recent years, due care has also found a use among information security and assurance professionals. Due care is the care that a reasonable person or management team takes to show responsibility for the activities that take place within the organization. Due care helps protect employees, resources, and the organization itself.

US federal government agencies must comply with laws and mandates, and exercising due care is part of civilian agencies' compliance with the Federal Information Systems Management Act (FISMA), as well as of military agencies' compliance with the Department of Defense Information Assurance Certification and Accreditation Process (DIACAP). And remember, most DoD regulations apply to both military agencies and contractors.

Due care sets the standard for determining legal duty. The United States Federal Sentencing Guidelines make it possible to hold officers liable for failing to exercise due care in the management of information systems. A negligent information security professional is likely to place his organization and management at risk of suffering direct and indirect losses, fines, loss of credibility, and reduced competitiveness.

You can exercise due care by effectively coordinating efforts to follow regulations, standards, and best practices. The practice of due care has no universal norm; however, it implies reasonable care and competence. Managers and their organizations have a duty to provide for information security and such obligations arise from the portion of US common law that deals with issues of negligence. One of the biggest challenges security professionals face in exercising due care is understanding what standard applies to a given circumstance. Refer to professional organizations such as the Systems Administration, Networking, and Security Institute (www.sans.org) for more information on due care standards.

The practice of due care must be part of a manager's day-to-day routine. Always keep best practices, governance, and federal laws and regulations in mind during the management of information systems. Do not forget you can always ask your agency's legal staff for an opinion on legal issues. Exercise due care with respect to all your organization's information resources.

Computing and Telecommunications Hardware and Software

Computing and telecommunications hardware and software form the core of information technology. Computing hardware is the computers, switches, servers, printers, and other devices we use. Computing software is the word processors, databases, payroll applications, operating systems, and other information that allow an agency or organization to do actual work. Telecommunications hardware is the routers, modems, fax machines, telephones, and other equipment we use to communicate with people in distant locations. Telecommunication software is the email, voice over IP (VoIP) programs, VPN applications, and other programs that make electronic communication possible. Today's federal agencies have all of these. They are our means of communication, but they are also the means by which opponents can attack, by detecting and stealing sensitive information. You must keep these components in mind when designing a security plan.

Computing and telecommunications hardware and software are essential to the pace of normal operations in federal agencies today. They are also the source of an information security specialist's job. They affect all three aspects of the traditional C-I-A security triad. Unauthorized or malicious users attack hardware and software to obtain sensitive or classified information. You need to keep them running properly to conduct business. Keep all of these objects and concerns in mind when designing a security plan for the agency. At the core of your plan should be how you will balance the need to run the business and do the work, on one hand, with the need to protect the information stored on and handled by all these objects, on the other.

Remember, civilian agencies must comply with the Federal Information Systems Management Act (FISMA). Military agencies must comply with the Department of Defense Information Assurance Certification and Accreditation Process (DIACAP). Your computing and telecommunications hardware and software is another part of your technology universe that must be aligned with these standards.

To do business in today's world, you need many pieces of hardware and software. All of them need to be secured from unauthorized access. You must patch software to close vulnerabilities. You must configure systems properly to restrict access. You must keep hardware in working condition to ensure availability. You must encrypt data stored on hardware or transmitted by software when necessary for confidentiality. You must install security devices like firewalls, intrusion detection systems, and antivirus programs, which are themselves computing hardware and software objects, where appropriate.

You must consider security concerns at the very beginning. Secure wiring properly against signal leaks and radiation. Protect all the devices on the network before they are installed. As patches for software become available, test and apply them to the network to maintain security. New threats and vulnerabilities appear regularly, so revise your security plans regularly to make sure they cover new issues.

Resource Misuse Prevention

Resource misuse prevention is the prevention of misuse of internal equipment. It is largely an internal control. Resource misuse can cause many problems for the agency leading to the loss of sensitive or classified data. You prevent resource misuse by policy as well as with specific security controls.

Resource misuse by agency personnel can cause many security issues ranging from infection to data leaks and more. Personnel doing unauthorized Web surfing may visit compromised sites and allow adversaries to acquire agency passwords. Clicking on links in phishing emails can lead to loss of login information or the downloading of malicious software. Unauthorized logins can lead to the leak of classified information.

Resource misuse prevention begins with a policy. An acceptable use policy (AUP) details exactly what actions the company will allow on its equipment. The policy should include what websites are allowed or not allowed. It should include how employees can use agency email and rules for other agency equipment like printers and fax machines. It must also include a warning when personnel activities are monitored. The policy should also include the penalties for noncompliance. Once you have written the policy, distribute it to all personnel. Include a recordable sign-off, so that you can verify that all personnel have read and agree to abide by the policy. Once you have accomplished this, put controls in place to enforce the rules.

Use firewall blacklisting—or blocking of specific sites—to enforce Web surfing policies. Use proper access control methods to restrict access to classified information. Use email spam filters to reduce spam. Monitor the network to ensure that personnel are complying with policy. Train people to ensure that they understand agency policy. Preventing resource misuse will greatly reduce risk to the agency of data leaks and other mishaps.

Write your acceptable use policy as early as possible during your network planning. This will allow for the definition of allowed behavior, and define the controls you need to enforce it. Review the AUP regularly for necessary updates. A comprehensive AUP with follow-up and constant monitoring is critical to information systems security, as the accompanying figure suggests.

FIGURE F-9

Follow-up and constant monitoring are critical to information systems security.

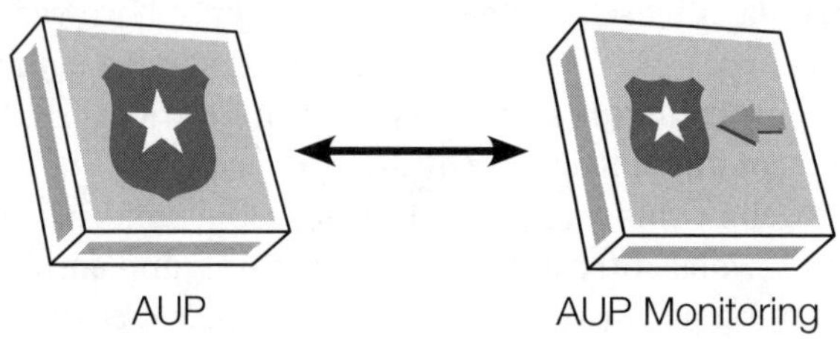

Anomalies and Integrity: Access Control Safeguards

Protected Distribution Systems

"Protected distribution system" or PDS, refers to the cabling of an agency. Specifically, PDS refers to cabling that has met shielding criteria to prevent/deter/detect intrusion attempts. A PDS is specifically required for networks transmitting classified National Security Information (NSI). A PDS is a system that has sufficient electrical, electromagnetic, and physical protection to allow transmission of unencrypted classified data through a non-classified area. A complete PDS is protected at both ends of the transmission as well as the entire length of the cabling carrying it.

A PDS is designed to carry classified high-security information. Normally, regulation requires that all classified information running through an unclassified area be encrypted. However, encryption increases overhead and increases bandwidth use. Installing a PDS allows transmission of high-security information through an unclassified area without encryption. This allows for greater freedom in designing networks for agencies that deal with multiple levels of classified information.

Setting up a system as a PDS requires approval from the authority designated for your agency. You must plan out the cabling and then get the OK. Run the cabling with required amounts of electronic, electromagnetic, and physical security to prevent access. Cable shielding must meet applicable TEMPEST standards. You must secure both ends of the communication to close the PDS. Also, the PDS must be able to detect attempts at unauthorized access. You should conduct random inspections depending on the highest level of classification of information the PDS handles.

Given the physical security and cable shielding requirements, a PDS is best implemented during the initial cable installation and termination. After installation, you need to maintain and inspect the system regularly.

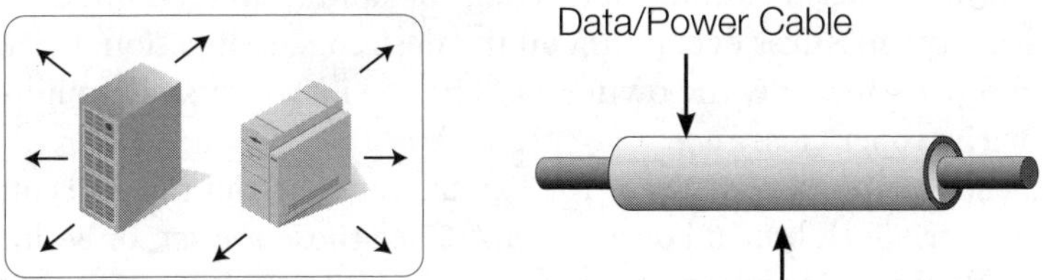

FIGURE F-10 The best time to implement a PDS is during the initial cable installation and termination.

Data Ownership and Custodianship

In information security, a clear chain of responsibility is necessary for sensitive and classified information. For classified information this is especially important. The data owner is the originator or ultimate responsible party for a document, hard or electronic. Data custodians are the people who take care of the documents and are responsible for their security while they have possession of them. For example, at Marine Corps Base Quantico, in Virginia, the Corps is the owner of the military classified information. The various contractor groups and Marine work groups are the custodians of the data while the data is in their possession.

Personally identifiable information (PII), which must also be secure, is slightly different. In this case, the owner of the data is the person it describes. The custodian is the entity possessing the data, usually the employing agency.

Owners of data are responsible for determining its classification. They set the original level of classification, whether Unclassified, Confidential, Secret, and Top Secret, as in the Department of Defense, or some other scheme. The different levels require different actions by the custodian. Top Secret documents require much more stringent security than confidential documents. The data custodians are responsible for keeping the data secure to that level for as long as it remains in their custody. This includes everything from the time they receive the data to disposal of the data, including archiving. Keeping the levels separate allows for maintaining a "need to know" status. Only people with the appropriate level of clearance can access the data. For PII, the security is mandated by regulation, and the custodians remain responsible for securing it throughout their care of the information. An information assurance professional will usually be the data custodian, responsible for the securing of any sensitive information the Agency works on. This includes such tasks as encrypting classified data, making sure only secure transmissions send classified data, and securing archived information.

Data ownership and custodianship in the case of classified data takes place through Mandatory Access Control (MAC). This method ensures that all information gets a classification level, and that only users at that level may access the information. Secret-level employees, for example, can access anything Secret and below pertaining to their job, but not Top Secret information. Individuals cannot grant access to someone who does not have the need to access and the appropriate clearance. The data owners mandate classification levels. Then the data custodian must use the appropriate security measures depending on the desired classification. Once a classification level has been set, only the owner can change it. The custodian allows access only to those with proper clearance.

You should use MAC during setup of the logical network. Set up levels of classification with appropriate rights and permissions. Once these are set, only the owner can change the classification of an object. Data archiving must continue to follow classification levels. Carry out periodic reviews of the system to ensure continued data confidentiality.

Administration

Access Control Policies: Modes of Operation

When you deploy a computer system to process classified information, you accredit it to operate in a particular "mode." The following four recognized modes represent either tighter security requirements on the data and user community or tighter requirements on the host computing system.

Dedicated: This mode places the fewest requirements on the computer itself, but places the most restrictions on the data processed and on the user community. A dedicated computer operates on data at or below one classification level. Everyone with access to that computer has clearance for the data it handles and must have a need to know for all data it handles. Almost any computer may be in dedicated mode. All security relies on physical protection. The operating system and hardware do not need to provide authentication, access control, or other security measures.

System high: In this mode, the system may process data at multiple classification levels. All users need clearance for the highest level present on the system, but they do not all require a need to know. The system must enforce need-to-know controls between users. Evaluate computers in system-high mode to ensure that they can in fact enforce need-to-know restrictions between users.

Compartmented or partitioned: In this mode, everyone who uses the system has clearance for Top Secret and for access to special program or intelligence data. However, the system contains data belonging to different compartments or possessing different intelligence or special program code words. Not all users have formal access permission to all compartments or code words. Users do not have clearance to see information marked with particular compartments or code words. Because all users have clearance for data above Top Secret, the risk of spillage is somewhat less than if a Secret user receives Top Secret information.

Multilevel: In this mode, the system may serve users with different security clearances and may store data for which some users do not have clearance to receive. The system needs a reliable and effective multilevel security mechanism. Today, multilevel servers often appear in two particular applications:

- **Multilevel servers**—server systems that provide information to clients operating at different classification levels.
- **Guards**—high-assurance firewalls that pass information between different security domains and environments.

The different modes reflect the different types of classified information that might be present on the system and the clearances of potential users.

The idea behind these applications is to easily provide data sharing in the low-to-high directions; in other words, users with lesser clearances can easily provide information to users with higher clearances. Modern military operations require an effective flow of information in the opposite direction as well: high-to-low.

For example, when a combat team receives orders to attack a target, the orders may be classified Confidential or Secret. However, an officer at a command post creates the Secret orders using online information from a Top Secret intelligence summary.

The use of modes of operation is merely a matter of structure. The civilian or military agency must use its data classification standard and determine which modes of operations it needs. US federal government agencies must comply with laws and mandates. Use of modes of operation must comply with the US federal government requirements for information system: Civilian agencies must comply with the Federal Information Systems Management Act (FISMA), and military agencies must comply with the Department of Defense Information Assurance Certification and Accreditation Process (DIACAPS). Most DoD regulations apply to both military agencies and contractors.

Access Control Countermeasures: Communications Security (COMSEC)

Communications Security (COMSEC) refers to cryptography within the US government and refers particularly to cryptosystems to protect critical government secrets. The Committee on National Security Systems (CNSS) has published policies, known collectively by their initials, CNSSP, on communications security and cryptography for national security systems. The CNSS also controls policies created by the National Security Telecommunications and Information Systems Security Committee, or NSTISSP. These include:

- Safeguarding Communications Security materials: CNSSP-1
- Granting access to classified crypto information: CNSSP-3

- Use of cryptography in high-risk environments: NCSC-5
- Wireless networking: CNSSP-17
- IPsec encryption: CNSSP-19
- Public key infrastructure: CNSSP-25
- Voice communications security: NSTISSP-101

Only National Security Agency/Central Security Service-approved communication security products and services can be used to secure classified information. Sensitive information and information unapproved for public release and processed on federal information systems are protected by products validated by the National Institute of Standards and Technology as meeting the criteria of applicable Federal Information Processing Standards, or by communication security products and services approved by the National Security Agency/Central Security Service.

Federal components acquire communication security products and services through the National Security Agency/Central Security Service, which serves as the centralized acquisition authority. If the products and services are unavailable through centralized procurement, the federal components must acquire them directly from commercial entities authorized by the National Security Agency/Central Security Service.

Validated communication security requirements for all federal information systems, including those integral to weapons systems and weapons support systems, apply throughout the system life cycle (e.g., concept definition, design and development, test and evaluation, procurement, installation, operation, maintenance, disposal, and archiving).

The ability to maintain the confidentiality, integrity, and availability of classified information and unclassified information unapproved for public release during transmission is of paramount importance for an effective security posture.

Using standardized COMSEC across an entire agency is a big job. Each agency has multiple organizations under its umbrella. As a security professional in such an agency, you must establish a security hierarchy. Each agency has a national COMSEC manager, whose job is to set the standards for COMSEC enforcement throughout that agency. Since one manager cannot specifically oversee each organization within an agency, each manager appoints an organizational manager. The organizational managers are responsible for using the national manager's designated COMSEC controls and security.

To maintain equal levels of security, as well as applications that can communicate with each other within an organization, you must establish a robust structure. Each agency will have a national COMSEC manager responsible for setting the IA standards required for the agency. Each organization with the agency will use these standards. The person responsible for managing each organization's IA activities is the organizational COMSEC manager. This person determines the applicable standards for the organization and directs the staff of the organization to use appropriate security measures.

Your use of COMSEC is merely a matter of structure. The agency must specify the national manager. Each organization specifies the organizational manager. These managers are responsible for use of COMSEC standards and procedures for their areas. All IA personnel for an organization report to the COMSEC manager. Organizational managers report to the national manager. This structure helps create standard use of COMSEC throughout an agency.

FIGURE F-11 The diagram shows an example of VPNs over the public network.

You must specify managers and responsibilities and define data ownership as soon as possible. You must ensure clear lines of communication and you must establish standard COMSEC use.

Access Control Countermeasures: Isolation and Mediation

Isolation and mediation is an access control mechanism that focuses on isolating each computing process within its own "island." The idea is to create a security domain in which each process will access its own RAM and CPU cycles. Isolation and mediation are concepts that apply to entire infrastructures if necessary. Isolation and mediation protects confidentiality, integrity, and availability.

By isolating the process, you create a security domain where the process has free rein without affecting any other running process. Restricting access to resources adds an extra layer of security where the operating system is in charge of mediating required access. Isolation and mediation is particularly critical with risky and sensitive processes. Protecting and isolating systems is particularly critical in military warfare and operations, intelligence gathering, and any other mission-critical task.

For the island to form its own security domain, you isolate the process or group of processes. You could use virtual machines as an example; each machine has its own RAM and CPU allocation. If one of the virtual machines crashes, it won't affect the host system or any other virtual machine running in the same system. One machine does not have access to the other's resources unless you deliberately configure it that way.

The practice of isolation and mediation as an access control mechanism depends on the sensitivity of the information and processes handled by the computer system. You do this with risky processes to restrict the damage they might do to an infrastructure. Identifying such processes and taking action to isolate and mitigate risk scenarios is critical. Always keep in mind the criticality of monitoring the system; in other words, constantly verify that the security domains are actually working.

The figure illustrates the basic idea behind isolation and mediation: independent and secure processes within the same system.

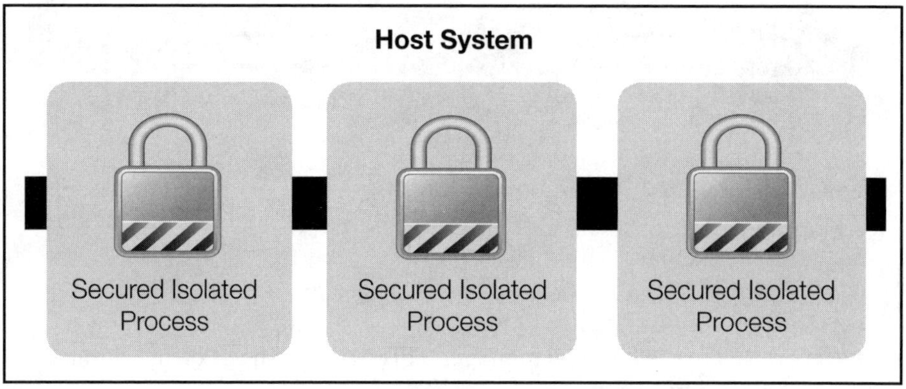

FIGURE F-12
The figure illustrates the basic idea behind isolation and mediation: independent and secure processes within the same system.

Glossary of Key Terms

10GigE | An abbreviation for 10 gigabit Ethernet LAN.

A

Acceptable use policy (AUP) | An organization-wide policy that defines what is allowed and disallowed regarding use of IT assets by employees.

Access controls | Methods used to restrict and allow access to resources.

Accountability | Associating actions with users for later reporting and research.

Accounting | In the context of monitoring information system activity, accounting is the process of recording events in log files.

Accreditation | The formal acceptance by the authorizing official of the risk of implementing the system.

Accredited | Refers to an educational institution that has successfully undergone evaluation by an external body to determine whether the institution meets applicable standards.

Actions | The activities that authorized users can perform on the resources.

Administrative controls | Controls involved in the process of developing and ensuring compliance with policy and procedures.

Adware | A software program that collects information about Internet usage and uses it to present targeted advertisements to users.

Algorithm | A mathematical process or series of structured steps for performing some function.

American National Standards Institute (ANSI) | A U.S. standards organization whose goal is to empower its members and constituents to strengthen the U.S. marketplace position in the global economy while helping to ensure the safety and health of consumers and the protection of the environment.

Analog central office (CO) switch | A switch used by the phone company to connect analog circuits and phone calls.

Annual loss expectancy (ALE) | The estimated loss due to a specific realized threat. The formula to calculate ALE is $ALE = SLE \times ARO$.

Annual rate of occurrence (ARO) | The annual probability that a stated threat will be realized.

Anomaly-based IDS | An intrusion detection system that compares current activity with stored profiles of normal (expected) activity.

Application convergence | The integration of applications to enhance productivity. Unified communications is an example of application convergence. Unified communications integrates recorded voice messages into e-mail so that voice messages are retrievable via e-mail.

Application proxy firewall | An advanced firewall that processes all traffic between two systems. Instead of allowing a direct connection between two systems, the proxy connects to each system separately and passes filtered traffic to the destination based on filtering rules.

Asset | Any item that has value to an organization or a person.

Asymmetric digital subscriber line (ADSL) | A DSL service where the bandwidth allocated is different for downstream and upstream traffic. ADSL transmits data on telephone lines using different frequencies. ADSL can support from 384Kbps to 20Mbps downstream using existing copper facilities. Bandwidth depends on physical distance, line conditions, and the type of DSL technology used.

Asymmetric key cryptography | A type of cryptography that uses a cipher with two separate keys, one for encryption and one for decryption, so that correspondents do not first have to exchange secret information to communicate securely.

Asynchronous token | An authentication token used to process challenge-response authentication with a server. The token takes the server's challenge value and calculates a response. The user enters the response to authenticate a connection.

Asynchronous transfer mode (ATM) | A high-speed broadband networking technology that uses a 53-byte cell to support real-time voice, video, or data communications. Service providers deployed ATM switches prior to the TCP/IP and Internet broadband era.

Attack | An attempt to exploit a vulnerability of a computer or network component.

Audio conferencing | A software-based audio conference-calling application that supports bridging callers into a common audio conference.

Authentication | The process of proving you are the person or entity you claim to be.

Authentication server | A server that provides second-level authentication for users desiring access.

Authority-level policy | An authorization method in which access to resources is decided by the user's authority level.

Authorization | The process of deciding who is approved for access to specific resources.

Authorization codes | Passwords or personal identification numbers (PINs) used on phone systems to provide authenticated access to a dial tone. Users have to enter their unique authorization code to make long-distance or toll calls from the organization's phone system.

Authorizing official (AO) | A senior manager who reviews a certification report and makes the decision to approve the system for implementation.

Availability | A mathematical formula that quantifies the amount of uptime for a system compared to the amount of downtime. Usually displayed as a ratio or percentage.

B

Backdoor | An undocumented and often unauthorized access method to a computer resource that bypasses normal access controls.

Baselines | Benchmarks used to make sure that a system provides a minimum level of security across multiple applications and across different products.

Benchmark | The standard by which your computer or device is compared to determine if it's securely configured.

Black-box testing | A method of security testing that isn't based directly on knowledge of a program's architecture.

Black-hat hacker | A computer attacker who tries to break IT security for the challenge and to prove technical prowess.

Biometric | A physiological or behavioral human-recognition system (i.e., a fingerprint reader, a retina scanner, a voice-recognition reader, etc.).

Bit error rate | The total number of errors divided by the total number of bits transmitted.

BlackBerry | A brand name for a line of smartphones and PDA handheld mobile devices.

Botnet | Robotically controlled network. A botnet consists of a network of compromised computers that attackers use to launch attacks and spread malware.

Brute-force password attack | A method that black-hat hackers use to attempt to compromise logon and password access controls. Brute-force password attacks usually follow a specific attack plan, including the use of social engineering to obtain user information.

Business associates | Under HIPAA, organizations that perform a health care activity on behalf of a covered entity.

Business continuity plan (BCP) | A plan for how to handle outages to IT systems, applications, and data access in order to maintain business operations.

Business drivers | The collection of components, including people, information, and conditions, that support business objectives.

Business impact analysis (BIA) | A prerequisite analysis for a business continuity plan that prioritizes mission-critical systems, applications, and data and the impact of an outage or downtime.

Business process reengineering | A term used to describe streamlining processes with automation or simplified steps. Business process reengineering is about designing a better mousetrap to enhance productivity.

Business to business (B2B) | A term used to describe a business that builds online systems with links for conducting business-to-business transactions, usually for integrated supply-chain purchases and deliveries.

Business to consumer (B2C) | A term used to describe an online storefront for consumers to purchase goods and services directly. An example of a B2C site is *http://www.amazon.com*.

C

Caesar cipher | One of the simplest substitution ciphers. It shifts each letter in the English alphabet a fixed number of positions, with Z wrapping back to A.

Call control | The software in a phone system that performs the call switching from an inbound trunk to a phone extension.

Call-detail recording (CDR) | A complete phone system usage report showing inbound and outbound dialing and usage per phone extension. CDR tracks usage of central office and direct inward dial trunks (phone lines) along with caller ID and inbound and outbound dialing.

Central office (CO) | A term used to describe where phone lines, also known as trunk lines, are cross-connected to customer facilities using existing copper cabling.

Certificate authority (CA) | A trusted entity that stores and distributes verified digital certificates.

Certificate of completion | A document that verifies a student has completed courses and earned a sufficient score on an assessment.

Certification | The technical evaluation of a system to provide assurance that you have implemented the system correctly. Also, an official statement that validates a person has satisfied specific requirements. Requirements often include possessing a certain level of experience, completing a course of study, and passing an examination.

Certified Information Systems Security Professional (CISSP) | A globally recognized information systems security professional certification offered by $(ISC)^2$.

Certifier | The individual or team responsible for performing the security test and evaluation (ST+E) for the system. The certifier also prepares the report for the AO on the risk of operating the system.

Change control | The process of managing changes to computer/device configuration or application software.

Change control committee | A group that oversees all proposed changes to systems and networks.

Characteristics | In authentication, this is a unique physical attribute or manner of expression, such as a fingerprint or a signature. Such attributes are often referred to as "something you are."

Checksum | The output of a one-way algorithm. A mathematically derived numerical representation of some input.

Children's Internet Protection Act (CIPA) | A federal law enacted by Congress to address concerns about access to offensive content over the Internet on school and library computers.

Cipher | An algorithm to encrypt or decrypt information.

Ciphertext | The opposite of cleartext. Data sent as ciphertext is not visible and not decipherable.

Class of service (COS) | A list of permissions that the phone extension is configured to perform. An executive's COS definitions may include international and long-distance dialing.

Clean desk/clear screen policy | A policy stating that users must never leave sensitive information in plain view on an unattended desk or workstation.

Cleartext | The opposite of ciphertext. Data sent as cleartext is visible and decipherable.

Clipping levels | Values used in security monitoring that tell controls to ignore activity that falls below a stated value.

Collaboration | A software-based application like WebEx that support audio conferencing and sharing of documents (text, spreadsheets, presentations, etc.) for real-time discussions with team members or colleagues.

Collusion | Two or more people working together to violate a security policy.

Committed information rate (CIR) | A guaranteed amount of bandwidth, offered by frame relay. CIR is like cruise control for a car. When you set the cruise control to a speed limit, the car accelerates to that guaranteed speed. Likewise, frame relay can support large bursts of traffic while providing a guaranteed CIR or throughput.

Compliance liaison | A person whose responsibility it is to ensure that employees are aware of and comply with an organization's security policies.

Confidentiality | The requirement to keep information private or secret.

Configuration control | The process of managing the baseline settings of a system device.

Constrained user interface | Software that allows users to enter only specific information.

Content filtering | The blocking of specific keywords or phrases in domain-name and URL lookups. Specific URLs and domain names can be prevented from being accessed with content filters.

Continuing education | An educational program that is generally associated with a college or university that provides formal courses that do not lead to degrees.

Continuing professional education (CPE) | A standard unit of credit that equals 50 minutes of instruction.

Continuous authentication | An authentication method in which a user is authenticated at multiple times or event intervals.

Convergence | A term used to describe the consolidation of voice, video, and data communications. Convergence can be application convergence, infrastructure convergence, or protocol convergence.

Cookie | A text file sent from a Web site to a Web browser to store for later use. Cookies contain details gleaned from visits to a Web site.

Corrective controls | Controls that mitigate or lessen the effects of the threat.

Countermeasures | Installed to counter or address a specific threat.

Covered entity | Health plans, health care clearinghouses, and any health care provider that transmits certain types of health information in electronic form. These entities must follow the HIPAA Security and Privacy Rules.

Covert act | An act carried out in secrecy.

Cracker | A computer attacker who has hostile intent, possesses sophisticated skills, and may be interested in financial gain.

Cryptography | The study or practice of hiding information.

Cybersecurity | The act of securing and protecting individuals, businesses, organizations, and governments that are connected to the Internet and the Web.

Cyberspace | The global online virtual world created by the Internet where individuals, businesses, organizations, and governments connect to one another.

D

Data classification standard | A definition of different data types.

Data Encryption Standard (DES) | Encryption cipher that is a product cipher with a 56-bit key consisting of 16 iterations of substitution and transformation. First published as a Federal Information Processing Standard (FIPS) in 1977.

Data infector virus | A type of virus that attacks document files containing embedded macro programming capabilities.

Decentralized access control | A system that put access control into the hands of people such as department managers who are closest to system users; there is no one centralized entity to process access requests in this system.

Decryption | The act of unscrambling ciphertext into plaintext.

Delphi method | An information- and opinion-c ollection method that employs formal anonymous surveys in multiple rounds.

Demilitarized zone (DMZ) | An exterior network that acts as a buffer zone between the public Internet and an organization's IT infrastructure (i.e., LAN-to-WAN Domain).

Denial of service (DoS) | An attack that uses ping or ICMP echo-request, echo-reply messages to bring down the availability of a server or system. DoS attacks are usually sourced from a single-host device.

Dense wavelength division multiplexing (DWDM) | A technique where multiple light streams can transmit data through a single strand of fiber.

Detective controls | Controls that identify that a threat has landed in your system.

Dictionary attack | An attack method that takes all the words from a dictionary file and attempts to log on by entering each dictionary entry as a password.

Differential cryptanalysis | Looking for patterns in vast amounts of ciphertext.

Digital central office (CO) switch | A switch used by the phone company to connect digital circuits and phone calls.

Digital signature | An object that uses asymmetric encryption to bind a message or data to a specific entity.

Digital subscriber line (DSL) | A high-speed digital broadband service that uses copper cabling for Internet access.

Digitized signature | An image of an electronically reproduced signature.

Direct inward dial (DID) | A phone company–assigned block of direct-dial phone numbers that enables outside callers to direct-dial phone extensions.

Direct inward system access (DISA) | An enabled feature within a PBX or phone system that permits a user to obtain access to a phone line for outbound dialing.

Directory information | Information that is publicly available about all students at a school.

Disaster recovery plan (DRP) | A written plan for how to handle major disasters or outages and recover mission-critical systems, applications, and data.

Disclosure | 1. Any instance of an unauthorized user accessing protected information. 2. Refers, under HIPAA, to how a covered entity shares PHI with other organizations.

Discretionary access control (DAC) | A means of restricting access to objects based on the identity of subjects and/or groups to which they belong.

Distance learning | Class environments where students are at a remote location for some or all of the instruction.

Distributed denial of service (DDoS) | An attack that uses ping or ICMP echo-request, echo-reply messages to bring down the availability of a server or system. DDoS attacks initiate from more than one host device.

Divestiture | A term used to describe the breakup of the AT&T monopoly on January 1, 1984.

Downtime | The amount of time that an IT system, application, or data is not available to users.

DS0 | A basic digital signaling rate that corresponds to one voice-frequency-equivalent channel. Although the true data rate for DS0 is 64 kbit/s, the effective data rate for a single voice channel when using DS0 is 56 kbit/s.

Dynamic Host Configuration Protocol (DHCP) | A protocol used on IP networks to provide configuration details automatically to client computers.

E

Eavesdropping | Listening to conversations without permission.

E-commerce | The buying and selling of goods and services online through a secure Web site, with payment by credit card or direct debit from a checking account.

Electronic protected health information (EPHI) | Patient health information that is computer based. It is PHI stored electronically.

Emergency operations center (EOC) | The place in which the recovery team will meet and work during a disaster.

Emergency operations group | A group that is responsible for protecting sensitive data in the event of a natural disaster or equipment failure, among other potential emergencies.

Encryption | The act of transforming cleartext data into undecipherable ciphertext.

Endpoint security | A term used to describe the A-I-C for handheld devices used by mobile workers such as cell phones, smartphones, PDA devices, laptops, and netbooks.

End user licensing agreement (EULA) | A software licensing agreement between the software manufacturer and purchaser, which limits the liability for software errors, bugs, or vulnerabilities.

Ethernet | An IEEE 802.3 CSMA/CD standard for Ethernet networking supporting speeds from 10Mbps to 10Gbps.

Ethical hacker | An information security or network professional who uses various penetration test tools to uncover or fix vulnerabilities. Also called a white-hat hacker.

Event | A measurable occurrence that has some impact on the business.

Event-based synchronization system | An authentication method in which a token's value is synchronized with a server based on each access request. The token's counter is increased each time a new value is requested.

Exposure factor (EF) | The percentage of loss for each realized threat.

F

False negative | Incorrectly identifying abnormal activity as normal.

False positive | Incorrectly identifying normal activity as abnormal.

Family Educational Rights and Privacy Act (FERPA) | A U.S. federal law that protects the private data of students, including their transcripts and grades, with which K–12 and higher-education institutions must comply.

Federal Communications Commission (FCC) | The federal agency responsible for defining laws, regulations, and mandates pertaining to telecommunication services.

Federal Information Security Management Act (FISMA) | A U.S. federal law that requires U.S. government agencies to protect citizens' private data and have proper security controls in place.

FICO | A publicly traded company that provides information used by the consumer credit reporting agencies Equifax, Experian, and TransUnion.

File infector virus | A type of virus that primarily infects executable programs.

File Transfer Protocol (FTP) | A non-secure file-transfer application that uses connection-oriented TCP transmissions with acknowledgements.

Firewall | A program or dedicated hardware device that inspects network traffic passing through it and denies or permits that traffic based on a set of rules you determine at configuration.

Frame relay | A packet-based WAN service capable of supporting one-to-many and many-to-many WAN connections. Frame relay provided a cloud-like WAN service offering, meaning organizations could connect to the cloud or network at the closest endpoint and ride on the service provider's backbone network. Frame relay was unique because it offered customers a guaranteed amount of bandwidth, called a committed information rate (CIR).

Functional policy | A statement of an organization's management direction for security in such specific functional areas as e-mail, remote access, and Internet surfing.

G

Gap analysis | A comparison of security controls in place and the controls that are needed to address all identified threats.

Generation Y | The generation composed of those born between 1980 and 2000 in the U.S. Members of Generation Y grew up with technologies that baby boomers did not have (i.e., cell phones, cable TV, Internet, iPods, etc.).

GigE | An abbreviation for Gigabit Ethernet LAN.

Gramm-Leach-Bliley Act (GLBA) | A U.S. federal law requiring banking and financial institutions to protect customers' private data and have proper security controls in place.

Gray-box testing | Security testing that is based on limited knowledge of an application's design.

Gray-hat hacker | A computer attacker with average abilities who may one day become a black-hat hacker. Gray-hat hackers are also called wannabes.

Group membership policy | An authorization method in which access to resources is decided by what group(s) you are in.

Guideline | A recommendation to purchase or how to use a product or system.

H

Hacker | A computer expert who explores computing environments to gain knowledge.

Hardened configuration | A computer or device in which you have turned off or disabled unnecessary services and protected the ones that are still running.

Hardening | A term that refers to ensuring the latest software revisions, security patches, and system configurations are installed properly.

Hash | The output of a one-way algorithm. A mathematically derived numerical representation of some input.

Health Insurance Portability and Accountability Act (HIPAA) | A U.S. federal law requiring health care institutions and insurance providers to protect patients' private data and have proper security controls in place.

High-value customer | A customer who purchases goods and services from a company multiple times—a big spender, in other words.

Hijacking | A type of attack in which the attacker takes control of a session between two machines and masquerades as one of them.

Honeynet | A group of honeypots made to simulate a real live network, but isolated from it.

Honeypot | A host or service deployed at the edge of a network to act as bait for potential hacking attacks. The purpose of the honeypot is to provide a controlled environment for attacks. This enables you to easily detect and analyze the attack to test the strength of the network.

Hub | A network device that connects network segments, echoing all received traffic to all other ports.

Human latency | the amount of time humans take to consider input or correspondence, take action, and then respond.

Hyper Text Transfer Protocol (HTTP) | An application layer protocol that allows users to communicate and access content via Web pages and browsers.

Hyper Text Transfer Protocol Secure (HTTPS) | The combination of HTTP and SSL/TLS encryption to provide security for data entry by users entering information on secure Web pages, like those found on online banking Web sites.

I

Identification | The process of providing credentials to claim to be a specific person or entity.

IEEE 802.3 CSMA/CD | An IEEE standard for local area networking that allows multiple computers to communicate using the same cabling. This is also known as Ethernet.

IM chat | An instant-messaging chat application. Examples include AOL IM, Yahoo! Messenger, and Google Talk.

Impact | The magnitude of harm that could be caused by a threat exercising a vulnerability.

Incident | An event that has a negative impact on operations.

Incident response team (IRT) | Teams of people organized to identify and respond to security incidents. An IRT is responsible for minimizing the impact of incidents and collecting any necessary evidence to analyze the incident.

Information security | The protection of data itself.

Information systems | The servers and application software on which information and data reside.

Information systems security | The protection of information systems, applications, and data.

Infrastructure convergence | This is the sharing of the same 4-pair, unshielded twisted-pair cabling and 100Mbps or GigE LAN switch connections. Workstations plug into IP phones sharing the same physical cabling. Commingled voice and data IP traffic traverses the shared workstation cabling. Separate voice and data VLANs segment traffic within the wiring closet and building backbone networks.

Institute of Electrical and Electronics Engineers (IEEE) | A standards body that defines specifications and standards for electronic technology.

Integrity | The validity of information or data. Data with high integrity has not been altered or modified.

Intellectual property (IP) | The unique knowledge a business possesses that gives it a competitive advantage over similar companies in similar industries

International Electrotechnical Commission (IEC) | The predominant organization for developing and publishing international standards for technologies related to electrical and electronic devices and processes.

International Information Systems Security Certification Consortium | *See* $(ISC)^2$.

International Organization for Standardization (ISO) | A nongovernmental international organization with the goal of developing and publishing international standards.

International Telecommunication Union (ITU) | The main United Nations agency responsible for managing and promoting information and technology issues.

Internet | A global network of computer networks that uses the TCP/IP family of protocols and applications to connect nearly two billion users.

Internet Architecture Board (IAB) | A subcommittee of the IETF comprised of independent researchers and professionals who have a technical interest the overall well-being of the Internet.

Internet Control Message Protocol (ICMP) | A management protocol for IP networks.

Internet Engineering Task Force (IETF) | A standards organization that develops and promotes Internet standards.

Internet Protocol (IP) | A network layer protocol that has a network layer address.

Intrusion detection system/intrusion prevention system (IDS/IPS) | Network security appliances typically installed within the LAN-to-WAN Domain at the Internet ingress/egress point to monitor and block unwanted IP traffic.

IP address | A 32-bit or 128-bit number that uniquely identifies a computer on a network.

IP default gateway router | The router interface's IP address that acts as your LAN's ingress/egress device.

IP-PBX | A hybrid digital PBX- and VoIP-capable phone switch.

IPSec | A suite of protocols designed to connect sites securely using IP networks.

IP stateful firewall | A device that examines the IP, TCP, and UDP layers within a packet to make blocking or forwarding decisions. Firewalls are placed at the ingress/egress points where networks interconnect.

(ISC)^2 | The International Information Systems Security Certification Consortium. A nonprofit organization dedicated to certifying information systems security professionals.

ISO 17799 | An international security standard that documents a comprehensive set of controls that represent information system best practices.

ISO/IEC 27002 | An update to the ISO 17799 standard.

IT security policy framework | A set of rules for security. The framework is hierarchical and includes policies, standards, procedures, and guidelines.

ITU Telecommunication Sector (ITU-T) | The committee of the ITU responsible for ensuring the efficient and effective production of standards covering all fields of telecommunications for \all nations.

J

Job rotation | A strategy to minimize risk by rotating employees between various systems or duties.

K

Key | A secret value a cipher uses to encrypt or decrypt information.

Key directory | A trusted repository of all public keys.

Key distribution | The process of issuing keys to valid users of a cryptosystem so they can communicate.

Key-encrypting key | An encryption key used to encrypt other keys before transmitting them.

Keylogger | Surveillance software or hardware that records to a log file every keystroke a user makes.

Key revocation | A situation in which someone is no longer trusted or allowed to use a cryptosystem. In a symmetric key system, where everyone shares the same key, compromising one copy of the key comprises all copies.

Keyspace | The set of all possible encryption keys.

Keyword mixed alphabet cipher | An encryption cipher that uses a cipher alphabet that consists of a keyword, less duplicates, followed by the remaining letters of the alphabet.

Knowledge | In authentication, this is something you know, such as a password, a passphrase, or a PIN.

L

Layer 2 switch | A network switch that examines the MAC-layer address of an Ethernet frame to determine where to send it. A Layer 2 switch supports LAN connectivity, typically via unshielded twisted-pair cabling at 10/100/1000 or 10Gbps Ethernet speeds.

Layer 3 switch | A network switch that examines the network layer address of an IP packet to determine where to route it. A Layer 3 switch supports LAN connectivity typically via unshielded twisted-pair cabling at 10/100/1000 or 10Gig Ethernet speeds and is the same thing as a router.

Likelihood | The probability that a potential vulnerability might be exercised within the construct of an associated threat environment.

Local area network (LAN) | A collection of computers that are connected to one another or to a common medium. Computers on a LAN are generally within an area no larger than a building.

Logic bomb | A program that executes a malicious function of some kind when it detects certain conditions.

Logical access control | A mechanism that limits access to computer systems and network resources.

Low-value customer | A customer who has purchased a product or service a single time. Low-value customers can become high-value customers through proper marketing and purchasing incentives, like discount coupons.

M

Macro virus | A type of virus that typically infects a data file and injects malicious macro commands.

Malicious code | Software written with malicious intent—for example, a computer virus.

Malicious software | Software designed to infiltrate one or more target computers and follow an attacker's instructions.

Malware | Short for malicious software. Software designed to infiltrate one or more target computers and follow an attacker's instructions.

Man-in-the-middle attack | An attack in which the attacker gets between two parties and intercepts messages before transferring them on to their intended destination.

Mandatory access control (MAC) | A means of restricting access to an object based on the object's classification and the user's security clearance.

Masquerade attack | An attack in which one user or computer pretends to be another user or computer.

Maximum tolerable downtime (MTD) | The greatest amount of time a business can survive without a particular critical system.

Mean time to failure (MTTF) | The average amount of time a device is expected to operate before encountering a failure.

Mean time to repair (MTTR) | The average amount of time required to repair a device.

Minimum necessary rule | A rule that covered entities may disclose only the amount of PHI absolutely necessary to carry out a particular function.

Mitigation activities | Any activities designed to reduce the severity of a vulnerability or remove it altogether.

Multimodal communications | Communication options for contacting an individual or business. Phone, fax, e-mail, text messaging, presence/availability, IM chat, audio conferencing, videoconferencing, and collaboration provide a multitude of communication options.

Multipartite virus | A type of virus that infects other files and spreads in multiple ways.

Multi-protocol label switching (MPLS) | A wide area network technology that operates at Layer 2 by inserting labels or tags in the packet header for creating virtual paths between endpoints in a WAN infrastructure. This is a faster method of transporting IP packets through the WAN without requiring routing and switching of IP packets.

N

National Centers of Academic Excellence in Information Assurance Education (CAEIAE) | Educational institutions that meet specific federal information assurance educational guidelines.

National Centers of Academic Excellence in Research (CAE-R) | Institutions that meet specific federal information assurance research guidelines.

National Institute of Standards and Technology (NIST) | A federal agency within the U.S. Department of Commerce whose mission is to "promote U.S. innovation and industrial competitiveness by advancing measurement science, standards, and technology in ways that enhance economic security and improve our quality of life."

Need-to-know | A property that indicates a specific subject needs access to a specific object. This is necessary to access the object in addition to possessing the proper clearance for the object's classification.

Netcat | A network utility program that reads from and writes to network connections.

Network Access Control (NAC) | A method to restrict access to a network based on identity or other rules.

Network Address Translation (NAT) | A method of IP address assignment that uses an alternate, public IP address to hide a system's real IP address.

Network infrastructure security | A term used to encompass the A-I-C for the LAN, LAN-to-WAN, WAN, and Remote Access domains.

Network interface card (NIC) | This is the physical interface between a computer and the Ethernet LAN. It contains a unique 6-byte MAC-layer address.

Network keys | Software encryption keys used for encrypting and decrypting keys.

Network mapping | Using tools to determine the layout and services running on an organization's systems and networks.

Network operations center (NOC) | The command control center for a telecommunication service provider's backbone network and customer networks. Customer trouble calls are answered by the NOC in support of managed services and SLAs.

Nonpublic Personal Information (NPI) | Any personally identifiable financial information that a consumer provides to a financial institution. This term is defined by the Gramm-Leach-Bliley Act.

Nonrepudiation | Prevents a party from denying a previous statement or action.

O

One-time pad cipher | The only unbreakable cryptographic cipher, also called a Vernam cipher.

One-way algorithm | An encryption algorithm that has no corresponding decryption algorithm.

Open Systems Interconnection (OSI) reference model | An internationally accepted framework of standards that governs how separate computer systems communicate using networks.

Operating system fingerprinting | A reconnaissance technique that enables an attacker to use port mapping to learn which operating system and version is running on a computer.

Opportunity cost | The amount of money a company loses due to downtime, either intentional or unintentional (also called true downtime cost).

Overt act | An act carried out in the open.

Ownership | In authentication, this is something you have, such as a smart card, key, badge, or token.

P

Packet-filtering firewall | A firewall that examines each packet it receives and compares the packet to a list of rules configured by the network administrator.

Packet sniffer | A software application that uses a hardware adapter card in promiscuous mode to capture all network packets sent across a network segment.

Passphrase | An authentication credential that is generally longer and more complex than a password. Passphrases can also contain multiple words.

Pattern- (signature-) based IDS | An intrusion detection system that uses pattern matching and stateful matching to compare current traffic with activity patterns (signatures) of known network intruders.

Payment Card Industry Data Security Standard (PCI DSS) | A standard, not a compliance law, for performing a security assessment along with use of proper security controls to reduce risk in handling customer privacy data.

Penetration testing | A testing method that tries to exploit a weakness in the system to prove that an attacker could successfully penetrate it.

Personal data assistant (PDA) | A handheld device that acts as a mobile computer device supporting cell phone, Internet browsing, and e-mail.

Personally identifiable information (PII) | Data that can be used to individually identify a person. It includes Social Security numbers, driver's license numbers, financial account data, and health data.

Pharming | An attack that seeks to obtain personal or private financial information through domain spoofing.

Phishing | A type of fraud in which an attacker attempts to trick the victim into providing private information.

Phishing scam | An identity theft scam that arrives via e-mail or instant message.

Phone phreaking | The art of exploiting bugs and weaknesses that exist in the telephone system.

Phreaking | The act of studying, experimenting with, or exploring telephone systems, telephone company equipment, and systems connected to public telephone networks.

Physical access control | A mechanism that limits access to physical resources, such as buildings or rooms.

Physically constrained user interface | A user interfaces that does not provide a physical means of entering unauthorized information.

Ping | Stands for "packet Internet groper." Ping uses the Internet Control Message Protocol (ICMP) echo-request and echo-reply communications to verify end-to-end IP connectivity.

Plaintext | Unencrypted information.

Point-to-Point Tunneling Protocol (PPTP) | A protocol to implement a VPN connection between two computers.

Polymorphic virus | A type of virus that includes a separate encryption engine that stores the virus body in encrypted format while duplicating the main body of the virus.

Pop-up | A type of window that appears on top of the browser window. Pop-ups generally contain ads. Although pop-ups are not strictly adware, many adware programs use them to interact with users.

Power over Ethernet (PoE) | A strategy that uses a device to provide electrical power for IP phones from the RJ-45 8-pin jacks directly to the workstation outlet.

Preventative controls | Controls that prevent threats from coming in contact with a weakness.

Private (symmetric) key | Encryption cipher that uses the same key to encrypt and decrypt information.

Privately held company | A company held by a small group of private investors.

Proactive change management | Initiating changes to avoid expected problems.

Procedures | Step-by-step actions to be performed to accomplish a security requirement, process, or objective.

Product cipher | Encryption cipher that is a combination of multiple ciphers. Each could be transposition or substitution.

Project Management Body of Knowledge (PMBOK) | A collection of the knowledge and best practices of the project management profession.

Project Management Institute (PMI) | A nonprofit international organization of project managers that promotes the field of project management.

Protected health information (PHI) | Any individually identifiable information about the past, present, or future health of a person. It includes mental and physical health data.

Protocol | A list of rules and methods for communicating.

Protocol convergence | When voice, video, multimedia, and data converge on the use of TCP/IP as its primary protocol. Today, TCP/IP has become the lowest common denominator protocol for voice, video, multimedia, and data communications.

Proxy server | A server that is placed on a DMZ LAN that acts as a middleman for data sharing between the outside world and a user. Proxy servers assume risk, threats, and vulnerabilities so that the workstations they're connected to don't have to.

Public (asymmetric) key | Encryption cipher that uses one key to encrypt and another key to decrypt information.

Public branch exchange (PBX) phone system | A term for a phone switch or phone system. PBXes are digital switches that can support both analog and digital ports and phones. Some PBXes support a VoIP migration strategy, allowing for a hybrid IP-PBX transition.

Public key cryptography | A system that allows correspondents to communicate only over a public channel using publicly known techniques.

Public key infrastructure (PKI) | A set of hardware, software, people, policies, and procedures needed to create, manage, distribute, use, store, and revoke digital certificates.

Publicly traded companies | Companies owned by a number of different investors, who own shares of their stock.

Q

Qualitative risk analysis | A risk-analysis method that uses relative ranking to provide further definition of the identified risks in order to determine responses to them.

Quality of service (QoS) | A method of prioritizing time-sensitive protocols such as VoIP and SIP through an IP WAN. You need QoS when there is congestion at WAN connections.

Quantitative risk analysis | A risk-analysis method that uses mathematical formulas and numbers to assist in ranking risk severity.

R

Reactive change management | Enacting changes in response to reported problems.

Real-time communications | Immediate communication conducted between two parties without the need for messaging.

Real-time monitoring | Analysis of activity as it is happening.

Reconnaissance | The process of gathering information.

Recovery time objective (RTO) | A defined metric for how long it must take to recover an IT system, application, and data access.

Reference monitor | Software that provides a central point of processing for all resource access requests.

Regional Bell Operating Company (RBOC) | A company formed after divestiture to create open competition in the telecommunications market throughout the U.S. In all, seven RBOCs emerged.

Relationships | Optional conditions that exist between users and resources. They are permissions granted to an authorized user, such as read, write, and execute.

Remediation | Fixing something that is broken or defective, such as by addressing or removing vulnerabilities.

Replay attack | An attack in which the attacker captures data packets from a network and retransmits them to produce an unauthorized effect.

Request for Comments (RFC) | A document produced by the IETF. RFCs contain standards as well as other specifications or descriptive contents.

Residual risk | Any risk that exists but has a defined response.

Resources | Protected objects in a computing system, such as files, computers, or printers.

Revocation | Stopping authorization for access to data.

"RFC 1087: Ethics and the Internet" | An acceptable-use policy statement as issued by the Internet Advisory Board and the U.S. government defining ethics and the Internet.

Risk | The likelihood that something bad will happen to an asset.

Risk management | The process of identifying, assessing, prioritizing, and addressing risks.

Risk methodology | A description of how you will manage overall risk. It includes the approach, required information, and techniques to address each risk.

Risk register | A list of identified risks that results from the risk-identification process.

Role based access control (RBAC) | An access control method that bases access control approvals on the jobs the user is assigned.

Rootkit | A type of malware that modifies or replaces one or more existing programs to hide the fact that a computer has been compromised.

Router | A device that connects two or more networks and selectively interchanges packets of data between them.

S

Safeguards | Built-in or used in a system to address gaps or weaknesses in the controls that could otherwise lead to an exploit.

Salt value | Random characters that you can combine with an actual input key to create the encryption key.

Sarbanes-Oxley Act (SOX) | A U.S. federal law requiring officers of publicly traded companies to have accurate and audited financial statements. SOX also requires proper security controls to protect financial records and insider information.

Screened subnet | A firewall device that has three NICs. One NIC connects to the Internet, the second NIC connects to the internal network, and the third NIC connects to a DMZ.

Script kiddie | A person with little or no computer-attack skills. Script kiddies simply follow directions or use a cookbook approach without fully understanding the meaning of the steps they are performing.

Second-level authentication | A second authentication requirement for users to gain access to more sensitive applications and data.

Secure shell (SSH) | An encrypted channel used for remote access to a server or system. Commonly used in Linux and UNIX servers and applications.

Secure Sockets Layer virtual private network (SSL-VPN) | SSL-VPN is a means of securing remote access to a secure Web site. In other words, it's a VPN that runs on Secure Sockets Layer and encrypts communications to a secure Web server via a secure browser connection.

Security administration | The group of individuals responsible for planning, designing, implementing, and monitoring an organization's security plan.

Security association (SA) | The basic element of ISAKMP key management. SA contains all the information needed to do a variety of network security services.

Security breach | Any event that results in a violation of any of the A-I-C security tenets.

Security event log | Recorded information from system events that describes security-related activity.

Security gap | The difference between the security controls you have in place and the controls you need to have in place in order to address all vulnerabilities.

Security Information and Event Management (SIEM) system | Software and devices that assist in collecting, storing, and analyzing the contents of log files.

Security kernel database | A database made up of rules that determine individual users' access rights.

Security operations and administration | One of the domains of the SSCP certification. Security operations and administration include the day-to-day roles, responsibilities, and tasks for maintaining and implementing security countermeasures.

Separation of duties | The process of dividing a task into a series of unique activities performed by different people, each of whom is allowed to execute only one part of the overall task.

Service level agreement (SLA) | A contractual commitment by a service provider or support organization to its customers or users.

Session hijacking | A network attack in which the attacker attempts to take over an existing connection between two network computers.

Session Initiation Protocol (SIP) | The multimedia communications protocol used by unified communication applications in a unicast (one-to-one) or multicast (one-to-many) capacity.

Simple Network Management Protocol (SNMP) | A non-secure connectionless UDP-based protocol that is used to transmit network-management data between IP devices and an SNMP network manager.

Simple substitution cipher | An encryption cipher that uniquely maps any letter to any other letter.

Single-factor authentication | An authentication method that uses only a single type of authentication credentials.

Single loss expectancy (SLE) | The expected loss for a single threat occurrence. The formula to calculate SLE is SLE = resource value × EF.

Social engineering | The act of persuading a person to reveal information.

Smart card | A plastic card with authentication credentials embedded in either a microchip or magnetic strip on the card.

Smartphone | A cell phone that runs mobile communications software and supports voice, Internet browsing, e-mail, and text messaging.

Smurfing | A DoS attack that uses a directed broadcast to create a flood of network traffic for the victim computer.

Sniffer | An application that captures traffic as it travels across a network.

Software vulnerability | An error or bug in software code that can be exploited.

Spam | Unwanted e-mail or instant messages.

Spear phishing | An e-mail or instant-message spoofing fraud attempt that targets a specific organization, seeking unauthorized access to confidential data.

Spoofing | A type of attack in which one person, program, or computer disguises itself as another person, program, or computer to gain access to some resource.

Spyware | Software that gathers user information through the user's Internet connection without the user's knowledge.

SSL handshake | A process that creates the first secure communications session between a client and a server.

Standards | Mandated requirements for hardware and software solutions that are used to deal with a security risk throughout the organization.

Stateful inspection firewall | A firewall that examines the state of a connection as well as simple address, port, and protocol rules to determine how to process a packet.

Stateful matching | A technique of matching network traffic with rules or signatures based on the appearance of the traffic and its relationship to other packets.

Stealth virus | A type of virus that uses a number of techniques to conceal itself from the user or detection software.

Store-and-forward communications | Voice mail and e-mail are examples of store-and-forward or non-real-time communications. Voice messages and e-mail messages are stored on a server and downloaded to endpoint devices.

Subnet mask address | The complement to an IP address that defines the IP network number and IP host address.

Substitution cipher | An encryption cipher that replaces bits, characters, or blocks of information with other bits, characters, or blocks.

Symmetric digital subscriber line (SDSL) | DSL service where the bandwidth allocated is the same for downstream and upstream traffic. SDSL can support from 384Kbps to 20Mbps using existing copper facilities. Bandwidth depends on physical distance, line conditions, and the type of DSL technology used.

Symmetric key cryptography | A type of cryptography that cannot secure correspondence until after the two parties exchange keys.

Synchronous token | A device used as a logon authenticator for remote users of a network.

SYN flood | A DoS attack that fills up a computer's connection table by sending a flood of unacknowledged connection requests. Once the connection table fills up, the computer cannot respond to any new legitimate connection requests.

System infector virus | A type of virus that targets key hardware and system software components in a computer, and is usually associated with system startup processes.

System owner | The person responsible for the daily operation of a system and for ensuring that the system continues to operate in compliance with the conditions set out by the AO.

Systems Security Certified Practitioner (SSCP) | A practitioner-level information systems security professional certification offered by $(ISC)^2$.

Switch | A network device that connects network segments, creating a direct connection between a sending and receiving port.

T

Technical control | A control that is carried out or managed by a computer system.

Technology protection measure (TPM) | Technology used to filter content from which children are to be protected.

Telnet | A non-secure application that supports remote terminal access in cleartext transmission.

Temporal isolation | A method of restricting resource access to specific periods of time.

Threat | Any action that could damage an asset.

Threat source | An intent or method targeted to intentionally exploit a vulnerability.

Threshold | Some value that indicates a change from normal to abnormal behavior. In the case of failed logon attempts, a threshold of five means that when a user fails to log on five times, the action should be considered abnormal.

Time-based synchronization system | An authentication method in which a token's internal clock is synchronized with a server's clock to generate matching values.

Timestamping | Providing an exact time when a producer creates or sends information.

Token | A physical device that transmits a secret code to a user to authenticate the user. Can be a hardware-device token or a software-generated token.

Toll calls | Long distance or international calls for which there is a separate charge in addition to basic telephone service fees.

Toll fraud | The theft of long-distance telephone service.

Traditional classroom | A classroom environment with an instructor leading the class in the same room as the students.

Traffic prioritization | Requires quality of service (QoS) to prioritize time-sensitive protocols such as VoIP and SIP through the WAN interface port prior to other types of IP traffic.

Transmission Control Protocol/Internet Protocol (TCP/IP) | A popular suite of protocols that operate at both the Network and Transport layers of the OSI reference model. TCP/IP governs all activity across the Internet and through most corporate and home networks.

Transposition cipher | An encryption cipher that rearranges characters or bits of data.

Trivial File Transfer Protocol (TFTP) | A connectionless, UDP-based file-transfer protocol used for quick and small file transfers between two IP devices.

Trojan | A malicious software code that appears benign to the user but actually performs a task on behalf of a perpetrator with malicious intent.

True downtime cost | The amount of money a company loses due to downtime, either intentional or unintentional. Also called opportunity cost.

Trunk access group restriction (TAGR) | A software setting for phone extensions allowing or restricting access to an outside trunk line for outbound dialing.

Two-factor authentication (TFA) | An authentication method that uses two types of authentication credentials.

U

Unified communications (UC) | A means of real-time communications between one-to-one or one-to-many. UC applications include IM chat, audio and video conferencing, and collaboration.

Uptime | The total amount of time the IT system, application and data was accessible.

USB token | A hardware device used for authentication that you plug into your computer's USB port. This device provides authentication credentials without the user having to type anything.

Use | How a covered entity shares or handles PHI within its organization. This term is defined by the Health Insurance Portability and Accountability Act.

User Datagram Protocol (UDP) | A communication protocol that is connectionless and is popular for exchanging small amounts of data or messages.

V

Vendor-neutral certification | This type of certification covers concepts and topics that are general in nature and do not focus on a specific product or product line.

Vendor-specific certification | This type of certification helps to identify professionals who possess in-depth product knowledge. Many organizations use these certifications, along with vendor-neutral certifications, when evaluating prospective employees and personnel.

Vernam cipher | The only unbreakable cryptographic cipher. Also called a one-time pad.

Videoconferencing | An application that supports bridging callers and their Web cam images into a common videoconference.

View-based access control (VBAC) | Limiting users' access to database views, as opposed to allowing users to access data in database tables directly.

Vigenère cipher | An encryption cipher that uses multiple encryption schemes in succession. For example, you could encrypt every fifth letter with its own substitution scheme.

Virtual LAN (VLAN) | The broadcast domain in Ethernet where all workstations are on the same logical LAN.

Virtual private networks (VPNs) | Methods of encrypting IP packets from one end to another, like in a tunnel.

Virus | A software program that attaches itself to or copies itself into another program for the purpose of causing the computer to follow instructions that were not intended by the original program developer.

Voice over IP (VoIP) | Voice communications supported over IP.

Vulnerability | A weakness that allows a threat to be realized or to have an effect on an asset.

Vulnerability assessment | A software review that identifies bugs or errors in software.

Vulnerability scanner | A software tool that collects information about any known weaknesses that exist on a target computer or network.

Vulnerability testing | A process of finding the weaknesses in a system and determining which places may be attack points.

Vulnerability window | The gap in time between when a software vendor releases a software or security patch and when you implement it.

W

Wannabe | A computer attacker who is of average abilities and could one day become a black hat. Wannabes are sometimes called gray-hat hackers.

Wardialer | A computer program used to identify the phone numbers that can successfully make a connection with a computer modem.

Waterfall model | A software development model that defines how development activities progress from one distinct phase to the next.

White-box testing | Security testing that is based on knowledge of the application's design and source code.

White-hat hacker | An information security or network professional who uses various penetration test tools to uncover or fix vulnerabilities. Also called an ethical hacker.

Wi-Fi Protected Access (WPA) | Current encryption for wireless networks. Much stronger than WEP, WPA is the recommended encryption for wireless use.

Wired Equivalent Privacy (WEP) | Legacy encryption for wireless networks. WEP is weak and does not provide sufficient protection for most traffic.

Wireless access point (WAP) | A radio transceiver device that transmits and receives IP communications via wireless LAN technology.

Wireless Fidelity (Wi-Fi) | An alliance among wireless manufacturers to brand certified products that interoperate with wireless LAN standards. A Wi-Fi hotspot is a wireless LAN access location.

Wireless LANs (WLANs) | LANs that use radio transmissions to connect computers and devices instead of wires or cables.

Wiretapping | Intercepting communication sent via a wired connection.

World Wide Web (WWW) | A collection of documents that are hyperlinked among one another and accessed using the Internet.

World Wide Web Consortium (W3C) | An organization formed in 1994 to develop and publish standards for the World Wide Web.

Worm | A self-replicating piece of malicious software that can spread from device to device.

Z

Zone transfer | A unique query of a DNS server that asks it for the contents of its zone.

References

Altholz, Nancy, and Larry Stevenson. *Rootkits for Dummies (For Dummies (Computer/Tech))*. New York: John Wiley and Sons Ltd., 2007.

Amoroso, Edward. *Cyber Security*. Summit, NJ: Silicon Press, 2006.

Aquilina, James M., Eoghan Casey, and Cameron H. Malin. *Malware Forensics: Investigating and Analyzing Malicious Code*. Burlington, MA: Syngress, 2008.

Bacik, Sandy. *Building an Effective Information Security Policy Architecture*. Boca Raton, FL: CRC Press, 2008.

Benantar, Messaoud. *Access Control Systems: Security, Identity Management and Trust Models*. New York: Spring, 2005.

Bhaiji, Yusuf. *Network Security Technologies and Solutions (CCIE Professional Development Series)*. Indianapolis: Cisco Press, 2008.

Biegelman, Martin T. and Daniel R. Biegelman. *Building a World-Class Compliance Program: Best Practices and Strategies for Success*. New York: Wiley, 2008.

Brotby, W. Krag. *Information Security Metrics: A Definitive Guide to Effective Security Monitoring and Measurement*. Chicago: Auerbach, 2008.

Bumiller, Elisabeth. "Bush Signs Bill Aimed at Fraud in Corporations," *The New York Times*, July 30, 2002. http://www.nytimes.com/2002/07/31/business/corporate-conduct-the-president-bush-signs-bill-aimed-at-fraud-in-corporations.html?pagewanted=1 (accessed April 16, 2010).

Calder, Alan, and Steve Watkins. *IT Governance: A Manager's Guide to Data Security and ISO 27001/ISO 27002*, 4th ed. London: Kogan Page, 2008.

Carpenter, Tom. *CWNA Certified Wireless Network Administrator & CWSP Certified Wireless Security Professional All-in-One Exam Guide (PWO-104 & PWO-204)*. New York: McGraw-Hill Osborne Media, 2010.

Chabrow, Eric. "Automated FISMA Reporting Tool Unveiled," GovInfoSecurity.com, October 30, 2009. http://www.govinfosecurity.com/articles.php?art_id=1894 (accessed April 24, 2010).

Chandramouli, Ramaswamy, David F. Ferraiolo, and D. Richard Kuhn. *Role-Based Access Control*, 2nd ed. Norwood, MA: Artech House Publishers, 2007.

Children's Internet Protection Act, The, Pub. L. No. 106-554, 114 Stat. 2763A-335 (codified in scattered sections of U.S. Code).

CISM Review Manual 2009. Chicago: Isaca Books, 2008.

Code of Federal Regulations, Title 45, sec. 160.103.

Code of Federal Regulations, Title 45, sec. 164.306.

Code of Federal Regulations, Title 45, sec. 164.316.

Code of Federal Regulations, Title 45, sec. 164.520.

Code of Federal Regulations, Title 45, sec. 164.530(f).

Code of Federal Regulations, Title 45, sec. 164.502(b).

Commission Guidance Regarding Management's Report on Internal Controls Over Financial Reporting, Code of Federal Regulations, Title 17, sec. 241.

Committee on Oversight and Government Reform, "Federal Information Security: Current Challenges and Future Policy Considerations," March 24, 2010. http://oversight.house.gov/images/stories/Hearings/Government_Management/032410_Federal_Info_Security/2010.FISMA.Kundra.testimony.final.pdf (accessed April 21, 2010). *See* prepared testimony of Mr. Vivek Kundra.

Davis, Chris, Mike Schiller, and Kevin Wheeler. *IT Auditing: Using Controls to Protect Information Assets*. New York: McGraw-Hill Osborne Media, 2006.

Douligeris, Christos, and Dimitrios N. Serpanos. *Network Security: Current Status and Future Directions*. New York: Wiley-IEEE Press, 2007.

Ernst & Young, "Emerging Trends in Internal Controls: Fourth Survey and Industry Insights," September 2005. http://www.sarbanes-oxley.be/aabs_emerging_trends_survey4.pdf (accessed April 16, 2010).

Faircloth, Jeremy, and Paul Piccard. *Combating Spyware in the Enterprise*. Burlington, MA: Syngress, 2006.

Federal Information Security Management Act, Title III of the E-Government Act of 2002, Pub. L. 107-347; U.S. Code Vol. 44, sec. 3541 et seq.

Free Software Foundation. http://www.fsf.org (accessed September 17, 2010).

GNU public license agreement Web site. http://www.gnu.org (accessed September 17, 2010).

Hampton, John J. *Fundamentals of Enterprise Risk Management: How Top Companies Assess Risk, Manage Exposure, and Seize Opportunity*. New York: AMACOM, 2009.

"Hazard Identification and Business Impact Analysis." Continuity Central (Portal Publishing Ltd.). http://www.continuitycentral.com/HazardIdentificationBusinessImpactAnalysis.pdf (accessed October 2, 2010).

Health Information Technology for Economic and Clinical Health Act (2009), Pub. L. No. 111-5, sec. 13402.

Hill, David G. *Data Protection: Governance, Risk Management, and Compliance*. Boca Raton, FL: CRC Press, 2009.

Hoopes, John. *Virtualization for Security: Including Sandboxing, Disaster Recovery, High Availability, Forensic Analysis, and Honeypotting*. Burlington, MA: Syngress, 2008.

Howard, Rick. *Cyber Fraud: Tactics, Techniques and Procedures*. Chicago: Auerbach, 2009.

Institute of Electrical and Electronics Engineers (IEEE). http://www.ieee.org (accessed September 17, 2010).

International Information Systems Security Certification Consortium $(ISC)^2$. http://www.isc2.org (accessed September 17, 2010).

Krause, Micki, and Harold F. Tipton. *Information Security Management Handbook*, 6th ed. $(ISC)^2$ Press. Chicago: Auerbach, 2007.

Kundra, Vivek. "Faster, Smarter Cybersecurity," The White House Blog, April 21, 2010, http://www.whitehouse.gov/blog/2010/04/21/faster-smarter-cybersecurity (accessed April 23, 2010).

Lauricella, Tom. "Investors Hope the '10s Beat the '00s," *The Wall Street Journal*, December 20, 2009. http://online.wsj.com/article/SB10001424052748704786204574607993448916718.html (accessed April 16, 2010).

Marcella, Albert J., "Electronically Stored Information and Cyberforensics," *Information Systems Control Journal*, Vol. 5 (2008). Available at http://www.isaca.org/Template.cfm?Section=Home&CONTENTID=52106&TEMPLATE=/ContentManagement/ContentDisplay.cfm (accessed April 16, 2010).

Mogollon, Manuel. *Cryptography and Security Services: Mechanisms and Applications*. London: Cybertech Publishing, 2008.

Moldovyan, Alex, and Nick Moldovyan. *Innovative Cryptography (Programming Series)*, 2nd ed. Rockland, MA: Charles River Media, 2006.

National Institute of Standards and Technology, SP 800-37, "Guide for Applying the Risk Management Framework to Federal Information Systems: A Security Life Cycle Approach" February 2010. http://csrc.nist.gov/publications/nistpubs/800-37-rev1/sp800-37-rev1-final.pdf (accessed May 21, 2010).

"Risk Management Framework." EPCB Risk Management Consulting Services (n.d.). http://www.emergencyriskmanagement.com/site/711336/page/248974 (accessed October 2, 2010).

Rose, Adam, and Linda S. Spedding. *Business Risk Management Handbook: A Sustainable Approach*. Oxford: Cima Publishing, 2007.

Sarbanes-Oxley Act of 2002, Pub. L. No. 107-204, 116 Stat. 745 (codified as amended in scattered sections of U.S. Code Vol. 15).

Senft, Sandra. *Information Technology Control and Audit*, 3rd ed. Chicago: Auerbach, 2008.

Standards for Insuring the Security Confidentiality, Integrity and Protection of Customer Records and Information ("Safeguards Rule"), Code of Federal Regulations, Title 16, sec. 314.

Stoneburner, Gary, Alice Goguen, and Alexis Feringa. *Risk Management Guide for Information Technology Systems* (NIST SP 800-30). National Institute for Standards and Technology, 2002. http://csrc.nist.gov/publications/nistpubs/800-30/sp800-30.pdf (accessed October 2, 2010).

Swenson, Christopher. *Modern Cryptanalysis: Techniques for Advanced Code Breaking*. New York: Wiley, 2008.

Tipton, Hal, Kevin Henry, and Steve Kalman, e-mail conversation with author, June 2008.

Total Disaster Risk Management Good Practice. Asian Disaster Reduction Center, 2009. http://www.adrc.asia/publications/TDRM2005/TDRM_Good_Practices/Index.html (accessed October 2, 2010).

U.S. Code Vol. 15, sec. 6801-6803.

U.S. Code Vol. 15, sec. 6801(b).

U.S. Code Vol. 15, sec. 7213m.

U.S. Code Vol. 15, sec. 7266.

U.S. Code Vol. 20, sec. 1232g.

U.S. Code Vol. 44, sec. 3542(b)(1).

U.S. Code Vol. 44, sec. 3544(a)(3)(A)(ii).

U.S. Government Accountability Office. *Federal Information System Controls Audit Manual*, 1999. http://www.gao.gov/special.pubs/ai12.19.6.pdf (accessed October 2, 2010).

U.S. Office of Management and Budget, Circular No. A-130, "Management of Federal Information Resources," December 2000. http://www.whitehouse.gov/omb/circulars_a130_a130trans4/ (accessed April 21, 2010).

U.S. Securities and Exchange Commission, "Information Matters," February 22, 2006, http://www.sec.gov/answers/infomatters.htm (accessed April 16, 2010).

Vacca, John R. *Computer and Information Security Handbook*. San Francisco: Morgan Kaufmann, 2009.

Verizon Business, *2009 Data Breach Investigations Report*, April 15, 2009. http://www.verizonbusiness.com/resources/security/reports/2009_databreach_rp.pdf (accessed March 1, 2010).

VoIP Security Alliance. http://www.voipsa.org (accessed September 17, 2010).

Whitman, M. E., and Matford, H. J. *Principles of Incident Response and Disaster Recovery*, p. 492. Boston: Course Technology, 2006.

Wright, Craig S. *The IT Regulatory and Standards Compliance Handbook: How to Survive Information Systems Audit and Assessments*. Burlington, MA: Syngress, 2008.

Wright, Steve. PCI DSS: *A Practical Guide to Implementation, 2nd Edition*. Rolling Meadows, IL: IT Governance Ltd, 2009.

Index

M

N

S